OXFORD
SCHOOL ATLAS

Prepared by
the Cartographic Department
of the Clarendon Press

under the general editorship of
D. P. BICKMORE and F. C. COUZENS

SECOND EDITION
Reprinted 1957, 1958
First edition 1955
Reprinted 1955

Second edition 1956
Reprinted 1957

OXFORD UNIVERSITY PRESS

1956

To get the best out of this atlas note well these points.

THE LEGEND is at the very front of the book. It is placed there so that you can find it easily. The legend is the "Highway Code" of the atlas and you will be in danger of misunderstanding the maps if you do not use the legend and know it almost by heart.

THE SCALE of a map is one of the most vital pieces of information about it. Make sure you have read the scale (from the title panel) before you start looking at the map. You will find that many of the scales in this atlas are the same or easily related; they are given as 1 inch to so many miles (and the black and white border round the panel is in quarter inches). Also remember that a small dot would cover the following distances on the ground at these different scales:

At	16 miles to the inch this dot	•	would be about	$\frac{1}{2}$ mile wide
,,	100	,,	,,	,,	,,	,,	,,	•	,,	,,	,,	3 miles ,,
,,	200	,,	,,	,,	,,	,,	,,	•	,,	,,	,,	6 ,, ,,
,,	300	,,	,,	,,	,,	,,	,,	•	,,	,,	,,	9 ,, ,,
,,	700	,,	,,	,,	,,	,,	,,	•	,,	,,	,,	22 ,, ,,

THE GRATICULE of a map is the framework of lines of latitude and longitude on which the map is built. On nearly all the maps we have shown the graticule at every 5°, so that you can find the same "5° squares" of country on maps of different scales and projections. The different shapes of these "squares" reflect the different projections that have been used. Notice that the name of the projection is shown at the lower left corner of each map.

THE ARRANGEMENT of the atlas and the sequence of the maps is shown opposite. Study this page carefully and often, or you may find that you are not using the map you really need. Remember that you can find out a great deal more about a place by consulting several of the maps; population and vegetation maps, for example, as well as the general map.

THE FIRST MAPS are of Britain. With the help of the National Grid you will easily be able to relate these maps at 16 miles to the inch to the Ordnance Survey maps of your home district e.g. at 1 mile to the inch. But to do this you must read the notes about the National Grid, facing page 138.

COLOURS. Notice that the same colours have been used to show the same things throughout the atlas. A tint of green or brown on a physical map means the same altitude anywhere in the world.

GAZETTEER. Often you will be able to find a place more quickly by looking it up in the Gazetteer—at the end of the atlas. But notice that there is one Gazetteer for the British Isles and another for the rest of the world. Positions are shown in Great Britain by the grid; in Ireland by letter and number; and the rest of the world by Latitude and Longitude to the nearest degree.

OTHER ATLASES. To know more about an area look it up in a bigger atlas. We have designed this atlas to lead on to the **Oxford Atlas** and the **Oxford Economic Atlases.**

Oxford University Press, Amen House, London, E.C. 4
Geoffrey Cumberlege, Publisher to the University

The maps have been compiled, drawn and photographed by the
Cartographic Department of the Clarendon Press, and printed
in Great Britain by Messrs. Cook, Hammond, and Kell, London.

CONTENTS

LEGEND on front endpaper

Map Scales are given as, e.g. 1 inch to 300 miles. Here they are abbreviated as e.g. " 300 miles ".

Ports and Canals

- ⊚ Major Ports handling over 20 million Net Registered Tonnage per year
- ○ Other important Ports handling 5–20 million N.R.T per year.
- ∘ Minor Ports & Packet Stations.
- ⌒ Canals & navigable rivers

Caledonian Canal

Glasgow

Newcastle upon Tyne

Aire and Calder Navigation

Liverpool

Hull

Trent Navigation

Manchester Ship Canal

Grand Union Canal

Swansea

London

Bristol

Southampton

Power

- Coalfields
- Hidden Coalfields
- Iron Ore
- ○○○ Coal Prodn.
- ▼ Oil Refineries
- + Atomic Power Centres
- ◻ Hydro-Electric Power

Haematite

1951 Population

One small dot represents a thousand persons.

The population of towns is shown by dots of graded size, e.g.

- • 50,000–100,000
- ● 400,000–500,000
- ⬤ 750,000–1,000,000

Urban Areas

Rural Areas

Sparsely settled Areas

⋈ Main railways

--- Main ferry and packet-boat services

Lerwick

Bergen & Oslo

55°N

Hamburg

Esbjerg

Hook

Göteborg

Ostend

Dunki.

Dieppe

St. Malo

POPULATION
and MAIN RAILWAYS
Scale 1:4,750,000 approx.
ONE INCH TO 75 MILES

ical Orthomorphic Projection

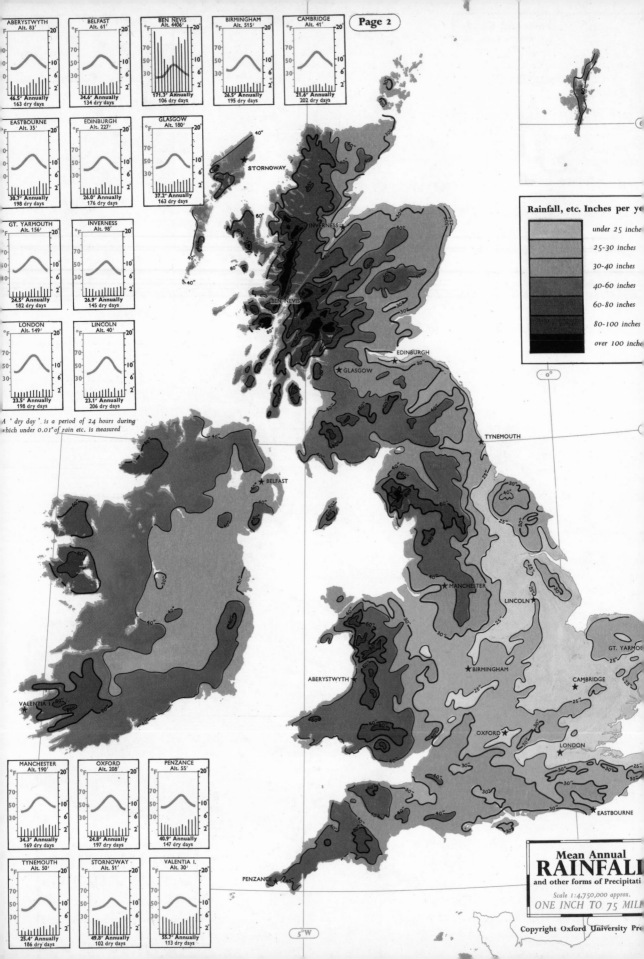

ABERYSTWYTH
Alt. 83'
46.5" Annually
163 dry days

BELFAST
Alt. 61'
34.6" Annually
134 dry days

BEN NEVIS
Alt. 4406'
171.3" Annually
106 dry days

BIRMINGHAM
Alt. 515'
26.5" Annually
195 dry days

CAMBRIDGE
Alt. 41'
21.6" Annually
202 dry days

EASTBOURNE
Alt. 35'
30.7" Annually
198 dry days

EDINBURGH
Alt. 227'
26.0" Annually
176 dry days

GLASGOW
Alt. 180'
37.2" Annually
163 dry days

GT. YARMOUTH
Alt. 156'
24.5" Annually
182 dry days

INVERNESS
Alt. 98'
26.9" Annually
145 dry days

LONDON
Alt. 149'
23.5" Annually
198 dry days

LINCOLN
Alt. 40'
23.1" Annually
206 dry days

A 'dry day' is a period of 24 hours during which under 0.01" of rain etc. is measured

MANCHESTER
Alt. 190'
34.3" Annually
169 dry days

OXFORD
Alt. 208'
24.8" Annually
197 dry days

PENZANCE
Alt. 55'
40.9" Annually
147 dry days

TYNEMOUTH
Alt. 50'
25.4" Annually
186 dry days

STORNOWAY
Alt. 51'
49.8" Annually
102 dry days

VALENTIA I.
Alt. 30'
55.7" Annually
113 dry days

Rainfall, etc. Inches per year

under 25 inches
25-30 inches
30-40 inches
40-60 inches
60-80 inches
80-100 inches
over 100 inches

Mean Annual
RAINFALL
and other forms of Precipitation

Scale 1:4,750,000 approx.
ONE INCH TO 75 MILES

Copyright Oxford University Press

Comparative frequency of
Bright Sunshine
in red tones
Thick Fog
in grey tones
Snow (lying)
in blue

Chief Urban Areas

Orchard and Nursery Gardens

Arable Land

Meadowland & Permanent Grass

Forest and Woodland

Heathland, Moorland
and Rough Pasture

55°N

January

38°
38°
39°
39°
39°
41°
42° 42°
43°
44°
39°
40°
41°
42°
43°
44°

No information available

*Mean Temperatures
Reduced to Sea Level*

*(by adding 1° F. for each
300' of altitude to the
average of actual
temperature in the
month concerned)*

July

54°
55°
56°
57°
58°
59°
59°
60°
61°
62°
63°
60°

LAND USE
Scale 1:4,750,000 approx.
ONE INCH TO 75 MILES

Conical Orthomorphic Projection

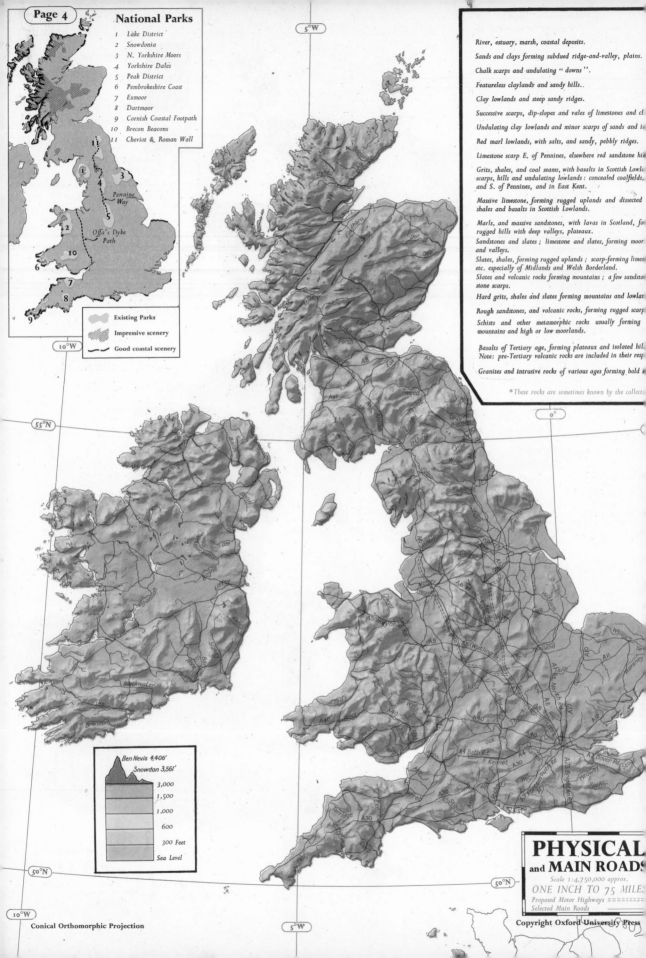

National Parks

1 Lake District
2 Snowdonia
3 N. Yorkshire Moors
4 Yorkshire Dales
5 Peak District
6 Pembrokeshire Coast
7 Exmoor
8 Dartmoor
9 Cornish Coastal Footpath
10 Brecon Beacons
11 Cheviot & Roman Wall

Pennine Way
Offa's Dyke Path

Existing Parks
Impressive scenery
Good coastal scenery

River, estuary, marsh, coastal deposits.

Sands and clays forming subdued ridge-and-valley, plains.

Chalk scarps and undulating " downs ".

Featureless claylands and sandy hills.

Clay lowlands and steep sandy ridges.

Successive scarps, dip-slopes and vales of limestones and cl

Undulating clay lowlands and minor scarps of sands and i

Red marl lowlands, with salts, and sandy, pebbly ridges.

Limestone scarp E. of Pennines, elsewhere red sandstone hi

Grits, shales, and coal seams, with basalts in Scottish Lowle
scarps, hills and undulating lowlands : concealed coalfields,
and S. of Pennines, and in East Kent.

Massive limestone, forming rugged uplands and dissected
shales and basalts in Scottish Lowlands.

Marls, and massive sandstones, with lavas in Scotland, fo
rugged hills with deep valleys, plateaux.

Sandstones and slates ; limestone and slates, forming moor
and valleys.

Slates, shales, forming rugged uplands ; scarp-forming limes
etc. especially of Midlands and Welsh Borderland.

Slates and volcanic rocks forming mountains ; a few sandsto
stone scarps.

Hard grits, shales and slates forming mountains and lowlar

Rough sandstones, and volcanic rocks, forming rugged scarp

Schists and other metamorphic rocks usually forming
mountains and high or low moorlands.

Basalts of Tertiary age, forming plateaux and isolated hil.
Note: pre-Tertiary volcanic rocks are included in their resp

Granites and intrusive rocks of various ages forming bold

*These rocks are sometimes known by the collecta

Ben Nevis 4,406'
Snowdon 3,561'

3,000
1,500
1,000
600
300 Feet
Sea Level

PHYSICAL and MAIN ROADS

Scale 1:4,750,000 approx.
ONE INCH TO 75 MILE
Proposed Motor Highways
Selected Main Roads

Conical Orthomorphic Projection

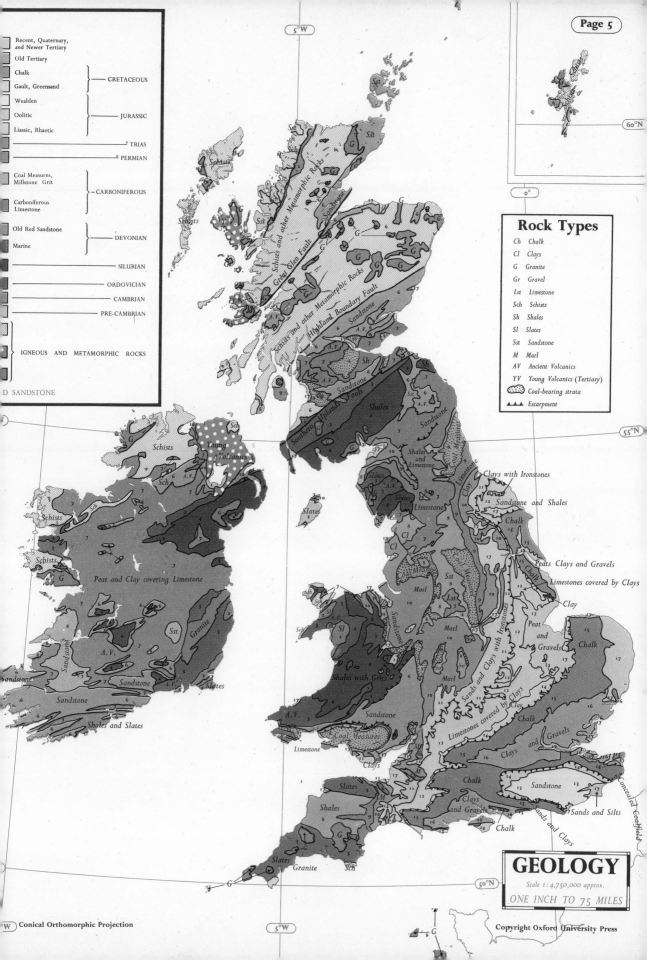

S.E. ENGLAND

Scale 1:1,000,000

ONE INCH TO 16 MILES APPROX.

0 Miles 5 10 15 20 25

Railways in red

National Parks

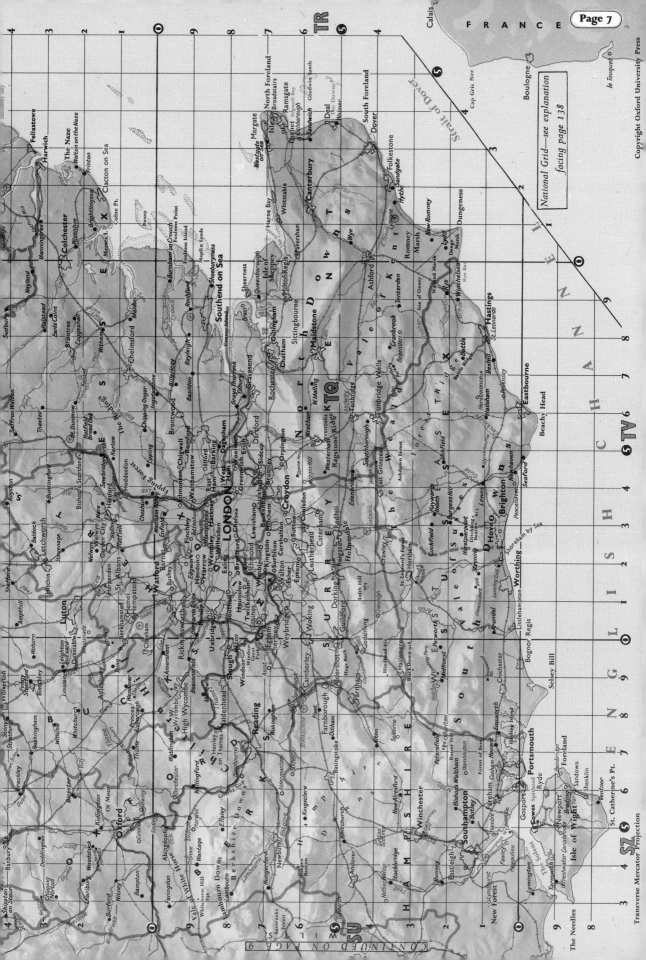

National Grid—see explanation
facing page 138

FRANCE

Calais
Boulogne
Cap Gris Nez
le Touquet

Strait of Dover

ENGLISH CHANNEL

Transverse Mercator Projection

CONTINUED ON PAGE 9

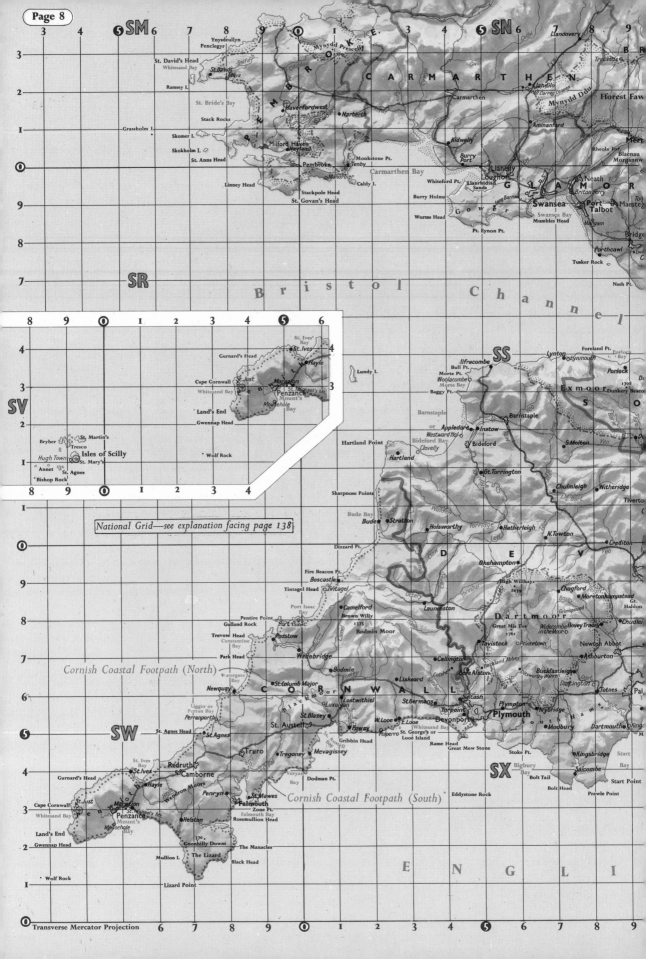

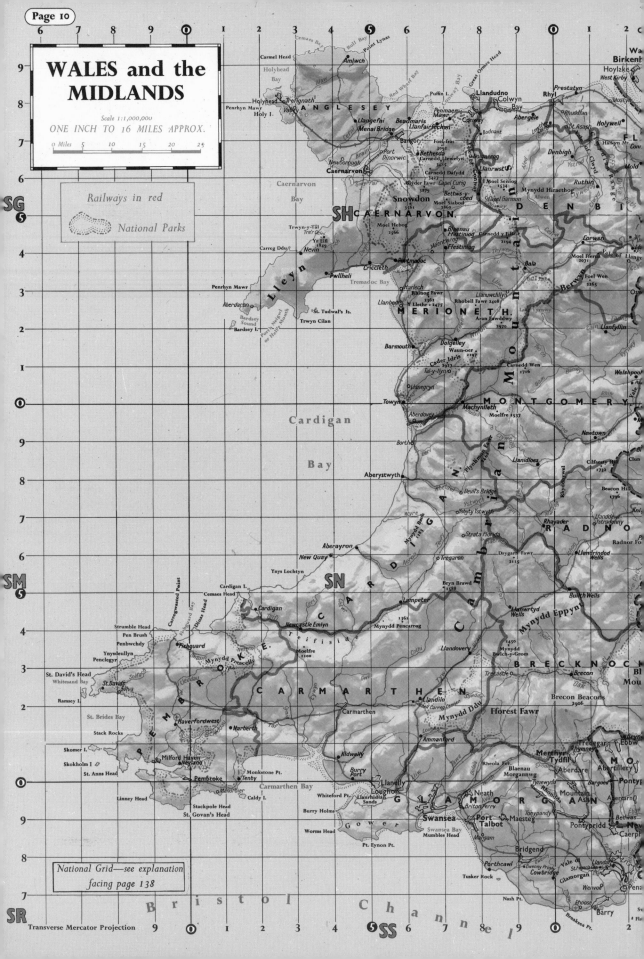

CONTINUED ON PAGE 14-15

NX
NY
DUMFRIESSHIRE

Milleur Pt.
Maxwelltown
Dumfries

KIRKCUDBRIGHT
Galloway
Fell of Fleet
Newton Stewart
Cairnsmore of Fleet
1329
Threave Castle
Castle Douglas
Dalbeattie
Criffell
1866
Annan
Gretna Green
Longtown

The Moors
WIGTOWNSHIRE
Stranraer
Cairn Pat 593
Loch Ryan
Lochinch
Castle L.
The Machers
Wigtown
1497
Cairnharrow
Bathgate House of Fleet
Dee
Southerness Point
Silloth
Wigton
Waver
Carlisle
Brampton

NW
Money Hd.
The Rhinns
Mull of Logan
Luce Bay
Wigtown Bay
Kirkcudbright
Little Ross
Suie Hill
Abbey Hd.
Balcary Point
Solway Firth
Inglewood
Forest

Mull of Galloway
Whithorn
Isle of Whithorn
Burrow Head
Maryport
Cockermouth
Skiddaw 3053
Saddleback 2847
Penrith
CUMBERLA

Railways in red
National Parks
Workington
Harrington
Whitehaven
St. Bees Head
St. Bees
Ennerdale Bridge
Buttermere
Cleator Moor
Egremont
Great Gable 2949
Wasdale Head
Sca Fell 3210
Langdales
Helvellyn 3118
Derwent Water
Keswick
Greenthwaite
Grasmere
Howtown
Ullswater
High Street 2663
Shap
Shap Fells
WESTMOR

Point of Ayre
Rue Point
Jurby Head
Ramsey Bay
Sulby
Ramsey
Snaefell 2034
Maughold Head
Laxey
Isle of Man
Laxey Bay
Clay Head
S. Barrule 1585
Douglas
Sellafield
Seascale
Ravenglass
Muncaster Castle
Eskdale Green
Whitfell 1881
Black Combe 1969
Broughton in Furness
Furness Fells
Coniston
Hawkshead
Ambleside
Troutbeck
Windermere
Bowness
Windermere
Winster
Kendal
Selker Bay

Peel
Ronaldsway
King Williams Coll.
Castletown
Port Erin
Calf of Man
Millom
Ulverston
Dalton in Furness
Barrow-in-Furness
Furness Abbey
Cartmel
Grange
Burto
Carnforth

SC
Isle of Walney
Hilpsford Point
Morecambe Bay
Morecambe
Heysham
Lancaste
Lune
Ward

SD
IRISH   SEA
Fleetwood
Rossall School
Preesall
Garstang
Cleveleys
Thornton
Poulton le Fylde
Wyre
Blackpool
Fylde
Kirkham
Brock

National Grid—see explanation facing page 138
St. Anne's on the Sea
Lytham
Preston
Walton
Leyland

Southport
Ribble

Formby Point
Formby
Ormskirk
Alt

Crosby
Bootle
Wallasey
Birkenhead
Hoylake
West Kirby
Liverpool Bay
Ashton in Makerfield
St. Helens
Liverpool
Warrin

Carmel Head
Amlwch
Point Lynas
Cemaes Bay
Bull Bay
Holyhead Bay
Puffin I.
Great Ormes Head
Llandudno
Colwyn Bay
Rhyl
Prestatyn
Mostyn
Port Sunlight
New Brighton
Bebington
Eastham
Neston
Ellesmere Port
Runco
Widn

Holyhead
Holy I.
Penrhyn Mawr
ANGLESEY
Llangefni
Menai Bridge
Beaumaris
Llanfairfechan
Penmaen Mawr
Conway
Abergele
Rhuddlan
St. Asaph
Holywell
Flint
FLINT
Connahs Quay
Chester
CH

Caernarvon Bay
Newborough
Port Dinorwic
Bangor
Bethesda
Foel-fras 3092
Carnedd Llewelyn 3485
Carnedd Dafydd 3427
Glyder Fawr 3279
Capel Curig
Bettws-y-coed
Capel Garmon
Llanrwst
Bodnant
Denbigh
Mold
Buckley
Halkin Mtn.
Ystrad

Caernarvon
Snowdon 3561
Moel Siabod 2860
Moel Hebog 2566
CAERNARVON
Carreg Ddu
Nevin
Yr Eifl 1849
Trwyn-y-Tâl
Tre'r Ceiri
Blaenau Ffestiniog
Ffestiniog
Maentwrog
Moel Seisiog 1534
Mynydd Hiraethog
Ruthin
Moel Siabod
Carnedd y Filiast 2194
Alwen
Corwen
Llangollen
DENBIGH
Clwyd
Offa's Dyke
Vale Crucis Abbey
Wrexham
FLINT

NORTHUMBERLAND

N. ENGLAND

Scale 1:1,000,000
ONE INCH TO 16 MILES APPROX.

0 Miles   5   10   15   20   25

NORTH

SEA

Whitley Bay
Woolsington
Gosforth
Newburn Newcastle Wallsend Tynemouth
Corbridge upon Tyne Jarrow South Shields
Hexham Poudhoe Blaydon Gateshead Southwick
Whickham Sunderland
Allendale Stanley Washington Birtley
Town Blackhill Annfield Plain Chester-le-Street Houghton le Spring
Blanchland Consett Seaham Harbour
Hetton Ill Hole
Durham Seaham Harbour
Peterlee
John's Chapel DURHAM
Stanhope Low Law Willington Hartlepool
Weardale Walsingham Crook WEST
Pawlaw Pike Spennymoor Bishop Auckland Hartlepool
1599 Sedgefield Billingham
Middleton Shildon Coatham Redcar
in Teesdale Raby Castle Stockton on Tees Grangetown Saltburn by the Sea
Barnard Castle Thornaby Middlesbrough Brotton
Stainmore on Tees Skelton Loftus
Darlington Yarm Guisborough
Cleveland
Whitby
Stokesley
Cleveland Hills
Rogan's Seat North Yorks. Moors
Reeth Swaledale Richmond The Wade's Causeway
Catterick Camp Northallerton Allerston Forest Scarborough
Askrigg Leyburn Rievaulx Filey
Middleham Bedale Kirkby Moorside Abbey Helmsley Pickering Hunmanby
Buckden Pike Masham Thirsk Ampleforth Flamborough Head
Grassington Ripon Howardian Hills Malton
Pateley Bridge Easingwold Bridlington
Ripley Boroughbridge
Knaresborough Gt. Driffield
Harrogate Spofforth
SE York Stamford Bridge
Bolton Abbey Wetherby Hornsea
Skipton Round Hill Ilkley Otley Harewood Pocklington
Craven Forest of Knaresborough Tadcaster Beverley
Earby Silsden Cawood Market Weighton
Keighley Bingley Baildon Yeadon Horsforth Selby Cottingham
Nelson Haworth Shipley Farsley Leeds Sherburn in Elmet S. Cave Hessle Kingston
Burnley Bradford Clayton Pudsey New Holland upon Hull
Hebden Shelf Low Moor Morley Rothwell Howden Barton upon Humber Withernsea
Bridge Halifax Somerset Birstall Castleford Goole Patrington
Sowerby Cleckheaton Batley Stanley Normanton Knottingley
Bridge Brighouse Dewsbury Ossett Wakefield Pontefract Snaith Winterton
Elland Grimsby
Rochdale Golcar Almondbury Horbury Thorne Crowle Scunthorpe Cleethorpes
Milnrow Slaithwaite Meltham Huddersfield Royston Spurn Head
Heywood Shaw Kirkburton Denby Dale Darton Cudworth Adwick le Street Brigg Caistor
Oldham Holmfirth Dodworth Barnsley Isle of Axholme
Ashton under Lyne Peniston Worsborough Wombwell Epworth
Stalybridge Bleaklow Hill Stocksbridge Hoyland Nether Wath Mexborough Doncaster Kirton in Lindsey
Manchester Glossop upon Dearne Conisbrough
Stockport Peak Rawmarsh Caistor
Marple Dovestone Tor Rotherham Bawtry Gainsborough
Haze Grove Kinder Scout District Sheffield Maltby Tickhill Market Rasen Louth
New Mills Whaley Bridge Dronfield Eckington Worksop Wragby Alford
Bollington Killamarsh Staveley East Retford Lincoln
Macclesfield Buxton Chesterfield Bakewell Bolsover The Dukeries Tuxford Horncastle Old Bolingbroke Spilsby
Clay Cross Market Warsop Ollerton Laxton Woodhall Spa Burgh le Mar
Matlock Mansfield Woodhouse Skeg
Biddulph Matlock Bath Sutton in Ashfield Newark upon Trent Wainfleet
Leek Alfreton Mansfield West Fen All Saint
Kidsgrove Wirksworth Kirkby in Ashfield Southwell Holland Fen
Burslem Ripley Belper Hucknall Cranwell Boston
Stoke on Trent Longton Ashbourne Heanor Torkard Sleaford
Cheadle Ilkeston Nottingham

STAFFORDSHIRE

Copyright Oxford University Press

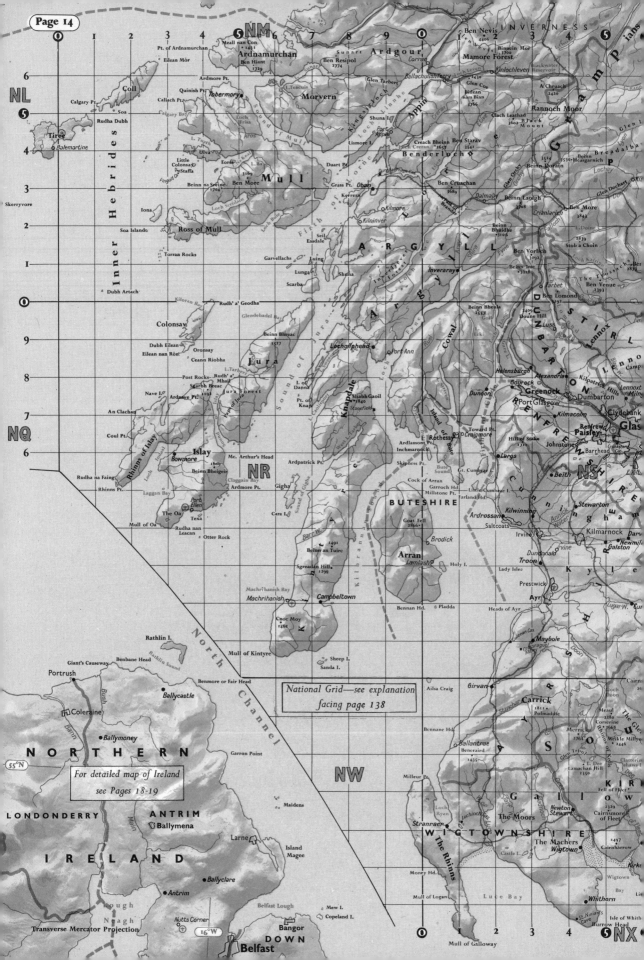

NM
NL
NQ
NR
NW
NX
NS

Pt. of Ardnamurchan
Eilean Mòr
Meall nan Con 1641
Ardnamurchan
Ben Hiant 1729

Sunart
Ben Resipol 2774
Ardgour
Corran
Ballachulishferry

INVERNESS
Ben Nevis 4406
Binnein Mòr 3700
Mamore Forest
Kinlochleven
Blackwater Reservoir
Glen Coe
A' Chruach 3426
Rannoch Moor
Clach Leathad 3602
Black Mount

Ardmore Pt.
Calgary Pt.
Coll
Quinish Pt.
Caliach Pt.
Tobermory

Morvern
Glen Tarbert
L. Teacuis
Appin
Creach Bheinn 2657
Ben Starav 3541
Benderloch
Ben Cruachan 3689
Dalmally
Beinn Laoigh 3708
Crianlarich
Ben More 3843

NL 5
Tiree
Balemartine
Rudha Dubh
Soa
Calgary Bay

Inner Hebrides
Sound of Mull
Ulva
L. Tuath
Eorsa
Little Colonsay
Staffa
Fingal's Cave
Beinn na Sreine 1704
Ben More 3169
Mull
L. Ba
L. na Keal
Loch Scridain
Duart Pc.
Grass Pt.
Kerrera
Oban
Port
Kilmore
Kilninver

Aros
L. Frisa
Loch Feochan
Kilvichewen

ARGYLL

Beinn Heasgarnich
Beinn Dorain
Breadalbane
Lochay
Glen Orchy
Glen Dochart
Glen Lochay

Skerryvore
Iona
Soa Islands
Ross of Mull
Loch Buie
Seil
Easdale
Luing
Garvellachs
Lunga
Scarba

Beinn Bhuidhe 3106
Ben Vorlich 3092
Beinn Ime 3318
Stob a Choin
Ben Vane 2685
Inveraray

Ben Lawers
Ben More 3843
L. Doine
2539
The Trossachs
Ben Venue 2393

ARGYLL

DUNBARTON
STIRL

Dubh Artach
Torran Rocks
Shuna
Dubh Eilean
Colonsay

Kiloran Bay
Rudh' a' Geodha
Glendebadel Bay

Beinn Bhreac 1527
Lochgilphead
Port Ann

Beinn Bheula 2557
Gott
Doune Hill
Luss
Loch Lomond

Lennox

Eilean nan Ròn
Oronsay
Ceann Riobha

Jura
Lochgilphead
Port Ann

Coval
Helensburgh
Alexandria
Kilpatrick Hills
Lennox
Gourock
Greenock
Port Glasgow
Dumbarton
Clydebank

Post Rocks
Rudh' a' Mhail
Sgarbh Breac
Nave I.
Ardnave Pt.
Jura Forest
Paps of Jura
Pt. of Knap
Knapdale
Sliabh Gaoil 1840
Stonefield

Dundon
Kilmacolm
Renfrew
Paisley
Johnstone
Barrhead

An Clachan
Coul Pt.
Rhinns of Islay
Bowmore
Islay
Beinn Bheigeir 1609
Mc. Arthur's Head
Ardpatrick Pt.
Gigha
Ardlamont Pt.
Inchmarnock
Rothesay
Island of Bute
Toward Pt.
Craigmore
Hill of Stake 1711
Largs

Rudha na Faing
Rhinns Pt.
Laggan Bay
Port Ellen
Claggain Bay
Ardmore Pt.
Skipness Pt.
Cock of Arran
Garroch Hd.
Millstone Pt.
Great Cumbrae
Little Cumbrae I.
Farland Hd.
Beith

The Oa
Texa
Cara I.
Sound of Gigha
BUTESHIRE
Kilwinning
Stewarton
Mull of Oa
Rudha nan Leacan
Otter Rock
Goat Fell 2866
Brodick
Ardrossan
Saltcoats
Irvine
Kilmarnock

NR
Barr W.
Beinn an Tuirc 1491
Arran
Lamlash
Holy I.
Dundonald
Troon
Lady Isle
Prestwick

Sgreadan Hill 1298
Machrihanish Bay
Machrihanish
Campbeltown
Bennan Hd.
Pladda
Heads of Ayr
Ayr

Cnoc Moy 1462
Maybole

Rathlin I.
Mull of Kintyre
Sheep I.
Sanda I.
Ailsa Craig
Girvan
Carrick
Polmaddie

Giant's Causeway
Benbane Head
Portrush
Rathlin Sound
Benmore or Fair Head
Coleraine
Ballycastle

North Channel

National Grid—see explanation facing page 138

Bennane Hd.
Ballantrae
Beneraird 1435
Merrick 2764
Corserine 2669
Meaul 2280

NW

NORTHERN
Ballymoney
Garron Point
55°N

Milleur Pt.
Galloway
The Moors
Newton Stewart

For detailed map of Ireland see Pages 18-19

LONDONDERRY
ANTRIM
Ballymena
Stranraer
Loch Ryan
The Rhinns
WIGTOWNSHIRE
The Machers
Wigtown

IRELAND
Maidens
Larne
Island Magee
Money Hd.
Luce Bay
Castle L.
Whithorn

Ballyclare
Antrim
Mull of Logan
Mull of Galloway

Nutts Corner
16°W
Belfast Lough
Mew I.
Copeland I.
Bangor
DOWN
Belfast

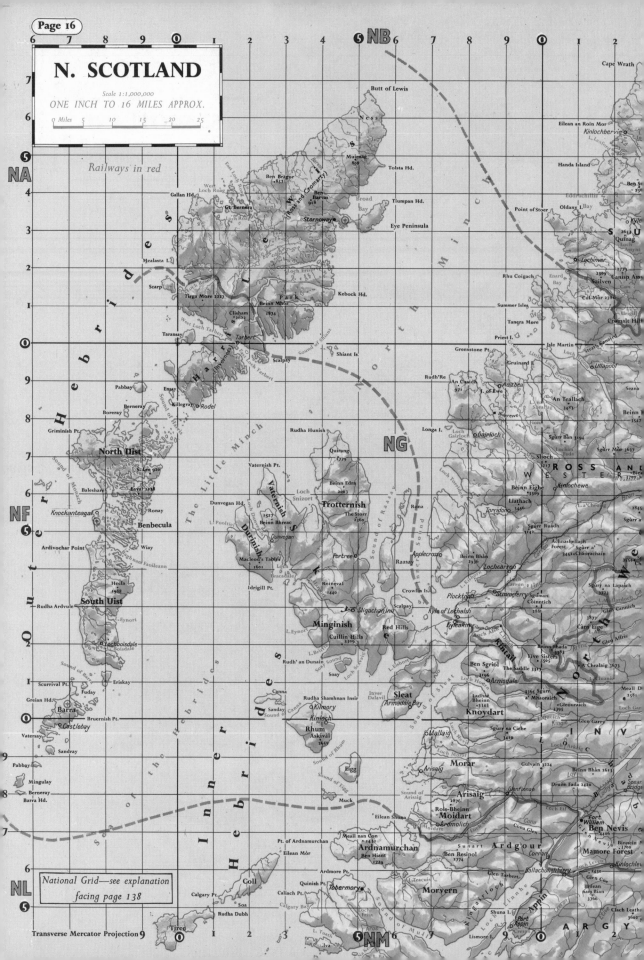

N. SCOTLAND

Scale 1:1,000,000
ONE INCH TO 16 MILES APPROX.

0 Miles 5 10 15 20 25

Railways in red

National Grid—see explanation
facing page 138

Transverse Mercator Projection

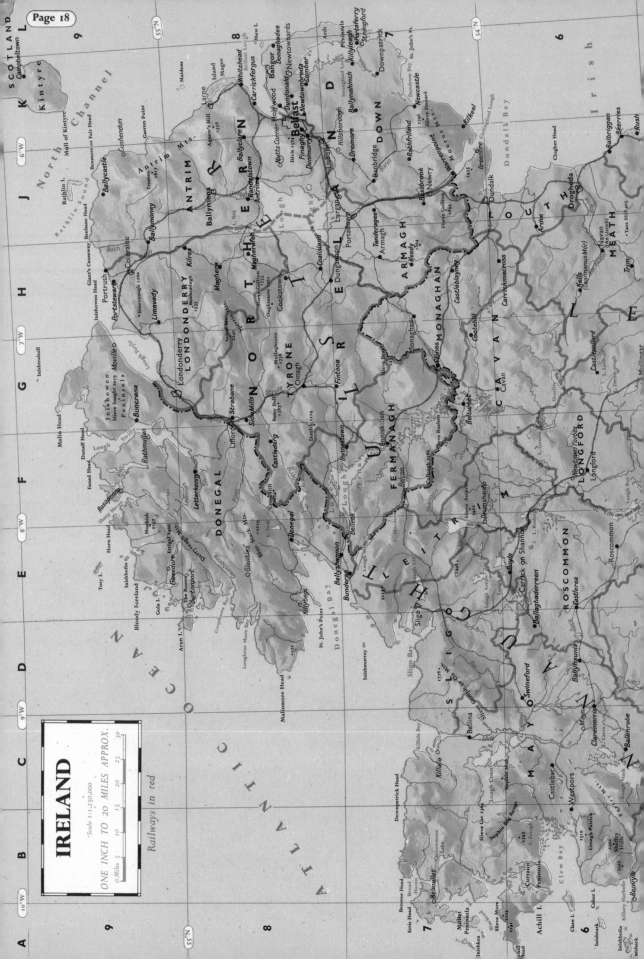

IRELAND

Scale 1:1,250,000

ONE INCH TO 20 MILES APPROX.

Railways in red

0 Miles 5 10 15 20 25 30

Conical Orthomorphic Projection

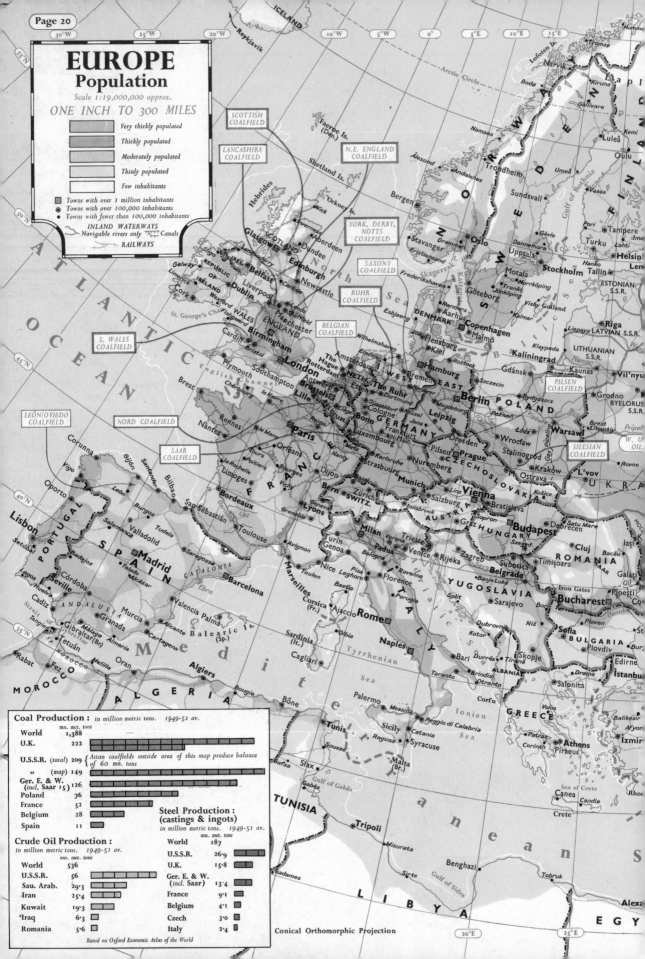

EUROPE
Population
Scale 1:19,000,000 approx.
ONE INCH TO 300 MILES

- Very thickly populated
- Thickly populated
- Moderately populated
- Thinly populated
- Few inhabitants

- Towns with over 1 million inhabitants
- Towns with over 100,000 inhabitants
- Towns with fewer than 100,000 inhabitants

INLAND WATERWAYS
Navigable rivers only — Canals
RAILWAYS

Coal Production: in million metric tons. 1949-51 av.

	mn. met. tons	
World	1,388	
U.K.	222	
U.S.S.R. (total)	209	Asian coalfields outside area of this map produce balance of 60 mn. tons
" (map)	149	
Ger. E. & W. (incl. Saar 15)	126	
Poland	76	
France	52	
Belgium	28	
Spain	11	

Crude Oil Production: in million metric tons. 1949-51 av.

	mn. met. tons
World	536
U.S.S.R.	56
Sau. Arab.	29·3
Iran	25·4
Kuwait	19·3
Iraq	6·3
Romania	5·6

Steel Production: (castings & ingots) in million metric tons. 1949-51 av.

	mn. met. tons
World	187
U.S.S.R.	26·9
U.K.	15·8
Ger. E. & W. (incl. Saar)	13·4
France	9·1
Belgium	4·1
Czech	3·0
Italy	2·4

Based on Oxford Economic Atlas of the World

Conical Orthomorphic Projection

EUROPE
Physical

Scale 1:19,000,000 approx.
ONE INCH TO 300 MILES

0 Miles   300   450

Altitude tints (layers) see p. 39

Maximum extent
of Glaciation

ICELAND

ATLANTIC

OCEAN

North Sea

Arctic Circle

NORWAY

SWEDEN

FINLAND

Gulf of Bothnia

Moray Firth

·1406

REPUBLIC
OF
IRELAND

·2414

GREAT BRITAIN

·3560

St. George's Chan.

English Channel

Skagerrak

Kattegat

DENMARK

L. Vänern

Baltic Sea

Neman

Bay of
Biscay

FRANCE

NETHERLANDS

BELGIUM

GERMANY

POLAND

Ems

Rhine

Seine

Marne

Meuse

Moselle

Oder

·5499

Vistula

Bug

Loire

Cher

Loire

Garonne

Lot

SWITZERLAND

·15,781

AUSTRIA

·12,457

CZECHOSLOVAKIA

Danube

Rhône

HUNGARY

Drava

Sava

Tisza

ROMANI

·8920

Danu

PORTUGAL

SPAIN

Douro

Tagus

Guadiana

Guadalquivir

Ebro

·11,168

·11,420

Gulf of
Lions

Strait
of Gibraltar

ITALY

·9583·

Tiber

Adriatic Sea

YUGOSLAVIA

·9055

ALBANIA

BULGARI

Maritsa

GREECE

·8067

Mediterranean

Tyrrhenian
Sea

·10,741·

Ionian
Sea

Aegean Sea

Sea of Crete

·5065

Gulf of Gabès

Gulf of Sidra

MOROCCO

Moulouya

ALGERIA

TUNISIA

LIBYA

Annual
Rainfall
and other forms of precipitation

	Under 10" each year
	10" — 20" ,, ,,
	20" — 40" ,, ,,
	Over 40"

Conical Orthomorphic Projection

Map labels

Barents Sea

40°E 45°E 60°E 65°E 70°E 75°E 80°E

60°N

White Sea

Pechora

North Dvina

Lake Onega

Sukhona

C. Vychegda

•5560

Rybinsk Reservoir

Volga

Volga

Kama

Belaya

U. S. S. R.

•5374

55°N

Oka

Tobol'

Ural

Don

Donets

50°N

Tsimlyansk Reservoir

Emba

Aral Sea

Sea of Azov

Caspian

Surface height 92 ft. below m.s.l.

18,468•

45°N

Kara-Bogaz-Gol

Kura

Black Sea

Araks

16,554•

Sea

40°N

Kizil Irmak

Lake Van

L. Urmia

•15,900

TURKEY

Euphrates

Tigris

IRAN (PERSIA)

Euphrates

SYRIA

IRAQ

35°N

Cyprus

LEBANON

5692•

ISRAEL

JORDAN

SAUDI ARABIA

KUWAIT

Persian G.

30°N

35°E 40°E 45°E

Copyright Oxford University Press

Climate graphs

ALGIERS Alt. 200' — 27·4" Ann.	ATHENS Alt. 351' — 15·6" Ann.	BARCELONA Alt. 25' — 21·2" Ann.
BASEL Alt. 1,040' — 32·2" Ann.	BERGEN Alt. 60' — 80·9" Ann.	BERLIN Alt. 115' — 22·2" Ann.
BORDEAUX Alt. 40' — 30·8" Ann.	BUCHAREST Alt. 276' — 23·2" Ann.	BUDAPEST Alt. 427' — 25" Ann.
CLERMONT-FERRAND Alt. 1,275' — 25·4" Ann.	COLOGNE Alt. 184' — 27·4" Ann.	CORUNNA Alt. 82' — 32" Ann.
HAMBURG Alt. 66' — 28·9" Ann.	ISTANBUL Alt. 30' — 28·9" Ann.	KIEV Alt. 590' — 21·1" Ann.
LENINGRAD Alt. 30' — 18·8" Ann.	LILLE Alt. 85' — 27·0" Ann.	LISBON Alt. 321' — 27·1" Ann.
MADRID Alt. 2,148' — 16·4" Ann.	MARSEILLES Alt. 246' — 22·5" Ann.	MILAN Alt. 450' — 39·8" Ann.
MOSCOW Alt. 480' — 21·0" Ann.	NICE Alt. 94' — 32·9" Ann.	PARIS Alt. 164' — 22·6" Ann.
PRAGUE Alt. 575' — 20·8" Ann.	ROME Alt. 208' — 32·6" Ann.	SEVILLE Alt. 98' — 19·5" Ann.
SONNBLICK (AUSTR.) Alt. 10,097' — 64·7" Ann.	SPLIT Alt. 420' — 34·5" Ann.	STOCKHOLM Alt. 144' — 21·6" Ann.
UTRECHT Alt. 43' — 28·7" Ann.	VALLETTA Alt. 231' — 19·95" Ann.	WARSAW Alt. 436' — 22·2" Ann.

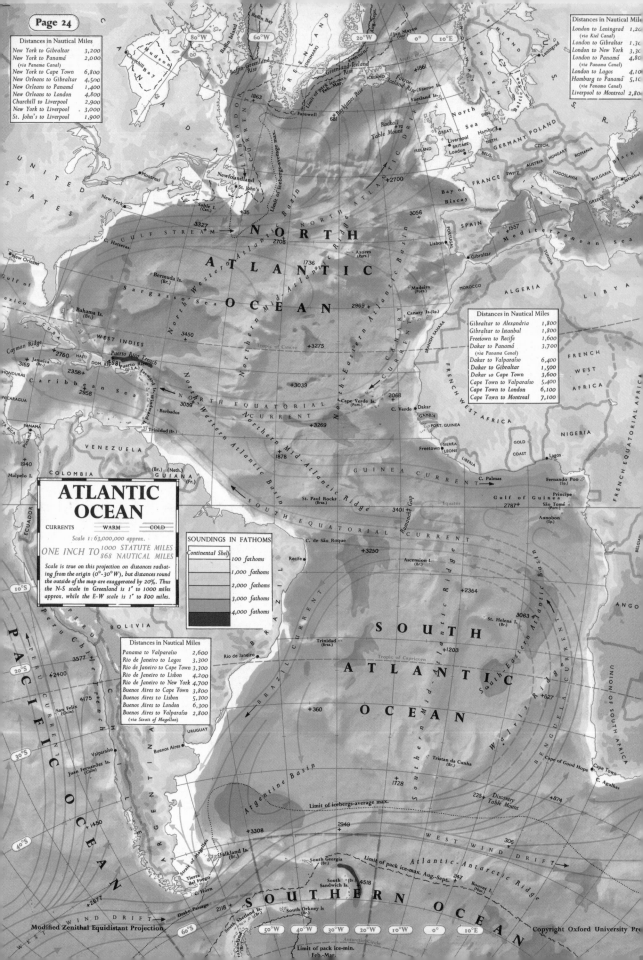

Distances in Nautical Miles

New York to Gibraltar	3,200
New York to Panamá	2,000
(via Panama Canal)	
New York to Cape Town	6,800
New Orleans to Gibraltar	4,500
New Orleans to Panamá	1,400
New Orleans to London	4,800
Churchill to Liverpool	2,900
New York to Liverpool	3,000
St. John's to Liverpool	1,900

Distances in Nautical Miles

London to Leningrad	1,2..
(via Kiel Canal)	
London to Gibraltar	1,3..
London to New York	3,3..
London to Panamá	4,8..
(via Panama Canal)	
London to Lagos	4,1..
Hamburg to Panamá	5,1..
Liverpool to Montreal	2,80..

Distances in Nautical Miles

Gibraltar to Alexandria	1,800
Gibraltar to Istanbul	1,800
Freetown to Recife	1,600
Dakar to Panamá	3,700
(via Panama Canal)	
Dakar to Valparaíso	6,400
Dakar to Gibraltar	1,500
Dakar to Cape Town	3,600
Cape Town to Valparaíso	5,400
Cape Town to London	6,100
Cape Town to Montreal	7,100

ATLANTIC OCEAN

CURRENTS ——— WARM ——— COLD

Scale 1: 63,000,000 approx.

ONE INCH TO 1000 STATUTE MILES / 868 NAUTICAL MILES

Scale is true on this projection on distances radiating from the origin (0°-30° W), but distances round the outside of the map are exaggerated by 20%. Thus the N-S scale in Greenland is 1" to 1000 miles approx. while the E-W scale is 1" to 800 miles.

SOUNDINGS IN FATHOMS

Continental Shelf	100 fathoms
	1,000 fathoms
	2,000 fathoms
	3,000 fathoms
	4,000 fathoms

Distances in Nautical Miles

Panama to Valparaíso	2,600
Rio de Janeiro to Lagos	3,300
Rio de Janeiro to Cape Town	3,300
Rio de Janeiro to Lisbon	4,200
Rio de Janeiro to New York	4,700
Buenos Aires to Cape Town	3,800
Buenos Aires to Lisbon	5,300
Buenos Aires to London	6,300
Buenos Aires to Valparaíso	2,800
(via Strait of Magellan)	

Modified Zenithal Equidistant Projection

Copyright Oxford University Pre..

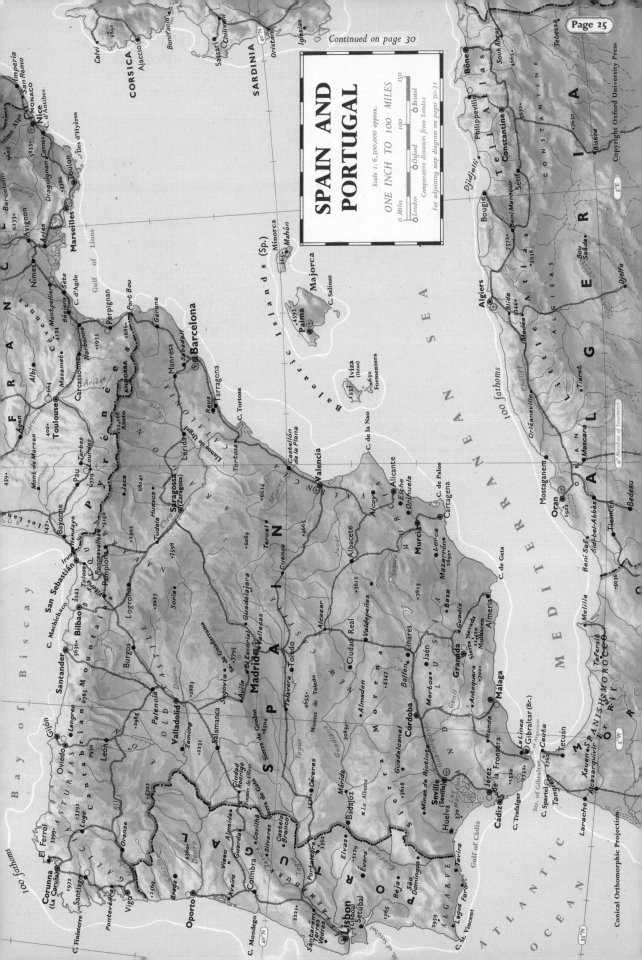

Continued on page 30

SPAIN AND PORTUGAL

Scale 1: 6,300,000 approx.

ONE INCH TO 100 MILES

0 Miles ⟶ 150

London ⟶ Oxford ⟶ Bristol
Comparative distances from London
For adjoining map diagram see pages 30-31

Copyright Oxford University Press

Conical Orthomorphic Projection

Continued on pages 34-35

RK
openhagen · Ringsted
Zealand
Malmö
Trelleborg
Bornholm
Nykøbing
Gedser
Lolland
Fehmarn
Grossenbrode
Neustrelitz
Rønne
C. Arkona
Sassnitz
Rügen
Greifswald
Pomeranian
Bay
Stralsund
177
Rostock
Wismar
Schwerin
410

Baltic
Sea
15°E
Gulf of
Danzig
20°E
Gdynia
587
Gdańsk
(Danzig)
Elbląg
Koszalin
725
Malbork
Olsztyn
1027
Tannenberg
Słupsk
Szczecinek
Chojnice
Grudziądz
Mława
692
Bydgoszcz
Toruń
146
Inowrocław
Włocławek

Soviétsk
(Tilsit)
Kaliningrad
(Königsberg)
Chernyakhovsk
(Insterburg)
Kaunas
LITH. S.S.R.
Vilnius
846
25°E
650
Mins

R. S. F. S. R.
170
961
Grodno
BYELORUSSIAN
Volkovysk
Baranovichi
Slutsk
Białystok
797
Slonim
Łomża
Ostrów Mazowiecki
Pripet
577
50°N
Pinsk
Pripet
Marshes

ANY
Neustrelitz
Wittenberge
Rathenow
Eberswalde
on Curtain
Stendal
sburg
EAST
Berlin
Spandau
Potsdam
Frankfurt
531
Magdeburg
Dessau
Halle
Eilenburg
ausen
599
Weimar
Jena
Gera
Zwickau
Leipzig
Dresden
Chemnitz

Oder
POLAND
Gorzów Wielkopolski
(Landsberg)
Warta
Gniezno
Poznań
613
Zielona Góra
(Grünberg)
547
Jarocin
Kalisz
Krotoszyn
Ostrów
Wielkopolski
961
Głogów
Piotrków
Łódź
Skierniewice
676

Warsaw
(Warszawa)
617
Biała Podlaska
Kutno
Kovel
Chełm
Lublin
Zamość
909
Brest Litovsk
Kobrin
David-Gorodok

UKRAINIAN
Vladimir
Volynskiy
Lutsk
Royno
Dubno
Kremenets
1332
50°N

Cottbus
521
Torgau
Eisenburg
Nysa)
Oder
SILESIA
Wrocław
(Breslau)
Brzeg
Częstochowa
Opole
Zawiercie
Bytom
Chorzów
Kamienna Góra
(Landeshut)
5259
Kłodzko
(Glatz)
Katowice
Gliwice
Zabrze
Sosnowiec
Kraków
Nowa Huta

Kielce
2006
Jędrzejów
Vistula

Rzeszów
Jarosław
1279
L'vov
Przemyśl
Jasło
Sanok
Sambor
Berezhany
Ternopol
1289
Bolekhov
Stanislav
1364

Bayreuth
Ezgebirge
Karlovy
Vary
Mariánské
Lázně
Cheb
Nuremberg
Regensburg
Bohemian
Forest
Klatovy
Pilsen
(Plzeň)
Písek
Ingolstadt
3448
Hof
Mid
Prague
Sadowa
Nymburk
Nučice
Pardubice
Liberec
Sudeten Mts.
Šumperk
Olomouc
Opava
Ostrava
Moravská
2746
Moravian Gate
Prostějov
Brno
Austerlitz
Znojmo
České Budějovice
1482
CZECHOSLOVAKIA
Gottwaldov
Cieszyn
Český Těšín
Nowy Sącz
4416
East
Beskids
Borislav
Spiš
3582
Košice
Uzhgorod
Chop
Mukachevo
Veretski Pass
Carpathia
Khust
Tatar
Pass
Chernovtsy
Kolomyya
4862

Passau
Danube (Donau)
3409
Matzen
Linz
Vienna
(Wien)
Steyr
Wiener-Neustadt
1732
Inn
Munich
Salzburg
8248
Eisenerz
7473
Niedere
Tauern
Leoben
Donawitz
Semmering P.
Bratislava
Komárno
Győr
Sopron
1060
Lučenec
Levice
Ózd
Miskolc
Tokaj
3081
3314
Gánt
Budapest
Esztergom
Jászberény
Debrecen
312
Nyíregyháza
Satu-Mare
Baia-Mare
7562
Câmpulung
Moldovenesc

Innsbruck
renner
Höhe Tauern
11,558
12,457
Lienz
Villach
Klagenfurt
7985
7034
Kotlach
Graz
Donawitz
Szombathely
2339
Úrkút
Veszprém
Balaton L.
Stalinvaros
Kecskemét
Kiskunfélegyháza
Szolnok
Dobreşti
Salonta
292
Oradea
758
Cluj
Turda
3199
Bistriţa
2096
Gheorghieni
Târgu
Mureş
5999
Odorhei
1890
Sighişoara
Mediaş

AUSTRIA
ALPS
Bolzano
10,705
8835
Merano
7700
Belluno
Venetian Alps
Dolomites
Udine
Gorizia
Julian Alps
8385
Villach
Dravograd
Maribor
Varaždin
3396
3481
Celje
5892
Karlovac
Ljubljana
SLOVENIA
Zagreb
Virovitica
981
Lispeszentadorján
Nagykanizsa
Kaposvár
2237
Pécs
Mohács
Sombor
Subotica
426
Hódmezővásárhely
Szeged
348
Arad
2746
HUNGARY
Timişoara
Lugoj
Caransebeş
8208
Deva
Reşiţa
Alba Iulia
Sebeş
Sibiu
8910
ROMANIA
TRANSYLVANIA
Târgu Jiu
Petroşani
Transylvanian Alps
Câmpulung
Râmnicu
Vâlcea
45°N
25°E

VENEZIA
Verona
Padua
(Padova)
Trieste
Venice
Gulf of
Venice
Chioggia
Mantua
1765
Pula
(Pola)
Cres
Krk
Rijeka
(Fiume)
Karlovac
Sisak
ISTRIA
CROATIA
Osijek
Brod
5413
Bihać
Banja Luka
6295
Ruma
Novi Sad
(Dunav)
Zrenjanin
(Petrovgrad)
430
Belgrade
(Beograd)
Sava
Požarevac
Bor
3940
Turnu Severin
Iron Gates
WALLACHI
Danube (Duna)
Vidin
Calafat
Oryakhovo
Bäileşti
Turnu
Măgurele
Craiova
Slatina
Piteşti
1027

eggio
l'Emilia
GNA
Ferrara
Ravenna
Bologna
Forli
5426
1457
Rimini
San Marino
THE MARCHES
Ancona
6434
5413
Spič
BOSNIA
Dinaric Alps
Dinara
2017
Šibenik
2221
Split
Brač
Šolta
Lastovo
Zadar
YUGOSLAVIA
HERCEGOVINA
Sarajevo
5042
Mostar
8314
Titovo Užice
Zlatibor
Kragujevac
Čačak
6617
Rankovićevo
(Kraljevo)
Kruševac
5118
Novi Pazar
Kosovska
Mitrovica
Trepča
Kopaonik
Niš
6594
Vratsa
BULGARIA
Botevgrad
1027

Florence
(Firenze)
Arezzo
Siena
Rapolano
Perugia
Assisi
Foligno
UMBRIA
8130
Macerata
Ascoli Piceno
Teramo
Pescara
5689
L. Trasimeno
Grosseto
3451
L.
Bolsena
Terni
Aquila
ABRUZZI
Chieti
Lanciano
MOLISE
Sulmona
8159
7490
100 fathoms
Sea
Dubrovnik
6217
Kotor (Cattaro)
Cetinje
MONTENEGRO
9524
Titograd
Dakovica
Prizren
Kukës
ALBANIA
Shkodër
(Scutari)
9055
MACEDONIA
Priština
Vranje
6309
Kyustendil
9593
Dimitrovo
(Pernik)
Dimitrovgrad
Pazardzh
7192

vitavecchia
Rome
(Roma)
Ostia
Tivoli
Frascati
Lepini Mts.
Anzio
LATIUM
Cassino
6726
Gaeta
Campobasso
15°E
3454
Termoli
C. Gargano
Foggia
Barletta
Cerignola
Molfetta
Bari
Durrës
(Durazzo)
Elbasan
3650
Tirane
(Tirana)
20°E
Prilep
Bitola
(Monastir)
Tito Veles
Štip
Strumica
Pirin
Drama
Serrai
Prespa
L.
Edhessa
MACEDONIA
Florina
GREECE
Salonica
(Thessaloniki)

Continued on pages 30-31

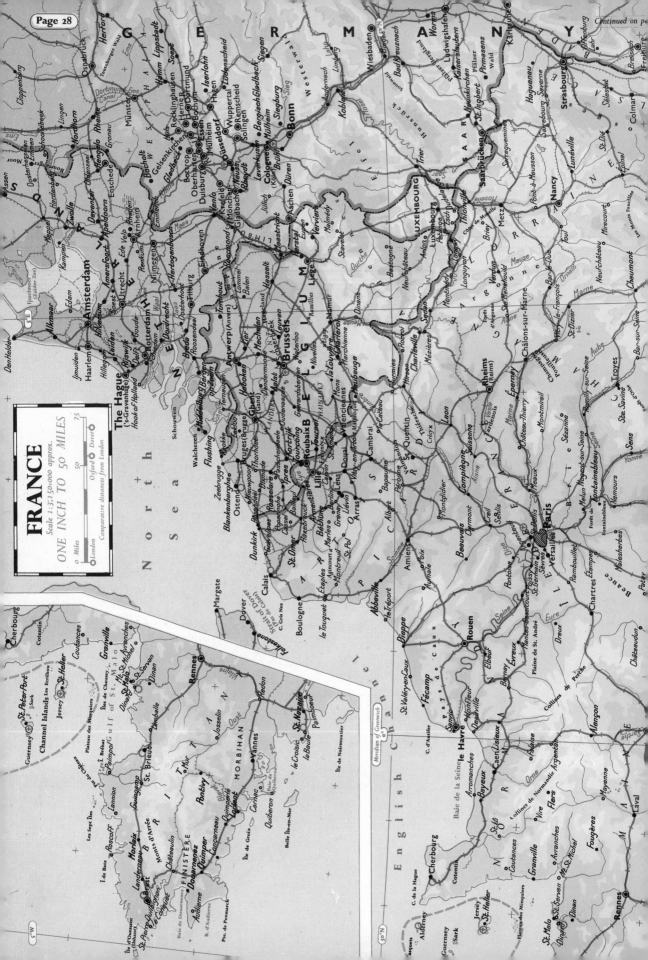

Continued on pa

FRANCE

Scale 1:3,150,000 approx.

ONE INCH TO 50 MILES

o Miles 50 75

Comparative distances from London

Oxford o o Dover

o London

SWITZERLAND ITALY

Conical Orthomorphic Projection

Meridian of Greenwich

Gulf of Lions

Bay of Biscay

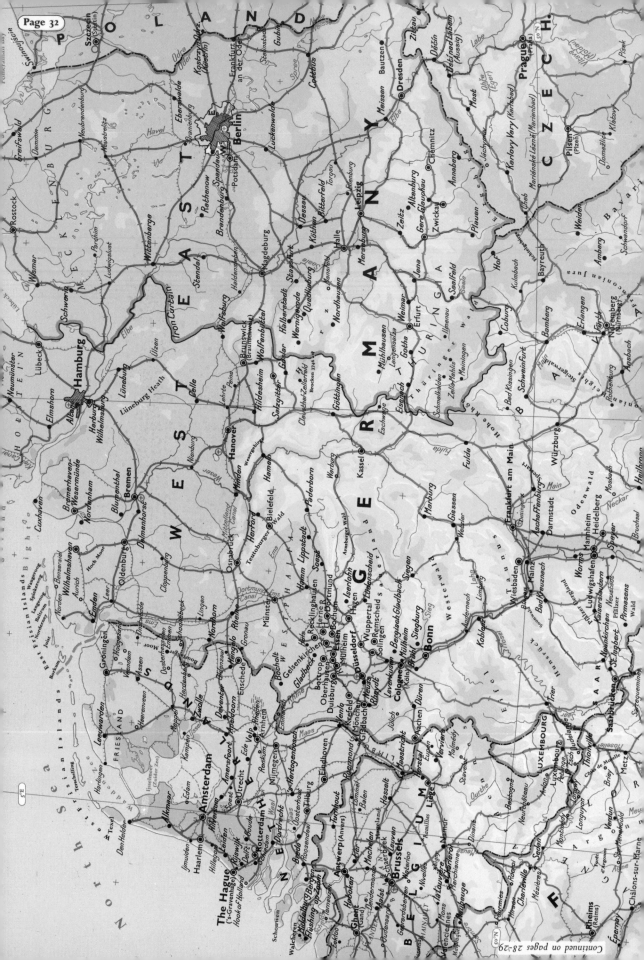

Continued on pages 28-29

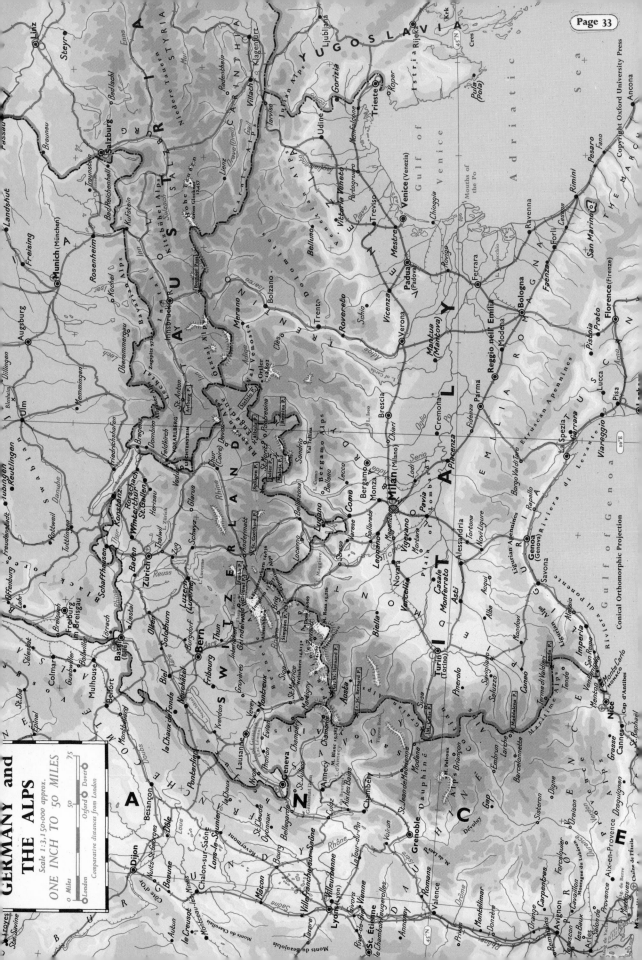

GERMANY and THE ALPS

Scale 1:3,150,000 approx.

ONE INCH TO 50 MILES

0 Miles   50   75

London ● Oxford ◐ Dover ◉

Comparative distances from London

Conical Orthomorphic Projection

Copyright Oxford University Press

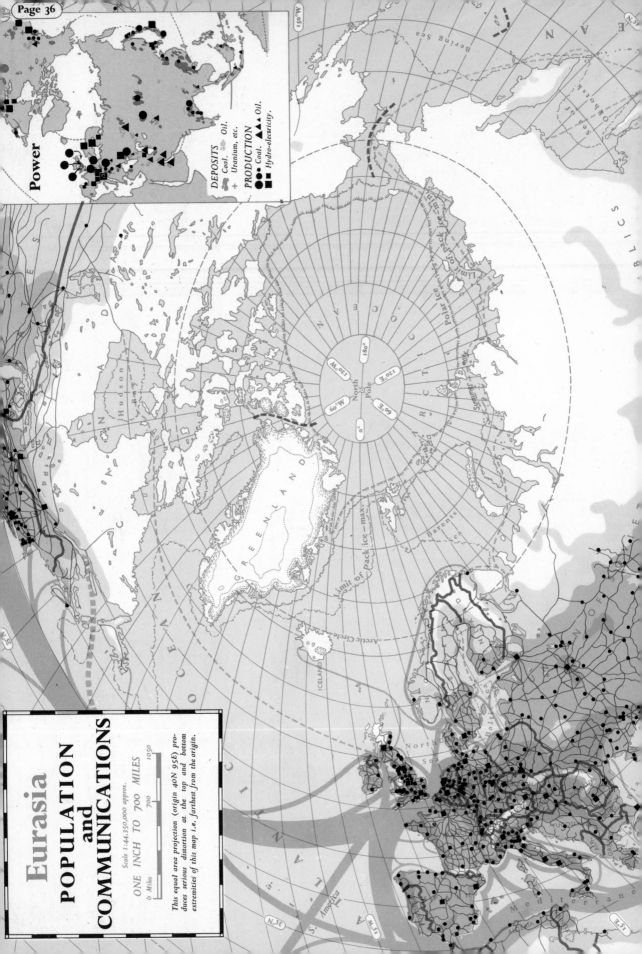

Power

DEPOSITS
- Coal.   Oil.
- + Uranium, etc.

PRODUCTION
- ●● Coal.   ▲▲ Oil.
- ●■ Coal.   ■ Hydro-electricity.

Eurasia
POPULATION and COMMUNICATIONS

Scale 1:44,350,000 approx.

ONE INCH TO 700 MILES

0 Miles   700   1050

This equal area projection (origin 40N 95E) produces serious distortion at the top and bottom
extremities of this map i.e. farthest from the origin.

North Pole

180°

130°W   120°E

60°W   60°E

0°

ARCTIC OCEAN

Limit of pack ice — max.

Limit of pack-ice — min.

Polar ice

Summer ice

Barents Sea

GREENLAND

ICELAND

Arctic Circle

Hudson Bay

CANADA

North Sea

Baltic Sea

Mediterranean

Bering Sea

REPUBLICS

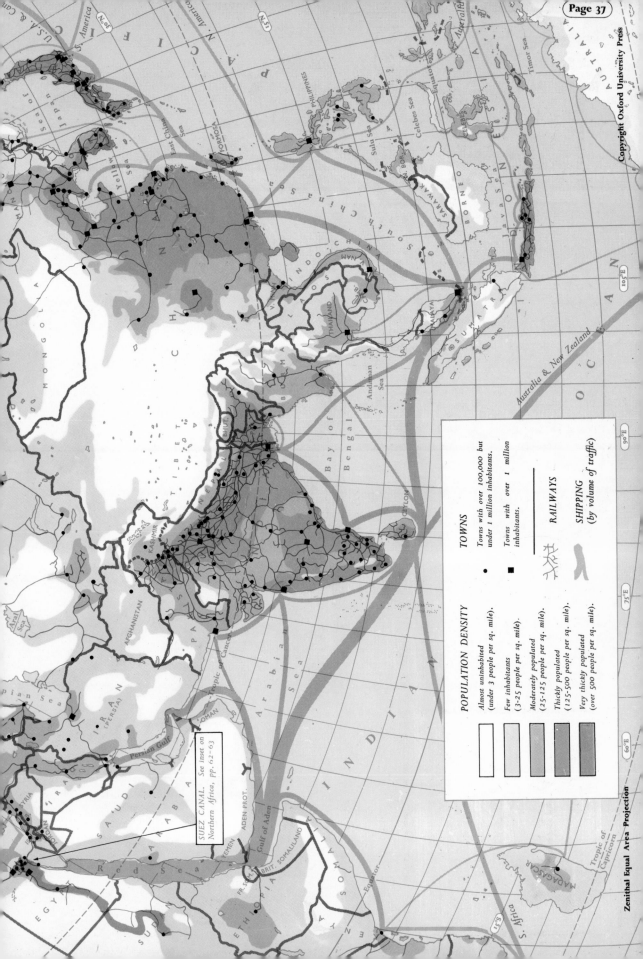

POPULATION DENSITY

Almost uninhabited
(under 3 people per sq. mile).

Few inhabitants
(3-25 people per sq. mile).

Moderately populated
(25-125 people per sq. mile).

Thickly populated
(125-500 people per sq. mile).

Very thickly populated
(over 500 people per sq. mile).

TOWNS

Towns with over 100,000 but
under 1 million inhabitants.   ●

Towns with over 1 million
inhabitants.   ■

RAILWAYS

_____

SHIPPING
(by volume of traffic)

SUEZ CANAL. See inset on
Northern Africa, pp. 62-63.

Zenithal Equal Area Projection

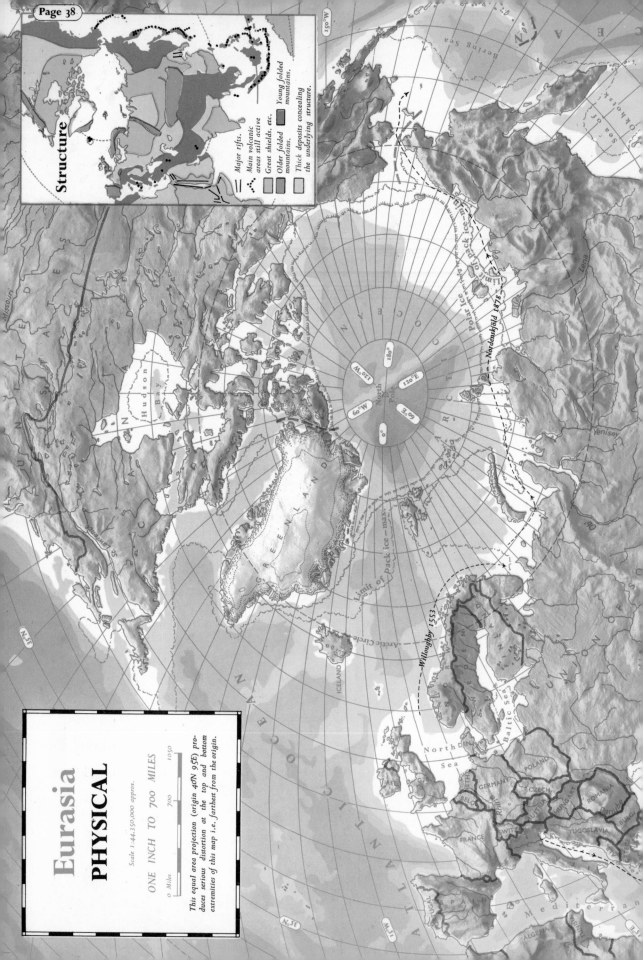

Structure

Major rifts.

Main volcanic
areas still active

Great shields, etc.

Older folded
mountains.

Young folded
mountains.

Thick deposits concealing
the underlying structure.

Eurasia
PHYSICAL

Scale 1:44,350,000 approx.

ONE INCH TO 700 MILES

0 Miles   700   1050

This equal area projection (origin 40°N 95°E) produces serious distortion at the top and bottom
extremities of this map i.e. farthest from the origin.

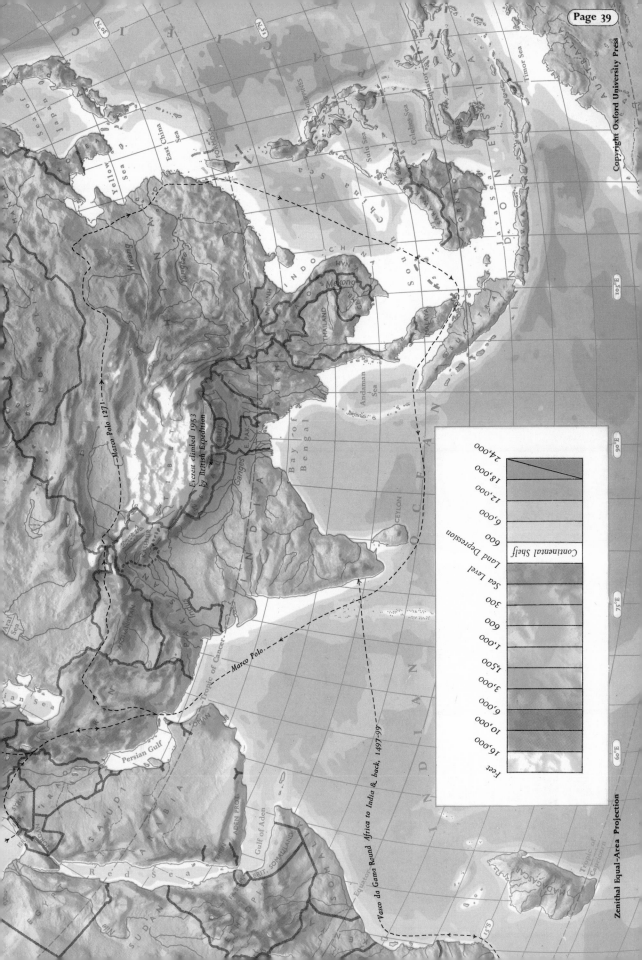

Zenithal Equal-Area Projection

Yellow Sea

East China Sea

FORMOSA

MANCHURIA

KOREA

Japan

Sea of Japan

MONGOLIA

Hwang

Yangtze

TIBET

— Marco Polo 1271 —

Everest climbed 1953
by British Expedition

BHUTAN

E. PAK.

Ganges

INDIA

PAKISTAN

Indus

Aral Sea

Caspian Sea

IRAN

IRAQ

Persian Gulf

OMAN

— Marco Polo.

Tropic of Cancer

SAUDI ARABIA

ADEN PROT.

Gulf of Aden

BRIT. SOMALILAND

ITAL. SOMALILAND

ABYSSINIA

ETHIOPIA

SUDAN

KENYA

Red Sea

Vasco da Gama Round Africa to India & back, 1497–99

Equator

Tropic of Capricorn

MADAGASCAR

INDIAN OCEAN

Bay of Bengal

CEYLON

Andaman Sea

BURMA

THAILAND

LAOS

INDO-CHINA

Mekong

ANNAM

SOUTH CHINA SEA

MALAYA

SUMATRA

BORNEO

JAVA SEA

Java

Sulu Sea

Celebes Sea

PHILIPPINES

CELEBES

TIMOR

Timor Sea

AUSTRALIA

PACIFIC OCEAN

15°N

15°S

105°E

90°E

75°E

60°E

Feet	
24,000	
18,000	
12,000	
6,000	
600	
Land Depression	
Sea Level	
Continental Shelf	
300	
600	
1,000	
1500	
3,000	
6,000	
10,000	
16,000	

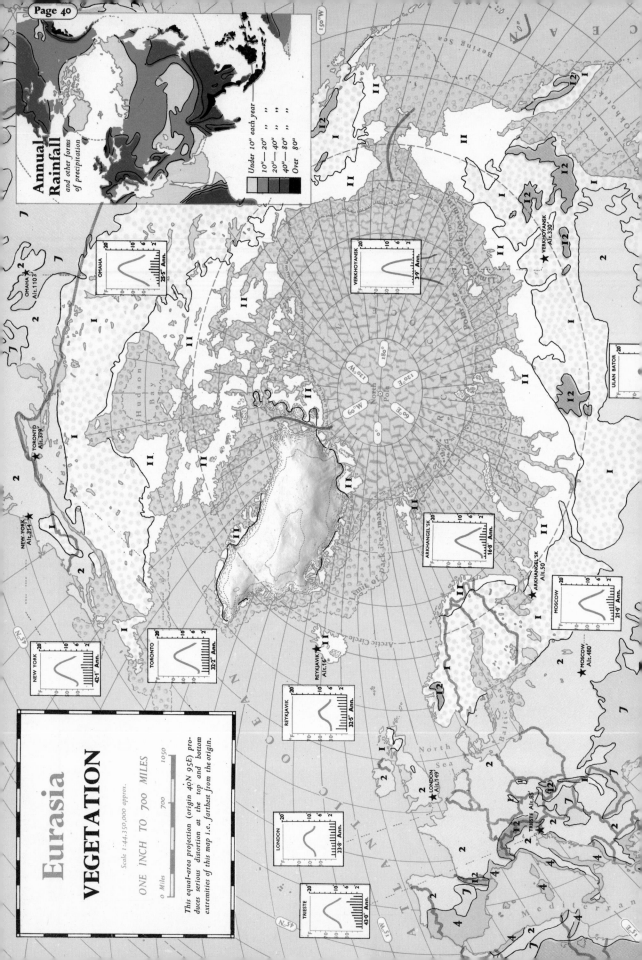

Eurasia
VEGETATION

Scale 1:44,350,000 approx.

ONE INCH TO 700 MILES

0 Miles   700   1050

*This equal-area projection (origin 40N 95E) pro-
duces serious distortion at the top and bottom
extremities of this map i.e. farthest from the origin.*

Annual Rainfall
*and other forms
of precipitation*

	Under 10" each year
	10"—20" " "
	20"—40" " "
	40"—80" " "
	Over 80" " "

OMAHA Alt.1103'
OMAHA   25·5" Ann.

VERKHOYANSK Alt.330'
VERKHOYANSK   3·9" Ann.

ULAN BATOR

ARKHANGEL'SK
ARKHANGEL'SK   16·8" Ann.

MOSCOW Alt.480'
MOSCOW   21·0" Ann.

NEW YORK Alt.31'
NEW YORK   42·1" Ann.

TORONTO Alt.379'
TORONTO   32·2" Ann.

REYKJAVIK Alt.16'
REYKJAVIK   32·5" Ann.

LONDON Alt.149'
LONDON   23·8" Ann.

TRIESTE Alt.85'
TRIESTE   43·0" Ann.

North Pole

Bering Sea

Hudson Bay

North Sea

Baltic Sea

Mediterranean

Arctic Circle

Limit of pack-ice max.

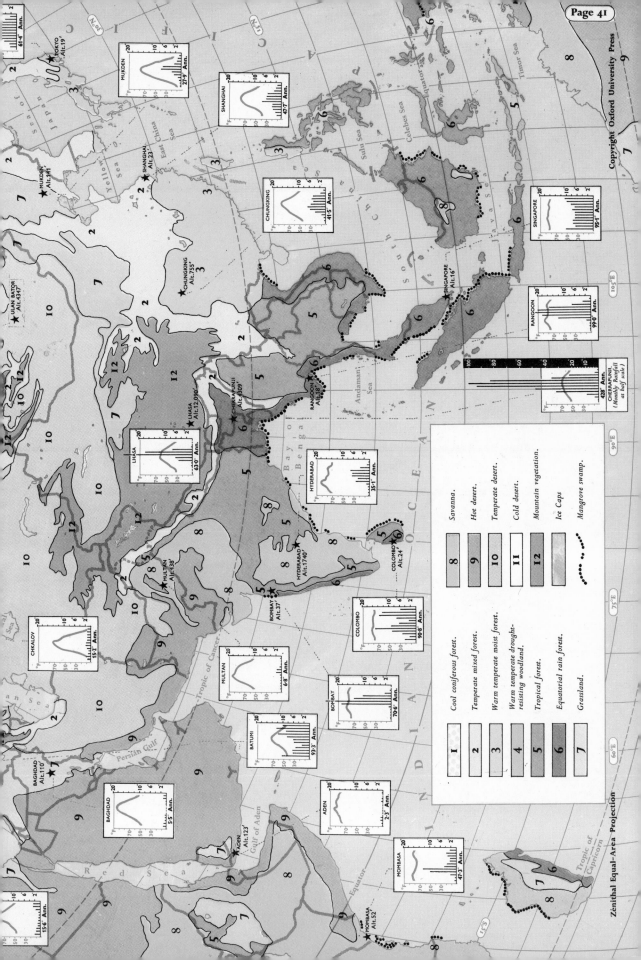

Zenithal Equal-Area Projection

Legend:

I	Cool coniferous forest.
2	Temperate mixed forest.
3	Warm temperate moist forest.
4	Warm temperate drought-resisting woodland.
5	Tropical forest.
6	Equatorial rain forest.
7	Grassland.
8	Savanna.
9	Hot desert.
IO	Temperate desert.
II	Cold desert.
I2	Mountain vegetation.
	Ice Caps
	Mangrove swamp.

TOKYO Alt.19' 61·4" Ann.

MUKDEN Alt.141' 27·9" Ann.

SHANGHAI Alt.23' 47·7" Ann.

CHUNGKING Alt.755' 41·5" Ann.

SINGAPORE Alt.16' 95·1" Ann.

RANGOON Alt.18' 99·0" Ann.

CHERRAPUNJI (Monthly Rainfall at half scale) 428" Ann.

ULAN BATOR Alt.4347'

LHASA Alt.12,090' 63·0" Ann.

HYDERABAD Alt.1740' 35·1" Ann.

COLOMBO Alt.24' 90·8" Ann.

CHKALOV 15·2" Ann.

MULTAN Alt.438' 6·8" Ann.

BOMBAY Alt.37' 70·6" Ann.

BATUMI 93·3" Ann.

BAGHDAD Alt.110' 5·5" Ann.

ADEN Alt.123' 2·3" Ann.

MOMBASA Alt.52' 47·3" Ann.

ALASKA

North Pole

180°

160°E

140°E

120°E

100°E

80°E

60°E

C. Lisburne

Seward Peninsula

Nome

Bering Strait

St. Lawrence I. (U.S.)

International Date Line

Wiese I. (Vize)

Severnaya Zemlya

Bol'shevik I.

C. Chelyuskin

Novosibirskiye Ostrova

Lyakhov Islands

Wrangel I.

Ayon I.

Ambarchik

Ostrovnoye

Markovo

Anadyr'

Kamenskoye

Kavacha

Kommandor Is.

Taymyr Penin.

L. Taymyr

Nordvik

Tiksi

Kazachye

Kolyma Plain

Yukagir Plateau

Gydan (Kolyma) Range

Kamchatka

Petropavlovsk-Kamchatsk

Karaul

Dudinka

Noril'sk

Khatanga

Verkhoyansk

Cherskiy Range

Susuman

Magadan

C. Tolstoy

Okhotsk

Igarka

Central

Putoran Mts.

Siberian

Sangar

Verkhoyansk Range

Lena

Sea of Okhotsk

Sale

Nizhnyaya Tunguska

El'gyey

Yakutsk

Buyaga

Aldan

Nikolayevsk

Aleksandrovsk

Sakhalin (USSR)

Korsakov

Kholmsk

Plateau

S O C I A L I S T   R E P U B L I C

Olekminsk

Dzherba

Aldan

F E D E R A T E D

S

Stony Tunguska

Vitim

Leninskiy

Angara

Vilyuy

Komsomol'sk

Khabarovsk

Soviet Harbour

Sikhote Alin'

Wakkanai

Sapporo

Hokkaido

Ust'-Kut

Never

Zeya

Tyda

Chekunda

Blagoveshchensk

Bureya

Birobidzhan

Voroshilov

Suchan

Muroran

Hakodate

Amoran

Honshu

Tomsk

Krasnoyarsk

Tayshet

Bratsk

Zhigalovo

Mogocha

C H I T A

Bukachacha

Shihchan

Nunkiang

Tsitsihar (Lungkiang)

Harbin (Pinkiang)

Vladivostok

Kemerovo

Abakan

Stalinsk

Minusinsk

Cheremkhovo

Usolye

Irkutsk

Ulan-Ude

Daresun

Nerchinsk

Sretensk

Sherlovaya Gora

Hulun

Great Khingan Mts.

Chuho

Mutankiang

Kirin

Biysk

Shalym

Kyzyl

Chita

Aksha

Erentsab

M A N C H U R I A

Ulanhoto

Changchun

Uldza

Choibalsan

Tamtsak Bulak

Mukden (Shenyang)

NORTH KOREA

Pyongyang

Ulangom

Bulagan

Ulan Bator (Urga)

Anshan

Yingkow

Chinnampo

Dzhibchalantu

M O N G O L I A

Sain Shanda

Chengteh (Jehol)

Dairen (Dai'niy)

SOUTH KOREA

Seoul

Pusan

Hiroshima

Kobe

Dzhargalantu

Altai Range

Gobi Desert

Changkiakow (Kalgan)

Peking (Peiping)

Port Arthur

Chefoo

Weihaiwei

Shimonoseki

Nagasaki

Kyushu

Urumchi

Turfan

Qomul (Hami)

Kweisui

Paotow

Tientsin

G. of Chihli

Tsinan

Tsingtao

Yellow Sea

Ansi

Alashan

Yinchwan (Ninghsia)

Taiyuan

Anyang

Süchow (Tungshan)

Altyn Tagh

C H I N A

Continued on pages 50-51

Sining (Kaolan)

Lanchow

Sian

Tungkwan

Loyang

Nanking

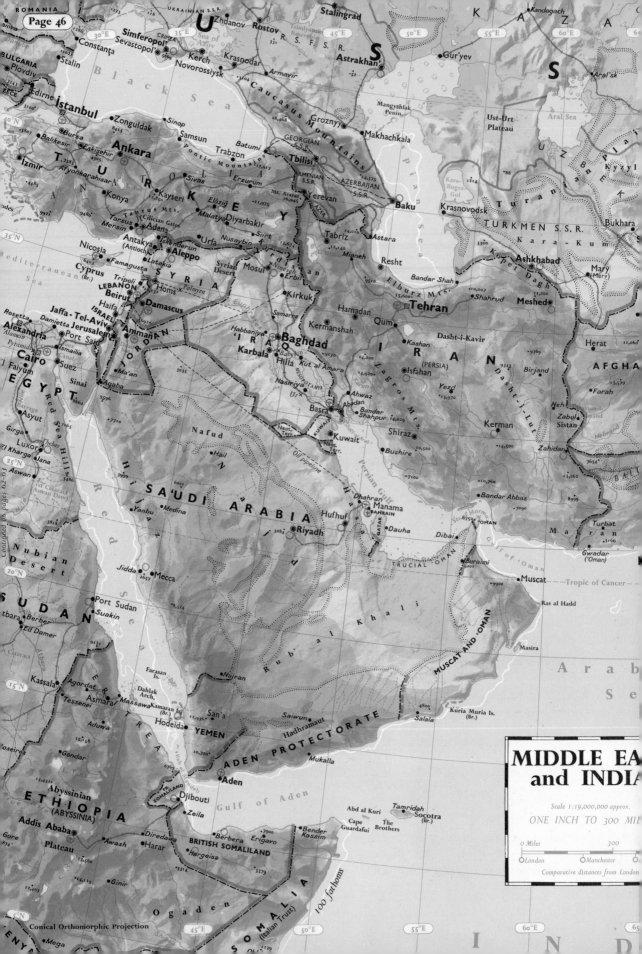

ROMANIA

BULGARIA
Plovdiv
Stalin
Edirne İstanbul
İzmir
Balikesir Eskişehir
Bursa
Nicosia
Cyprus
(Br.)

U R S S

Zhdanov Rostov Stalingrad Kandagach
Simferopol R.S.F.S.R.
Sevastopol Kerch Krasnodar Armavir
Novorossiysk Gur'yev Aral'sk
Black Sea Caucasus Mountains Groznyy Makhachkala
Sinop Samsun Trabzon Batumi GEORGIAN S.S.R. Mangyshlak Aral Sea Ust-Urt
Zonguldak Pontic Mountains Tbilisi Penin. Plateau
Ankara ANATOLIA Erzurum ARMENIAN AZERBAIJAN Kara- U Z B E
Sivas S.S.R. Bogaz Krasnovodsk Bukhara
Aryonkarahisar Kayseri Mt. Ararat Yerevan Gol TURKMEN S.S.R.
Konya TURKEY Elâzığ AZER. Baku Kara-Kum Ashkhabad
Tarsus Taurus Mts. Malatya Diyarbakir Tabriz Astara Kopet Dagh Mary
Mersin Adana Siirt Urmi Mianeh (Mery)
Antakya İskenderun Urfa Nusaybin Resht Bandar Shah Shahrud Meshed
(Antioch) Aleppo Kurdistan Mosul Erbil Elburz Mts. Tehran
Latakia Syrian Nineveh Hamadan Qum
Famagusta Desert Kirkuk Kermanshah Dasht-i-Kavir Herat
Tripoli Homs Palmyra Samarra Kashan Birjand AFGHA
LEBANON Damascus Isfahan IRAN
Beirut Habbaniya Baghdad (PERSIA) Dasht-i-Lut
Haifa Baby lon Karbala Kut al Amara Yezd
Jaffa - Tel-Aviv ISRAEL Amman IRAQ Hilla Ahwaz Kerman
Jerusalem JORDAN Nasiriya Basra Abadan Shiraz Zahidan
Damietta Ur Bandar
Port Said Ma'an Shahpur BAL
Rosetta Aqaba MESOPOTAMIA KUWAIT Bushire
Alexandria Neut. Kuwait Bandar Abbas Turbat
Ismailia Terr. Oil pipeline Neut. Str of Hormuz
Cairo Suez Nafud Terr. Persian Gulf OMAN Gwadar
EGYPT Sinai Hail Dhahran Manama ('Oman) Matran
Faiyum BAHRAIN Dauha Muscat
Asyut SAUDI ARABIA Hufhuf QATAR Dibai TRUCIAL OMAN Tropic of Cancer
Luxor Yanbu Buraimi Ras al Hadd
Aswan Medina Riyadh
Nubian MUSCAT AND OMAN Masira
Desert Rub al Khali
SUDAN Jidda Mecca Najran
Port Sudan ERITREA
Suakin Farasan San'a Saiwun Salala
Kassala Is. Hadhramaut
Agordat Dahlak Kamaran Is. ADEN PROTECTORATE Mukalla
Asmara Arch. (Br.) YEMEN
Tessenei Massawa Hodeida
Aduwa Abd al Kuri Tamridah
ETHIOPIA Aden Socotra The
(ABYSSINIA) FR. Djibouti Gulf of Aden Cape (Br.) Brothers
SOMALILAND Zeila Guardafui
Addis Ababa Bender
Plateau Harar Kassim
BRITISH SOMALILAND Hargeisa
Ogaden SOMALIA
Gore Mega (Italian Trust) 100 farthoms
Conical Orthomorphic Projection
KEN

Arab
Se

100 fathoms

MIDDLE EA
and INDIA
Scale 1:19,000,000 approx.
ONE INCH TO 300 MIL
0 Miles   300
London   Manchester
Comparative distances from London

Continued on pages 50/51

INDIAN OCEAN

CURRENTS — WARM — COLD

Scale 1 : 63,000,000

ONE INCH TO 1000 STATUTE MILES / 868 NAUTICAL MILES

Modified Zenithal Equidistant Projection Origin 0°, 70° E

SOUNDINGS IN FATHOMS

Continental Shelf
- 100 fathoms
- 1,000 fathoms
- 2,000 fathoms
- 3,000 fathoms
- 4,000 fathoms

Rainfall during the Summer Monsoon

- 5 Very heavy rainfall
- 4 Heavy rainfall
- 3 Moderate rainfall
- 2 Light rainfall
- 1 Practically no rain

Distances in Nautical Miles

Aden to Bombay	1,700	Colombo to Bombay	880	Mombasa to Fremantle	4,700
Aden to Durban	3,200	Colombo to Mombasa	2,600	Rangoon to Djakarta	1,600
Aden to Port Said	1,400	Durban to Colombo	3,600	Rangoon to Madras	1,000
Aden to Mombasa	2,100	Durban to Mombasa	1,800	Rangoon to Colombo	1,200
Alexandria to Suez	250	Fremantle to Durban	4,400	Rangoon to Durban	4,700
Basra to Bombay	1,600	Fremantle to Aden	4,900	Shanghai to Durban	7,000
Bombay to Durban	3,800	Fremantle to Singapore	2,200	Shanghai to Fremantle	4,300
Calcutta to Fremantle	3,700	Fremantle to Colombo	3,100	Singapore to Hong Kong	1,400
Colombo to Aden	2,100	Istanbul to Suez	890	Singapore to Durban	5,000
Colombo to Calcutta	1,200	Karachi to Basra	1,500	Singapore to Calcutta	1,600
Colombo to Djakarta	1,800	Karachi to Calcutta	2,600	Singapore to Colombo	1,600
Colombo to Hong Kong	3,000	Karachi to Fremantle	4,500	Suez to Aden	1,300
Colombo to Karachi	1,300			Suez to Karachi	2,800

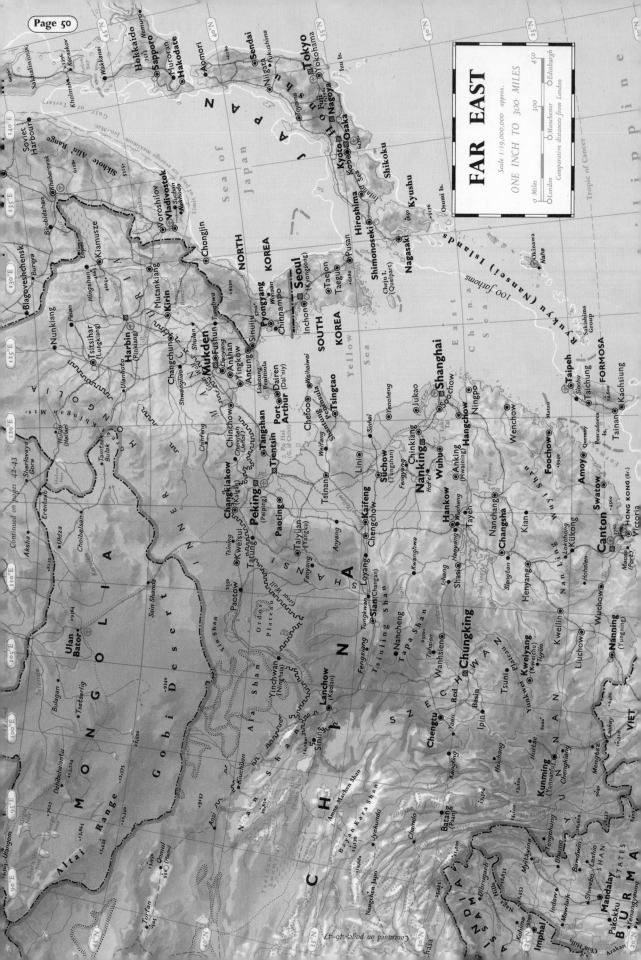

FAR EAST

Scale 1:19,000,000 approx.

ONE INCH TO 300 MILES

Comparative distances from London

Continued on pages 42-43

Continued on pages 46-47

Caroline

Islands
(U.S. Trust.)

Palau
Is.

Biak

Manokwari

Japen

NETHERLANDS

NEW

Berau Peninsula

GUINEA

New Guinea

Waigeo

Misoöl

Aru
Is.

Kai Is.

Tanimbar
Is.

Arafura

Sea

Mobile

Morotai

Halmahera

Ternate

Moluccas
(Maluku)

Obi Is.

Buru

Amboina

Ambon

Ceram

Wetar

Alor

Babar
Is.

Dili

Timor (Port.)

Mindanao

Davao

Basilan

Jolo

Tawitawi

Celebes

Sea

Manado

Talaud
Is.

Sula Is.

Bandar

Lombor

Kupang

Timor

100 fathoms

Copyright Oxford University Press

PHILIPPINE

ISLANDS

Samar

Leyte

Cebu

Bacolod

Bohol

Iloilo

Panay

Negros

Zamboanga

Gulf of
Tomini

Celebes
(Sulawesi)

Gulf
of
Bone

Butung

Muna

Kabaena

Banda Sea

Maumere

Flores

Waingapu

Savu Sea

Sumba

Savu

Continued on pages 58–59

Luzon

Manila

Aparri

San Fernando

Bataan
Peninsula

Mindoro

Calamian
Group

Palawan

Sulu
Sea

Makassar

Strait of Makassar

Laut

Sumbawa

Singaradja

Bali
Sea

Kangean

INDONESIA

Paracel
Is. (China)

Mt.
Kinabalu

NORTH

BORNEO

Kudat

Jesselton

Labuan

Weston

Brunei

BRUNEI

Sandakan

Tarakan

Samarinda

Balikpapan

Bandjarmasin

Borneo
(Kalimantan)

Java

Sea

Madura

Bali

Lombok

South

China

Sea

100 fathoms

Bunguran Is. (Indon.)
(Natuna)

SARAWAK

Sibu

BRITISH

Simanggang

Serian

Kuching

Pontianak

Belitung
(Billiton)

Bangka

Semarang

Surabaja

Madiun

Malang

Surakarta

Bandung

Jogjakarta

Java

INDOCHINA

Tourane

Hue

VIET NAM

Saigon

Cholon

COCHIN
CHINA

Binhdinh

Phanrang

CAMBODIA

Kratié

Phompenh

x Angkor

Phnom

Anambas
Is. (Indon.)

Riau
Archipelago

Bintan

Lingga

Singkep

Teluk Betung

Krakatau

Palembang

Djakarta

Sumatra

THAILAND
(Siam)

Bangkok

Ayutthaya

Nakhon
Ratchasima

Ubon

Udon Thani

Dongrak

Mekong

Range

Saravakhet

Moulmein

Tavoy

Mergui

Tenasserim

Range

Chumphon

Chanthaburi

Gulf
of
Siam

Songkhla
(Singora)

Alor Star

George Town

Penang

Taiping

Ipoh

Kuala
Lumpur

Seremban

Malacca

MALAYA
(British)

Johore Bahru

Singapore

Kota Bharu

Kuantan

Medan

Strait of Malacca

Padang

Engganno

Mentawai Is.

Batu
Is.

Nias

Conical Orthomorphic Projection

Railways
under construction
Roads
Tracks

130°E · 135°E · 45°N · 140°E · Rishiri

Mutankiang · Lishuchen · Spassk Dal'niy · Sikhote Alin Range · Tetyukhe · Embetsu · Nav

Ningan · Mulingchen · Grodekovo · Tetyukhe-Pristan' · Asahikaw · Su

CHINA · Tungning · U · S · S · R · Otaru · Sapporo

Voroshilov · Ol'ga · 100 fathoms · Suttsu · Tomakomai

Wangching · Artem · Margaritovo · HOKKAIDO · Uchiura Bay · Muroran

Yenki · Hunchun · Vladivostok · 6080 · Suchan · Okushiri I. · Esashi · 5915

Hoeryong · Posyet · Nakhodka · Fukuyama · Hakodate · Ohata

Unggi · Limit of pack ice average maximum (Feb.-Mar.) · 3517 · Tsugaru Channel

Chongjin · NORTH · Misawa · Aomori · Hachi

KOREA · Hirosaki · Kosaka · Z

Kilchu · Noshiro · 6693 · M

Songjin · Sea of Japan · Akita · Morioka · 6280 · Ka

A · Yokote · Kitaki Mountains

Sakata · On Mts. · Ishino

Tsuruoka · Shinjo

Yamagata · Sendai

P · Sado · Yonezawa · Shibata · Niigata · 6640 · Fukushima

Wajima · Sanjo · Nagaoka · Wakamatsu · Koriyama · Taira

A · Noto Peninsula · Kashiwazaki · Shirakawa · 3814 · 100 fathoms

Take Islands · Nanao · HONSHU · Takada · 6994 · Abukuma Mts.

J · Takaoka · 9622 · Miakmi Mts. · Nikko · Hitachi

A · Kanazawa · Toyama · Nagano · Utsunomiya

SOUTH · Yongdok · Oki Is. · Fukui · 8865 · Maebashi · Kiryu · Mito

KOREA · Pohang · Takasaki · Matsumoto · Chichibu · Kawagoe · Choshi

Kyongju · Kyoga Point · Wakasa Bay · 9698 · Kofu · Tokyo · Urawa · Chiba

Matsue · Tottori · Tsuruga · 10,466 · Hachioji · Kawasaki · Boso Peninsula

Hamada · Chugoku Mountains · 3008 · Gifu · Ichinomiya · Fuji · Yokohama

3995 · Tsuyama · 3081 · Ogaki · Yokkaichi · Omiya · Yokosuka · Numazu · Tateyama

Okayama · Otsu · Nagoya · 12,390 · Shizuoka · Sagami Gulf

Hiroshima · Kurashiki · 1656 · Himeji · Kyoto · Okazaki · 3368 · Izu Islands

Tsu · Yamaguchi · 2267 · Kobe · Osaka · Ueno · Nara · Toyohashi · Totomi Gulf

Islands · Kure · Iwakuni · Harima Gulf · Uji-Yamada · Hamamatsu · PACIFIC

Shimonoseki · Takamatsu · Sumoto · Anjo

Yawata · Moji · Ube · Imabari · Tokushima · Wakayama

Nogata · Kokura · Matsuyama · Shikoku Mts. · Kii Mts. · 6420

Fukuoka · Takawa · Iyo Gulf · Tanabe · Shingu

Sasebo · Kurume · Oita · Kochi · Tosa Bay

asaki · Usuki · Yawatahama · C. Muroto

Omuta · 5865 · Uwajima · SHIKOKU

Kumamoto · Shimabara · C. Ashizuri

Minamata · Nobeoka · Kyushu Mts. · 5650 · KYUSHU

Miyazaki

Kagoshima · Zenithal Equidistant Projection

Kanoya · 135°E · 140°E

Makurazaki

POPULATION
of Japan
85½ million approx.

JAPAN

Scale 1:6,300,000 approx.

ONE INCH TO 100 MILES

0 Miles · 100 · 150

◊London · ◊Oxford · ◊Bristol

Comparative distances from London

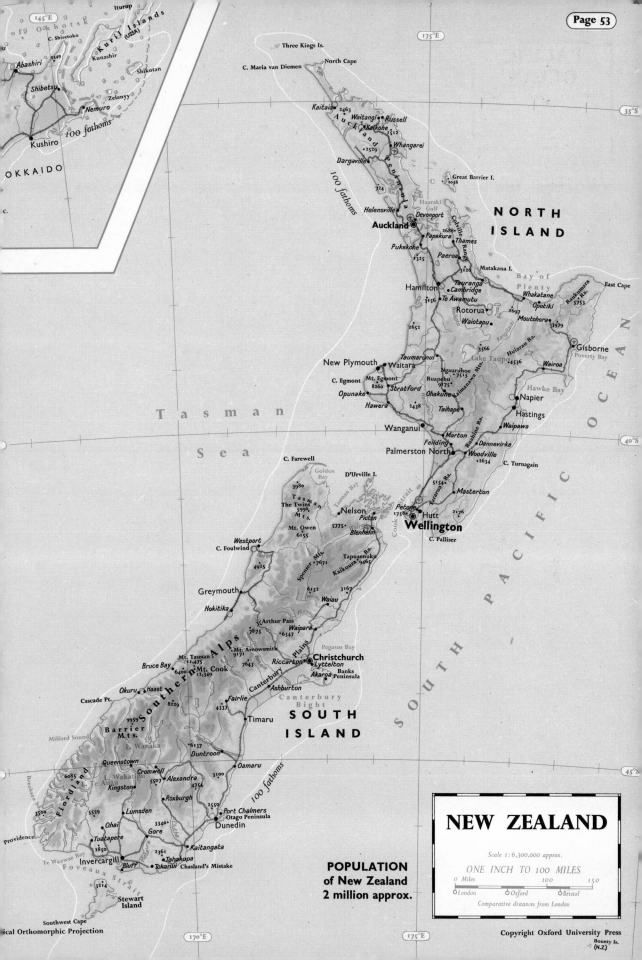

NEW ZEALAND

Scale 1 : 6,300,000 approx.

ONE INCH TO 100 MILES

0 *Miles*   100   150

○ *London*   ○ *Oxford*   ○ *Bristol*

Comparative distances from London

**POPULATION
of New Zealand
2 million approx.**

**NORTH
ISLAND**

**SOUTH
ISLAND**

T a s m a n

S e a

S O U T H   P A C I F I C   O C E A N

Southern Alps

Fiordland

Barrier Mts.

Stewart Island

OKKAIDO

Kuril Islands (USSR)

ical Orthomorphic Projection

Copyright Oxford University Press

Bounty Is. (N.Z.)

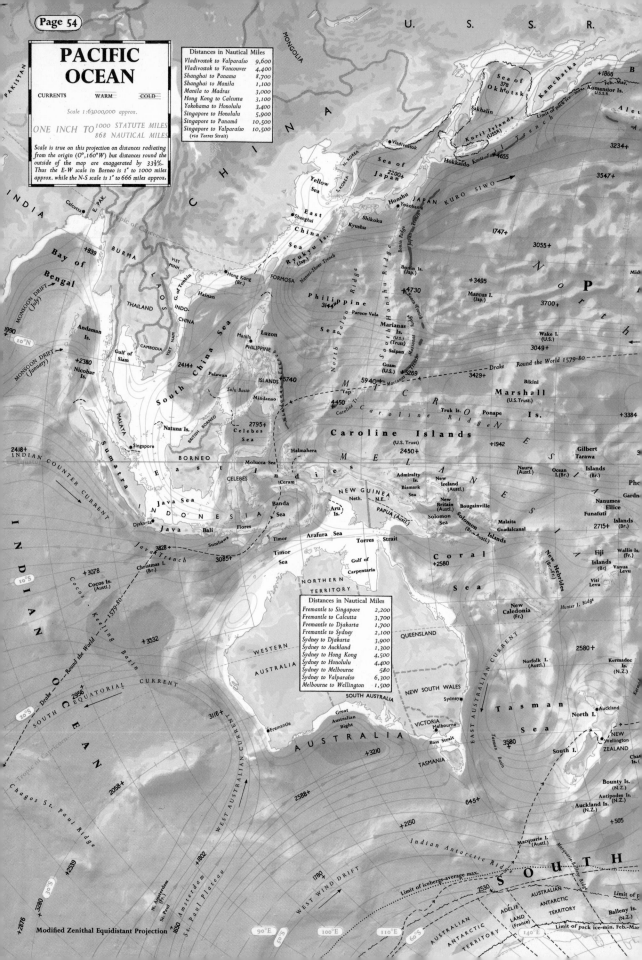

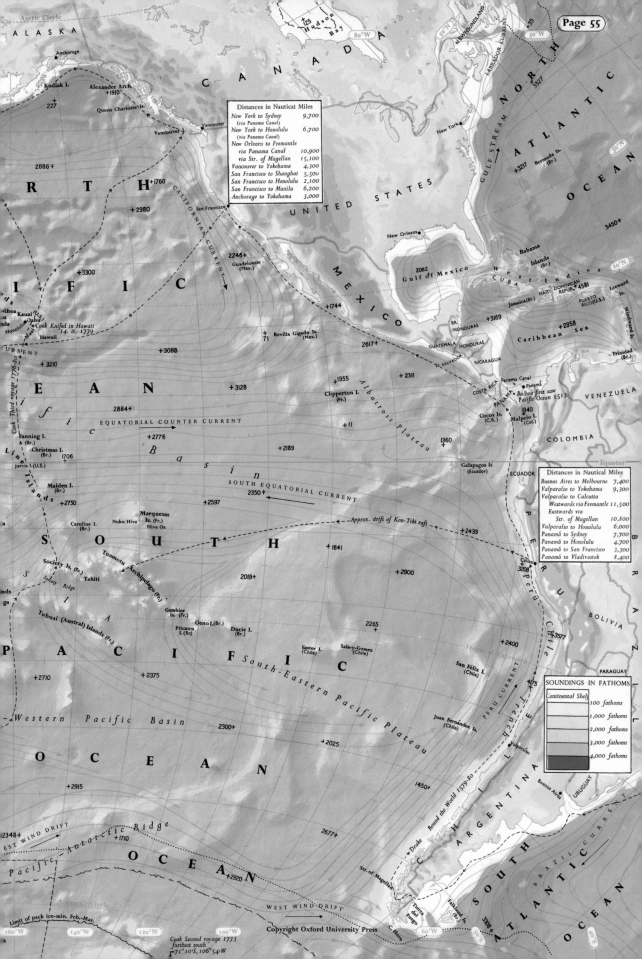

Arctic Circle

ALASKA

CANADA

Hudson Bay

NORTH ATLANTIC OCEAN

Anchorage

Kodiak I.
+227

Alexander Arch.
+1910

Queen Charlotte Is.

Vancouver

NEWFOUNDLAND

LABRADOR CURRENT

+35

2886+

+2980

+1760

CALIFORNIAN CURRENT

San Francisco

New York

GULF STREAM

+3217

Bermuda Is.
(Br.)

3327

3450+

Distances in Nautical Miles

New York to Sydney *(via Panama Canal)*	9,700
New York to Honolulu *(via Panama Canal)*	6,700
New Orleans to Fremantle	
via Panama Canal	10,900
via Str. of Magellan	15,100
Vancouver to Yokohama	4,300
San Francisco to Shanghai	5,500
San Francisco to Honolulu	2,100
San Francisco to Manila	6,200
Anchorage to Yokohama	3,000

UNITED STATES

MEXICO

New Orleans

Gulf of Mexico

2062

Bahama Islands (Br.)

West Indies

CUBA

HAITI

DOMINICAN REPUB.

PUERTO RICO (U.S.) +4581

Leeward Is.

Jamaica (Br.)

+3169

Caribbean Sea

+2958

Trinidad (Br.)

Windward Is.

+3300

P A C I F I C

Niihau

Kauai

Oahu

Honolulu

Maui

Hawaii

Cook Knifed in Hawaii 14. II. 1779

+3210

CURRENT

2246+
Guadeloupe (Mex.)

+1744

+3088

Revilla Gigedo Is. (Mex.)
71

2617+

BR. HONDURAS

GUATEMALA

HONDURAS

EL SALVADOR

NICARAGUA

COSTA RICA

Panama Canal

Panamá

Balboa first saw Pacific Ocean 1513

VENEZUELA

E A N

Cook Third voyage 1776-80

Line Islands

Fanning I. (Br.)

Christmas I. (Br.)
1706

Jarvis I. (U.S.)

2884+

EQUATORIAL COUNTER CURRENT

+2776

+3128

+2189

+1955

Clipperton I. (Fr.)

+2311

+11

Albatross Plateau

1360

Galapagos Is. (Ecuador)

Equator

ECUADOR

Cocos Is. (C.R.)

1940

Malpelo I. (Col.)

COLOMBIA

S O U T H

Malden I. (Br.)

+2750

Caroline I. (Br.)

Nuku Hiva

Marquesas Is. (Fr.)

Hiva Oa

2350

SOUTH EQUATORIAL CURRENT

+2597

Approx. drift of Kon-Tiki raft

+2439

+1841

Callao

3208+

Distances in Nautical Miles

Buenos Aires to Melbourne	7,400
Valparaíso to Yokohama	9,300
Valparaíso to Calcutta	
Westwards via Fremantle	11,500
Eastwards via Str. of Magellan	10,800
Valparaíso to Honolulu	6,000
Panamá to Sydney	7,700
Panamá to Honolulu	4,700
Panamá to San Francisco	3,300
Panamá to Vladivostok	8,400

Society Is. (Fr.)

Tahiti

Tuamotu Archipelago (Fr.)

Society Ridge

2019+

+2900

PERU CURRENT

PERU CHILE

BOLIVIA

B R A Z I L

Tubuai (Austral) Islands (Fr.)

Gambier Is. (Fr.)

Oeno I. (Br.)

Ducie I. (Br.)

Pitcairn I. (Br)

2265

PARAGUAY

S O U T H

+2710

+2375

Easter I. (Chile)

Sala-y-Gomez (Chile)

San Félix I. (Chile)

+2400

Tropic of Capricorn

4175

+3577

SOUNDINGS IN FATHOMS

Continental Shelf
100 fathoms
1,000 fathoms
2,000 fathoms
3,000 fathoms
4,000 fathoms

South-Eastern Pacific Plateau

Juan Fernández Is. (Chile)

Valparaíso

P A C I F I C

Western Pacific Basin

2300+

+2025

+2915

1450+

Round the World 1579-80

CHILE TRENCH

ARGENTINA

Buenos Aires

URUGUAY

SOUTH ATLANTIC OCEAN

2348+

EAST WIND DRIFT

Pacific

Antarctic Ridge

+1710

O C E A N

+2920

2677+

Drake

Str. of Magellan

Tierra del Fuego

Falkland Is. (Br.)

C. Horn

3308+

BRAZIL CURRENT

Antarctic Circle

Limit of pack ice-min. Feb.-Mar.

160°W

140°W

120°W

100°W

WEST WIND DRIFT

Cook Second voyage 1773 furthest south 71° 10' S, 106° 54' W

60°W

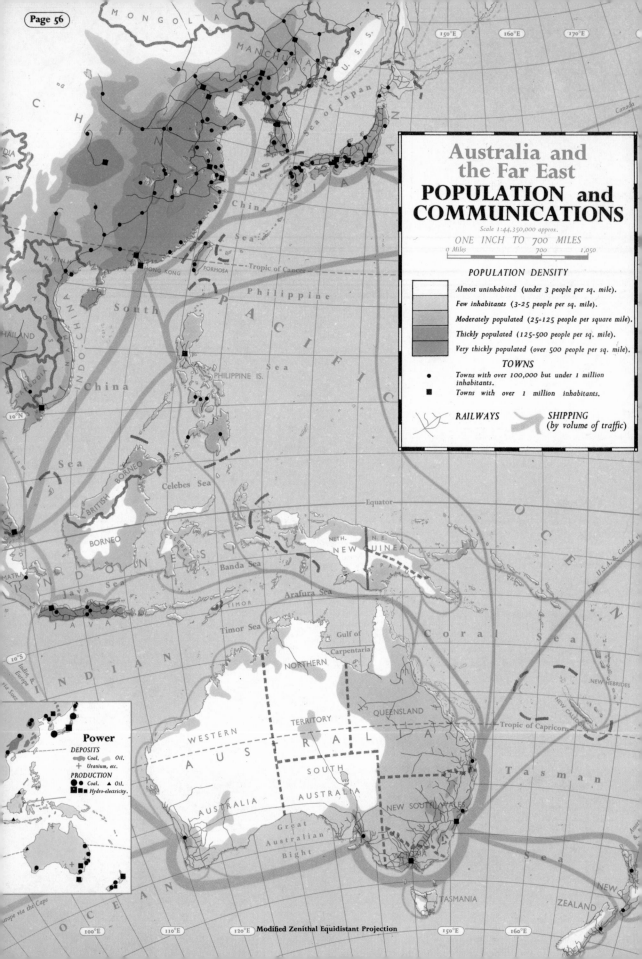

MONGOLIA

MANCHURIA

U.S.S.R.

C H I N A

Sea of Japan

V.MIN.&c.

HONG KONG

FORMOSA

Tropic of Cancer

East China Sea

China Sea

J A P A N

Philippine Sea

P A C I F I C

THAILAND

INDO-CHINA

China

CAMBODIA

LAOS

South

10°N

Sea

PHILIPPINE IS.

BRITISH BORNEO

Celebes Sea

BORNEO

CELEBES

I N D O N E S I A

SUMATRA

Java Sea

JAVA

Banda Sea

TIMOR

Equator

NETH. | N.E.
NEW GUINEA
PAPUA

Arafura Sea

Timor Sea

OCEAN

U.S.A. & Canada &c.

Coral

Sea

NEW HEBRIDES

NEW CALEDONIA

Gulf of Carpentaria

NORTHERN

TERRITORY

QUEENSLAND

Tropic of Capricorn

WESTERN

A U S T R A L I A

SOUTH

AUSTRALIA

Tasman

AUSTRALIA

NEW SOUTH WALES

Sea

India & Europe via Suez

I N D I A N

O C E A N

Great Australian Bight

VICTORIA

TASMANIA

NEW
ZEALAND

Europe via the Cape

Australia and the Far East
POPULATION and COMMUNICATIONS

Scale 1:44,350,000 approx.
ONE INCH TO 700 MILES

0 Miles   700   1,050

POPULATION DENSITY

Almost uninhabited (under 3 people per sq. mile).

Few inhabitants (3-25 people per sq. mile).

Moderately populated (25-125 people per square mile).

Thickly populated (125-500 people per sq. mile).

Very thickly populated (over 500 people per sq. mile).

TOWNS

● Towns with over 100,000 but under 1 million inhabitants.

■ Towns with over 1 million inhabitants.

RAILWAYS   SHIPPING
(by volume of traffic)

Power

DEPOSITS
⌒ Coal.   + Oil.
+ Uranium, etc.
PRODUCTION
● Coal.   ▲ Oil.
■ Hydro-electricity.

150°E   160°E   170°E

Canada

100°E   110°E   120°E   Modified Zenithal Equidistant Projection   150°E   160°E

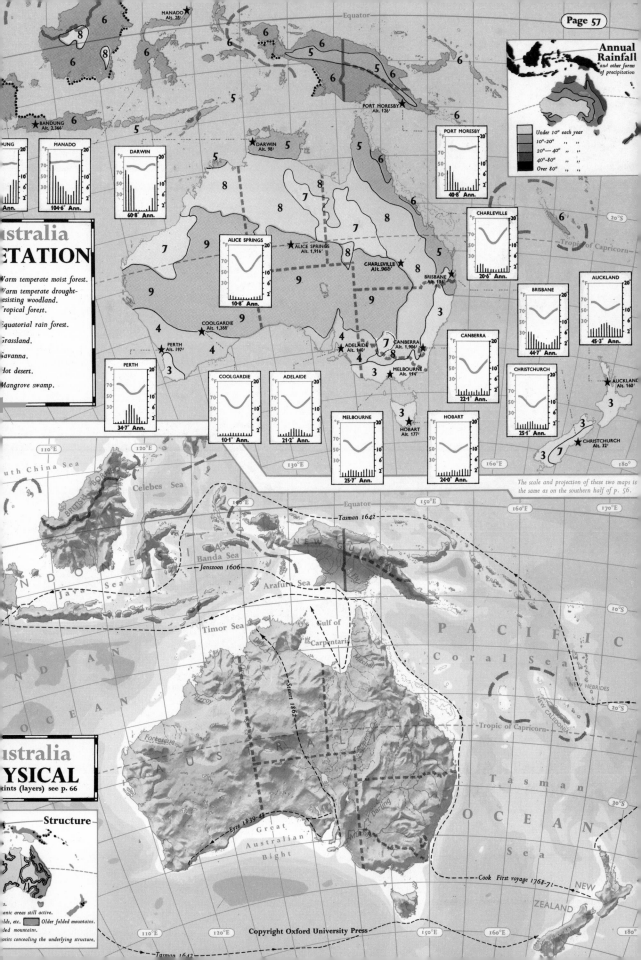

Annual Rainfall and other forms of precipitation

Under 10" each year
10"–20" "
20"–40" "
40"–80" "
Over 80" "

MANADO
Alt. 28'

BANDUNG
Alt. 2,366'

Equator

PORT MORESBY
Alt. 126'

DARWIN
Alt. 98'

PORT MORESBY
40·8" Ann.

CHARLEVILLE
20·6" Ann.

Tropic of Capricorn

20°S

BUNG
Ann.

MANADO
104·6" Ann.

DARWIN
60·8" Ann.

ALICE SPRINGS
Alt. 1,916'

ALICE SPRINGS
10·8" Ann.

CHARLEVILLE
Alt. 965'

BRISBANE
Alt. 134'

CHARLEVILLE
Alt. 965'

AUCKLAND
45·3" Ann.

BRISBANE
44·7" Ann.

AUCKLAND
Alt. 160'

ustralia
ETATION

Varm temperate moist forest.
Varm temperate drought-
esisting woodland.
ropical forest.

Equatorial rain forest.

Grassland.

Savanna.

Hot desert.

Mangrove swamp.

COOLGARDIE
Alt. 1,388'

PERTH
Alt. 197'

ADELAIDE
Alt. 140'

CANBERRA
Alt. 1,906'

MELBOURNE
Alt. 114'

CANBERRA
22·1" Ann.

CHRISTCHURCH
25·1" Ann.

PERTH
34·7" Ann.

COOLGARDIE
10·1" Ann.

ADELAIDE
21·2" Ann.

MELBOURNE
25·7" Ann.

HOBART
Alt. 177'

HOBART
24·0" Ann.

AUCKLAND
Alt. 160'

CHRISTCHURCH
Alt. 32'

160°E

180°

The scale and projection of these two maps is the same as on the southern half of p. 56.

110°E   120°E   130°E

uth China Sea   Celebes Sea   Banda Sea   140°E   Equator   150°E   160°E   170°E

Janszoon 1606   Arafura Sea   NEW GUINEA   Tasman 1642

Timor Sea   Gulf of Carpentaria   PACIFIC   10°S

ustralia
YSICAL

ints (layers) see p. 66

NDIAN   OCEAN   Fortescue   Stuart 1862   AUSTRALIA   Coral Sea   NEW HEBRIDES

Tropic of Capricorn   20°S

Eyre 1839-41   Darling   Murray   NEW CALEDONIA   Tasman   OCEAN   30°S

Structure

anic areas still active.
lds, etc.   Older folded mountains.
mountains,
sits concealing the underlying structure.

Great Australian Bight

Cook First voyage 1768-71   NEW ZEALAND

Copyright Oxford University Press

Tasman 1642

110°E   120°E   150°E   160°E   180°

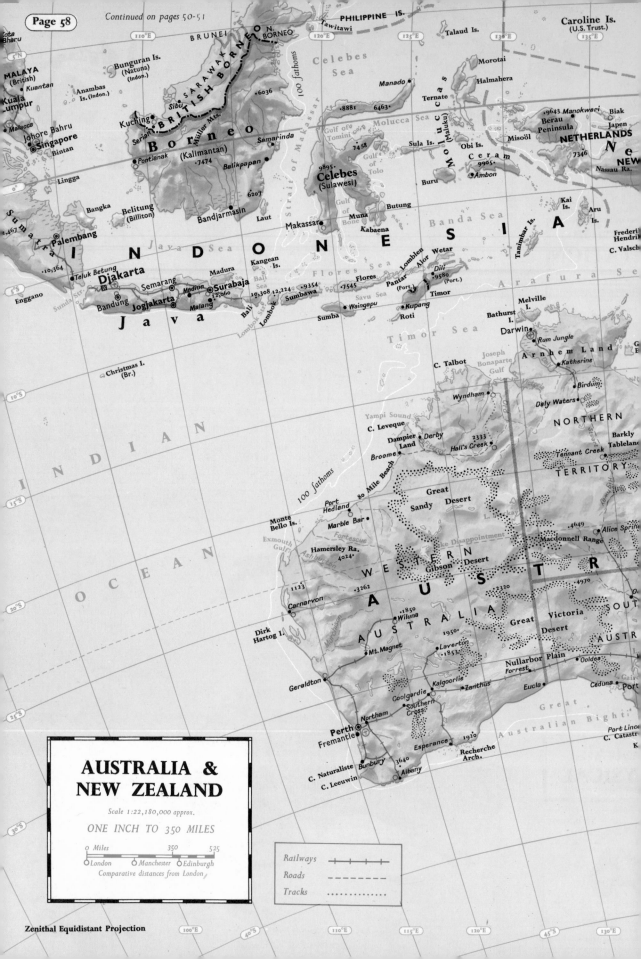

Continued on pages 50-51

PHILIPPINE IS.

Caroline Is.
(U.S. Trust.)

Kota
Bharu

MALAYA
(British)

Kuala
Lumpur

Kuantan

BRUNEI
BORNEO

SARAWAK BRITISH BORNEO

Tawitawi

Talaud Is.

Celebes
Sea

Morotai

Halmahera

Manado

Ternate

Berau
Peninsula

Manokwari

Biak

Japen

NETHERLANDS
N

NEW

Nassau Ra.

Anambas
Is. (Indon.)

Bunguran Is.
(Natuna)
(Indon.)

Sibu

Kuching

Serian

Müller Mts.

6036

Gulf of
Tomini

8881

6463

Molucca Sea

Sula Is.

Obi Is.

Misööl

7346

Malacca

Johore Bahru

Singapore

Bintan

Lingga

Pontianak

Borneo
(Kalimantan)

7474

Samarinda

Balikpapan

7458

Gulf
of
Tolo

Ceram

9905

Buru

Ambon

9643

Sumatra
2,467

Palembang

10,364

Bangka

Belitung
(Billiton)

6207

Bandjarmasin

Laut

9895

Celebes
(Sulawesi)

Makassar

Gulf
of
Bone

Muna

Kabaena

Butung

Banda Sea

Kai
Is.

Aru
Is.

Frederi
Hendri

C. Valsch

Teluk Betung

Djakarta

Semarang

Djava Sea

Madura

Kangean Is.

Flores Sea

Flores

Pantar
(Port.)

Alor

Wetar

Lomblen

Dili
(Port.)

9580

Tanimbar Is.

Arafura Sea

Enggano

Bandung

Jogjakarta

Medan

12,060

Malang

Surabaja

10,308 12,224

Sumbawa

9354

7545

Waingapu

Timor

Kupang

Roti

Melville
I.

Bathurst
I.

Darwin

Rum Jungle

Arnhem Land

Katherine

Java

Bali

Lombok

Lombok Str.

Sumba

Savu Sea

Timor Sea

C. Talbot

Joseph
Bonaparte
Gulf

Birdum

Daly Waters

NORTHERN

Christmas I.
(Br.)

Wyndham

Yampi Sound

C. Leveque

Dampier
Land

Derby

2333

Hall's Creek

Broome

Barkly
Tableland

Tennant Creek

TERRITORY

INDIAN

100 fathoms

Port
Hedland

80 Mile Beach

Great
Sandy Desert

Monte
Bello Is.

Marble Bar

Fortescue

Exmouth
Gulf

Hamersley Ra.
4024

Ashburton

Lake Disappointment

4649

Alice Sprin

Macdonnell Range

OCEAN

1123

3262

Carnarvon

WESTERN

Gibson Desert

AUSTR

2320

470

Dirk
Hartog I.

1850

Wiluna

AUSTRALIA

Great Victoria
Desert

SOUT

AUSTR

Mt. Magnet

1950

Laverton

1853

Nullarbor Plain

Forrest

Ooldea

Geraldton

Coolgardie

Kalgoorlie

Zanthus

Eucla

Caduna

Gair

Port

Southern
Cross

Northam

Perth

Fremantle

Esperance

1920

Recherche
Arch.

Great

Australian Bight

Port Lince

C. Catastr

C. Naturaliste

Bunbury

364

Albany

C. Leeuwin

AUSTRALIA &
NEW ZEALAND

Scale 1:22,180,000 approx.

ONE INCH TO 350 MILES

0 Miles   350   525

London   Manchester   Edinburgh
Comparative distances from London

Railways	———	——	——	———
Roads	– – – – – – –
Tracks	· · · · · · · · · · · ·

Zenithal Equidistant Projection

Equator

Tarawa **Gilbert**

Nauru
(Austl.)   Ocean I.
                 (Br.)   **Islands**
                                                   (Br)

Admiralty Is.
Manus
TERRITORY   OF   NEW   Kavieng
          (Australian Trust)   GUINEA
                     New
                     Ireland   0°
Bismarck Archipelago   Rabaul

6053 New Britain

EAST NEW GUINEA   10,171   *Solomon Islands*
rck Ra.
           Lae •Finschhafen   Bougainville Choiseul   **(British)**   5°S
NEA Owen Stanley Ra. 13,230   Shortland Is. 2407   Santa
U 8497   Ganongga   New   Ysabel   3900   **Ellice**
(Austl.)   12,041   Georgia Vangunu
Gulf of   D'Entrecasteaux Is.   Honiara Malaita   Stewart Is.
Papua   Port   Guadalcanal 8005   Ulawa
York Moresby   100 fathoms   San Cristobal   Funafuti
                      Louisiade Arch.   Rennell I.   **Islands**
                          •2750   (Br.)   10°S
-3-   Santa Cruz Is.
    1922   Cherry I.
nsula   •Cooktown   C o r a l   Mitre I.
        4552•
yth •Cairns •Herberton   S e a   Espiritu   *Fiji Is.* (Br.)   15°S
Townsville   Santo   Vanua Levu
                                                     Malekula
Hughenden   3460•   Mackay   Chesterfield Is.   Efate   Viti Levu
Winton   (Fr.)   Eromanga   Suva
ongreach Rockhampton   2069•   New   Lau
Yaraka   Caledonia Nouméa   Group
Quilpie   •2240 Bundaberg   Tropic of Capricorn   (Fr.)   20°S
     1293• Charleville   Maryborough
Cunnamulla   Toowoomba •Brisbane
              Ipswich   •Lismore   Norfolk I.   25°S
        •Bourke   5100   •Grafton   (Austl.)
NEW   5279•
ken Hill •1706 Dubbo •4902   Maitland
SOUTH   4180• •Newcastle
     Orange Lithgow
Mildura WALES Katoomba •Sydney   30°S
Swan   Goulburn Wollongong
Hill Echuca •6263 Canberra   North Cape
VICTORIA Albury Wangaratta   •2529 Keikoho
Bendigo •6102   Cape Howe   T a s m a n   Auckland
Ballarat Geelong   Hamilton   35°S
King I. Bass Furneaux   S e a   NORTH ISLAND
        Strait Group   New Plymouth 5753•
Burnie •5160 St. Mary's   8265   •9275 Gisborne
Launceston   Napier
TASMANIA •4720   Westport 3980•   NEW
Hobart   SOUTH ISLAND Nelson   Wellington
              Greymouth 7671•
          12,349• Southern Alps ZEALAND   40°S
          9959•   •Christchurch
Invercargill •Dunedin
Stewart I.

South West AUSTRALIA

SAME SCALE

QUEENSLAND

WESTERN AUSTRALIA

Tropic of Capricorn

Coral Sea

Great Barrier Reef

Marion Reef

Abington Reef

Flinders Reef

Palm Is.

Magnetic I.
Townsville
3980

C. Bowling Green
Home Hill
Ayr
Ravenswood
Burdekin

Merinda
Proserpine
Hook I.
Whitsunday I.
Shaw I.
Repulse B.
Clarke Ra.
Owens Creek
Mackay
Cumberland Is.

Northumberland Islands
Long I.
Percy Is.
Broad Sd.
Shoalwater I.
Townshend I.
Port Clinton
C. Manifold

Leichhardt Ra.
Denham Ra.
Sutor
Belyando
Sellheim

Swain Reefs

Capricorn Channel
Curtis Channel
Gt. Keppel I.
Capricorn Group
Lady Elliot I.
Sandy Cape
Hervey Bay

Fraser or Great Sandy I.
Morton Bay
Sandgate

Rockhampton 1336
Mt. Morgan
Gladstone
Jambin
Lawgi
Nagoorin
Mackenzie
Dawson
2060
Marlborough

Expedition Ra.
Springsure
Emerald
Clermont
Buckland Tableland
Carnarvon Ra.
Great Dividing Range

Taroom
Surat
Roma
Mitchell
Chinchilla
Condamine
Dalby
Toowoomba
Darling
Bogne
3611
Crow's Nest
Redcliffe
Brisbane
Ipswich

Burnett Heads
Bundaberg
Childers
Maryborough
Gympie
1300
Nambour
Nanango
Kingaroy
Murgon
Murrego

Tambo
Augathella
1293
Charleville
Mitchell

Quilpie
Bulloo
Eromanga

Simpson Desert
Lake Yamma Yamma
Cooper's Creek
Wilson

Laverton
Leonora
Menzies
Kalgoorlie
Boulder
Coolgardie
Lake Cowan
Norseman
Lake Barlee
Southern Cross
Merredin
Goomalling
Cunderdin
Northam
Midland
Perth
Fremantle
Rottnest I.
Darling Ra.
Swan
Narrogin
Wagin
Boyup Brook
Katanning
Collie
Bridgetown
Bunbury
Augusta
Cape Leeuwin
Blackwood
Northcliffe
Nornalup
Stirling Ra. 3640
Albany
Point D'Entrecasteaux
Newdegate
Esperance 151
Recherche Archipelago
Hood Point
100 fathoms

Blue
Mt. Magnet
2156
1850
1195
1910
Mullewa
Three Springs
Northampton
Ajana 939
Geraldton
Houtman Abrolhos
Greenough
Dongara
Nangerr

INDIAN OCEAN

P. Naturaliste

100 fathoms

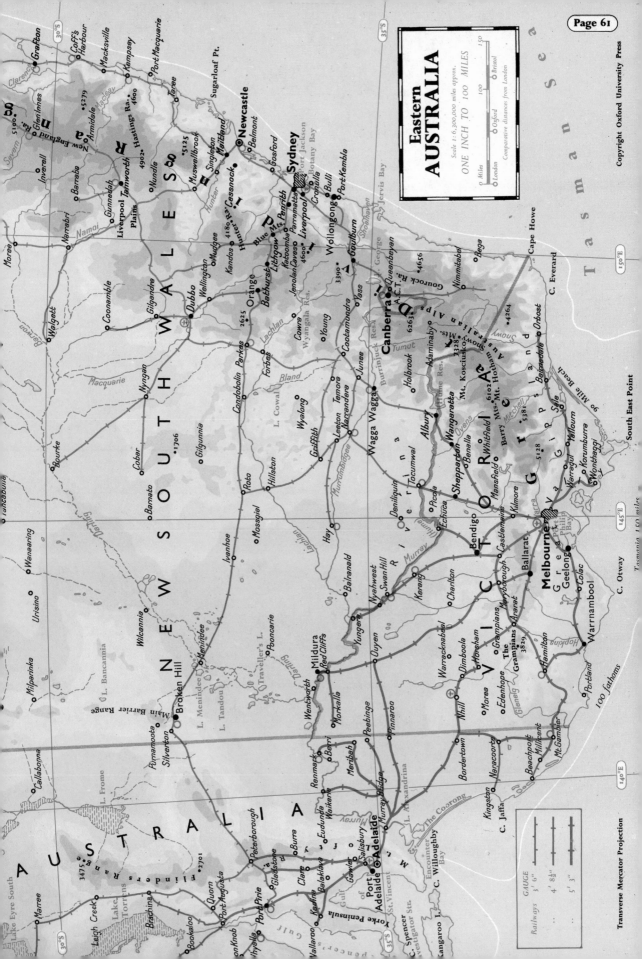

Eastern
AUSTRALIA

Scale 1:6,300,000 miles approx.
ONE INCH TO 100 MILES

Comparative distances from London

Transverse Mercator Projection

South East Point

GAUGE
Railways   3' 6"
    "   4' 8½"
    "   5' 3"

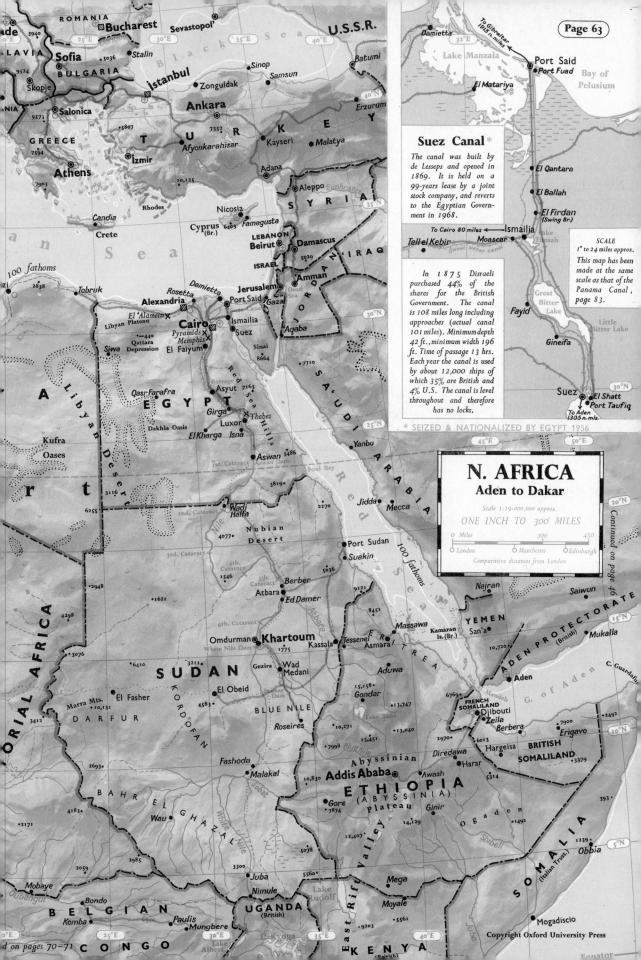

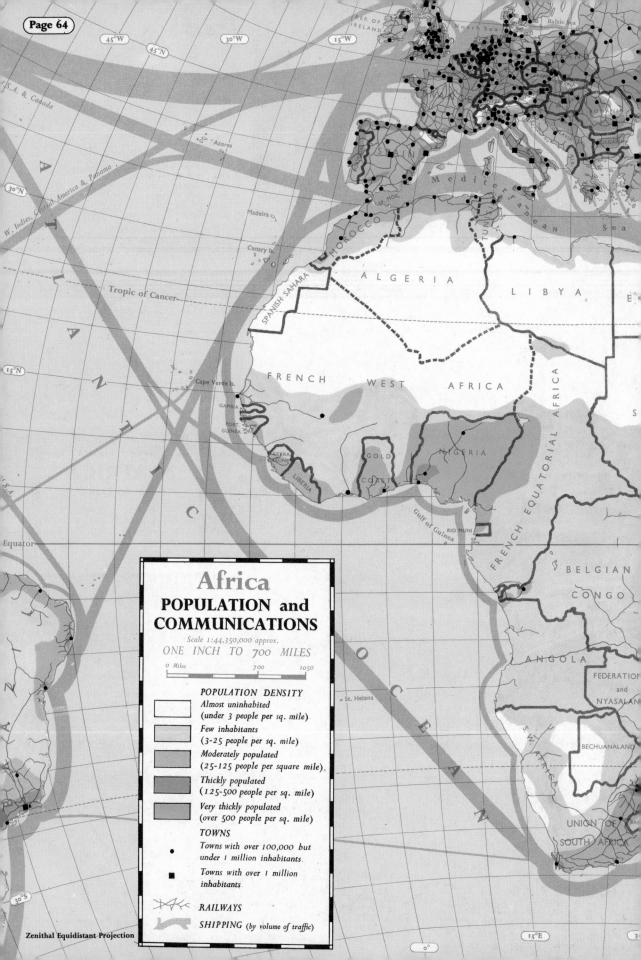

Africa
POPULATION and COMMUNICATIONS
Scale 1:44,350,000 approx.
ONE INCH TO 700 MILES

0 Miles   700   1050

POPULATION DENSITY
Almost uninhabited
(under 3 people per sq. mile).

Few inhabitants
(3-25 people per sq. mile)

Moderately populated
(25-125 people per square mile).

Thickly populated
(125-500 people per sq. mile)

Very thickly populated
(over 500 people per sq. mile)

TOWNS
• *Towns with over 100,000 but under 1 million inhabitants*

■ *Towns with over 1 million inhabitants*

RAILWAYS

SHIPPING (by volume of traffic)

Zenithal Equidistant Projection

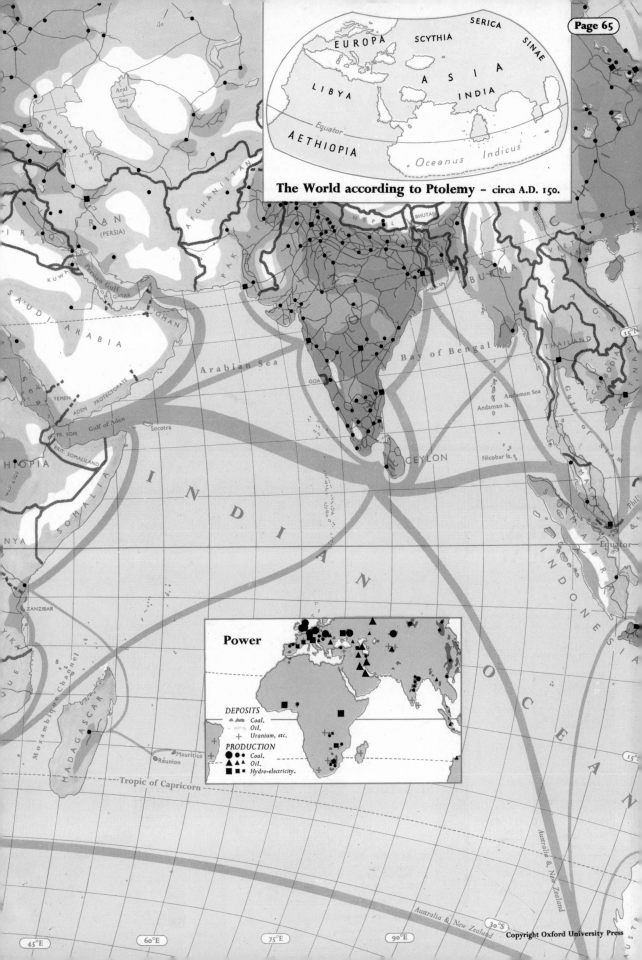

The World according to Ptolemy – circa A.D. 150.

EUROPA
SCYTHIA
SERICA
SINAE
LIBYA
A S I A
INDIA
AETHIOPIA
Equator
Oceanus Indicus

Aral Sea

Caspian Sea

IRAN (PERSIA)

IRAQ

KUWAIT

AFGHANISTAN

PAKISTAN

NEPAL

BHUTAN

BURMA

VIET

LAOS

THAILAND

CAMBODIA

Persian Gulf

QATAR

OMAN

SAUDI ARABIA

YEMEN

ADEN PROTECTORATE

FR. SOM.

BRIT. SOMALILAND

Gulf of Aden

Socotra

Arabian Sea

GOA

Bay of Bengal

Andaman Sea

Andaman Is.

CEYLON

Nicobar Is.

Gulf of Siam

ETHIOPIA

SOMALIA

NYA

ZANZIBAR

IKA

UE

Mozambique Channel

MADAGASCAR

Mauritius

Réunion

I N D I A N

O C E A N

INDONESIA

SUMATRA

Equator

Phil

Tropic of Capricorn

Australia & New Zealand

Australia & New Zealand

Power

DEPOSITS
- Coal.
- Oil.
- + Uranium, etc.

PRODUCTION
- ● Coal.
- ▲ Oil.
- ■ Hydro-electricity.

45°E   60°E   75°E   90°E

15°N

30°S

15°S

Mungo Park 1805

Park drowned

Marchand 1898

Bruce 1768

Speke & Grant 1861

Stanley & Livingstone met, 1871

Livingstone 1866

Livingstone died 1873

Livingstone 1853-56

Vasco da Gama Round Africa to India & back, 1497-99

Livingstone 1849

Tropic of Cancer

Equator

Tropic of Capricorn

Africa
PHYSICAL

Scale 1:44,350,000 approx.

ONE INCH TO 700 MILES

0 Miles   700   1,050

London   Geneva   Rome

Comparative distances from London

	Feet
	16,000
	10,000
	6,000
	3,000
	1,500
	1,000
	600
	300
	Sea Level
	Land Depression
Continental Shelf	600
	6,000
	12,000
	18,000
	24,000

Zenithal Equal-Area Projection

Structure

Major rifts.

Main volcanic areas still active.

Great shields, etc.

Older folded mountains.

Young folded mountains.

Thick deposits concealing the underlying structure.

Annual Rainfall
and other forms of precipitation

Under 10" each year

10" — 20"   ,,   ,,

20" — 40"   ,,   ,,

40" — 80"   ,,   ,,

Over 80"

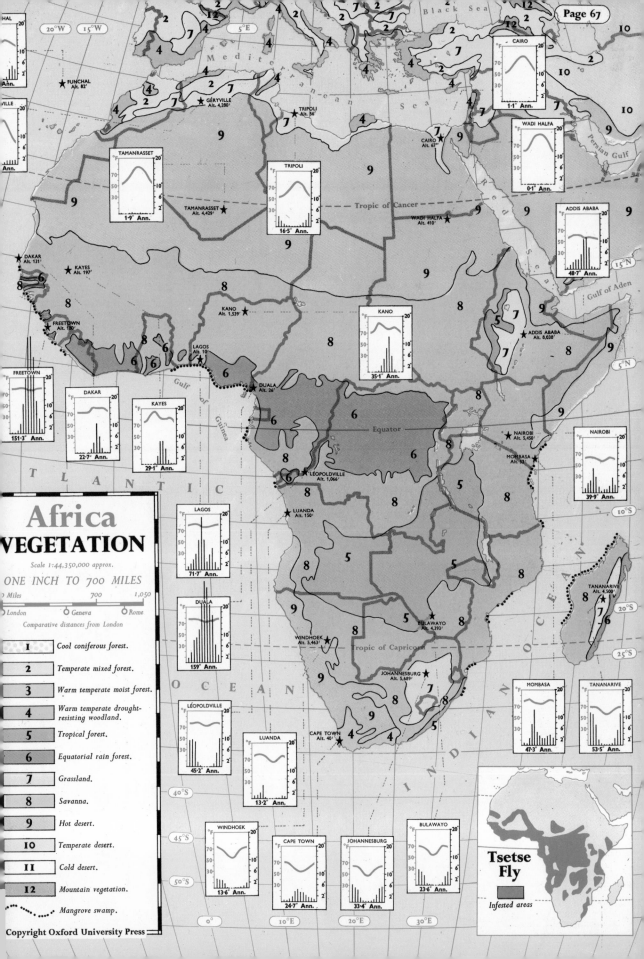

Africa
VEGETATION

Scale 1:44,350,000 approx.

ONE INCH TO 700 MILES

0 Miles	700	1,050

London Geneva Rome

Comparative distances from London

1	Cool coniferous forest.
2	Temperate mixed forest.
3	Warm temperate moist forest.
4	Warm temperate drought-resisting woodland.
5	Tropical forest.
6	Equatorial rain forest.
7	Grassland.
8	Savanna.
9	Hot desert.
10	Temperate desert.
11	Cold desert.
12	Mountain vegetation.
••••••	Mangrove swamp.

Copyright Oxford University Press

Tsetse Fly

Infested areas

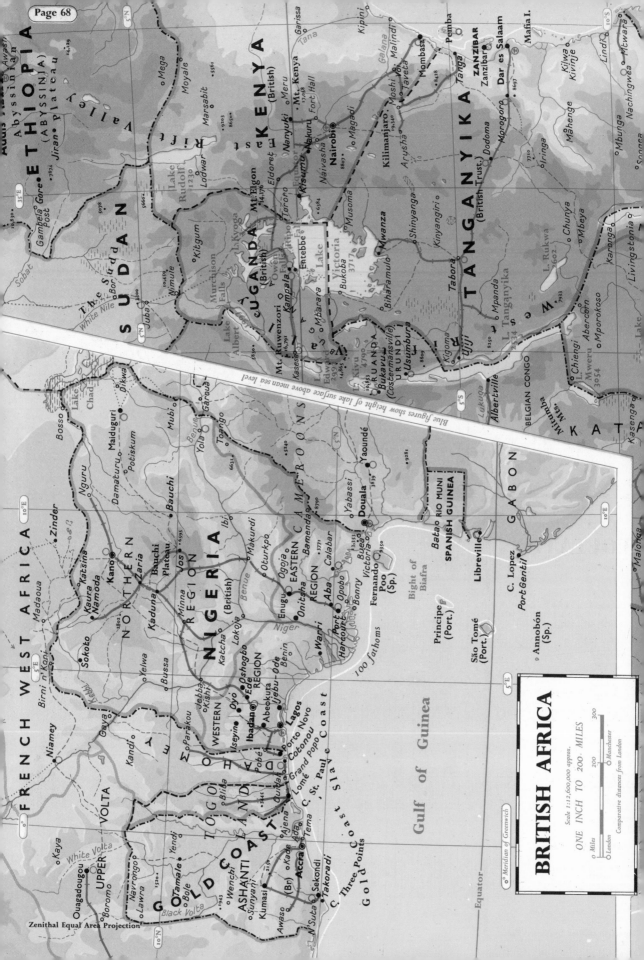

ETHIOPIA
(ABYSSINIA)

Abyssinian Rift
Jiran Plateau

Addis Ababa •
Awash

Gore •
Gambela •
Post

KENYA
(British)

Mega •
Moyale •

Mansabit •

Mt. Kenya
17058

Meru •

Nanyuki •
Nyeri •
Nakuru
Fort Hall

Lodwar •
Lake Rudolf
1130

Mt. Elgon
14176

Eldoret •

Kitgum •

Kisumu •
Kericho •

NAIROBI

Kilimanjaro
19340

Moshi •
Taveta •

Voi •
Malindi •

Mombasa

ZANZIBAR
Zanzibar

Dar es Salaam

Pemba

Tanga

Mafia I.

SUDAN

L. Kyoga

Murchison
Falls

UGANDA
(British)

KAMPALA
Entebbe

Owen
Falls

Jinja •

Lake Victoria
3717

Musoma •

Mwanza •

Shinyanga •

TANGANYIKA
(British Trust.)

Dodoma

Morogoro

Kilwa Kivinje

White Nile

Juba •

Nimule •

Lake
Albert

Mt. Ruwenzori
16791

L. Edward
2994

L. Kivu
4700

RUANDA
Bukavu
(Costermansville)

Usumbura

URUNDI

Kigoma
Ujiji

Tabora •

Mpanda •

L. Tanganyika
2534

Iringa •

Mbeya •

Chunya •

L. Rukwa
2602

Mahenge •

Mbunga •

Nachingwea •

Lindi

Mtwara

The figures show height of lake surface above mean sea level

FRENCH WEST AFRICA

Zinder •

Madaoua •

Nguru •

Damaturu •
Maiduguri

Potiskum •

NORTHERN
REGION

Kano

Zaria •

Bauchi •

Jos •
Plateau

Makurdi •

EASTERN
CAMEROONS

Yabassi •

Douala

Yaoundé •

GABON

BELGIAN CONGO

KATANGA

Mubi •

Dikwa •

Lake Chad

Bosso •

Kaduna •

Minna •

NIGERIA
(British)

WESTERN
REGION

Ibadan

Abeokuta •

LAGOS

Enugu •

Onitsha •

Aba •

Opobo •

Port Harcourt

Calabar •

Victoria •
Buea •

RIO MUNI
SPANISH GUINEA

Bata •

Fernando Poo
(Sp.)

Bight of Biafra

Principe
(Port.)

São Tomé
(Port.)

C. Lopez
Port Gentil

Libreville

Annobón
(Sp.)

Sokoto •

Katsina •
Kaura
Namoda •

Katcha •

Oyo •
Ede •
Oshogbo •

Ijebu-Ode •

Ado •
Benin •

Warri •

Porto Novo
Cotonou •
Lomé

Niger

FRENCH WEST AFRICA

Niamey •

UPPER VOLTA

Ouagadougou •

TOGO

White Volta

Kaya •

Navrongo •

GOLD COAST

ASHANTI

Kumasi •

Tamale •

Yendi •

Black Volta

Wenchi •

Sunyani •

Sekondi
Takoradi

Accra
(Br.)

C. Three Points

C. St. Paul

Slave Coast

Grand Popo Coast

Gold Coast

Gulf of Guinea

Equator

Meridian of Greenwich

100 Fathoms

BRITISH AFRICA

Scale 1:12,600,000 approx.

ONE INCH TO 200 MILES

0   Miles   100   200   300

London   Manchester

Comparative distances from London

Zenithal Equal Area Projection

Continued on page 46

E. AFRICA
Cape to Cairo

Scale 1:19,000,000 approx.
ONE INCH TO 300 MILES

Comparative distances from London

○ Edinburgh
○ Manchester
○ London

0 Miles

Indian Ocean
page 49

Atlantic Ocean
page 24

Africa
700 mile
pages 64–7

SAUDI ARABIA

IRAQ (PERSIA)

Bushire

Kuwait

KUWAIT

JORDAN

Gaza

Aqaba

Sinai

Suez

Port Said

Ismailia

Alexandria

Cairo

Memphis

Pyramids

El Faiyum

EGYPT

Qasr Farafra

Dakhla Oasis

El Kharga

Siwa

Qattara Depression

Libyan Plateau

El Alamein

Tobruk

Gulf of Benghazi

Gulf of Sidra

Sirte

Jofra Oasis

Soda Mts.

Sebha Oasis

L I B Y A

Libyan Desert

Kufra Oases

S a h a r a   D e s e r t

Tibesti

Emi Koussi

Bodélé Depression

Tarso Muri

Gadames

ALGERIA

A i r

F R E N C H   W E S T   A F R I C A

Bosso

Nguru

Maiduguri

NORTHERN REGION

NIGERIA (British)

Kano

Zaria

Bauchi Plateau

Enugu

EASTERN REGION

Douala

CAMEROONS

Yaoundé

SPANISH GUINEA

Fernando Poo (Sp.)

Principe (Port.)

Bight of Biafra

Garoua

Fort Lamy

Lake Chad

Lake Chad Basin

Chari

Bahr el Ghazal

F R E N C H   E Q U A T O R I A L   A F R I C A

Zongo

Bangui

Oubangui

Mongbere

Bondo

Komba

Mene

Mobaye

Paulis

Red Sea

Tropic of Cancer

100 fathoms

Yanbu

Medina

Mecca

e Jidda

Foul Bay

Saiwun

Mukalla

ADEN PROTECTORATE

Najran

Sana'a

YEMEN

Kamaran Is. (Br.)

Massawa

Aden

Bab el Mandeb

G. of Aden

C. Guardafui

Obbia

Erigavo

Berbera

Hargeisa

BRITISH SOMALILAND

Zeila

Djibouti

FRENCH SOMALILAND

Diredawa

Harar

O g a d e n

S O M A L I A   (Italian Trust.)

Mogadiscio

Juba

Shibeli

ETHIOPIA (ABYSSINIA)

Addis Ababa

Gore

Gondar

Lake Tana

Aduwa

Asmara

Tessenei

ERITREA

Kassala

Port Sudan

Suakin

Berber

Ed Damer

Atbara

A t b a r a

Nubian Desert

Wadi Halfa

4th. Cataract

5th. Cataract

6th. Cataract

Khartoum

Omdurman

White Nile Dam

Wad Medani

Gezira

Sennar Dam

Roseires

BLUE NILE

Blue Nile

Abyssinian Plateau

Mega

Moyale

Lake Rudolf

East Rift Valley

K E N Y A

UGANDA

Lake Albert

Lake Kyoga

Juba

Nimule

Malakal

Fashoda

Sobat

White Nile

B A H R   E L   G H A Z A L

Wau

S U D A N

El Obeid

K O R D O F A N

El Fasher

Marra Mts.

D A R F U R

Gezira

Thebes

Luxor

Isna

Ginga

Asyut

Aswan

Aswan Dam

1st. Cataract

2nd. Cataract

3rd. Cataract

Nile

Continued on page 62

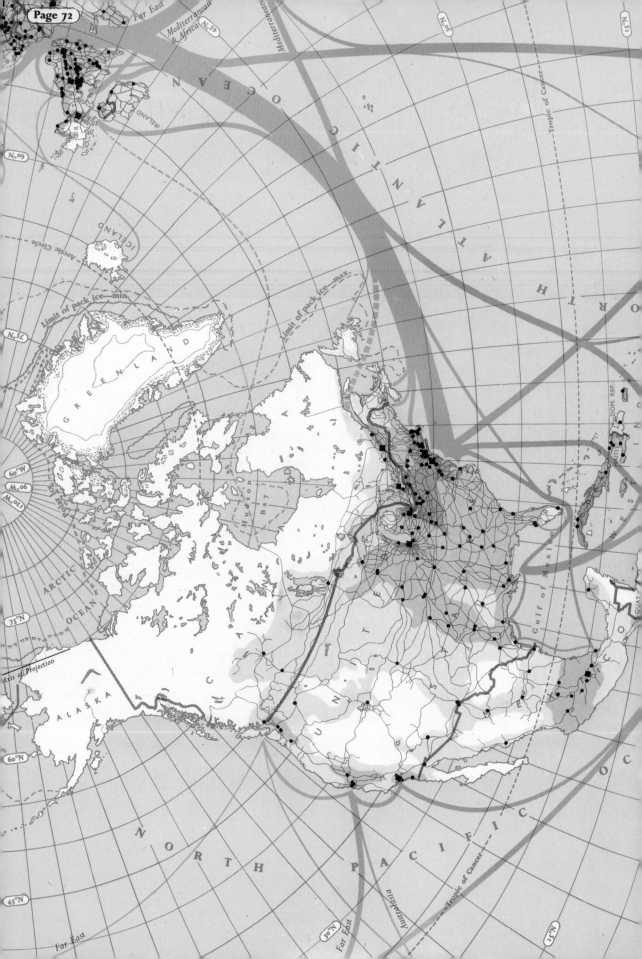

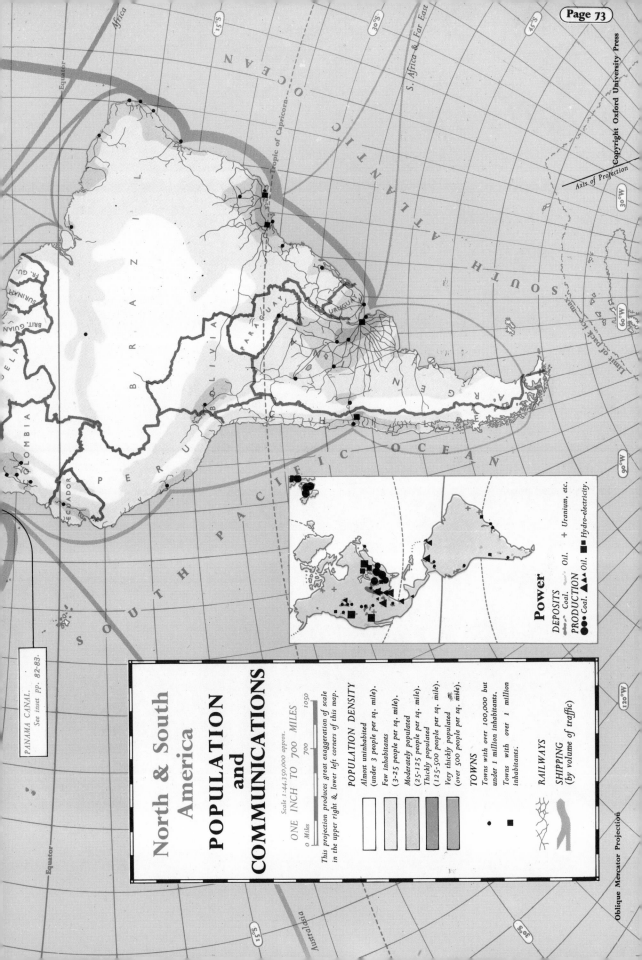

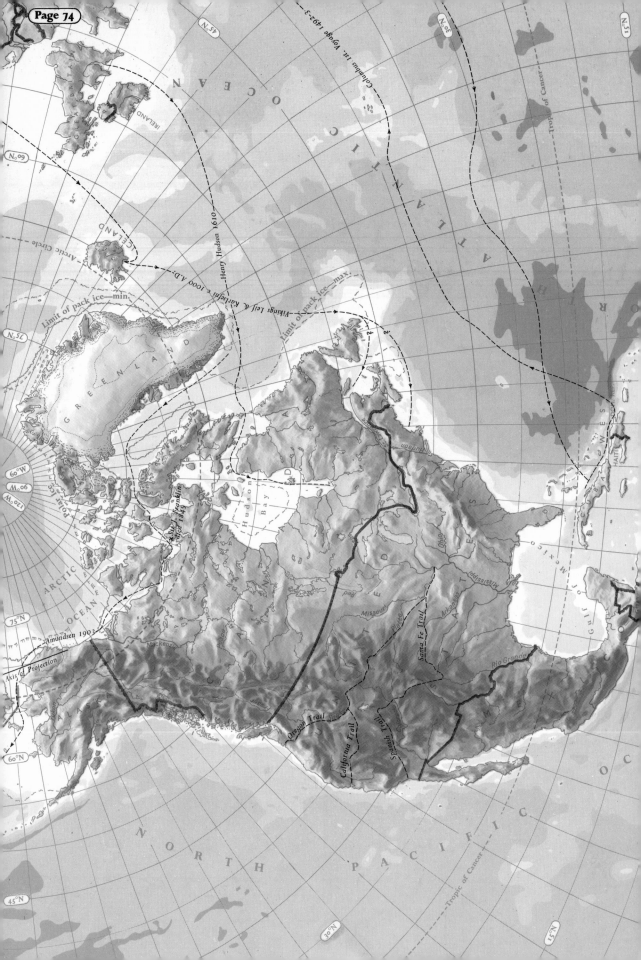

ARCTIC OCEAN

ATLANTIC OCEAN

NORTH ATLANTIC

NORTH PACIFIC OCEAN

GREENLAND

ICELAND

IRELAND

Arctic Circle

Limit of pack ice — min.

Limit of pack ice — max.

Henry Hudson 1610

Vikings Leif & Karlsefni c. 1000 A.D.

Columbus 1st. Voyage 1492-3

Tropic of Cancer

Hudson Bay

Sir J. Franklin died 1847

Polar Sea

Axis of Projection

Amundsen 1903

Mackenzie

Oregon Trail

California Trail

Spanish Trail

Santa Fe Trail

Missouri

Platte

Arkansas

Mississippi

Ohio

Red

Rio Grande

Gulf of Mexico

CUBA

HAITI

WEST INDIES

MEXICO

Tropic of Cancer

45°N

60°N

75°N

90°W

120°W

60°W

30°N

15°N

30°E

45°N

55°N

75°N

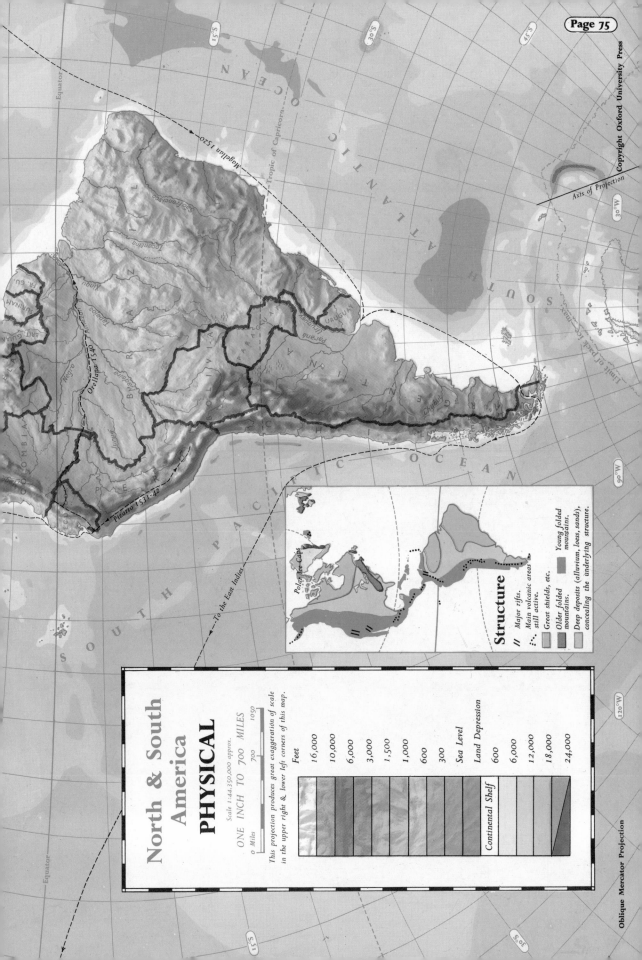

North & South America
PHYSICAL

Scale 1:44,350,000 approx.

ONE INCH TO 700 MILES

0 Miles   350   700   1050

This projection produces great exaggeration of scale in the upper right & lower left corners of this map.

Feet

16,000
10,000
6,000
3,000
1,500
1,000
600
300
Sea Level
Land Depression
600
6,000
12,000
18,000
24,000

Continental Shelf

Structure

// Major rifts.
⋯ Main volcanic areas still active.

Great shields, etc.
Older folded mountains.
Young folded mountains.
Deep deposits (alluvium, loess, sands), concealing the underlying structure.

Polar Ice Caps

Equator
Tropic of Capricorn
15°S
30°S
45°S
30°W
90°W
120°W
45°S
30°S

SOUTH ATLANTIC OCEAN

SOUTH PACIFIC OCEAN

Magellan 1520
Orellana 1540
Pizarro 1531-42
To the East Indies

Axis of Projection

Limit of pack ice, max.

Oblique Mercator Projection

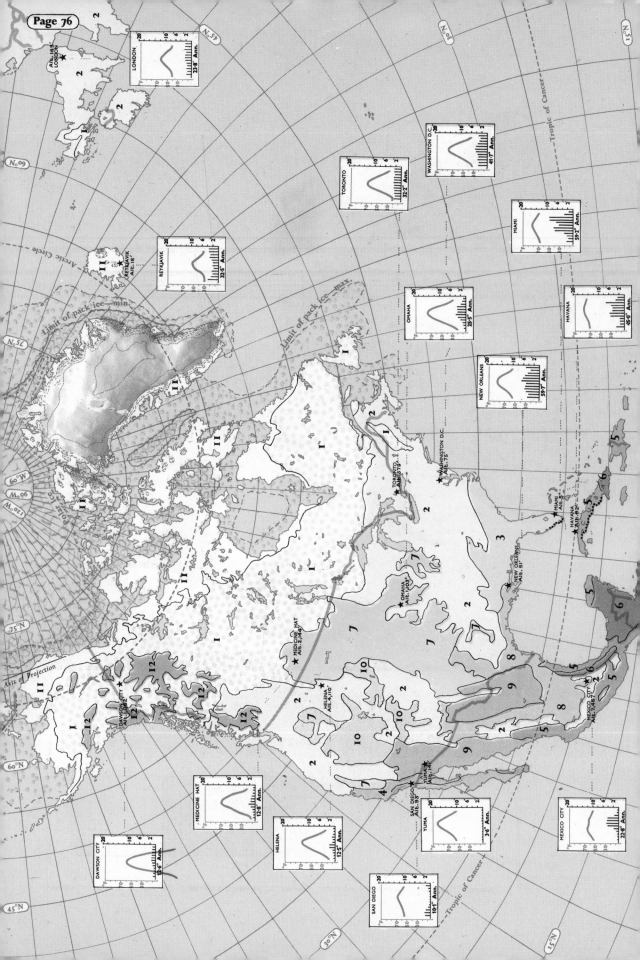

North & South America
VEGETATION

Scale 1:44,350,000 approx.

ONE INCH TO 700 MILES

| 0 Miles | 350 | 700 | 1050 |

This projection produces great exaggeration of scale in the upper right & lower left corners of this map.

I	Cool coniferous forest.
2	Temperate mixed forest.
3	Warm temperate moist forest.
4	Warm temperate drought-resisting woodland.
5	Tropical forest.
6	Equatorial rain forest.
7	Grassland.
8	Savanna.
9	Hot desert.
IO	Temperate desert.
II	Cold desert.
I2	Mountain vegetation.
	Ice Caps
	Mangrove swamp.

Annual Rainfall
and other forms of precipitation

	Under 10" each year
	10"—20" ,, ,,
	20"—40" ,, ,,
	40"—80" ,, ,,
	Over 80"

Oblique Mercator Projection

Copyright Oxford University Press

Axis of Projection

Tropic of Capricorn

Equator

RECIFE Alt. 91'
CUIABÁ Alt. 54.7'
RIO DE JANEIRO Alt. 201'
BUENOS AIRES Alt. 89'
MENDOZA Alt. 2,625'
PUNTA ARENAS Alt. 92'
VALPARAISO Alt. 135'
ANTOFAGASTA Alt. 308'
LA PAZ Alt. 11,916'
BOGOTÁ Alt. 8,727'

RECIFE 63·4' Ann.
CUIABÁ 54·9' Ann.
RIO DE JANEIRO 44·7' Ann.
BUENOS AIRES 37·4' Ann.
MENDOZA 7·5' Ann.
PUNTA ARENAS 14·6' Ann.
VALPARAISO 19·5' Ann.
ANTOFAGASTA 0·5' Ann.
LA PAZ 22·6' Ann.
89·7' Ann.
41·6' Ann.

Limit of pack ice max.

ICELAND

CANADA

Scale 1:19,000,000 approx.
ONE INCH TO 300 MILES

0 Miles   300   450

◦ London   ◦ Manchester   ◦ Edinburgh
Comparative distances from London

The North Magnetic Pole moves about, slowly (and unpre-
dictably) in central arctic Canada. In 1946 it was at 74°N
96°W approx.; and see map for 1951 position. This move-
ment affects "Magnetic Variation from True North"—i.e.
the angle between true north and "compass" north. For
example in London in 1820 a compass would have pointed
approximately 24° west of true north; in 1951, 8° west.

Railways ————————
Roads   ------------------

United States Ra.

Island

Ellesmere

Humboldt
Glacier

G R E E N L A N D

Thule

(Denmark)

Devon I.

Bylot I.

Pond Inlet

Lancaster Sound

Melville
Bay

Baffin Island

Tugssåq

Disko

Mt. Forel
11,022

Sukkertoppen

Søndre
Strömfjord

Arctic Circle

Godthaab

Cape Farewell

10,000

6,000

3,550

8,571

9,055

Davis Strait

Cumberland Sound

T E R R I T O R I E S

Arctic Circle

Foxe Basin

Southampton
Island

Chesterfield

Frobisher Bay

Hudson Strait

Resolution I.

Ungava
Peninsula

Ungava Bay

Nain

H u d s o n

D A

Ice-free

Churchill

Bay

Knob Lake

Goose Bay

Battle Harbour

Strait of Belle Isle

Limit of pack ice—average max. (spring)

Limit of pack ice—average max. (spring)

Limit of pack ice—average min. (autumn)

Limit of pack ice—average max. (spring)

James Bay

L A B R A D O R

Grand Falls

Gander

Wabana

St. John's

BA

Nelson

Fort Albany

Moosonee

Lake
Mistassini

Chibougamau

Ashuanipi

Q U E B E C

Seven Islands

Anticosti I.

Corner
Brook

Grand Falls

NEWFOUNDLAND

Port-
aux-Basques

Miquelon
(Fr.)

C. Race

Grand Banks

100 fathoms

O C E A N

Dolbeau

Chicoutimi

Gaspé

Gaspé
Peninsula

Gulf of St. Lawrence

Magdalen Is.

Cape Breton I.

Sydney Mines

Sydney

Canso

Placentia Bay

Kapuskasing

O N T A R I O

S. Porcupine

Timmins

Kirkland Lake

Cobalt

Noranda
Rouyn

Quebec

Trois
Rivières

Thetford
Mines

NEW
BRUNSWICK

Newcastle

Fredericton

Charlottetown

PRINCE
EDWARD I.

Pictou

THE

NOVA SCOTIA

Halifax

Lake of
the Woods

Port Arthur

Fort William

Lake Nipigon

Sudbury

Sault Ste
Marie

Montreal

Ottawa

Kingston

Saint John

Bangor

Bay of Fundy

Cape Sable

MARITIME

Duluth

Iron Mountain

St. Paul

Georgian
Bay

Midland

Lake
Huron

Utica

Albany

Manchester

Portland

Boston

Providence

Fall River

ATLANTIC

apolis

Toronto

Hamilton

Niagara Falls

Lake Ontario

Rochester

Syracuse

Hartford

New Haven

Madison

Milwaukee

Grand
Rapids

Flint

Detroit

Windsor

Cleveland

Lake Erie

Buffalo

Pittsburgh

Scranton

Jersey
City

Trenton

New York

Chicago

Cedar
Rapids

Des Moines

Toledo

Fort Wayne

Columbus

Lake Michigan

Gary

Appalachians

Wilmington

Baltimore

Philadelphia

Washington

D

T E S

Peoria

maha

Falls

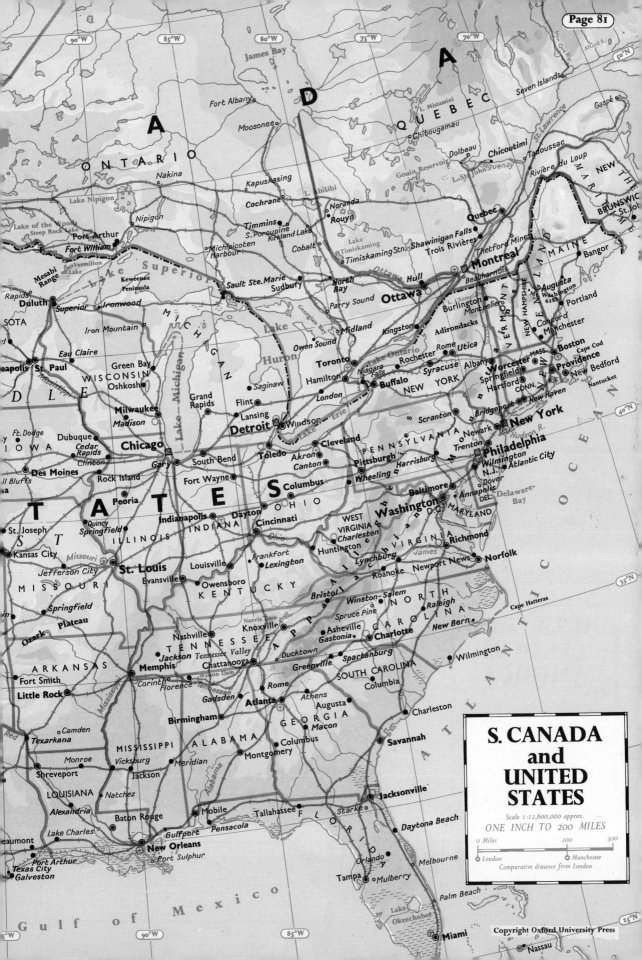

S. CANADA
and
UNITED
STATES

Scale 1:12,600,000 approx.
ONE INCH TO 200 MILES

0 Miles   200   300

London   Manchester
Comparative distance from London

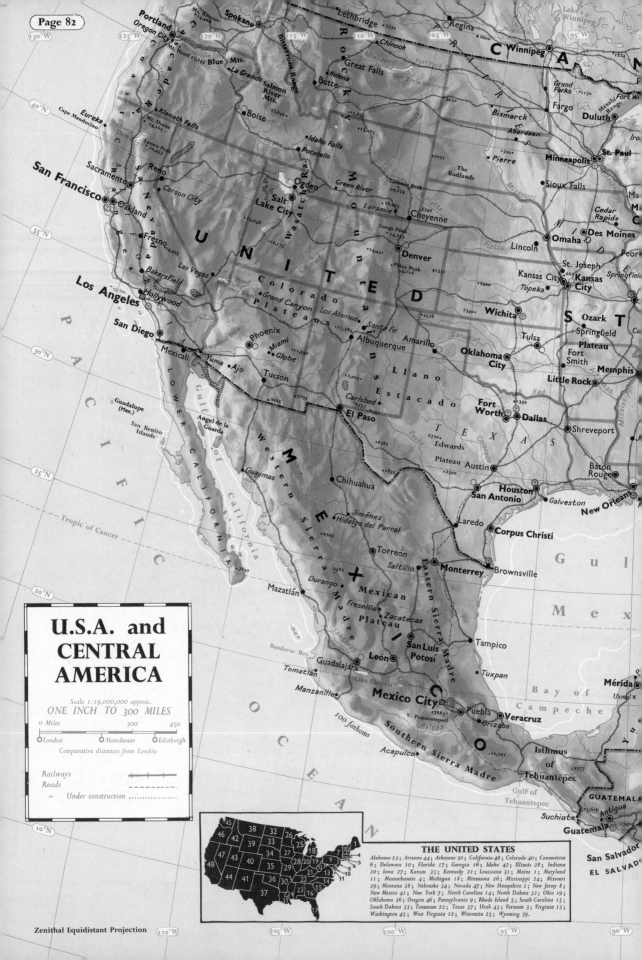

U.S.A. and CENTRAL AMERICA

Scale 1:19,000,000 approx.
ONE INCH TO 300 MILES

0 Miles   300   450

o London   o Manchester   o Edinburgh
Comparative distances from London

Railways
Roads
,,   Under construction

THE UNITED STATES

Alabama 23; Arizona 44; Arkansas 30; California 48; Colorado 40; Connecticut 6; Delaware 10; Florida 17; Georgia 16; Idaho 42; Illinois 28; Indiana 20; Iowa 27; Kansas 35; Kentucky 21; Louisiana 31; Maine 1; Maryland 11; Massachusetts 4; Michigan 18; Minnesota 26; Mississippi 24; Missouri 29; Montana 38; Nebraska 34; Nevada 47; New Hampshire 2; New Jersey 8; New Mexico 41; New York 7; North Carolina 14; North Dakota 32; Ohio 19; Oklahoma 36; Oregon 46; Pennsylvania 9; Rhode Island 5; South Carolina 15; South Dakota 33; Tennessee 22; Texas 37; Utah 43; Vermont 3; Virginia 13; Washington 45; West Virginia 12; Wisconsin 25; Wyoming 39.

Zenithal Equidistant Projection

Panama Canal

One inch to 24 miles approx.
Vertical Interval 10 times

PANAMA The canal, opened 1914, is 50 miles long including approaches (actual canal 40 miles). Minimum depth 41 ft. minimum width 300 ft. (Gaillard Cut). Time of passage 7 hours. About 6,000 ships use the canal each year of which 30% are U.S. and 18% British.

Continued on pages 86/87

THE ST. LAWRENCE SEAWAY (scheduled for completion in 1959). The main obstacles to navigation on the St. Lawrence are the rapids between Prescott and Montreal at present by-passed by canals only suitable for ships of 14 ft. draught. The Seaway project will make the river navigable by ships of 28 ft. draught. Canals will by-pass the rapids at Montreal and Beauharnois, and dams will be built at Cornwall and Iroquois. These will make the level of the river down to Cornwall the same as that of Lake Ontario, and will form a huge lake between Prescott and Cornwall. Between Montreal and the Seaway lake ships will be lifted about 230 ft. through six locks. To enable ocean-going ships to go further than Lake Ontario the existing Welland and Sault Ste. Marie canals and the St. Clair river are being deepened to take ships of 28 ft. draught.

GREAT LAKES

Scale 1:6,336,000 approx.
ONE INCH TO 100 MILES

0 Miles   100   150

London   Oxford   Bath
Comparative distances from London

THIS MAP EMPHASIZES TRANSPORT

RAILWAYS. Thicknesses ———— show relative importance.

ROADS are too numerous to show without obscuring the map, but road transport is an important factor.

CANALS:━━━━━ LAKE ROUTES:
See also note on the St. Lawrence Seaway.

OCEAN ROUTES. Thicknesses indicate approximate flow of traffic.

PORTS. Three sizes ⚓ ⚓ ⚓ based on net registered tonnage handled each year. Only about 25 ports in the world are in the top class.

PRINCIPAL MINING AREAS

Coal   Iron ore

Nova Scotia

Same scale

55°W　50°W　45°W　40°W　35°W　30°W　15°W

S. AMERICA
(North)

Scale 1:19,000,000 approx.
ONE INCH TO 300 MILES

0 Miles　　　300　　　450

◯ London　◯ Manchester　◯ Edinburgh
Comparative distances from London

Canada pages 78-9

N. & S. America
700 mile
pages 72-7

pages 82-3

Pacific Ocean, pp 54-5

pages 88-9

Atlantic Ocean
page 24

Railways
Roads
" Under construction

10°N

5°N

Equator

5°S

10°S

15°S

20°S

A　T　L　A　N　T　I　C

100 fathoms

O　C　E　A　N

Georgetown
New
Amsterdam
ckenzie
Dam
SURINAM
(NETH. GUIANA)
3050
Paramaribo
Moengo
Cayenne
FRENCH GUIANA
1969

highland
1148
2064
Obidos
1180
I. of Marajó
Pará
Belém (Pará)
Fordlândia
1300
São Luís (Maranhão)
Parnaíba
Camocim
Fortaleza (Ceará)
Cascavel
Fernando de Noronha
3451
Cáxias
Teresina
C. de São Roque
Natal
Z I L
2100
Floriano
Carolina
3609
João Pessoa
Canudos
1624
2067
Recife (Pernambuco)
1980
Paulistana
Paulo Afonso Falls
827
Maceió
1053
3707
Aracajú
Angical
4357
Feira de Santana
Nazaré
4035
Salvador (Bahia)
1968
Plateau
Poções
of
Goiás
Itabuna
Ilhéus
Cuiabá
Mato Grosso
Goiás
Massif
4913
2953
Anápolis
2953
Goiânia
Jequitinhonha
3450
Montes Claros
Corumbá
Brazilian
Diamantina
Caravelas
1716
MINAS
Campo Grande
Dôres do Indaiá
GERAIS
4101
Uberaba
Itabira
4625
Colatina
Belo Horizonte
2904
Ribeirão Prêto
Plateau
Vitória
ESPIRITO SANTO
Ponta Porã
9251
Juiz de Fora
6160
Volta Redonda
Petrópolis
Campinas
Niterói
Trinidad
São Paulo
Rio de Janeiro
Santos
Asuncion
Paraná
Curitiba
Platea

Tapajós
Tocantins
Xingu
Araguaia
Tocantins
Serra Geral de Goiás
São Francisco
Serra Geral
Serra dos Aimorés

Copyright Oxford University Press

Tropic of Capricorn

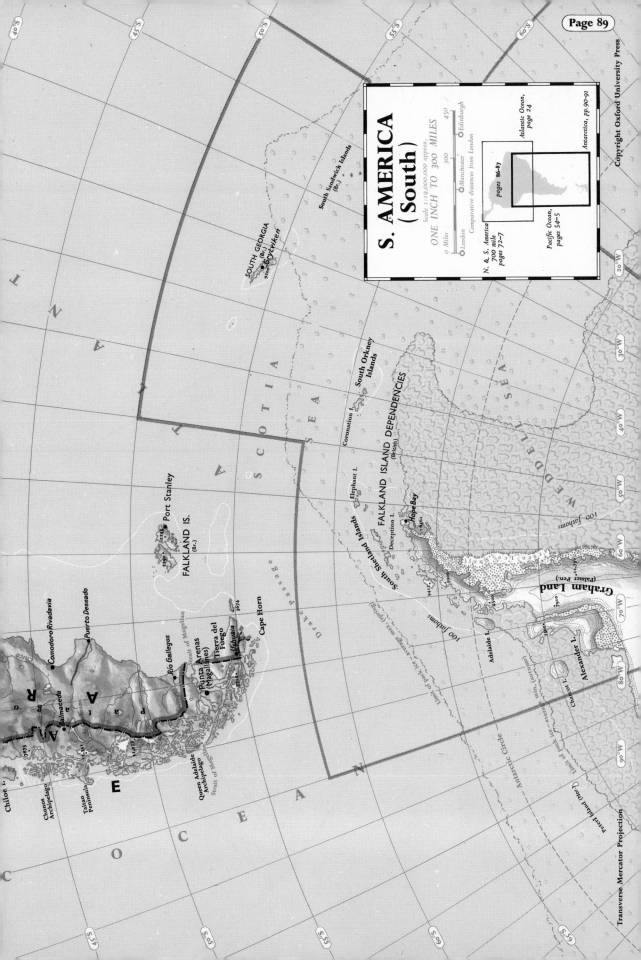

S. AMERICA (South)

Scale 1:19,000,000 approx.

ONE INCH TO 300 MILES

0 Miles   150   300   450

○ London
○ Manchester
○ Edinburgh

Comparative distances from London

N. & S. America
700 mile
pages 72-7

pages 86-87

Atlantic Ocean,
Page 24

Pacific Ocean,
pages 54-5

Antarctica, pp. 90-91

South Sandwich Islands (Br.)

SOUTH GEORGIA (Br.)
Grytviken
9300

A T L A N T I C

S C O T I A   S E A

Coronation I.
South Orkney
Islands

Elephant I.

South Shetland Islands

FALKLAND ISLAND DEPENDENCIES
(British)

Deception I.
Hope Bay
4501

W E D D E L L   S E A

100 fathoms

100 fathoms

Graham Land
(Palmer Pen.)

Adelaide I.

Alexander I.

Charcot I.

Antarctic Circle

Limit of pack ice max. (autumn)

Limit of pack ice min. (autumn)

Peter I Island (Nor.)

Port Stanley

FALKLAND IS.
(Br.)

2290

Drake Passage

Cape Horn
3674

Comodoro Rivadavia

Puerto Deseado

Río Gallegos

Strait of Magellan

Punta Arenas
(Magallanes)

Tierra del
Fuego

Ushuaia

Queen Adelaide
Archipelago

Strait of Magellan

Chiloé I.

Chonos
Archipelago

Taitao
Peninsula

Balmaceda

2675

3744

A R

A   G   E

P A C I F I C   O C E A N

40°S
45°S
50°S
55°S
60°S

50°S
55°S
60°S   65°S   59°S

20°W
30°W
40°W
50°W
60°W
70°W
80°W
90°W

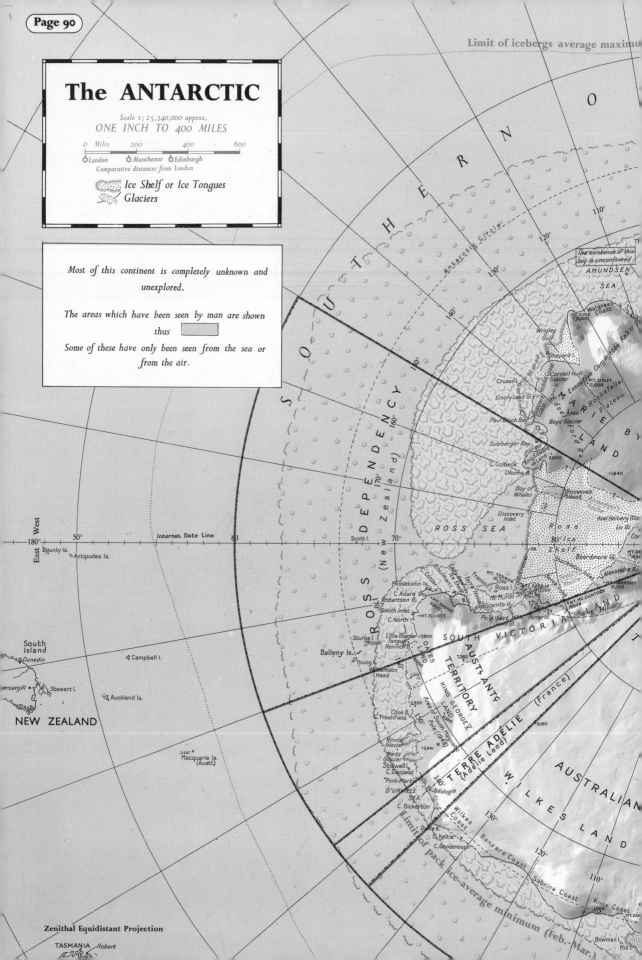

The ANTARCTIC

Scale 1; 25,340,000 approx.
ONE INCH TO 400 MILES

0 Miles   200   400   600

○ London   ○ Manchester   ○ Edinburgh
Comparative distances from London

Ice Shelf or Ice Tongues
Glaciers

Most of this continent is completely unknown and
unexplored.

The areas which have been seen by man are shown
thus

Some of these have only been seen from the sea or
from the air.

Limit of icebergs average maximu

SOUTHERN O

Antarctic Circle

AMUNDSEN
SEA

The existence of this
bay is unconfirmed

MT. SIPLE
15,000

Walgreen

Wrigley
Gulf

Shepard I.

Cordell Hull
Glacier

MT. SIDLEY
12,000

Cruzen I.

Emory Land Gl.

4,460

MARIE

Rockefeller
Plateau

Paul Block Bay

Boyd Glacier

Sulzberger Bay

King Edward
VII Land   2,600

●1,840

C. Colbeck
Okuma B.

Roosevelt
Island

Axel Heiberg Gla.
Liv Gl.

Bay of
Whales

Amundsen
Route

Discovery
Inlet

ROSS SEA

ROSS
ICE
SHELF

80

Beardmore Gl.

MT. DI
13,3

Alexandra Ra.

Scott I.

70

58.

Shackleton Inlet

SOUTH DEPENDENCY (New Zealand)
160°

MT. MARKHAM
15,100

Possession Is.

C. Cotter

C. Adare

Coulman I.

Franklin
I.

MT. TERROR
10,750

Ross I.

MT. MC.CLINTOCK
13,928

Mt. Hilary

Robertson B.

Smith Inlet

MT. SABINE
9,850

MT. ELLIOTT

C. North

Terra Nova
Bay

MT. EREBUS
13,200

McMurdo Sd.
Granite Hr.

Pr. Albert Mtns. Terra Gl.
Drond Gl.

Lillie Glacier
Tongue

7,800

SOUTH VICTORIA LAND

Sturge I.
5,000

Rennick B.

OATES LAND

Young I.

Williamson
Head

King George V
Land

Area of
South Magnetic
Pole (1918)

SOUTH ANT.
TERRITORY

7,260

Balleny Is.

Cook B.
C. Freshfield

2,350

Area of South Magnetic
Pole (1948) +

9,180

TERRE ADÉLIE (France)
(Adélie Land)

AUSTRALIAN

Ninnis
Glacier

Mertz
Glacier

Stillwell I.
C. Denison

2,441

WILKES LAND

"Port-Martin"
Pt. Géologie

130°

D'URVILLE
SEA

C. Bickerton

Wilkes
Coast

Davis B.

C. Keltie

Banzare Coast

120°

C. Goodenough

110°

Sabrina Coast

Knox Coast
1,000

MT. SA

Bowman I.

Mill I.

Limit of pack ice average minimum (Feb.-Mar.)

South
Island

○ Dunedin

West   50°
East   180°

Internat. Date Line   60°

ercargill ●   ● Stewart I.

Bounty Is.
Antipodes Is.

Campbell I.

Auckland Is.

NEW ZEALAND

Macquarie Is.
(Aust.)

Zenithal Equidistant Projection

TASMANIA   Hobart

110°

120°

130°

140°

150°

SOUTH AMERICA

C. Horn

Port Stanley
Falkland Islands (Br.)

Drake Passage

SCOTIA

F A L K L A N D

South Shetland Islands
King George I. Admiralty Bay
Livingston I.
Deception I. *3500* Elephant I.
Bransfield Str. Clarence I.
Palmer Arch. Trinity I.
Anvers I. Hope Bay
Port Lockroy Joinville I.
James Ross I.
Biscoe Snow Hill I.
Is. Robertson I.
Adelaide I. 70°
Stonington I. *7154*
Marguerite *12200*
Bay C. Agassiz
Charcot I. *5900*
10300 C. WAKEFIELD
5200 *9400*
2570 Hearst I.
Alexander *2580*
Land Boggs I.
Dolleman I.
Steele I.
Knowles
3920 Violante Inlet
New Bedford Inlet
Nantucket Inlet

D E P E N D E N C I E S (British)

Shag Rocks

South Georgia
Grytviken
MT. PAGET 9200

Coronation Island
South Orkney Islands
Laurie I.

SEA

South Sandwich Islands
Candlemas
2650 Saunders
9128 Montagu I.
Bristol I.

W E D D E L L
S E A

COATS
Vahsel Bay
Kulh cold Coast
Caird Coast
Stancomb Wills Promontory

LD

KRON PRINSESSE MARTHA COAST
C. Norvegia
Maudheim

Fuchs 1957-58

KING HAAKON VII SEA

Bouvet I. (Nor.)

Amundsen 14.12.11.
Scott 18.1.12.
8530

INCOGNITA

QUEEN MAUD LAND
(Dronning Maud Land)
Mühlig-Hofmann Mts. *9128*
10825
Wohlthat Massif *9675*
PRINSESSE ASTRID COAST *8200*
PRINSESSE RAGNHILD COAST *10500*
PRINS HARALD COAST
KRON PRINS OLAF COAST
Lützow-Holm Bay

ARCTIC TERRITORY
KEMP LAND
ENDERBY LAND
MAC-ROBERTSON LAND Scott Ra.
PRINCESS ELIZABETH LAND
Prince Charles Mts.
Munro-Kerr Mts. *4000*
5216 BAILLEAU PEAK
Lars Christensen Coast *2260* *6200*
Douglas Is.
Ingrid Christensen Coast
MACKENZIE LAND
Prydz Bay
BAY
C. Darnley 70°
80°
West Ice Shelf
Amundsen Bay
C. Ann *6100*
4985
Proclamation I.
Mawson
Magnet Bay

Meridian of Greenwich
60° West 0° East 50°

S O U T H E R N   O C E A N

Limit of pack ice—average maximum (Aug.-Sept.)

AFRICA

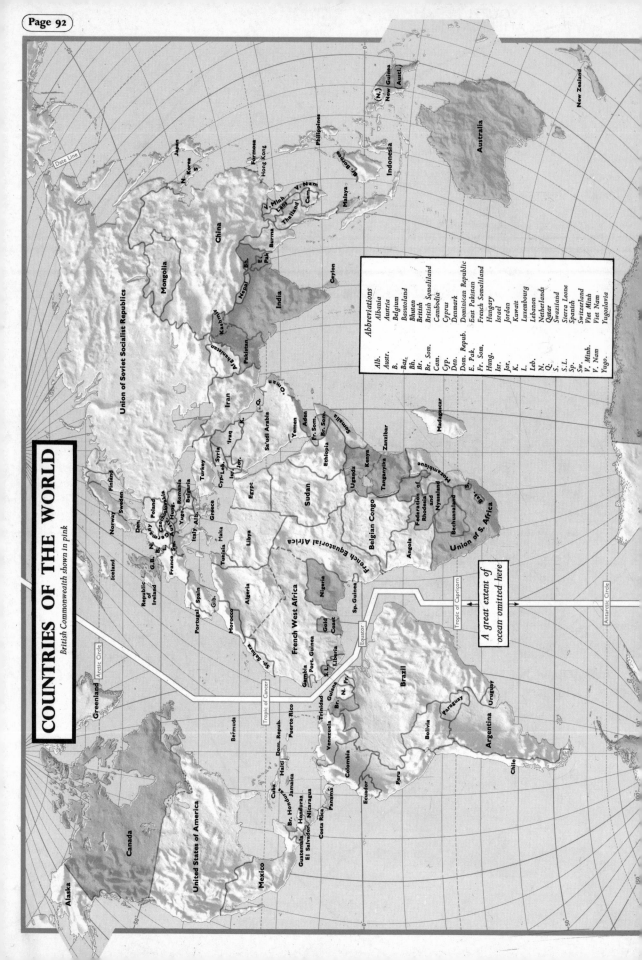

COUNTRIES OF THE WORLD
British Commonwealth shown in pink

A great extent of ocean omitted here

	Abbreviations
Alb.	Albania
Austr.	Austria
B.	Belgium
Bas.	Basutoland
Bh.	Bhutan
Br.	British
Br. Som.	British Somaliland
Cam.	Cambodia
Cyp.	Cyprus
Den.	Denmark
Dom. Repub.	Dominican Republic
E. Pak.	East Pakistan
Fr. Som.	French Somaliland
Hung.	Hungary
Isr.	Israel
Jor.	Jordan
K.	Kuwait
L.	Luxembourg
Leb.	Lebanon
N.	Netherlands
Q.	Qatar
S.	Swaziland
S.L.	Sierra Leone
Sp.	Spanish
Sw.	Switzerland
V. Minh.	Viet Minh
V. Nam	Viet Nam
Yugo.	Yugoslavia

Alaska

Canada

Greenland

Iceland

Republic of Ireland

G.B.

Norway

Sweden

Finland

Den.

Poland

N. Ger.

B.

Lux.

France

Spain

Portugal

Gib.

Czechoslovakia

Austr.

Hung.

Yugo.

Romania

Bulgaria

Italy

Alb.

Greece

Malta

Tunisia

Morocco

Algeria

Libya

Egypt

Union of Soviet Socialist Republics

Mongolia

China

N. Korea

S. Korea

Japan

Formosa

Hong Kong

Turkey

Cyp.

Syria

Leb.

Isr.

Jor.

'Iraq

Iran

Afghanistan

Saudi Arabia

Kuwait

Q.

Yemen

Aden

Fr. Som.

Br. Som.

Somalia

Ethiopia

Sudan

Pakistan

Kashmir

Nepal

Bh.

India

E. Pak.

Burma

Thailand

Laos

Cam.

V. Minh.

V. Nam

Malaya

Br. Borneo

Philippines

Indonesia

New Guinea (N.)

New Guinea (Austl.)

Australia

New Zealand

Madagascar

French Equatorial Africa

French West Africa

Sp. Sahara

Gambia

Port. Guinea

S.L.

Liberia

Gold Coast

Guinea

Nigeria

Sp. Guinea

Belgian Congo

Uganda

Kenya

Tanganyika

Zanzibar

Angola

Mozambique

Federation of Rhodesia and Nyasaland

Bechuanaland

S.

Bas.

Union of S. Africa

United States of America

Mexico

Bermuda

Cuba

Haiti

Dom. Repub.

Puerto Rico

Jamaica

Br. Hond.

Guatemala

Honduras

El Salvador

Nicaragua

Costa Rica

Panama

Colombia

Venezuela

Trinidad

Br. Guiana

N. Fr.

Ecuador

Peru

Brazil

Bolivia

Paraguay

Chile

Argentina

Uruguay

Ceylon

Arctic Circle

Tropic of Cancer

Equator

Tropic of Capricorn

Antarctic Circle

Date Line

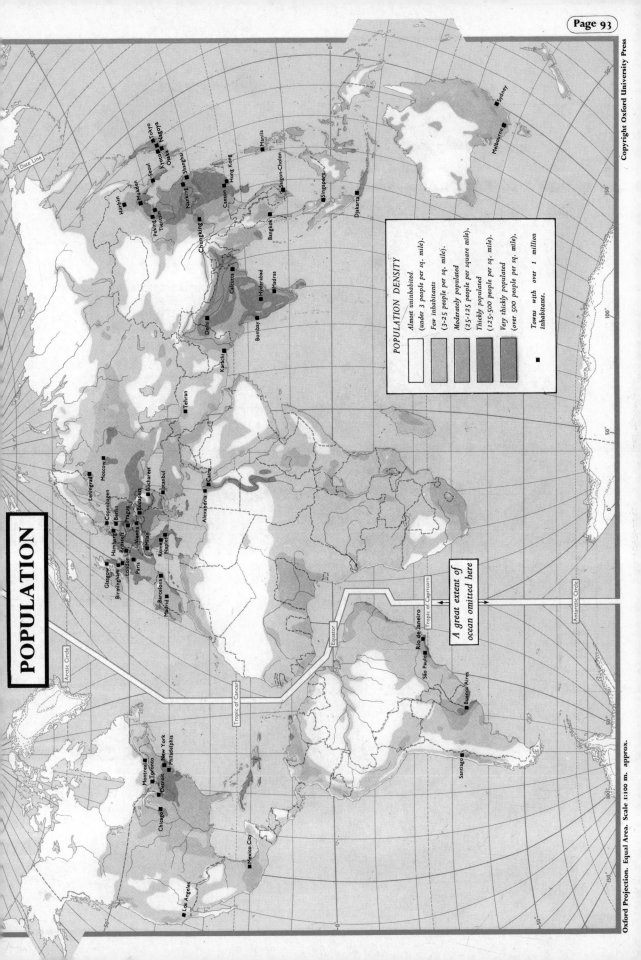

POPULATION

Oxford Projection. Equal Area. Scale 1:100 m. approx.

POPULATION DENSITY

Almost uninhabited.
(under 3 people per sq. mile).

Few inhabitants
(3–25 people per sq. mile).

Moderately populated
(25–125 people per square mile).

Thickly populated
(125–500 people per sq. mile).

Very thickly populated
(over 500 people per sq. mile).

Towns with over 1 million
inhabitants.

A great extent of
ocean omitted here

Date Line
Arctic Circle
Tropic of Cancer
Equator
Tropic of Capricorn
Antarctic Circle

Sydney
Melbourne

Tokyo
Nagoya
Osaka
Kyoto
Seoul
Mukden
Harbin
Peking
Tientsin
Nanking
Shanghai
Chungking
Canton
Hong Kong
Manila
Saigon-Cholon
Singapore
Djakarta
Bangkok
Madras
Hyderabad
Calcutta
Bombay
Delhi
Karachi
Tehran

Moscow
Leningrad
Copenhagen
Berlin
Prague
Budapest
Bucharest
Istanbul
Vienna
Milan
Rome
Naples
Hamburg
Brussels
Glasgow
Birmingham
London
Paris
Barcelona
Madrid
Alexandria
Cairo

Montreal
Toronto
Detroit
New York
Chicago
Philadelphia
Los Angeles
Mexico City

Rio de Janeiro
São Paulo
Buenos Aires
Santiago

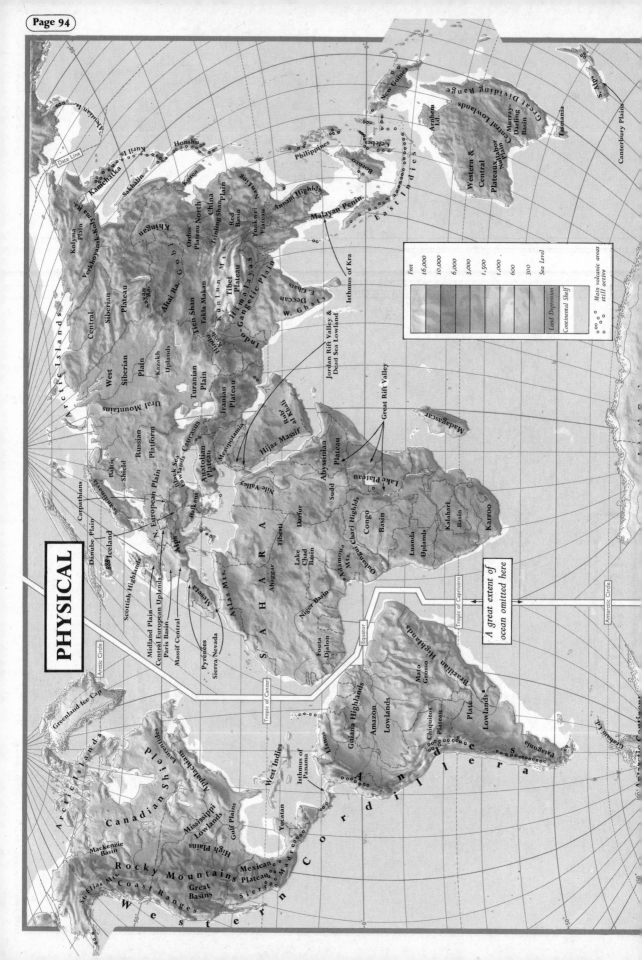

PHYSICAL

Feet
16,000
10,000
6,000
3,000
1,500
1,000
600
300
Sea Level

Land Depression

Continental Shelf

Main volcanic areas
still active

A great extent of
ocean omitted here

Arctic Circle

Tropic of Cancer

Equator

Tropic of Capricorn

Antarctic Circle

Date Line

Aleutian Is.

Greenland Ice Cap

Arctic Islands

Canadian Shield

Laurentides

Appalachians

Mackenzie Basin

Rocky Mountains

High Plains

Great Basins

Mississippi Lowlands

Gulf Plains

Yucatan

Mexican Plateau

Sierra Madre

St. Elias Mts.

Coast Ranges

W e s t e r n

C o r d i l l e r a

West Indies

Isthmus of Panama

Guiana Highlands

Amazon Lowlands

Llanos

Chiquitos Plateau

Mato Grosso

Brazilian Highlands

Plate Lowlands

A n d e s

Patagonia

S.

Kolyma Range

Kamchatka

Kuril Is.

Sakhalin

Verkhoyansk Ra.

Korea

Honshu

Central Siberian Plateau

Sayan

Altai Ra.

Gobi

Khingan

Ordos Plateau

North China Plain

Tsingling Shan

Nan Shan

Red Basin

Yunkwei Plateau

West Siberian Plain

Kazakh Uplands

Turanian Plain

Ural Mountains

Russian Platform

Tien Shan

Takla Makan

Kunlun Mts.

Tibet Plateau

Himalayas

Indo-Gangetic Plain

Deccan

W. Ghats

E. Ghats

Iranian Plateau

Caucasus

Black Sea Lowlands

Anatolian Plateau

Mesopotamia

Nile Valley

Rub' al Khali

Hijaz Massif

Jordan Rift Valley &
Dead Sea Lowland

Great Rift Valley

Abyssinian Plateau

Sudd

Darfur

Lake Plateau

Congo Basin

Luanda Uplands

Kalahari Basin

Karroo

Madagascar

Chari Basin

Ubangui

Adamoua Mts.

Lake Chad Basin

Tibesti

Ahaggar

Niger Basin

Fouta Djalon

S A H A R A

Atlas Mts.

Meseta

Pyrénées

Sierra Nevada

Massif Central

Paris Basin

Central European Uplands

Midland Plain

Alps

N. European Plain

Balkans

Carpathians

Danube Plain

Scandinavia

Scottish Highlands

Iceland

888

Baltic Shield

Amman Highlds

Malayan Penin.

Isthmus of Kra

East Indies

Borneo

Celebes

Philippines

New Guinea

Arnhem Ld.

Western &
Central
Plateaux

Nullarbor Plain

Central Lowlands

Murray Darling Basin

Great Dividing Range

Tasmania

S. Alps

Canterbury Plain

A great extent of
ocean omitted here

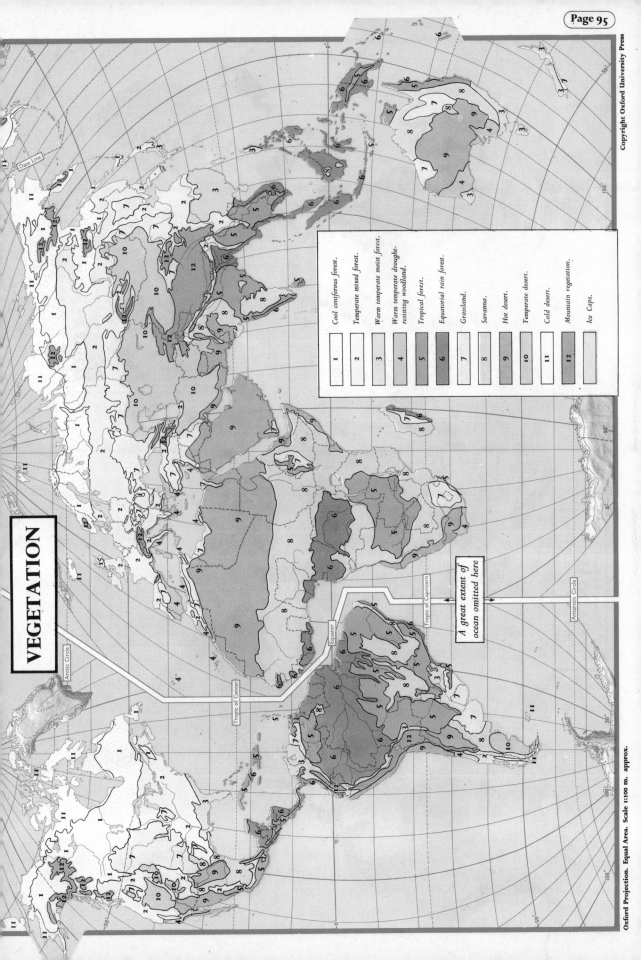

VEGETATION

Cool coniferous forest.
Temperate mixed forest.
Warm temperate moist forest.
Warm temperate drought-resisting woodland.
Tropical forest.
Equatorial rain forest.
Grassland.
Savanna.
Hot desert.
Temperate desert.
Cold desert.
Mountain vegetation.
Ice Caps.

1 2 3 4 5 6 7 8 9 10 11 12

A great extent of ocean omitted here

Date Line

Arctic Circle
Tropic of Cancer
Equator
Tropic of Capricorn
Antarctic Circle

Oxford Projection. Equal Area. Scale 1:100 m. approx.

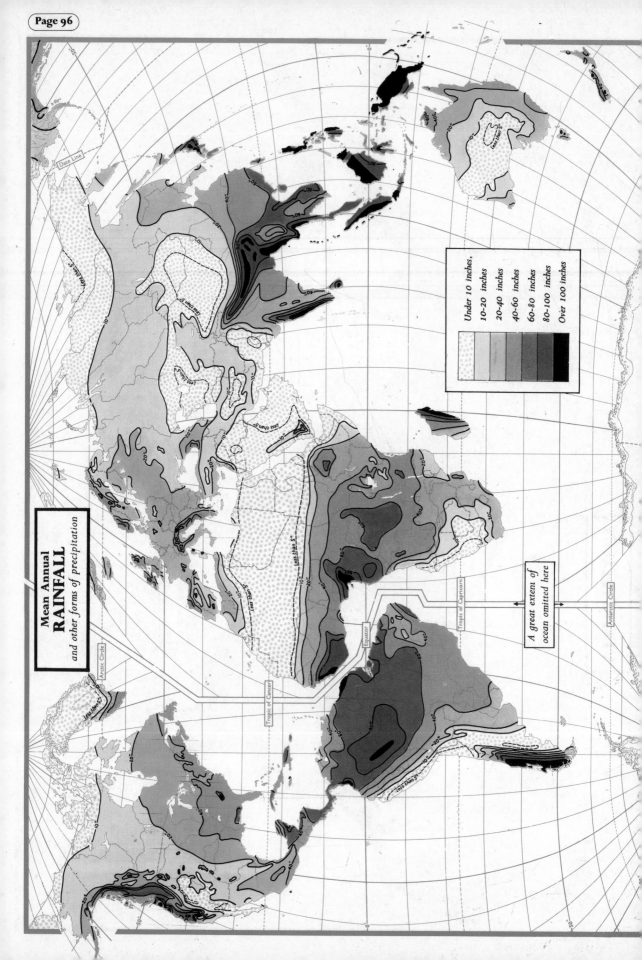

Mean Annual
RAINFALL
and other forms of precipitation

Under 10 inches.
10-20 inches
20-40 inches
40-60 inches
60-80 inches
80-100 inches
Over 100 inches

A great extent of
ocean omitted here

Date Line

Arctic Circle

Tropic of Cancer

Equator

Tropic of Capricorn

Antarctic Circle

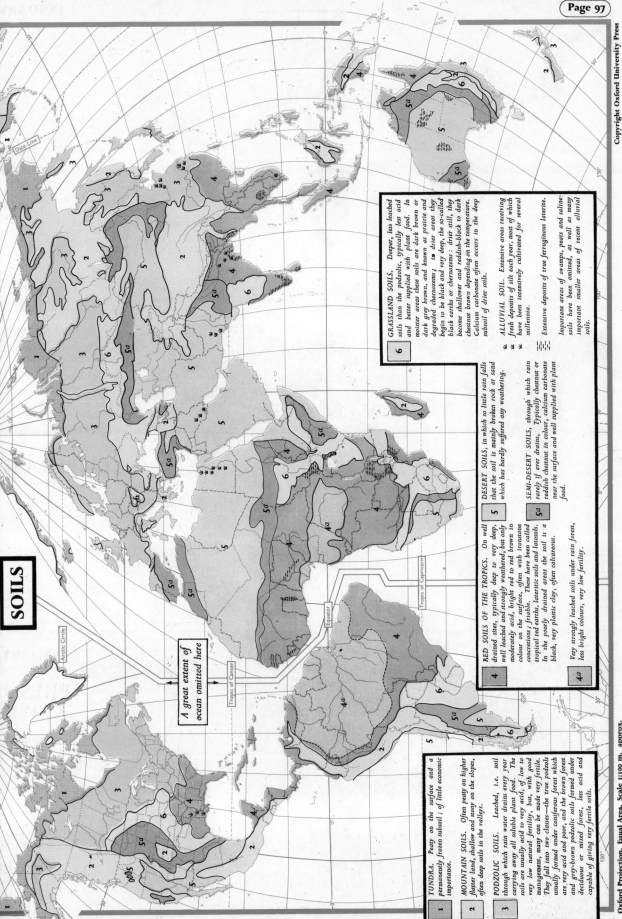

SOILS

A great extent of ocean omitted here

1 TUNDRA. Peaty on the surface and a permanently frozen subsoil; of little economic importance.

2 MOUNTAIN SOILS. Often peaty on higher flatter land, shallow and stony on the slopes, often deep soils in the valleys.

3 PODZOLIC SOILS. Leached, i.e. soil through which rain water drains every year carrying away all soluble plant food. The soils are usually acid to very acid, of low to very low natural fertility, but, with good management, may can be made very fertile. They fall into two classes—the true podzols usually formed under coniferous forest which are very acid and poor, and the brown forest and grey-brown podzolic soils formed under deciduous or mixed forest, less acid and capable of giving very fertile soils.

4 RED SOILS OF THE TROPICS. On well drained sites, typically deep to very deep, well leached and strongly weathered, but only moderately acid, bright red to red brown in colour on the surface, often with ironstone concretions; friable. These have been called tropical red earths, lateritic soils and latosols. In the poorly drained areas the soil is a black, very plastic clay, often calcareous.

4a Very strongly leached soils under rain forest, less bright colours, very low fertility.

5 DESERT SOILS, in which so little rain falls that the soil is mainly broken rock or sand which has hardly suffered any weathering.

5a SEMI-DESERT SOILS, through which rain rarely if ever drains. Typically chestnut or reddish chestnut in colour, calcium carbonate near the surface and well supplied with plant food.

6 GRASSLAND SOILS. Deeper, less leached soils than the podzolic, typically less acid and better supplied with plant food. In moister areas these soils are dark brown or dark grey brown, and known as prairie and degraded chernozems; in drier areas they begin to be black and very deep, the so-called black earths or chernozems: drier still, they become shallower and reddish-black to dark chestnut brown depending on the temperature. Calcium carbonate often occurs in the deep subsoil of drier soils.

ALLUVIAL SOIL. Extensive areas receiving fresh deposits of silt each year, most of which have been intensively cultivated for several millennia.

Extensive deposits of true ferruginous laterite.

Important areas of swamps, peats and saline soils have been omitted, as well as many important smaller areas of recent alluvial soils.

Oxford Projection. Equal Area. Scale 1:100 m. approx.

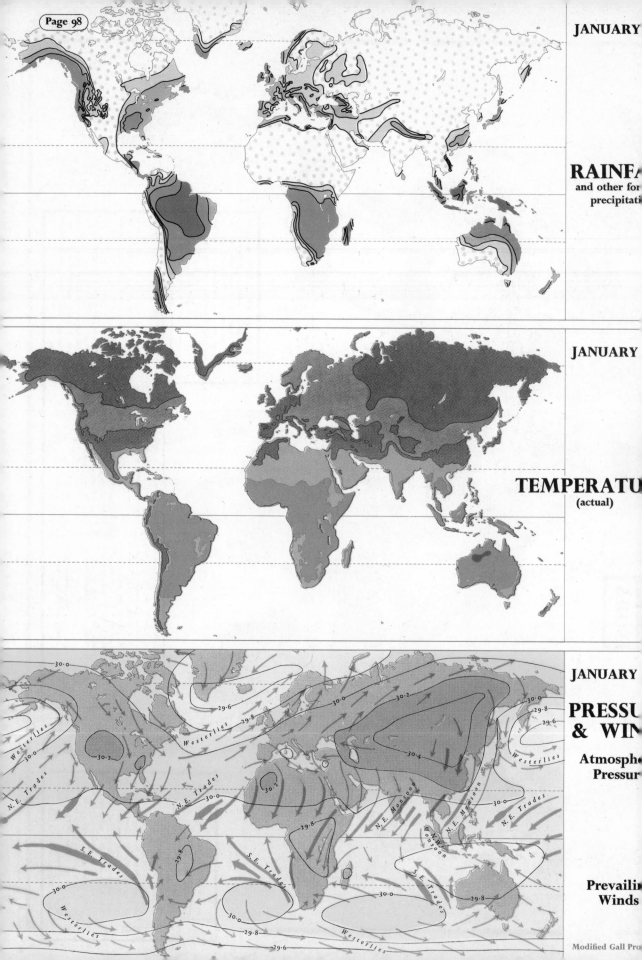

JANUARY

RAINF
and other for
precipitati

JANUARY

TEMPERATU

(actual)

JANUARY

PRESS
& WIN

Atmosph
Pressur

Prevailin
Winds

30.0
29.6
Westerlies
29.8
30.0
Westerlies
29.8
30.2
30.0
30.0
29.8
29.6
30.2
N.E. Trades
30.2
N.E. Trades
30.0
N.E. Monsoon
N.E. Monsoon
Monsoon
N.E. Trades
30.0
Westerlies
30.2
29.8
S.E. Trades
29.8
S.E. Trades
S.E. Trades
29.8
30.0
Westerlies
30.0
29.8
Westerlies
29.6

Modified Gall Pro

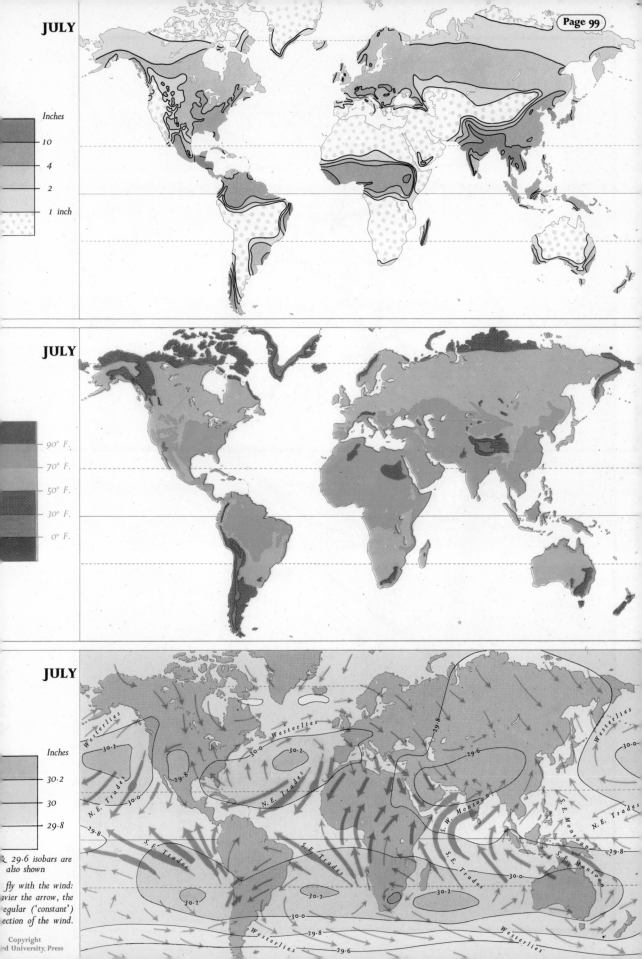

JULY

Inches

— 10
— 4
— 2
— 1 inch

JULY

90° F.
70° F.
50° F.
30° F.
0° F.

JULY

Inches

— 30·2
— 30
— 29·8

& 29·6 isobars are
also shown

*fly with the wind:
ivier the arrow, the
egular ('constant')
ection of the wind.*

Copyright
rd University, Press

Westerlies   30·2   30·0   30·2   29·8   Westerlies   29·8   30·0   30·2   Westerlies   30·0

N.E. Trades   30·0   29·8   N.E. Trades   S.W. Monsoon   S.E. Monsoon   N.E. Trades   29·8

29·8   S.E. Trades   S.E. Trades   S.E. Trades   S.E. Monsoon

30·2   30·2   30·2   30·0

Westerlies   29·8   29·6   Westerlies

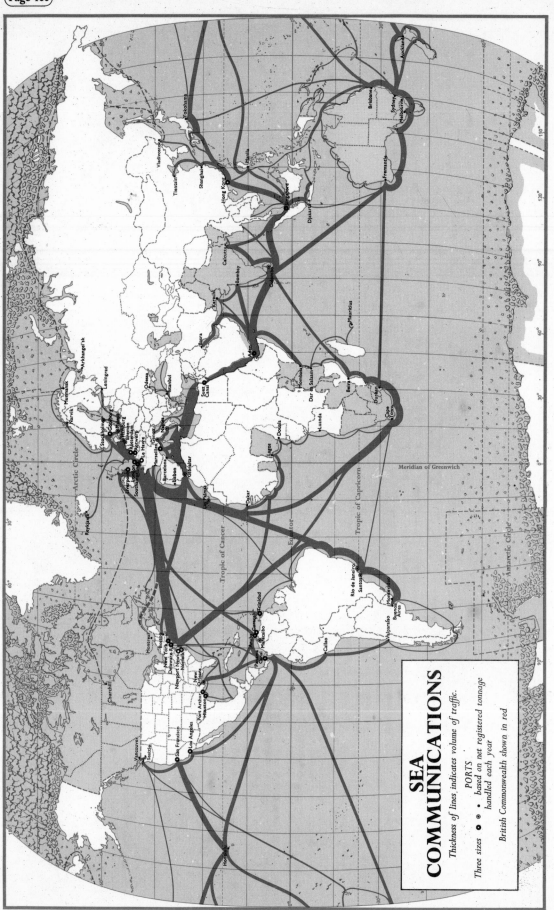

TRAVEL TIMES from LONDON by AIR and SURFACE TRANSPORT
(Times of less than 2 days are given in hours)

SEA COMMUNICATIONS

Thickness of lines indicates volume of traffic.

PORTS

Three sizes ⊙ ◉ •   *based on net registered tonnage handled each year*

British Commonwealth shown in red

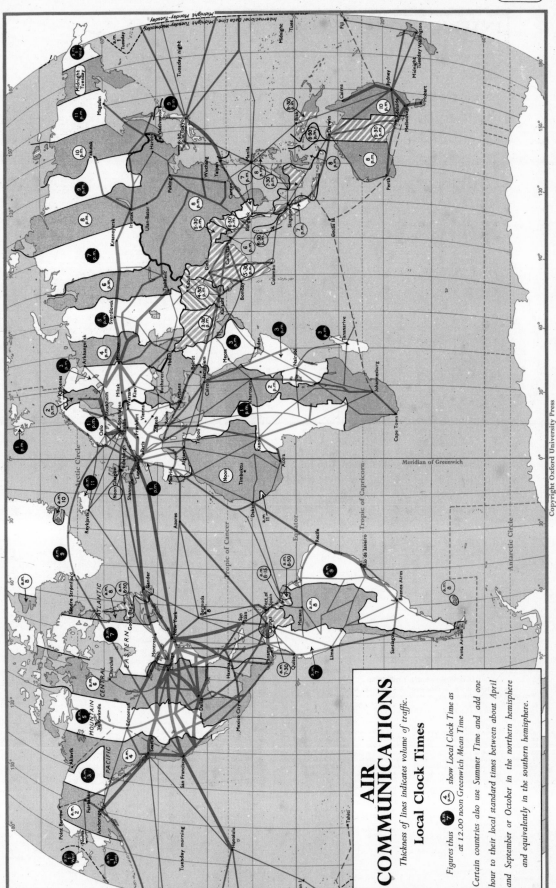

INTERNATIONAL BLOCS
1956

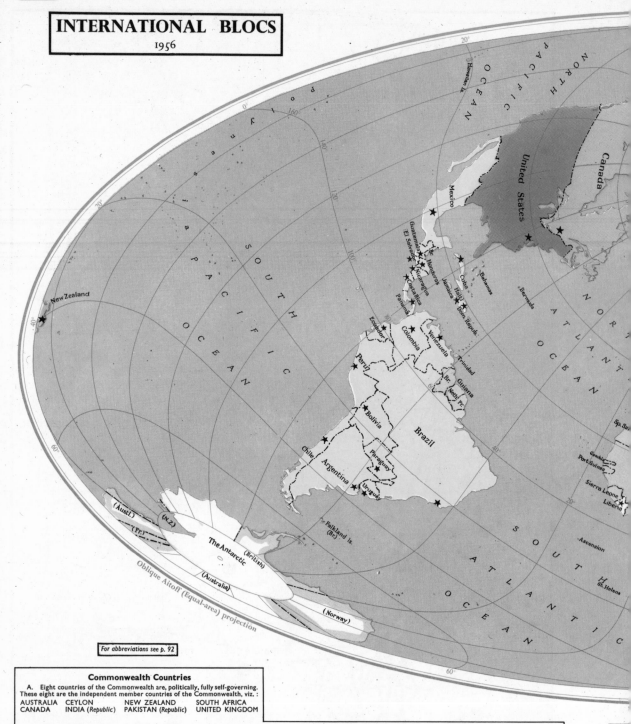

Oblique Aitoff (Equal-area) projection

For abbreviations see p. 92

Commonwealth Countries

A. Eight countries of the Commonwealth are, politically, fully self-governing. These eight are the independent member countries of the Commonwealth, viz. :

AUSTRALIA	CEYLON	NEW ZEALAND	SOUTH AFRICA
CANADA	INDIA (*Republic*)	PAKISTAN (*Republic*)	UNITED KINGDOM

B. Most of these eight members have, to a greater or less extent, other Commonwealth countries dependent upon them. The degree of dependence varies and is often difficult to calculate. If the dependent countries are in a procession towards self-government, the order of procession cannot always be precisely stated. Certain countries are, however, clearly at the head of the procession :

Caribbean Federation to be formed 1958 consisting of colonies of Barbados, Jamaica, Leeward Is., Trinidad & Tobago, and Windward Is.
Federation of Rhodesia & Nyasaland
Gold Coast (including Togoland‡)
Malaya (Federation of 9 states and 2 settlements)
Malta
Nigeria (including Cameroons‡)
Singapore

C. Some others have a substantial measure of self-government, shown often by the fact that there is a majority of elected members in the legislature, or because the native administration is given a fairly free hand. In this category may be placed, in alphabetical order :

Bahamas (*colony*)
Bermuda (*colony*)
Brunei (*protected state*)
Channel Is.
Fiji
Isle of Man
Mauritius

Sierra Leone (*colony & protectorate*)
Tonga (*protected state*)
Zanzibar (*protectorate*)

D. Next may be grouped those dependent countries in which the inhabitants have some share in the legislation, through unofficial members, elected or nominated. The extent of self-government in practice in these countries varies considerably and bears no necessary relationship to the formal constitution. In this group may be placed :

Aden Protectorate
British Honduras (*colony*)
Falkland Islands (*colony*)
Gambia (*colony & protectorate*)
Gibraltar (*colony*)

Kenya (*colony & protectorate*)
Sarawak
Seychelles (*colony*)
Tanganyika‡
Uganda (*protectorate*)

E. At the latter end of the procession probably would come the following countries, whose order would be difficult to determine :

Aden (*colony*)
Basutoland*
Bechuanaland Protectorate*
British Guiana (*colony*)
British Solomon Is. (*protectorate*)
Cyprus (*colony*)
Gilbert & Ellice Is. (*colony*)
Hong Kong (*colony*)
Nauru‡ (*Austl.*)
New Hebrides (*Anglo-French condominium*)

North Borneo (*colony*)
Papua & New Guinea‡ (*Austl.*)
Pitcairn I.
St. Helena and Ascension (*colony*)
Somaliland Protectorate*
Swaziland*
Tristan da Cunha (*colony*)
West Samoa‡ (*N.Z.*)

* High Commission territory.
‡ Trust territory.

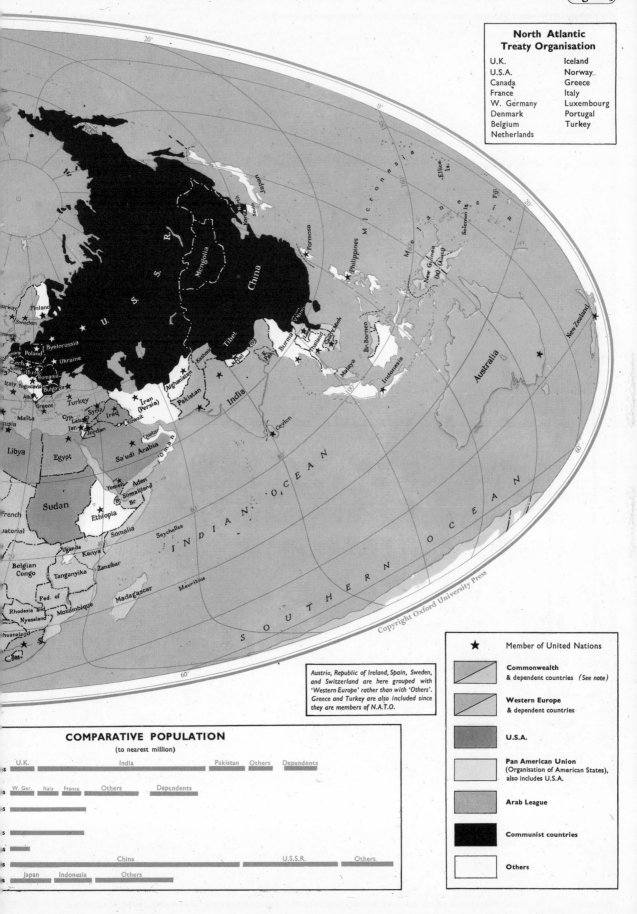

North Atlantic Treaty Organisation

U.K.	Iceland
U.S.A.	Norway
Canada	Greece
France	Italy
W. Germany	Luxembourg
Denmark	Portugal
Belgium	Turkey
Netherlands	

Austria, Republic of Ireland, Spain, Sweden, and Switzerland are here grouped with 'Western Europe' rather than with 'Others'. Greece and Turkey are also included since they are members of N.A.T.O.

Copyright Oxford University Press

★ Member of United Nations

Commonwealth & dependent countries *(See note)*

Western Europe & dependent countries

U.S.A.

Pan American Union (Organisation of American States), also includes U.S.A.

Arab League

Communist countries

Others

COMPARATIVE POPULATION
(to nearest million)

U.K.   India   Pakistan   Others   Dependents

W. Ger.   Italy   France   Others   Dependents

China   U.S.S.R.   Others

Japan   Indonesia   Others

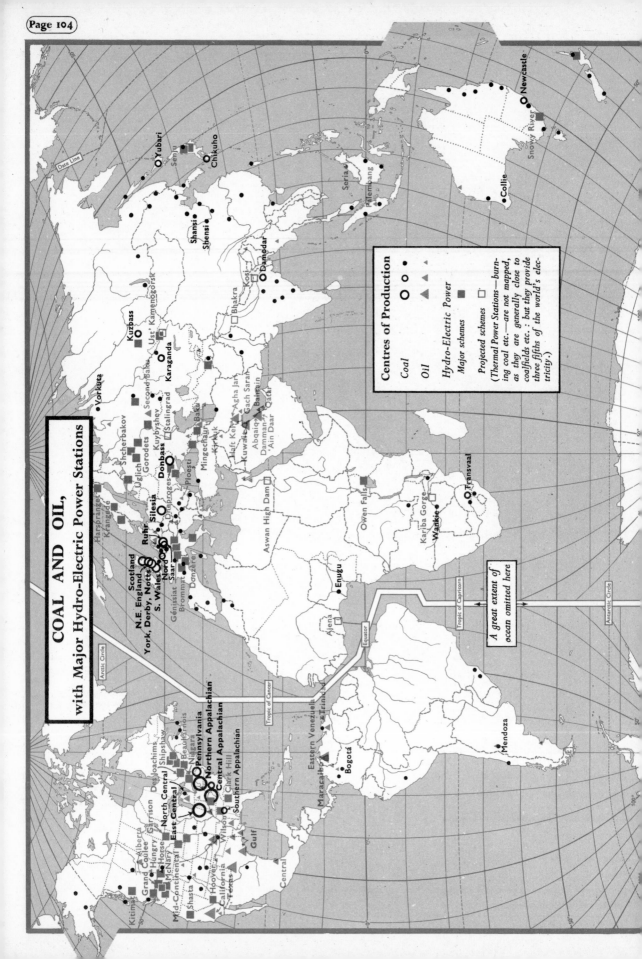

COAL AND OIL,
with Major Hydro-Electric Power Stations

Centres of Production

Coal ● ○ ◐

Oil ▲ ◗ ◤

Hydro-Electric Power
Major schemes ■
Projected schemes □

(Thermal Power Stations—burning coal etc.—are not mapped, as they are generally close to coalfields etc.; but they provide three fifths of the world's electricity.)

A great extent of ocean omitted here

Date Line

Arctic Circle

Tropic of Cancer

Equator

Tropic of Capricorn

Antarctic Circle

Newcastle
Snowy River
Collie
Seria
Palembang
Yubari
Senju
Chikuho
Shansi
Shensi
Damodar
Kosi
Bhakra
Kuzbass
Ust' Kamenogorsk
Vorkuta
Second Baku
Karaganda
Shcherbakov
Kuybyshev
Stalingrad
Uglich
Gorodets
Donbass
Ploesti
Baku
Mingechaur
Kirkuk
Haft Kel
Agha Jari
Kuwait
Gach Saran
Abqaiq
'Ain Daar
Damman
Bahrain
Qatar
Dniproges
Silesia
Ruhr
Saar
Nord
Harspränget
Krangede
Brommat
Génissiat
Donzère
Scotland
N.E. England
York, Derby, Notts.
S. Wales
Aswan High Dam
Owen Falls
Kariba Gorge
Wankie
Transvaal
Enugu
Ajena
Bogotá
Maracaibo
Eastern Venezuela
Trinidad
Mendoza
Kitimat
Grand Coulee
Alberta
Hungry Horse
Garrison
McNary
Shasta
Hoover
California
Mid-Continental
Texas
North Central
East Central
Desjoachims
Shipshaw
Beauharnois
Niagara
Pennsylvania
Northern Appalachian
Central Appalachian
Southern Appalachian
Clark Hill
Gulf
Central

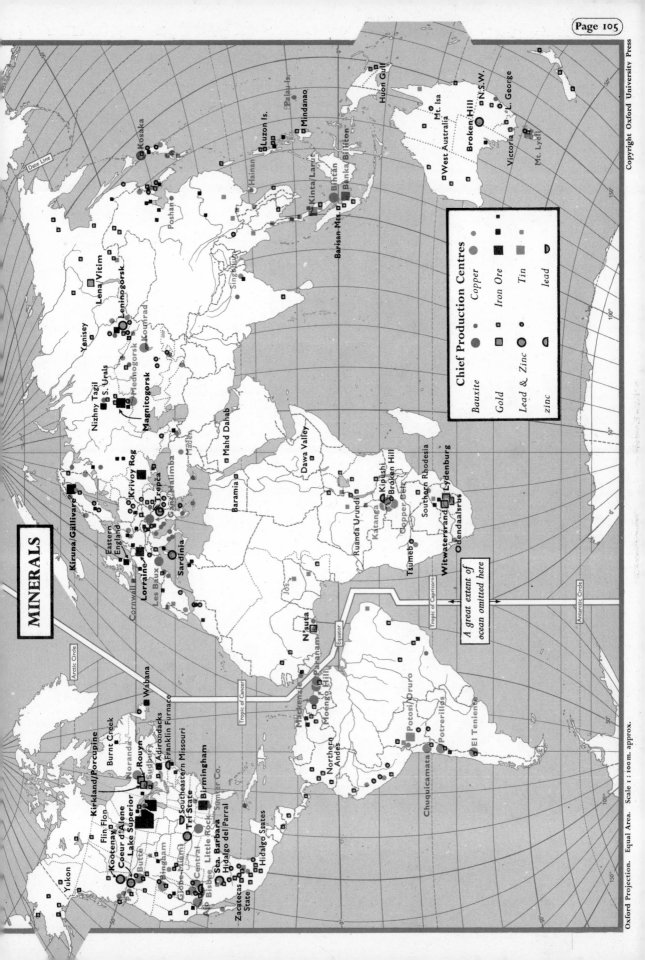

MINERALS

Chief Production Centres

		Copper
Bauxite		
Gold		Iron Ore
Lead & Zinc		Tin
zinc		lead

A great extent of ocean omitted here

Oxford Projection. Equal Area. Scale 1 : 100 m. approx.

Date Line

Arctic Circle

Tropic of Cancer

Equator

Tropic of Capricorn

Antarctic Circle

Kosaka
Palau Is.
Luzon Is.
Mindanao
Hainan
Bihtan
Kinta/Larut
Banka/Billiton
Barisan Mts.
Huon Gulf
Mt. Isa
N.S.W.
Broken Hill
West Australia
Victoria
L. George
Mt. Lyell

Poshan
Singburi
Lena/Vitim
Leninogorsk
Kounrad
Yenisey
Nizhny Tagil
S. Urals
Magnitogorsk
Hednogorsk
Krivoy Rog
Trepča
Gan/Halimba
Sardinia

Kiruna/Gällivare
Eastern England
Cornwall
Lorraine
Les Baux

Maden
Mahd Dahab
Dawa Valley
Baramia
Jos

Kilubi
Broken Hill
Kitanga
Ruanda Urundi
Copper Belt
Southern Rhodesia
Lydenburg
Witwatersrand
Odendaalsrus
Tsumeb

N'suta
Paranam
Mackenzie
Moengo Hill
Northern Andes
Potosi
Oruro
Potrerillos
El Teniente
Chuquicamata
Zacatecas State

Yukon
Flin Flon
Burnt Creek
Wabana
Kirkland/Porcupine
Kootenay
Coeur d'Alene
Lake Superior
Butte
Noranda
Rouyn
Sudbury
Adirondacks
Franklin Furnace
Southeastern Missouri
Tri State
Birmingham
Bingham
Globe-Miami
Central
Little Rock
Bisbee
Sta. Barbara
Hidalgo del Parral
Hidalgo States
Sumter Co.

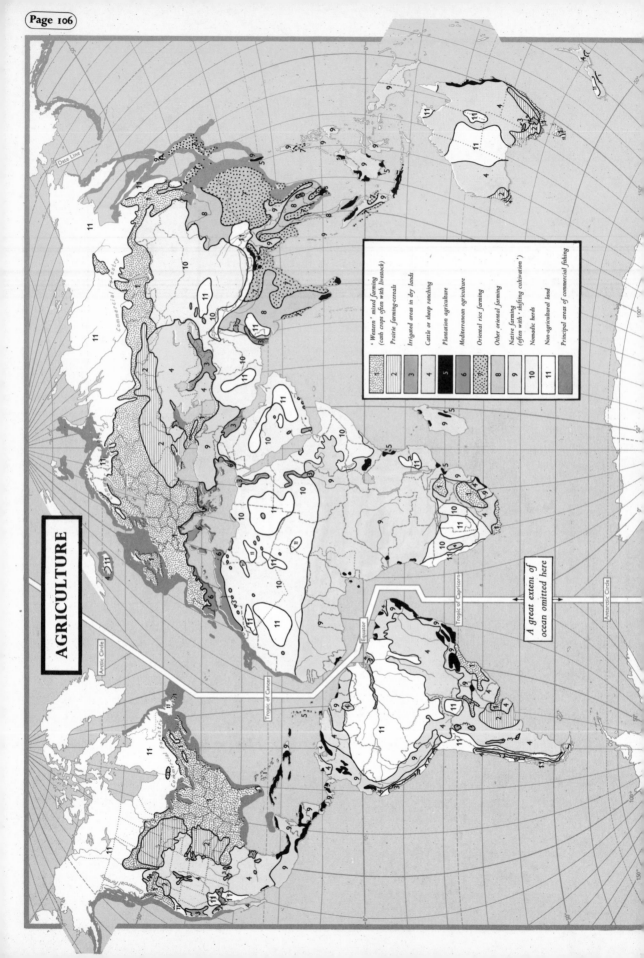

AGRICULTURE

1 'Western' mixed farming (cash crops often with livestock)
2 Prairie farming-cereals
3 Irrigated areas in dry lands
4 Cattle or sheep ranching
5 Plantation agriculture
6 Mediterranean agriculture
7 Oriental rice farming
8 Other oriental farming
9 Native farming (often with 'shifting cultivation')
10 Nomadic herds
11 Non-agricultural land
Principal areas of commercial fishing

A great extent of ocean omitted here

ABBREVIATIONS

used on the Maps and in the Gazetteers

Aber.	Aberdeen
A.C.T.	Australian Capital Territory
Admin.	Administrative
Afghan.	Afghanistan
Afr.	Africa
Alb.	Albania
Alg.	Algeria
Ang.	Angola
Ann.	Annual
Antarc.	Antarctica
Arch.	Archipelago
Arg.	Argentina
Ark.	Arkansas
Arm.	Armagh
Atl. O.	Atlantic Ocean
Austl.	Australia
Austr.	Austria
Auton.	Autonomous
Ayr	Ayrshire
B.	Bay
Basuto.	Basutoland
Bech.	Bechuanaland
Beds	Bedfordshire
Belg.	Belgium, Belgian
Ber.	Berwickshire
Berks	Berkshire
Bol.	Bolivia
Br.	British
Braz.	Brazil
Breck.	Brecknockshire
Bucks	Buckinghamshire
Bulg.	Bulgaria
Bute.	Buteshire
C., c.	Cape
Caer.	Caernarvonshire
Caith.	Caithness
Camb.	Cambodia
Cambs.	Cambridgeshire
Can.	Canada
Card.	Cardiganshire
Carm.	Carmarthenshire
Cen. Am.	Central America
Chan.	Channel
Ches.	Cheshire
Clack.	Clackmannan
Co.	County
Col.	Colombia
Col.	Colony
Corn.	Cornwall
C.R.	Costa Rica
Cumb.	Cumberland
Czech.	Czechoslovakia
D.C.	District of Columbia
Del.	Delaware
Den.	Denmark, Danish
Denb.	Denbighshire
Dept.	Department
Derby.	Derbyshire
Devon.	Devonshire
Dist.	District
Divis.	Division
Dom. Repub.	Dominican Republic
Don.	Donegal
Dumf.	Dumfriesshire
Dunb.	Dunbarton
Dur.	Durham
E.	East(ern)
E. Loth.	East Lothian
Ec.	Ecuador
El Sal.	El Salvador
Eng.	England
Eq.	Equatorial
Étg.	Étang (lagoon)
Eth.	Ethiopia
Falk. Is.	Falkland Is.
Fd.	Fjord
Fed.	Federal
Ferm.	Fermanagh
Fin.	Finland
Flint.	Flintshire
Fla.	Florida
For. for.	Forest
Fr.	France, French
Ft.	Fort
Gal.	Galway
G.B.	Great Britain
Gd.	Grand
Ger.	Germany
Glam.	Glamorgan
Glos	Gloucestershire
Gp.	Group
Grc.	Greece
Grnld	Greenland
Gt.	Great
Gu.	Guiana
Guin.	Guinea
Hants	Hampshire
Harb.	Harbour
Hd.	Head
Hebr.	Hebrides
Here.	Herefordshire
Herts	Hertfordshire
Hond.	Honduras
Hung.	Hungary
Hunts	Huntingdonshire
Î.	Île (island)
I.(s) i.(s)	Isle Island(s) island(s)
Ice.	Iceland
Ill.	Illinois
Ind.	India
Ind.	Indiana (U.S.A.)
Indon.	Indonesia
Ins.	Inset
Inv.	Inverness
Irel.	Ireland
Isr.	Israel
It.	Italy
Jap.	Japan(ese)
Jor.	Jordan
Junc.	Junction
Kans.	Kansas
Kash.	Kashmir
Kild.	Kildare
Kilk.	Kilkenny
Kinc.	Kincardine
Kinr.	Kinross
Kirkc.	Kirkcudbright
Ky.	Kentucky
L., l.	Lake, Loch, Lough, Lac, Lago
Lan.	Lanark
Lancs	Lancashire
Ld.	Land
Leb.	Lebanon
Leics.	Leicestershire
Leit.	Leitrim
Lim.	Limerick
Lincs	Lincolnshire
Lit.	Little
Lon.	Londonderry
Long.	Longford
Lr.	Lower
Lux.	Luxembourg
Madag.	Madagascar
Mal.	Malaya
Mass.	Massachusetts
Md.	Maryland
Medit.	Mediterranean Sea
Mer.	Merionethshire
Mex.	Mexico
Mich.	Michigan
Middx.	Middlesex
Midloth.	Midlothian
Minn.	Minnesota
Miss.	Mississippi
Mo.	Missouri
Mon.	Monmouthshire
Mor.	Morocco
Montg.	Montgomeryshire
Moray.	Morayshire
Moz.	Mozambique
Mt.(n)., mtn.	Mount(ain)
N.	North(ern)
Nairn.	Nairnshire
Nat.	National
Nat. Mon.	National Monument
N.C.	North Carolina
Neth.	Netherlands
Neth. N. Guin.	Netherlands New Guinea
N.H.	New Hampshire
Nic.	Nicaragua
N.J.	New Jersey
Nor.	Norway, Norwegian
Norf.	Norfolk
Northants	Northamptonshire
Northumb.	Northumberland
Notts	Nottinghamshire
N.Sc.	Nova Scotia
N.Y.	New York State
Nyasa.	Nyasaland
N.Z.	New Zealand
O.	Ocean
Ont.	Ontario
Oreg.	Oregon
Ork. Is.	Orkney Is.
Oxon.	Oxfordshire
Pa.	Pennsylvania
Pac. O.	Pacific Ocean
Peeb.	Peeblesshire
Pak.	Pakistan
P.E.I.	Prince Edward I.
Pemb	Pembrokeshire
Penin., penin.	Peninsula
Perth.	Perthshire
Phil.	Philippines
Pk.	Peak
Plat.	Plateau
Pol.	Poland
Port.	Portugal, Portuguese
P.R.	Puerto Rico
Prot.	Protectorate
Prov.	Province
Pt(e)	Point(e)
Queens.	Queensland
R., r.	River
Rad.	Radnorshire
Reg.	Region
Renf.	Renfrew
Rep., Repub.	Republic
R. of Irel.	Republic of Ireland
Res.	Reservoir
Rhod.	Rhodesia
Rom.	Romania
Rosc.	Roscommon
R. & Crom.	Ross & Cromarty
Rox.	Roxburgh
Rut.	Rutland
S.	South(ern)
Salop	Shropshire
S. Am.	South America
Sau. Arab.	Sa'udi Arabia
S.C.	South Carolina
Sd.	Sound
Selk.	Selkirk
Shet. Is.	Shetland Is.
Som.	Somerset
Sp.	Spain, Spanish
S.S.R.	Soviet Socialist Republic
St.	Saint
Staffs	Staffordshire
Stirl.	Stirling
Stn.	Station
Str.	Strait
Suff.	Suffolk
Suther.	Sutherland
Swazi.	Swaziland
Swed.	Sweden, Swedish
Switz.	Switzerland
Syr.	Syria
Tangan.	Tanganyika
Tenn.	Tennessee
Territ.	Territory
Thai.	Thailand
Tip.	Tipperary
Trin.	Trinidad
Trust.	Trusteeship
Tur.	Turkey
Tyr.	Tyrone
U.N.	United Nations
Up.	Upper
U.S.A.	United States of America
U.S.S.R.	Union of Soviet Socialist Republics
V.	Vulcan (volcano)
Va.	Virginia
Val., val.	Valley
Venez.	Venezuela
Vict.	Victoria
V. Minh	Viet Minh
V. Nam	Viet Nam
Volc.	Volcano
Vt.	Vermont
W.	West(ern)
War	Warwickshire
Wat.	Waterford
Westmor.	Westmorland
Wex.	Wexford
Wick.	Wicklow
Wig.	Wigtownshire
Wilts.	Wiltshire
Wis.	Wisconsin
W. Loth.	West Lothian
Worcs	Worcestershire
Yorks	Yorkshire
Yugo.	Yugoslavia

WORLD

AABENRAA — BALIKESIR

	Page	Lat.	Long.
Aabenraa: Denmark	**35**	55N	9E
Aachen: Germany	**32**	51N	6E
Aalborg: Denmark	**35**	57N	10E
Aalst: Belgium	**28**	51N	4E
Aare: *r.*, Switz.	**33**	47N	8E
Aarhus: Denmark	**35**	56N	10E
Abadan: Iran	**46**	30N	48E
Abakan: U.S.S.R.	**45**	54N	91E
Abancay: Peru	**86**	13S	73W
Abashiri: Japan	**52**	44N	144E
Abbeville: France	**28**	50N	2E
Abbottabad: W. Pak.	**48**	34N	73E
Abeokuta: Nigeria	**68**	7N	3E
Abercorn: N.Rhod.	**68**	9S	32E
Aberdeen: U.S.A.	**80**	45N	98W
Abidjan: Fr.W.Afr.	**62**	5N	4W
Abilene: U.S.A.	**80**	32N	100W
Abington Reef: Coral Sea	**60**	18S	150E
Abisko: Sweden	**34**	68N	19E
Abitibi, L.: Canada	**84**	48N	80W
Åbo: Finland	**35**	60N	22E
Abruzzi Molise: Italy	**30**	42N	14E
Abu: India	**48**	25N	73E
Abukuma Mts.: Japan	**52**	37N	141E
ABYSSINIA *see* ETHIOPIA			
Abyssinian Plateau	**63**	10N	37E
Acapulco: Mexico	**82**	17N	100W
Accra: Gold Coast	**68**	5N	0
Aci, L.: Turkey	**31**	38N	30E
Aconcagua: *mtn.*, Arg.	**88**	33S	70W
Acqui: Italy	**33**	45N	8E
Ada: Gold Coast	**68**	6N	0
Adam's Bridge: Ceylon/Ind.	**48**	9N	80E
Adana: Turkey	**46**	37N	35E
Adapazarı: Turkey	**31**	41N	30E
Addis Ababa: Ethiopia	**63**	9N	39E
Adelaide: Austl.	**61**	35S	139E
Aden: & *gulf*	**63**	13N	45E
ADEN PROTECTORATE	**63**	15N	47E
Adige: *r.*, Italy	**33**	45N	11E
Adirondack Mts.: U.S.A.	**85**	44N	74W
Admiralty Is.: Pac.O.	**54**	2S	147E
Adour: *r.*, France	**29**	44N	1W
Adrian: U.S.A.	**84**	42N	84W
Adrianople: Turkey	**31**	42N	27E
Adriatic Sea	**30**	—	—
Aduwa: Ethiopia	**67**	14N	39E
Aegean Is.: & *sea*	**31**	38N	26E
AFGHANISTAN	**46**	—	—
Afyonkarahisar: Turkey	**31**	39N	30E
Agadir: Morocco	**62**	30N	10W
Agartala: India	**49**	24N	91E
Agde, Cap d': France	**29**	43N	3E
Agen: France	**29**	44N	1E
Agenais: France	**29**	44N	1E
Agincourt: France	**29**	51N	2E
Agra: India	**48**	27N	78E
Agrigento: Sicily	**30**	37N	14E
Agulhas, C.: S.Afr.	**71**	35S	20E
Ahaggar: Algeria	**62**	23N	6E
Ahmadabad: India	**48**	23N	73E
Ahvenanmaa: *is.*, Finland	**35**	60N	20E
Ahwaz: Iran	**46**	31N	49E
Aiguesmortes: & *gulf*, Fr.	**29**	44N	4E
Aïn Sefra: Algeria	**62**	33N	1W
Aïr: Fr.W.Afr.	**62**	18N	8E
Aisne: *r.*, France	**28**	49N	3E
Aix-en-Provence: France	**29**	44N	5E
Aix-les-Bains: France	**29**	46N	6E
Ajaccio: Corsica	**30**	42N	9E
Ajena: Gold Coast	**68**	6N	0E
Ajmer: India	**48**	26N	75E
Ajo: U.S.A.	**80**	32N	113E
Akaishi Mts.: Japan	**52**	35N	138W
Akaroa: N.Z.	**53**	44S	173E
Akhisar: Turkey	**31**	39N	28E
Akita: Japan	**52**	40N	140E
Aklavik: Canada	**78**	68N	135E
Akmolinsk: U.S.S.R.	**45**	51N	71W
Akola: India	**48**	21N	77E
Akritas, C.: Greece	**31**	37N	22E
Akron: U.S.A.	**84**	41N	82E
Akşehir: Turkey	**31**	38N	32W
Aksha: U.S.S.R.	**43**	50N	113E
Aktyubinsk: U.S.S.R.	**45**	50N	57E
Akureyri: Iceland	**34**	66N	18E
Akyab: Burma	**47**	20N	93W
Alabama: *r.*, U.S.A.	**81**	32N	87E
Alabama: *State*, U.S.A.	**81**	33N	87W
Alai Range: U.S.S.R.	**45**	39N	70W
Ala Kul': U.S.S.R.	**45**	46N	82E
Åland Is.: Finland	**35**	60N	20E
Alapayevsk: U.S.S.R.	**45**	58N	62E
Ala Shan: *mtns.*, China	**50**	40N	103E
Alaska: *Territ.*, U.S.A.	**78**	65N	150E
Alaska, Gulf of: Alaska	**78**	58N	145W
Alaskan Highway: U.S.A.	**78**	61N	140W
Alaska Peninsula: Alaska	**78**	56N	160W
Alassio: Italy	**33**	44N	8W
Alba: Italy	**33**	45N	8E
Albacete: Spain	**25**	39N	2W
Alba Iulia: Romania	**31**	46N	24E
ALBANIA	**31**	—	—
Albany: Austl.	**60**	35S	118E
Albany: U.S.A.	**85**	43N	74W
Albemarle Sound: U.S.A.	**85**	36N	76W
Albert: France	**28**	50N	3E
Albert, Lake: Uganda	**68**	3N	30E
Alberta: *Prov.*, Canada	**78**	55N	115W
Albert Lea: U.S.A.	**84**	44N	94W
Albertville: Belg. Congo	**68**	6S	29E
Albi: France	**29**	44N	2E
Albret, Pays d': France	**29**	44N	1W
Albuera *see* La Albuera			
Albula Pass: Switz.	**33**	47N	10E
Albuquerque: U.S.A.	**80**	35N	107W
Albury: Austl.	**61**	36S	147E
Alcazar: Spain	**25**	39N	3W
Alcazarquivir: Morocco	**25**	35N	6W
Alcoy: Spain	**25**	39N	1W
Aldan: & *r.*, U.S.S.R.	**43**	58N	130E
Alegranza: *i.*, Canary Is.	**62**	29N	13W
Aleksandrov Gay: U.S.S.R.	**44**	50N	49E
Aleksandrovsk: U.S.S.R.	**43**	51N	142E
Alençon: France	**28**	48N	0
Aleppo: Syria	**44**	36N	37E
Alès: France	**29**	44N	4E
Alessandria: Italy	**33**	45N	9E
Ålesund: Norway	**34**	62N	6E
Aletschhorn: *mtn.*, Switz.	**33**	46N	8E
Aleutian Is.: Alaska	**54**	50N	170W
Aleutian Range: Alaska	**78**	60N	155W
Alexander I.: Antarctica	**89**	71S	72W
Alexandra: N.Z.	**53**	45S	169E
Alexandria: Egypt	**63**	31N	30E
Alexandria: U.S.A.	**81**	31N	92W
Alexandrina, L.: Austl.	**61**	35S	139E
Alexandroúpolis: Greece	**31**	41N	26E
Algarve: *Prov.*, Portugal	**25**	37N	8W
Algeciras, Bay of: Spain	**25**	36N	5W
ALGERIA	**62**	—	—
Algiers: & *Prov.*, Algeria	**62**	37N	3E
Algoa Bay: S. Africa	**69**	34S	26E
Algonquin Park: Canada	**85**	46N	78W
Alicante: Spain	**25**	38N	1W
Alice Springs: Austl.	**58**	24S	134E
Aligarh: India	**48**	28N	78E
Alingsås: Sweden	**35**	57N	13E
Alkmaar: Neth.	**32**	53N	5E
Allahabad: India	**48**	25N	82E
Allard Lake: Canada	**79**	50N	63W
Allegheny Mts.: U.S.A.	**85**	37N	81W
Allentown: U.S.A.	**85**	41N	75W
Alleppey: India	**48**	9N	76E
Allgäuer Alps: Austr./Ger.	**33**	47N	10E
Alliance: U.S.A.	**84**	41N	81W
Allier: *r.*, France	**29**	47N	3E
Alma-Ata: U.S.S.R.	**45**	43N	77E
Almaden: Spain	**25**	39N	5W
Almeida: Portugal	**25**	41N	7W
Almeria: Spain	**25**	37N	2W
Alor Star: Malaya	**51**	6N	100E
Alpena: U.S.A.	**84**	45N	83W
Alps, The: *mtns.*, Europe	**30**	—	—
Alsace: *Old Prov.*, France	**28**	48N	7E
Alta: Norway	**34**	70N	23E
Altai Range: Mongolia	**50**	46N	93E
Altenburg: Germany	**32**	51N	12E
Altiplano: *plat.*, S. America	**88**	17S	69W
Alton: U.S.A.	**84**	39N	90W
Altona: Germany	**32**	54N	10E
Altoona: U.S.A.	**85**	41N	78W
Altyn Tagh: *mtns.*, China	**47**	37N	85E
Alwar: India	**48**	28N	77E
Amarillo: U.S.A.	**80**	35N	102W
Amazon: *r.*, S. America	**86**	4S	60W
Ambala: India	**48**	30N	77E
Ambarchik: U.S.S.R.	**43**	70N	162E
Amberg: Germany	**32**	49N	12E
Amboina: Indonesia	**51**	4S	128E
Amboise: France	**29**	47N	1E
Amersfoort: Neth.	**32**	52N	5E
Amherst: Canada	**85**	46N	64W
Amiens: France	**28**	50N	2E
'Amman: Jordan	**46**	32N	36E
Amne Machen Shan: China	**50**	35N	100E
Amoy: China	**50**	24N	117E
Amritsar: India	**48**	32N	75E
Amsterdam: Netherlands	**32**	52N	5E
Amu Darya: *r.*, U.S.S.R.	**42**	37N	65E
Amur: *r.*, U.S.S.R./China	**43**	52N	138E
Anadyr': & *gulf*, U.S.S.R.	**43**	65N	178W
Anaimudi: *mtn.*, India	**48**	10N	77E
Anambas Is.: Indonesia	**50**	3N	106E
Anan'yev: U.S.S.R.	**44**	48N	30E
Anápolis: Brazil	**87**	16S	49W
Ancenis: France	**29**	47N	1W
Anchorage: Alaska	**78**	61N	150W
Ancona: Italy	**33**	44N	14E
Åndalsnes: Norway	**34**	62N	8E
Andalusia: Spain	**25**	37N	5W
Andaman Is.: & *sea*, India	**47**	12N	93E
Andermatt: Switz.	**33**	47N	9E
Andernach: Germany	**32**	50N	7E
Anderson: U.S.A.	**84**	40N	86W
Andes: *range*, S. America	**89**	—	—
Andizhan: U.S.S.R.	**45**	41N	73E
ANDORRA: & *town*	**29**	43N	2E
Andreyevka: U.S.S.R.	**45**	46N	81E
Andros: *i.*, Greece	**31**	38N	25E
Aneto: *mtn.*, Spain	**29**	43N	1E
Angara: *r.*, U.S.S.R.	**43**	58N	95E
Angel de la Guarda: *i.*, Mex.	**82**	30N	113W
Angel Falls: Venezuela	**86**	6N	62W
Angers: France	**29**	47N	1W
Angical: Brazil	**87**	12S	45W
Angkor: *ruins*, Indo-China	**51**	13N	104E
Anglooedl: Austl.	**61**	29S	148E
ANGOLA	**71**	—	—
Angoulême: France	**29**	46N	0
Angoumois: *Old Prov.*, France	**29**	46N	0
Angren: U.S.S.R.	**45**	41N	70E
Aniak: Alaska	**78**	62N	160W
Aniva Bay: U.S.S.R.	**43**	46N	143E
Anjou: *Old Prov.*, France	**29**	48N	1W
Ankara: Turkey	**46**	40N	33E
Ankarata Mts.: Madag.	**71**	20S	47E
Anking: China	**50**	31N	117E
Annaberg: Germany	**32**	51N	13E
Annam Range: Indo-China	**51**	18N	105E
Annapolis: U.S.A.	**85**	39N	76W
Annapolis Royal: Canada	**85**	45N	66W
Ann Arbor: U.S.A.	**84**	42N	84W
Annecy: France	**29**	46N	6E
Annonay: France	**29**	45N	5E
Ansbach: Germany	**32**	4911	11E
Anshan: China	**50**	41N	123E
Ansi: China	**43**	40N	95E
Antakya (Antioch): Turkey	**46**	36N	36E
Antalya: Turkey	**31**	37N	31E
Antequera: Spain	**25**	37N	4W
Anti-Atlas: *mtns.*, Morocco	**62**	30N	8W
Antibes: France	**29**	44N	7E
Anticosti I.: Canada	**79**	49N	63W
Antifer, Cap d': France	**28**	50N	0
Antigua: Guatemala	**82**	15N	91W
Antigua: *i.*, W. Indies	**83**	17N	62W
Antofagasta: Chile	**88**	24S	70W
Antsirane: Madag.	**71**	12S	49E
Antung: China	**50**	40N	125E
Antwerp (Anvers): Belg.	**28**	51N	4E
Anyang: China	**50**	36N	114E
Anzhero-Sudzhensk: U.S.S.R.	**45**	56N	86E
Anzio: Italy	**30**	41N	13E
Aoiz: Spain	**29**	43N	1W
Aomori: Japan	**52**	41N	141E
Aosta: Italy	**33**	46N	7E
Apeldoorn: Netherlands	**32**	52N	6E
Apennines: *mtns.*, Italy	**30**	—	—
Apostle Is.: U.S.A.	**84**	47N	91W
Appalachian Mts.: U.S.A.	**84/5**	—	—
Appleton: U.S.A.	**84**	44N	88W
Apulia: Italy	**30**	41N	16E
Apurimac: *r.*, Peru	**88**	12S	74W
'Aqaba: Jordan	**46**	29N	35E
Aquila: Italy	**30**	42N	13E
Aquiles Serdán: Mexico	**80**	28N	106W
Aquitaine: *Old Prov.*, Fr.	**29**	45N	0
ARABIA *see* SA'UDI ARABIA			
Arabian Sea	**46**	—	—
Aracajú: Brazil	**87**	11S	37W
Arad: Romania	**31**	46N	21E
Arafura Sea	**58**	—	—
Aragon: Spain	**25**	42N	0
Araguaia: *r.*, Brazil	**87**	12S	51W
Arakan Yoma: Burma	**50**	21N	94E
Araks (Araxes): *r.*, U.S.S.R./Iran	**44**	39N	48E
Aral Sea: U.S.S.R.	**45**	45N	60E
Aral'sk: U.S.S.R.	**45**	47N	62E
Ararat, Mt.: Turkey	**46**	40N	44E
Arauca: Colombia	**86**	7N	71W
Arcachon: France	**29**	45N	1W
Arcot: India	**48**	13N	79E
Arctic Ocean	**42/3**	—	—
Ardèche: *r.*, France	**29**	44N	4E
Ardennes: *mtns.*, Belgium	**28**	50N	5E
Arendal: Norway	**35**	58N	9E
Arequipa: Peru	**88**	17S	72W
Arezzo: Italy	**30**	43N	12E
Argaum: India	**48**	21N	77E
Argentan: France	**28**	49N	0
Argenteuil: France	**28**	49N	2E
ARGENTINA	**88/9**	—	—
Argonne, Forêt d': France	**28**	49N	5E
Argos: Greece	**31**	37N	23E
Argostolion: Cephalonia	**31**	38N	20E
Argyrokastro: Albania	**31**	40N	20E
Arica: Chile	**86**	18S	70W
Ariège: *r.*, France	**29**	43N	2E
Arizona: *State*, U.S.A.	**80**	35N	112W
Arkansas: *r.* & *State*, U.S.A.	**81**	35N	93W
Arkhangel'sk: U.S.S.R.	**42**	64N	40E
Arkona, C.: Germany	**27**	55N	14E
Arlberg Pass: Austria	**33**	47N	10E
Arles: France	**29**	44N	5E
Arlon: Belgium	**28**	50N	6E
Armavir: U.S.S.R.	**44**	45N	41E
Armenian S.S.R.: U.S.S.R.	**44**	40N	45E
Armentières: France	**28**	51N	3E
Armidale: Austl.	**61**	31S	152E
Arnhem: Netherlands	**32**	52N	6E
Arnhem Land: Austl.	**58**	14S	133E
Arno: *r.*, Italy	**33**	44N	11E
Arnsberger Wald: Germany	**32**	51N	8E
Arras: France	**28**	50N	3E
Arrée, Mts. d': France	**28**	48N	4W
Arromanches: France	**28**	49N	1W
Arrowsmith, Mt.: N.Z.	**53**	43S	172E
Arta: Greece	**31**	39N	21E
Arthur Pass: N.Z.	**53**	43S	172E
Artois: *Old Prov.*, France	**28**	50N	2E
Artsiz: U.S.S.R.	**31**	46N	29E
Aruba: *i.*, S. America	**86**	12N	70W
Aru Is.: Indonesia	**51**	6S	134E
Arusha: Tangan.	**68**	3S	37E
Arvida: Canada	**85**	48N	71W
Arvidsjaur: Sweden	**34**	66N	19E
Arvika: Sweden	**35**	60N	13E
Arys': U.S.S.R.	**45**	42N	69E
Asahikawa: Japan	**52**	44N	142E
Asansol: India	**48**	24N	87E
Ascension I.: Atlantic O.	**24**	9S	15W
Aschaffenburg: Germany	**32**	50N	9E
Ascoli Piceno: Italy	**30**	43N	14E
Asenovgrad: Bulgaria	**31**	42N	25E
Ashanti: Gold Coast	**68**	7N	2W
Ashburton: N.Z.	**53**	44S	172E
Ashburton: *r.*, Austl.	**58**	23S	115W
Asheville: U.S.A.	**81**	36N	82W
Ashizuri, C.: Japan	**52**	33N	133E
Ashkhabad: U.S.S.R.	**45**	38N	58E
Ashland: Ky., U.S.A.	**84**	38N	83W
Ashland: Ohio, U.S.A.	**84**	41N	82W
Ashland: Oreg., U.S.A.	**80**	42N	123W
Ashland: Wis., U.S.A.	**84**	47N	91W
Ashtabula: U.S.A.	**84**	42N	81W
Ashuanipi, L.: Canada	**79**	52N	66W
Asmara: Ethiopia	**63**	15N	39E
Assam: India	**49**	27N	93E
Assaye: India	**48**	20N	76E
Assen: Netherlands	**32**	53N	76E
Assiniboia: Canada	**80**	50N	106W
Assiniboine: *r.*, Canada	**80**	50N	106W
Assisi: Italy	**30**	43N	13E
Astara: U.S.S.R.	**44**	39N	49E
Asti: Italy	**33**	54N	8S
Astipalaia: , *i.*, Greece	**31**	37N	26E
Astoria: U.S.A.	**80**	46N	124W
Astrakhan': U.S.S.R.	**44**	46N	48E
Asturias: *Old Prov.*, Spain	**25**	43N	7W
Asunción: Paraguay	**88**	25S	58W
Aswan: & *dam*, Egypt	**63**	24N	33E
Asyut: Egypt	**63**	27N	31E
Atacama Desert: S. America	**88**	22S	69W
Atasuskiy: U.S.S.R.	**45**	49N	72E
Atbara: & *r.*, Sudan	**63**	18N	34E
Atbasar: U.S.S.R.	**45**	52N	68E
Athabasca, L.: & *r.*, Canada	**78**	59N	110W
Athens (Athenai): Greece	**31**	38N	24W
Athens: U.S.A.	**81**	34N	83E
Athos: *penin.*, Greece	**31**	40N	24W
Atlanta: U.S.A.	**81**	34N	84W
Atlantic City: U.S.A.	**85**	39N	75
Atlantic Ocean	**24**	—	—E
Aubagne: France	**29**	43N	6E
Aube: *r.*, France	**28**	48N	4E
Aubrac, Mts. d': France	**29**	45N	3W
Auburn: Maine, U.S.A.	**85**	44N	70W
Auburn: N.Y., U.S.A.	**85**	43N	77W
Aubusson: France	**29**	46N	2E
Auch: France	**29**	44N	1E
Auckland: N.Z.	**53**	37S	175E
Aude: *r.*, France	**29**	43N	3E
Audierne: & *bay*, France	**28**	48N	5W
Augsburg: Germany	**33**	48N	11E
Augusta: Austl.	**60**	34S	115E
Augusta: Georgia, U.S.A.	**81**	33N	82W
Augusta: Maine, U.S.A.	**85**	44N	70W
Aumale: France	**28**	50N	2E
Aunis: *Old Prov.*, France	**29**	46N	1W
Aurangabad: India	**48**	20N	75E
Aurich: Germany	**32**	53N	7E
Aurignac: France	**29**	43N	1E
Aurillac: France	**29**	45N	2E
Aurora: U.S.A.	**84**	42N	88W
Aussig: Czech.	**32**	51N	14E
Austerlitz: Czech.	**27**	49N	17E
Austin: Minn., U.S.A.	**84**	44N	93W
Austin: Nevada, U.S.A.	**80**	39N	117W
Austin: Texas, U.S.A.	**80**	30N	98W
Austral: *is.*, Pacific O.	**55**	22S	150W
AUSTRALIA	**58/9**	—	—
Australian Capital Territory	**61**	35S	149E
AUSTRIA	**26/7**	—	—
Autun: France	**29**	47N	4E
Auvergne: *Old Prov.* & *mtns.*, France	**29**	45N	3E
Auxerre: France	**28**	48N	4E
Avallon: France	**29**	47N	4E
Aveiro: Portugal	**25**	41N	9W
Avellaneda: Argentina	**88**	35S	58W
Aveyron: *r.*, France	**29**	44N	2E
Avignon: France	**29**	44N	5E
Ávila: Spain	**25**	41N	5W
Avranches: France	**28**	49N	1W
Awash: Ethiopia	**63**	9N	40E
Axel-Heilberg I.: Canada	**79**	80N	90W
Ayacucho: Peru	**86**	13S	74W
Ayaguz: U.S.S.R.	**45**	48N	80E
Aydın: Turkey	**31**	38N	28E
Aylmer, L.: Canada	**78**	64N	107W
Ayon I.: U.S.S.R.	**43**	70N	168E
Ayutthaya: Thailand	**51**	14N	100E
Ayvalık: Turkey	**31**	39N	27E
Azerbaijan S.S.R.: U.S.S.R.	**44**	41N	47E
Azores: *is.*, Atlantic O.	**24**	39N	29W
Azov, Sea of: U.S.S.R.	**44**	46N	37E
Babar Is: Indonesia	**51**	8S	130E
Bab el Mandeb: *str.*, Eth./Arabia	**62**	13N	43E
Bacău: Romania	**31**	47N	27E
Bacolod: Phil.	**51**	11N	123E
Badajoz: Spain	**25**	39N	7W
Baden: *Old Prov.*, Germany	**33**	49N	8E
Baden: Switzerland	**33**	47N	8E
Baden-Baden: Germany	**33**	49N	8E
Bad Ischl: Austria	**33**	48N	14E
Bad Kissingen: Germany	**32**	50N	10E
Bad Kreuznach: Germany	**32**	50N	8E
Bad Reichenhall: Ger.	**33**	48N	13E
Baffin Bay: Canada	**79**	73N	70E
Baffin I.: Canada	**79**	70N	75W
Baghdad: Iraq	**46**	34N	45E
Bagheria: Sicily	**30**	38N	14E
Bahama Is.: West Indies	**83**	25N	75W
Bahawalpur: W. Pakistan	**48**	29N	72E
Bahia: Brazil	**87**	13S	39W
Bahía Blanca: Argentina	**88**	39S	62W
Bahraich: India	**48**	28N	82E
Bahrain I.: Sa'udi Arabia	**46**	26N	50E
Bahr el Ghazal: *r.*, Fr. Eq. Afr.	**62**	14N	17E
Bahr el Ghazal: *Prov.* & *r.*, Sudan	**70**	10N	27E
Baia-Mare: Romania	**27**	48N	24E
Bailen: Spain	**25**	38N	4W
Băilesti: Romania	**31**	44N	23E
Bailleul: France	**28**	51N	3E
Bakersfield: U.S.A.	**80**	35N	119W
Bakony Forest: Hungary	**27**	47N	18E
Baku: U.S.S.R.	**44**	40N	50E
Balaghat: India	**48**	22N	80E
Balaklava: Austl.	**61**	34S	138E
Balaklava: U.S.S.R.	**44**	45N	34E
Balashov: U.S.S.R.	**44**	51N	43E
Balasore: India	**48**	21N	87E
Balaton, L.: Hungary	**27**	47N	18E
Balboa: Panama	**83**	*Inset*	
Bâle: Switzerland	**33**	48N	8E
Balearic Is.: Spain	**25**	—	—
Balen: Belgium	**28**	51N	5E
Bali: *i.*, Indonesia	**51**	8S	115E
Balıkesir: Turkey	**31**	40N	28E

WORLD

BALIKPAPAN — BURDEKIN

	Page	Lat.	Long.
Balikpapan: Borneo	51	1S	117E
Balkan Mts.: Bulgaria	31	43N	25E
Balkhash: & *l.*, U.S.S.R.	45	47N	75E
Ballarat: Austl.	61	38S	144E
Ballina: Austl.	61	29S	154E
Balmaceda: Chile	89	46S	72W
Balovale: N. Rhodesia	69	14S	23E
Balranald: Austl.	61	35S	144E
Balsas: *r.*, Mexico	82	18N	99W
Balta: U.S.S.R.	31	48N	30E
Baltic Sea:	35	—	—
Baltimore: U.S.A.	85	39N	77W
Baltrum: *i.*, Germany	32	54N	7E
Baluchistan: W. Pak.	48	27N	66E
Bamako: Fr. W. Africa	62	13N	8W
Bamba: Fr. W. Africa	62	17N	2W
Bamberg: Germany	32	50N	11E
Bamenda: Nigeria	68	6N	10E
Banat: Romania	31	45N	21E
Banaras: India	48	25N	83E
Bancannia, L.: Austl.	61	31S	142E
Bandar Abbas: Iran	46	27N	56E
Bandar Shah: Iran	46	37N	54E
Bandar Shahpur: Iran	46	30N	49E
Banda Sea: Indonesia	51	6S	127E
Banderas Bay: Mexico	82	21N	106W
Bandirma: Turkey	31	40N	28E
Bandjarmasin: Borneo	51	3S	115E
Bandra: India	48	19N	73E
Bandung: Java	51	7S	107E
Banff: Canada	80	51N	115W
Bangalore: India	48	13N	78E
Bangka: *i.*, Indonesia	51	2S	106E
Bangkok: Thailand	51	14N	100E
Bangor: U.S.A.	85	45N	69W
Bangui: Fr. Eq. Africa	70	4N	18E
Bangweulu, L.: N. Rhod.	68	11S	31E
Banja Luka: Yugoslavia	30	45N	17E
Banks I.: Canada	78	73N	120W
Bannu: W. Pakistan	48	33N	71E
Bapaume: France	28	50N	3E
Baranovichi: U.S.S.R.	44	53N	26E
Barbados: *i.*, W. Indies	83	13N	60W
Barbuda: *i.*, W. Indies	83	18N	62W
Barcelona: Spain	25	41N	2E
Barcelona: Venezuela	86	10N	65W
Barcelonnette: France	29	44N	7E
Barcoo: *r.*, Austl.	59	24S	144E
Bareilly: India	48	28N	80E
Barents Sea: U.S.S.R.	42	72N	40E
Bar Harbor: U.S.A.	85	44N	68W
Bari: Italy	30	41N	17E
Barkly Tableland: Austl.	58	18S	135E
Barkly West: S. Africa	69	28S	25E
Bârlad: Romania	31	46N	28E
Bar-le-Duc: France	28	49N	5E
Barlee, L.: Austl.	60	29S	119E
Barletta: Italy	30	41N	16E
Barlin: France	20	50N	3E
Barnato: Austl.	61	32S	145E
Barnaul: U.S.S.R.	45	53N	84E
Baroda: India	48	22N	73E
Barquisimeto: Venez.	86	10N	69W
Barraba: Austl.	61	30S	151E
Barrackpore: India	48	23N	88E
Barranquilla: Colombia	86	11N	75W
Barrier Mts.: N.Z.	53	45S	168E
Barrow, Point: Alaska	78	72N	156W
Barry Mts.: Austl.	61	37S	147E
Bar-sur-Seine: France	28	48N	4E
Basel: Switzerland	33	48N	8E
Basilicata: *Reg.*, Italy	30	41N	16E
Baskatong Reservoir: Can.	85	47N	76W
Basra: 'Iraq	46	30N	48E
Bassein: & *r.*, Burma	47	17N	95E
Basse-Terre: Guadeloupe	83	16N	62W
Bass Strait: Austl.	61	40S	145E
Bastia: Corsica	30	43N	9E
Bastogne: Belgium	28	50N	6E
Bastuträsk: Sweden	34	65N	20E
BASUTOLAND	69	29S	27E
Bata: Sp. Guinea	68	2N	10E
Bataan Penin.: Phil.	51	15N	120E
Batang: China	50	30N	99E
Batavia *see* Djakarta			
Bathurst: Austl.	61	33S	150E
Bathurst: Canada	85	48N	66W
Bathurst: Gambia	62	13N	17W
Bathurst, Cape: Canada	78	71N	128W
Bathurst I.: Austl.	58	12S	130E
Bathurst I.: Canada	78	76N	100W
Baton Rouge: U.S.A.	81	31N	91W
Batticaloa: Ceylon	48	8N	82E
Battle Creek: *city*, U.S.A.	84	42N	85W
Battle Harbour: Canada	79	52N	55W
Batumi: U.S.S.R.	46	42N	42E
Batz, Î. de: France	28	49N	4W
Bauchi: & *plat.*, Nigeria	68	10N	10E
Bautzen: Ger.	32	51N	14E
Bavaria: *Prov.*, Germany	33	48N	11E
Bawdwin: Burma	47	23N	97E
Bayan Kara Shan: *mtns.*, China	50	34N	99E
Bay City: U.S.A.	84	44N	84W
Bayeux: France	28	49N	1W
Baykal, L.: U.S.S.R.	43	53N	107E
Baykonur: U.S.S.R.	45	47N	66E
Baymak: U.S.S.R.	44	53N	58E
Bayonne: France	29	43N	1W
Bayreuth: Germany	32	50N	12E
Baza: Spain	25	37N	3W
Beachport: Austl.	61	38S	140E
Bear I.: U.S.S.R.	42	74N	20E
Béarn: *Old Prov.*, France	29	43N	1W
Beas: *r.*, India	48	32N	76E
Beauce: France	28	48N	2E
Beaufort Sea	78	73N	140W
Beaufort West: S. Africa	69	32S	23E
Beauharnois: Canada	85	45N	74W

	Page	Lat.	Long.
Beaujolais, Mts. du: Fr.	29	46N	4E
Beaumont: U.S.A.	81	30N	94W
Beaune: France	29	47N	5E
Beauvais: France	28	49N	2E
Beaver Lodge Lake: Can.	78	60N	108W
BECHUANALAND	69	—	—
Bedford: U.S.A.	84	39N	87W
Bega: Austl.	61	37S	150E
Begovat: U.S.S.R.	45	40N	69E
Beira: Mozambique	69	20S	35E
Beirut: Lebanon	46	34N	35E
Beit Bridge: S. Rhod.	69	22S	30E
Beja: Portugal	25	38N	8W
Bela: W. Pakistan	48	26N	66E
Belaya: *r.*, U.S.S.R.	44	54N	56E
Bélem: Brazil	87	1S	48W
Belfort: France	29	48N	7E
Belgaum: India	48	16N	75E
BELGIAN CONGO	70/1	—	—
BELGIUM	28	—	—
Belgrade: Yugoslavia	31	45N	20E
Belitung: *i.*, Indon.	51	3S	108E
Belize: Br. Honduras	82	17N	88W
Bellac: France	29	46N	1E
Bellano: Italy	33	46N	9E
Bellary: India	48	15N	77E
Bellegarde: France	29	46N	6E
Belle Île-en-Mer: France	28	47N	3W
Belle Isle: Canada	79	52N	55W
Belleville: Canada	85	44N	77W
Belleville: U.S.A.	84	39N	90W
Bellingham: U.S.A.	80	49N	123W
Bellinzona: Switz.	33	46N	9E
Belluno: Italy	33	46N	12E
Belmont: Austl.	61	33S	152E
Belo Horizonte: Brazil	88	20S	44W
Beloit: U.S.A.	84	43N	89W
Bel'tsy: U.S.S.R.	31	47N	28E
Belyando: *r.*, Austl.	60	22S	146E
Belyy I.: U.S.S.R.	42	73N	70E
Bemidji: Canada	84	47N	95W
Benalla: Austl.	61	37S	146E
Benares *see* Banaras			
Bend: U.S.A.	80	44N	121W
Bendery: U.S.S.R.	31	47N	30E
Bendigo: Austl.	61	37S	144E
Benevento: Italy	30	41N	15E
Bengal: & *bay*, Ind./Pak.	49	—	—
Benghazi: Libya	63	32N	20E
Benguela: Angola	68	13S	13E
Beni: *r.*, Bolivia	86	13S	67W
Beni Mansour: Algeria	25	36N	4E
Benin: Nigeria	68	6N	6E
Benin, Bight of: Africa	66	4N	3E
Beni Saf: Algeria	25	35N	1W
Bensersiel: Germany	32	54N	8E
Benue: *r.*, Africa	68	9N	12E
Beograd: Yugo.	31	45N	20E
Berar: India	48	21N	77E
Berau Penin.: Neth. N. Guin.	51	1S	132E
Berber: Sudan	63	18N	34E
Berbera: Br. Somaliland	63	10N	45E
Berdichev: U.S.S.R.	44	50N	29E
Berezhany: U.S.S.R.	27	49N	25E
Berezovka: U.S.S.R.	31	47N	31E
Berezovo: U.S.S.R.	45	64N	65E
Bergama: Turkey	31	39N	27E
Bergamo: Italy	33	46N	10E
Bergamo Alps: Italy	33	46N	10E
Bergen: Norway	35	60N	5E
Bergen-op-Zoom: Neth.	32	51N	4E
Bergerac: France	29	45N	0
Bergisch Gladbach: Ger.	32	51N	7E
Berhampore: India	48	24N	88E
Bering Str.: U.S.S.R./U.S.A.	78	65N	170W
Berislav: U.S.S.R.	31	47N	34E
Berlin: Germany	32	53N	13E
Berlin: U.S.A.	85	44N	71W
Bermuda: *is.*, Atlantic O.	83	32N	65W
Bern: Switzerland	33	47N	7E
Bernay: France	28	49N	1E
Bernese Alps: Switz.	33	46N	8E
Bernina Pass: Switz.	33	46N	10E
Berre, Étg. de: France	29	43N	5E
Berri: Austl.	61	34S	141E
Berry: *Old Prov.*, France	29	47N	2E
Besançon: France	29	47N	6E
Bessarabia: U.S.S.R.	31	46N	29E
Bessèges: France	29	44N	4E
Bessines: France	29	46N	1E
Bethlehem: Jordan	21	32N	35E
Bethlehem: U.S.A.	85	41N	75W
Béthune: France	28	51N	3E
Betwa: *r.*, India	48	26N	80E
Beuvron: *r.*, France	29	48N	2E
Beyşehir, L.: Turkey	31	38N	32E
Béziers: France	29	43N	3E
Bhagalpur: India	48	25N	88E
Bhamo: Burma	47	24N	97E
Bhaunagar: India	48	22N	72E
Bhima: *r.*, India	48	17N	76E
Bhopal: India	48	23N	77E
Bhubaneswar: India	48	20N	86E
Bhuj: India	48	23N	70E
BHUTAN	49	27N	90E
Biafra, Bight of: G. of Guinea	68	3N	8E
Biak: *i.*, Neth. N. Guinea	51	1S	136E
Biała Podlaska: Poland	27	52N	23E
Białystok: Poland	35	53N	23E
Biarritz: France	29	43N	2W
Biddeford: U.S.A.	85	44N	70W
Biel: Switzerland	33	47N	7E
Bielefeld: Germany	32	52N	9E
Biella: Italy	33	46N	8E
Big Eau Pleine Res.: U.S.A.	84	45N	90W
Biggar: Canada	80	52N	108W
Bighorn Mts.: U.S.A.	80	44N	107W
Bihać: Yugoslavia	30	45N	16E
Bihar: *State*, India	48	25N	85E

	Page	Lat.	Long.
Bikaner: India	48	28N	73E
Bikini: *i.*, Pacific Ocean	54	12N	165E
Bilaspur: India	48	22N	82E
Bilbao: Spain	25	43N	3W
Billings: U.S.A.	80	46N	109W
Billiton: *i.*, Indonesia	51	3S	108E
Bingham: U.S.A.	85	45N	70W
Binghamton: U.S.A.	85	42N	76W
Binhdinh: Viet Nam	51	14N	109E
Birdum: Austl.	58	16S	133E
Birjand: Iran	46	33N	59E
Birmingham: U.S.A.	81	33N	87W
Birni n'Koni: Fr. W. Afr.	68	14N	5E
Birobidzhan: U.S.S.R.	43	49N	133E
Bisbee: U.S.A.	80	31N	110W
Biscay, Bay of: Spain	25	—	—
Biskotasi Lake: Canada	84	47N	82W
Biskra: Algeria	66	35N	6E
Bismarck: U.S.A.	80	47N	101W
Bismarck Arch.: N. Guinea	59	5S	145E
Bismarck Sea	54	5S	152E
Bissau: Port. Guinea	62	12N	16W
Bistriţa: Romania	31	47N	24E
Bitola: Yugoslavia	31	41N	21E
Bitterfeld: Germany	32	52N	12E
Bitterfontein: S. Afr.	69	31S	18E
Bitter Lakes: Egypt	63	*Inset*	
Bitterroot Range: U.S.A.	80	46N	114W
Biwa, L.: Japan	52	35N	136E
Biysk: U.S.S.R.	45	53N	85E
Bizerta: Tunisia	30	37N	10E
Bjøllånes: Norway	34	66N	15E
Björneborg: Finland	34	61N	22E
Black Forest: Germany	33	48N	8E
Black Sea: U.S.S.R.	44	43N	35E
Black Volta: *r.*, Fr. W. Afr.	68	10N	2W
Blackwood: *r.*, Austl.	60	34S	117E
Blagoveshchensk: U.S.S.R.	43	50N	127E
Blanc, C.: Sp. Sahara	62	20N	17W
Blanc, Mt.: Fr./Switz.	33	46N	7E
Bland: *r.*, Austl.	61	34S	148E
Blankenberghe: Belgium	28	51N	3E
Blantyre: Nyasaland	69	16S	35E
Blavet: *r.*, France	28	48N	3W
Blaye: France	29	45N	1W
Blenheim: Germany	33	49N	10E
Blenheim: N.Z.	53	42S	174E
Blida: Algeria	25	36N	3E
Blita: Fr. W. Afr.	68	8N	1E
Bloemfontein: S. Afr.	69	29S	26E
Blois: France	29	48N	1E
Bloomington: Ill., U.S.A.	84	40N	89W
Bloomington: Ind., U.S.A.	84	39N	87W
Bluefield: U.S.A.	84	37N	81W
Blue Mts.: Austl.	61	33S	105E
Blue Mts.: U.S.A.	78	45N	119W
Blue Nile: *r.*, Africa	63	10N	35E
Blue Ridge: U.S.A.	84	36N	82W
Bluff: N.Z.	53	47S	168E
Blumenthal: Germany	32	53N	9E
Blythe: U.S.A.	80	34N	115W
Blytheville: U.S.A.	84	36N	90W
Bo: Sierra Leone	62	8N	12W
Boa Vista: Brazil	86	3N	61W
Bobo Dioulasso: Fr. W. Afr.	62	12N	4W
Bocholt: Germany	32	52N	7E
Bochum: Germany	32	51N	7E
Bodelé Depres.: Fr. Eq. Africa	70	17N	17E
Boden: Sweden	34	66N	22E
Bodensee *see* Constance, L.			
Bodø: Norway	34	67N	14E
Bogotá: Colombia	86	5N	74W
Bohemia: *Old Prov.*, Czech.	26/7	—	—
Bohol: *i.*, Philippines	51	10N	124E
Boise: U.S.A.	80	44N	116W
Bojador, C.: Sp. Sahara	66	26N	15W
Bokn Fd.: Norway	35	59N	6E
Bolama: Port. Guinea	62	12N	15W
Bolan Pass: W. Pak.	48	30N	67E
Bold Eagle Lake: U.S.A.	84	48N	92W
Bolekhov: U.S.S.R.	27	49N	24E
Bolgrad: U.S.S.R.	31	46N	29E
Boling: U.S.A.	81	29N	96W
BOLIVIA	86	15S	65W
Bollwiller: France	28	48N	7E
Bologna: Italy	33	44N	11E
Bolsena, L.: Italy	30	43N	12E
Bol'shevik I.: U.S.S.R.	43	78N	102E
Bolzano: Italy	33	47N	11E
Boma: Belgian Congo	70	6S	13E
Bombay: India	48	19N	73E
Bon, C.: Tunisia	30	37N	11E
Bône: Algeria	25	37N	8E
Bonifacio: & *str.*, Corsica	30	41N	9E
Bonin Is.: Japan	54	27N	142E
Bonn: W. Germany	32	51N	7E
Bonneville Dam: U.S.A.	80	46N	122W
Bonny: Nigeria	68	4N	7E
Bookaloo: Austl.	61	32S	137E
Bor: Yugoslavia	31	44N	22E
Borås: Sweden	35	58N	13E
Bordeaux: France	29	45N	1W
Bordertown: Austl.	61	36S	141E
Borgholm: Sweden	35	57N	17E
Borgo Val di Taro: Italy	33	44N	10E
Borislav: U.S.S.R.	27	49N	23E
Borisoglebsk: U.S.S.R.	44	51N	42E
Borkum: *i.*, Germany	32	54N	7E
Borlänge: Sweden	35	60N	15E
Borneo: *i.*, Indonesia	51	0	115E
Bornholm: *i.*, Denmark	35	55N	15E
Boromo: Fr. W. Afr.	68	12N	3W
Bosnia: Yugoslavia	30	45N	17E
Boso Peninsula: Japan	52	35N	140E
Bosporus: Turkey	31	41N	29E
Bosso: Fr. W. Afr.	68	14N	13E
Boston: U.S.A.	85	42N	71W
Botany Bay: Austl.	61	34S	151E
Botevgrad: Bulgaria	31	43N	24E

	Page	Lat.	Long.
Bothnia, Gulf of	34	63N	20E
Botoşani: Romania	31	47N	26E
Bottrop: Germany	32	52N	7E
Bougainville: *i.*, Solomon Is.	59	7S	155E
Bougie: Algeria	25	37N	5E
Boulder: Austl.	60	31S	122E
Boulder Dam *see* Hoover Dam			
Boulogne: France	28	51N	2E
Bourbonnais: *Old Prov.*, Fr.	29	46N	3E
Bourg: France	29	46N	5E
Bourges: France	29	47N	2E
Bourget, Lac du: France	29	46N	6E
Bourke: Austl.	61	30S	146E
Bourtanger Moor: Neth./Ger.	32	53N	7E
Bou Saâda: Algeria	25	35N	4E
Boussac: France	29	46N	2E
Bow: *r.*, Can.	78	51N	115W
Bowling Green: U.S.A.	84	37N	86W
Bowling Green, C.: Austl.	60	19S	147E
Boyne: *r.*, Austl.	60	26S	151E
Boyup Brook: Austl.	60	34S	116E
Brabant: *Old Prov.*, Belgium	28	51N	4E
Brač: *i.*, Yugoslavia	30	43N	16E
Bradford: England	26	54N	2W
Braga: Portugal	25	42N	8W
Brahmani: *r.*, India	48	21N	86E
Brahmaputra: *r.*, India/Pak.	49	26N	93E
Brăila: Romania	31	45N	28E
Branco: *r.*, Brazil	86	1N	62W
Brandenburg: Germany	32	52N	13E
Brandon: Canada	80	50N	100W
Brantford: Canada	84	43N	80W
Bras d'Or Lake: Canada	85	46N	61W
Braşov: Romania	31	46N	26E
Bratislava: Czech.	27	48N	17E
Bratsk: U.S.S.R.	43	56N	102E
Braunau: Czech.	33	48N	13E
Braunschweig: Germany	32	52N	10E
BRAZIL	86/7	—	—
Brazil Plateau	88	19S	44W
Brazoria: U.S.A.	81	29N	96W
Brazos: *r.*, U.S.A.	81	30N	96W
Brazzaville: Fr. Eq. Afr.	71	4S	15E
Breaksea Sound: N.Z.	53	46S	167E
Breda: Netherlands	32	52N	5E
Bregenz: Austria	33	47N	10E
Bréhat, Î.: France	28	49N	3W
Breisach: Germany	33	48N	8E
Bremen: Germany	32	53N	9E
Bremerhaven-Wesermünde: Germany	32	54N	9E
Brenner Pass: Austr./Italy	33	47N	12E
Brescia: Italy	33	46N	10E
Breslau: Poland	35	51N	17E
Bressuire: France	29	47N	0
Brest: France	28	48N	4W
Brest Litovskiy: U.S.S.R.	35	52N	24E
Briançon: France	29	45N	7E
Bridgeport: U.S.A.	85	41N	73W
Brie: France	28	49N	3E
Brienz, Lake: Switz.	33	47N	8E
Briey: France	28	49N	6E
Brig: Switz.	33	46N	8E
Brindisi: Italy	30	41N	18E
Brisbane: Austl.	60	27S	153E
Bristol: U.S.A.	84	37N	82W
Bristol Bay: Alaska	78	58N	160W
BRITISH BORNEO	51	5N	115E
British Columbia: *Prov.*, Can.	78	53N	125W
BRITISH GUIANA	87	7N	58W
BRITISH HONDURAS	82	17N	88W
BRITISH SOMALILAND	63	10N	45E
Brittany: *Old Prov.*, France	28	48N	3W
Brive: France	29	45N	2E
Brno: Czech.	27	49N	17E
Brocken: *mtn.*, Germany	32	52N	11E
Brod: Yugoslavia	31	45N	18E
Broken Hill: Austl.	61	32S	141E
Broken Hill: N. Rhod.	69	15S	29E
Brooks Range: Alaska	78	67N	150W
Broome: Austl.	58	18S	122E
Brownsville: Mexico	82	26N	97W
Bruce Bay: N.Z.	53	44S	170E
Bruchsal: Germany	32	49N	9E
Bruges (Brugge): Belgium	28	51N	3E
Brühl: Germany	32	51N	7E
Brunei: Br. Borneo	51	4N	114E
Brunswick: Germany	32	52N	10E
Brussels (Bruxelles): Belg.	28	51N	4E
Bryansk: U.S.S.R.	44	53N	34E
Brzeg: Poland	27	51N	17E
Bucaramanga: Colombia	86	7N	73W
Bucharest (Bucuresti): Rom.	31	44N	26E
Buckland Tableland: Austl.	60	25S	148E
Budapest: Hungary	27	48N	19E
Budweis: Czech.	33	49N	15E
Buea: Nigeria	68	4N	9E
Buenaventura: Colombia	86	4N	77W
Buenos Aires: Argentina	88	35S	58W
Buffalo: U.S.A.	85	43N	79W
Bug: *r.*, Pol./U.S.S.R.	31	47N	32E
Buganda: Uganda	68	0	32E
Bukachacha: U.S.S.R.	43	53N	117E
Bukama: Belg. Congo	71	9S	26E
Bukavu: Belg. Congo	68	3S	29E
Bukhara: U.S.S.R.	45	40N	65E
Bukoba: Tangan.	68	1S	32E
Bulagan: Mongolia	43	49N	103E
Bulawayo: S. Rhodesia	69	20S	29E
BULGARIA	31	—	—
Buller: *r.*, N.Z.	53	42S	172E
Bulli: Austl.	61	34S	151E
Bulloo: *r.*, Austl.	60	26S	143E
Bulloo, L.: Austl.	61	28S	142E
Bull Run: U.S.A.	85	39N	77W
Bumtang: Bhutan	49	27N	91E
Bunbury: Austl.	60	33S	116E
Bundaberg: Austl.	60	25S	152E
Burdekin: *r.*, Austl.	60	20S	147E

WORLD

BURDUR — COPLEY

	Page	Lat.	Long.
Burdur: & *l.*, Turkey	**31**	38N	30E
Bureya: U.S.S.R.	**43**	50N	130E
Burgas: & *gulf*, Bulgaria	**31**	42N	27E
Burgdorf: Switz.	**33**	47N	8E
Burgos: Spain	**25**	42N	4W
Burgundy: *Old Prov.*, France	**29**	47N	5E
Burlington: Iowa, U.S.A.	**84**	41N	91W
Burlington: N.C., U.S.A.	**85**	36N	79W
Burlington: Vt., U.S.A.	**85**	44N	73W
BURMA	**49**	—	—
Burnett: *r.*, Austl.	**60**	25S	152E
Burnett Heads: Austl.	**60**	25S	152E
Burnie: Tasmania	**59**	41S	146E
Burra: Austl.	**61**	34S	139E
Burrinjuck Res.: Austl.	**61**	35S	149E
Bursa: Turkey	**31**	40N	29E
Buru: *i.*, Indonesia	**51**	3S	126E
Bushire: Iran	**46**	29N	51E
Bussa: Nigeria	**68**	10N	5E
Butte: U.S.A.	**80**	46N	113W
Butung: *i.*, Indonesia	**51**	5S	123E
Buxar: India	**48**	25N	85E
Buyaga: U.S.S.R.	**43**	60N	127E
Buzău: Romania	**31**	45N	27E
Bydgoszcz: Poland	**35**	53N	18E
Byelorussian S.S.R.: U.S.S.R.	**44**	53N	27E
Bylot I.: Canada	**79**	73N	78W
Bytom: Poland	**27**	51N	19E
Cabawin: Australia	**60**	27S	150E
Cabinda: Angola	**70**	5S	12E
Cabonga Reservoir: Canada	**85**	47N	76W
Cabot Strait: Canada	**79**	47N	60W
Čačak: Yugoslavia	**31**	44N	20E
Cáceres: Spain	**25**	39N	6W
Cádiz: Spain	**25**	37N	6W
Caen: France	**28**	49N	0
Caernarvon: Wales	**26**	53N	4W
Cagliari: Sardinia	**30**	39N	9E
Cahors: France	**29**	44N	1E
Caicos Is.: Bahamas	**83**	22N	72W
Cairns: Austl.	**59**	17S	146E
Cairo: Egypt	**63**	30N	31E
Cairo: U.S.A.	**84**	37N	89W
Cajamarca: Peru	**86**	7S	78W
Calabar: Nigeria	**68**	5N	8E
Calabozo: Venezuela	**86**	9N	67W
Calabria: *Reg.*, Italy	**30**	39N	16E
Calafat: Romania	**31**	44N	23E
Calais: France	**28**	51N	2E
Calamian Group: Phil.	**51**	12N	120E
Călăraşi: Romania	**31**	44N	27E
Calcutta: India	**48**	22N	88E
Caldera: Chile	**88**	27S	71W
Calexico: U.S.A.	**80**	33N	115W
Calgary: Canada	**80**	51N	114W
Cali: Colombia	**86**	3N	77W
California: *State*, U.S.A.	**80**	36N	118W
California, Gulf of: Mex.	**82**	27N	113W
Callao: Peru	**86**	12S	77W
Caltanissetta: Sicily	**30**	37N	14E
Calvi: Corsica	**30**	43N	9E
Calvinia: S. Afr.	**69**	32S	20E
Camagüey: Cuba	**83**	21N	78W
Camargue: France	**29**	44N	4E
Cambay, Gulf of: India	**48**	21N	72E
CAMBODIA: Indo-China	**51**	13N	105E
Cambrai: France	**28**	50N	3E
Cambridge: Md., U.S.A.	**85**	38N	76W
Cambridge: Mass., U.S.A.	**85**	42N	71W
Cambridge: N.Z.	**53**	38S	175E
Cambridge: Ohio, U.S.A.	**84**	40N	82W
Camden: Ark., U.S.A.	**81**	34N	93W
Camden: N.J., U.S.A.	**85**	40N	75W
Cameroons: Africa	**62**	6N	12E
Camocim: Brazil	**87**	3S	41W
Camooweal: Austl.	**58**	20S	138E
Campania: *Reg.*, Italy	**30**	41N	15E
Campeche, Bay of: Mexico	**82**	20N	93W
Campine: Belg.	**26**	51N	5E
Campinas: Brazil	**88**	23S	47W
Campobasso: Italy	**30**	42N	15E
Campo Grande: Brazil	**88**	20S	55W
Câmpulung: Romania	**31**	45N	25E
Câmpulung Moldovenesc: Romania	**31**	48N	26E
CANADA	**78/9**	—	—
Canadian: *r.*, U.S.A.	**80**	36N	101W
Çanakkale: Turkey	**31**	40N	26E
Cananea: Mexico	**80**	31N	110W
Canary Islands: Atl. O.	**62**	28N	15W
Canberra: Austl.	**61**	35S	149E
Candia: Crete	**31**	35N	25E
Canea: Crete	**31**	36N	24E
Cannes: France	**29**	44N	7E
Canso: & *cape*, Canada	**85**	45N	61W
Cantabrian Mts.: Spain	**25**	43N	6W
Canterbury Bight: N.Z.	**53**	44S	172E
Canterbury Plains: N.Z.	**53**	44S	172E
Canton: China	**50**	23N	113E
Canton: U.S.A.	**84**	41N	81W
Canudos: Brazil	**87**	7S	58W
Cape Breton Highlands National Park: Canada	**85**	47N	61W
Cape Breton I.: Canada	**85**	46N	61W
Cape Girardeau: *city*, U.S.A.	**84**	37N	90W
Cape of Good Hope: S. Afr.	**69**	35S	18E
Cape Province: S. Africa	**69**	—	—
Cape Town: S. Africa	**69**	34S	18E
Cape Verde Is.: Atlantic O.	**24**	18N	22W
Capodistra *see* Kopar			
Capri: *i.*, Italy	**30**	40N	14E
Capricorn Channel: Austl.	**60**	23S	152E
Capua: Italy	**30**	41N	14E
Caracas: Venezuela	**86**	10N	67W
Caransebeş: Romania	**31**	45N	22E
Caravelas: Brazil	**87**	18S	39W

	Page	Lat.	Long.
Carcassonne: France	**29**	43N	2E
Caribbean Sea	**83**	—	—
Cariboo Mts.: Canada	**78**	53N	121W
Carinthia: Austria	**33**	47N	14E
Carlsbad: U.S.A.	**80**	32N	104W
Carmarthen: Wales	**26**	52N	4W
Carmaux: France	**29**	44N	2E
Carnac: France	**28**	48N	3W
Carnarvon: Austl.	**58**	25S	114E
Carnarvon Range: Austl.	**60**	25S	148E
Carnic Alps: Austr./Italy	**33**	47N	13E
Carolina: Brazil	**87**	7S	47W
Caroline I.: Pacific Ocean	**55**	10S	150W
Caroline Is.: Pacific Ocean	**54**	—	—
Caroni: *r.*, Venezuela	**86**	5N	62W
Carpathian Mts.: U.S.S.R.	**27**	47N	24E
Carpentaria, G. of: Austl.	**58**	15S	138E
Carpentras: France	**29**	44N	5E
Carrara: Italy	**33**	44N	10E
Carson City: U.S.A.	**80**	39N	120W
Cartagena: Colombia	**86**	10N	75W
Cartagena: Spain	**25**	38N	1W
Carthage: Tunisia	**30**	37N	10E
Carvin: France	**28**	50N	3E
Caryapundy Swamp: Austl.	**61**	29S	143E
Casablanca: Morocco	**62**	34N	8W
Casale Monteferrato: Italy	**33**	45N	8E
Casamozza: Corsica	**30**	42N	9E
Cascade Pt.: N.Z.	**53**	44S	168E
Cascade Range: U.S.A.	**80**	46N	123W
Cascavel: Brazil	**87**	4S	38W
Caserta: Italy	**30**	41N	14E
Casino: Australia	**61**	29S	153E
Casiquiare: *r.*, Venez.	**86**	3N	66W
Caspian Sea: Europe	**44**	—	—
Cassel: France	**28**	51N	2E
Cassino: Italy	**30**	42N	14E
Castellón de la Plana: Sp.	**25**	40N	0°
Castelo Branco: Portugal	**25**	40N	8W
Castlemaine: Austl.	**61**	37S	144E
Castile *see* Old & New			
Castres: France	**29**	44N	2E
Çatalca: Turkey	**31**	41N	28E
Catalonia: *Old Prov.*, Spain	**25**	41N	1E
Catamarca: Argentina	**88**	28S	66W
Catania: Sicily	**30**	38N	15E
Catanzaro: Italy	**30**	39N	17E
Catastrophe, C.: Austl.	**59**	35S	136E
Catoche, Cape: Mexico	**83**	22N	87W
Catskill Mts.: U.S.A.	**85**	42N	75W
Cattaro: Yugoslavia	**31**	42N	19E
Cauca: *r.*, Colombia	**86**	8N	75W
Caucasus Mts.: U.S.S.R.	**44**	43N	45E
Cauvery: *r.*, India	**48**	12N	77E
Caux, Pays de: France	**28**	50N	1E
Cavaillon: France	**29**	44N	5E
Cawnpore *see* Kanpur			
Cáxias: Brazil	**87**	5S	43W
Cayenne: French Guiana	**87**	5N	52W
Ceará: Brazil	**87**	4S	38W
Cebu: & *i.*, Indon.	**51**	10N	124E
Cedar Falls: U.S.A.	**84**	43N	92W
Cedar Rapids: U.S.A.	**82**	42N	92W
Ceduna: Austl.	**58**	32S	134E
Celebes: *i.* & *sea*, Indonesia	**51**	3S	120E
Celje: Yugoslavia	**30**	46N	15E
Celle: Germany	**32**	53N	10E
Central Siberian Plateau: U.S.S.R.	**43**	—	—
Cephalonia: *i.*, Greece	**31**	38N	21E
Ceram: *i.* & *sea*, Indonesia	**51**	3S	129E
Cerignola: Italy	**30**	41N	16E
Cerigo: *i.*, Greece	**31**	36N	23E
Cerro Bolívar: *mtn.*, Venez.	**86**	7N	63W
Cerro de Pasco: Peru	**86**	11S	76W
Cesena: Italy	**33**	44N	12E
České Budejovice: Czech.	**27**	49N	14E
Česky Těšin: Czech.	**27**	50N	18E
Cessnock: Austl.	**61**	33S	151E
Cetinje: Yugoslavia	**31**	42N	19E
Ceuta: Morocco	**25**	36N	5W
Cévennes: *mtns.*, France	**29**	44N	4E
CEYLON	**48**	—	—
Chablis: France	**28**	48N	4E
Chad, Lake: Africa	**68**	13N	14E
Chalcis: Greece	**31**	38N	24E
Chaleur, Baie de: Canada	**85**	48N	65W
Chalon-sur-Saône: France	**29**	47N	5E
Châlons-sur-Marne: France	**28**	49N	4E
Chaman: W. Pakistan	**48**	31N	66E
Chamba: India	**48**	32N	76E
Chambal: *r.*, India	**48**	26N	77E
Chamberlain Lake: U.S.A.	**85**	46N	69W
Chambersburg: U.S.A.	**85**	40N	78W
Chambéry: France	**29**	46N	6E
Chamdo: China	**50**	31N	97E
Chamonix: France	**29**	46N	7E
Champagne: *Old Prov.*, Fr.	**28**	49N	4E
Champagne Pouilleuse: Fr.	**28**	49N	4E
Champaign: U.S.A.	**84**	40N	88W
Champéry: Switzerland	**33**	46N	7E
Champlain, Lake: U.S.A.	**85**	45N	73W
Chanaral: Chile	**88**	26S	71W
Changan: China	**50**	34N	109E
Changchun: China	**50**	44N	125E
Changkiakow: China	**50**	41N	115E
Changsha: China	**50**	28N	113E
Chanthaburi: Thailand	**51**	13N	102E
Chany, Lake, U.S.S.R.	**45**	55N	77E
Chaoyangchen: China	**43**	43N	126E
Chapala, Lake: Mexico	**82**	20N	103W
Chapayevsk: U.S.S.R.	**44**	53N	50E
Chapel Hill: *city*, U.S.A.	**85**	36N	79W
Chapra: India	**48**	26N	85E
Chardzhou: U.S.S.R.	**45**	39N	64E
Charente: *r.*, France	**29**	46N	0
Chari: *r.*, Fr. Eq. Afr.	**70**	11N	16E
Chariton: U.S.A.	**84**	41N	94W
Charleroi: Belgium	**28**	50N	4E

	Page	Lat.	Long.
Charles, Cape: U.S.A.	**85**	37N	76W
Charles City: U.S.A.	**84**	43N	93W
Charleston: S.C., U.S.A.	**81**	33N	80W
Charleston: W.Va., U.S.A.	**85**	38N	82W
Charleville: Austl.	**60**	26S	146E
Charleville: France	**28**	50N	5E
Charlotte: U.S.A.	**81**	35N	81W
Charlottesville: U.S.A.	**85**	38N	78W
Charlottetown: Canada	**85**	46N	63W
Charlton: Austl.	**61**	36S	143E
Charollais, Mts. du: France	**29**	46N	4E
Charolles: France	**29**	46N	4E
Chartres: France	**28**	48N	1E
Chasland's Mistake: *c.*, N.Z.	**53**	47S	170E
Château, Pte. du: France	**28**	49N	3W
Châteaubriant: France	**28**	48N	1W
Châteaudun: France	**28**	48N	1E
Châteaulin: France	**28**	48N	4W
Château Renault: France	**29**	48N	1E
Châteauroux: France	**29**	47N	2E
Château-Thierry: France	**28**	49N	3E
Châtellerault: France	**29**	47N	1E
Chatham: Canada	**84**	42N	82W
Chatham Is.: N.Z.	**54**	44S	177E
Châtillon-sur-Seine: France	**28**	48N	5E
Chatrapur: India	**48**	19N	85E
Chattanooga: U.S.A.	**81**	35N	85W
Chaumont: France	**28**	48N	5E
Chausey, Îles de: France	**28**	49N	2W
Chautauqua Lake: U.S.A.	**85**	42N	79W
Cheb: Czechoslovakia	**32**	50N	12E
Chedabucto Bay: Canada	**85**	45N	61W
Cheduba: *i.*, Burma	**47**	19N	94E
Chefoo: China	**50**	38N	121E
Cheju: *i.*, Korea	**50**	33N	126E
Chekunda: U.S.S.R.	**43**	51N	132E
Chéliff: *r.*, Algeria	**25**	36N	1E
Chelkar-Tengiz, L.: U.S.S.R.	**45**	48N	63E
Chełm: Poland	**27**	51N	24E
Cheleken: U.S.S.R.	**44**	39N	54E
Chelyabinsk: U.S.S.R.	**45**	55N	61E
Chelyuskin, C.: U.S.S.R.	**43**	77N	105E
Chemnitz: Germany	**32**	51N	13E
Chenab: *r.*, Ind./W. Pak.	**48**	33N	75E
Chengchow: China	**50**	35N	113E
Chengkiang: China	**50**	25N	103E
Chengteh: China	**50**	41N	118E
Chengtu: China	**50**	31N	104E
Cher: *r.*, France	**29**	47N	1E
Cherbourg: France	**28**	50N	2W
Cheremkhovo: U.S.S.R.	**43**	53N	103E
Cherepovets: U.S.S.R.	**44**	59N	38E
Chernigov: U.S.S.R.	**44**	52N	31E
Chernogorsk: U.S.S.R.	**45**	54N	91E
Chernovtsy: U.S.S.R.	**27**	48N	26E
Chernyakhovsk: U.S.S.R.	**35**	55N	22E
Cherrapunji: India	**49**	25N	92E
Cherry I.: Pac. Ocean	**59**	12S	170E
Cherskiy Range: U.S.S.R.	**43**	65N	145E
Chesapeake Bay: U.S.A.	**85**	38N	76W
Chester: U.S.A.	**85**	40N	75W
Chesterfield: Canada	**79**	63N	91W
Chesterfield Is.: Coral Sea	**59**	20S	158E
Cheyenne: U.S.A.	**80**	41N	105W
Chhindwara: India	**48**	22N	79E
Chiang Mai: Thailand	**51**	19N	99E
Chiang Rai: Thailand	**51**	20N	100E
Chiari: Italy	**33**	46N	10E
Chiba: Japan	**52**	36N	140E
Chicago: U.S.A.	**84**	42N	88W
Chicagof I.: Alaska	**78**	57N	136W
Chichén Itzá: Mexico	**82**	21N	89W
Chichibu: Japan	**52**	36N	139E
Chiclayo: Peru	**86**	7S	80W
Chico: *r.*, Argentina	**89**	45S	67W
Chicoutimi: Canada	**85**	48N	71W
Chief Joseph Dam: U.S.A.	**80**	48N	120W
Chiemsee: *l.*, Germany	**33**	48N	12E
Chieti: Italy	**30**	42N	14E
Chigneto Bay: Canada	**85**	45N	65W
Chihli, G. of: China	**50**	38N	120E
Chihuahua: & *Prov.*, Mexico	**80**	29N	106W
CHILE	**88/9**	—	—
Chilivani: Sardinia	**30**	41N	9E
Chillán: Chile	**88**	36S	72W
Chillicothe: U.S.A.	**84**	39N	83W
Chiloé I.: Chile	**89**	43S	64W
Chimborazo: *volc.*, Ecuador	**86**	1S	79W
Chimbote: Peru	**86**	9S	79W
Chimkent: U.S.S.R.	**45**	42N	70E
CHINA	**50**	—	—
Chinchow: China	**50**	41N	121E
Chindwin: *r.*, Burma	**50**	23N	94E
Chin Hills: Burma	**50**	22N	93E
Chinkiang: China	**50**	32N	120E
Chinon: France	**29**	47N	0
Chinook: U.S.A.	**80**	49N	109W
Chioggia: Italy	**33**	45N	12E
Chios: *i.*, Greece	**31**	38N	26E
Chiquitos Plat., Argentina	**88**	17S	62W
Chira: China	**48**	37N	81E
Chita: & *Prov.*, U.S.S.R.	**43**	52N	113E
Chitral: W. Pak.	**48**	36N	72E
Chittagong: E. Pakistan	**49**	22N	92E
Chkalov: U.S.S.R.	**44**	52N	55E
Choibalsan: Mongolia	**43**	48N	114E
Chojnice: Poland	**27**	54N	18E
Cholet: France	**29**	47N	1W
Chongjin: N. Korea	**51**	42N	130E
Chonos Arch.: Chile	**89**	45S	74W
Chop: U.S.S.R.	**31**	48N	22E
Chorzów: Poland	**27**	50N	19E
Chott Djerid: *salt lake*, Tunisia	**62**	34N	8E
Christchurch: N.Z.	**53**	44S	173E
Christmas I.: Indian Ocean	**54**	11S	106E
Christmas I.: Pacific Ocean	**54**	2N	157W
Chu: U.S.S.R.	**45**	44N	74E
Chubut: *r.*, Argentina	**89**	43S	66W

	Page	Lat.	Long.
Chugoku Mts.: Japan	**52**	35N	133
Chuguchak: China	**45**	47N	83
Chuho: China	**43**	45N	128
Chukchi Sea: U.S.S.R.	**43**	70N	175
Chumphon: Thailand	**51**	10N	99
Chungking: China	**50**	30N	107
Chunya: Tanganyika	**68**	9S	34
Chuquicamata: Chile	**88**	22S	69
Chur: Switzerland	**33**	47N	10
Churchill: Canada	**79**	59N	94
Churchill: *r.*, Canada	**79**	57N	96
Cienfuegos: Cuba	**83**	22N	81
Cieszyn: Poland	**27**	50N	18
Cilician Gates: Turkey	**46**	37N	35
Cincinnati: U.S.A.	**84**	39N	84
Ciudad Bolívar: Venezuela	**86**	8N	64
Ciudad Juárez: Mexico	**80**	32N	106
Ciudad Real: Spain	**25**	39N	4
Ciudad Rodrigo: Spain	**25**	41N	7
Ciudad Trujillo: Dom. Repub.	**83**	19N	70
Civitavecchia: Italy	**30**	42N	12
Clamecy: France	**29**	47N	3
Clare: Austl.	**61**	34S	139
Clarence: *r.*, Austl.	**61**	30S	153
Clarke Range: Austl.	**60**	20S	148
Clarksburg: U.S.A.	**84**	39N	80
Clausthal Zellerfeld: Ger.	**32**	52N	10
Clermont: Austl.	**60**	23S	148
Clermont: France	**28**	49N	2
Clermont-Ferrand: France	**29**	46N	3
Clès: Italy	**33**	46N	11
Cleveland: U.S.A.	**84**	42N	82
Clifton Forge: U.S.A.	**84**	38N	80
Clinch Mts.: U.S.A.	**84**	36N	83
Clinton: U.S.A.	**84**	42N	90
Cloncurry: Austl.	**59**	21S	140
Cloppenburg: Germany	**32**	53N	8
Clovis: U.S.A.	**80**	34N	103
Cluj: Romania	**31**	47N	24
Clutha: *r.*, N.Z.	**53**	46S	169
Coast Mts.: Canada	**78**	55N	130
Coast Range: Austl.	**60**	26S	152
Coast Ranges: U.S.A.	**78**	42N	123
Cobalt: Canada	**85**	47N	80
Cobar: Austl.	**61**	32S	146
Cobequid Mts.: Canada	**85**	45N	64
Cobourg: Canada	**85**	44N	78
Coburg: Germany	**32**	50N	11
Cochabamba: Bolivia	**86**	17S	66
Cochin: India	**48**	10N	76
Cochin China: Viet Nam	**51**	10N	106
Cochrane: Canada	**81**	49N	81
Cochrane, L.: Chile	**89**	47S	72
Cocos Is.: Ind. O.	**49**	11S	97
Cocos Is.: Costa Rica	**86**	5N	88
Cod, Cape: U.S.A.	**85**	42N	70
Coeur d'Alene: U.S.A.	**80**	48N	117
Coff's Harbour: Austl.	**61**	30S	153
Cognac: France	**29**	46N	0
Cohoes: U.S.A.	**85**	43N	74
Coimbatore: India	**48**	11N	77
Coimbra: Portugal	**25**	40N	8
Coire: Switzerland	**33**	47N	10
Colac: Austl.	**61**	38S	144
Colatina: Brazil	**87**	20S	41
Collie: Austl.	**60**	33S	116
Collingwood: Canada	**84**	45N	80
Colmar: France	**28**	48N	7
Cologne: Germany	**32**	51N	7
Colomb Béchar: Algeria	**62**	32N	2
COLOMBIA	**86**	—	—
Colombo: Ceylon	**48**	7N	80
Colón: Panamá	**83**	9N	80
Colorado: *r.*, Argentina	**88**	39S	65
Colorado: *r.*, Texas, U.S.A.	**80**	30N	97
Colorado: *r.*, U.S.A.	**80**	37N	111
Colorado: *State*, U.S.A.	**80**	39N	105
Colorado Plateaux: U.S.A.	**80**	36N	110
Colorado Springs: U.S.A.	**80**	39N	105
Columbia: Mo., U.S.A.	**84**	39N	92
Columbia: S.C., U.S.A.	**81**	34N	81
Columbia: *r.*, U.S.A.	**80**	46N	120
Columbus: Georgia, U.S.A.	**81**	32N	85
Columbus: Ohio, U.S.A.	**84**	40N	83
Colville Lake: Canada	**78**	67N	126
Colville Range: N.Z.	**53**	37S	176
Comacchio, Lake: Italy	**33**	45N	12
Comilla: E. Pakistan	**49**	23N	91
Comino, Cape: Sardinia	**30**	40N	10
Como: & *lake*, Italy	**33**	46N	9
Comodoro Rivadavia: Arg.	**89**	46S	67
Comorin, Cape: India	**48**	8N	77
Compiègne: France	**28**	49N	3
Conakry: Fr. W. Afr.	**62**	10N	14
Concarneau: France	**28**	48N	4
Concepción: Chile	**88**	37S	73
Concord: U.S.A.	**85**	43N	71
Condamine: *r.*, Austl.	**60**	27S	151
Condobolin: Austl.	**61**	33S	147
Congo: *r.*, Africa	**70**	2N	21
Conneaut: U.S.A.	**84**	42N	81
Connecticut: *State*, U.S.A.	**85**	42N	72
Constance, L.: Switz./Ger.	**33**	48N	9
Constanţa: Romania	**31**	44N	29
Constantine: & *Prov.*, Alg.	**62**	37N	7
Constantinople: Turkey	**31**	41N	29
Cooch Behar: India	**48**	26N	90
Cook Is.: Pacific Ocean	**54**	20S	160
Cook, Mt.: N.Z.	**53**	44S	170
Cook Strait: N.Z.	**53**	41S	174
Cooktown: Austl.	**59**	15S	145
Coolangatta: Austl.	**60**	28S	153
Coolgardie: Austl.	**60**	31S	121
Cooper's Creek: Austl.	**61**	27S	140
Coorong, The: Austl.	**61**	36S	139
Cootamundra: Austl.	**61**	35S	148
Copenhagen: Denmark	**35**	56N	13
Copiapó: Chile	**88**	27S	70
Copley: Austl.	**61**	31S	138

WORLD

COPPERMINE — EVANSVILLE

	Page	Lat.	Long.
oppermine: Canada	78	68N	115W
oquilhatville: Belg. Congo	70	0°	18E
oquimbo: Chile	88	30S	71W
oral Sea	59	—	—
orbières: *mtns.*, France	28	43N	2E
ordillera Central: Col.	86	5N	75W
ordillera de Mérida: Venez.	86	9N	71W
ordillera Occidental: Col.	86	4N	77W
ordillera Oriental: Col.	86	5N	74W
órdoba: Argentina	88	32S	64W
órdoba: Spain	25	38N	5W
ordova: Alaska	78	61N	145W
orfu: *i.*, Greece	31	40N	20E
orinth: & *gulf*, Greece	31	38N	23E
orinth: U.S.A.	81	35N	89W
orlu: Turkey	31	41N	28E
orner Brook: Can.	79	49N	58W
ornwall: Canada	85	45N	75W
orocoro: Bolivia	88	17S	69W
oromandel Coast: India	48	13N	81E
oronation Gulf: Canada	78	68N	110W
oronel: Chile	88	37S	73W
orpus Christi: U.S.A.	80	28N	97W
orrientes: Argentina	88	27S	59W
orsica: *i.*, Medit. Sea	30	—	—
orsicana: U.S.A.	81	32N	96W
orumbá: Brazil	87	19S	57W
orunna: Spain	25	43N	8W
os: *i.*, Greece	31	37N	27E
osenza: Italy	30	39N	16E
osne: France	29	47N	3E
OSTA RICA	86	10N	85W
ostermansville: Belg. Congo	68	3S	29E
ôte d'Azur: France	29	43N	6E
ôte d'Or: France	29	47N	5E
otentin: France	28	49N	2W
ôtes de Moselle: France	28	49N	6E
otonou: Fr. W. Africa	68	6N	3E
otopaxi: *volc.*, Ecuador	86	1S	78W
ottbus: Germany	32	52N	14E
ottian Alps: Fr./Italy	33	45N	7E
oubre, Pte. de la: France	29	46N	1W
ouncil Bluffs: U.S.A.	80	41N	96W
ourtrai *see* Kortrijk			
outances: France	28	49N	1W
ovilhã: Portugal	25	40N	7W
ovington: U.S.A.	84	39N	84W
owal, Lake: Austl.	61	34S	147E
owan, Lake: Austl.	60	32S	122E
owra: Austl.	61	34S	149E
ox's Bazar: E. Pakistan	49	21N	92E
raiova: Romania	31	44N	24E
ranbrook: Canada	80	49N	116W
récy: France	28	50N	4E
reil: France	28	49N	2E
remona: Italy	33	45N	10E
res: *i.*, Yugoslavia	30	45N	14E
rete: *i. & sea*, Greece	31	35N	25E
reuse: *r.*, France	29	47N	1E
rimea: U.S.S.R.	44	45N	34E
roatia: Yugoslavia	30	45N	17E
romwell: N.Z.	53	45S	169E
ronulla: Austl.	61	34S	151E
rosby: U.S.A.	84	46N	94W
rotone: Italy	30	39N	17E
row's Nest: Austl.	60	27S	152E
rowsnest Pass: Canada	80	49N	115W
ruzeiro do Sul: Brazil	86	8S	73W
sepel: Hungary	27	47N	19E
UBA	83	22N	80W
ubango: *r.*, Angola	69	17S	18E
úcuta: Colombia	86	8N	73W
uddalore: India	48	12N	80E
uddapah: India	48	15N	79E
uenca: Spain	25	40N	2W
uiabá: Brazil	88	16S	56W
uito: *r.*, Angola	69	17S	19E
ulebra Cut: Panama	83	*Inset*	
uloz: France	29	46N	6E
umaná: Venezuela	86	10N	64W
umberland: U.S.A.	85	40N	79W
umberland Is.: Austl.	60	21S	149E
umberland Mts.: U.S.A.	84	37N	83W
umberland Sound: Canada	79	65N	65W
underdin: Austl.	60	32S	117E
uneo: Italy	33	44N	8E
unnamulla: Austl.	60	28S	146E
uraçao: *i.*, Caribbean Sea	86	12N	69W
uricó: Chile	88	35S	71W
uritiba: Brazil	88	25S	49W
urtis Channel: Austl.	60	24S	153E
usco (Cuzco): Peru	86	14S	72W
uttack: India	48	20N	86E
uxhaven: Germany	32	54N	9E
yclades: *is.*, Greece	31	37N	25E
yprus: *i.*, Medit. Sea	46	35N	33E
ZECHOSLOVAKIA	27	—	—
zestochowa: Poland	27	51N	19E
acca: E. Pakistan	49	24N	90E
ahlak Archipelago: Red Sea	46	16N	40E
ahomey: *Prov.*, Fr. W. Afr.	68	10N	3E
airen (Dal'niy): China	50	39N	122E
ajarra: Austl.	58	22S	140E
akar: Fr. W. Africa	62	15N	17W
akhla Oasis: Egypt	63	25N	29E
akovica: Yugoslavia	31	42N	20E
alby: Austl.	60	27S	151E
alhousie: India	48	33N	76E
alhousie, Cape: Canada	78	70N	130W
allas: U.S.A.	80	33N	97W
ltonganj: India	48	24N	84E
ly Waters: Austl.	58	16S	133E
m: Surinam	87	5N	55W
mão: Port. India	48	20N	73E
mascus: Syria	46	34N	36E
mietta: Egypt	63	31N	32E
Dampier Land: Austl.	58	17S	123E
Danbury: U.S.A.	85	41N	73W
Danilovka: U.S.S.R.	45	53N	71E
Dannemora: Sweden	35	60N	18E
Dannevirke: N.Z.	53	40S	176E
Danville: Illinois, U.S.A.	84	40N	88W
Danville: Virginia, U.S.A.	85	37N	79W
Danube, *r.*, Europe	31	—	—
Danushkodi: India	48	9N	80E
Danzig: & *gulf*, Poland	27	54N	19E
Darasun: U.S.S.R.	43	53N	116E
Dardanelles: Turkey	31	40N	26E
Dar es Salaam: Tanganyika	68	7S	40E
Darfur: *Prov.*, Sudan	63	13N	25E
Dargaville: N.Z.	53	36S	174E
Darien, G. of: Colombia	86	9N	77W
Darjeeling: India	48	27N	88E
Darling: *r.*, Austl.	61	31S	145E
Darling Downs: Austl.	60	27S	151E
Darling Range: Austl.	60	32S	116E
Darmstadt: Germany	32	50N	9E
Dartmouth: Canada	85	45N	64W
Darwin: Austl.	58	12S	131E
Dasht-i-Kavir: *desert*, Iran	46	34N	55E
Dasht-i-Lut: *desert*, Iran	46	32N	57E
Daugavpils: U.S.S.R.	35	56N	26E
Dauphiné: *Old Prov.*, France	29	45N	6E
Dauphiné Alps: France	29	46N	6E
Davao: Mindanao	51	7N	126E
David-Gorodok: U.S.S.R.	35	52N	27E
Davis Strait: Can./Greenland	79	67N	60W
Davos: Switzerland	33	47N	10E
Dawna Range: Burma/Thai.	47	13N	98E
Dawson: Canada	78	64N	139W
Dawson: *r.*, Austl.	60	25S	150E
Dawson Creek: *town*, Canada	78	56N	120W
Dax: France	29	44N	1W
Dayton: U.S.A.	84	40N	84W
Daytona Beach: U.S.A.	81	29N	81W
De Aar: South Africa	69	31S	24E
Dead Sea: Israel/Jordan	46	32N	36E
Dearborn: U.S.A.	84	42N	83W
Deauville: France	28	49N	0
Debrecen: Hungary	27	48N	22E
Decatur: U.S.A.	84	40N	89W
Decazeville: France	29	45N	2E
Deccan: India	48/9	—	—
Děčín: Czechoslovakia	32	51N	14E
Dedeagach: Greece	31	41N	26E
Dehra Dun: India	48	30N	78E
Delaware: *r.*, U.S.A.	85	41N	75W
Delaware: *State*, & *bay*, U.S.A.	85	39N	75W
Delft: Netherlands	32	52N	4E
Delhi: India	48	29N	77E
Delmenhorst: Germany	32	53N	9E
Demarcation Point: Alaska	78	70N	141W
Demavend: *mtn.*, Turkey	44	36N	52E
Demmin: Germany	32	54N	13E
Dendermonde: Belgium	28	51N	4E
Denham Range: Austl.	60	22S	148E
Den Helder: Netherlands	32	53N	5E
Deniliquin: Austl.	61	36S	145E
Denizli: Turkey	31	38N	29E
DENMARK	35	—	—
D'Entrecasteaux Is.: New Guinea	59	10S	151E
D'Entrecasteaux, Pt: Austl.	60	35S	116E
Denver: U.S.A.	80	40N	105W
Dera Ghazi Khan: W. Pak.	48	30N	70E
Dera Ismail Khan: W. Pak.	48	32N	71E
Derby: Austl.	58	17S	123E
Des Joachims: Canada	85	46N	78W
Des Moines: U.S.A.	81	42N	94W
Dessau: Germany	32	52N	12E
Detroit: U.S.A.	84	42N	83W
Dettingen: Germany	32	50N	9E
Deva: Romania	31	46N	23E
Deventer: Netherlands	32	52N	6E
Dévoluy: *mtns.*, France	29	45N	6E
Devon I.: Canada	79	75N	85W
Devonport: N.Z.	53	37S	175E
Dhahran: Sa'udi Arabia	46	26N	50E
Dharwar: India	48	15N	75E
Dhulia: India	48	21N	75E
Diamantina: Brazil	87	18S	44W
Dibrugarh: India	47	28N	95E
Dieppe: France	28	50N	1E
Digby: Canada	85	45N	66W
Digne: France	29	44N	6E
Dijon: France	29	47N	5E
Dili: Port. Timor	50	8S	126E
Dillingen: Germany	33	49N	10E
Dimboola: Austl.	61	36S	142E
Dimitrovgrad: Bulgaria	31	42N	26E
Dimitrovgrad: Yugoslavia	31	43N	23E
Dimitrovo: Bulgaria	31	43N	23E
Dinajpur: E. Pakistan	48	25N	89E
Dinan: France	28	48N	2W
Dinant: Belgium	28	50N	5E
Dinard: France	28	49N	2W
Dinaric Alps: Yugoslavia	30	44N	16E
Dinkelsbühl: Germany	32	49N	10E
Diomede Is.: Bering Strait	78	66N	169W
Dir: W. Pak.	48	35N	72E
Diredawa: Ethiopia	63	10N	42E
Dirk Hartog I.: Austl.	58	26S	114E
Disko: *i.*, Greenland	79	69N	54W
Diu: Port. India	48	21N	71E
Divriği: Turkey	44	40N	38E
Dixmude: Belgium	28	51N	3E
Diyarbakir: Turkey	46	38N	40E
Djakarta: Java	51	6S	107E
Djerba I.: Tunisia	62	34N	11E
Djibouti: Fr. Som.	46	12N	43E
Djidjelli: Algeria	25	37N	6E
Dneprodzerzhinsk: U.S.S.R.	44	48N	35E
Dnepropetrovsk: U.S.S.R.	44	48N	35E
Dnieper: *r.*, U.S.S.R.	44	—	—
Dniester: *r.*, U.S.S.R.	44	—	—
Dobreşti: Romania	31	47N	22E
Dobruja: Romania	31	44N	28E
Dodecanese: *is.*, Greece	31	37N	27E
Dodge City: U.S.A.	80	38N	100W
Dodoma: Tanganyika	68	6S	36E
Dôle: France	29	47N	5E
Dolomites: *mtns.*, Italy	33	46N	12E
Domažlice: Czechoslovakia	32	49N	13E
Dombås: Norway	34	62N	9E
Dominica: *i.*, West Indies	83	15N	61W
DOMINICAN REPUBLIC	83	19N	70W
Don: *r.*, U.S.S.R.	44	—	—
Donau: *r.*, Europe	33	—	—
Donauwörth: Germany	33	49N	11E
Donawitz: Austria	30	47N	15E
Dondra Head: Ceylon	48	6N	81E
Donets: *r.*, U.S.S.R.	44	49N	38E
Dongara: Austl.	60	29S	115E
Donzère: France	29	44N	5E
Dordogne: *r.*, France	29	45N	0
Dordrecht: Netherlands	32	52N	5E
Dore: *r.*, France	29	46N	4E
Dôres do Indaiá: Brazil	87	20S	46W
Dornbirn: Austria	33	47N	10E
Dortmund: Germany	32	52N	7E
Douai: France	28	50N	3E
Douala: Fr. Eq. Africa	68	4N	10E
Douarnenez: & *bay*, France	28	48N	5W
Doubs: *r.*, France	29	47N	6E
Douro: *r.*, Spain/Port.	25	41N	8W
Dover: U.S.A.	85	39N	76W
Dovrefjell: Norway	34	62N	10E
Draguignan: France	29	44N	6E
Drakensberg: *mtns.*, S. Afr.	69	31S	28E
Drama: Greece	31	41N	24E
Drammen: Norway	35	60N	10E
Drava (Drau or Drave): *r.*, Europe	31	—	—
Dravograd: Yugoslavia	30	47N	15E
Dre: *r.*, China	50	34N	94E
Dresden: Germany	32	51N	14E
Dreux: France	28	49N	1E
Drôme: *r.*, France	29	45N	5E
Drummondville: Canada	85	46N	72W
Dubbo: Austl.	61	32S	149E
Dubno: U.S.S.R.	27	50N	26E
Dubrovnik: Yugoslavia	30	43N	18E
Dubuque: U.S.A.	84	43N	91W
Duck: *r.*, U.S.A.	84	36N	87W
Ducktown: U.S.A.	81	35N	84W
Dudelange: Luxembourg	32	50N	6E
Dudinka: U.S.S.R.	43	70N	85E
Duisburg: Germany	32	51N	7E
Dulce: *r.*, Argentina	88	29S	64W
Duluth: U.S.A.	84	47N	92W
Dunedin: N.Z.	53	46S	171E
Dunkerque (Dunkirk): Fr.	28	51N	2E
Duntroon: N.Z.	53	45S	171E
Duquesne: U.S.A.	84	40N	80W
Durance: *r.*, France	29	44N	5E
Durango: Mexico	82	24N	105W
Durazzo: Albania	31	41N	19E
Durban: S. Africa	69	30S	31E
Düren: Germany	32	51N	6E
Durge Nor: *l.*, Mongolia	50	48N	94E
Durham: U.S.A.	85	36N	79W
Durrës: Albania	31	41N	19E
D'Urville I.: N.Z.	53	41S	174E
Düsseldorf: Germany	32	51N	7E
Dvina, N.: *r.*, U.S.S.R.	42	63N	43E
Dvina, W.: *r.*, U.S.S.R.	35	57N	26E
Dza: *r.*, China	47	32N	97E
Dzaudzhikau: *see* Ordzhonikidze			
Dzerzhinsk: U.S.S.R.	44	56N	43E
Dzhambul: U.S.S.R.	45	43N	71E
Dzhargalantu: Mongolia	43	48N	91E
Dzherba: U.S.S.R.	43	60N	116E
Dzhetygara: U.S.S.R.	45	52N	61E
Dzhezkazgan: U.S.S.R.	45	48N	68E
Dzhibchalantu: Mongolia	43	47N	97E
Dzungaria: China	45	45N	85E
Dzungaria Gate: China/U.S.S.R.	45	45N	82E
Eagle Pass: *city*, U.S.A.	80	29N	100W
East Beskids: *mtns.*, Czech.	27	49N	22E
East Cape: N.Z.	53	38S	178E
East China Sea	50	30N	125E
Eastern Ghats: *mtns.*, India	48	—	—
Eastern Sierra Madre: *range*, Mexico	82	24N	100W
East London: S. Afr.	69	33S	28E
East Pakistan: *Prov.*, Pak.	49	—	—
Eastport: U.S.A.	85	45N	67W
East Rift Valley: Kenya/Ethiopia	63	5N	37E
East St. Louis: U.S.A.	84	39N	90W
East Siberian Sea: U.S.S.R.	43	73N	160W
Eau Claire: U.S.A.	84	45N	92W
Eauze: France	29	44N	0
Eberswalde: Germany	32	53N	14E
Ebi Nor: *l.*, China	46	45N	83E
Ebro: *r.*, Spain	25	42N	1W
Echuca: Austl.	61	36S	145E
ECUADOR	86	1S	77W
Edam: Netherlands	32	53N	5E
Ed Damer: Sudan	63	17N	34E
Ede: Netherlands	32	52N	6E
Edenhope: Austl.	61	37S	141E
Edhessa: Greece	31	41N	22E
Edirne: Turkey	31	42N	27E
Edmonton: Canada	80	54N	113W
Edmundston: Canada	85	47N	68W
Edremit: Turkey	31	40N	27E
Edward, Lake: Africa	68	0	30E
Edwards Plateau: U.S.A.	80	31N	100W
Eekloo: Belgium	28	51N	4E
Efate: *i.*, New Hebrides	59	18S	168E
Eger: *r.*, Czech.	32	50N	14E
Egersund: Norway	35	58N	6E
Egmont, C.: N.Z.	53	39S	174E
Egmont, Mt.: N.Z.	53	39S	174E
Eğridir, L.: Turkey	31	38N	31E
EGYPT	62/3	—	—
Eifel: *mtns.*, Germany	32	50N	7E
Eighty Mile Beach: Austl.	58	20S	120E
Eilenburg: Germany	35	51N	13E
Eindhoven: Netherlands	32	51N	5E
Eisenach: Germany	32	51N	10E
El 'Alamein: Egypt	63	31N	29E
Elâziğ: Turkey	44	39N	39E
Elba: *i.*, Italy	30	43N	10E
Elbasan: Albania	31	41N	20E
Elbe: *r.*, Germany	32	53N	10E
Elbeuf: France	28	49N	1E
Elbląg: Poland	27	54N	20E
El'brus: *mtn.*, U.S.S.R.	44	43N	42E
Elburz Mts.: Iran	46	36N	52E
Elche: Spain	25	38N	1W
Eldoret: Kenya	68	1N	35E
El Escorial: Spain	25	41N	4W
El Faiyum: Egypt	63	29N	31E
El Fasher: Sudan	63	14N	25E
El Ferrol: Spain	25	43N	8W
Elgin: U.S.A.	84	42N	88W
Elgon, Mt.: Kenya	70	1N	35E
El'gyay: U.S.S.R.	43	62N	117E
Elisabethville: Belg. Congo	68	12S	27E
Elizabeth Point: S.W. Afr.	69	27S	15E
Elizabethton: U.S.A.	84	36N	82W
El Kharga: Egypt	63	25N	30E
Elkhart: U.S.A.	84	42N	86W
Elko: U.S.A.	80	41N	116W
Ellesmere I.: Canada	79	80N	80W
Ellice Is.: Pacific Ocean	54	8S	180
Elmira: U.S.A.	85	42N	77W
Elmshorn: Germany	32	54N	10E
El Obeid: Sudan	63	13N	30E
El Paso: U.S.A.	80	32N	106W
El Qantara: Egypt	63	31N	32E
EL SALVADOR	82	14N	88W
Elvas: Portugal	25	39N	7W
Emba: U.S.S.R.	45	49N	58E
Embrun: France	29	45N	6E
Emden: Germany	32	53N	7E
Emerald: Austl.	60	23S	148E
Emi Koussi: *mtn.*, Fr. Eq. Afr.	70	20N	19E
Emilia Romagna: *Reg.*, Italy	33	44N	11E
Emmen: Netherlands	32	53N	7E
Emmerich: Germany	32	52N	6E
Ems: *r.*, Germany	32	53N	7E
Encounter Bay: Austl.	61	36S	139E
Enfidaville: Tunisia	30	36N	10E
Enggano: *i.*, Indon.	51	5S	102E
Enns: *r.*, Austria	33	47N	14E
Enschede: Netherlands	32	52N	7E
Ensenada: Mexico	80	32N	116W
Entebbe: Uganda	68	0	33E
Entre Rios: Mozambique	69	15S	38E
Enugu: Nigeria	68	6N	8E
Épernay: France	28	49N	4E
Épinal: France	28	48N	6E
Epirus: Greece	31	39N	21E
Erbil: 'Iraq	44	36N	44E
Erebus, Mt.: Antarctica	90	78S	168E
Erentsab: Mongolia	43	50N	115E
Erfurt: Germany	32	51N	11E
Erie: U.S.A.	84	42N	80W
Erie, Lake: Can./U.S.A.	84	42N	81W
Erigavo: Br. Som.	46	11N	47E
Erimo, C.: Japan	53	42N	143E
Eritrea: *Prov.*, Eth.	63	15N	40E
Erlangen: Germany	33	50N	11E
Ermoupolis: *i.*, Greece	31	37N	25E
Eromanga, *i.*, New Hebrides	59	19S	169E
Er Rif: *mtns.*, Morocco	25	35N	5W
Erzgebirge: *mtns.*, Germany	32	50N	13E
Erzurum: Turkey	46	40N	41E
Esashi: Japan	52	42N	140E
Esbjaerg: Denmark	35	55N	8E
Escanaba: U.S.A.	84	46N	87W
Esch: Luxembourg	32	50N	6E
Eschwege: Germany	32	51N	10E
Eshowe: S. Africa	69	29S	32E
Eskilstuna: Sweden	35	59N	17E
Eskişehir: Turkey	31	40N	30E
Esnagi Lake: Canada	84	49N	84W
Esperance: Austl.	60	34S	122E
Espinouse, Mts. de l': Fr.	29	44N	3E
Espírito Santo: *Prov.*, Brazil	88	20S	40W
Espiritu Santo: *i.*, New Hebr.	59	15S	167E
Essen: Germany	32	51N	7E
Essequibo: *r.*, Br. Guiana	87	5N	58W
Esslingen: Germany	33	49N	9E
Estats, Pic d': France	29	43N	1E
Estevan: Canada	80	49N	103W
Estonian S.S.R.: U.S.S.R.	35	58N	26E
Estremadura: *Prov.*, Port.	25	39N	9W
Esztergom: Hungary	27	48N	19E
Étampes: France	28	48N	2E
Étaples: France	28	51N	2E
Etawah: India	48	27N	79E
ETHIOPIA	63	—	—
Etna: *volc.*, Sicily	30	38N	15E
Étoile, Chaîne de l': Fr.	29	43N	6E
Etosha Pan: S.W. Afr.	69	19S	16E
Etruscan Apennines: Italy	33	44N	10E
Euboea: & *gulf*, Greece	31	38N	24E
Eucla: Austl.	58	32S	129E
Eudunda: Austl.	61	34S	139E
Eugene: U.S.A.	80	44N	123W
Eupen: Belgium	28	51N	6E
Euphrates: *r.*, Syria	46	35N	40E
Eure: *r.*, France	28	48N	1E
Eureka: U.S.A.	80	41N	124W
Evanston: U.S.A.	84	42N	88W
Evansville: U.S.A.	84	38N	88E

WORLD

EVERARD, C. — GUARDAFUI, C.

	Page	Lat.	Long.
Everard, C.: Austl.	**61**	38S	149E
Everest: *mtn.*, Himalayas	**49**	28N	87E
Everett: U.S.A.	**80**	48N	122W
Evian: France	**29**	46N	7E
Évora: Portugal	**25**	39N	8W
Évreux: France	**28**	49N	1E
Exmouth Gulf: Austl.	**58**	22S	114E
Expedition Range: Austl.	**60**	24S	149E
Eyre, Lake: Austl.	**58**	28S	137E
Faenza: Italy	**33**	44N	12E
Faeroe-Iceland Rise	**24**	65N	10W
Faeroe Is.: Denmark	**24**	62N	7W
Fagersta: Sweden	**35**	60N	16E
Faguibine, Lake: Fr. W. Afr.	**62**	16N	4W
Fairbanks: Alaska	**78**	65N	148W
Faizabad: Afghan	**47**	37N	70E
Falaise: France	**28**	49N	0
Falkland Is.: Atlantic O.	**89**	52S	60W
Falköping: Sweden	**35**	58N	13E
Fall River: *city*, U.S.A.	**85**	42N	71W
False Bay: S. Africa	**69**	34S	19E
Falun: Sweden	**35**	61N	16E
Famagusta: Cyprus	**63**	35N	34E
Fano: Italy	**33**	44N	13E
Farah: Afghan	**46**	32N	62E
Farasan Is.: Red Sea	**46**	17N	41E
Farewell: Alaska	**78**	63N	154W
Farewell, Cape: Greenland	**79**	60N	43W
Farewell, Cape: N.Z.	**53**	40S	173E
Fargo: U.S.A.	**80**	47N	97W
Faro: Portugal	**25**	37N	8W
Faxa Bay: Iceland	**34**	64N	23W
Fécamp: France	**28**	50N	0
FEDERATION OF RHODESIA & NYASALAND	**68/9**	—	—
Feilding: N.Z.	**53**	40S	176E
Feira de Santana: Brazil	**87**	12S	39W
Feldkirch: Austria	**33**	47N	10E
Fengsiang: China	**50**	35N	107E
Fengyang: China	**50**	33N	117E
Fenouillèdes: *mtns.*, France	**29**	43N	2E
Fenyang: China	**50**	37N	112E
Fergana: U.S.S.R.	**45**	40N	72E
Fernando de Noronha: *i.*, Brazil	**87**	4S	32W
Fernando Poo: *i.*, G. of Guin.	**62**	4N	9E
Ferrara: Italy	**33**	45N	12E
Ferret, Cap: France	**29**	45N	1W
Ferryville: Tunisia	**30**	37N	10E
Feteşti: Romania	**31**	44N	28E
Fethiye: Turkey	**31**	36N	29E
Fez: Morocco	**62**	34N	5W
Fianarantsoa: Madag.	**71**	22S	47E
Fichtelgebirge: *mtns.*, Ger.	**32**	50N	12E
Fidenza: Italy	**33**	45N	10E
Figeac: France	**29**	45N	2E
Fiji Is.: Pacific Ocean	**59**	18S	178E
Finistère: *Dept.*, France	**28**	48N	4W
Finisterre, Cape: Spain	**25**	43N	9W
FINLAND	**34/5**	—	
Finschhafen: N.E. New Guin.	**59**	7S	148E
Finsteraarhorn: *mtn.*, Switz.	**33**	47N	8E
Fiordland: N.Z.	**53**	45S	167E
Firenze: Italy	**33**	44N	11E
Fitchburg: U.S.A.	**85**	43N	72W
Fitzpatrick: Canada	**85**	47N	73W
Fitzroy: *r.*, Queens., Austl.	**60**	23S	150E
Fitzroy: *r.*, W. Austl.	**58**	19S	125E
Fiume: Yugoslavia	**27**	45N	15E
Flanders: *Old Prov.*, Belgium	**28**	51N	4E
Flensburg: Germany	**35**	55N	9E
Flers: France	**28**	49N	1W
Flinders: *r.*, Austl.	**59**	20S	141E
Flinders Range: Austl.	**61**	32S	139E
Flinders Reefs: Coral Sea	**60**	18S	149E
Flint: U.S.A.	**84**	43N	84W
Florence: Italy	**33**	44N	11E
Florence: U.S.A.	**81**	35N	88W
Florencia: Colombia	**86**	1N	75W
Flores: *i. & sea*, Indonesia	**51**	9S	122E
Floreshty: U.S.S.R.	**31**	47N	28E
Floriano: Brazil	**87**	7S	43W
Florianópolis: Brazil	**88**	28S	49W
Florida: *State*, U.S.A.	**81**	30N	83W
Florida, Straits of: U.S.A.	**83**	24N	80W
Florida Keys: *is.*, U.S.A.	**83**	25N	81W
Florina: Greece	**31**	41N	21E
Florø: *i.*, Norway	**34**	62N	5E
Flushing: Netherlands	**32**	51N	4E
Foggia: Italy	**30**	41N	16E
Foix: *& Old Prov.*, France	**29**	43N	2E
Foligno: Italy	**30**	43N	13E
Fond du Lac: U.S.A.	**84**	44N	88W
Fontainebleau: France	**28**	48N	3E
Fontainebleau, Forêt de: Fr.	**28**	48N	3E
Fontenoy: Belgium	**28**	51N	3E
Foochow: China	**50**	26N	118E
Forbes: Austl.	**61**	33S	148E
Forcalquier: France	**29**	44N	6E
Fordlândia: Brazil	**87**	4S	55W
Forel, Mt.: Greenland	**79**	67N	37W
Forez, Monts du: France	**29**	45N	4E
Forli: Italy	**33**	44N	12E
Formentera: *i.*, Balearic Is.	**25**	38N	1E
Formosa: *i. & strait*, China	**50**	24N	121E
Forsayth: Austl.	**59**	19S	144E
Fort Albany: Canada	**81**	52N	81W
Fortaleza: Brazil	**87**	4S	38W
Fort de France: Martinique	**83**	15N	61W
Fort Dodge: U.S.A.	**81**	43N	94W
Fortescue: *r.*, Austl.	**58**	22S	119E
Fort Hall: Kenya	**68**	1S	37E
Fort Jameson: N. Rhod.	**69**	14S	33E
Fort Johnston: Nyasa.	**69**	15S	35E
Fort Lamy: Fr. Eq. Afr.	**70**	12N	15E
Fort Macleod: Canada	**80**	50N	113W
Fort McMurray: Canada	**78**	57N	111W
Fort Madison: U.S.A.	**84**	41N	91W
Fort Nelson: Canada	**78**	59N	122W
Fort Peck Reservoir: U.S.A.	**80**	48N	107W
Fort Rosebery: N. Rhod.	**68**	11S	29E
Fort Sandeman: W. Pak.	**48**	31N	70E
Fort Simpson: Canada	**78**	62N	121W
Fort Smith: U.S.A.	**81**	35N	94W
Fort Wayne: U.S.A.	**84**	41N	85W
Fort William: Canada	**84**	48N	89W
Fort Worth: U.S.A.	**80**	33N	97W
Fort Yukon: Alaska	**78**	66N	145W
Fostoria: U.S.A.	**84**	41N	84W
Fougères: France	**28**	48N	1W
Foul Bay: Red Sea	**63**	23N	37E
Foulwind, C.: N.Z.	**53**	42S	172E
Fourmies: France	**28**	50N	4E
Foveaux Strait: N.Z.	**53**	47S	168E
Foxe Basin: Canada	**79**	66N	80W
FRANCE	**28/9**	—	—
Franche Comté: *Old Prov.*, Fr.	**29**	47N	6E
Francistown: Bechuanaland	**69**	21S	27E
Franconian Jura: *mtns.*, Ger.	**32**	49N	12E
Frankfort: U.S.A.	**84**	38N	85W
Frankfurt am Main: Ger.	**32**	50N	9E
Frankfurt an der Oder: Ger.	**32**	52N	15E
Franz Josef Land: U.S.S.R.	**42**	80N	55E
Frascati: Italy	**30**	42N	13E
Fraser: *r.*, Canada	**78**	52N	122W
Fraser I.: Austl.	**60**	25S	153E
Fray Bentos: Uruguay	**88**	33S	58W
Frederik Hendrik I.: Neth. New Guinea	**58**	8S	138E
Fredericia: Denmark	**35**	56N	10E
Fredericksburg: U.S.A.	**85**	38N	78W
Fredericton: Canada	**85**	46N	67W
Frederikshavn: Denmark	**35**	57N	11E
Fredrikstad: Norway	**35**	59N	11E
Freeport: U.S.A.	**84**	42N	90W
Freetown: Sierra Leone	**62**	7N	13W
Freiburg im Breisgau: Ger.	**33**	48N	8E
Freising: Germany	**33**	48N	12E
Fréjus: France	**29**	43N	7E
Fremantle: Austl.	**60**	32S	116E
FRENCH EQUATORIAL AFRICA	**70**	—	—
FRENCH GUIANA	**87**	4N	53W
FRENCH SOMALILAND	**67**	13N	43E
French Sudan: Fr. W. Afr.	**62**	17N	3W
FRENCH WEST AFRICA	**62**	—	—
Fresnillo: Mexico	**82**	23N	103W
Fresno: U.S.A.	**80**	37N	120W
Freudenstadt: Germany	**33**	48N	8E
Fribourg: Switz.	**33**	47N	7E
Friedrichshafen: Germany	**33**	48N	9E
Friesland: *Prov.*, Neth.	**32**	53N	6E
Frisian Is., East: Germany	**32**	54N	7E
Frisian Is., North: Germany	**35**	55N	8E
Frisian Is. West: Neth.	**32**	53N	5E
Frobisher Bay: Canada	**79**	63N	65W
Frome, Lake: Austl.	**61**	31S	140E
Frunze: U.S.S.R.	**45**	43N	75E
Fuentes de Oñoro: Spain	**25**	41N	7W
Fuerteventura: *i.*, Can. Is.	**62**	29N	14W
Fuji: *mtn.*, Japan	**52**	35N	139E
Fuji: *r.*, Japan	**52**	35N	138E
Fukui: Japan	**52**	36N	136E
Fukuoka: Japan	**52**	34N	130E
Fukushima: Japan	**52**	38N	140E
Fukuyama: Japan	**52**	41N	140E
Fulda: *& r.*, Germany	**32**	51N	10E
Fulton: U.S.A.	**84**	36N	89W
Funchal: Madeira	**62**	33N	17W
Fundy, Bay of: Canada	**85**	45N	66W
Funen: *i.*, Denmark	**35**	55N	10E
Furka Pass: Switz.	**33**	47N	8E
Furneaux Group: Austl.	**58**	40S	148E
Fürth: Germany	**32**	49N	11E
Fushun: China	**50**	42N	124E
Gabès: *& gulf*, Tunisia	**62**	34N	11E
Gabon: *Prov.*, Fr. Eq. Afr.	**70**	1S	12E
Gabrovo: Bulgaria	**31**	43N	25E
Gadames: Libya	**62**	30N	10E
Gadsden: U.S.A.	**81**	34N	86W
Gaeta: Italy	**30**	41N	14E
Gafsa: Tunisia	**62**	35N	8E
Gail: *r.*, Austria	**33**	47N	13E
Gairdner, Lake: Austl.	**58**	32S	136E
Galapagos Is.: Ecuador	**86**	0	90W
Galaţi: Romania	**31**	45N	28E
Galena: Alaska	**78**	65N	157W
Galesburg: U.S.A.	**84**	41N	90W
Galicia: *Old Prov.*, Spain	**25**	43N	8W
Gallarate: Italy	**33**	46N	9E
Galle: Ceylon	**48**	6N	80E
Gallegos: *r.*, Arg.	**89**	52S	71W
Gallinas, Cape: Colombia	**86**	13N	72W
Gallipoli: Turkey	**31**	40N	27E
Gällivare: Sweden	**34**	67N	21E
Galveston: U.S.A.	**81**	29N	95W
Gambela Post: Ethiopia	**68**	8N	35E
GAMBIA: *& r.*	**62**	13N	15W
Gamlakarleby: Finland	**34**	64N	23E
Gand: Belgium	**28**	51N	4E
Gandak: *r.*, India	**48**	27N	85E
Gander: Canada	**79**	49N	55W
Ganges: France	**29**	44N	4E
Ganges: *r.*, India/Pak.	**48**	25N	88E
Ganongga: *i.*, Solomon Is.	**59**	8S	157E
Gánt: Hungary	**31**	47N	18E
Gap: France	**29**	45N	6E
Gard: *r.*, France	**29**	44N	4E
Garda, L. of: Italy	**33**	46N	11E
Gardez: Afghan.	**48**	34N	69E
Gargano, C.: Italy	**30**	42N	16E
Garian: Libya	**62**	32N	13E
Garissa: Kenya	**68**	1S	40E
Garonne: *r.*, France	**29**	45N	0
Garoua: Fr. Eq. Afr.	**68**	9N	13E
Garrigues: *mtns.*, France	**29**	44N	4E
Garry, Lake: Canada	**78**	66N	100W
Gartok: China	**48**	32N	80E
Gary: U.S.A.	**84**	42N	87W
Gascony: *Old Prov.*, France	**29**	44N	0
Gaspé: Canada	**79**	49N	64W
Gaspé Peninsula: Canada	**79**	48N	65W
Gastonia: U.S.A.	**81**	35N	81W
Gata, C. de: Spain	**25**	37N	2W
Gata, Sierra de: Spain	**25**	40N	7W
Gâtine, Hauteurs de: *hills*, France	**29**	47N	1W
Gatooma: S. Rhod.	**69**	18S	30E
Gatun Lake: *& dam*, Panamá	**83**	*Inset*	
Gauhati: India	**49**	26N	92E
Gävle: Sweden	**35**	61N	17E
Gawler: Austl.	**61**	35S	139E
Gaya: Fr. W. Afr.	**68**	12N	4E
Gaya: India	**48**	25N	85E
Gaza: Egypt	**21**	31N	34E
Gaziantep: Turkey	**44**	37N	37E
Gdańsk: Poland	**27**	54N	19E
Gdov: U.S.S.R.	**35**	59N	28E
Gdynia: Poland	**27**	55N	18E
Gedser: Denmark	**35**	54N	12E
Geelong: Austl.	**61**	38S	144E
Geerardsbergen: Belgium	**28**	51N	4E
Gelidonya, Cape: Turkey	**31**	36N	30E
Gelsenkirchen: Germany	**32**	52N	7E
Geneva: *& l.*, Switz.	**33**	46N	6E
Genil: *r.*, Spain	**25**	37N	4W
Genissiat Dam: France	**29**	46N	6E
Genoa: *& gulf*, Italy	**33**	44N	9E
Genova: Italy	**33**	44N	9E
George: S. Afr.	**69**	34S	22E
George, Lake: Austl.	**61**	35S	149E
George Bay: Canada	**85**	46N	62W
Georgetown: Br. Guiana	**87**	7N	58W
George Town: Malaya	**51**	5N	100E
Georgia: *State*, U.S.A.	**81**	33N	83W
Georgian Bay: Canada	**84**	45N	81W
Georgian S.S.R.: U.S.S.R.	**44**	43N	43E
Gera: Germany	**32**	51N	12E
Geraldton: Austl.	**60**	29S	115E
GERMANY	**32/3**	—	—
Gerona: Spain	**25**	42N	3E
Gers: *r.*, France	**29**	44N	1E
Gettysburgh: U.S.A.	**85**	40N	77W
Gezira: Sudan	**63**	14N	33E
Ghardaïa: Alg.	**62**	33N	4E
Ghazipur: India	**48**	26N	83E
Ghent: Belgium	**28**	51N	4E
Gheorgheni: Romania	**31**	47N	26E
Gibraltar: *& strait*	**25**	36N	5W
Gibson Desert: Austl.	**58**	25S	125E
Gien: France	**29**	47N	3E
Giessen: Germany	**32**	51N	9E
Gifu: Japan	**52**	35N	137E
Gijón: Spain	**25**	44N	6W
Gila: *r.*, U.S.A.	**80**	33N	111W
Gilbert: *r.*, Austl.	**59**	17S	142E
Gilbert Is.: Pac. O.	**54**	0	175E
Gilgandra: Austl.	**61**	32S	149E
Gilgit: Kashmir	**47**	36N	74E
Gilgunnia: Austl.	**61**	32S	146E
Ginir: Ethiopia	**63**	7N	41E
Gippsland: Austl.	**61**	38S	148E
Girga: Egypt	**63**	26N	32E
Gironde: *r.*, France	**29**	45N	1W
Gisborne: N.Z.	**53**	39S	178E
Giurgiu: Romania	**31**	44N	26E
Givors: France	**29**	46N	5E
Gjinokastër: Albania	**31**	40N	20E
Glace Bay:	**85**	46N	60W
Gladbeck: Germany	**32**	52N	7E
Gladstone: Queens., Austl.	**60**	24S	151E
Gladstone: S. Austl.	**61**	34S	138E
Glåma: *r.*, Norway	**35**	61N	12E
Glarus: Switz.	**33**	47N	9E
Glauchau: Germany	**32**	51N	13E
Glazov: U.S.S.R.	**44**	58N	53E
Glenelg: *r.*, Austl.	**61**	37S	141E
Glen Innes: Austl.	**61**	30S	152E
Gliwice: Poland	**27**	50N	19E
Globe: U.S.A.	**80**	33N	111W
Głogów: Poland	**27**	52N	16E
Gloversville: U.S.A.	**85**	43N	74W
Gniezno: Poland	**27**	53N	18E
Goa: Port. India	**48**	15N	74E
Gobi Desert: Mongolia	**43**	43N	105E
Godavari: *r.*, India	**48**	18N	80E
Goderich: Canada	**84**	44N	82W
Godthaab: Greenland	**79**	64N	52W
Godwin Austen, Mt. *see* K2			
Gogra: *r.*, India	**48**	26N	83E
Goiânia: Brazil	**88**	17S	49W
Goiás: Brazil	**88**	16S	50W
Goiás Massif: Brazil	**88**	15S	48W
Gol: Norway	**35**	61N	9E
GOLD COAST	**62**	7N	0
Golden: Canada	**80**	51N	117W
Golden Lake: Canada	**85**	46N	77W
Goldsboro: U.S.A.	**85**	35N	78W
Gomel': U.S.S.R.	**44**	53N	31E
Gondar: Eth.	**63**	13N	37E
Good Hope, Cape of: S. Afr.	**69**	34S	18E
Goomalling: Austl.	**60**	31S	117E
Goondiwindi: Austl.	**61**	29S	150E
Goose Bay: *settlement*, Can.	**79**	53N	60W
Göppingen: Germany	**33**	49N	10E
Gorakhpur: India	**48**	27N	83E
Gore: Ethiopia	**68**	8N	36E
Gore: N.Z.	**53**	46S	169E
Goree: Fr. W. Africa	**62**	14N	17W
Gorizia: Italy	**33**	46N	14E
Gor'kiy: U.S.S.R.	**44**	56N	44E
Görlitz: Germany	**32**	51N	15E
Gorno-Altaysk: U.S.S.R.	**45**	52N	86E
Gorzów Wielkopolski: Pol.	**27**	53N	15E
Gosford: Austl.	**61**	33S	151E
Goslar: Germany	**32**	52N	10E
Gospić: Yugoslavia	**30**	45N	15E
Göteborg: Sweden	**35**	58N	12E
Gotha: Germany	**32**	51N	11E
Gotland: *i.*, Sweden	**35**	57N	19E
Göttingen: Germany	**32**	52N	10E
Gottwaldov: Czech.	**27**	49N	18E
Gouda: Netherlands	**32**	52N	5E
Gouin Reservoir: Canada	**81**	49N	75W
Goulburn: Austl.	**61**	35S	150E
Gourock Range: Austl.	**61**	36S	149E
Goyllarisquizga: Peru	**86**	11S	77W
Gozo: *i.*, Medit. Sea	**30**	36N	14E
Graaff Reinet: S. Afr.	**69**	32S	25E
Gracias a Dios, C.: Nic.	**86**	15N	83W
Grafton: Austl.	**61**	30S	153E
Grahamland: Antarctica	**91**	66S	65W
Grahamstown: S. Afr.	**69**	33S	26E
Graian Alps: Fr./Italy	**33**	45N	7E
Grain Coast: Fr. W. Afr.	**62**	5N	10W
Grammont: Belgium	**28**	51N	4E
Grampians: *mtns.*, Austl.	**61**	37S	142E
Granada: Spain	**25**	37N	4W
Granby: Canada	**85**	45N	73W
Gran Canaria: *i.*, Can. Is.	**66**	28N	15W
Gran Chaco: Arg./Paraguay	**88**	25S	61W
Grand Banks: Can.	**79**	45N	53W
Grand Canyon: U.S.A.	**80**	36N	112W
Grand Coulee Dam: U.S.A.	**80**	48N	119W
Grand Falls: *falls*, Canada	**79**	53N	64W
Grand Falls: *town*, N.B., Can.	**85**	47N	68W
Grand Falls: *town*, Newf., Canada	**79**	49N	56W
Grand Forks: U.S.A.	**80**	48N	97W
Grand Junction: U.S.A.	**80**	39N	109W
Grand Popo: Fr. W. Afr.	**68**	6N	2E
Grand Rapids: Mich., U.S.A.	**84**	43N	86W
Grand Rapids: Minn., U.S.A.	**84**	47N	94W
Grane: Norway	**34**	66N	13E
Grant, Mt.: U.S.A.	**80**	38N	119W
Granville: France	**28**	49N	2W
Grasse: France	**29**	44N	7E
Grave, Pte. de: France	**29**	46N	1W
Gravelines: France	**28**	51N	2E
Great Australian Bight	**58**	—	—
Great Barrier I.: N.Z.	**53**	36S	175E
Great Barrier Reef: Austl.	**60**	20S	150E
Great Bear Lake: Canada	**78**	66N	120W
Great Belt: Denmark	**35**	55N	11E
Great Dividing Range: Austl.	**60**	—	—
Greater Antilles: W. Indies	**83**	18N	75W
Great Eastern Erg: *desert*, Alg.	**66**	30N	8E
Great Falls: *city*, U.S.A.	**80**	47N	111W
Great Himalayan Range	**48/9**	—	—
Great Karroo: *plat.*, S. Afr.	**69**	33S	23E
Great Keppel I.: Austl.	**60**	23S	151E
Great Khingan Mts.: China	**51**	50N	122E
Great Salt Lake: U.S.A.	**80**	41N	113W
Great Sandy Desert: Austl.	**58**	21S	124E
Great Sandy I.: Austl.	**60**	25S	153E
Great Slave Lake: Canada	**78**	62N	115W
Great Victoria Desert: Austl.	**58**	28S	129E
Gredos, Sierra de: Spain	**25**	40N	5W
GREECE	**31**	—	—
Green: *r.*, U.S.A.	**80**	40N	110W
Greenough: *r.*, Austl.	**60**	28S	115E
Green Bay: *& city*, U.S.A.	**84**	45N	88W
GREENLAND	**79**	—	—
Green Mtns.: U.S.A.	**85**	44N	73W
Green River: *city*, U.S.A.	**80**	42N	110W
Greensboro: U.S.A.	**84**	36N	80W
Greensburg: U.S.A.	**85**	40N	80W
Greenville: U.S.A.	**81**	35N	82W
Greifswald: Germany	**32**	54N	13E
Grenada: *i.*, W. Indies	**83**	12N	62W
Grenadines: *is.*, W. Indies	**83**	12N	61W
Grenay: France	**28**	50N	3E
Grenoble: France	**29**	45N	6E
Greymouth: N.Z.	**53**	42S	171E
Grey Range: Austl.	**61**	28S	143E
Griffith: Austl.	**61**	34S	146E
Grimsel Pass: Switz.	**33**	47N	8E
Griqualand: S. Afr.	**69**	29S	24E
Griquatown: S. Afr.	**69**	29S	25E
Gris Nez: *cape*, France	**28**	51N	2E
Grodekovo: U.S.S.R.	**52**	44N	131E
Grodno: U.S.S.R.	**44**	54N	24E
Groix, Île de: France	**28**	48N	3W
Gronau: Germany	**32**	52N	7E
Grong: Norway	**34**	64N	12E
Groningen: Neth.	**32**	53N	7E
Groote Eylandt: *i.*, Austl.	**58**	14S	137E
Grootfontein: S.W. Afr.	**69**	20S	18E
Grossenbrode: Germany	**35**	54N	11E
Grosseto: Italy	**30**	43N	11E
Gross Glockner: *mtn.*, Austr.	**33**	47N	13E
Groznyy: U.S.S.R.	**44**	43N	46E
Grudziądz: Poland	**27**	53N	18E
Grünberg: Poland	**27**	52N	16E
Gruyères: Switz.	**33**	46N	7E
Guadalajara: Mexico	**82**	21N	103W
Guadalajara: Spain	**25**	41N	3W
Guadalcanal: Spain	**25**	38N	6W
Guadalcanal: *i.*, Pac. O.	**59**	10S	160E
Guadalquivir: *r.*, Spain	**25**	37N	6W
Guadalupe: *i.*, Mexico	**82**	29N	118W
Guadarrama, Sierra de: Sp.	**25**	41N	4W
Guadeloupe: *i.*, W. Indies	**83**	17N	61W
Guadiana: W., Sp./Port.	**25**	38N	8W
Guadix: Spain	**25**	37N	3W
Guajará-mirim: Brazil	**86**	11S	65W
Guam: *i.*, Pac. O.	**54**	14N	145E
Guarda: Portugal	**25**	41N	7W
Guardafui, C.: Somalia	**46**	12N	51E

WORLD

GUATEMALA — JÖRN

	Page	Lat.	Long.
GUATEMALA: *& city*	82	15N	91W
Guayaquil: *& gulf*, Ecuador	86	2S	80W
Guaymas: Mexico	80	28N	111W
Gubakha: U.S.S.R.	44	58N	57E
Guebwiller: France	28	48N	7E
Guelph: Canada	84	44N	80W
Guéret: France	29	46N	2E
Guernsey: *i.*, Chan. Is.	28	49N	3W
Guiana Highlands: S. Am.	86/7	—	—
Guienne: *Old Prov.*, France	29	45N	0
Guinea, G. of	68	—	—
Guinea Highlands: Fr. W. Afr.	66	10N	10W
Guingamp: France	28	49N	3W
Gujranwala: W. Pak.	48	32N	74E
Gulfport: U.S.A.	81	30N	89W
Gumti: *r.*, India	48	26N	82E
Gunnedah: Austl.	61	31S	150E
Guntur: India	48	16N	80E
Gurgan: Iran	44	37N	55E
Gur'yev: U.S.S.R.	44	47N	52E
Gwadar: W. Pak.	46	25N	62E
Gwalior: India	48	26N	78E
Gwelo: S. Rhod.	69	20S	30E
Gyangtse: China	47	29N	90E
Gydan Range: U.S.S.R.	43	62N	160E
Gyda Peninsula: U.S.S.R.	43	70N	80E
Gympie: Austl.	60	26S	153E
Györ: Hungary	27	48N	18E
Haarlem: Neth.	32	52N	5E
Haast: N.Z.	53	44S	169E
Hachinohe: Japan	52	40N	141E
Hachioji: Japan	52	36N	140E
Hadhramaut: Aden	46	16N	48E
Hageland: Belgium	28	51N	5E
Hagen: Germany	32	51N	7E
Hagerstown: U.S.A.	85	40N	78W
Hague, Cap de la: France	28	50N	2W
Hague, The: Neth.	32	52N	4E
Haguenau: France	28	49N	8E
Haifa: Israel	46	33N	35E
Hail: Sa'udi Arabia	46	27N	42E
Hailar: China	50	50N	118E
Hainan: *i. & str.*, China	51	19N	110E
Hainault: *Old Prov.*, Belgium	28	51N	4E
Haiphong: Viet Minh	51	21N	107E
HAITI	83	19N	73W
Hakodate: Japan	52	42N	141E
Halberstadt: Germany	32	52N	11E
Haldensleben: Germany	32	52N	11E
Halifax: Canada	85	44N	63W
Halle: Germany	32	51N	12E
Halmahera: *i.*, Indonesia	51	1N	128E
Halmstad: Sweden	35	57N	13E
Hälsingborg: Sweden	35	56N	13E
Hamada: Japan	52	35N	132E
Hamadan: Iran	46	35N	49E
Hamamatsu: Japan	52	35N	138E
Hamar: Norway	35	61N	11E
Hamburg: Germany	32	54N	10E
Hämeenlinna: Finland	34	61N	24E
Hameln: Germany	32	52N	9E
Hamersley Ra.: Austl.	58	22S	118E
Hami: China	50	43N	93E
Hamilton: Austl.	61	38S	142E
Hamilton: Canada	84	43N	80W
Hamilton: N.Z.	53	38S	175E
Hamilton: U.S.A.	84	39N	85W
Hamm: Germany	32	52N	8E
Hammamet, Gulf of: Tunisia	30	36N	11E
Hammerfest: Norway	34	71N	24E
Hamun-i-Helmand: *l.*, Iran/ Afghanistan	46	31N	61E
Hangchow: China	50	30N	120E
Hangö (Hanko): Finland	35	60N	23E
Hankow: China	50	31N	114E
Hannibal: U.S.A.	84	40N	91W
Hanö Bay: Sweden	35	56N	15E
Hanoi: Viet Minh	50	21N	106E
Hanover: Germany	32	52N	10E
Hanyang: China	50	31N	114E
Haogoundou, L.: Fr. W. Afr.	62	15N	3W
Harar: Ethiopia	63	9N	42E
Harbin: China	50	46N	127E
Harburg-Wilhelmsburg: Ger.	32	53N	10E
Hardanger Fd.: Norway	35	60N	6E
Hardangervidda: Norway	35	60N	8E
Hardenberg: Neth.	32	53N	7E
Hargeisa: Br. Somaliland	63	10N	44E
Harima Gulf: Japan	52	34N	135E
Harlingen: Neth.	32	53N	5E
Härnösand: Sweden	34	63N	18E
Harrisburg: Ill., U.S.A.	84	38N	88W
Harrisburg: Pa., U.S.A.	85	40N	77W
Harrismith: S. Afr.	69	28S	29E
Harsprånget: Sweden	34	67N	20E
Harstad: Norway	34	69N	16E
Hartford: U.S.A.	85	42N	73W
Harz: *mtns.*, Germany	32	52N	11E
Hasa: Sa'udi Arabia	46	27N	48E
Hassan: India	48	13N	76E
Hasselt: Belgium	28	51N	5E
Hässleholm: Sweden	35	56N	14E
Hastings: N.Z.	53	40S	177E
Hastings Range: Austl.	61	31S	152E
Hat nh: Laos	51	19N	106E
Hatiteras, Cape: U.S.A.	81	35N	76W
Haugesund: Norway	35	59N	5E
Hauraki Gulf: N.Z.	53	36S	175E
Havana: Cuba	83	23N	82W
Havel: *r.*, Germany	32	53N	13E
Haverhill: U.S.A.	85	43W	71W
Havre, Le: France	28	50N	0
Havre de Grace: U.S.A.	85	39N	76W
Hawaii: *i.*, Pacific Ocean	55	20N	155W
Hawaiian Is.: Pac. O.	54/5	—	—
Hawera: N.Z.	53	40S	174E
Hawke Bay: N.Z.	53	39S	177E
Hay: Austl.	61	34S	145E
Hazaribagh: India	48	24N	85E
Hazebrouck: France	28	51N	3E
Hazelton: Canada	78	55N	127W
Heard Is.: Southern O.	49	53S	73E
Heerenveen: Neth.	32	53N	6E
Heidelberg: Germany	32	49N	9E
Heidelberg: S. Africa	69	26S	28E
Heilbronn: Germany	32	49N	9E
Hekla: *mtn.*, Iceland	34	64N	19W
Helena: U.S.A.	80	47N	112W
Helensville: N.Z.	53	37S	174E
Heligoland: *i. & bight*, Ger.	35	54N	8E
Helles, Cape: Turkey	31	40N	26E
Helsinki (Helsingfors): Fin.	35	60N	25E
Helsingør: Denmark	35	56N	13E
Hendaye: France	25	43N	2W
Henderson: U.S.A.	84	38N	88W
Hengelo: Neth.	32	52N	7E
Herat: Afghan.	46	34N	62E
Hérault: *r.*, France	29	44N	4E
Herberton: Austl.	59	18S	145E
Hercegovina: Yugo.	30	44N	18E
Herford: Germany	32	52N	9E
Herisau: Switz.	33	47N	9E
Hermosillo: Mexico	80	29N	111W
Herne: Germany	32	52N	7E
Herning: Denmark	35	56N	9E
Herschel I.: Canada	78	70N	139W
Herstal: Belgium	28	51N	6E
Hervey Bay: Austl.	60	25S	153E
Hibbing: U.S.A.	84	47N	93W
Hidaka Mts.: Japan	52	42N	143E
Hidalgo del Parral: Mexico	82	27N	106W
Hida Mts.: Japan	52	36N	138E
High Atlas: *mtns.*, Morocco	62	31N	7W
High Plateaux: Algeria	62	34N	0
High Veld: S. Afr.	69	30S	28E
Hijaz: Sa'udi Arabia	46	25N	39E
Hildesheim: Germany	32	52N	10E
Hilla: 'Iraq	46	33N	44E
Hillegom: Neth.	32	52N	5E
Hillston: Austl.	61	34S	146E
Hilversum: Neth.	32	52N	5E
Himalayas *see* Great Himalayan Range			
Himeji: Japan	52	35N	135E
Hinckley: U.S.A.	84	46N	93W
Hindu Kush: *mtns.*, Afghan.	47	35N	70E
Hingshan: China	50	47N	130E
Hirosaki: Japan	52	41N	140E
Hiroshima: Japan	52	34N	132E
Hirson: France	28	50N	4E
Hispaniola: W. Indies	83	18N	72W
Hitachi: Japan	52	37N	140E
Hjørring: Denmark	35	57N	10E
Hobart: Tasmania	59	43S	147E
Hoboken: Belgium	28	51N	4E
Hoboken: U.S.A.	85	40N	75W
Hoch Moor: Germany	32	53N	8E
Hodeida: Yemen	46	15N	43E
Hódmezövásárhely: Hungary	27	46N	20E
Hof: Germany	32	50N	12E
Hofei: China	50	32N	117E
Hofsjökull: *mtn.*, Iceland	34	65N	19W
Hohe Rhön: *mtns.*, Germany	32	50N	10E
Hohe Tauern: *mtns.*, Austr.	33	47N	12E
Hohsien: China	51	24N	112E
Hoihow: China	51	20N	110E
Hokitika: N.Z.	53	43S	171E
Hokkaido: *i.*, Japan	50	43N	143E
Holbaek: Denmark	35	56N	12E
Holbrook: Austl.	61	36S	147E
Holland *see* Netherlands			
Hollandia: New Guinea	58	3S	141E
Hollywood: U.S.A.	80	34N	118W
Holstebro: Denmark	35	56N	9E
Holstein: *Old Prov.*, Ger.	32	54N	10E
Holyoke: U.S.A.	85	42N	73W
Home Hill: Austl.	60	20S	147E
Homs: Libya	62	33N	14E
Homs: Syria	46	35N	37E
HONDURAS	83	15N	87W
Hønefoss: Norway	35	60N	10E
Honfleur: France	28	49N	0
Hong Kong: China	50	22N	114E
Honiara: Guadalcanal	59	10S	160E
Honolulu: Hawaiian Is.	55	21N	158W
Honshu: *i.*, Japan	52	—	—
Hood, Mt.: U.S.A.	78	45N	122W
Hood, Point: Austl.	60	34S	120E
Hoogezand: Neth.	32	53N	7E
Hooghly: *r.*, India	48	22N	88E
Hook I., Austl.	60	20S	149E
Hook of Holland: Neth.	32	52N	4E
Hoover Dam: U.S.A.	80	36N	115W
Hopkins: *r.*, Austl.	61	38S	143E
Hopkinsville: U.S.A.	84	37N	88W
Hormuz, Str. of: Iran	46	27N	56E
Horn, Cape: Chile	89	56S	67W
Hornsby: Austl.	61	34S	151E
Horsham: Austl.	61	37S	142E
Hoshangabad: India	48	23N	78E
Hotham, Mt.: Austl.	61	37S	147E
Hoting: Sweden	34	64N	16E
Houeisai: Laos	47	20N	100E
Hourtin, Étg. d': France	29	45N	1W
Houston: U.S.A.	80	30N	95W
Howe, Cape: Austl.	61	38S	150E
Howrah: India	48	23N	88E
Hoyo Str.: Japan	52	33N	132E
Hsichang: China	50	28N	102E
Huallaga: *r.*, Peru	86	8S	76W
Huancavelica: Peru	86	13S	75W
Huancayo: Peru	86	12S	75W
Huánuco: Peru	86	10S	76W
Huarás: Peru	86	10S	78W
Hubli: India	48	15N	75E
Hudson: *r.*, U.S.A.	85	41N	74W
Hudson Bay: Canada	79	60N	85W
Hudson Bay: *town*, Canada	80	53N	102W
Hudson Strait: Canada	79	63N	70W
Hué: Viet Nam	51	16N	107E
Huelva: Spain	25	37N	7W
Huesca: Spain	25	42N	0
Hufhuf: Sa'udi Arabia	46	25N	49E
Hughenden: Austl.	59	21S	144E
Huiarau Range: N.Z.	53	39S	177E
Huitse: China	50	26N	103E
Hull: Canada	85	45N	76W
Hüls: Germany	32	52N	7E
Hulun: China	50	49N	120E
Hulun Nor: *l.*, China	50	49N	118E
Humboldt Glacier: Greenland	79	80N	63W
Hume: *r.*, Austl.	61	36S	145E
Hume Reservoir: Austl.	61	36S	147E
HUNGARY	30	—	—
Hunsrück: *mtns.*, Germany	32	50N	7E
Hunter: *r. & range*, Austl.	61	33S	151E
Huntington: U.S.A.	84	38N	82W
Huron, Lake: Can./U.S.A.	84	45N	83W
Hurunui: *r.*, N.Z.	53	43S	172E
Huskvarna: Sweden	35	58N	14E
Hutchinson: U.S.A.	80	38N	98W
Hutt: N.Z.	53	41S	175E
Hwaining: China	50	31N	117E
Hwang (Yellow): *r.*, China	50	37N	106E
Hyderabad: India	48	17N	78E
Hyderabad: W. Pak.	48	25N	68E
Hyères: France	29	43N	6E
Hyères, Îles d': France	29	43N	6E
Iaşi: Romania	31	47N	28E
Ibadan: Nigeria	68	7N	4E
Ibagué: Colombia	86	4N	75W
Ibi: Nigeria	68	8N	10E
Ibiza: *i.*, Balearic Is.	25	39N	2E
Ica: Peru	86	14S	76W
ICELAND	34	—	—
Ichang: China	50	31N	111E
Ichinomiya: Japan	52	35N	137E
Idaho: *State*, U.S.A.	80	44N	114W
Idaho Falls: U.S.A.	80	43N	112W
Ifni: *Territ.*, Sp. Mor.	62	29N	10W
Igarka: U.S.S.R.	42	67N	86E
Iglesias: Sardinia	30	39N	8E
Iharhar: *r.*, Algeria	62	27N	5E
Iisalmi: Finland	34	64N	27E
Ijebu-Ode: Nigeria	68	7N	4E
Ijmuiden: Neth.	32	52N	5E
Ijssel: *r.*, Neth.	32	53N	6E
Ijsselmeer: Neth.	32	53N	5E
Ikaria: *i.*, Greece	31	38N	26E
Île de France: *Old Prov.*, Fr.	28	49N	2E
Ilhéus: Brazil	87	15S	39W
Iliamna Lake: Alaska	78	59N	155W
Iliodhromia: *i.*, Greece	31	39N	24E
Illimani: *mtn.*, Bolivia	86	17S	68W
Illinois: *r.*, U.S.A.	84	40N	90W
Illinois: *State*, U.S.A.	81	39N	89W
Il'men', L.: U.S.S.R.	44	58N	32E
Ilmenau: Germany	32	51N	11E
Imabari: Japan	52	34N	133E
Imatra: Finland	35	61N	29E
Imperia: Italy	33	44N	8E
Imperial Dam: U.S.A.	80	33N	114W
Imphal: India	47	25N	94E
Imroz: *i.*, Turkey	31	40N	26E
Inari, L.: Finland	34	69N	28E
INDIA	48/9	—	—
Indiana: *State*, U.S.A.	81	39N	86W
Indianapolis: U.S.A.	84	40N	86W
Indian Ocean	49	—	—
Indo-China	51	—	—
INDONESIA	51	—	—
Indore: India	48	23N	76E
Indre: *r.*, France	29	47N	1E
Indus: *r.*, W. Pak.	48	27N	68E
Ingolstadt: Germany	33	49N	11E
Inhambane: Mozambique	69	24S	35E
Inhaminga: Mozambique	69	18S	35E
Inkerman: U.S.S.R.	44	45N	34E
Inn: *r.*, Germany/Austria	33	48N	12E
Inner Mongolia: China	50	45N	120E
Innsbruck: Austria	33	47N	11E
Inowrocław: Poland	27	53N	18E
Insterburg: U.S.S.R.	27	55N	22E
Interlaken: Switz.	33	47N	8E
International Rapids: Can./ U.S.A.	85	45N	75W
Invercargill: N.Z.	53	46S	168E
Inverell: Austl.	61	30S	151E
Inverness: Canada	85	46N	61W
Investigator Strait: Austl.	61	35S	137E
Ionian Is.: Greece	31	38N	20E
Ionian Sea	31	—	—
Ios: *i.*, Greece	31	37N	25E
Iowa: *State*: U.S.A.	81	42N	93W
Iowa City: U.S.A.	84	42N	92W
Iowa Falls: U.S.A.	84	42N	94W
Ipin: China	50	29N	105E
Ipoh: Malaya	51	5N	101E
Ipswich: Austl.	60	28S	153E
Iquique: Chile	88	20S	70W
Iquitos: Peru	86	4S	73W
Iraklion: Crete	31	35N	25E
IRAN	46	—	—
IRAQ	46	—	—
Iringa: Tanganyika	68	8S	36E
Irkutsk: U.S.S.R.	43	52N	105E
Iron Gates: Yugo./Romania	31	45N	23E
Iron Knob: Austl.	61	33S	137E
Iron Mt.: Utah, U.S.A.	80	38N	114W
Iron Mtn.: *city*, Wis. U.S.A.	84	46N	88W
Ironton: U.S.A.	84	39N	83W
Ironwood: U.S.A.	84	46N	90W
Iroquois: Canada	85	45N	75W
Irrawaddy: *r.*, Burma	47	19N	95E
Irtysh: *r.*, U.S.S.R.	45	57N	73E
Irun: Spain	25	43N	2W
Isabela I.: Pacific Ocean	86	0	92W
Isafjördhur: Iceland	34	66N	23W
Isar: *r.*, Germany	33	48N	12E
Isarco: *r.*, Italy	33	47N	12E
Ischia: *i.*, Italy	30	41N	14E
Ise Bay: Japan	52	35N	137E
Iseo, Lake: Italy	33	46N	10E
Isère: *r.*, France	29	45N	5E
Iserlohn: Germany	32	51N	8E
Isfahan: Iran	46	33N	52E
Ishikari: *r.*, Japan	52	43N	141E
Ishim: *r.*, U.S.S.R.	45	54N	68E
Ishimbay: U.S.S.R.	44	53N	56E
Ishinomaki: Japan	52	38N	141E
İskenderun: Turkey	46	36N	36E
Ismailia: Egypt	63	30N	32E
Isna: Egypt	63	25N	33E
Isonzo: *r.*, Italy	33	46N	14E
ISRAEL	46	32N	35E
Issigeac: France	29	45N	1E
Issoudun: France	29	47N	2E
Issyk Kul': *l.*, U.S.S.R.	45	42N	77E
İstanbul: Turkey	31	41N	29E
Istria: *penin.*, Yugoslavia	33	45N	14E
Itabira: Brazil	88	20S	43W
Itabuna: Brazil	87	15S	39W
ITALY	30/31	—	—
Ithaca: U.S.A.	85	42N	77W
Ithaca (Ithaki): *i.*, Greece	31	38N	21E
Ivailovgrad: Bulgaria	31	42N	26E
Ivanhoe: Austl.	61	33S	144E
Ivanovo: U.S.S.R.	44	57N	41E
Ivdel': U.S.S.R.	45	61N	60E
Iviza: *i.*, Balearic Is.	25	39N	2E
Ivory Coast: Fr. W. Afr.	62	7N	6W
Iwakuni: Japan	52	34N	132E
Iyo Gulf: Japan	52	34N	132E
Izhevsk: U.S.S.R.	44	57N	53E
Izmail: U.S.S.R.	31	45N	29E
İzmir: Turkey	31	38N	27E
Izu Islands: Japan	52	34N	139E
Jaca: Spain	25	43N	1W
Jáchymov: Czech.	32	50N	13E
Jackson: Mich., U.S.A.	84	42N	84W
Jackson: Miss., U.S.A.	81	32N	90W
Jackson: Tenn., U.S.A.	84	36N	89W
Jacksonville: Fla., U.S.A.	81	30N	82W
Jacksonville: Ill., U.S.A.	84	40N	90W
Jacobabad: W. Pak.	48	28N	69E
Jadotville: Belg. Congo	71	11S	27E
Jaén: Spain	25	38N	4W
Jaffa-Tel Aviv: Israel	46	32N	35E
Jaffa, C.: Austl.	61	37S	140E
Jaffna: Ceylon	48	10N	80E
Jaipur: India	48	27N	76E
Jaisalmer: India	48	27N	71E
Jakobstad: Finland	34	64N	23E
Jalalabad: Afghan.	48	34N	70E
JAMAICA	83	18N	77W
Jambin: Austl.	60	24S	150E
James: *r.*, U.S.A.	85	37N	78W
James Bay: Canada	81	53N	80W
Jamestown: U.S.A.	85	42N	79W
Jammu: Kashmir	48	33N	75E
Jamshedpur: India	48	23N	86E
Janesville: U.S.A.	84	43N	89W
JAPAN	52	—	—
Japan, Sea of	52	—	—
Jarocin: Poland	27	52N	18E
Jarosław: Poland	27	50N	23E
Jasło: Poland	27	50N	22E
Jászberény: Hungary	31	47N	20E
Java: *i. & sea*, Indonesia	51	7S	110E
Jaxartes: *r.*, U.S.S.R.	45	43N	67E
Jebba: Nigeria	68	9N	4E
Jedrzejów: Poland	27	51N	20E
Jefferson City: U.S.A.	84	39N	92W
Jehol: China	50	41N	118E
Jena: Germany	32	51N	12E
Jenolan Caves: Austl.	61	34S	150E
Jequitinhonha: *r.*, Brazil	89	16S	40W
Jerez de la Frontera: Sp.	25	37N	6W
Jersey City: U.S.A.	85	41N	74W
Jerusalem: Isr./Jordan	46	32N	35E
Jervis Bay: Austl.	61	35S	151E
Jesselton: N. Borneo	51	6N	116E
Jessore: E. Pak.	48	23N	89E
Jhansi: India	48	25N	79E
Jhelum: *r.*, W. Pak.	48	31N	72E
Jidda: Sa'udi Arabia	46	22N	39E
Jiménez: Mexico	82	27N	105W
Jiran: Ethiopia	68	7N	37E
João Pessoa: Brazil	87	7S	35W
Jodhpur: India	48	26N	73E
Joensuu: Finland	34	63N	30E
Jofra Oasis: Libya	62	30N	15E
Jogjakarta: Java	51	8S	110E
Johannesburg: S. Africa	69	26S	28E
Johnson City: U.S.A.	84	36N	82W
Johnstown: U.S.A.	85	40N	79W
Johore Bahru: Malaya	51	1N	104E
Joliet: U.S.A.	84	42N	88W
Joliette: Canada	85	46N	73W
Jolo: *i.*, Philippines	51	6N	121E
Jonesboro: U.S.A.	84	36N	91W
Jönköping: Sweden	35	58N	14E
Jonquière: Canada	85	48N	71W
Joplin: U.S.A.	81	37N	94W
JORDAN: *& r.*	46	32N	37E
Jorhat: India	49	27N	94E
Jörn: Sweden	34	65N	20E

	Page	Lat.	Long.
Jos: Nigeria	**68**	10N	9E
Joseph Bonaparte Gulf: Austl.	**58**	14S	128E
Josselin: France	**28**	48N	3W
Jostedals Bre: *mtn.*, Norway	**34**	62N	7E
Jotunheimen: *mtns.*, Norway	**35**	61N	9E
Juan Fernández Is.: Chile	**88**	34S	79W
Juba: Sudan	**63**	5N	32E
Juba: *r.*, Somalia	**63**	2N	42E
Jubbulpore: India	**48**	23N	80E
Jucar: *r.*, Spain	**25**	39N	1W
Juist: *i.*, Germany	**32**	54N	7E
Juiz de Fóra: Brazil	**38**	22S	43W
Jujuy: Argentina	**88**	24S	65W
Julian Alps: Italy/Yugo.	**30**	46N	13E
Julich: Germany	**32**	51N	6E
Julier Pass: Switz.	**33**	46N	10E
Jullundur: India	**48**	31N	76E
Jumna: *r.*, India	**48**	25N	81E
Juneau: Alaska	**78**	58N	134W
Junee: Austl.	**61**	35S	148E
Jungfrau: *mtn.*, Switz.	**33**	47N	8E
Jura: *mtns.*, Fr./Switz.	**33**	47N	6E
Juruá: *r.*, Brazil	**86**	5S	67W
Jussey: France	**28**	48N	6E
Jutland: *penin.*, Denmark	**35**	56N	9E
Jyväskylä: Finland	**34**	62N	26E
K2: *mtn.*, Kashmir	**47**	36N	77E
Kabaena: *i.*, Indon.	**58**	5S	122E
Kabalo: Belg. Congo	**70**	6S	27E
Kabul: *& r.*, Afghan.	**48**	35N	69E
Kade: Gold Coast	**68**	6N	1W
Kadina: Austl.	**61**	34S	138E
Kaduna: Nigeria	**68**	10N	8E
Kafue: *& r.*, N. Rhod.	**69**	15S	28E
Kagoshima: Japan	**52**	32N	131E
Kagul: U.S.S.R.	**31**	46N	28E
Kaieteur Falls: Br. Guiana	**87**	5N	59W
Kaifeng: China	**50**	35N	115E
Kaikohe: N.Z.	**53**	35S	174E
Kaikoura: *mtns.*, N.Z.	**53**	42S	173E
Kailas Range: China	**48**	31N	82E
Kaimanawa Mts.: N.Z.	**53**	39S	176E
Kairouan: Tunisia	**30**	36N	10E
Kaiserslautern: Germany	**32**	49N	8E
Kaitaia: N.Z.	**53**	35S	173E
Kaitangata: N.Z.	**53**	46S	170E
Kajaani: Finland	**34**	64N	28E
Kakinada: India	**48**	17N	82E
Kalabagh: W. Pak.	**48**	33N	72E
Kalachinsk: U.S.S.R.	**45**	55N	75E
Kalahari Desert: Bech.	**69**	24S	23E
Kalamata: Greece	**31**	37N	22E
Kalamazoo: U.S.A.	**84**	42N	86W
Kalat: W. Pakistan	**48**	29N	67E
Kalgoorlie: Austl.	**60**	31S	122E
Kalimnos: *i.*, Greece	**31**	37N	27E
Kalinin: U.S.S.R.	**44**	57N	36E
Kaliningrad: U.S.S.R.	**27**	55N	20E
Kalmar: Sweden	**35**	57N	16E
Kaluga: U.S.S.R.	**44**	55N	36E
Kama: *r.*, U.S.S.R.	**44**	55N	50E
Kamaishi: Japan	**52**	39N	142E
Kamaran Is.: Red Sea	**46**	15N	42E
Kamchatka: U.S.S.R.	**43**	55N	160E
Kamchatka Bay: U.S.S.R.	**43**	55N	163E
Kamenskoye: U.S.S.R.	**43**	63N	165E
Kamensk-Uralskiy: U.S.S.R.	**45**	57N	62E
Kamet: *mtn.*, Ind./China	**48**	31N	80E
Kamienna Góra: Poland	**27**	51N	16E
Kamina: Belg. Congo	**70**	9S	25E
Kamloops: Canada	**80**	51N	120W
Kampala: Uganda	**68**	0	33E
Kampen: Neth.	**32**	53N	6E
Kanazawa: Japan	**52**	37N	136E
Kandagach: U.S.S.R.	**44**	49N	57E
Kandahar: Afghan.	**46**	32N	66E
Kandalaksha: U.S.S.R.	**34**	67N	32E
Kandi: Fr. W. Afr.	**68**	11N	3E
Kandla: India	**48**	23N	70E
Kandos: Austl.	**61**	33S	150E
Kandy: Ceylon	**48**	7N	81E
Kane Basin: Canada	**79**	79N	70W
Kangaroo I.: Austl.	**61**	36S	137E
Kangchenjunga: *mtn.*, Nepal/ Sikkim	**49**	28N	88E
Kangean Is.: Indonesia	**51**	7S	116E
Kanin, C.: U.S.S.R.	**42**	68N	45E
Kankanee: U.S.A.	**84**	41N	88W
Kano: Nigeria	**68**	12N	8E
Kanpur: India	**48**	26N	80E
Kansas: *State*, U.S.A.	**80**	38N	99W
Kansas City: Kans., U.S.A.	**81**	39N	95W
Kansas City: Mo., U.S.A.	**81**	39N	95W
Kansk: U.S.S.R.	**45**	56N	95E
Kaohsiung: China	**51**	23N	120E
Kaposvár: Hungary	**27**	46N	18E
Kapurthaa: India	**48**	31N	75E
Kapuskasilng: *& r.*, Can.	**84**	49N	83W
Kara: U.S.S.R.	**42**	69N	65E
Kara-Bogaz-Gol: *l.*, U.S.S.R.	**44**	42N	54E
Karabük: Turkey	**44**	41N	33E
Karachi: W. Pak.	**48**	25N	67E
Karaganda: U.S.S.R.	**45**	50N	73E
Karakoram: *& pass.*, Kashmir	**48**	36N	76E
Kaa-Kum: U.S.SR.	**44**	39N	60E
Karrasberg: S.W. Afr.	**69**	28S	19E
Kara Sea: U.S.S.R.	**42**	72N	62E
Kara-Tau: U.S.S.R.	**45**	44N	68E
Karaul: U.S.S.R.	**43**	70N	83E
Karbala: 'Iraq	**46**	33N	44E
Karelo - Finnish S.S.R.: U.S.S.R.	**42**	65N	34E
Kargil: Kashmir	**48**	35N	76E
Kariba Gorge: N. Rhod.	**69**	17S	29E
Karibib: S.W. Afr.	**69**	22S	16E
Karkinitsky Bay: U.S.S.R.	**31**	46N	33E
Karlovac: Yugoslavia	**30**	45N	16E
Karlovy Vary (Karlsbad): Czech.	**32**	50N	13E
Karlshamn: Sweden	**35**	56N	15E
Karlskoga: Sweden	**35**	59N	15E
Karlskrona: Sweden	**35**	56N	16E
Karlsruhe: Germany	**32**	49N	8E
Karlstad: Sweden	**35**	59N	13E
Karpathos: *i.*, Greece	**31**	36N	27E
Kartaly: U.S.S.R.	**45**	53N	60E
Karwar: India	**48**	15N	74E
Kaş: Turkey	**31**	36N	30E
Kasai: *r.*, Belg. Congo	**71**	4S	19E
Kasba Lake: Canada	**78**	60N	102W
Kasenga: Belg. Congo	**68**	10S	29E
Kasese: Uganda	**68**	0	30E
Kashgar: China	**45**	40N	76E
KASHMIR & JAMMU	**48**	35N	76E
Kasos: *i & str.*, Greece	**31**	35N	27E
Kassala: Sudan	**67**	15N	36E
Kassel: Germany	**32**	51N	9E
Kasserine: Tunisia	**30**	35N	9E
Kastellorizo: Turkey	**31**	36N	29E
Katahdin, Mt.: U.S.A.	**85**	46N	69W
Katakolon: Greece	**31**	38N	21E
Katanga: Belg. Congo	**68**	12S	27E
Katanning: Austl.	**60**	34S	118E
Kathiawar: *penin.*, India	**48**	22N	71E
Katmandu: Nepal	**48**	28N	85E
Katoomba: Austl.	**61**	34S	150E
Katowice: Poland	**27**	50N	19E
Katrineholm: Sweden	**35**	59N	16E
Katsina: Nigeria	**68**	13N	8E
Kattegat: *str.*, Den./Swed.	**35**	57N	11E
Kaunas: U.S.S.R.	**44**	55N	24E
Kaura Namoda: Nigeria	**68**	13N	7E
Kautokeino: Norway	**34**	69N	23E
Kavacha: U.S.S.R.	**43**	60N	170E
Kavalla: Greece	**31**	41N	24E
Kavieng: New Ireland	**59**	3S	152E
Kawasaki: Japan	**52**	35N	140E
Kaya: Fr. W. Afr.	**68**	14N	1W
Kayes: Fr. W. Afr.	**66**	14N	11W
Kayseri: Turkey	**44**	39N	35E
Kazach'ye: U.S.S.R.	**43**	71N	136E
Kazakh S.S.R.: U.S.S.R.	**45**	—	—
Kazan': U.S.S.R.	**44**	56N	49E
Kazanlik: Bulgaria	**31**	43N	25E
Kazvin: Iran	**44**	36N	50E
Kea: *i.*, Greece	**31**	38N	24E
Kebbi: *r.*, Nigeria	**68**	12N	4E
Kecskemét: Hungary	**27**	47N	20E
Keetmanshoop: S.W. Afr.	**69**	26S	18E
Kefallinia: *i.*, Greece	**31**	38N	21E
Keflavik: Iceland	**34**	64N	22W
Kemerovo: U.S.S.R.	**45**	55N	86E
Kemi: *& r.*, Finland	**34**	66N	25E
Kempsey: Austl.	**61**	31S	153E
Kennebec: *r.*, U.S.A.	**85**	45N	70W
Kennicott: Alaska	**78**	62N	143W
Kentucky: *State*, U.S.A.	**81**	37N	85W
Kentucky: *r.*, U.S.A.	**84**	38N	84W
KENYA	**68**	—	—
Kenya, Mt.: Kenya	**68**	0	37E
Keokuk: U.S.A.	**84**	40N	92W
Keppel Bay: Austl.	**60**	23S	151E
Kerang: Austl.	**61**	36S	144E
Kerch': U.S.S.R.	**44**	45N	36E
Kerguelen: *is.* Southern O.	**49**	50S	70E
Kerkira: *i.*, Greece	**31**	40N	20E
Kermanshah: Iran	**46**	34N	47E
Kerme, Gulf of: Turkey	**31**	37N	28E
Kerulen: *r.*, Mong.	**50**	48N	112E
Kewanee: U.S.A.	**84**	41N	90W
Key West: U.S.A.	**83**	25N	82W
Khabarovsk: U.S.S.R.	**43**	48N	135E
Khairpur: W. Pak.	**48**	28N	69E
Khalkis: Greece	**31**	38N	24E
Khandwa: Ind.	**48**	22N	77E
Khania: Crete	**31**	36N	24E
Khanka, L.: U.S.S.R.	**43**	45N	133E
Khan Tengri: *mtn.*, China	**45**	42N	80E
Khanty-Mansiysk: U.S.S.R.	**45**	61N	69E
Kharagpur: India	**48**	22N	87E
Khar'kov: U.S.S.R.	**44**	50N	36E
Khartoum: Sudan	**67**	16N	33E
Khasi Hills: India	**49**	25N	92E
Khaskovo: Bulgaria	**31**	42N	26E
Khatanga: U.S.S.R.	**43**	72N	102E
Kherson: U.S.S.R.	**44**	47N	33E
Khiuma: *i.*, U.S.S.R.	**35**	59N	23E
Khiva: U.S.S.R.	**45**	41N	60E
Khobso Gol: *l.* Mong.	**50**	51N	100E
Khodzheyli: U.S.S.R.	**45**	42N	60E
Kholmsk: U.S.S.R.	**43**	47N	142E
Khorog: U.S.S.R.	**45**	37N	72E
Khotan: China	**48**	37N	80E
Khrom-Tau: U.S.S.R.	**44**	50N	58E
Khust: U.S.S.R.	**31**	48N	23E
Khyber Pass: Afghan./Pak.	**48**	34N	71E
Kiamusze: China	**50**	47N	130E
Kicking Horse Pass: Can.	**80**	51N	116W
Kiel: *& bay*, Germany	**35**	54N	10E
Kiel Canal: Germany	**32**	54N	10E
Kielce: Poland	**35**	51N	21E
Kiev: U.S.S.R.	**44**	51N	30E
Kigoma: Tanganyika	**68**	5S	30E
Kii: *mtns. & str.*, Japan	**52**	34N	136E
Kilaya: U.S.S.R.	**31**	46N	29E
Kilimanjaro: Tangan.	**68**	3S	37E
Kilmore: Austl.	**61**	37S	145E
Kimberley: S. Afr.	**69**	29S	25E
Kindu: Belg. Congo	**71**	3S	26E
Kingaroy: Austl.	**60**	27S	152E
King I.: Austl.	**58**	40S	143E
Kingsport: U.S.A.	**84**	37N	83W
Kingston: Austl.	**61**	37S	140E
Kingston: Canada	**85**	44N	76W
Kingston: Jamaica	**83**	18N	77W
Kingston N.Z.	**53**	45S	169E
Kingston: U.S.A.	**85**	42N	74W
King William I.: Canada	**79**	69N	96W
King William's Town: S. Afr.	**69**	33S	27E
Kinsha: *r.*, China	**50**	31N	99E
Kinyargiri: Tangan.	**68**	5S	35E
Kiølen Mts.: Norway	**34**	66N	14E
Kipawa, Lake: Canada	**85**	47N	79W
Kipushi: Belg. Congo	**69**	12S	27E
Kirchheim: Germany	**33**	49N	9E
Kirgiz Nor: *l.*, Mongolia	**50**	49N	94E
Kirgiz S.S.R.: U.S.S.R.	**42**	42N	75E
Kirin: China	**51**	44N	126E
Kirkenes: Norway	**34**	70N	30E
Kirkland Lake: *town*, Can.	**84**	48N	80W
Kırklareli: Turkey	**31**	42N	27E
Kirksville: U.S.A.	**84**	40N	93W
Kirkuk: 'Iraq	**46**	35N	44E
Kirov: U.S.S.R.	**44**	59N	50E
Kirovabad: U.S.S.R.	**44**	41N	46E
Kirovograd: U.S.S.R.	**44**	49N	32E
Kirovsk: U.S.S.R.	**45**	38N	60E
Kiruna: Sweden	**34**	68N	20E
Kiryu: Japan	**52**	36N	139E
Kishinev: U.S.S.R.	**31**	47N	29E
Kishm: Afghan.	**45**	37N	70E
Kiskunfélegyháza: Hungary	**27**	47N	20E
Kismayu: Somalia	**70**	0	42E
Kisújszállás: Hungary	**31**	47N	21E
Kisumu: Kenya	**68**	0	35E
Kitaka Mts.: Japan	**52**	39N	142E
Kitchener: Canada	**84**	43N	80W
Kithira: *i.*, Greece	**31**	36N	23E
Kithirai Strait: Crete	**31**	36N	24E
Kithnos: *i.*, Greece	**31**	37N	24E
Kitimat: Canada	**78**	54N	128W
Kitzbühel Alps: Austria	**33**	47N	12E
Kiuchüan: China	**50**	40N	99E
Kivak: U.S.S.R.	**43**	65N	174W
Kivu, L.: Belgian Congo	**68**	2S	29E
Klagenfurt: Austria	**33**	47N	14E
Klamath Falls: U.S.A.	**80**	42N	122W
Klatovy: Czech.	**33**	49N	13E
Klaypeda: U.S.S.R.	**35**	56N	21E
Klepp: Norway	**35**	59N	6E
Klipplaat: S. Afr.	**69**	33S	24E
Kłodzko: Poland	**27**	50N	17E
Knob Lake: Can.	**79**	55N	67W
Knokke: Belgium	**28**	51N	3E
Knoxville: U.S.A.	**84**	36N	84W
Kobe: Japan	**52**	35N	135E
København: Denmark	**35**	56N	13E
Koblenz: Germany	**32**	50N	8E
Kobrin: U.S.S.R.	**35**	52N	24E
Kochel: Germany	**33**	48N	11E
Kochi: Japan	**52**	34N	134E
Kodiak I.: Alaska	**78**	57N	153W
Kofu: Japan	**52**	36N	138E
Kohat: W. Pak.	**48**	34N	71E
Kohima: India	**49**	26N	94E
Kokand: U.S.S.R.	**45**	40N	71E
Kokkola: Finland	**34**	64N	23E
Kokomo: U.S.A.	**84**	41N	86W
Koko Nor: *l.*, China	**50**	37N	100E
Kokura: Japan	**52**	34N	131E
Kola Peninsula: U.S.S.R.	**42**	67N	38E
Kolarovgrad: Bulgaria	**31**	43N	27E
Kolhapur: India	**48**	17N	74E
Köln: Germany	**32**	51N	7E
Kolomna: U.S.S.R.	**44**	55N	39E
Kolomyya: U.S.S.R.	**27**	48N	25E
Kolyma Plain: U.S.S.R.	**43**	68N	155E
Kolyma Range: U.S.S.R.	**43**	63N	160E
Kolyuchin, G. of: U.S.S.R.	**43**	67N	175W
Kolyvan': U.S.S.R.	**45**	51N	83E
Kolyvan': U.S.S.R.	**45**	55N	83E
Komandor Is.: U.S.S.R.	**43**	55N	166E
Komárno: Czech.	**31**	48N	18E
Komatipoort: S. Afr.	**69**	25S	32E
Komsomol'sk: U.S.S.R.	**43**	51N	137E
Kongola: Belg. Congo	**70**	5S	27E
Kongsvinger: Norway	**35**	60N	12E
Königsberg: U.S.S.R.	**27**	55N	20E
Konosha: U.S.S.R.	**44**	61N	40E
Konotop: U.S.S.R.	**44**	51N	33E
Konstanz: Switz.	**33**	48N	9E
Konya: Turkey	**5**	38N	32E
Kootenay, Lake: Canada	**80**	50N	116W
Kopaonik Mts.: Yugo.	**31**	43N	21E
Kopar: Yugoslavia	**33**	46N	14E
Kopet Dagh: *range*, Iran U.S.S.R.	**46**	38N	57E
Korcë: Albania	**31**	41N	21E
Kordofan: *Prov.*, Sudan	**67**	13N	30E
KOREA, N. & S.	**50**	38N	128E
Koritsa: Albania	**31**	41N	21E
Koriyama: Japan	**52**	37N	140E
Korsakov: U.S.S.R.	**43**	47N	143E
Kortrijk: Belgium	**28**	51N	3E
Korumburra: Austl.	**61**	38S	146E
Kos: *i.*, Greece	**31**	37N	27E
Kosaka: Japan	**52**	40S	140E
Kosciusko: Mt.: Austl.	**61**	36N	148E
Kosh-Agach: U.S.S.R.	**45**	50N	89E
Kosi: *r.*, Nepal/India	**48**	26N	87E
Košice: Czech.	**27**	49N	21E
Kosovska Mitrovica: Yugo.	**21**	43N	21E
Kostamo: Finland	**34**	67N	27E
Kostroma: U.S.S.R.	**44**	57N	41E
Kostrzyn Odrzanski: Poland	**32**	53N	15E
Koszalin: Poland	**42**	56N	4W
Kota Bharu: Malaya	**51**	6N	102E
Kotah: India	**48**	25N	76E
Köhen: Germany	**32**	52N	12E
Kotka: Finland	**35**	60N	27E
Kotlas: U.S.S.R.	**44**	61N	47E
Kotor: Yugoslavia	**30**	42N	19E
Kotri: W. Pak.	**48**	25N	68E
Kounradskiy: U.S.S.R.	**45**	47N	75E
Kovel': U.S.S.R.	**27**	51N	25E
Kovrov: U.S.S.R.	**44**	56N	41E
Kozani: Greece	**31**	40N	22E
Kozhikode: India	**48**	11N	76E
Kra, Isthmus of: Thailand	**51**	10N	99E
Kragujevac: Yugo.	**31**	44N	21E
Krakatau: *volc.*, Indon.	**51**	6S	105E
Kraków: Poland	**27**	50N	20E
Kraljevo: Yugo.	**31**	44N	21E
Kramfors: Sweden	**34**	63N	18E
Krasnodar: U.S.S.R.	**44**	45N	39E
Krasnovodsk: U.S.S.R.	**44**	40N	53E
Krasnoyarsk: U.S.S.R.	**45**	56N	93E
Krasnyy Kut: U.S.S.R.	**44**	51N	47E
Krasnyy Luch: U.S.S.R.	**44**	48N	38E
Kratié: Cambodia	**51**	13N	106E
Krefeld: Germany	**32**	51N	6E
Kremenchug: U.S.S.R.	**44**	49N	33E
Kremenets: U.S.S.R.	**27**	50N	26E
Krishna: *r.*, India	**48**	16N	78E
Krishnagar: India	**48**	23N	88E
Kristiansand: Norway	**35**	58N	8E
Kristianstad: Sweden	**35**	56N	14E
Kristiansund: Norway	**34**	63N	8E
Kristinehamn: Sweden	**35**	59N	14E
Krivoy Rog: U.S.S.R.	**44**	48N	33E
Krk: Yugo.	**30**	45N	15E
Kronotsky Bay: U.S.S.R.	**43**	54N	162E
Kronshtadt: U.S.S.R.	**35**	60N	30E
Krotoszyn: Poland	**27**	52N	18E
Kruševac: Yugo.	**31**	44N	21E
Kuala Lumpur: Malaya	**51**	3N	102E
Kuantan: Malaya	**51**	4N	103E
Kuching: Sarawak	**51**	2N	110E
Kufra Oases: Libya	**63**	25N	22E
Kufstein: Austria	**33**	48N	12E
Kukës: Albania	**31**	42N	20E
Kükong: China	**50**	25N	113E
Kulmbach: Germany	**32**	50N	11E
Kulunda Steppe: U.S.S.R.	**45**	53N	77E
Kulundinskoye, L.: U.S.S.R.	**42**	53N	80E
Kumamoto: Japan	**52**	33N	31E
Kumasi: Gold Coast	**68**	7N	12W
Kunene: *r.*, Ang./S.W. Afr.	**69**	17S	13E
Kunlun Mts.: China	**47**	35N	80E
Kunming: China	**50**	25N	103E
Kuopio: Finland	**34**	63N	28E
Kupang: Indonesia	**51**	10S	124E
Kurashiki: Japan	**52**	35N	134E
Kurdistan	**46**	37N	44E
Kure: Japan	**52**	34N	133E
Kurgan: U.S.S.R.	**45**	55N	65E
Kuria Muria Is.: Arab. Sea	**49**	18N	56E
Kuril Is.: U.S.S.R.	**43**	45N	150E
Kurnool: India	**48**	16N	78E
Kursk: U.S.S.R.	**44**	52N	36E
Kurume: Japan	**52**	33N	130E
Kushiro: Japan	**52**	43N	144E
Kushka: U.S.S.R.	**45**	35N	62E
Küstrin: Poland	**32**	53N	15E
Kütahya: Turkey	**31**	39N	30E
Kutaisi: U.S.S.R.	**44**	42N	42E
Kut al Amara: 'Iraq	**46**	32N	47E
Kutaradja: Sumatra	**47**	5N	95E
Kutch, G. of: India	**48**	23N	69E
Kutno: Poland	**27**	52N	19E
Kuusjärvi: Finland	**34**	63N	29E
KUWAIT: *& town*	**46**	29N	48E
Kuybyshev: U.S.S.R.	**45**	55N	78E
Kuybyshev: U.S.S.R.	**44**	53N	50E
Kuznetsk *see* Stalinsk			
Kweichu: China	**50**	26N	107E
Kweilin: China	**50**	25N	110E
Kweisui: China	**50**	41N	112E
Kweiyang: China	**50**	26N	107E
Kyoga Point: Japan	**52**	36N	135E
Kyongju: S. Korea	**52**	36N	129E
Kyongsong: S. Korea	**50**	38N	127E
Kyoto: Japan	**52**	35N	136E
Kyushu: *i.*, Japan	**52**	33N	131E
Kyzyl: U.S.S.R.	**43**	52N	95E
Kyzyl-Kum: *desert*, U.S.S.R.	**45**	43N	64E
La Albuera: Spain	**25**	39N	7W
La Bastide: France	**29**	45N	1W
La Baule: France	**28**	47N	2E
Labrador: Canada	**79**	55N	60W
Labuan: Br. Borneo	**51**	5N	115E
La Cabrière: *mtns.*, France	**29**	44N	6E
Lacapelle-Marival: France	**29**	45N	2E
Lacaune, Mts. de: France	**29**	44N	3E
Laccadive: *is. & sea*, India	**49**	12N	73E
La Chârtre: France	**29**	47N	2E
La Chaux: France	**29**	46N	6E
La Chaux-de-Fonds: Switz.	**33**	47N	7E
Lachlan: *r.*, Austl.	**61**	33S	148E
La Ciotat: France	**29**	43N	6E
Lackawanna: U.S.A.	**85**	43N	79W
La Coruña: Spain	**25**	43N	8W
Lacq: France	**29**	43N	1W
La Crosse: U.S.A.	**84**	44N	91W
Ladakh Range: Kashmir	**48**	34N	77E
Ladismith: S. Afr.	**69**	34S	21E
Ladoga, Lake: U.S.S.R.	**44**	61N	31E
Lady Elliot I.: Austl.	**60**	24S	153E
Ladysmith: S. Afr.	**69**	28S	30E
Ladysmith: U.S.A.	**84**	45N	91W
Lae: N.E. New Guin.	**59**	7S	147E
Lafayette: U.S.A.	**84**	41N	86W
La Flèche: France	**28**	48N	0
Laghouat: Algeria	**62**	34N	3E
Lagos: Nigeria	**68**	6N	3E
Lagos: Portugal	**25**	37N	9W
La Gouette: Tunisia	**30**	37N	10E
La Grande: U.S.A.	**80**	45N	118W
La Guaira: Venez.	**86**	10N	67W
Lahn: *r.*, Germany	**32**	50N	8E

WORLD

LAHORE — MANAAR

	Page	Lat.	Long.
Lahore: W. Pak.	48	32N	75E
Lahr: Germany	33	48N	8E
Lahti: Finland	34	61N	26E
La Junta: U.S.A.	80	38N	104W
Lake Charles: *city*, U.S.A.	81	30N	93W
Lakhimpur: India	48	28N	81E
La Linea: Spain	25	36N	5W
La Louvière: Belgium	28	50N	4E
Lamballe: France	28	48N	3W
Lamia: Greece	31	39N	22E
La Montana: Peru	86	12S	72W
Lampedusa: *i.*, Italy	30	36N	13E
Lanak Pass: China/Kashmir	48	34N	80E
Lancaster: Ohio, U.S.A.	84	40N	83W
Lancaster: Pa., U.S.A.	85	40N	76W
Lancaster Sound: Canada	79	74N	85W
Lanchow: China	50	36N	104E
Lanciano: Italy	30	42N	14E
Landerneau: France	28	48N	4W
Landeshut: Poland	27	51N	16E
Landsberg: Poland	27	53N	15E
Lands End: England	26	50N	6W
Landshut: Germany	33	49N	12E
Langensalza: Germany	32	51N	11E
Langeoog: *i.*, Germany	32	54N	8E
Langon: France	29	45N	0
Langreo: Spain	25	43N	6W
Langres: France	28	48N	5E
Langres, Plateau de: Fr.	28	48N	5E
Languedoc: *Old Prov.*, Fr.	29	44N	4E
Lannion: France	28	49N	4W
Lans, Mts. de: France	29	45N	6E
Lansing: U.S.A.	84	43N	85W
Lanzarote: *i.*, Can. Is.	62	29N	13W
Laokay: Viet Minh	51	22N	104E
Laon: France	28	50N	4E
La Oroya: Peru	86	12S	76W
LAOS: Indo-China	51	18N	105E
Lapalisse: France	29	46N	4E
La Paz: Bolivia	86	17S	68E
Lapland: Scandinavia	34	68N	24E
La Plata: Argentina	88	35S	58W
Lappeenranta: Finland	34	61N	28E
Laptev Sea: U.S.S.R.	43	75N	125E
Laptev Str. U.S.S.R.	43	73N	142E
Larache: Morocco	25	35N	6W
Laramie: & *mtn.*, U.S.A.	80	41N	105W
Larche: France	29	44N	7E
Laredo: U.S.A.	80	27N	99W
La Rioja: Argentina	88	29S	67W
Larisa: Greece	31	40N	22E
La Rochelle: France	29	46N	1W
La Roche sur Yon: France	29	47N	1W
Larzac, Causse du: France	29	44N	3E
La Serena: Chile	88	30S	71W
La Seyne-sur-mer: France	29	43N	6E
Lashio: Burma	50	23N	98E
Las Marismas: *marsh*, Spain	25	37N	6W
Las Palmas: Canary Is.	62	28N	15W
La Spezia: Italy	33	44N	10E
Lassalle: France	29	44N	4E
Lassen Peak: U.S.A.	80	40N	122W
Lastoursville: Fr. Eq. Afr.	71	1S	13E
Lastovo: *i.*, Yugoslavia	30	43N	17E
Las Vegas: U.S.A.	80	36N	115W
Las Yungas: *mtns.*, Bol.	88	16S	66W
Latakia: Syria	46	35N	36E
Latium: Italy	30	42N	12E
La Tour-du-Pin: France	29	46N	5E
La Trappe: Canada	85	46N	74W
La Tuque: Canada	85	47N	73W
Latvian S.S.R.: U.S.S.R.	35	57N	25E
Lau Group: Fiji Is.	59	17S	181E
Launceston: Tasmania	59	41S	147E
Laurentide Park: Canada	85	48N	71W
Lausanne: Switz.	33	47N	7E
Laut: *i.*, Indonesia	51	4S	116E
Laval: France	28	48N	1W
La Vega: Dom. Repub.	83	19N	70W
Laverton: Austl.	60	29S	123E
Lawrence: U.S.A.	85	43N	71W
Leamington: Canada	84	42N	83W
LEBANON	46	33N	36E
Lebanon: U.S.A.	85	40N	76W
Le Blanc: France	29	47N	1E
Lebu: Chile	88	38S	74W
Le Cateau: France	28	50N	4E
Lecce: Italy	31	40N	18E
Lecco: Italy	33	46N	9E
Lech: *r.*, Ger./Austria	33	48N	11E
Le Chambon-Feugerolles: Fr.	29	45N	4E
Le Conquet: France	28	48N	5W
Le Creusot: France	29	47N	4E
Le Croisic: France	28	47N	2W
Lectoure: France	29	44N	1E
Leeds: England	26	54N	2W
Leer: Germany	32	53N	7E
Leeton: Austl.	61	35S	146E
Leeuwarden: Neth.	32	53N	6E
Leeuwin, Cape: Austl.	60	34S	115E
Leeward Is.: W. Indies.	83	17N	63W
Legaspi: Phil.	51	13N	124E
Leghorn: Italy	30	44N	10E
Legnano: Italy	33	46N	9E
Leh: Kashmir	48	34N	78E
Le Havre: France	28	50N	0
Lehrte: Germany	32	52N	10E
Leicester: England	26	53N	1W
Leichhardt Range: Austl.	60	21S	148E
Leiden: Neth.	32	52N	4E
Leikanger: Norway	34	61N	7E
Leipzig: Germany	32	51N	12E
Le Kef: Tunisia	30	36N	9E
Léman, L.: Switz./France	33	46N	7E
Le Mans: France	28	48N	0
Lemnos: *i.*, Greece	31	40N	25E
Le Monastier: France	29	45N	4E
Lena: *r.*, U.S.S.R.	43	64N	126E
Leninabad: U.S.S.R.	45	40N	70E
Leninakan: U.S.S.R.	44	41N	44E
Leningrad: U.S.S.R.	44	60N	30E
Leninogorsk: U.S.S.R.	45	50N	84E
Lenin Pk.: U.S.S.R.	45	39N	73E
Leninskiy: U.S.S.R.	43	58N	115E
Leninsk-Kuznetskiy: U.S.S.R.	45	55N	86E
Lens: France	28	50N	3E
Leoben: Austria	30	47N	15E
León: Mexico	82	21N	102W
León: & *Old Prov.*, Spain	25	43N	6W
Leonora: Austl.	60	29S	121E
Leopold II, Lake: Belg. Congo	71	2S	17E
Léopoldville: Belg. Congo	71	4S	15E
Lepini Mts.: Italy	30	42N	13E
Lepontine Alps: Switz./Italy	33	46N	8E
Le Puy: France	29	45N	4E
Lérida: Spain	25	42N	1E
Leros: *i.*, Greece	31	37N	27E
Les Bains du Mont Dore: Fr.	29	46N	3E
Les Baux: France	29	44N	5E
Lesbos: *i.*, Greece	31	39N	26E
Les Ecréhou: *is.*, Chan. Is.	28	49N	2W
Les Landes: France	29	44N	1W
Les Monts Faucilles: Fr.	28	48N	6E
Les Sables d'Olonne: Fr.	29	47N	2W
Les Saintes Maries: France	29	43N	4E
Les Sept Îles: France	28	49N	3W
Lesser Antilles: *arch.*, W. Ind.	83	15N	62W
Lethbridge: Canada	80	50N	113W
Leticia: Colombia	86	4S	70W
Le Touquet: France	28	51N	2E
Le Tréport: France	28	50N	1E
Leuven: Belgium	28	51N	5E
Levante, Riviera di: Italy	33	44N	9E
Leveque, C.: Austl.	58	17S	123E
Le Verdon: France	29	46N	1W
Leverkusen: Germany	32	51N	7E
Levice: Czech.	27	48N	18E
Le Vigan: France	29	44N	4E
Lévis: Canada	85	47N	71W
Lewiston: U.S.A.	85	44N	70W
Lewistown: U.S.A.	85	41N	78W
Lexington: Ky., U.S.A.	84	38N	84W
Lexington: Mass., U.S.A.	85	43N	71W
Lexington: N.C., U.S.A.	84	36N	80W
Leyburn: Austl.	60	28S	152E
Leydsdorp: S. Afr.	69	24S	31E
Leyre: *r.*, France	29	45N	1W
Leyte: *i.*, Philippines	51	11N	125E
Lhasa: China	49	30N	91E
L'Hospitalet: France	29	43N	2E
Liaotung Penin.: China	50	40N	123E
Liaoyang: China	50	42N	124E
Liberec: Czechoslovakia	27	51N	15E
LIBERIA	66	7N	10W
Libourne: France	29	45N	0
Libreville: Fr. Eq. Afr.	70	0	10E
LIBYA	66/7	—	—
Libyan Desert: Libya/Egypt	67	25N	25E
Licata: Sicily	30	37N	14E
Lichtenburg: S. Afr.	69	26S	26E
Lida: U.S.S.R.	27	54N	25E
Lidköping: Sweden	35	58N	13E
LIECHTENSTEIN	33	47N	10E
Liège: Belgium	28	51N	6E
Lieksa: Finland	34	63N	30E
Lienz: Austria	33	47N	13E
Liepaya: U.S.S.R.	35	57N	21E
Lier: Belgium	28	51N	5E
Liestal: Switz.	33	47N	8E
Liévin: France	28	50N	3E
Ligny: Belgium	28	50N	5E
Liguria: *Reg.*, Italy	33	45N	9E
Ligurian Alps: Italy	33	44N	8E
Ligurian Sea: Italy	30	43N	9E
Lille: France	28	51N	3E
Lillehammer: Norway	34	61N	11E
Lillooet: Canada	80	51N	122W
Lilongwe: Nyasaland	68	14S	34E
Lima: Peru	86	12S	77W
Lima: U.S.A.	84	41N	84W
Limagne: France	29	46N	3E
Limburg: Germany	32	50N	8E
Limburg: *Prov.*, Neth.	28	51N	6E
Limoges: France	29	46N	1E
Limousin: *Old Prov.*, Fr.	29	46N	1E
Limpopo: *r.*, Moz.	69	23S	33E
Linares: Spain	25	38N	4W
Linaro, C.: Italy	30	42N	12E
Lincoln: U.S.A.	80	41N	97W
Lindi: Tangan.	68	10S	40E
Lingen: Germany	32	53N	7E
Lingga: *i.*, Indonesia	51	0	105E
Linköping: Sweden	35	58N	16E
Linz: Austria	33	48N	14E
Lions, G. of: France	29	43N	4E
Lipari Is.: Italy	30	38N	15E
Lipetsk: U.S.S.R.	44	53N	40E
Lippstadt: Germany	32	52N	8E
Lisbon: Portugal	25	39N	9W
Lisburne, Cape: Alaska	78	69N	166W
Lisieux: France	28	49N	0
Lismore: Austl.	61	29S	153E
Lispeszentadorján: Hungary	31	47N	17E
Lithgow: Austl.	61	33S	150E
Lithuanian S.S.R.: U.S.S.R.	35	55N	24E
Little Belt: *str.*, Denmark	35	55N	10E
Little Current: Canada	84	46N	82W
Little Rock: U.S.A.	81	35N	93W
Liuchow: China	50	24N	109E
Liverpool: Austl.	61	34S	151E
Liverpool Plains: Austl.	61	31S	150E
Livingstone: N. Rhod.	69	18S	26E
Livingstone Falls: B. Congo	70	5S	14E
Livingstonia: Nyasa.	68	11S	34E
Livorno: Italy	30	44N	10E
Livradois, Massif du: *mtns.*, France	29	45N	3E
Lizard Point: England	26	50N	5W
Ljubljana: Yugoslavia	30	46N	14E
Ljunga: *r.*, Sweden	34	62N	17E
Llano Estacado: U.S.A.	80	34N	103W
Llanos de Guarayos: Bolivia	86	15S	63W
Llanos de Urgel: Spain	25	41N	0
Lobito: Angola	69	12S	14E
Locarno: Switz.	33	46N	9E
Lodi: Italy	33	45N	10E
Łódź: Poland	35	52N	19E
Lofoten Is.: Norway	34	68N	13E
Logan, Mt.: Canada	78	60N	140W
Logansport: U.S.A.	84	41N	86W
Logroño: Spain	25	42N	2W
Loir: *r.*, France	29	48N	0
Loire: *r.*, France	28	47N	1W
Lója: Ecuador	86	4S	79W
Lokchong: China	50	25N	113E
Lokoja: Nigeria	68	8N	7E
Lolland: *i.*, Denmark	35	55N	11E
Lombardy: Plain of: Italy	33	45N	9E
Lomblen: *i.*, Indonesia	51	8S	123E
Lombok: *i.*, Indonesia	51	8S	116E
Lomé: Fr. W. Afr.	68	6N	1E
Lommel: Belgium	28	51N	5E
Łomża: Poland	27	53N	22E
London: Canada	84	43N	81W
Long Beach: U.S.A.	80	34N	118W
Long I.: Austl.	60	22S	150E
Long I.: U.S.A.	85	41N	73W
Longreach: Austl.	59	23S	144E
Longs Peak: U.S.A.	80	40N	106W
Longuyon: France	28	49N	6E
Longwy: France	28	50N	6E
Lønsdal: Norway	34	67N	16E
Lons-le-Saunier: France	29	47N	6E
Lopei: China	50	48N	131E
Lopez, C.: Fr. Eq. Africa	71	1S	9E
Lop Nor: *l.*, China	46	40N	90E
Lorain: U.S.A.	84	42N	82W
Lorca: Spain	25	38N	2W
Lörrach: Germany	33	48N	8E
Lorraine: *Old Prov.*, Fr.	28	49N	6E
Los Alamos: U.S.A.	80	36N	106W
Los Andes: Chile	88	33S	71W
Los Angeles: U.S.A.	80	34N	118W
Lot: *r.*, France	29	44N	1E
Loue: *r.*, France	29	47N	6E
Louisburg: Canada	85	46N	60W
Louisiade Arch.: Coral Sea	59	12S	153E
Louisiana: *State*, U.S.A.	81	32N	92W
Louis Trichardt: S. Afr.	69	23S	30E
Louisville: U.S.A.	84	38N	86W
Loukhi: U.S.S.R.	34	66N	33E
Lourdes: France	29	43N	0
Lourenço Marques: Moz.	71	26S	33E
Louvain *see* Leuven			
Lowell: U.S.A.	85	42N	71W
Lower California: *Territ.*, Mexico	82	30N	115W
Lower Red Lake: U.S.A.	84	48N	94W
Lower Tunguska: *r.*, U.S.S.R.	43	64N	95E
Loyalty Is.: Pac. O.	59	20S	168E
Loyang: China	50	35N	112E
Lu: *r.*, China	50	30N	97E
Lualaba: *r.*, Belg. Congo	70	6S	26E
Luanda: Angola	71	9S	13E
Luangprabang: Laos	51	20N	102E
Luanshya: N. Rhod.	68	13S	28E
Lubbock: U.S.A.	80	34N	102W
Lübeck: & *bay*, Germany	32	54N	11E
Lubéron, Mont du: France	29	44N	5E
Lublin: Poland	27	51N	23E
Lucca: Italy	33	44N	11E
Lučenec: Czech.	27	48N	20E
Lucerne: & *lake.*, Switz.	33	47N	8E
Luckenwalde: Germany	32	52N	13E
Lucknow: India	48	27N	81E
Lüdenscheid: Germany	32	51N	8E
Lüderitz: S.W. Afr.	69	27S	15E
Ludhiana: India	48	31N	76E
Ludington, U.S.A.	84	44N	86W
Ludvika: Sweden	35	60N	15E
Ludwigsburg: Germany	33	49N	9E
Ludwigshafen: Germany	32	49N	8E
Ludwigslust: Germany	32	53N	11E
Luga: U.S.S.R.	35	59N	30E
Lugano: Switz.	33	46N	9E
Lugo: Spain	25	43N	8W
Lugoj: Romania	31	46N	22E
Luichow Peninsula: China	51	21N	110E
Lukuga: *r.*, Belg. Congo	68	6S	28E
Luleå: Sweden	34	66N	22E
Lüleburgaz: Turkey	31	41N	27E
Luluabourg: Belg. Congo	71	6S	22E
Lumsden: N.Z.	53	46S	168E
Lund: Sweden	35	56N	13E
Lüneburg: Germany	32	53N	10E
Lüneburg Heath: Germany	32	53N	10E
Lunéville: France	28	49N	6E
Lungkiang: China	50	47N	124E
Lure: France	28	48N	6E
Lusaka: N. Rhod.	68	15S	28E
Lusambo: Belg. Congo	71	5S	23E
Lussac-les-Châteaux: Fr.	29	46N	1E
Lutsk: U.S.S.R.	27	51N	25E
LUXEMBOURG: & *town*	32	50N	6E
Luxor: Egypt	63	26N	33E
Luzern: Switz.	33	47N	8E
Luzon: *i.*, Philippines	51	15N	121E
Luzy: France	29	47N	4E
L'vov: U.S.S.R.	27	50N	24E
Lyakhov Is.: U.S.S.R.	43	73N	142E
Lyallpur: W. Pak.	48	31N	73E
Lydenburg: S. Afr.	69	25S	30E
Lyell, Mt.: Tasmania	59	42S	145E
Lynchburg: U.S.A.	85	37N	79W
Lynn: U.S.A.	85	42N	71W
Lynn Lake: *settlement*, Can.	78	57N	101W
Lyonnais: *Old Prov.*, Fr.	29	46N	4E
Lyons (Lyon): France	29	46N	5E
Lys: *r.*, Belgium	28	51N	3E
Lys'va: U.S.S.R.	45	58N	58E
Lyttleton: N.Z.	53	44S	173E
Lytton: Canada	80	50N	121W
Ma'an: Jordan	46	30N	36E
Maarianhamina: Finland	35	60N	20E
Maas: *r.*, Neth.	32	52N	5E
Maastricht: Neth.	32	51N	6E
Macão: China	50	22N	114E
Macchu Picchu: Peru	86	13S	73W
Macdonnell Range: Austl.	59	24S	132E
Macedonia: *Old Prov.*, Yugo./Greece	31	41N	22E
Maceió: Brazil	87	10S	36W
Macequece: Mozambique	69	19S	33E
Macerata: Italy	30	43N	13E
Machichaco, C.: Spain	25	43N	3W
Mackay: Austl.	60	21S	149E
Mackenzie: Br. Gu.	87	6N	58W
Mackenzie: *r.*, Austl.	60	24S	150E
Mackenzie: *r.*, Canada	78	67N	131W
Mackenzie Bay: Canada	78	69N	137W
Mackenzie Mts.: Canada	78	63N	130W
Mackinac, Straits of: U.S.A.	84	46N	85W
Mackinaw City: U.S.A.	84	46N	85W
McKinley, Mt.: Alaska	78	63N	151W
Macksville: Austl.	61	31S	153E
McMurdo Sound: Antarctica	90	78S	168E
McNary Dam: U.S.A.	80	46N	119W
Mâcon: France	29	46N	5E
Macon: U.S.A.	81	33N	84W
Macquarie: *r.*, Austl.	61	32S	148E
Macquarie I.: Pac. O.	54	55S	159E
MADAGASCAR	71	—	—
Madame I.: Canada	85	46N	61W
Madaoua: Fr. W. Afr.	68	15N	6E
Maddalena Pass: Fr./Switz.	33	44N	7E
Madeira: *i.*, Atlantic Ocean	66	33N	17W
Madeira: *r.*, Brazil	86	5S	61W
Madeleine I.: U.S.A.	84	47N	91W
Madera: Mexico	80	29N	108W
Madison: U.S.A.	84	43N	89W
Madisonville: U.S.A.	84	37N	88W
Madiun: Java	51	8S	112E
Madras: India	48	13N	80E
Madrid: Spain	25	40N	4W
Madura: *i.*, Indonesia	51	7S	113E
Madurai: India	48	10N	78E
Maebashi: Japan	52	36N	139E
Mafeking: S.W. Afr.	69	26S	25E
Mafia: *i.*, Tangan.	68	8S	40E
Magadan: U.S.S.R.	43	60N	150E
Magadi: Kenya	68	2S	36E
Magallanes: Chile	89	53S	71W
Magdalena: *r.*, Colombia	86	7N	74W
Magdalen Is.: Canada	85	47N	62W
Magdeburg: Germany	32	52N	12E
Magellan, Str. of: Chile/Argentina	89	53S	71W
Magenta: Italy	33	45N	9E
Maggiore, Lake: It./Switz.	33	46N	9E
Magnetic I.: Austl.	60	19S	147E
Magnitogorsk: U.S.S.R.	44	53N	59E
Magude: Mozambique	69	25S	33E
Magwe: Burma	47	20N	95E
Mahanadi: *r.*, India	48	21N	85E
Mahón: Minorca	25	40N	4E
Maiduguri: Nigeria	68	12N	13E
Maimana: Afghan.	46	36N	65E
Main: *r.*, Germany	32	50N	9E
Main Barrier Range: Austl.	61	32S	141E
Maine: *Old Prov.*, France	28	48N	1W
Maine: *State*, U.S.A.	85	46N	69W
Maine, Gulf of: U.S.A.	85	43N	69W
Mainz: Germany	32	50N	8E
Maitland: Austl.	61	33S	152E
Majorca: *i.*, Balearic Is.	25	39N	3E
Majunga: Madag.	71	16S	46E
Makarikari Salt Pan: Bech.	69	21S	26E
Makassar: & *str.*, Indon.	51	5S	120E
Makeyevka: U.S.S.R.	44	48N	38E
Makhachkala: U.S.S.R.	44	43N	48E
Makran: Iran/W. Pak.	46	26N	62E
Makurdi: Nigeria	68	8N	8E
Makushino: U.S.S.R.	45	55N	67E
Malabar Coast: India	48	12N	75E
Malacca: & *str.*, Malaya	51	2N	102E
Maladetta Massif: Spain	29	43N	1E
Málaga: Spain	25	37N	4W
Malaita: *i.*, Solomon Is.	54	9S	161E
Malakal: Sudan	63	10N	32E
Malakand: India	48	35N	72E
Malange: Angola	71	9S	16E
Mälar, L.: Sweden	34	59N	17E
Malatya: Turkey	44	38N	38E
MALAYA	51	—	—
Malbork: Poland	27	54N	19E
MALDIVE IS.: Indian Ocean	47	7N	73E
Malekula: *i.*, New Hebrides	59	17S	167E
Malesherbes: France	28	48N	2E
Malindi: Kenya	68	3S	40E
Malines *see* Mechelen			
Malmberget: Sweden	34	67N	20E
Malmédy: Belg.	28	50N	6E
Malmesbury: S. Africa	69	33S	19E
Malmö: Sweden	35	56N	13E
Maloja Pass: Switz.	33	46N	10E
Malonga: Belg. Congo	68	10S	23E
Malpelo I.: Colombia	86	4N	82W
Malplaquet: France	28	50N	4E
Malta: *i.* & *chan.*, Medit. Sea	30	36N	14E
Malvan: India	48	16N	73E
Mammoth Cave Nat. Park.: U.S.A.	84	37N	86W
Manaar: & *gulf*, Ceylon	48	9N	80E

	Page	Lat.	Long.
Manado: Celebes	**51**	2N	125E
Managua: Nicaragua	**83**	12N	86W
Manama: Bahrain	**46**	26N	50E
Mana Pass: China	**48**	31N	80E
Manaus (Manáos): Brazil	**86**	3S	60W
Manchester: Iowa, U.S.A.	**84**	43N	91W
Manchester: N. H., U.S.A.	**85**	43N	71W
Manchuria: China	**50**	45N	125E
Mandalay: Burma	**47**	22N	96E
Mandasor: India	**48**	24N	75E
Mangalore: India	**48**	13N	75E
Mangyshlak Peninsula: U.S.S.R.	**42**	44N	51E
Manifold, Cape: Austl.	**60**	23S	151E
Manila: Phil.	**51**	15N	121E
Manitoba: *Prov.*, Canada	**78**	55N	95W
Manitoba, L.: Canada	**80**	51N	98W
Manitoulin I.: Canada	**84**	45N	82W
Manitowoc: U.S.A.	**84**	44N	88W
Manizales: Colombia	**86**	5N	76W
Manjra: *r.*, India	**48**	18N	76E
Mankato: U.S.A.	**84**	44N	94W
Mankoya: N. Rhod.	**68**	15S	25E
Mannheim: Germany	**32**	49N	8E
Manokwari: Neth. N. Guin.	**51**	1S	134E
Manresa: Spain	**25**	42N	2E
Mansfeld: Germany	**32**	52N	11E
Mansfield: Austl.	**61**	37S	146E
Mansfield: U.S.A.	**84**	41N	82W
Manta: Ecuador	**86**	1S	81W
Mantes-Gassicourt: France	**28**	49N	2E
Mantua (Mantova): Italy	**33**	45N	11E
Manus: *i.*, New Guinea	**59**	3S	147E
Manzanillo: Mexico	**82**	19N	104W
Maracaibo: & *lake*, Venez.	**86**	11N	72W
Maracay: Venezuela	**83**	10N	68W
Marajó, I. of: Brazil	**87**	1S	50W
Marampa: Sierra Leone	**62**	8N	12W
Maranhão: Brazil	**87**	3S	44W
Marañón: *r.*, Peru	**86**	5S	77W
Maraş: Turkey	**44**	38N	37E
Marathon: Greece	**31**	38N	24E
Marble Bar: Austl.	**58**	21S	120E
Marburg: Germany	**32**	51N	9E
Marche: *Old Prov.*, France	**29**	46N	2E
Marches, The: *Reg.*, Italy	**30**	43N	13E
Marchienne: Belgium	**28**	50N	4E
Mar del Plata: Arg.	**88**	38S	58W
Mardin: Turkey	**44**	37N	41E
Margarita: *i.*, Venez.	**86**	11N	64W
Margeride, Monts de la: Fr.	**29**	44N	4E
Marianas Is.: Pacific O.	**54**	18N	145E
Mariánské Lázně: Czech.	**32**	50N	13E
Maribor: Yugoslavia	**30**	47N	16E
Marie Byrd Land: Antarctica	**90**	80S	130W
Marienbad: Czech.	**32**	50N	13E
Mariental: S.W. Afr.	**69**	25S	18E
Mariinsk: U.S.S.R.	**45**	56N	88E
Marinette: U.S.A.	**84**	45N	88W
Marion: Ind., U.S.A.	**84**	41N	86W
Marion: Ohio, U.S.A.	**84**	41N	83W
Maritime Alps: France	**29**	44N	7E
Maritimes, The: U.S.A.	**81**	42N	65W
Maritsa: *r.*, Bulgaria	**31**	42N	26E
Markovo: U.S.S.R.	**43**	65N	170E
Marlborough: Austl.	**60**	23S	150E
Marles: France	**28**	51N	2E
Marmande: France	**29**	44N	0
Marmara, Sea of: Turkey	**31**	41N	28E
Marne: *r.*, France	**28**	49N	4E
Marquesas Is.: Pac. O.	**55**	10S	140W
Marquette: U.S.A.	**84**	47N	87W
Marrakesh: Morocco	**62**	32N	8W
Marra Mts.: Sudan	**63**	13N	24E
Marree: Austl.	**61**	30S	138E
Marsala: Sicily	**30**	38N	12E
Marseilles (Marseille): Fr.	**29**	43N	5E
Marshall Is.: Pac. O.	**54**	10N	166E
Marshalltown: U.S.A.	**84**	42N	93W
Martaban, G. of: Burma	**47**	16N	97E
Martha's Vineyard: *i.*, U.S.A.	**85**	41N	71W
Martigny: Switzerland	**33**	46N	7E
Martigues: France	**29**	43N	5E
Martinique: *i.*, W. Indies	**83**	15N	61W
Martinsburg: U.S.A.	**85**	39N	78W
Marton: N.Z.	**53**	40S	175E
Martos: Spain	**25**	38N	4W
Mary: U.S.S.R.	**45**	38N	62E
Maryborough: Queens., Austl.	**60**	25S	153E
Maryborough: Vict., Austl.	**61**	37S	144E
Maryland: *State*, U.S.A.	**81**	39N	76W
Mascara: Algeria	**25**	35N	0
Maseru: Basutoland	**69**	29S	28E
Masira: *i.*, Muscat & 'Oman	**46**	20N	59E
Mason City: U.S.A.	**84**	43N	93W
Massachusetts: *State*, U.S.A.	**85**	42N	72W
Massachusetts Bay: U.S.A.	**85**	42N	70W
Massawa: Ethiopia	**63**	16N	39E
Massif Central: France	**29**	46N	3E
Masterton: N.Z.	**53**	41S	176E
Mastung: W. Pak.	**48**	30N	67E
Masulipatam: India	**48**	16N	81E
Matadi: Belg. Congo	**71**	6S	14E
Matakana I.: N.Z.	**53**	38S	176E
Matapan, C.: Greece	**31**	36N	22E
Mataura: *r.*, N.Z.	**53**	46S	169E
Matera: Italy	**30**	41N	17E
Mateur: Tunisia	**30**	37N	9E
Mathura: India	**48**	27N	78E
Mato Grosso, Plat. of: Braz.	**88**	15S	49W
Matopo Hills. S. Rhod.	**69**	21S	30E
Matsang: *r.*, China	**47**	29N	86E
Matsue: Japan	**52**	35N	133E
Matsumoto: Japan	**52**	36N	138E
Matsuyama: Japan	**52**	34N	133E
Matterhorn: *mtn.*, Switz.	**33**	46N	8E
Mattoon: U.S.A.	**84**	40N	88W
Maturín: Venez.	**86**	10N	63W
Matzen: Austria	**30**	48N	17E
Maubeuge: France	**28**	50N	4E
Maumere: Indon.	**51**	8S	122E
Maun: Bech.	**69**	20S	23E
Mauritania: *Col.*, Fr. W. Afr.	**66**	20N	10W
Mauritius: *i.*, Ind. O.	**49**	20S	58E
Mawlaik: Burma	**47**	24N	94E
Mayenne: & *r.*, France	**28**	48N	1W
Maykop: U.S.S.R.	**44**	45N	40E
Mayoumba: Fr. Eq. Afr.	**71**	4S	11E
Maywood: U.S.A.	**84**	42N	88W
Mazamet: France	**29**	43N	2E
Mazar-i-Sharif: Afghan.	**45**	37N	67E
Mazarrón: Spain	**25**	38N	2W
Mazatlán: Mexico	**82**	23N	106W
Mazoe: S. Rhodesia	**69**	17S	31E
Mbeya: Tangan.	**68**	9S	33E
M'Clintock Channel: Can.	**78**	72N	102W
Mead, Lake: U.S.A.	**80**	36N	114W
Meaux: France	**28**	49N	3E
Mecca: Sa'udi Arabia	**46**	21N	40E
Mechelen: Belgium	**28**	51N	4E
Mecklenburg: *Old Prov.*, Ger.	**32**	54N	12E
Medan: Sumatra	**51**	4N	99E
Medéa: Algeria	**25**	36N	3E
Medellín: Colombia	**86**	6N	76W
Mediaş: Romania	**31**	46N	25E
Medicine Hat: Canada	**80**	50N	110W
Medina: Sa'udi Arabia	**46**	25N	40E
Mediterranean Sea	**30/31**	—	—
Medjerda: *r.*, Tunisia	**30**	37N	9E
Medjez-el-Bab: Tunisia	**30**	37N	10E
Mednogorsk: U.S.S.R.	**44**	51N	58E
Médoc: France	**29**	45N	1W
Meerut: India	**48**	29N	78E
Mega: Ethiopia	**68**	4N	38E
Megara: Greece	**31**	38N	23E
Meiningen: Germany	**32**	51N	10E
Meissen: Germany	**32**	51N	14E
Mekong (Dza): *r.*, China/Indo-China	**47**	33N	96E
Melanesia: Pacific Ocean	**54**	—	—
Melbourne: Austl.	**61**	38S	145E
Melbourne: U.S.A.	**81**	28N	80W
Melilla: Morocco	**25**	35N	3W
Melun: France	**28**	49N	3E
Melville Bay: Greenland	**79**	76N	62W
Melville I.: Austl.	**58**	12S	131E
Melville I.: Canada	**78**	76N	110W
Memel: U.S.S.R.	**35**	56N	21E
Memmingen: Germany	**33**	48N	10E
Memphis: Egypt	**63**	30N	31E
Memphis: U.S.A.	**81**	35N	90W
Menderes: *r.*, Turkey	**31**	38N	29E
Mendocino, Cape: U.S.A.	**78**	40N	125W
Mendoza: Arg.	**88**	33S	69W
Mène: Fr. Eq. Afr.	**70**	2N	16E
Menemen: Turkey	**31**	39N	27E
Mengtsz: China	**50**	23N	103E
Menindee: & *lake*, Austl.	**61**	32S	142E
Mentawai Is.: Indonesia	**51**	3S	100E
Menton: France	**29**	44N	7E
Menzies: Austl.	**60**	30S	121E
Meppel: Neth.	**32**	53N	6E
Merano: Italy	**33**	47N	11E
Merauke: Neth. N. Guin.	**58**	9S	140E
Mercara: India	**48**	12N	76E
Mergui: Burma	**47**	12N	99E
Mergui Arch.: Burma	**51**	12N	98E
Meribah: Austl.	**61**	35S	141E
Mérida: Mexico	**82**	21N	90W
Mérida: Spain	**25**	39N	6W
Meridian: U.S.A.	**81**	32N	89W
Merinda: Austl.	**60**	20S	148E
Merredin: Austl.	**60**	31S	118E
Merrimack: *r.*, U.S.A.	**85**	43N	71W
Merseburg: Germany	**32**	51N	12E
Mersin: Turkey	**46**	37N	35E
Meru: Kenya	**68**	0	38E
Merv: U.S.S.R.	**45**	38N	62E
Mesabi Range: U.S.A.	**84**	48N	93W
Meshed: Iran	**46**	36N	60E
Mesolongion: Greece	**31**	38N	21E
Mesopotamia: 'Iraq	**46**	32N	45E
Messina: & *str.*, Sicily	**30**	38N	16E
Messina: S. Africa	**69**	23S	30E
Mesta: *r.*, Bulgaria	**31**	41N	24E
Mestre: Italy	**33**	45N	12E
Mettur: India	**48**	12N	78E
Metz: France	**28**	49N	6E
Meuse: *r.*, France/Belg.	**28**	50N	5E
Mexicali: Mexico	**80**	33N	115W
Mexican Plateau: Mexico	**82**	23N	103W
MEXICO	**82**	—	—
Mexico: U.S.A.	**84**	39N	92W
Mexico, Gulf of: Mexico	**82**	25N	90W
Mexico City: Mexico	**82**	19N	99W
Mézières: France	**28**	50N	5E
Miami: Ariz., U.S.A.	**80**	34N	111W
Miami: Fla., U.S.A.	**81**	26N	80W
Mianeh: Iran	**46**	37N	47E
Michaud Point: Canada	**85**	46N	61W
Michigan: *State*, U.S.A.	**81**	45N	85W
Michigan, Lake: U.S.A./Can.	**84**	44N	87W
Michigan City: U.S.A.	**84**	42N	87W
Michipicoten Harbour: Can.	**84**	48N	85W
Micronesia: Pacific Ocean	**54**	—	—
Middelburg: Neth.	**32**	51N	4E
Middelburg: S. Africa	**69**	26S	30E
Middlesboro: U.S.A.	**84**	36N	84W
Middletown: N.Y., U.S.A.	**85**	41N	74W
Middletown: Ohio, U.S.A.	**84**	40N	84W
Midland: Austl.	**60**	32S	116E
Midland: Canada	**84**	45N	80W
Midnapore: India	**48**	22N	87E
Midway I.: Pacific Ocean	**54**	29N	179W
Mijares: *r.*, Spain	**25**	40N	0
Mikkeli: Finland	**34**	62N	27E
Mikuni Mts.: Japan	**52**	37N	139E
Milan (Milano): Italy	**33**	44N	9E
Mildura: Austl.	**61**	34S	142E
Milford Sound: N.Z.	**53**	44S	168E
Milk. *r.*, U.S.A.	**80**	48N	109W
Millau: France	**29**	44N	3E
Mille Lacs Lake: U.S.A.	**84**	46N	93W
Millicent: Austl.	**61**	38S	141E
Milos: *i.*, Greece	**31**	37N	24E
Milparinka: Austl.	**61**	30S	142E
Milwaukee: U.S.A.	**84**	43N	88W
Minamata: Japan	**52**	32N	130E
Minaragra: Peru	**86**	11S	77W
Minas Basin: Canada	**85**	45N	64W
Minas de Riotinto: Spain	**25**	38N	7W
Minas Gerais: *State*, Brazil	**88**	18S	45W
Mindanao: *i.*, Philippines	**51**	8N	125E
Minden: Germany	**32**	52N	9E
Mindoro: *i.*, Philippines	**51**	13N	121E
Minho: *r.*, Spain	**25**	42N	8W
Minna: Nigeria	**68**	10N	7E
Minneapolis: U.S.A.	**84**	45N	93W
Minnesota: *State*, U.S.A.	**81**	47N	95W
Minorca: *i.*, Balearic Is.	**25**	40N	4E
Minot: U.S.A.	**80**	48N	101W
Minquiers, Plateau de: *is.*, Fr.	**28**	49N	2W
Minsk: U.S.S.R.	**44**	54N	28E
Minusinsk: U.S.S.R.	**45**	54N	92E
Miquelon: *i.*, N. America	**79**	47N	57W
Miraflores Lock: Panama	**83**	*Inset*	
Miram Shah: W. Pak.	**48**	33N	70E
Mirande: France	**29**	44N	0
Mirecourt: France	**28**	48N	6E
Mirtoon Sea	**31**	37N	24E
Mirzapur: India	**48**	25N	82E
Misawa: Japan	**52**	41N	141E
Miskolc: Hungary	**27**	48N	21E
Misoöl: *i.*, Neth. New Guin.	**51**	2S	130E
Missinaibi Lake: Canada	**84**	48N	83W
Mississippi: *r.*, U.S.A.	**81**	35N	91W
Mississippi: *State*, U.S.A.	**81**	33N	90W
Missoula: U.S.A.	**80**	47N	114W
Missouri: *r.*, U.S.A.	**80**	47N	111W
Missouri: *State*, U.S.A.	**81**	38N	93W
Mistassini, Lake: Canada	**81**	51N	74W
Misurata: Libya	**62**	32N	15E
Mitchell: *r.*, Queens., Austl.	**59**	16S	142E
Mitchell: *r.*, Vict., Austl.	**61**	38S	147E
Mitilini: Lesbos	**31**	39N	27E
Mito: Japan	**52**	36N	140E
Mitre I.: Pac. O.	**59**	12S	170E
Mitú: Colombia	**86**	1N	70W
Mitumba Mts.: Belg. Congo	**68**	8S	27E
Miyazaki: Japan	**52**	32N	131E
Mizque: Bolivia	**86**	18S	65W
Mjøsa Lake: Norway	**35**	61N	11E
Mława: Poland	**27**	53N	20E
Mobaye: Fr. Eq. Afr.	**70**	4N	22E
Moberly: U.S.A.	**84**	39N	92W
Mobile: U.S.A.	**81**	31N	88W
Mocimboa: Mozambique	**68**	11S	40E
Moctezuma: Mexico	**80**	30N	110W
Modane: France	**29**	45N	7E
Modder River: S. Afr.	**69**	29S	25E
Modena: Italy	**33**	45N	11E
Mogadiscio: Somalia	**63**	2N	45E
Mogador: Morocco	**62**	31N	10W
Mogilev Podol'skiy: U.S.S.R.	**31**	48N	28E
Mogocha: U.S.S.R.	**43**	53N	120E
Mohács: Hungary	**27**	46N	19E
Mohawk: *r.*, U.S.A.	**85**	43N	75W
Mointy: U.S.S.R.	**45**	47N	74E
Moji: Japan	**52**	34N	131E
Mokambo: Belg. Congo	**69**	12S	29E
Moldau: *r.*, Europe	**32**	50N	14E
Moldavian S.S.R.: U.S.S.R.	**31**	47N	28E
Molfetta: Italy	**30**	41N	17E
Molières: France	**29**	44N	1E
Molde: Norway	**34**	63N	7E
Mollendo: Peru	**88**	17S	72W
Mölndal: Sweden	**35**	58N	12E
Molodechno: U.S.S.R.	**35**	54N	27E
Molopo: *r.*, S. Africa	**69**	26S	23E
Molotov: U.S.S.R.	**44**	57N	55E
Moluccas: *is.*, Indon.	**51**	0	127E
Molucca Sea	**51**	0	125E
Mombasa: Kenya	**68**	4S	40E
Mombetsu: Japan	**53**	44N	143E
MONACO	**33**	44N	7E
Mona Passage: W. Indies	**83**	18N	67W
Monastir: Yugoslavia	**31**	41N	21E
Monchegorsk: U.S.S.R.	**34**	68N	33E
Mönchen-Gladbach: Ger.	**32**	51N	6E
Moncton: Canada	**85**	46N	65W
Mondego, C.: Portugal	**25**	40N	9W
Mondovi: Italy	**33**	44N	8E
Monessen: U.S.A.	**85**	40N	80W
Monfalcone: Italy	**33**	46N	14E
MONGOLIA	**43**	—	—
Mongu: N. Rhodesia	**69**	15S	23E
Monroe: U.S.A.	**81**	33N	92W
Monrovia: Liberia	**62**	6N	11W
Mons: Belgium	**28**	50N	4E
Montague I.: Alaska	**78**	60N	147W
Montana: *State*, U.S.A.	**80**	47N	110W
Montargis: France	**28**	48N	3E
Montauban: France	**29**	44N	1E
Montbéliard: France	**29**	47N	7E
Montceau-les-Mines: Fr.	**29**	47N	4E
Mont Cenis Pass: Fr./Italy	**33**	45N	7E
Mont de Marsan: France	**29**	44N	1W
Montdidier: France	**28**	50N	3E
Monte Bello Is.: Austl.	**58**	20S	115E
Monte Carlo: Monaco	**29**	44N	7E
Monte Cristo: *i.*, Italy	**30**	42N	10E
Montego Bay: *town.*, Jamaica	**83**	18N	78W
Montélimar: France	**29**	45N	5E
Montenegro: Yugo.	**31**	43N	19E
Monterey: U.S.A.	**80**	37N	122W
Monterrey: Mexico	**82**	26N	100W
Montes Claros: Brazil	**88**	17S	44W
Montevideo: Uruguay	**88**	35S	56W
Montgomery: U.S.A.	**81**	32N	86W
Mont Joli: Canada	**85**	49N	68W
Montluçon: France	**29**	46N	3E
Montmédy: France	**28**	50N	5E
Montmirail: France	**28**	49N	4E
Montpelier: U.S.A.	**85**	44N	72W
Montpellier: France	**29**	44N	4E
Montreal: Canada	**85**	45N	74W
Montreuil: France	**28**	50N	2E
Montreuil Bellay: France	**29**	47N	0
Montreux: Switzerland	**33**	46N	7E
Mont St. Michel: France	**28**	49N	2W
Montserrat: *i.*, W. Indies	**83**	17N	62W
Mont Tremblant Park: Can.	**85**	47N	75W
Montvalier, Pic de: Sp./Fr.	**29**	43N	1E
Monza: Italy	**33**	46N	9E
Moosehead Lake: U.S.A.	**85**	46N	70W
Moose Jaw: Canada	**80**	50N	105W
Moose Lake: *city*, U.S.A.	**84**	46N	93W
Moosonee: Canada	**81**	51N	80W
Moradabad: India	**48**	29N	79E
Moravska Ostrava: Czech.	**27**	50N	18E
Morbihan: *Dept.*, France	**28**	48N	3W
Morea: Austl.	**61**	37S	141E
Morea: Greece	**31**	38N	22E
Moree: Austl.	**61**	29S	150E
Moreton Bay: Austl.	**60**	27S	153E
Morgantown: U.S.A.	**85**	40N	80W
Morioka: Japan	**52**	40N	141E
Morjärv: Sweden	**34**	66N	23E
Morkalla: Austl.	**61**	34S	141E
Morlaix: France	**28**	49N	4W
MOROCCO	**62**	—	—
Morogoro: Tangan.	**68**	7S	38E
Morona: *r.*, Ec./Peru	**86**	3S	77W
Morotai: *i.*, Indonesia	**51**	3N	128E
Morristown: U.S.A.	**84**	36N	83W
Mortara: Italy	**33**	45N	9E
Morvan: France	**29**	47N	4E
Mosbach: Germany	**32**	49N	9E
Moscow: U.S.S.R.	**44**	56N	38E
Mosel: *r.*, Germany	**32**	50N	7E
Moselle: *r.*, France	**28**	49N	6E
Moshi: Tangan.	**69**	3S	37E
Moss: Norway	**35**	59N	11E
Mossâmedes: Angola	**69**	15S	12E
Mossel Bay: *town*, S. Afr.	**69**	34S	22E
Mossgiel: Austl.	**61**	33S	145E
Most: Czech.	**32**	51N	14E
Mostaganem: Algeria	**25**	36N	0
Mostar: Yugoslavia	**30**	43N	18E
Mosul: 'Iraq	**46**	36N	43E
Motala: Sweden	**35**	59N	15E
Motte, Lac la: Canada	**85**	48N	78W
Moulins: France	**29**	47N	3E
Moulmein: Burma	**47**	16N	98E
Moulouya: *r.*, N. Afr.	**62**	35N	3W
Mount Desert I.: U.S.A.	**85**	44N	68W
Mount Eba: *town*, Austl.	**58**	30S	136E
Mount Gambier: *town*, Austl.	**61**	38S	141E
Mount Isa: *town*, Austl.	**58**	21S	140E
Mount Lofty Range: Austl.	**61**	35S	138E
Mount Magnet: *town*, Austl.	**58**	28S	118E
Mount Morgan: *town*, Austl.	**60**	24S	150E
Mount Vernon: *city*, U.S.A.	**84**	38N	88W
Moutohora: N.Z.	**53**	38S	178E
Moyale: Kenya	**68**	4N	39E
MOZAMBIQUE	**69**	—	—
Mozambique: & *channel*, Moz.	**69**	15S	41E
Mpanda: Tangan.	**68**	6S	31E
Mtwara: Tangan.	**68**	10S	40E
Muchinga Mts.: N. Rhod.	**68**	13S	32E
Mudros: Lemnos	**31**	40N	25E
Muğla: Turkey	**31**	37N	28E
Mühlhausen: Germany	**32**	51N	10E
Mukachevo: U.S.S.R.	**27**	48N	23E
Mukalla: Aden	**46**	15N	49E
Mukden: China	**50**	42N	124E
Mulberry: U.S.A.	**81**	28N	82W
Mulhacen: *mtn.*, Spain	**25**	37N	3W
Mülheim: (*Cologne*), Germany	**32**	51N	7E
Mülheim: (*Ruhr*), Germany	**32**	51N	7E
Mulhouse: France	**28**	48N	7E
Müller Mts.: Borneo	**51**	1N	114E
Mullewa: Austl.	**60**	28S	115E
Multan: W. Pak.	**48**	30N	71E
Muna: *i.*, Indon.	**58**	5S	122E
München (Munich): Germany	**33**	48N	12E
Muncie: U.S.A.	**84**	40N	85W
Münster: Germany	**32**	52N	8E
Muonio: *r.*, Finland	**34**	68N	24E
Mur: France	**28**	48N	3W
Murat: France	**29**	45N	3E
Murchison: *r.*, Austl.	**58**	27S	116E
Murchison Falls: Uganda	**68**	2N	32E
Murcia: & *Old Prov.*, Spain	**25**	38N	1W
Muret: France	**29**	43N	1E
Murfreesboro: U.S.A.	**84**	36N	86W
Murgon: Austl.	**60**	26S	152E
Murmansk: U.S.S.R.	**42**	69N	33E
Muroran: Japan	**52**	42N	141E
Muroto, C.: Japan	**52**	33N	134E
Murray: *r.*, Austl.	**61**	34S	140E
Murray (Hume): *r.*, Austl.	**61**	36S	145E
Murray Bridge: Austl.	**61**	35S	139E
Murree: India	**48**	34N	73E
Murrumbidgee: *r.*, Austl.	**61**	35S	146E
Murwillumbah: Austl.	**60**	28S	153E
Muscat: Muscat & 'Oman	**46**	24N	59E
MUSCAT AND 'OMAN	**46**	—	—
Muskegon: U.S.A.	**84**	43N	86W
Muskogee: U.S.A.	**80**	36N	95W
Musoma: Tangan.	**68**	2S	34E
Mussoorie: India	**48**	30N	78E
Mustafa Kemalpaşa: Turkey	**31**	40N	28E
Muswellbrook: Austl.	**61**	32S	151E
Mutankiang: China	**50**	45N	130E
Mutano: Angola	**69**	17S	15E

WORL

MUYUN KUM — OTRANTO

	Page	Lat.	Long.
Muyun Kum: U.S.S.R.	45	44N	71E
Muzaffarpur: India	48	26N	85E
Mwanza: Tangan.	68	3S	33E
Mweru, L.: N. Rhod.	68	9S	29E
Mycenae: Greece	31	38N	23E
Myitkyina: Burma	47	26N	97E
Mymensingh: E. Pak.	49	25N	90E
Mysore: India	48	12N	77E
Nacala: Moz.	69	15S	40E
Nachingwea: Tangan.	68	10S	38E
Nacozari: Mexico	80	30N	110W
Naestved: Denmark	35	55N	12E
Nafud: Sa'udi Arabia	46	28N	42E
Naga Hills: Ind./Burma	49	27N	95E
Nagano: Japan	52	37N	138E
Nagaoka: Japan	52	37N	139E
Nagapattinam: India	48	11N	80E
Nagasaki: Japan	52	33N	130E
Nagoorin: Austl.	60	24S	151E
Nagoya: Japan	52	35N	136E
Nagpur: India	48	21N	79E
Nagykanizsa: Hungary	27	46N	17E
Nain: Canada	79	57N	62W
Naini Tal: India	48	29N	80E
Nairobi: Kenya	68	2S	37E
Naivasha: Kenya	68	1S	36E
Najd: Sa'udi Arabia	46	25N	44E
Najran: Sa'udi Arabia	63	17N	44E
Nakhon Ratchasima: Thai.	51	15N	102E
Nakina: Canada	81	50N	87W
Namangan: U.S.S.R.	45	41N	72E
Nambour: Austl.	60	27S	153E
Namib Desert: S.W. Africa	69	23S	15E
Nampula: Mozambique	69	15S	40E
Namsos: Norway	34	64N	11E
Namur: Belgium	28	50N	5E
Nanaimo: Canada	80	49N	124W
Nanao: Japan	52	37N	137E
Nanchang: China	50	28N	116E
Nancheng: China	50	33N	107E
Nancy: France	28	49N	6E
Nanda Devi: *mtn.*, India	48	30N	80E
Nanga Parbat: *mtn.*, Kashmir	45	35N	75E
Nangchen Japo: *mtn.*, China	50	33N	94E
Nanking: China	50	32N	119E
Nan Ling: China	50	25N	112E
Nanning: China	50	23N	108E
Nansei Is.: Japan	51	27N	127E
Nan Shan: China	50	38N	100E
Nantes: France	29	47N	2W
Nanticoke: U.S.A.	85	41N	76W
Nantucket: *i. & sound*, U.S.A.	85	41N	70W
Nao, C. de la: Spain	25	39N	0
Napanee: Canada	85	44N	77W
Napier: N.Z.	53	39S	177E
Naples (Napoli): Italy	30	41N	14E
Nara: Japan	52	35N	136E
Naracoorte: Austl.	61	37S	141E
Narbada: *r.*, India	48	22N	75E
Narbonne: France	29	43N	3E
Narrabri: Austl.	61	30S	150E
Narrandera: Austl.	61	35S	147E
Narrogin: Austl.	60	33S	117E
Narva: U.S.S.R.	35	59N	28E
Narvik: Norway	34	68N	17E
Nar'yan-Mar: U.S.S.R.	42	67N	53E
Nashua: U.S.A.	85	43N	71W
Nashville: U.S.A.	81	36N	87W
Nasik: India	48	20N	74E
Nasiriya: 'Iraq	46	31N	46E
Nassau: Bahama Islands	83	25N	77W
Nassau Range: Neth. New Guinea	58	4S	136E
Nässjö: Sweden	35	58N	15E
Natal: Brazil	87	6S	35W
Natal: *Prov.*, S. Africa	69	28S	31E
Natchez: U.S.A.	81	32N	91W
Natuna Is.: Indonesia	51	4N	108E
Naturaliste, C.: Austl.	60	33S	115E
Nauplia: Greece	31	38N	23E
Nauru: *i.*, Pac. O.	54	1S	167E
Navanagar: India	48	22N	70E
Navarin, C.: U.S.S.R.	43	62N	179E
Navarino, Bay of: Greece	31	37N	22E
Navarra: *Old Prov.*, Spain	25	42N	2W
Navoro: Japan	52	44N	142E
Naxos: *i.*, Greece	31	37N	26E
Nazaré: Brazil	87	13S	39W
Nazareth: Israel	21	33N	35E
Ndola: N. Rhodesia	68	13S	29E
Nebit-Dag: U.S.S.R.	44	40N	55E
Nebraska: *State*, U.S.A.	80	42N	100W
Neckar: *r.*, Germany	32	49N	9E
Negro: *r.*, Arg.	88	40S	65W
Negro: *r.*, Brazil	86	2S	64W
Negros: *i.*, Phil.	51	10N	123E
Neh: Iran	46	32N	60E
Neisse: *r.*, Poland/Germany	32	52N	15E
Neiva: Colombia	86	3N	75W
Nellore: India	48	14N	80E
Nelson: N.Z.	53	41S	173E
Neman: *r.*, U.S.S.R.	27	53N	25E
Nemours: France	28	48N	3E
Nemuro: Japan	53	43N	145E
Nenana: Alaska	78	64N	149W
NEPAL	48	—	—
Nerchinsk: U.S.S.R.	43	52N	116E
Neskaupstadhur: Iceland	34	65N	14W
Nestos: *r.*, Greece	31	41N	24E
NETHERLANDS	32	—	—
NETH. NEW GUINEA	58	—	—
Neubrandenburg: Germany	32	54N	13E
Neuchâtel: *& lake*, Switz.	33	47N	7E
Neufchâteau: Belgium	28	50N	5E
Neufchâteau: France	28	48N	6E
Neumünster: Germany	32	54N	10E

	Page	Lat.	Long.
Neunkirchen: Saar	32	49N	7E
Neuquén: Argentina	88	39S	68W
Neuss: Germany	32	51N	7E
Neustadt: Germany	32	49N	8E
Neustrelitz: Germany	32	53N	13E
Nevada: *State*, U.S.A.	80	39N	117W
Never: U.S.S.R.	43	54N	124E
Nevers: France	29	47N	4E
Nevis: *i.*, West Indies	83	17N	63W
New Albany: U.S.A.	84	38N	86W
New Amsterdam: Br. Gu.	87	6N	57W
New Amsterdam: *i.*, Ind. O.	49	38S	78E
Newark: N. J., U.S.A.	85	41N	74W
Newark: Ohio, U.S.A.	84	40N	82W
New Bedford: U.S.A.	85	42N	71W
New Bern: U.S.A.	81	35N	77W
New Britain: *i.*, Pac. O.	54	6S	150E
New Brunswick: U.S.A.	85	40N	74W
New Brunswick: *Prov.*, Can.	79	47N	67W
Newburgh: U.S.A.	85	41N	74W
New Caledonia: *i.*, Pac. O.	54	21S	165E
New Castile: *Old Prov.*, Spain	25	39N	4W
Newcastle: Austl.	61	33S	152E
Newcastle: Canada	85	47N	65W
Newcastle: S. Afr.	69	28S	30E
New Castle: U.S.A.	84	41N	80W
Newdegate: Austl.	60	33S	119E
New England: U.S.A.	81	42N	72W
New England Range: Austl.	61	30S	152E
Newenham, Cape: Alaska	78	59N	162W
Newfoundland: *Prov.*, Can.	79	48N	55W
New Georgia, *i.*, Solomon Is.	59	8S	157E
New Guinea: *i.*, E. Indies	59	5S	140E
New Hampshire: *State*, U.S.A.	85	44N	72W
New Haven: U.S.A.	85	41N	73W
New Hebrides: *is.*, Pac. O.	54	15S	168E
New Ireland: *i.*, Pac. O.	54	3S	153E
New Jersey: *State*, U.S.A.	85	40N	75W
New Kensington: U.S.A.	85	41N	80W
New London: U.S.A.	85	41N	72W
New Mexico: *State*, U.S.A.	80	34N	107W
New Orleans: U.S.A.	81	30N	90W
New Plymouth: N.Z.	53	39S	174E
Newport: Ky., U.S.A.	84	39N	85W
Newport: R.I., U.S.A.	85	41N	71W
Newport News: U.S.A.	85	37N	76W
New South Wales: *State*, Austl.	61	32S	146E
New Westminster: Canada	80	49N	123W
New York: U.S.A.	85	41N	74W
New York: *State*, U.S.A.	81	42N	77W
NEW ZEALAND	53	—	—
Ngami, Lake: Bech.	69	21S	23E
Ngauruhoe: *mtn.*, N.Z.	53	39S	175E
Nguru: Nigeria	68	13N	10E
Nhill: Austl.	61	36S	142E
Niagara Falls: Can./U.S.A.	85	43N	79W
Niamey: Fr. W. Africa	68	14N	2E
NICARAGUA	83	13N	85W
Nicaragua, Lake: Nic.	83	11N	85W
Nice: France	29	44N	7E
Nicobar Is.: India	47	7N	94E
Nicosia: Cyprus	46	35N	33E
Niedere Tauern: *mtns.*, Austr.	27	47N	14E
Nienburg: Germany	32	53N	9E
Nieuwpoort: Belgium	28	51N	3E
Niger: *Prov.*, Fr. W. Africa	63	16N	8E
Niger: *r.*, Fr. W. Afr./Nig.	62	8N	6E
NIGERIA	68	—	—
Niigata: Japan	52	38N	139E
Nijmegen: Netherlands	32	52N	6E
Nikolayev: U.S.S.R.	44	47N	32E
Nikolayevsk: U.S.S.R.	43	53N	142E
Nikopol': U.S.S.R.	44	48N	34E
Nile: *r.*, Egypt/Sudan	63	—	—
Niles: U.S.A.	84	42N	86W
Nilgiri Hills: Ind.	48	12N	77E
Nîmes: France	29	44N	4E
Nimmitabel: Austl.	61	36S	149E
Nimule: Sudan	68	4N	32E
Ninety Mile Beach: Austl.	61	38S	147E
Ninghsia: China	50	39N	106E
Ningpo: China	50	30N	122E
Niort: France	29	46N	0
Nipigon: *& lake*, Canada	81	49N	88W
Nipissing, Lake: Canada	85	46N	80W
Niš: Yugoslavia	31	43N	22E
Nisiros: *i.*, Greece	31	37N	27E
Niterói: Brazil	88	23S	43W
Nivelles: Belgium	28	51N	4E
Nivernais: *Old Prov.*, Fr.	29	47N	3E
Nizhniy-Tagil: U.S.S.R.	45	58N	60E
Nkana: N. Rhod.	68	13S	28E
Nobeoka: Japan	52	32N	132E
Noccundra: Austl.	60	28S	142E
Nogales: Mexico	80	31N	111W
Nogent-sur-Seine: France	28	48N	4E
Noirmoutier, Île de: Fr.	28	47N	2W
Nome: Alaska	78	65N	165W
Nonacho Lake: Canada	78	62N	109W
Nootka Sound: Canada	80	49N	127W
Noranda: Canada	85	48N	79W
Norden: Germany	32	54N	7E
Nordenham: Germany	32	53N	8E
Norderney: *i.*, Germany	32	54N	7E
Nordhausen: Germany	32	51N	11E
Nordhorn: Germany	32	52N	7E
Nördlingen: Germany	33	49N	11E
Nordvik: U.S.S.R.	43	74N	110E
Norfolk: U.S.A.	85	37N	76W
Norfolk I.: Austl.	59	29S	168E
Noril'sk: U.S.S.R.	43	69N	90E
Norman: *r.*, Austl.	59	19S	142E
Normandy: *Old Prov.*, Fr.	28	49N	0
Normanton: Austl.	59	18S	141E
Nornalup: Austl.	60	35S	117E
Norris Dam: U.S.A.	84	36N	84W
Norrköping: Sweden	35	59N	16E
Norseman: Austl.	60	32S	122E

	Page	Lat.	Long.
North Adams: U.S.A.	85	43N	73W
Northam: Austl.	60	32S	117E
Northampton: Austl.	60	28S	115E
North Battleford: Canada	80	53N	108W
North Bay: *town*, Canada	85	46N	79W
North Borneo: *Prov.*, Br. Borneo	51	5N	117E
North Cape: Norway	34	71N	26E
North Carolina: *State*, U.S.A.	81	36N	80W
North Channel: Canada	84	46N	83W
Northcliffe: Austl.	60	35S	116E
North Dakota: *State*, U.S.A.	80	47N	100W
North Dvina: *r.*, U.S.S.R.	42	63N	43E
North East New Guinea	54	5S	145E
Northern Mid-Atlantic Ridge	24	—	—
Northern Rhodesia: *State*, Fed. of Rhod.	68/9	—	—
Northern Sporades: *is.*, Grc.	31	39N	24E
Northern Territory: Austl.	58	—	—
North Island: N.Z.	53	—	—
NORTH KOREA	50	—	—
North Platte: U.S.A.	80	41N	100W
North Platte: *r.*, U.S.A.	78	42N	104W
North Sea	26	—	—
North Stradbroke I.: Austl.	60	28S	154E
North Tonawanda: U.S.A.	85	43N	79W
Northumberland Is.: Austl.	60	22S	150E
Northumberland Strait: Can.	85	46N	63W
Northwest Territories: Can.	78/9	—	—
Norton Sound: Alaska	78	64N	163W
NORWAY	34	—	—
Norwood: U.S.A.	84	39N	84W
Noshiro: Japan	52	40N	140E
Nossob: *r.*, S. Africa	69	26S	21E
Nosy Bé: *i.*, Madag.	71	13S	48E
Noto Peninsula: Japan	52	37N	137E
Notre Dame Mts.: Canada	85	48N	67W
Nouméa: New Caledonia	59	22S	167E
Nova Lisboa: Angola	71	13S	16E
Novara: Italy	33	45N	9E
Nova Scotia: *Prov.*, Canada	79	45N	63W
Novaya Zemlya: *is.*, U.S.S.R.	42	75N	60E
Novgorod: U.S.S.R.	44	58N	31E
Novi Ligure: Italy	33	45N	9E
Novi Pazar: Yugoslavia	31	43N	20E
Novi Sad: Yugoslavia	31	45N	20E
Novocherkassk: U.S.S.R.	44	47N	40E
Novograd Volynskiy: U.S.S.R.	35	51N	28E
Novogrudok: U.S.S.R.	27	54N	26E
Novonazyvayevka: U.S.S.R.	45	56N	72E
Novo Redondo: Angola	68	11S	14E
Novorossiysk: U.S.S.R.	44	45N	38E
Novosibirsk: U.S.S.R.	45	55N	83E
Novosibirskiye Ostrova: U.S.S.R.	43	76N	140E
Novouzensk: U.S.S.R.	44	50N	48E
Novyy Port: U.S.S.R.	42	67N	73E
Nowa Huta: Poland	27	50N	20E
Nowy Sącz: Poland	27	50N	21E
N'Suta: Gold Coast	68	5N	2W
Nubian Desert: Sudan	63	21N	33E
Nučice: Czech.	27	50N	14E
Nueva Rosita: Mexico	80	28N	101W
Nuits-St. Georges: France	29	47N	5E
Nuku Hiva: *i.*, Pac. O.	55	9S	140W
Nullarbor Plain: Austl.	58	30S	128E
Nundle: Austl.	61	32S	151E
Nunivak: *i.*, Alaska	78	60N	166W
Nuoro: Sardinia	30	40N	9E
Nuremberg (Nürnberg): Ger.	32	49N	11E
Nusaybin: Turkey	46	37N	41E
Nuwara Eliya: Ceylon	48	7N	81E
Nyahwest: Austl.	61	35S	143E
Nyasa, Lake: Nyasa.	68	13S	35E
Nyasaland: *State*, Fed. of Rhod.	68/9	—	—
Nyenchen Tanglha Range: China	47	30N	90E
Nyíregyháza: Hungary	31	48N	22E
Nykøbing: Denmark	35	55N	12E
Nyköping: Sweden	35	59N	17E
Nymburk: Czech.	27	50N	15E
Nyngan: Austl.	61	32S	147E
Nyon: Switz.	33	46N	6E
Nysa: Poland	27	51N	18E
Nysa: *r.*, Poland/Germany	32	51N	15E
Oakland: U.S.A.	80	38N	122W
Oak Ridge: U.S.A.	84	36N	84W
Oamaru: N.Z.	53	45S	171E
Ob': *r.*, U.S.S.R.	42	63N	65E
Oberammergau: Germany	33	48N	11E
Oberhausen: Germany	32	51N	7E
Obidos: Brazil	87	2S	56W
Obihiro: Japan	53	43N	143E
Ochakov: U.S.S.R.	31	47N	32E
Odda: Norway	35	60N	7E
Ödemiş: Turkey	31	38N	28E
Odense: Denmark	35	55N	10E
Odenwald: *hills*, Germany	32	49N	9E
Oder (Odra): *r.*, Ger./Pol.	32	53N	14E
Odessa: U.S.S.R.	44	46N	31E
Odorhei: Romania	31	46N	25E
Offenburg: Germany	33	48N	8E
Ofot Fiord: Norway	34	68N	17E
Ogaden: Eth.	63	7N	45E
Ogaki: Japan	52	35N	137E
Ogden: U.S.A.	80	41N	112W
Oglio: *r.*, Italy	33	45N	10E
Ogoja: Nigeria	68	7N	9E
Ohai: N.Z.	53	46S	168E
Ohakune: N.Z.	53	39S	175E
Ohio: *r.*, U.S.A.	81	39N	84W
Ohio: *State*, U.S.A.	81	40N	83W
Ohře: *r.*, Czech.	32	50N	14E
Oil City: U.S.A.	84	41N	80W

	Page	Lat.	Long.
Oise: *r.*, France	28	49N	2E
Oita: Japan	52	33N	132E
Oka: *r.*, U.S.S.R.	44	55N	40E
Okanogan: *r.*, U.S.A.	80	49N	120W
Okayama: Japan	52	35N	134E
Okeechobee, L.: U.S.A.	81	27N	81W
Okhotsk: U.S.S.R.	43	59N	143E
Okhotsk, Sea of	43	55N	150E
Oki Is.: Japan	52	36N	133E
Okinawa: *i.*, Japan	50	27N	128E
Oklahoma: *State*, U.S.A.	80	36N	97W
Oklahoma City: U.S.A.	80	35N	98W
Okovango: *r.*, Ang./S.W. Afr.	69	18S	21E
Okovango Basin: Bech.	69	19S	23E
Okuru: N.Z.	53	44S	169E
Öland: *i.*, Sweden	35	57N	17E
Olbia: Sardinia	30	41N	9E
Old Castile: *Old Prov.*, Sp.	25	42N	5W
Oldenburg: Germany	32	53N	8E
Oldenzaal: Neth.	32	52N	7E
Olean: U.S.A.	85	42N	78W
Olekminsk: U.S.S.R.	43	60N	120E
Olenëk: *r.*, U.S.S.R.	43	71N	120E
Oléron, Île d': France	29	46N	1W
Olomouc: Czech.	27	50N	17E
Olonzac: France	29	43N	3E
Oloron-Ste.-Marie: France	29	43N	1W
Olsztyn: Poland	27	54N	20E
Olten: Switzerland	33	47N	8E
Olympia: Greece	31	38N	22E
Olympia: U.S.A.	80	47N	123W
Olympus: *mtn.*, Greece	31	40N	22E
Omaha: U.S.A.	80	41N	96W
'Oman, G. of:	46	25N	58E
Omdurman: Sudan	63	16N	32E
Omiya: Japan	52	35N	139E
Omsk: U.S.S.R.	45	55N	73E
Omu: Japan	52	45N	143E
Omuta: Japan	52	33N	130E
Omutinskoye: U.S.S.R.	45	56N	68E
Onega, Lake: U.S.S.R.	44	63N	35E
Oneida Lake: U.S.A.	85	43N	76W
Onekotan: *i.*, U.S.S.R.	43	50N	155E
Onitsha: Nigeria	68	6N	6E
Onstwedde: Neth.	32	53N	7E
Ontario: *Prov.*, Canada	79	51N	90W
Ontario, Lake: Can./U.S.A.	85	43N	78W
Oodnadatta: Austl.	58	27S	135E
O'Okiep: S. Afr.	69	30S	18E
Ooldea: Austl.	58	30S	132E
Oosterhesselen: Neth.	32	53N	7E
Oosterhout: Neth.	32	52N	5E
Ootacamund: India	48	11N	77E
Opava: Czech.	27	50N	18E
Opeongo Lake: Canada	85	46N	78W
Opole: Poland	27	51N	18E
Oporto: Portugal	25	41N	9W
Opotiki: N.Z.	53	38S	177E
Opunake: N.Z.	53	39S	174E
Oradea: Romania	31	47N	22E
Oraison: France	29	44N	6E
Oran: *& Prov.*, Algeria	25	36N	1W
Orange: Austl.	61	33S	149E
Orange: France	29	44N	5E
Orange: *r.*, S. Africa	69	28S	18E
Orange Free State: *Prov.*, S. Africa	69	29S	27E
Oranienburg: Germany	32	53N	13E
Orasul Stalin: Romania	31	46N	26E
Ordos Plateau: China	50	39N	108E
Ordzhonikidze: U.S.S.R.	44	43N	45E
Örebro: Sweden	35	59N	15E
Oregon: *State*, U.S.A.	80	44N	120W
Oregon City: U.S.A.	80	45N	123W
Orekhovo-Zuyevo: U.S.S.R	44	55N	39E
Orel: U.S.S.R.	44	53N	36E
Orense: Spain	25	42N	8W
Orgeyev: U.S.S.R.	31	48N	29E
Orihuela: Spain	25	38N	1W
Orillia: Canada	85	45N	79W
Orinoco: *r.*, Venez.	86	8N	63W
Orissa: *State*, India	48	20N	85E
Oristano: Sardinia	30	40N	9E
Orizaba: Mexico	82	19N	97W
Orlando: U.S.A.	81	28N	82W
Orléanais: *Old Prov.*, Fr.	28	48N	2E
Orléans: France	28	48N	2E
Orléans, Île d': Canada	85	47N	71W
Orléansville: Algeria	25	36N	1E
Ornain: *r.*, France	28	49N	5E
Orne: *r.*, France	28	49N	0
Orsk: U.S.S.R.	45	51N	59E
Orthez: France	29	43N	1W
Ortler: *mtn.*, Italy	33	47N	10E
Oruro: Bolivia	88	18S	67W
Oryakhovo: Bulgaria	31	44N	24E
Osaka: *& bay*, Japan	52	35N	135E
Osh: U.S.S.R.	45	41N	73E
Oshawa: Canada	85	44N	79W
Oshkosh: U.S.A.	84	44N	88W
Oshogbo: Nigeria	68	8N	5E
Osijek: Yugo.	31	46N	19E
Oskarshamn: Sweden	35	57N	16E
Oslo: *& fiord*, Norway	35	60N	11E
Osmanabad: India	48	18N	76E
Osnabrück: Germany	32	52N	8E
Osorno: Chile	88	40S	73W
Ostend: Belgium	28	51N	3E
Östersund: Sweden	34	63N	15E
Ostia: Italy	30	42N	12E
Ostrovnoye: U.S.S.R.	43	68N	164E
Ostrów Mazowiecka: Poland	27	53N	22E
Ostrów Wielkopolski: Pol.	27	52N	18E
Osumi Is.: Japan	50	31N	131E
Oswego: U.S.A.	85	43N	76W
Otago Peninsula: N.Z.	53	46S	171E
Otaru: Japan	52	43N	141E
Othe, Forêt d': France	28	48N	4E
Otranto: *& str.*, Italy	31	40N	18E

ORLD

OTSU — RACINE

	Page	Lat.	Long.
Otsu: Japan	52	35N	136E
Ottawa: Canada	85	45N	76W
Ottawa: U.S.A.	84	41N	89W
Ottawa: *r.*, Canada	79	46N	77W
Ottingen: Germany	33	49N	11E
Ottumwa: U.S.A.	84	41N	92W
Otway, Cape: Austl.	61	39S	144E
Ötztal Alps: Austria	33	47N	11E
Ou: *mtns.*, Japan	52	39N	141E
Ouagadougou: Fr. W. Afr.	68	12N	2W
Ouargla: Algeria	62	32N	5E
Oubangui: *r.*, Africa	70	4N	21E
Oudenaarde: Belgium	28	51N	4E
Oudtshoorn: S. Africa	69	34S	22E
Ouessant, Î. d': France	28	48N	5W
Oulu: *& lake*, Finland	34	65N	25E
Ourthe: *r.*, Belgium	28	50N	6E
Oust: *r.*, France	28	48N	2W
Outjo: S.W. Africa	69	20S	17E
Ouyen: Austl.	61	35S	142E
Ovens: *r.*, Austl.	61	36S	147E
Oviedo: Spain	25	43N	6W
Owen, Mt.: N.Z.	53	42S	172E
Owen Falls: Uganda	68	0	33E
Owensboro: U.S.A.	84	38N	87W
Owens Creek: *town*, Austl.	60	21S	149E
Owen Sound: *town*, Canada	84	45N	81W
Owen Stanley Range: New Guinea	58	9S	147E
Owosso: U.S.A.	84	43N	84W
Oxus: *r.*, U.S.S.R.	45	37N	65E
Oyonnax: France	29	46N	6E
Ozark Plateau: U.S.A.	81	37N	93W
Ozarks, Lake of the: U.S.A.	84	38N	92W
Ózd: Hungary	27	48N	20E
Paarl: S. Africa	69	34S	19E
Pacific Ocean	54/5	—	—
Padang: Sumatra	51	1S	100E
Paderborn: Germany	32	52N	9E
Padua (Padova): Italy	33	45N	12E
Paducah: U.S.A.	84	37N	88W
Paeroa: N.Z.	53	37S	176E
Pagoda Pt.: Burma	47	16N	94E
Paimboeuf: France	29	47N	2E
Paimpol: France	28	49N	3W
PAKISTAN	46	—	—
Pakokku: Burma	47	21N	95E
Palau Is.: Caroline Is.	51	7N	135E
Palawan: *i.*, Philippines	51	10N	119E
Palembang: Sumatra	51	3S	105E
Palencia: Spain	25	42N	5W
Palermo: Sicily	30	38N	13E
Palghat: India	48	11N	77E
Palk Strait: India/Ceylon	48	10N	80E
Palliser, C.: N.Z.	53	42S	175E
Palma: Majorca	25	40N	3E
Palmas, C.: Liberia	62	4N	8W
Palm Beach: U.S.A.	81	27N	80W
Palm Is.: Austl.	60	19S	147E
Palmerston North: N.Z.	53	40S	176E
Palmyra: Syria	46	35N	38E
Palos, C. de: Spain	25	38N	1W
Paltamo: Finland	34	64N	28E
Pamiers: France	29	43N	2E
Pamirs: U.S.S.R./Afghan.	45	37N	73E
Pamlico Sound: U.S.A.	85	35N	76W
Pampas de la Plata: Arg.	88	33S	64W
Pamplona: Spain	25	43N	2W
PANAMÁ	86	8N	80W
Panama Canal Zone	83	*Inset*	
Panay: *i.*, Philippines	51	11N	122E
Pangong Range: China	48	34N	80E
Panjim: Goa, India	48	15N	74E
Pantar: *i.*, Indonesia	58	8S	124E
Pantellaria: *i.*, Italy	30	37N	12E
Paoting: China	50	39N	115E
Paotow: China	50	41N	110E
Papakura: N.Z.	53	37S	175E
Papua: *& gulf*, New Guinea	58	7S	145E
Pará: *& r.*, Brazil	87	1S	48W
Paracel Is.: S. China Sea	51	16N	112E
PARAGUAY	88	23S	58W
Paraguay: *r.*, S. America	88	26S	58W
Parakou: Fr. W. Afr.	68	9N	3E
Paramaribo: Surinam	87	6N	55W
Paramushir: *i.*, U.S.S.R.	43	51N	155E
Paraná: Argentina	88	32S	60W
Paraná: *r. & plat.*, S. Am.	88	25S	55W
Parbati: *r.*, India	48	23N	77E
Parchim: Germany	32	53N	12E
Pardubice: Czech.	27	50N	16E
Parecis, Serra dos: Braz.	86	12S	61W
Paris: France	28	49N	2E
Parkersburg: U.S.A.	84	39N	82W
Parkes: Austl.	61	33S	148E
Parma: Italy	33	45N	10E
Parnaíba: Brazil	87	3S	42W
Parnassus: *mtn.*, Greece	31	38N	22E
Paros: *i.*, Greece	31	37N	25E
Parramatta: Austl.	61	34S	151E
Parry, Cape: Canada	78	70N	125W
Parry Is.: Canada	78	77N	107W
Parry Sound: Canada	84	45N	80W
Parthenay: France	29	47N	0
Pasadena: U.S.A.	80	34N	118W
Passau: Germany	33	49N	13E
Passchendaele: Belgium	28	51N	3E
Passero, C.: Sicily	30	37N	15E
Pasto: Colombia	86	1N	77W
Patagonia: Argentina	89	45S	70W
Patay: France	28	48N	2E
Paterson: U.S.A.	85	41N	74W
Pathfinder Dam: U.S.A.	80	42N	107W
Patiala: India	48	30N	77E
Patmos: *i.*, Greece	31	37N	26E
Patna: India	48	26N	85E

	Page	Lat.	Long.
Patras: *& gulf*, Greece	31	38N	22E
Pau: France	29	43N	0
Paulis: Belgian Congo	70	3N	28E
Paulistana: Brazil	87	8S	41W
Paulsboro: U.S.A.	85	40N	75W
Pavia: Italy	33	45N	9E
Pavlodar: U.S.S.R.	45	52N	77E
Pawtucket: U.S.A.	85	42N	71W
Paysandú: Uruguay	88	32S	58W
Pays d'Albret: France	29	44N	1W
Pazardzhik: Bulgaria	31	42N	24E
Peace: *r.*, Canada	78	58N	114W
Peace River: *town*, Canada	78	56N	117W
Peary Channel: Canada	79	79N	100W
Pechenga: U.S.S.R.	34	70N	31E
Pechora: *r.*, U.S.S.R.	44	63N	56E
Pecos: *r.*, U.S.A.	80	31N	102W
Pécs: Hungary	27	46N	18E
Pedro, Pt.: Ceylon	48	10N	80E
Pedro Miguel Locks: Panama	83	*Inset*	
Peebinga: Austl.	61	35S	141E
Pegasus Bay: N.Z.	53	44S	173E
Pegu: Burma	47	17N	97E
Peian: China	50	48N	127E
Peine: Germany	32	52N	10E
Peipus, L.: U.S.S.R.	35	59N	27E
Pekin: U.S.A.	84	40N	90W
Peking (Peiping): China	50	40N	116E
Pelican Lake: U.S.A.	84	48N	93W
Pelican Pt.: S.W. Africa	69	23S	14E
Peloponnese: Greece	31	38N	22E
Pelotas: Brazil	88	32S	52W
Pelusium, B. of: Egypt	63	31N	32E
Pelvoux, Mont: France	29	45N	6E
Pemba: N. Rhodesia	69	17S	27E
Pemba: *i.*, Zanzibar	68	5S	40E
Pembroke: Canada	85	46N	77W
Penang: *i.*, Malaya	51	5N	100E
Pendembu: Sierra Leone	62	8N	11W
Penmarch, Pte. de: France	28	48N	4W
Pennar: *r.*, India	48	14N	77E
Pennine Alps: Switz./Italy	33	46N	8E
Pennsylvania: *State*, U.S.A.	81	41N	77W
Penobscot: *r.*, U.S.A.	85	45N	69W
Penrith: Austl.	61	34S	151E
Pensacola: U.S.A.	81	30N	87W
Penza: U.S.S.R.	44	53N	45E
Peoria: U.S.A.	84	41N	90W
Perche, Collines du: Fr.	28	49N	1E
Percy Is.: Austl.	60	22S	150E
Perdu, Mont: France/Spain	29	43N	0
Pergamino: Argentina	88	34S	61W
Périgord: France	29	45N	1E
Périgueux: France	29	45N	1E
Perm: U.S.S.R.	44	57N	55E
Pernambuco: Brazil	87	8S	35W
Pernik: Bulgaria	31	43N	23E
Péronne: France	28	50N	3E
Perpignan: France	29	43N	3E
PERSIA	46	—	—
Persian Gulf	46	27N	50E
Perth: Austl.	60	32S	116E
PERU	86	—	—
Peru: U.S.A.	84	41N	86W
Perugia: Italy	30	43N	12E
Pervomaysk: U.S.S.R.	31	48N	31E
Pesaro: Italy	33	44N	13E
Pescadores Is.: Formosa	50	24N	120E
Pescara: Italy	30	42N	14E
Peshawar: W. Pak.	47	34N	71E
Pessac: France	29	45N	1W
Petange: Luxembourg	32	50N	6E
Peterborough: Austl.	61	33S	139E
Peterborough: Canada	85	44N	78W
Petersburg: U.S.A.	85	37N	77W
Petone: N.Z.	53	41S	175E
Petrich: Bulgaria	31	41N	23E
Petropavlovsk: U.S.S.R.	45	55N	69E
Petropavlovsk-Kamchatski: U.S.S.R.	43	53N	159E
Petrópolis: Brazil	88	23S	43W
Petroşani: Romania	31	45N	23E
Petrovgrad: Yugoslavia	31	45N	20E
Petrozavodsk: U.S.S.R.	42	62N	35E
Petsamo: U.S.S.R.	34	70N	31E
Petukhovo: U.S.S.R.	45	55N	68E
Pfälzer Bergland: Germany	32	50N	8E
Pforzheim: Germany	32	49N	9E
Phanom Dongrak: Thailand	51	14N	104E
Phanrang: Viet Nam	51	12N	109E
Philadelphia: U.S.A.	85	40N	75W
PHILIPPINE ISLANDS	51	10N	125E
Philippine Sea	51	20N	130E
Philippeville: Algeria	30	37N	7E
Philippopolis: Bulgaria	31	42N	25E
Phoenix: U.S.A.	80	34N	112W
Phuket I.: Thailand	51	8N	98E
Piacenza: Italy	33	45N	10E
Piatra-Neamt: Romania	31	47N	26E
Piave: *r.*, Italy	33	46N	13E
Picardy: *Old Prov.*, France	28	50N	2E
Picola: Austl.	61	36S	145E
Picton: N.Z.	53	41S	174E
Pictou: *& i.*, Canada	85	46N	63W
Piedmont: *Reg.*, Italy	33	45N	8E
Pierre: U.S.A.	80	44N	100W
Pietarsaari: Finland	34	64N	23E
Pietermaritzburg: S. Afr.	69	30S	30E
Pilcomayo: *r.*, S. America	88	23S	62W
Pilsen: Czech.	27	50N	13E
Pindus Mts.: Greece	31	40N	21E
Pinerolo: Italy	33	45N	7E
Piney River: *city*, U.S.A.	85	38N	79W
Pinkiang: China	50	46N	127E
Pinsk: U.S.S.R.	27	52N	26E
Piotrków: Poland	27	51N	20E
Piqua: U.S.A.	84	40N	84W
Piraeus: Greece	31	38N	24E
Pirgos: Greece	31	38N	22E

	Page	Lat.	Long.
Pirin Mts.: Bulgaria	31	42N	23E
Pirmasens: Germany	32	49N	8E
Pisa: Italy	33	44N	10E
Pisagua: Chile	86	20S	70W
Pisek: Czech.	32	49N	14E
Pistoia: Italy	33	44N	11E
Pitcairn I.: Pac. O.	55	25S	130W
Piteşti: Romania	31	45N	25E
Pittsburgh: U.S.A.	85	40N	80W
Pittsfield: U.S.A.	85	42N	73W
Piura: Peru	86	5S	81W
Placentia Bay: Canada	79	47N	55W
Plantaurel, Mts. du: Fr.	29	43N	1E
Plassey: India	48	23N	88E
Plate: *r.*, South America	88	35S	57W
Platte: *r.*, U.S.A.	80	41N	99W
Plattling: Germany	33	49N	13E
Plauen: Germany	32	50N	12E
Plenty, Bay of: N.Z.	53	38S	177E
Pleven: Bulgaria	31	43N	25E
Ploeşti: Romania	31	45N	26E
Plomb du Cantal: *mtn.*, Fr.	29	45N	3E
Plombières: France	28	48N	6E
Plön: Germany	32	54N	10E
Plovdiv: Bulgaria	31	42N	25E
Plumtree: S. Rhod.	69	20S	28E
Plymouth: U.S.A.	85	42N	71W
Plzeň: Czech.	27	50N	13E
Pnompenh: Cambodia	51	12N	105E
Po: *r.*, Italy	33	45N	10E
Pobé: Fr. W. Africa	68	7N	3E
Pocatello: U.S.A.	80	43N	112W
Poções: Brazil	87	15S	40W
Po Hai: *gulf*, China	50	38N	120E
Pohang: S. Korea	52	36N	129E
Pointe Noire: Fr. Eq. Afr.	70	5S	12E
Poissy: France	28	49N	2E
Poitiers: France	29	47N	0
Poitou: *Old Prov.*, France	29	47N	1W
Poix: France	28	50N	2E
Pola: Yugoslavia	30	45N	14E
POLAND	27	—	—
Polatli: Turkey	31	40N	32E
Poliyiros: Greece	31	40N	23E
Polotsk: U.S.S.R.	35	55N	29E
Poltava: U.S.S.R.	44	50N	35E
Polynesia: Pac. O.	54	—	—
Pomeranian Bay: Germany	35	54N	14E
Pomona: S.W. Africa	69	27S	15E
Pompeii: Italy	30	41N	14E
Pondicherry: India	48	12N	80E
Ponente, Riviera di: Italy	33	44N	8E
Pont-à-Mousson: France	28	49N	6E
Ponta Porã: Brazil	88	22S	56W
Pontarlier: France	29	47N	6E
Pontevedra: Spain	25	42N	9W
Ponthierville: Belg. Congo	71	0	25E
Pontiac: U.S.A.	84	43N	83W
Pontianak: Borneo	51	0	109E
Pontic Mts.: Turkey	44	42N	37E
Pontivy: France	28	48N	3W
Pontoise: France	28	49N	2E
Pontresina: Switzerland	33	46N	10E
Poona: India	48	18N	74E
Pooncarie: Austl.	61	33S	143E
Poopó, L.: Bolivia	88	18S	67W
Poperinghe: Belgium	28	51N	3E
Poplar Bluff: U.S.A.	84	37N	90W
Popocatepetl: *volc.*, Mex.	82	19N	99W
Porbandar: Ind.	48	22N	70E
Pori: Finland	34	61N	22E
Porkkala: U.S.S.R.	35	60N	24E
Port Adelaide: Austl.	61	35S	139E
Portalegre: Portugal	25	39N	7W
Port Alfred: Canada	85	48N	71W
Port Alfred: S. Africa	69	34S	27E
Port Arthur: Canada	84	48N	89W
Port Arthur: China	50	39N	121E
Port Arthur: U.S.A.	81	30N	94W
Port Augusta: Austl.	61	32S	138E
Port-au-Prince: Haiti	83	18N	72W
Port-aux-Basques: Canada	79	47N	59W
Port Bou: Spain	25	42N	3E
Port Clinton: Austl.	60	22S	151E
Port Colborne: Canada	85	43N	79W
Port Elizabeth: S. Africa	69	34S	26E
Port Francqui: B. Congo	71	4S	21E
Port Gentil: Fr. Eq. Afr.	68	1S	9E
Port Harcourt: Nigeria	68	5N	7E
Port Hedland: Austl.	58	20S	119E
Port Huron: U.S.A.	84	43N	82W
Port Kembla: Austl.	61	34S	151E
Portland: Austl.	61	38S	142E
Portland: Maine, U.S.A.	81	44N	70W
Portland: Oreg., U.S.A.	80	46N	123W
Port Lincoln: Austl.	61	35S	136E
Port Lyautey: Morocco	66	34N	7W
Port Macquarie: Austl.	61	31S	153E
Port Moresby: New Guinea	59	9S	147E
Port Nolloth: S. Africa	69	29S	17E
Pôrto Alegre: Brazil	88	30S	51W
Pôrto Alexandre: Angola	69	16S	12E
Pôrto Amélia: Mozambique	69	13S	40E
Portobello: Panamá	86	10N	80W
Port of Spain: W. Indies	83	11N	61W
Portogruaro: Italy	33	46N	13E
Porto Novo: Fr. W. Afr.	68	6N	3E
Porto Novo: India	48	12N	80E
Pôrto Velho: Brazil	86	9S	64W
Port Phillip Bay: Austl.	61	38S	145E
Port Pirie: Austl.	61	33S	138E
Port Radium: Canada	78	66N	117W
Port Said: Egypt	63	31N	32E
Port Shepstone: S. Africa	69	31S	31E
Portsmouth: N.H., U.S.A.	85	43N	71W
Portsmouth: Ohio, U.S.A.	84	39N	83W
Portsmouth: Va., U.S.A.	85	37N	76W
Port Stanley: Falkland Is.	89	52S	58W
Port Sudan: Sudan	63	20N	37E

	Page	Lat.	Long.
Port Sulphur: U.S.A.	81	29N	90W
PORTUGAL	25	—	—
Portuguese Guinea: Africa	62	12N	15W
Port Vendres: France	29	43N	3E
Posadas: Argentina	88	27S	56W
Postmasburg: S. Africa	69	28S	23E
Potenza: Italy	30	41N	16E
Potgiertersrus: S. Africa	69	24S	29E
Potomac: *r.*, U.S.A.	85	39N	77W
Potosí: Bolivia	88	20S	66W
Potrerillos: Chile	88	26S	69W
Potsdam: Germany	32	52N	13E
Pottsville: U.S.A.	85	41N	76W
Poughkeepsie: U.S.A.	85	42N	74W
Poverty Bay: N.Z.	53	39S	178E
Powder: *r.*, U.S.A.	80	44N	106W
Poyang, L.: China	50	29N	116E
Požarevac: Yugoslavia	31	45N	21E
Poznań: Poland	27	52N	17E
Prades: France	29	43N	2E
Prague (Praha): Czech.	27	50N	14E
Prato: Italy	33	44N	11E
Prescott: Canada	85	45N	76W
Presque Isle: U.S.A.	85	47N	68W
Pretoria: S. Africa	71	26S	28E
Preveza: Greece	31	39N	21E
Pribilof Is.: U.S.A.	54	57N	170W
Prilep: Yugoslavia	31	41N	22E
Prince Albert: Canada	80	53N	105W
Prince Edward I.: Canada	85	47N	63W
Prince George: Canada	78	54N	123W
Prince of Wales I.: Canada	79	73N	100W
Prince Patrick I.: Canada	78	77N	120W
Prince Rupert: Canada	78	54N	130W
Princeton: Canada	80	49N	120W
Princeton: U.S.A.	85	40N	75W
Principe: *i.*, G. of Guin.	68	2N	7E
Pripet: *r. & marshes*, U.S.S.R.	44	52N	30E
Priština: Yugoslavia	31	43N	21E
Privas: France	29	45N	5E
Prizren: Yugoslavia	31	42N	21E
Progreso: Mexico	82	21N	90W
Prokop'yevsk: U.S.S.R.	43	54N	86E
Prome: Burma	47	19N	95E
Proserpine: Austl.	60	20S	149E
Prostějov: Czech.	27	50N	17E
Provence: *Old Prov.*, France	29	44N	6E
Providence: U.S.A.	85	42N	72W
Provincetown: U.S.A.	85	42N	70W
Provo: U.S.A.	80	40N	112W
Prut: *r.*, U.S.S.R.	31	48N	27E
Przemysl: Poland	27	50N	23E
Pskov: U.S.S.R.	44	58N	28E
Puebla: Mexico	82	19N	98W
Pueblo: U.S.A.	80	38N	105W
Puerto Ayacucho: Venez.	86	6N	66W
Puerto Cabello: Venez.	86	10N	68W
Puerto Deseado: Arg.	89	48S	66W
Puerto Montt: Chile	89	41S	73W
Puerto Rico: C. America	83	18N	67W
Pukekohe: N.Z.	53	37S	175E
Pula: Yugoslavia	30	45N	14E
Pulaski: U.S.A.	85	37N	81W
Punakha: Bhutan	49	28N	90E
Punjab: Pak./Ind.	48	32N	75E
Puno: Peru	88	16S	70W
Punta Arenas: Chile	89	53S	71W
Puri: India	48	20N	86E
Purnamoota: Austl.	61	32S	141E
Purnea: India	48	26N	88E
Purús: *r.*, Brazil	86	5S	64W
Pusan: S. Korea	50	35N	129E
Pushkin: U.S.S.R.	44	60N	30E
Putoran Mts.: U.S.S.R.	43	69N	95E
Putumayo: *r.*, S. America	86	2S	72W
Puy de Sancy: *mtn.*, France	29	45N	3E
Pyatigorsk: U.S.S.R.	44	44N	43E
Pyongyang: N. Korea	50	39N	126E
Pyramids: Egypt	63	30N	31E
Pyrénées: *mtns.*, Sp./Fr.	25	43N	0
Qasr Farafrā: Egypt	63	27N	28E
QATAR	46	25N	51E
Qattara Depression: Egypt	63	29N	28E
Qila Saifullah: Pakistan	48	31N	68E
Qomul: China	50	43N	93E
Queanbeyan: Austl.	61	35S	149E
Quebec: *& Prov.*, Canada	79	47N	71W
Quedlinburg: Germany	32	52N	11E
Queen Adelaide Arch.: Chile	89	52S	75W
Queen Charlotte Is.: *& sound*, Canada	78	53N	132W
Queen Elizabeth Is.: Can.	78	77N	105W
Queensland: *State*, Austl.	59	23S	145E
Queenstown: N.Z.	53	45S	169E
Quelimane: Mozambique	69	18S	37E
Quelpart I.: Korea	50	33N	126E
Que Que: S. Rhodesia	69	19S	30E
Quesnel: Canada	80	53N	122W
Quetta: W. Pakistan	48	30N	67E
Quiberon: *& bay*, France	28	47N	3W
Quilpie: Austl.	60	27S	144E
Quimper: France	28	48N	4W
Quimperlé: France	28	48N	4W
Quincy: U.S.A.	84	40N	91W
Quinze, Lac des: Canada	85	48N	79W
Quito: Ecuador	86	0	78W
Qum: Iran	46	35N	50E
Quorn: Austl.	61	32S	138E
Rabat: Gozo	30	36N	14E
Rabat: Morocco	62	34N	7W
Rabaul: New Britain	59	4S	153E
Race, C.: Canada	79	47N	53W
Racine: U.S.A.	84	43N	88W

WORL

RAGUSA — SAVIGLIANO

	Page	Lat.	Long.
Ragusa: Sicily	30	37N	15E
Raichur: India	48	16N	77E
Rainier, Mt.: U.S.A.	80	47N	122W
Raipur: India	48	21N	82E
Rajahmundry: India	48	17N	82E
Rajkot: India	48	22N	71E
Rajshahi: E. Pak.	48	24N	89E
Rakaia: *r.*, N.Z.	53	44S	172E
Raleigh: U.S.A.	85	36N	79W
Rambouillet: France	28	49N	2E
Ramillies: Belgium	28	51N	5E
Râmnicu Sărat: Romania	31	45N	27E
Râmnicu Vălcea: Romania	31	45N	24E
Rampur: India	48	29N	79E
Rancagua: Chile	88	34S	71W
Ranchi: India	48	23N	85E
Randers: Denmark	35	56N	10E
Rangitaiki: *r.*, N.Z.	53	39S	177E
Rangoon: Burma	47	17N	96E
Rangpur: E. Pakistan	48	26N	89E
Raniganj: India	48	24N	87E
Rankovićevo: Yugo.	31	44N	21E
Rann of Kutch: Pak./Ind.	48	24N	69E
Rapallo: Italy	33	44N	9E
Rapolano: Italy	30	43N	12E
Rappahannock: *r.*, U.S.A.	85	38N	77W
Ras al Hadd: *c.*, Muscat & 'Oman	46	23N	60E
Rastatt: Germany	32	49N	8E
Rathenow: Germany	32	53N	13E
Ratisbon *see* Regensburg			
Ratlam: India	48	23N	75E
Ratnagiri: Ind.	48	17N	73E
Raton: U.S.A.	80	37N	105W
Raukumara Range: N.Z.	53	38S	178E
Ravenna: Italy	33	44N	12E
Ravenswood: Austl.	60	20S	147E
Ravi: *r.*, W. Pakistan	48	31N	72E
Rawalpindi: W. Pakistan	48	34N	73E
Rawson: Argentina	89	43S	65W
Razdel'naya: U.S.S.R.	31	47N	30E
Ré, Île de: France	29	46N	1W
Reading: U.S.A.	85	40N	76W
Recherche Arch.: Austl.	58	34S	123E
Recife: Brazil	87	8S	35W
Recklinghausen: Germany	32	52N	7E
Red: *r.*, Canada/ U.S.A.	79	49N	97W
Red: *r.*, China	50	23N	102E
Red: *r.*, U.S.A.	81	34N	94W
Red Basin: China	50	30N	105E
Red Bluff: U.S.A.	80	40N	122W
Redcliffe: Austl.	60	27S	153E
Red Cliffs: Austl.	61	34S	142E
Redon: France	28	48N	2W
Red Sea	46	—	—
Red Sea Hills: Egypt	63	27N	33E
Redwater: Canada	80	54N	113W
Regensburg: Germany	32	49N	12E
Reggio di Calabria: Italy	30	38N	16E
Reggio nell'Emilia: Italy	33	45N	11E
Regina: Canada	80	50N	105W
Reims: France	28	49N	4E
Reindeer Lake: Canada	78	57N	102W
Remoulins: France	29	44N	5E
Remscheid: Germany	32	51N	7E
Renkum: Netherlands	32	52N	6E
Renmark: Austl.	61	34S	141E
Rennell I.: Solomon Is.	59	12S	160E
Rennes: France	28	48N	2W
Reno: U.S.A.	80	39N	120W
Repulse Bay: Austl.	60	21S	149E
Resht: Iran	46	37N	50E
Resistencia: Argentina	88	27S	59W
Reşiţa: Romania	31	45N	22E
Resolution I.: Canada	79	62N	65W
Rethimnon: Crete	31	35N	25E
Réunion: *i.*, Ind. O.	49	21S	55E
Reus: Spain	25	41N	1E
Reuss: *r.*, Switzerland	33	47N	8E
Reutlingen: Germany	33	48N	9E
Revelstoke: Canada	80	51N	118W
Revermont: France	29	46N	5E
Revilla Gigedo Is.: Mexico	55	19N	112W
Rewari: India	48	28N	77E
Reykjavik: Iceland	34	64N	22W
Rezekne: U.S.S.R.	35	56N	28E
Rhaetian Alps: Switz./It.	30	47N	10E
Rheden: Netherlands	32	52N	6E
Rheims: France	28	49N	4E
Rheine: Germany	32	52N	7E
Rheydt: Germany	32	51N	6E
Rhine (Rhein): *r.*, Europe	32	52N	6E
Rhode Island: *State*, U.S.A.	85	42N	72W
Rhodes: *i.*, Greece	31	36N	28E
Rhodope Mts.: Bulgaria	31	42N	24E
Rhône: *r.*, Europe	29	45N	5E
Ribeirão Prêto: Brazil	88	21S	48W
Riberalta: Bolivia	86	11S	66W
Riccarton: N.Z.	53	44S	173E
Richelieu: *r.*, Canada	85	46N	73W
Richmond: Calif. U.S.A.	80	38N	122W
Richmond: Ind., U.S.A.	84	40N	85W
Richmond: Va., U.S.A.	85	38N	77W
Rideau Lake: Canada	85	45N	76W
Riga: *& gulf*, U.S.S.R.	35	57N	24E
Rijeka: Yugoslavia	30	45N	15E
Rijswijk: Netherlands	32	52N	4E
Rimini: Italy	33	44N	13E
Ringsted: Denmark	35	55N	12E
Riobamba: Ecuador	86	2S	79W
Rio Branco: Brazil	86	10S	68W
Rio de Janeiro: Brazil	88	23S	43W
Rio Gallegos: Argentina	89	52S	69W
Rio Grande: Brazil	88	32S	52W
Rio Grande: *r.*, U.S.A./Mex.	82	29N	101W
Rio Grande do Sul: *State*, Brazil	88	30S	53W
Riom: France	29	46N	3E
Rio Muni: *Col.*, Sp. Guinea	70	2N	10E

	Page	Lat.	Long.
Ripon Falls: Uganda	68	1N	33E
Rishiri: *i.*, Japan	52	45N	141E
Rive-de-Gier: France	29	46N	5E
Rivera: Uruguay	88	31S	56W
Riverina: Austl.	61	36S	145E
Rivière du Loup: Canada	85	48N	70W
Riyadh: Sa'udi Arabia	46	25N	47E
Roanne: France	29	46N	4E
Roanoke: *& r.*, U.S.A.	85	37N	80W
Rochechouart: France	29	46N	1E
Rochefort-sur-Mer: France	29	46N	1W
Rochester: Minn., U.S.A.	84	44N	92W
Rochester: N.Y., U.S.A.	85	43N	78W
Rockall: *i.*, Atl. O.	24	58N	14W
Rockford: U.S.A.	84	42N	89W
Rockhampton: Austl.	60	23S	151E
Rock Island: *city*, U.S.A.	84	41N	91W
Rock Springs: U.S.A.	80	42N	109W
Rocky Mount: *city*, U.S.A.	85	36N	78W
Rocky Mts.: N. America	78	—	—
Rocroi: France	28	50N	5E
Rødberg: Norway	35	60N	9E
Rodez: France	29	44N	3E
Roermond: Neth.	32	51N	6E
Roeselare: Belgium	28	51N	3E
Rogers City: U.S.A.	84	46N	84W
Rolla: U.S.A.	84	38N	92E
Roma: Austl.	60	27S	149E
Roman: Romania	31	47N	26E
ROMANIA	31	—	—
Romans: France	29	45N	5E
Rome: Italy	30	42N	12E
Rome: Ga., U.S.A.	81	34N	85W
Rome: N.Y., U.S.A.	85	43N	75W
Romilly-sur-Seine: France	28	49N	4E
Roncesvalles: Spain	25	43N	1W
Ronda: Spain	25	37N	5W
Rønne: Denmark	35	55N	15E
Roosendaal: Neth.	32	52N	4E
Roquefort: France	29	44N	0
Roquefort: France	29	44N	3E
Roraima: *mtn.*, Venez.	86	5N	61W
Rorschach: Switz.	33	47N	9E
Rørvik: Norway	34	65N	11E
Rosa, Monte: Switz./Italy	33	46N	8E
Rosario: Argentina	88	33S	61W
Roscoff: France	28	49N	4W
Roseires: Sudan	63	12N	34E
Rosendaël: France	28	51N	2E
Rosenheim: Germany	33	48N	12E
Rose Point: Canada	85	44N	64W
Rosetta: Egypt	63	31N	30E
Rossignol, L.: Canada	85	44N	65W
Ross Sea: Antarctica	90	76S	175W
Rostock: Germany	32	54N	12E
Rostov: U.S.S.R.	44	47N	40E
Rothenburg: Germany	32	49N	10E
Roto: Austl.	61	33S	146E
Rotorua: N.Z.	53	38S	176E
Rotterdam: Neth.	32	52N	4E
Rottnest I.: Austl.	60	32S	115E
Rottweil: Germany	33	48N	9E
Roubaix: France	28	51N	3E
Rouen: France	28	49N	1E
Roulers *see* Roeselare			
Round L.: Canada	85	45N	77W
Roussillon: *Old Prov.*, Fr.	29	43N	3E
Rouyn: Canada	85	48N	79W
Rovaniemi: Finland	34	66N	26E
Rovereto: Italy	33	46N	11E
Rovigo: Italy	33	45N	12E
Rovno: U.S.S.R.	27	51N	26E
Roxburgh: N.Z.	53	46S	169E
Roxo, C.: Port. Guinea	62	12N	17W
Royale, Isle: U.S.A.	84	48N	89W
Royan: France	29	46N	1W
Ruahine Range: N.Z.	53	40S	176E
RUANDA URUNDI: Afr.	68	3S	30E
Ruapehu: *mtn.*, N.Z.	53	39S	176E
Rub' al Khali: Sa'udi Arabia	46	20N	50E
Rubtsovsk: U.S.S.R.	45	52N	81E
Rudok: China	48	34N	80E
Rudolf, L.: Kenya	68	4N	36E
Ruffec: France	29	46N	0
Rügen: *i.*, Germany	35	54N	13E
Ruhr: *district*, Germany	32	51N	8E
Ruhrort: Germany	32	51N	7E
Rukwa, L.: Tangan.	68	8S	32E
Ruma: Yugoslavia	31	45N	20E
Rum Jungle: Austl.	58	13S	131E
Ruschuk (Ruse): Bulgaria	31	44N	26E
Russell: N.Z.	53	35S	174E
RUSSIAN SOVIET FEDERATED SOCIALIST REPUBLIC	44/5	—	—
Rutland: U.S.A.	85	44N	73W
Ruvuma: *r.*, Africa	68	11S	37E
Ruwenzori, Mt.: Uganda	68	1N	30E
Ruzomberok: Czech.	27	49N	19E
Ryazan': U.S.S.R.	44	55N	40E
Rybach'ye: U.S.S.R.	45	42N	76E
Rybinsk Reservoir: U.S.S.R.	44	58N	38E
Rybnitsa: U.S.S.R.	31	48N	29E
Ryukyu Is.: Japan	50	27N	127E
Rzeszów: Poland	27	50N	22E
Rzhev: U.S.S.R.	44	56N	35E
Saale: *r.*, Germany	32	51N	12E
Saalfeld: Germany	32	51N	11E
SAAR: Europe	32	49N	7E
Saar: *r.*, Saar	32	50N	7E
Saarbrücken: Saar	32	49N	7E
Sabadell: Spain	25	42N	2E
Sable, Cape: Canada	85	43N	66W
Sacramento: *& r.*, U.S.A.	80	38N	121W
Sá da Bandeira: Angola	69	15S	14E
Sado: *i.*, Japan	52	38N	138E

	Page	Lat.	Long.
Sadowa: Czech.	27	50N	16E
Safi: Morocco	62	32N	9W
Sagami Gulf: Japan	52	35N	139E
Saginaw: *& bay*, U.S.A.	84	44N	84W
Saguenay: *r.*, Canada	85	48N	70W
Sahara Desert: N. Africa	62/3	—	—
Saharanpur: India	48	30N	78E
Sai: *r.*, India	48	26N	82E
Saigon: Viet Nam	51	11N	107E
Sain Shanda: Mongolia	43	45N	110E
St. Affrique: France	29	44N	3E
St. Amand: France	28	50N	3E
St. Amand-Mont-Rond: Fr.	29	47N	2E
St. André, Plaine de: Fr.	28	49N	1E
St. Anton: Austria	33	47N	10E
St. Bernard Pass, Great: Switz./Italy	33	46N	7E
St. Bernard Pass, Little: France/Italy	33	46N	7E
St. Brieuc: France	28	49N	3W
St. Chamond: France	29	45N	5E
St. Clair: *r.*, U.S.A./Can.	84	43N	82W
St. Claude: France	29	46N	6E
St. Cloud: U.S.A.	84	46N	94W
St. Croix: *i.*, W. Indies	83	18N	65E
St. Croix: *r.*, U.S.A./Can.	84	46N	93W
St. David's Head: Wales	26	52N	5W
St. Denis: France	28	49N	2E
St. Dié: France	28	48N	7E
St. Dizier: France	28	49N	5E
St. Elias, Mt.: *& mtns.*, Alaska/Canada	78	60N	140W
Saintes: France	29	46N	1W
Ste. Savine: France	28	48N	4E
Saintes, Les: *is.*, W. Indies	83	16N	62W
St. Étienne: France	29	45N	4E
St. Flour: France	29	45N	3E
St. Francis, C.: S. Africa	69	34S	25E
St. Francis, Lake: Canada	85	46N	71W
St. Gallen: Switzerland	33	47N	9E
St. George: U.S.A.	80	37N	114W
St. George's Channel: Eng.	26	52N	6W
St. Germain: France	28	49N	2E
St. Gotthard Pass: Switz.	33	47N	9E
St. Helena: *i.*, Atl. O.	24	16S	8W
St. Helena Bay: S. Africa	69	32S	18E
St. Hyacinthe: Canada	85	46N	73W
St. Ingbert: Saar	32	49N	7E
St. Jean: Canada	85	45N	73W
St. Jean-de-Luz: France	29	43N	2W
St. Jean de Maurienne: Fr.	29	45N	6E
St. Jean Pied-de-Port: Fr.	29	43N	1W
Saint John: Canada	85	45N	66W
St. John, L.: Canada	85	49N	72W
St. John's: Canada	79	48N	53W
St. Joseph: U.S.A.	81	40N	95W
St. Julien: France	29	46N	6E
St. Junien: France	29	46N	1E
St. Kitts: W. Indies	83	17N	63W
St. Lawrence: *i.*, Alaska	78	63N	170W
St. Lawrence: *r.*, Can./U.S.A.	85	48N	70W
St. Lawrence, Gulf of: Can.	79	48N	63W
St. Lô: France	28	49N	1W
St. Louis: U.S.A.	84	39N	90W
St. Louis: Fr. W. Africa	62	16N	16W
St. Lucia: *i.*, W. Indies	83	14N	61W
St. Malo: *& gulf*, France	28	49N	2W
St. Martin: *i.*, W. Indies	83	18N	63W
Saint Mary's: Tasmania	59	42S	148E
St. Matthew: *i.*, Alaska	78	60N	172W
St. Maurice: Switz.	33	46N	7E
Ste. Menehould: France	28	49N	5E
St. Moritz: Switz.	33	46N	10E
St. Nazaire: France	28	47N	2W
St. Omer: France	28	51N	2E
Saintonge: *Old Prov.*, Fr.	29	45N	1W
St. Paul: *i.*, Ind. O.	49	39S	78E
St. Paul: U.S.A.	84	45N	93W
St. Paul, C.: Gold Coast	68	6N	1E
St. Paul Rocks: Atlantic O.	24	0	30W
St. Peter Port: Guernsey	28	49N	3W
St. Peter, L.: Canada	85	46N	73W
St. Pierre-Quilbignon: Fr.	28	48N	5W
St. Pol: France	28	50N	2E
St. Pons: France	29	43N	3E
St. Quentin: France	28	50N	3E
St. Raphaël: France	29	43N	7E
St. Servan: France	28	49N	2W
St. Thomas: Canada	84	43N	81W
St. Thomas: *i.*, W. Indies	83	18N	65W
St. Tropez: France	29	43N	7E
St. Valery en Caux: France	28	50N	1E
St. Veit: Austria	33	47N	13E
St. Vincent, C.: Port.	25	37N	9W
St. Vincent: *gulf*, Austl.	61	35S	138E
St. Vincent: *i.*, W. Indies	83	13N	61W
Sakania: Belgian Congo	68	12S	28E
Sakata: Japan	52	39N	140E
Sakawa: Japan	52	33N	133E
Sakhalin: *i.*, U.S.S.R.	43	50N	143E
Salado: *r.*, Arg.	88	30S	61W
Salala: Muscat & 'Oman	46	17N	55E
Salamanca: Spain	25	41N	6W
Sala-y-Gomez: *i.*, Pac. O.	55	26S	105W
Sale: Austl.	61	38S	147E
Salekhard: U.S.S.R.	42	66N	65E
Salem: India	48	12N	78E
Salem: U.S.A.	80	45N	123W
Salerno: Italy	30	41N	15E
Salima: Nyasa.	69	14S	35E
Salinas, C.: Majorca	25	39N	3E
Salisbury: Austl.	61	35S	139E
Salisbury: S. Rhodesia	69	18S	31E
Salisbury: U.S.A.	85	38N	75W
Salmon: *r.*, U.S.A.	80	46N	115W
Salmon River Mts.: U.S.A.	80	45N	115W
Salon de Provence: France	29	44N	5E
Salonica: Greece	31	41N	23E
Salonta: Romania	31	47N	22E

	Page	Lat.	Long.
Salpaus Selkä: Sweden	35	61N	25E
Salta: Argentina	88	25S	65W
Saltillo: Mexico	82	25N	101W
Salt Lake City: U.S.A.	80	41N	112W
Salto: Uruguay	88	31S	58W
Salt Range: W. Pakistan	48	33N	73E
Saluzzo: Italy	33	45N	7E
Salvador: Brazil	87	13S	39W
Salween: *r.*, Burma	47	17N	98E
Salzach: *r.*, Austria	33	47N	12E
Salzburg: *& Prov.*, Austria	33	48N	13E
Salzgitter: Germany	32	52N	10E
Samah: China	51	18N	110E
Samar: *i.*, Philippines	51	12N	125E
Samarinda: Borneo	51	0	117E
Samarkand: U.S.S.R.	45	40N	67E
Sambalpur: India	48	22N	84E
Sambor: U.S.S.R.	27	50N	23E
Sambre: *r.*, France/Belg.	28	50N	4E
Samnan: Iran	44	35N	53E
Samoa: *i.*, Pacific Ocean	54	12S	172W
Samos: *i.*, Greece	31	38N	27E
Samothrace: *i.*, Greece	31	40N	26E
Samsun: Turkey	44	41N	36E
San'a: Yemen	46	15N	44E
San Angelo: U.S.A.	80	32N	100W
San Antonio: U.S.A.	80	29N	98W
San Benito Is.: Mexico	82	28N	115W
San Bernardino: U.S.A.	80	34N	117W
San Carlos de Bariloche: Arg.	89	41S	72W
Sancerre: France	29	47N	3E
San Cristobal: Pac. O.	86	1S	90W
San Cristobal: *i.*, Solomon Is.	59	11S	162E
San Cristóbal: Venez.	86	8N	72W
Sandakan: N. Borneo	51	6N	118E
Sandane: Norway	34	62N	6E
Sandgate: Austl.	60	27S	153E
San Diego: U.S.A.	80	33N	117W
Sandusky: U.S.A.	84	41N	83W
San Félix: *i.*, Chile	55	26S	80W
San Fernando: Chile	88	35S	71W
San Francisco: U.S.A.	80	38N	122W
Sangar: U.S.S.R.	43	64N	127E
San Joaquin: *r.*, U.S.A.	80	37N	120W
San José: Costa Rica	86	10N	84W
San Juan: Argentina	88	32S	69W
San Juan: Puerto Rico	83	18N	66W
San Luis: Argentina	88	33S	66W
San Luis Potosí: Mexico	82	22N	101W
SAN MARINO	33	44N	12E
Sanok: Poland	27	50N	22E
San Rafael: Argentina	88	35S	68W
San Remo: Italy	33	44N	8E
San Salvador: El Salvador	82	14N	89W
San Salvador: *i.*, Bahama Is.	83	24N	75W
San Sebastian: Spain	25	43N	2W
San Severo: Italy	30	42N	15E
Santa Barbara: U.S.A.	80	34N	120W
Santa Cruz: Bolivia	86	18S	63W
Santa Cruz de Tenerife: Canary Islands	62	28N	16W
Santa Fé: Argentina	88	32S	61W
Santa Fe: U.S.A.	80	36N	106W
Santa Maria: Brazil	88	30S	54W
Santa Marta: Colombia	86	11N	74W
Santander: Spain	25	43N	4W
Santarém: Portugal	25	39N	9W
Santa Rosa: Argentina	88	37S	64W
Santa Ysabel: *i.*, Solomon Is.	59	8S	159E
Santiago: Chile	88	33S	71W
Santiago: Spain	25	43N	9W
Santiago: *r.*, Mexico	82	21N	104W
Santiago de Cuba: Cuba	83	20N	76W
Santiago del Estero: Arg.	88	28S	64W
Santo Antônio: Brazil	86	9S	64W
Santos: Brazil	88	24S	46W
Sanvic: France	28	49N	0
São Domingos: Portugal	25	38N	7W
São Francisco: *r.*, Brazil	87	12S	43W
São Leopoldo: Brazil	88	30S	51W
São Luis: Brazil	87	3S	44W
Saône: *r.*, France	28	46N	5E
São Paulo: Brazil	88	24S	47W
São Roque, C. de: *cape*, Braz.	87	5S	35W
Sapporo: Japan	52	43N	141E
Saragossa: Spain	25	42N	1W
Sarajevo: Yugoslavia	31	44N	18E
Saratoga Springs: U.S.A.	85	43N	74W
Saratov: U.S.S.R.	44	52N	46E
Sarawak: Br. Borneo	51	3N	113E
Sardinia: *i.*, Medit. Sea	30	—	—
Sarema: *i.*, U.S.S.R.	35	58N	23E
Sargasso Sea	24	30N	60W
Sarnia: Canada	84	43N	82W
Sarny: U.S.S.R.	27	51N	27E
Sarpsborg: Norway	35	59N	11E
Sarrebourg: France	28	49N	7E
Sarreguemines: France	28	49N	7E
Sarthe: *r.*, France	28	48N	0
Sasebo: Japan	52	33N	130E
Saskatchewan: *Prov. & r.*, Canada	78	55N	105W
Saskatoon: Canada	80	52N	106W
Sassari: Sardinia	30	41N	9E
Sassnitz: Germany	27	54N	14E
Satpura Range: India	48	23N	77E
Satu-Mare: Romania	31	48N	23E
SA'UDI ARABIA	46	—	—
Sauerland: Germany	32	51N	8E
Saugor: India	48	24N	79E
Sault Ste. Marie: U.S.A./Can.	84	46N	84W
Saumur: France	29	47N	0
Sauternes: France	29	45N	0
Sava: *r.*, Yugo.	30	45N	17E
Savannah: U.S.A.	81	32N	81W
Savannakhet: Laos	51	17N	105E
Savaştepe: Turkey	31	39N	28E
Saverne: France	28	49N	7E
Savigliano: Italy	33	45N	8E

ORLD

SAVONA — SZOMBATHELY

	Page	Lat.	Long.
Savona: Italy	33	44N	8E
Savonlinna: Finland	34	62N	29E
Savoy: *Old Prov.*, France	29	46N	6E
Saxony: *Prov.*, Germany	27	51N	13E
Scania: Sweden	35	56N	14E
Schaerbeek: Belgium	28	51N	4E
Schaffhausen: Switz.	33	48N	9E
Scheldt: *r.*, Belgium	28	51N	4E
Schenectady: U.S.A.	85	43N	74W
Schiedam: Neth.	32	52N	4E
Schio: Italy	33	46N	11E
Schleswig: Germany	35	54N	10E
Schmalkalden: Germany	32	51N	10E
Schoonebeek: Neth.	32	53N	7E
Schouwen: *i.*, Neth.	32	52N	4E
Schwäbisch-Gmünd: Ger.	33	49N	10E
Schwandorf: Germany	32	49N	12E
Schweinfurt: Germany	32	50N	10E
Schwerin: Germany	32	54N	11E
Schwyz: Switzerland	33	47N	9E
Scoresby Sound: Greenland	79	71N	23W
Scottsbluff: U.S.A.	80	42N	104W
Scranton: U.S.A.	85	41N	76W
Scugog, L.: Canada	85	44N	79W
Scutari: Albania	31	42N	20E
Scutari: Turkey	31	41N	29E
Seal, C.: S. Africa	69	34S	24E
Seattle: U.S.A.	80	48N	122W
Sebeş: Romania	31	46N	24E
Sebha Oasis: Libya	62	27N	15E
Sechura Desert: Peru	86	6S	80W
Sedalia: U.S.A.	84	38N	93W
Sedan: France	28	50N	5E
Seeheim: S.W. Africa	69	27S	18E
Segovia: Spain	25	42N	4W
Segovia: *r.*, Nicaragua	83	15N	85W
Segre: *r.*, Spain	25	42N	1E
Seguia Hamra: Sp. Sahara	62	27N	12W
Segura: *r.*, Spain	25	38N	2W
Seine: *r.*, France	28	49N	1E
Seine, Baie de la: France	28	49N	1W
Sekondi: Gold Coast	68	5N	2W
Selenga: *r.*, Mongolia	43	49N	101E
Sélestat: France	28	48N	7E
Selety-Tengiz, L.: U.S.S.R.	45	53N	73E
Selkirk Mts.: Canada	80	52N	117W
Selukwe: S. Rhodesia	69	20S	30E
Selvas: Brazil	86	6S	65W
Semarang: Java	51	7S	110E
Seminoe Dam: U.S.A.	80	42N	107W
Semiozernoye: U.S.S.R.	45	52N	64E
Semipalatinsk: U.S.S.R.	45	50N	80E
Sendai: Japan	52	38N	141E
Seneca L.: U.S.A.	85	42N	77W
Senegal: *Col.*, Fr. W. Afr.	62	15N	15W
Senja: *i.*, Norway	34	69N	18E
Senlis: France	28	49N	3E
Sennar Dam: Sudan	63	13N	34E
Sens: France	28	48N	3E
Seoul: S.Korea	50	38N	127E
Serbia: Yugoslavia	31	44N	21E
Seremban: Malaya	51	3N	102E
Serio: *r.*, Italy	33	45N	10E
Serov: U.S.S.R.	45	60N	60E
Serowe: Bechuanaland	69	23S	27E
Serra dos Aimorés: *mtns.*, Brazil	87	18S	41W
Serra Geral: *mtns.*, Brazil	88	17S	43W
Serra Geral de Goias: *mtns.*, Brazil	87	13S	46W
Serrai: Greece	31	41N	24E
Sète: France	29	43N	4E
Sétif: Algeria	25	36N	5E
Setúbal: *& bay*, Portugal	25	38N	9W
Sevastopol': U.S.S.R.	44	45N	34E
Seven Islands: *town*, Can.	79	50N	66W
Severn: *r.*, Austl.	61	30S	151E
Severnaya Zemlya: *i.*, U.S.S.R.	43	79N	95E
Sevevoural'sk: U.S.S.R.	45	60N	60E
Seville (Sevilla): Spain	25	37N	6W
Sèvre Nantaise: *r.*, France	29	47N	1W
Sèvre Niortaise: *r.*, France	29	46N	1W
Sèvres: France	28	49N	2E
Seward: Alaska	78	60N	150W
Seward Peninsula: Alaska	78	66N	165W
Seychelles: *i.*, Ind. O.	49	10S	60E
Seydhisfjörjur: Iceland	34	65N	14W
Sézanne: France	28	49N	4E
Sfântu Gheorghe: Romania	31	46N	26E
Sfax: Tunisia	30	35N	11E
's-Gravenhage: Neth.	32	52N	4E
Shahjahanpur: India	48	28N	80E
Shahrud: Iran	46	36N	55E
Shakhty: U.S.S.R.	44	48N	40E
Shalym: U.S.S.R.	45	53N	88E
Shamokin: U.S.A.	85	41N	77W
Shamva: S. Rhodesia	69	17S	32E
Shangani: *r.*, S. Rhod.	69	19S	28E
Shanghai: China	50	31N	121E
Shan States: Burma	50	22N	98E
Shantung Penin.: China	50	37N	120E
Sharon: U.S.A.	84	41N	80W
Shasta, Mt.: U.S.A.	80	42N	122W
Shasta Dam: U.S.A.	80	41N	123W
Shaw I.: Austl.	60	20S	149E
Shawinigan Falls: *town*, Can.	85	47N	73W
Shcherbakov: U.S.S.R.	44	58N	39E
Sheboygan: U.S.A.	84	44N	88W
Shelby: U.S.A.	80	49N	112W
Shelbyville: U.S.A.	84	39N	86W
Shelekhov Bay: U.S.S.R.	43	60N	157E
Shenandoah: Pa., U.S.A.	85	41N	76W
Shenandoah: *& r.*, Va., U.S.A.	85	39N	78W
Shenandoah National Park: U.S.A.	85	39N	78W
Shepparton: Austl.	61	36S	145E
Sherbrooke: Canada	85	45N	72W
Sherlovaya Gora: U.S.S.R.	43	51N	116E
's-Hertogenbosch: Neth.	32	52N	5E
Shibeli: *r.*, Africa	63	6N	43E
Shibetsu: Japan	53	44N	145E
Shickshock Mts.: Canada	85	49N	66W
Shigatse: China	47	29N	89E
Shihchan: China	43	51N	126E
Shikoku: *i.*, Japan	52	34N	134E
Shikoku Mts.: Japan	52	34N	133E
Shikotan: *i.*, U.S.S.R.	53	44N	147E
Shillong: India	49	26N	92E
Shimbara Gulf: Japan	52	33N	130E
Shimoga: India	48	14N	76E
Shimonoseki: Japan	52	34N	131E
Shinano: *r.*, Japan	52	37N	138E
Shingu: Japan	52	34N	136E
Shinjo: Japan	52	39N	140E
Shipka Pass: Bulgaria	31	43N	25E
Shipki Pass: India/China	48	32N	79E
Shiraz: Iran	46	30N	53E
Shire: *r.*, Nyasaland	69	16S	35E
Shiretoko, C.: Japan	52	44N	145E
Shizuoka: Japan	52	35N	138E
Shkoder: Albania	31	42N	20E
Shoalhaven: *r.*, Austl.	61	35S	150E
Shoalwater Bay: Austl.	60	22S	150E
Sholapur: India	48	18N	76E
Shortland Is.: Solomon Is.	59	7S	155E
Shreveport: U.S.A.	81	32N	94W
Shufu: China	45	40N	76E
Shumen: Bulgaria	31	43N	27E
Shwangliao: China	50	44N	123E
Shwebo: Burma	47	23N	96E
Shyaulyay: U.S.S.R.	35	56N	23E
Si: *r.*, China	50	23N	112E
Sialkot: W. Pakistan	48	32N	75E
SIAM	51	—	—
Siam, Gulf of	51	10N	102E
Sian: China	50	34N	109E
Šibenik: Yugoslavia	30	44N	16E
Sibi: W. Pakistan	48	30N	68E
Sibiu: Romania	31	46N	25E
Sicilian Channel	30	37N	12E
Sicily: *i. & Reg.*, Italy	30	—	—
Sidi-bel-Abbès: Algeria	25	35N	1W
Sidra, Gulf of: Libya	63	32N	17E
Sieg: *r.*, Germany	32	51N	8E
Siegburg: Germany	32	51N	7E
Siegen: Germany	32	51N	8E
Siena: Italy	30	43N	11E
SIERRA LEONE	62	8N	12W
Sierra Morena: *mtns.*, Spain	25	38N	5W
Sierra Nevada: *mtns.*, Spain	25	37N	3W
Sierra Nevada: *mtns.*, U.S.A.	80	38N	120W
Sighişoara: Romania	31	46N	25E
Siglufjördhur: Iceland	34	66N	19W
Siirt: Turkey	44	38N	42E
Sikhote Alin' Range: U.S.S.R.	43	47N	137E
Sikkim: *State*, India	48	27N	88E
Silchar: India	49	25N	93E
Silesia: *Old Prov.*, Poland	27	51N	17E
Silistra: Bulgaria	31	44N	27E
Silva Porto: Angola	69	13S	17E
Silvares: Portugal	25	40N	8W
Silverton: Austl.	61	32S	141E
Simcoe, L.: Canada	85	44N	79W
Simferopol': U.S.S.R.	44	45N	34E
Simla: India	48	31N	77E
Simonstown: S. Africa	69	34S	18E
Simplon Pass: Switz.	33	46N	8E
Sinai: *penin.*, Egypt	63	28N	34E
Sind: *Prov.*, W. Pak.	48	26N	68E
Singapore: Malaya	51	1N	104E
Singaradja: Indon.	51	8S	115E
Singkep: *i.*, Indonesia	51	1S	104E
Singleton: Austl.	61	33S	151E
Singora: Thailand	51	7N	101E
Sinhai: China	50	35N	120E
Sining: China	50	36N	102E
Sinkiang: *Prov.*, China	45	40N	80E
Sinuiju: N. Korea	50	40N	124E
Sion: Switz.	33	46N	7E
Sioux City: U.S.A.	81	42N	96W
Sioux Falls: *city*, U.S.A.	80	44N	97W
Sirte: Libya	63	31N	17E
Sisak: Yugoslavia	30	45N	16E
Sistan: Iran/Afghan.	46	31N	61E
Sisteron: France	29	44N	6E
Sitapur: India	48	28N	81E
Sittang: *r.*, Burma	47	18N	97E
Sivas: Turkey	44	40N	37E
Siwa: Egypt	63	29N	25E
Skadovsk: U.S.S.R.	31	46N	33E
Skagerrak: *str.*, Denmark/Norway	35	57N	8E
Skagway: Alaska	78	59N	135W
Skaw, The: *cape*, Denmark	35	58N	11E
Skeena: *r.*, Canada	78	54N	128W
Skellefte: *r.*, Sweden	34	65N	20E
Skellefteå: Sweden	34	65N	21E
Skien: Norway	35	59N	10E
Skierniewice: Poland	27	52N	20E
Skiros: *i.*, Greece	31	39N	25E
Skive: Denmark	35	57N	9E
Skjold: Norway	35	60N	6E
Skopelos: *i.*, Greece	31	39N	24E
Skopje: Yugoslavia	31	42N	21E
Skövde: Sweden	35	58N	14E
Slatina: Romania	31	44N	24E
Slave: *r.*, Canada	78	60N	113W
Slave Coast: Nigeria	68	5N	3E
Sliven: Bulgaria	31	43N	26E
Slonim: U.S.S.R.	27	53N	25E
Slovakia: Czech.	27	48N	20E
Slovenia: Yugoslavia	30	46N	15E
Slutsk: U.S.S.R.	27	53N	28E
Smoky Mts.: U.S.A.	84	36N	83W
Smolensk: U.S.S.R.	44	55N	32E
Smyrna: Turkey	31	38N	27E
Snake: *r.*, U.S.A.	80	47N	118W
Snowy: *mtns. & r.*, Austl.	61	37S	148E
Sobat: *r.*, Sudan	68	9N	33E
Soche: China	45	38N	77E
Sochi: U.S.S.R.	44	44N	40E
Society Is.: Pac. O.	55	17S	150W
Socotra: *i.*, Arabian Sea	46	12N	54E
Soda Mts.: Libya	62	29N	15E
Söderhamn: Sweden	34	61N	17E
Soest: Germany	32	52N	8E
Soest: Netherlands	32	52N	5E
Sofala: Mozambique	69	20S	35E
Sofia (Sofiya): Bulgaria	31	43N	23E
Sogne Fd.: Norway	35	61N	6E
Söğüt, L.: Turkey	31	37N	30E
Soissons: France	28	49N	3E
Sokoto: Nigeria	68	13N	5E
Solikamsk: U.S.S.R.	44	60N	57E
Solimoes: *r.*, S. America	86	4S	69W
Solingen: Germany	32	51N	7E
Sologne: France	28	48N	2E
Solomon Is.: Pac. O.	54	10S	160E
Solothurn: Switz.	33	47N	8E
Šolta: *i.*, Yugoslavia	30	43N	16E
SOMALIA	63	—	—
Sombor: Yugoslavia	31	46N	19E
Sombrero: *i.*, W. Indies	83	18N	63W
Somerset I.: Canada	79	73N	93W
Somme: *r.*, France	28	50N	2E
Sommières: France	29	44N	4E
Son: *r.*, India	48	24N	81E
Sondre Strømfjord: Grnld	79	67N	52W
Sondrio: Italy	33	46N	10E
Songea: Tanganyika	69	11S	36E
Songkhla: Thailand	51	7N	101E
Soochow: China	50	32N	121E
Soonwald: *mtns.*, Germany	32	50N	8E
Sopron: Hungary	31	48N	16E
Sorel: Canada	85	46N	73W
Soria: Spain	25	42N	2W
Sosnowiec: Poland	27	50N	19E
Souk Ahras: Algeria	30	36N	8E
Souris: Man., Canada	80	50N	101W
Souris: N.Sc., Canada	85	46N	62W
Sousse: Tunisia	30	36N	11E
SOUTH AFRICA	69	—	—
Southampton I.: Canada	79	64N	85W
South Australia: *State*, Austl.	58/9	—	—
South Bend: U.S.A.	84	42N	86W
South Carolina: *State*, U.S.A.	81	34N	80W
South China Sea	51	—	—
South Dakota: *State*, U.S.A.	80	45N	100W
Southern Alps: N.Z.	53	43S	170E
Southern Cross: Austl.	60	31S	119E
Southern Ocean	24	—	—
Southern Rhodesia: *State*, Fed. of Rhod.	69	—	—
Southern Sierra Madre: Mex.	82	17N	100W
South Georgia: *i.*, Atl. O.	89	54S	37W
South Island: N.Z.	53	—	—
SOUTH KOREA	50	—	—
South Porcupine: Canada	84	49N	81W
South Sandwich Is.: Antarc.	89	57S	27W
South Shetland Is.: Antarc.	89	62S	60W
SOUTH WEST AFRICA	69	—	—
Southwest Cape: Stewart I.	53	47S	168E
Sovetsk: U.S.S.R.	27	55N	22E
Soviet Harbour: U.S.S.R.	43	49N	140E
SPAIN	25	—	—
Spandau: Germany	32	53N	13E
Spanish Guinea, *Col.*, Africa	70	2N	10E
Spanish Morocco: Mor.	25	35N	5W
Spanish Sahara: N.W.Afr.	62	25N	14W
Spanish Town: Jamaica	83	18N	77W
Sparrows Point: *city*, U.S.A.	85	39N	77W
Sparta: Greece	31	37N	22E
Spartanburg: U.S.A.	81	35N	82W
Spartel, C.: Tangier	25	36N	6W
Spartivento, C.: Italy	30	38N	16E
Spasskoye: U.S.S.R.	45	52N	69E
Spatha, C.: Crete	31	36N	24E
Speedwell, C.: U.S.S.R.	42	75N	55E
Spencer, C.: Austl.	61	35S	137E
Spencer's Gulf: Austl.	61	34S	137E
Spenser Mts.: N.Z.	53	42S	173E
Spessart: *hills*, Germany	32	50N	9E
Spetsai: *i.*, Greece	31	37N	23E
Speyer: Germany	32	49N	8E
Spiekeroog: *i.*, Germany	32	54N	8E
Spiš: *Region*, Czech.	27	49N	21E
Spitsbergen: *i.*, Arctic O.	42	78N	20E
Split: Yugoslavia	30	44N	16E
Splügen Pass: Switz./Italy	33	47N	9E
Spokane: U.S.A.	80	48N	117W
Sporades: *is.*, Greece	31	37N	27E
Spree: *r.*, Germany	32	52N	14E
Springbok: S. Africa	69	30S	18E
Springfield: Ill., U.S.A.	84	40N	90W
Springfield: Mass, U.S.A.	85	42N	73W
Springfield: Mo., U.S.A.	81	37N	93W
Springfield: Ohio, U.S.A.	84	40N	84W
Springsure: Austl.	60	24S	148E
Spruce Pine: U.S.A.	84	36N	82W
Spungabera: Mozambique	69	20S	33E
Squamish: Canada	80	50N	123W
Sretensk: U.S.S.R.	43	52N	118E
Srinagar: Kashmir	48	34N	75E
Stadskanaal: Neth.	32	53N	7E
Stalin: Bulgaria	31	43N	28E
Stalinabad: U.S.S.R.	45	39N	69E
Stalingrad: U.S.S.R.	44	49N	45E
Stalino: U.S.S.R.	44	48N	38E
Stalinogorsk: U.S.S.R.	44	54N	38E
Stalinogrod: Poland	27	50N	19E
Stalin Pk.: U.S.S.R.	45	39N	72E
Stalinsk: U.S.S.R.	45	54N	87E
Stalinstadt: Germany	33	52N	15E
Stanislav: U.S.S.R.	27	49N	25E
Stanley Falls: Belg. Congo	70	0	25E
Stanley Pool: *l.*, Belgian Congo/Fr. Eq. Africa	71	4S	15E
Stanleyville: Belg. Congo	70	1N	25E
Stanthorpe: Austl.	61	29S	152E
Stara Zagora: Bulgaria	31	42N	26E
Starke: U.S.A.	81	30N	82W
Stassfurt: Germany	32	52N	12E
Staten I.: U.S.A.	85	41N	74W
Staunton: U.S.A.	85	38N	79W
Stavanger: Norway	35	59N	6E
Stavelot: Belgium	28	50N	6E
Stavropol': U.S.S.R.	44	45N	42E
Steep Rock Lake: Canada	84	48N	92W
Steigerwald: *mtns.*, Germany	32	50N	11E
Steinkjer: Norway	34	64N	11E
Stellenbosch: S. Africa	69	34S	19E
Stelvio Pass: Switz./Italy	33	47N	10E
Stendal: Germany	32	53N	12E
Sterling: U.S.A.	84	42N	90W
Sterlitamak: U.S.S.R.	44	54N	56E
Stettin: Poland	27	53N	15E
Steubenville: U.S.A.	84	40N	81W
Stewart I.: N.Z.	53	47S	168E
Stewart Is.: Solomon Is.	59	8S	163E
Steyr: Austria	33	48N	14E
Stip: Yugoslavia	31	42N	22E
Stirling Range: Austl.	60	34S	118E
Stjernøy: *i.*, Norway	34	70N	23E
Stockholm: Sweden	35	59N	18E
Stockton: U.S.A.	80	38N	121W
Stor L.: Sweden	34	63N	14E
Storuman: Sweden	34	65N	17E
Stralsund: Germany	35	54N	13E
Stranca Mts.: Turkey	31	42N	28E
Strasbourg: France	28	49N	8E
Stratford: Canada	84	43N	81W
Stratford: N.Z.	53	39S	174E
Straubing: Germany	33	49N	13E
Streator: U.S.A.	84	41N	89W
Stresa: Italy	33	46N	9E
Stromboli: *i.*, Italy	30	39N	15E
Strömstad: Sweden	35	59N	11E
Struma: *r.*, Bulgaria	31	42N	23E
Strumica: Yugoslavia	31	41N	23E
Sturt Desert: Austl.	60	28S	141E
Stuttgart: Germany	33	49N	9E
Styria: *Prov.*, Austria	33	47N	15E
Suakin: Sudan	63	19N	37E
Subotica: Yugoslavia	31	46N	20E
Suceava: Romania	31	48N	26E
Suchan: U.S.S.R.	43	43N	133E
Suchiate: Mexico	82	15N	92W
Süchow: China	50	34N	117E
Sucre: Bolivia	88	19S	65W
SUDAN	63	—	—
Sudbury: Canada	84	46N	81W
Sudeten Mts.: Czech.	27	51N	16E
Suez: *& gulf.*, Egypt	63	30N	32E
Suez Canal: Egypt	63	31N	32E
Sugarloaf Pt.: Austl.	61	32S	153E
Sukhona: *r.*, U.S.S.R.	44	60N	42E
Sukhumi: U.S.S.R.	44	43N	41E
Sukkur: W. Pakistan	48	28N	69E
Sula: *is.*, Indonesia	51	2S	125E
Sulaiman Range: W. Pak.	48	30N	70E
Sulina: Romania	44	45N	30E
Sulmona: Italy	30	42N	14E
Sultan Mts.: Turkey	31	38N	31E
Sulu Sea	51	8N	120E
Sumatra: *i.*, Indonesia	51	0	100E
Sumba: *i.*, Indonesia	51	10S	120E
Sumbawa: *i.*, Indonesia	51	8S	118E
Sumgait: U.S.S.R.	44	40N	50E
Summit: Alaska	78	63N	149W
Sumperk: Czech.	27	50N	17E
Sunda Str.: Indonesia	51	6S	106E
Sundarbans: Ind./Pak.	49	22N	90E
Sundsvall: *l.*, Sweden	34	62N	17E
Sungari Reservoir: China	50	43N	127E
Suo Gulf: Japan	52	34N	131E
Superior: U.S.A.	84	47N	92W
Superior, L.: U.S.A./Can.	84	48N	88W
Surabaja: Java	51	7S	113E
Surakarta: Java	51	7S	111E
Surat: Austl.	60	27S	149E
Surat: India	48	21N	73E
SURINAM	87	4N	56W
Susa: Italy	33	45N	7E
Susquehanna: *r.*, U.S.A.	85	40N	76W
Susuman: U.S.S.R.	43	63N	148E
Sutlej: *r.*, Pak./India	48	31N	80E
Suttor: *r.*, Austl.	60	21S	147E
Suttsu: Japan	52	43N	140E
Svalbard: *i.*, Arctic O.	42	78N	20E
Svendborg: Denmark	35	55N	11E
Sverdlovsk: U.S.S.R.	45	57N	61E
Sverdrup Is.: Canada	78	78N	100W
Svir': *r.*, U.S.S.R.	44	61N	34E
Svishtov: Bulgaria	31	44N	25E
Swabian Jura: *mtns.*, Ger.	33	48N	9E
Swain Reefs: Austl.	60	21S	152E
Swakopmund: S.W. Africa	69	23S	14E
Swatow: China	50	23N	117E
SWAZILAND	69	27S	32E
SWEDEN	34/5	—	—
Swellendam: S. Africa	69	34S	20E
Świnoujście: Poland	27	54N	14E
SWITZERLAND	33	—	—
Sydney: Austl.	61	34S	151E
Sydney: Canada	85	46N	60W
Sylhet: E. Pakistan	49	25N	92E
Syracuse: Sicily	30	37N	15E
Syracuse: U.S.A.	85	43N	76W
Syr Darya: *r.*, U.S.S.R.	45	43N	67E
SYRIA	46	35N	38E
Syzran': U.S.S.R.	44	53N	48E
Szczecin: Poland	27	53N	15E
Szczecinek: Poland	27	54N	17E
Szeged: Hungary	27	46N	20E
Szolnok: Hungary	31	47N	20E
Szombathely: Hungary	27	47N	17E

WORL

TABORA — UWAJIMA

	Page	Lat.	Long.
Tabora: Tanganyika	68	5S	33E
Tabriz: Iran	46	38N	46E
Tacna: Peru	88	18S	70W
Tacoma: U.S.A.	80	47N	123W
Taconic Range: U.S.A.	85	42N	74W
Tadoussac: Canada	85	48N	70W
Tadzhik S.S.R.: U.S.S.R.	45	38N	72E
Taegu: S. Korea	50	36N	127E
Taejon: S. Korea	50	37N	127E
Tafersit: Morocco	25	35N	4W
Tafilalet: Morocco	62	31N	4W
Taganrog: U.S.S.R.	44	47N	39E
Tagliamento: *r.*, Italy	33	46N	13E
Tagus: *r.*, Sp./Port.	25	40N	8W
Tahawus: U.S.A.	85	44N	74W
Taihape: N.Z.	53	40S	176E
Tainan: Formosa	50	23N	120E
Taipeh: Formosa	50	25N	122E
Taiping: Malaya	51	5N	101E
Taira: Japan	52	37N	141E
Taitao Penin: Chile	89	47S	75W
Tak: Thailand	51	17N	99E
Takada: Japan	52	37N	138E
Takamatsu: Japan	52	34N	134E
Takaoka: Japan	52	37N	137E
Takasaki: Japan	52	36N	139E
Take: *i.*, Japan	52	37N	132E
Takla Makan: *desert*, China	47	39N	80E
Takoradi: Gold Coast	68	5N	2W
Talara: Peru	86	5S	81W
Talaud Is.: Indonesia	51	4N	127E
Talavera: Spain	25	40N	5W
Talbot, C.: Australia	58	14S	127E
Tallahassee: U.S.A.	81	30N	84W
Tallin: U.S.S.R.	44	59N	25E
Taltal: Chile	88	25S	71W
Tamale: Gold Coast	68	9N	1W
Tamatave: Madagascar	71	18S	49E
Tambo: Austl.	60	25S	146E
Tambov: U.S.S.R.	44	53N	41E
Tammisaari: Finland	35	60N	23E
Tampa: U.S.A.	81	28N	83W
Tampere: Finland	34	61N	24E
Tampico: Mexico	82	22N	98W
Tamridah: Socotra	46	13N	54E
Tamtsak Bulak: Mongolia	43	47N	117E
Tamworth: Austl.	61	31S	151E
Tana: *& Fd.*, Norway	34	70N	28E
Tana, L.: Ethiopia	63	12N	37E
Tanana: Alaska	78	65N	152W
Tananarive: Madagascar	71	19S	47E
Tandil: Argentina	88	37S	59W
Tandou, L.: Austl.	61	33S	142E
Tanezrouft: Algeria	62	23N	0
Tanga: Tanganyika	68	5S	39E
TANGANYIKA: (*Brit. Trusteeship*)	68	—	—
Tanganyika, L.: Africa	68	8S	30E
TANGIER	25	36N	6W
Tanimbar Is.: Indonesia	51	7S	131E
Tanjore: India	48	11N	79E
Tannenberg: Poland	27	53N	20E
Tapajos: *r.*, Brazil	87	6S	57W
Tapti: *r.*, India	48	22N	75E
Tapuaenuku: *mtn.*, N.Z.	53	42S	174E
Tarakan: Borneo	51	3N	118E
Taranto: *& gulf*, Italy	30	40N	17E
Tarare: France	29	46N	4E
Tararua Range: N.Z.	53	41S	175E
Tarascon: France	29	44N	5E
Tarbes: France	29	43N	0
Tardenois: *hills*, France	28	49N	4E
Taree: Austl.	61	32S	152E
Târgu Jiu: Romania	31	45N	23E
Târgu Mureş: Romania	31	46N	25E
Tarija: Bolivia	88	22S	65W
Tarim: *r.*, China	45	41N	82E
Tarkhankut, C.: U.S.S.R.	31	46N	33E
Tarko-Sale: U.S.S.R.	43	65N	78E
Tarn: *r.*, France	29	44N	2E
Tarragona: Spain	25	41N	1E
Tarso Muri: *mtn.*, Libya	63	21N	19E
Tarsus: Turkey	46	37N	35E
Tartary, Gulf of: U.S.S.R.	43	50N	140E
Tartu: U.S.S.R.	35	58N	27E
Tarviso: Italy	33	46N	14E
Taschereau: Canada	85	49N	79W
Tashkent: U.S.S.R.	45	41N	69E
Tasman Bay: *& sea*, N.Z.	53	41S	173E
Tasman, Mt.: *& mtns.*, N.Z.	53	44S	170E
Tasmania: *i. & State*, Austl.	59	42S	146E
Tassili-n-Ajjer: *plat.*, Alg.	62	26N	8E
Tatar Pass: U.S.S.R.	27	48N	25E
Tatry: *mtns.*, Czech.	27	49N	20E
Tatung: China	50	40N	113E
Taumarunui: N.Z.	53	39S	175E
Taupo, L.: N.Z.	53	39S	176E
Tauranga: N.Z.	53	38S	176E
Taurus Mts.: Turkey	44	37N	35E
Tavda: *& r.*, U.S.S.R.	45	58N	65E
Taveta: Kenya	68	3S	38E
Tavira: Portugal	25	37N	8W
Tavoy: Burma	47	14N	98E
Tawitawi: *i.*, Phil.	51	5N	120E
Tayeh: China	50	30N	115E
Taymyr Penin.: U.S.S.R.	43	75N	105E
Tayshet: U.S.S.R.	43	56N	98E
Tbilisi (Tiflis): U.S.S.R.	44	42N	45E
Te Anau, L.: N.Z.	53	45S	168E
Te Awamatu: N.Z.	53	38S	175E
Tecuci: Romania	31	46N	27E
Tegucigalpa: Honduras	83	14N	87W
Tehran: Iran	46	35N	51E
Tehuantepec: *gulf & isthmus*, Mexico	82	16N	95W
Tekely: U.S.S.R.	45	45N	79E
Tekirdağ: Turkey	31	41N	27E
Tel Aviv: Israel	46	32N	35E
Tell Atlas: *mtns.*, Algeria	62	37N	7E
Tell el Kebir: Egypt	63	31N	32E
Tellina, Val: Italy	33	46N	10E
Teluk Betung: Sumatra	51	5S	105E
Temerin: Yugoslavia	31	45N	20E
Temir-Tau: U.S.S.R.	45	50N	73E
Temora: Austl.	61	34S	148E
Temuco: Chile	88	39S	73W
Tenda Pass: France/Italy	33	44N	7E
Tende: France	29	44N	8E
Tenerife: Canary Is.	62	28N	16W
Tengchung: China	50	25N	98E
Tengiz, L.: China	45	50N	69E
Tennant Creek: *town.*, Austl.	58	20S	134E
Tennessee: *r. & State*, U.S.A.	81	36N	87W
Tennessee Valley: U.S.A.	81	35N	86W
Tenterfield: Austl.	61	29S	152E
Teramo: Italy	30	43N	14E
Teresina: Brazil	87	5S	43W
Terme di Valdieri: Italy	33	44N	7E
Termez: U.S.S.R.	45	37N	67E
Termoli: Italy	30	42N	15E
Ternate: *i.*, Indonesia	51	1N	127E
Terneuzen: Netherlands	32	51N	4E
Terni: Italy	30	43N	13E
Ternopol': U.S.S.R	27	50N	26E
Terre Haute: U.S.A.	84	39N	87W
Terschelling: *i.*, Neth.	32	53N	5E
Teruel: Spain	25	40N	1W
Tete: Mozambique	69	16S	34E
Tetuán: Morocco	25	36N	5W
Teutoburger Wald: Germany	32	52N	8E
Texarkana: U.S.A.	81	33N	94W
Texas: *State*, U.S.A.	80	32N	100W
Texas City: U.S.A.	81	29N	95W
Texel: *i.*, Netherlands	32	53N	5E
Tezpur: India	49	27N	93E
Thabazimbi: S. Africa	69	25S	27E
THAILAND	51	15N	100E
Thal: W. Pak.	48	32N	72E
Thalwil: Switz.	33	47N	9E
Thames: N.Z.	53	37S	176E
Thar Desert: Ind./Pak.	48	27N	72E
Thasos: *i.*, Greece	31	41N	25E
Thebes: Egypt	63	26N	33E
The Hague *see* Hague			
Thermai: G. of: Greece	31	40N	23E
Thermia: *i.*, Greece	31	37N	24E
Thermopylae: Greece	31	39N	22E
The Sound: *str.*, Den./Swe.	35	56N	13E
Thessaloniki: Greece	31	41N	23E
Thessaly: *Division*, Greece	31	39N	22E
Thetford Mines: Canada	85	46N	71W
The Twins: *mtns.*, N.Z.	53	41S	172E
Thiérache: France	28	50N	4E
Thiers: France	29	46N	4E
Thionville: France	28	49N	6E
Thira: *i.*, Greece	31	36N	25E
Thomson's Falls: Kenya	68	0	36E
Thonon: France	29	46N	7E
Thore: *r.*, France	29	44N	2E
Thorhout: Belgium	28	51N	3E
Thouars: France	29	47N	0
Thousand Is.: Canada	85	44N	76W
Thrace: *Division*, Greece	31	41N	25E
Three Points, C.: G. Coast	68	5N	2W
Three Springs: Austl.	60	30S	116E
Thule: Greenland	79	76N	68W
Thun: *& l.*, Switz.	33	47N	8E
Thur: *r.*, Switz.	33	48N	9E
Thuringia: *Prov.*, Germany	32	51N	11E
Thursday I.: Austl.	59	11S	142E
Tiaret: Algeria	25	35N	1E
Tiber: *r.*, Italy	30	43N	12E
Tibesti: *highlands*, Fr. Eq. Afr.	63	20N	17E
Tibet: *Territ.*, China	47	—	—
Ticino: *r.*, Italy	33	46N	9E
Ticonderoga: U.S.A.	85	44N	73W
Tien Shan: *range*, China	47	42N	80E
Tientsin: China	50	39N	117E
Tierra del Fuego: *Territ.*, Argentina	89	54S	67W
Tiffin: U.S.A.	84	41N	83W
Tiflis *see* Tbilisi			
Tignes Reservoir: France	29	45N	7E
Tigris: *r.*, Turkey/Iraq	46	35N	44E
Tihwa: China	47	44N	88E
Tijuana: Mexico	80	32N	117W
Tiksi: U.S.S.R.	43	72N	129E
Tilburg: Netherlands	32	52N	5E
Tilos: *i.*, Greece	31	36N	27E
Tilsit: U.S.S.R.	27	55N	22E
Timaru: N.Z.	53	44S	171E
Timbuktu: Fr. W. Africa	62	17N	3W
Timiskaming, L.: Canada	85	47N	79W
Timiskaming Station: Canada	85	47N	79W
Timişoara: Romania	31	46N	21E
Timmins: Canada	84	48N	81W
Timor: *i. & sea*, S.E. Asia	51	10S	125E
Tintic: U.S.A.	80	40N	112W
Tirana (Tiranë): Albania	31	41N	20E
Tiraspol': U.S.S.R.	31	47N	30E
Tire: Turkey	31	38N	28E
Tirnovo: Bulgaria	31	43N	26E
Tiruchirappalli: India	48	11N	79E
Tirunelveli: India	48	9N	78E
Tista: *r.*, E. Pakistan	48	27N	89E
Tisza: *r.*, Europe	31	46N	20E
Titicaca, L.: Peru/Bolivia	88	16S	69W
Titograd: Yugoslavia	31	42N	19E
Titovo Užice: Yugoslavia	31	44N	20E
Titov Veles: Yugoslavia	31	42N	22E
Tivoli: Italy	30	42N	13E
Tlemcen: Algeria	25	35N	1W
Toango: Nigeria	68	8N	12E
Tobago: *i.*, W. Indies	83	11N	61W
Tobol': *r.*, U.S.S.R.	45	56N	66E
Tobol'sk: U.S.S.R.	45	58N	68E
Tobruk: Libya	67	32N	24E
Tocantins: *r.*, Brazil	87	3S	50W
Tocumwal: Austl.	61	36S	146E
Togoland: Africa	62	8N	1E
Tokaj: Hungary	27	48N	21E
Tokushima: Japan	52	34N	135E
Tokyo: Japan	52	36N	140E
Tolbukhin: Bulgaria	31	44N	28E
Toledo: *& mtns.*, Spain	25	40N	4W
Toledo: U.S.A.	84	42N	84W
Tolosa: Spain	25	43N	2W
Tolstoy, C.: U.S.S.R.	43	59N	155E
Tomakomai: Japan	52	43N	142E
Tomatlán: Mexico	82	20N	105W
Tomini, G. of: Indon.	51	0	121E
Tomsk: U.S.S.R.	45	56N	85E
Tonga Is.: Pac. O.	54	20S	175W
Tonkin, G. of: Viet Nam	50	20N	107E
Tonle L.: Cambodia	51	13N	104E
Tønsberg: Norway	35	59N	11E
Toowoomba: Austl.	60	28S	152E
Topeka: U.S.A.	81	39N	96W
Topozero: *l.*, U.S.S.R.	34	66N	32E
Torgau: Germany	32	52N	13E
Torino: Italy	33	45N	8E
Torne: *l. & r.*, Swed./Fin.	34	68N	19E
Tornio: Finland	34	66N	24E
Toronto: Canada	85	44N	79W
Tororo: Uganda	68	1N	34E
Torrens, L.: Austl.	58	31S	137E
Torreón: Mexico	82	26N	103W
Torres Strait: Austl.	59	10S	142E
Torres Vedras: Portugal	25	39N	9W
Tortona: Italy	33	45N	9E
Tortosa: *& cape*, Spain	25	41N	1E
Toruń: Poland	35	53N	19E
Tosa Bay: Japan	52	33N	134E
Totomi Gulf: Japan	52	34N	138E
Tottori: Japan	52	35N	134E
Touggourt: Algeria	62	33N	6E
Toul: France	28	49N	6E
Toulon: France	29	43N	6E
Toulouse: France	29	44N	1E
Toungoo: Burma	47	19N	96E
Touraine: *Old Prov.*, Fr.	29	47N	1E
Tourane: Viet Nam	51	16N	108E
Tourcoing: France	28	51N	3E
Tournai: Belgium	28	51N	3E
Tours: France	29	47N	1E
Townshend I.: Austl.	60	22S	151E
Townsville: Austl.	60	19S	147E
Toyama: Japan	52	37N	137E
Toyohashi: Japan	52	35N	137E
Trabzon: Turkey	46	41N	40E
Trafalgar, C.: Spain	25	36N	6W
Tranås: Sweden	35	58N	15E
Transvaal: *Prov.*, Union of South Africa	69	25S	29E
Transylvania: *Prov.*, Rom.	31	46N	24E
Transylvanian Alps: Rom.	31	45N	24E
Trapani: Sicily	30	38N	12E
Trasimeno, L.: Italy	30	43N	12E
Traunstein: Germany	33	48N	13E
Travancore: *State*, India	48	9N	77E
Traveller's L.: Austl.	61	33S	142E
Traverse City: U.S.A.	84	45N	86W
Trelleborg: Sweden	35	55N	13E
Trentino: *Reg.*, Italy	33	46N	11E
Trento: Italy	33	46N	11E
Trenton: Canada	85	44N	78W
Trenton: U.S.A.	85	40N	75W
Trepca: Yugoslavia	31	43N	21E
Trèves (Trier): Germany	32	50N	7E
Treviso: Italy	33	46N	12E
Trieste: Italy	30	46N	14E
Trikkala: Greece	31	40N	22E
Trincomalee: Ceylon	48	8N	81E
Trinidad: *i.*, W. Indies	83	10N	61W
Tripoli: Lebanon	46	35N	36E
Tripoli: Libya	63	33N	13E
Tripolis: Greece	31	38N	22E
Tristan da Cunha: *i.*, Atl. O.	24	38S	12W
Trivandrum: Ind.	48	8N	77E
Trois Rivières: Canada	85	46N	73W
Trollhättan: Sweden	35	58N	12E
Tromsø: Norway	34	70N	19E
Trondheim: *& fd.*, Norway	34	63N	11E
Trout Lake: Canada	78	61N	122W
Troy: Turkey	31	40N	26E
Troyes: France	28	48N	4E
TRUCIAL 'OMAN	46	24N	55E
Trujillo: Honduras	83	16N	86W
Trujillo: Peru	86	8S	79W
Truro: Canada	85	45N	63W
Truth or Consequences: U.S.A.	80	33N	107W
Tsaidam Swamps: China	50	37N	95E
Tsangpo: *r.*, China	47	29N	94E
Tsetserlig: Mongolia	50	47N	102E
Tsimlyansk Res.: U.S.S.R.	44	48N	43E
Tsinan: China	50	37N	117E
Tsing Hai: *l.*, China	50	37N	100E
Tsingtao: China	50	36N	120E
Tsinling Shan: China	50	34N	108E
Tsitsihar: China	50	47N	124E
Tsu: Japan	52	35N	136E
Tsugaru Channel: Japan	52	41N	140E
Tsumeb: S.W. Africa	69	19S	18E
Tsuruga: Japan	52	36N	136E
Tsuyama: Japan	52	35N	134E
Tsyurupinsk: U.S.S R	31	47N	33E
Tuapse: U.S.S.R.	44	44N	39E
Tuatapere: N.Z.	53	46S	168E
Tübingen: Germany	33	49N	9E
Tucson: U.S.A.	80	32N	111W
Tucumán: Argentina	88	27S	65W
Tucupita: Venez.	83	9N	62W
Tudela: Spain	25	42N	2W
Tula: U.S.S.R.	44	54N	37E
Tulare: U.S.A.	80	36N	119W
Tul'chin: U.S.S.R.	31	49N	29E
Tulle: France	29	45N	2E
Tulsa: U.S.A.	81	36N	96W
Tumaco: Colombia	86	2N	79W
Tumkur: India	48	13N	77E
Tungabhadra: *r.*, India	48	16N	76E
Tunghwa: China	50	42N	126E
Tung Ting, L.: China	50	29N	112E
Tunis: *& gulf*, Tunisia	30	37N	10E
TUNISIA	62	37N	10E
Tunja: Colombia	86	5N	73W
Turanian Plain: U.S.S.R.	45	43N	60E
Turbat: W. Pakistan	46	26N	63E
Turda: Romania	31	47N	24E
Turfan: China	50	43N	89E
Turgay: U.S.S.R.	45	50N	64E
Turgutlu: Turkey	31	39N	28E
Turin: Italy	33	45N	8E
Turkestan: U.S.S.R.	45	43N	68E
TURKEY	46	—	—
Turkmen S.S.R.: U.S.S.R.	45	39N	60E
Turku: Finland	35	60N	22E
Turner Valley: *settlement*, Canada	80	50N	114W
Turnhout: Belgium	28	51N	5E
Turnu Măgurele: Romania	31	44N	25E
Turnu Severin: Romania	31	45N	23E
Tuscany: *Reg.*, Italy	30	44N	11E
Tuttlingen: Germany	33	48N	9E
Tuxpan: Mexico	82	21N	97W
Tuyün: China	50	26N	107E
Tuz, L.: Turkey	44	38N	33E
Two Harbors: U.S.A.	84	47N	92W
Tygda: U.S.S.R.	43	53N	126E
Tyrol: *Prov.*, Austria	33	47N	11E
Tyrrhenian Sea	30	—	—
Tyumen': U.S.S.R.	45	57N	65E
Ube: Japan	52	34N	131E
Uberaba: Brazil	88	20S	48W
Ubon: Thailand	51	15N	105E
Ubsa Nor: *l.*, Mongolia	50	50N	93E
Ucayali: *r.*, Peru	86	7S	75W
Uchiura Bay: Japan	52	42N	140E
Udaipur: India	48	25N	74E
Uddevalla: Sweden	35	58N	12E
Udd L.: Sweden	34	66N	18E
Udine: Italy	33	46N	13E
Udon Thani: Thailand	51	18N	103E
Uele: *r.*, Belg. Congo	71	6S	25E
Ufa: *& r.*, U.S.S.R.	44	55N	56E
UGANDA	68	—	—
Uji-Yamada: Japan	52	34N	137E
Ujiji: Tanganyika	68	5S	30E
Ujjain: India	48	23N	76E
Ukhta: U.S.S.R.	44	63N	54E
Ukrainian S.S.R.: U.S.S.R.	42	50N	30E
Ulan Bator: Mongolia	43	47N	107E
Ulangom: Mongolia	43	50N	92E
Ulanhoto: China	43	46N	122E
Ulan Ude: Mongolia	43	52N	107E
Ulawa: *i.*, Solomon Is.	59	10S	162E
Uleåborg: Finland	34	65N	25E
Ulm: Germany	33	48N	10E
Ulundi: S. Afr.	69	28S	32E
Ulu-Tau: *range*, U.S.S.R.	45	49N	67E
Ul'yanovsk: U.S.S.R.	44	54N	48E
Ulyungur Nor: *l.*, China	47	47N	87E
Ülzen: Germany	32	53N	10E
Umarkot: W. Pakistan	48	25N	70E
Umeå: Sweden	34	64N	20E
Umtali: S. Rhodesia	69	19S	33E
Ungava Bay: *& penin.*, Can.	79	60N	67W
Uniondale: S. Africa	69	34S	23E
UNION OF SOUTH AFRICA	70/1	—	—
UNION OF SOVIET SOCIALIST REPUBLICS	42/3	—	—
Uniontown: U.S.A.	84	40N	80W
UNITED STATES OF AMERICA	80/1	—	—
United States Range: Can.	79	82N	75W
Upper Volta: Fr. W. Afr.	68	12N	0
Uppsala: Sweden	35	60N	18E
Ural: *r.*, U.S.S.R.	44	52N	53E
Ural Mts.: U.S.S.R.	45	55N	58E
Ural'sk: U.S.S.R.	44	51N	51E
Urawa: Japan	52	36N	140E
Urbana: U.S.A.	84	40N	88W
Urdos: France	29	43N	1W
Urfa: Turkey	46	37N	39E
Urga: Mongolia	43	47N	107E
Urisino: Austl.	61	30S	144E
Úrkút: Hungary	27	47N	17E
Urmia, L.: Iran	46	37N	46E
Uruguaiana: Brazil	88	30S	57W
URUGUAY	88	—	—
Uruguay: *r.*, S. Am.	88	28S	56W
Urumchi: China	47	44N	88E
Uşak: Turkey	31	39N	30E
Ushant: France	28	48N	5W
Ushuaia: Argentina	89	55S	68W
Üsküdar: Turkey	31	41N	29E
Usol'ye: U.S.S.R.	43	53N	103E
Uspallata Pass: Chile/Arg.	88	33S	70W
Uspenskiy: U.S.S.R.	45	49N	73E
Ústí nad Labem: Czech.	32	51N	14E
Ust'-Kamenogorsk: U.S.S.R.	45	50N	83E
Ust'-Kut: U.S.S.R.	43	57N	105E
Ust'-Urt Plateau: U.S.S.R.	44	44N	57E
Usuki: Japan	52	33N	132E
Usumbura: Ruanda Urundi	68	3S	29E
Utah: *State*, U.S.A.	80	39N	112W
Utica: U.S.A.	85	43N	75W
Utrecht: Neth.	32	52N	5E
Utsunomiya: Japan	52	37N	140E
Uttaradit: Thailand	51	18N	100E
Uwajima: Japan	52	33N	132E

WORLD

UXMAL — ZYRYANOVSK

	Page	Lat.	Long.
Uxmal: Mexico	82	20N	90W
Uyuni: Bolivia	88	21S	67W
Uzbek S.S.R.: U.S.S.R.	42	41N	62E
Uzhgorod: U.S.S.R.	27	49N	22E
Vaal: *r.*, S. Africa	69	27S	28E
Vaasa: Finland	34	63N	22E
Vaccarès, Étang de: Fr.	29	44N	5E
Vaduz: Liechtenstein	33	47N	9E
Vahsel Bay: Antarctica	91	78S	35W
Valday Hills: U.S.S.R.	44	57N	33E
Valdepeñas: Spain	25	39N	3W
Valdés Penin: Arg.	89	43S	64W
Valdez: Alaska	78	61N	146W
Valdivia: Chile	88	40S	74W
Valence: France	29	45N	5E
Valencia: *& Old Prov.*, Sp.	25	39N	0
Valencia: Venezuela	86	10N	68W
Valenciennes: France	28	50N	4E
Valladolid: Spain	25	42N	5W
Vallecas: Spain	25	40N	4W
Valletta: Malta	30	36N	14E
Valleyfield: Canada	85	45N	74W
Valona: Albania	31	40N	20E
Valparaiso: Chile	88	33S	72W
Valsch, C.: New Guinea	58	8S	137E
Van, L.: Turkey	46	39N	43E
Vancouver: *& i.*, Canada	80	49N	123W
Vancouver: U.S.A.	80	46N	123W
Vancouver, Mt.: Alaska/Can.	78	60N	140W
Väner, L.: Sweden	35	59N	13E
Vänersborg: Sweden	35	58N	12E
Vannes: France	28	48N	3W
Vannøy: *i.*, Norway	34	70N	20E
Vansbro: Sweden	35	60N	14E
Varanger Penin.: *& fd.*, Nor.	34	71N	29E
Varaždin: Yugoslavia	30	46N	16E
Vardar: *r.*, Yugo./Greece	31	41N	22E
Vardø: Norway	34	70N	31E
Varese: Italy	33	46N	9E
Värnamo: Sweden	35	57N	14E
Vaslui: Romania	31	47N	28E
Västerås: Sweden	35	60N	17E
Västervik: Sweden	35	58N	17E
Vatnajökull: Iceland	34	64N	17W
Vätter, L.: Sweden	35	58N	14E
Vaupés: *r.*, Colombia	86	1N	72W
Växjö: Sweden	35	57N	15E
Vaygach I.: U.S.S.R.	42	70N	59E
Veendam: Neth.	32	53N	7E
Vega: *& i.*, Norway	34	66N	12E
Velikiye Luki: U.S.S.R.	44	56N	30E
Vellore: India	48	13N	79E
Velmandois: France	28	50N	3E
Velp: Neth.	32	52N	6E
Venado Tuerto: Arg.	88	34S	62W
Vendée: France	29	47N	1W
Vendôme: France	28	48N	1E
Venetian Alps: Italy	33	46N	13E
Venezia: *& Reg.*, Italy	33	46N	12E
VENEZUELA	86	—	—
Venezuela, Gulf of	86	11N	71W
Venice: *& gulf*, Italy	33	45N	12E
Venlo: Neth.	32	51N	6E
Venosta, Val: Italy	33	47N	11E
Ventimiglia: Italy	33	44N	8E
Ventspils: U.S.S.R.	44	57N	22E
Veracruz: Mexico	82	19N	96W
Vercelli: Italy	33	45N	8E
Verde: C.: Fr. W. Africa	62	15N	17W
Verdon: *r.*, France	29	44N	6E
Verdun: France	28	49N	5E
Verkhoyansk Range: U.S.S.R.	43	65N	130E
Vermilion: Canada	80	53N	110W
Vermilion L.: U.S.A.	84	48N	92W
Vermont: *State*, U.S.A.	85	44N	73W
Verona: Italy	33	45N	11E
Versailles: France	28	49N	2E
Verviers: Belgium	28	51N	6E
Vesle: *r.*, France	28	49N	4E
Vesoul: France	29	48N	6E
Vesterålen: *i.*, Norway	34	69N	15E
Vest Fiord: Norway	34	68N	15E
Vesuvius: *volc.*, Italy	30	41N	15E
Veszprém: Hungary	27	47N	18E
Vevey: Switz.	33	46N	7E
Viareggio: Italy	33	44N	10E
Viborg: Denmark	35	56N	9E
Vicenza: Italy	33	46N	12E
Vichy: France	29	46N	3E
Vicksburg: U.S.A.	81	32N	91W
Victoria: Canada	80	48N	123W
Victoria *r.*, Austl.	58	16S	130E
Victoria: *State*, Austl.	59	37S	145E
Victoria Falls: Rhodesia	69	18S	26E
Victoria I.: Canada	78	70N	110W
Victoria, L.: Africa	68	1S	33E
Victoriaville: Canada	85	46N	72W
Victoria West: S. Africa	69	31S	23E
Vidin: Bulgaria	31	44N	23E
Viella: Spain	29	43N	1E
Vienna: Austria	27	48N	16E
Vienne: France	29	46N	5E
Vienne: *r.*, France	29	47N	1E
Vientiane: Laos	51	18N	103E
Vierzon-Ville: France	29	47N	2E
VIET MINH: Indo China	50	21N	105E
VIET NAM: Indo China	51	12N	108E
Vigevano: Italy	33	45N	9E
Vigo: Spain	25	42N	9W
Vijayawada: India	48	16N	81E
Vikna: *i.*, Norway	34	65N	11E
Vilaine: *r.*, France	28	48N	2W
Villach: Austria	33	47N	14E
Villa Cisneros: Sp. Sahara	62	24N	16W
Villefranche-sur-Saône: Fr.	29	46N	5E
Villeneuve-sur-Lot: Fr.	29	44N	1E
Villeurbanne: France	29	46N	5E

	Page	Lat.	Long.
Vil'nyus: U.S.S.R.	44	55N	25E
Viña del Mar: Chile	88	33S	72W
Vincennes: U.S.A.	84	39N	87W
Vindel: *r.*, Sweden	34	65N	18E
Vindhya Range: India	48	23N	77E
Vinh: Viet Minh	51	19N	106E
Vinnitsa: U.S.S.R.	44	49N	28E
Vire: France	28	49N	1W
Virginia: *State*, U.S.A.	81	37N	78W
Virgin Is.: W. Indies	83	19N	64W
Visakhapatnam: India	49	18N	83E
Visby: Sweden	35	58N	18E
Viscount Melville Sd.: Can.	78	73N	110W
Viseu: Portugal	25	41N	8W
Vistula: *r.*, Poland	27	53N	21E
Vitebsk: U.S.S.R.	44	55N	30E
Vitim: U.S.S.R.	43	60N	113E
Vitória: Brazil	88	20S	40W
Vitoria: Spain	25	43N	3W
Vitry-en-Artois: France	28	50N	3E
Vitry-le-François: France	28	49N	5E
Vittoria Veneto: Italy	33	46N	12E
Vizianagaram: India	49	18N	83E
Vladimir: U.S.S.R.	44	56N	40E
Vladimir-Volinskiy: U.S.S.R.	27	51N	24E
Vladivostok: U.S.S.R.	43	43N	132E
Vlissingen *see* Flushing			
Vlonë: Albania	31	40N	20E
Vltava: *r.*, Czech.	32	50N	14E
Voiron: France	29	45N	6E
Volga: *r.*, U.S.S.R.	44	49N	45E
Vologda: U.S.S.R.	44	59N	40E
Volos: Greece	31	39N	23E
Vol'sk: U.S.S.R.	44	52N	47E
Volta, Black: *r.*, W. Africa	62	10N	3W
Volta, White: *r.*, W. Africa	62	12N	4W
Volta Redonda: Brazil	88	23S	44W
Vorarlberg: *Prov.*, Austr.	33	47N	10E
Vorkuta: U.S.S.R.	42	67N	64E
Voronezh: U.S.S.R.	44	52N	39E
Voroshilov: U.S.S.R.	43	44N	132E
Voroshilovgrad: U.S.S.R.	44	48N	40E
Vosges: *mtns.*, France	28	48N	7E
Voss: Norway	34	61N	6E
Voznesensk: U.S.S.R.	31	48N	31E
Vranje: Yugoslavia	31	43N	22E
Vratsa: Bulgaria	31	43N	24E
Vryburg: S. Africa	71	27S	25E
Vulcano: *i.*, Italy	30	38N	15E
Vyaz'ma: U.S.S.R.	44	55N	34E
Vyborg: U.S.S.R.	44	61N	29E
Vyshniy Volochek: U.S.S.R.	44	58N	35E
Waal: *r.*, Neth.	32	52N	5E
Wabana: Newfoundland	79	48N	53W
Wabash: *r.*, U.S.A.	84	40N	87W
Waco: U.S.A.	80	32N	97W
Wadden Zee: Neth.	26	53N	5E
Wadi Halfa: Sudan	63	22N	31E
Wad Medani: Sudan	63	14N	34E
Wagga Wagga: Austl.	61	35S	147E
Wagin: Austl.	60	33S	117E
Waiau: *& r.*, N.Z.	53	43S	173E
Waigeo: *i.*, Neth. New Guin.	51	0	131E
Waikerie: Austl.	61	34S	140E
Waingapu: Indon.	51	10S	120E
Waiotapu: N.Z.	53	38S	176E
Waipara: N.Z.	53	43S	173E
Waipawa: N.Z.	53	40S	177E
Wairau: *r.*, N.Z.	53	42S	173E
Wairoa: N.Z.	53	39S	177E
Waitaki: *r.*, N.Z.	53	45S	171E
Waitangi: N.Z.	53	35S	174E
Wakamatsu: Japan	52	38N	140E
Wakasa Bay: Japan	52	36N	136E
Wakatipu, L.: N.Z.	53	45S	168E
Wakayama: Japan	52	34N	135E
Wake I.: Pacific Ocean	54	20N	167E
Wakkanai: Japan	50	45N	142E
Walcheren: *i.*, Neth.	32	51N	4E
Walgett: Austl.	61	30S	148E
Wallachia: *Old Reg.*, Rom.	27	44N	25E
Wallaroo: Austl.	61	34S	138E
Wallis Is.: Pacific Ocean	54	13S	176W
Walvis Bay: S.W. Africa	69	23S	14E
Wanaaring: Austl.	61	30S	144E
Wanaka, L.: N.Z.	53	44S	169E
Wanapitei L.: Canada	84	47N	81W
Wandiwash: India	48	13N	79E
Wanganui: *& r.*, N.Z.	53	40S	175E
Wangaratta: Austl.	61	36S	146E
Wangeroog: *i.*, Germany	32	54N	8E
Wanhsien: China	50	31N	109E
Wankie: S. Rhodesia	69	18S	26E
Warangal: India	48	18N	80E
Warburg: Germany	32	51N	9E
Warmbad: S.W. Africa	69	28S	19E
Warracknabeal: Austl.	61	36S	142E
Warragul: Austl.	61	38S	146E
Warrego: *r.*, Austl.	60	28S	146E
Warren: Idaho, U.S.A.	80	45N	116W
Warren: Ohio, U.S.A.	84	41N	81W
Warren: Pa., U.S.A.	85	42N	79W
Warrnambool: Austl.	61	38S	143E
Warsaw (Warszawa): Poland	27	52N	21E
Warwick: Austl.	60	28S	152E
Wasatch Range: U.S.A.	82	41N	111W
Washington: *State*, U.S.A.	80	47N	120W
Washington D.C.: U.S.A.	85	38N	77W
Washington, Mt.: U.S.A.	85	44N	71W
Waterbury: U.S.A.	85	42N	73W
Waterloo: Belgium	28	51N	4E
Waterloo: U.S.A.	84	42N	92W
Watertown: U.S.A.	85	44N	76W
Watling: *i.*, Bahama Is.	83	24N	75W
Watson Lake: *town*, Canada	78	60N	129W
Waukegan: U.S.A.	84	42N	88W
Waukesha: U.S.A.	84	43N	88W

	Page	Lat.	Long.
Wausau: U.S.A.	84	45N	90W
Wauwatosa: U.S.A.	84	43N	88W
Waynesboro: U.S.A.	85	38N	79W
Webster Groves: U.S.A.	84	38N	90W
Weddell Sea: Antarctica	91	70S	40W
Weiden: Germany	32	50N	12E
Weihaiwei: China	50	38N	122E
Weimar: Germany	32	51N	11E
Weisshorn: *mtn.*, Switz.	33	46N	8E
Wellesley Is.: Austl.	58	17S	139E
Wellington: Austl.	61	33S	149E
Wellington: N.Z.	53	41S	175E
Wenchi: Gold Coast	68	7N	1W
Wenchow: China	50	28N	120E
Wernigerode: Germany	32	52N	11E
Weser: *r.*, Germany	32	53N	9E
Wesergebirge: *mtns.*, Ger.	32	52N	9E
West Dvina: *r.*, U.S.S.R.	44	56N	28E
Western Australia	58	—	—
Western Ghats: *range*, India	48	—	—
Western Sayan Mts.: U.S.S.R.	45	52N	91E
Western Sierra Madre: Mex.	82	25N	105W
Westerwald: Germany	32	51N	8E
West Indies	83	20N	70W
West Nicholson: S. Rhod.	69	21S	30E
Weston: N. Borneo	51	5S	116E
Westphalia: *Old Prov.*, Ger.	32	52N	7E
West Point: *city*, U.S.A.	85	41N	74W
Westport: N.Z.	53	42S	172E
West Rift Valley: Afr.	68	3S	30E
West Siberian Plain: U.S.S.R.	45	—	—
West Virginia: *State*, U.S.A.	81	39N	80W
Wetzlar: Germany	32	51N	8E
Whakatane: N.Z.	53	38S	177E
Whangarei: N.Z.	53	36S	174E
Wheeling: U.S.A.	84	40N	80W
Whitehorse: Canada	78	61N	135W
White Mts.: U.S.A.	85	44N	71W
White Nile: *r.*, Sudan	67	7N	32E
White Sea: U.S.S.R.	42	65N	37E
White Volta: *r.*, Fr. W. Afr.	62	12N	2W
Whitfield: Austl.	61	37S	146E
Whitsunday I.: Austl.	60	20S	149E
Whyalla: Austl.	61	33S	138E
Wichita: U.S.A.	80	38N	97W
Wichita Falls: *city*, U.S.A.	80	34N	98W
Wien: Austria	27	48N	16E
Wiesbaden: Germany	32	50N	8E
Wilcannia: Austl.	61	32S	143E
Wilhelmshaven: Germany	32	54N	8E
Wilkes-Barre: U.S.A.	85	41N	76W
Williamsburg: U.S.A.	85	37N	77W
Williamsport: U.S.A.	85	41N	77W
Williston: U.S.A.	80	48N	104W
Willoughby, C.: Austl.	61	36S	138E
Willow Run: U.S.A.	84	42N	84W
Wilmington: Del., U.S.A.	85	40N	75W
Wilmington: N.C., U.S.A.	81	34N	78W
Wilson Dam: U.S.A.	81	35N	87W
Wiluna: Austl.	58	27S	120E
Winchester: U.S.A.	85	39N	78W
Windhoek: S.W. Africa	69	22S	17E
Windsor: N. Sc., Canada	85	45N	64W
Windsor: Ont., Canada	84	42N	83W
Windward Is.: W. Indies	83	13N	62W
Winnibigoshish L.: U.S.A.	84	47N	94W
Winnipeg: Canada	80	50N	97W
Winnipeg, L.: Canada	80	53N	97W
Winnipegosis: *& l.*, Canada	80	52N	100W
Winona: U.S.A.	84	44N	92W
Winston-Salem: U.S.A.	84	36N	80W
Winterthur: Switz.	33	47N	9E
Winton: Austl.	59	22S	143E
Wisconsin: *State*, U.S.A.	81	44N	90W
Wisconsin: *r.*, U.S.A.	84	44N	90W
Wismar: Germany	32	54N	11E
Witbank: S. Africa	69	26S	29E
Witdraai: S. Africa	69	27S	21E
Wittenberge: Germany	32	53N	12E
Włocławek: Poland	27	52N	19E
Wolfenbüttel: Germany	32	52N	11E
Wolfsburg: Germany	32	52N	11E
Wollaston L.: Canada	78	58N	103W
Wollongong: Austl.	61	34S	151E
Wonthaggi: Austl.	61	39S	146E
Woods, Lake of the: Can./U.S.A.	81	49N	94W
Woodville: N.Z.	53	40S	176E
Woomera: Austl.	58	31S	137E
Woonsocket: U.S.A.	85	42N	71W
Worcester: U.S.A.	85	42N	72W
Worcester: S. Africa	69	34S	20E
Worms: Germany	32	50N	8E
Wrangel I.: E. Siberian Sea	43	72N	180°
Wrocław: Poland	35	51N	17E
Wuchang: China	50	30N	115E
Wuhu: China	50	31N	118E
Wuppertal: Germany	32	51N	7E
Würzburg: Germany	32	50N	10E
Wuyi Shan: *mtns.*, China	50	27N	117E
Wyalong: Austl.	61	34S	147E
Wyangala Res.: Austl.	61	34S	149E
Wyndham: Austl.	58	15S	128E
Wyoming: *State*, U.S.A.	80	43N	107W
Xanthi: Greece	31	41N	25E
Xauen: Morocco	25	35N	5W
Xingu: *r.*, Brazil	87	8S	53W
Yaan: China	50	30N	103E
Yabassi: Fr. Eq. Afr.	68	5N	10E
Yakima: U.S.A.	80	46N	120W
Yakutsk: U.S.S.R.	43	62N	130E
Yallourn: Austl.	61	38S	146E
Yalta: U.S.S.R.	44	45N	34E
Yamagata: Japan	52	38N	140E
Yamaguchi: Japan	52	34N	131E

	Page	Lat.	Long.
Yamal Peninsula: U.S.S.R.	42	70N	70E
Yamatu: China	45	46N	84E
Yambol: Bulgaria	31	42N	26E
Yampi Sound: Austl.	58	16S	123E
Yanbu: Sa'udi Arabia	46	24N	38E
Yangku: China	50	38N	113E
Yangtze (Dre): *r.*, China	50	34N	94E
Yangtze (Kinsha): *r.*, China	50	32N	98E
Yannina: Greece	31	40N	21E
Yantabulla: Austl.	61	29S	145E
Yaoundé: Fr. Eq. Africa	68	4N	11E
Yap: *i.*, Pacific Ocean	54	10N	138E
Yaqui: *r.*, Mexico	80	29N	110W
Yaraka: Austl.	59	25S	144E
Yarkand: *& r.*, China	45	38N	77E
Yarmouth: Canada	85	44N	66W
Yaroslavl': U.S.S.R.	44	58N	40E
Yass: Austl.	61	35S	149E
Yatsushiro Bay: Japan	52	32N	130E
Yawata: Japan	52	34N	131E
Yawatahama: Japan	52	33N	132E
Yellowhead Pass: Canada	80	53N	118W
Yellowknife: Canada	78	62N	115W
Yellow Sea: China	50	35N	124E
Yellowstone: *r.*, U.S.A.	80	47N	107W
YEMEN	46	15N	44E
Yenakiyevo: U.S.S.R.	44	48N	38E
Yenangyaung: Burma	47	20N	95E
Yenisey: *r.*, U.S.S.R.	43	63N	90E
Yenisey, G. of: U.S.S.R.	43	72N	83E
Yeniseysk: U.S.S.R.	45	58N	92E
Yenki: China	52	43N	129E
Yerevan: U.S.S.R.	44	40N	44E
Yevpatoriya: U.S.S.R.	31	45N	33E
Yezd: Iran	46	32N	54E
Yingkow: China	50	40N	122E
Yin Shan: China	50	42N	108E
Yokkaichi: Japan	52	35N	136E
Yokohama: Japan	52	35N	140E
Yokosuka: Japan	52	35N	140E
Yokote: Japan	52	39N	141E
Yola: Nigeria	68	9N	13E
Yonezawa: Japan	52	38N	140E
Yongdok: S. Korea	52	36N	129E
Yonkers: U.S.A.	85	41N	74W
Yonne: *r.*, France	28	48N	3E
York: U.S.A.	85	40N	77W
York: *cape & penin.*, Austl.	59	15S	143E
Yorke Penin: Austl.	61	35S	138E
Yorkton: Canada	80	51N	102W
Yorktown: U.S.A.	85	37N	76W
Yoshkar-Ola: U.S.S.R.	44	57N	48E
Young: Austl.	61	34S	148E
Youngstown: U.S.A.	84	41N	81W
Ypres: Belgium	28	51N	3E
Yuan: *r.*, China	50	29N	110E
Yuan (Red): *r.*, China/Viet Minh	50	23N	102E
Yubari: Japan	52	43N	142E
Yucatan: Mexico	82	20N	88W
YUGOSLAVIA	30/31	—	
Yukagir Plateau: U.S.S.R.	43	66N	157E
Yukon: *r.*, Can./Alaska	78	63N	159W
Yukon: *Territ.*, Canada	78	62N	135W
Yuma: U.S.A.	80	33N	115W
Yungning: China	50	23N	108E
Yunkwei Plateau: China	50	27N	106E
Yunnan: China	50	25N	103E
Yverdon: Switz.	33	47N	7E
Zabrze: Poland	27	50N	19E
Zabul: Iran	46	31N	62E
Zacatecas: Mexico	82	23N	103W
Zadar: Yugoslavia	30	44N	15E
Zagreb: Yugoslavia	30	46N	16E
Zahidan: Iran	46	29N	61E
Zakinthos: *i.*, Greece	31	38N	21E
Zama: Tunisia	30	36N	9E
Zambezi: *r.*, S. Africa	69	16S	31E
Zamora: Spain	25	41N	6W
Zamość: Poland	27	51N	23E
Zanesville: U.S.A.	84	40N	82W
Zante: *i.*, Greece	31	38N	21E
Zanthus: Austl.	58	31S	123E
Zanzibar: *& Prot.*, E. Afr.	68	6S	39E
Zaporozh'ye: U.S.S.R.	44	48N	35E
Zaragoza: Spain	25	42N	1W
Zaria: Nigeria	68	11N	8E
Zaysan, L.: U.S.S.R.	45	48N	84E
Zealand: *i.*, Denmark	35	56N	12E
Zeebrugge: Belgium	28	51N	3E
Zeila: Br. Som.	46	11N	43E
Zeitz: Germany	32	51N	12E
Zelenyy: *i.*, U.S.S.R.	53	43N	146E
Zella-Mehlis: Germany	32	51N	11E
Zermatt: Switz.	33	46N	8E
Zeya: U.S.S.R.	43	54N	127E
Zezere: *r.*, Portugal	25	40N	8W
Zhdanov: U.S.S.R.	44	47N	37E
Zhitomir: U.S.S.R.	44	50N	29E
Zielona Góra: Poland	27	52N	16E
Zimbabwe: S. Rhod.	69	20S	32E
Zinder: Fr. W. Afr.	68	14N	9E
Zittau: Germany	32	51N	15E
Zlatograd: Bulgaria	31	41N	25E
Zlatoust: U.S.S.R.	45	55N	60E
Znojmo: Czech.	27	49N	16E
Zomba: Nyasa.	69	15S	35E
Zongo: Belg. Congo	70	4N	18E
Zonguldak: Turkey	31	41N	32E
Zrenjanin: Yugoslavia	31	45N	20E
Zug: Switz.	33	47N	9E
Zugspitz: *mtn.*, Ger./Austr.	33	47N	11E
Zuider Zee: Neth.	32	53N	5E
Zürich: *& l.*, Switz.	33	47N	9E
Zwickau: Germany	32	51N	12E
Zwolle: Neth.	32	53N	6E
Zyryanovsk: U.S.S.R.	45	50N	84E

GAZETTEER OF GREAT BRITAIN & IRELAND

Names in italics are not shown on maps 6—19, but their precise positions can be found from the four-figure Grid references. Notes on the use of the Grid are at the end of this gazetteer.

Abberton: Essex TM 0019
Abbey Cwmhir: Rad. SO 0571
Abbey Dore: Here. SO 3830
Abbeyfeale: Lim. **19 C3**
Abbey Hd.: Kirkc. **15 NX74**
Abbey St. Bathans: Ber. NT 7762
Abbey Town: Cumb. NY 1750
Abbots' Bromley: Staffs SK 0824
Abbotsbury: Dorset **9 SY58**
Abbotsford: Rox. **15 NT53**
Abbotsley: Hunts TL 2256
Aber: Caer. SH 6572
Aberader: Inv. NN 5489
Aberaman: Glam. SO 0101
Aberayron: Card. **10 SN46**
Abercarn: Mon. **10 ST29**
Aberchirder: Banff **17 NJ65**
Abercorn: W. Loth. NT 0878
Aberdalgie: Perth. NO 0720
Aberdare: Glam. **10 SO00**
Aberdaron: Caer. **10 SH12**
ABERDEEN: *Co.*, Scot. **17 NJ90**
Aberdour: Fife NT 1885
Aberdovey: Card. **10 SN69**
Aberdulais: Glam. SS 7799
Aberedw: Rad. SO 0747
Aber-fan: Glam. SO 0600
Aberfeldy: Perth. **17 NN84**
Aberffraw: Anglesey SH 3568
Aberford: Yorks SE 4336
Aberfoyle: Perth. NN 5200
Abergavenny: Mon. **10 SO21**
Abergele: Denb. **10 SH97**
Abergorlech: Carm. SN 5833
Abergynolwyn: Mer. SH 6706
Aberhosan: Montg. SN 8197
Aberlemno: Angus NO 5255
Abernethy: Perth. **15 NO11**
Abernethy Forest: Inv. NH 9718
Abernyte: Perth. NO 2531
Aberporth: Card. SN 2651
Abersoch: Caer. SH 3128
Abersychan: Mon. **10 SO20**
Aberthaw, E.&W.: Glam. ST 0266
Abertillery: Mon. **10 SO20**
Aberuthven: Perth. NN 9715
Aberystwyth: Card. **10 SN58**
Abingdon: Berks **11 SU49**
Abinger: Surrey TQ 1145
Abington: Lan. NS 9323
Aboyne: Aber. **17 NO59**
Abriachan: Inv. NH 5535
Accrington: Lancs **13 SD72**
Achahoish: Argyll NH 7877
Achanalt: Ross & Crom. NH 2661
Acharacle: Argyll NM 6767
Achill: *i. & head*, Mayo **18 A6**
Achiltibuie: Suther. NC 0208
Achintraid: Ross&Crom. NG 8438
Achmore: Lewis NB 3029
Achnacroish: Argyll NM 8541
Achnasheen: Ross&Crom. NH 1658
Achnashellach Forest: Ross & Crom. **16 NH04**
A Chralaig: *mtn.*, Ross & Crom. **16 NH11**
A Chruach: *mtn.*, Perth. **16 NN35**
Achuvoldrach: Suther. NC 5659
Acklam: Yorks SE 7861
Acklington: Northumb. NU 2201
Acle: Norf. **6 TG41**
Acomb: Northumb. NY 9366
Acton: Middx. TQ 1980
Acton Burnell: Salop SJ 5202
Acton Scott: Salop SO 4589
Acton Turville: Glos. ST 8080
Add: *r.* **14 NR89**
Addingham: Yorks SE 0749
Adel: Yorks SE 2840
Adlington: Ches. SJ 9180
Adlington: Lancs. SD 5912
Adur: *r.* **7 TQ14**
Advie: Moray NJ 1234
Adwick le Street: Yorks **13 SE50**
Aeron: *r.* **10 SN65**
Affric: *r.* **16 NH11**
Afon Wen: Caer. SH 4437
Agnew's Hill: Antrim **18 K8**
Aherlow: *r.* **19 E3**
Aikton: Cumb. NY 2753
Ailsa Craig: *i.*, Ayr **14 NX09**
Ainsdale: Lancs SD 3111
Ainstable: Cumb. NY 5346
Aintree: Lancs **12 SJ39**
Aird, The: Inv. **17 NH54**
Aird Barvas: Lewis NB 3553
Aird Brenish: Lewis NA 9726
Aird Dell: Lewis NB 4762
Aird of Sleat: Skye NG 5900
Airdrie: Lan. **15 NS76**
Aire: *r.*, Yorks **13 SE62**
Airmyn: Yorks SE 7224
Airor: Inv. NG 7205
Airth: Stirl. NS 8987
Aislaby: Yorks NZ 8508
Aith: Shet. Is. **17 HU35**
Alaw: *r.* **10 SH38**
Alcester: War **11 SP05**
Alchester: Oxon. **11 SP52**
Alconbury: Hunts TL 1875
Aldborough: Yorks. SE 4065
Aldbourne: Wilts. SU 2675
Aldbrough: Yorks **13 TA23**
Alde: *r.* **6 TM36**
Aldeburgh: Suff. **6 TM45**
Alderbury: Wilts. SU 1827
Alderholt: Dorset SU 1212
Alderley Edge: Ches. **11 SJ87**
Aldermaston: Berks **11 SU56**
Alderney: *i.*, Chan. Is. **9 Ins.**
Aldershot: Hants **7 SU85**
Alderton: Glos SP 0033
Aldford: Ches. SJ 4159
Aldingham: Lancs SD 2870
Aldridge: Staffs SK 0500
Aldsworth: Glos SP 1509
Aled, *r.* **10 SH96**
Ale Water: *r.* **15 NT41**
Alexandria: Dunb. **14 NS38**
Alfold: Surrey TQ 0333
Alford: Aber. NJ 5715
Alford: Lincs **6 TF47**
Alfreton: Derby. **11 SK45**
Alfriston: Sussex TQ 5103
Alham: *r.* **9 ST63**
Alkborough: Yorks SE 8721
Allanton: Ber. NT 8654
Allen: *r.*, Corn. **8 SX07**
Allen: *r.*, Dorset **9 SU00**
Allen: *r.*, Northumb. **13 NY86**
Allen, L.: Rosc./Leit. **18 E7**
Allendale Town: Northumb. **13 NY85**
Allen Water: *r.* **15 NN80**
Allerston Forest: Yorks **13 SE98**
Allhallows: Cumb. NY 2041
Allhallows: Kent TQ 8377
Alloa: Clack. **15 NS89**
Allonby: Cumb. NY 0842
All Stretton: Salop SO 4395
Almeley: Here. SO 3351
Almond: *r.*, Perth. **15 NN92**
Almond: *r.*, W. Loth. **15 NT07**
Almondbank: Perth. NO 0626
Almondbury: Yorks **13 SE11**
Almondsbury: Glos ST 6083
Aln: *r.* **15 NU11**
Alne: *r.* **11 SP16**
Alness: *& r.*, Ross&Crom. **17 NH66**
Alnham: Northumb. NT 9910
Alnmouth: Northumb. NU 2410
Alnwick: Northumb. **15 NU11**
Alphington: Devon. SX 9190
Alrewas: Staffs SK 1715
Alsager: Ches. **11 SJ75**
Alston: Cumb. **13 NY74**
Alstonfield: Staffs SK 1355
Alt: *r.* **12 SD30**
Altarnun: Corn. SX 2281
Althorne: Essex TQ 9098
Althorp: Northants **11 SP66**
Altnabreac: Caith. ND 0045
Altnaharra: Suther. NC 5635
Alton: Ayr NS 4938
Alton: Hants **7 SU73**
Altrincham: Ches. **11 SJ78**
Alun: *r.* **10 SJ26**
Alva: Clack. **15 NS89**
Alvechurch: Worcs SP 0272
Alverdiscott: Devon. SS 5225
Alverley: Salop **11 SO78**
Alveston: War SP 2256
Alvie: Inv. **17 NH80**
Alwalton: Hunts TL 1395
Alwen: *lake*, Denb. **10 SH95**
Alwinton: Northumb. NT 9206
Alyth: Perth. **17 NO24**
Amberley: Sussex TQ 0313
Amble: Northumb. **15 NU20**
Amblecote: Staffs SO 8885
Ambleside: Westmor. **12 NY30**
Ambleston: Pemb SN 0026
Amersham: Bucks **11 SU99**
Amesbury: Wilts. SU 1541
Amlwch: Anglesey **10 SH49**
Ammanford: Carm. **10 SN61**
Ampleforth: Yorks **13 SE57**
Ampthill: Beds **7 TL03**
Amroth: Pemb SN 1608
Amulree: Perth. NN 8936
Ancaster: Lincs SK 9843
Ancholme: *r.* **13 SE90**
An Clachan: *c.*, Islay **14 NR27**
Ancrum: Rox. NT 6224
An Cuaidh: Ross&Crom. **16 NG78**
Andover: Hants **7 SU34**
Andoversford: Glos SP 0219
Andreas: I. of Man SC 4199
Angarsk: Perth. NO 1510
Angle: Pemb SM 8603
Anglers' Retreat: Card. SN 7492
ANGLESEY: *Co.*, Wales **10 SH47**
Angmering: Sussex TQ 0704
ANGUS: *Co.*, Scotland **15 NO46**
Anker: *r.* **11 SP39**
Annan: *& r.*, Dumf. **15 NY16**
Annandale: Dumf. **15 NY09**
Annbank: Ayr NS 4022
Annet: *i.*, Scilly Is. **8 SV80**
Annfield Plain: Dur. **13 NZ15**
Annick Water: *r.* **14 NS34**
Anstey: Leics. SK 5408
Anstiebury: Surrey TQ 1643
Anston: Yorks SK 5184
Anstruther: Fife **15 NO50**
An Teallach: *mtn.*, Ross & Crom. **16 NH08**
ANTRIM: *Co.*, N. Irel. **18 J8**
Antrim Mts. **18 J9**
An Uaimh: Meath **18 H6**
Anwick: Lincs TF 1150
Anworth: Kirkc. NX5856
Appin: Argyll **16 NM95**
Appleby: Lincs SE 9414
Appleby: Westmor. **12 NY62**
Appleby Bridge: Lancs SD 5208
Appleby Magna: Leics. SK 3109
Applecross: *& for.*, Ross & Crom. **16 NG74**
Appledore: Devon. **8 SS43**
Appledore: Kent TQ 9529
Applethwaite: Cumb. NY 2625
Appleton: Berks SP 4401
Aran Fawddwy: Mer. **10 SH82**
Aran I.: Don. **18 D8**
Aran Is.: Gal. **19 B5**
Aray: *r.* **14 NN11**
Arbirlot: Angus NO 6040
Arbor Low: Derby. **11 SK16**
Arbroath: Angus **15 NO64**
Arbury: War **11 SP38**
Arbuthnott: Kinc. NO 8074
Archarn: Perth. NN 7743
Archiestown: Moray. NJ 2344
Ardbeg: Islay NR 4146
Ardclach: Nairn. NH 9445
Ardee: Louth **18 H6**
Ardentinny: Argyll NS 1887
Ardeonaig: Perth. NN 6635
Ardersier: Ross & Crom. **17 NH75**
Ardessie: Ross & Crom. NH 0589
Ardfern: Argyll NM 8004
Ardgartan: Argyll NN 2702
Ardgay: Ross & Crom. NH 6090
Ardgour: Argyll **16 NM96**
Ardingly: Sussex TQ 3429
Ardivochar Pt.: S. Uist **16 NF74**
Ardlamont Pt.: Bute. **14 NS06**
Ardle: *r.* **17 NO15**
Ardleigh: Essex TM 0529
Ardler: Perth. NO 2641
Ardley: Oxon. SP 5427
Ardlui: Dunb. NN 3115
Ardlussa: Jura NR 6487
Ardminish: Gigha NR 6448
Ardmolich: Inv. **16 NM77**
Ardmore Point: Islay **14 NR45**
Ardmore Point: Mull **16 NM45**
Ardnamurchan: Argyll **16 NM56**
Ardnave Point: Islay **14 NR27**
Ardoch: Perth. **15 NN80**
Ardpatrick: Argyll NR 7560
Ardpatrick Pt.: Argyll. **14 NR75**
Ardrishaig: Argyll NR 8585
Ardroil: Lewis NB 0331
Ardrossan: Ayr **14 NS24**
Ards Peninsula: Down **18 L7**
Ardtalnaig: Perth. NN 7039
Ardwell: Wig. NX 1045
ARGYLL: *Co.*, Scotland **14 —**
Aridhglas: Mull NM 3123
Arinagour: Coll NM 2257
Arisaig: Inv. **16 NM68**
Arkendale: Yorks SE 3860
Arkengarthdale: Yorks **13 NZ09**
Arkle: mtn., Suther. NC 3046
Arkleton Hill: Dumf. **15 NY49**
Arklow: Wick. **19 J4**
Arlecdon: Cumb. NY 0419
Arlesey: Beds TL 1935
Arlington: Devon. SS 6140
Armadale: Suther. NC 7864
Armadale: W. Loth. **15 NS96**
Armadale Bay: Skye **16 NG60**
ARMAGH: *Co.*, N. Irel. **18 H7**
Armathwaite: Cumb. NY 5046
Armitage: Staffs SK 0816
Armley: Yorks SE 2533
Armthorpe: Yorks SE 6105
Arne: Dorset SY 9788
Arnisdale: Inv. **16 NG81**
Arnish: Raasay NG 5948
Arnold: Notts SK 5745
Arnside: Westmor. SD 4578
Aros: *r.* **16 NM54**
Arran: *i.*, Bute. **14 NR93**
Arrochar: Dunb. NN 2904
Arrow, Lough: Sligo **18 E7**
Arrow: *r.* **10 SO35**
Arthog: Mer. SH 6414
Artro: *r.* **10 SH62**
Arun: *r.* **7 TQ02**
Arundel: Sussex **7 TQ00**
Ascog: Bute. NS 1063
Ascot: Berks **7 SU96**
Ascrib Is.: Inv. NG 3063
Asfordby: Leics. SK 7018
Ash: Kent TR 2958
Ash: *r.* **7 TL21**
Ashbourne: Derby **11 SK14**
Ashburton: Devon. **8 SX77**
Ashbury: Berks SU 2685
Ashby: Lincs SE 8908
Ashby de la Zouch: Leics. **11 SK31**
Ashby Magna: Leics. SP 5690
Ashchurch: Glos SO 9233
Ashdown Forest: Sussex **7 TQ43**
Ashford: Derby. SK 1969
Ashford: Devon. SS 5335
Ashford: Kent **7 TR04**
Ashford Carbonell; Salop SO 5270
Ashill: Norf. TF 8804
Ashington: Northumb. **15 NZ28**
Ashkirk: Selk. NT 4722
Ashmore: Dorset ST 9117
Ashprington: Devon. SX 8157
Ashridge: Herts **11 SP91**
Ashton in Makerfield: Lancs **12 SJ59**
Ashton Keynes: Wilts. SU 0494
Ashton under Hill: Worcs. SO 9938
Ashton under Lyne: Lancs **13 SJ99**
Ashwater: Devon. SX 3895
Ashwell: Herts TL 2639
Ashwell: Rutland SK 8613
Askam in Furness: Lancs SD 2177
Askern: Yorks SE 5613
Askham: Westmor. NY 5123
Askham Bryan: Yorks SE 5548
Askival: *mtn.*, Rhum **16 NM39**
Askrigg: Yorks **13 SD99**
Aspatria: Cumb. NY 1442
Astbury: Ches. SJ 8461
Aston: Herts TL 2722
Aston: War SP 0789
Aston Clinton: Bucks SP 8712
Astwood: Bucks SP 9547
Astwood Bank: Worcs SP 0362
Atcham: Salop SJ 5409
Atherington: Devon. SS 5923
Atherstone: War **11 SP39**
Atherton: Lancs **12 SD60**
Athlone: Westmeath **19 F5**
Athy: Kild. **19 H4**
Attingham Park: Salop. SJ 5409
Attleborough: Norf. **6 TM09**
Atwick: Yorks TA 1850
Atworth: Wilts. ST 8565
Auchencairn: Kirkc. NX 7951
Auchinblae: Kinc. NO 7278
Auchinleck: Ayr. NS 5422
Auchmithie: Angus NO 6744
Auchterarder: Perth. **15 NN91**
Auchterderran: Fife NT 2195
Auchtermuchty: Fife **15 NO21**
Auchtertool: Fife. NT 2190
Audlem: Ches. SJ 6543
Audley: Staffs SJ 7950
Audley End House: Essex TL 5136
Aughrim: Wick. **19 J4**
Aughton: Yorks SE 7038
Aultbea: Ross & Crom. **16 NG88**
Aust: Glos. **9 ST58**
Austrey: War SK 2906
Avan: *r.* **10 SS89**
Avebury: Wilts. **9 SU06**
Aviemore: Inv. **17 NH81**
Avoca: *& r.*, Wick. **19 J4**
Avoch: Ross & Crom. NH 7055
Avon: Hants **9 SZ19**
Avon: *r.*, Banff **17 NJ11**
Avon: *r.*, Devon. **8 SX75**
Avon: *r.*, Glos **9 ST66**
Avon: *r.*, Stirl. **15 NS97**
Avon: *r.*, War. **11 SP04**
Avon: *r.*, Wilts. **9 SU12**
Avonmouth: Glos **9 ST57**
Avon Water: *r.* **14 NS74**
Avon Wick: Devon. SX 7158
Awbeg: *r.* **19 D3**
Axbridge: Som. **9 ST45**
Axe: *r.*, Dorset **9 ST30**
Axe Edge: Derby **13 SK06**
Axminster: Devon. **9 SY29**
Axmouth: Devon. SY 2591
Aycliffe: Dur. NZ 2822
Aylesbury: Bucks **11 SP81**
Aylesford: Kent TQ 7359
Aylesham: Kent TR 2352
Aylsham: Norf. **6 TG12**
Aynho: Northants SP 5133
Ayr: Ayr **14 NS32**
Ayr: *r.* **14 NS62**
AYRSHIRE: Scot. **14 NS—**
Aysgarth: Yorks SE 0088
Ayton: Ber. NT 9260
Ayton: Yorks SE 9884

Babbacombe Bay: Devon. **9 SX96**
Babingley: *r.* **6 TF72**
Back: Lewis NB 4840
Backaland: Ork. Is. HY 5630
Backbarrow: Lancs SD 3584
Backwell: Som. ST 4868
Baconsthorpe: Norf. TG 1237
Bacton: Norf. TG 3233
Bacup: Lancs **13 SD82**
Badachro: Ross & Crom. NG 7873
Badby: Northants SP 5559
Badcall: Suther. NC 1541
Badenoch: Inv. **17 NN79**
Badrallach: Ross & Crom. NH 0691
Badsworth: Yorks SE 4614
Bagborough: Som. ST 1733
Bagenalstown: Carlow. **19 H4**
Baggy Pt.: Devon. **8 SS44**
Bagh nam Faoileann: N/S. Uist **16 NF84**
Bagillt: Flint. SJ 2175
Baginton: War SP 3474
Baildon: Yorks **13 SE13**
Baile Átha Cliath: Dublin **19 J5**
Baillieston: Lanark NS 6764
Bain: *r.*, Lincs **13 TF26**
Bain: *r.*, Yorks **13 SD98**
Bakewell: Derby. **13 SK26**
Bala: *& l.*, Mer. **10 SH93**
Balbriggan: Dublin **18 J6**
Balcary Point: Kirkc. **15 NX84**
Balcombe: Sussex TQ 3130
Balder: *r.* **13 NY90**
Baldock: Herts **7 TL23**
Balemartine: Tiree **16 NL94**
Baleshare: Uist **16 NF76**
Ballachulish Ferry: Inv. **16 NN05**
Ballaghaderreen: Rosc. **18 D6**
Ballantrae: Ayr. **14 NX08**
Ballater: Aber. **17 NO39**
Ballina: Mayo **18 C7**
Ballinasloe: Gal. **19 E5**
Ballinrobe: Mayo **18 C6**
Balloch: Dunb. NS 3981
Ballycastle: Antrim **18 J9**
Ballyclare: Antrim **18 J8**
Ballydavid Head: Kerry **19 Ins.**
Ballygrant: Islay NR 3966
Ballyhaunis: Mayo **18 D6**
Ballyheige Bay: Kerry **19 B3**
Ballyhoura Hills: Irel. **19 E3**
Ballymena: Antrim **18 J8**
Ballymoney: Antrim **18 H9**
Ballynahinch: Down **18 K7**
Ballyshannon: Don. **18 E8**
Ballyteige Bay: Wex. **19 H3**
Balmacaan Forest; Inv. NH 4025
Balmacara: Ross & Crom. NG 8028
Balmedie: Aber. NJ 9617
Balmerino: Fife NO 3524
Balmoral Castle: Aber. **17 NO29**
Balmoral For.: Aber. **17 NO28**
Balnagown: *r.* **17 NH77**
Balnaguard: Perth. NN 9451
Balquhidder: Perth. NN 5320
Balsall: War SP 2376
Baltimore: Cork **19 C1**
Bamber Bridge: Lancs SD 5624
Bamburgh: Northumb. **15 NU13**
Bamford: Derby. SK 2083
Bampton: Devon. **8 SS92**
Bampton: Oxon. **11 SP30**
Banavie: Inv. NN 1177
Banbridge: Down **18 J7**
Banbury: Oxon. **11 SP44**
Banchory: Kinc. **17 NO79**
Bandon: *& r.*, Cork **19 D2**
BANFF: *Co.*, Scot. **17 NJ66**
Bangor: Caer. **10 SH57**
Bangor: Down **18 K8**
Bangor-is-y-Coed: Flint. SJ 3945
Banham: Norf. TM 0688
Bankend: Dumf. NY 0268
Bankhead: Aber. NJ 8910
Bann: *r.*, Down **18 J7**
Bann: *r.*, N. Irel. **18 H9**
Bann: *r.*, Wex. **19 J4**
Bannockburn: Stirl. **15 NS89**
Banstead: Surrey TQ 2559
Bantry: *& bay*, Cork **19 C2**
Banwell: Som. ST 3959
Banwy: *r.* **10 SJ00**
Barbon: Westmor. SD 6282
Bardney: Lincs TF 1169
Bardsea: Lancs SD 3074
Bardsey: *i.&sound*, Caer. **10 SH12**
Bardwell: Suff. TL 9473
Barford: War SP 2660
Bargoed: Glam. **10 SO10**
Barham: Kent TR 2050
Barking: Essex **7 TQ48**
Barking: Suff. TM 0653
Barkston: Lincs SK 9241
Barkway: Herts TL 3835
Barlborough: Derby. SK 4777
Barlby: Yorks SE 6334
Barle: *r.* **8 SS83**
Barley: Lancs SD 8240
Barling: Essex TQ 9289
Barmouth: Mer. **10 SH61**
Barnack: Northants TF 0705
Barnard Castle: Dur. **13 NZ01**
Barnby: Suff. TM 4789
Barnby Moor: Notts SK 6684
Barnet: Herts **7 TQ29**
Barnetby le Wold: Lincs TA 0509
Barnham: Suff. TL 8779
Barnham: Sussex SU 9604
Barningham: Suff. TL 9676
Barningham: Yorks NZ 0810

G.B. & IRELAND

BARNOLDSWICK — BRENDON HILLS

Barnoldswick: Yorks . 13 SD84
Barnsley: Glos . . SP 0705
Barnsley: Yorks . . 13 SE30
Barnstaple: & bay, Devon. 8 SS53
Barnston: Ches. . SJ 2783
Barnt Green: Worcs . SP 0073
Barnwell: Northants . TL 0485
Barpa Langass: N. Uist NF 8565
Barra: i., Inv. . 16 NF60
Barra Hd.: Berneray . 16 NL57
Barrhead: Renf. . 14 NS55
Barrhill: Ayr . . NX 2382
Barrington: Som. . ST 3918
Barrisdale: Inv. . NG 8604
Barrmill: Ayr . . NS 3651
Barrock: Caith. . ND 2671
Barrow: Lancs . . SD 7338
Barrow: Suff. . . TL 7663
Barrow: r. . . 19 H4
Barrowden: Rutland . SK 9400
Barrowford: Lancs . 13 SD83
Barrow in Furness: Lancs 12 SD16
Barrow upon Soar: Leics. SK 5717
Barr Water: r. . . 14 NR63
Barry: Glam. . . 10 ST16
Barshill: Dumf. . 15 NY08
Bartlow: Cambs. . TL 5845
Barton: Yorks . . NZ 2208
Barton Bendish: Norf. . TF 7105
Barton in the Clay: Beds TL 0831
Barton Mills: Suff. . TL 7273
Barton upon Humber: Yorks . . 13 TA02
Barvas: r., Lewis . 16 NB34
Baschurch: Salop . SJ 4222
Basildon: Essex . 7 TQ79
Basing: Hants . . SU 6652
Basingstoke: Hants . 7 SU65
Baslow: Derby. . . SK 2572
Bassenthwaite: Cumb. . 12 NY22
Bassingbourn: Cambs. . TL 3344
Bassingham: Lincs . SK 9059
Bass Rock: F. of Forth 15 NT68
Baston: Lincs . . TF 1114
Batcombe: Som. . ST 6838
Batemans: Sussex . TQ 6823
Bath: Som. . . 11 ST76
Bathford: Som. . ST 7866
Bathgate: W. Loth. . 15 NS96
Batley: Yorks . . 13 SE22
Battle: & ridge, Sussex. 7 TQ71
Battlefield: Salop . SJ 5117
Battlesbury: Wilts . ST 8945
Battock, Mt.: Angus . 17 NO58
Baumber: Lincs . . TF 2174
Bawburgh: Norf. . TG 1508
Bawden Rocks: Corn. . SW 6953
Bawdeswell: Norf. . TG 0420
Bawdsey: Suff. . . TM 3440
Bawtry: Yorks . . 13 SK69
Baydon: Wilts. . . SU 2877
Bayfordbury: Herts . 7 TL31
Baystonhill: Salop . SJ 4809
Bayton: Worcs . . SO 6973
Beachy Head: Sussex . 7 TV59
Beacon Hill: Rad. . 10 SO17
Beaconsfield: Bucks . 11 SU99
Beadlam: Yorks . . SE 6584
Beadnell Bay: Northumb. 15 NU22
Beal: Northumb. . NU 0642
Beaminster: Dorset . 9 ST40
Beane: r. . . 7 TL22
Bearsden: Dunb. . NS 5471
Bearsted: Kent . . TQ 8055
Beaufort: Mon. . . SO 1611
Beaulieu: Hants . 9 SU30
Beauly: r. & firth, Inv. . 17 NH54
Beaumaris: Anglesey . 10 SH67
Beaworthy: Devon. . SX 4699
Bebington: Ches. . 10 SJ38
Beccles: Suff. . . 6 TM49
Beckenham: Kent . 7 TQ36
Beckford: Worcs. . SO 9735
Beckingham: Lincs . SK 8753
Beckingham: Notts . SK 7790
Beckington: Som. . ST 8051
Beck Row: Suff. . . TL 6977
Bedale: Yorks . . 13 SE28
Bedford: Beds . . 7 TL04
BEDFORDSHIRE: Eng. 7 TL—
Bedgebury Park: Kent. 7 TQ73
Bedlington: Northumb. 15 NZ28
Bedrule: Rox. . . NT 6017
Bedstone: Salop . SO 3675
Bedwellty: Mon. . SO 1600
Bedwas: Mon. . . 10 ST18
Bedworth: War . . SP 3587
Beeford: Yorks . . TA 1254
Beela: r. . . . 12 SD58
Beeley: Derby. . . SK 2667
Beer Head: Devon. . 9 SY28
Beeston: Ches. . . 11 SJ55
Beeston: Notts . . 11 SK53
Beeswing: Kirkc. . NX 8969
Beg, Lough: N. Irel. . 18 J8
Beguildy: Rad. . . SO 1979
Beighton: Derby. . SK 4183
Beinn a'Bhuird: Aber. 17 NO09
Beinn A'Chuallaich: Perth 17 NN66
Beinn A'Ghlo: Perth. . 17 NN97
Beinn an Tuirc: Argyll. 14 NR73
Beinn Bhàn: R. & Crom. 16 NG84
Beinn Bhàn: Inv. . 16 NN18
Beinn Bheigeir: Islay . 14 NR45
Beinn Bheula: Argyll . 14 NS19
Beinn Bhreac: Jura . 14 NR59
Beinn Bhreac: Skye . 16 NG25
Beinn Bhuidhe: Argyll. 14 NN21
Beinn Dearg: Perth. . 17 NN87
Beinn Dearg: R.&Crom. 16 NH28
Beinn Dhorain: Suther. 17 NC91
Beinn Dorain: Argyll . 14 NN33
Beinn Edra: Skye . 16 NG46
Beinn Eighe: R. & Crom. 16 NG95
Beinn Fhada: R.&Crom. 16 NH01
Beinn Heasgarnich: Perth 14 NN43
Beinn Ime: Argyll . 14 NN20
Beinn Iutharn Mhòr: Perth . . 17 NO07
Beinn Laoigh: Perth. . 14 NN22
Beinn Mhòr: Lewis . 16 NB20
Beinn nam Bad Mor: Caith. . . 17 NC95
Beinn na Sreine: Mull . 14 NM43
Beinn Spionnaidh: Suther. NC 3657
Beinn Stumanadh: Suther. 17 NC64
Beinn Tharsuinn: Ross & Crom. . 17 NH67
Beinn Udlamain: Inv. 17 NN57
Beith: Ayr . . 14 NS35
Belchford: Lincs . . TF 2975
Belcoo: Ferm. . . 18 F7
Belfast: & l., N. Irel. . 18 K8
Belford: Northumb. . 15 NU13
Belhaven: E. Loth. . NT 6678
Belhelvie: Aber. . . NJ 9417
Bell Crags: Northumb. 15 NY77
Belleek: Ferm. . . 18 E7
Bellehiglash: Banff . NJ 1837
Bellerby: Yorks . . SE 1192
Bellingham: Northumb. 15 NY88
Belmont: Lancs . . SD 6715
Belmullet: Mayo . 18 B7
Belper: Derby. . . 11 SK34
Belsay: Northumb. . NZ 1078
Belton: Lincs . . SE 7806
Belturbet: Cavan . 18 G7
Belvoir Castle: Leics . 11 SK83
Bembridge: I. of Wight 7 SZ68
Bempton: Yorks . . TA 1972
Ben Aigan: Banff . 17 NJ34
Ben Alder: Inv. . . 17 NN47
Ben Armine: Suther. . NC 6828
Ben Avon: Banff . . NJ 1401
Benbane Head: Antrim 18 J9
Ben Barvas: Lewis . 16 NB33
Benbecula: i., Inv. . 16 NF85
Benbradagh: Lon. . 18 H8
Ben Bragor: Lewis . 16 NB24
Ben Chonzie: Perth. . 15 NN73
Ben Cruachan: Argyll . 14 NN03
Ben-damph Forest: Ross & Crom. . NG 8852
Benderloch: Argyll . 14 NN93
Benenden: Kent . . 7 TQ83
Beneraird: Ayr. . . 14 NX17
Ben Griam More: Suther. 17 NC83
Ben Hee: Suther. . 17 NC43
Ben Hiant: Argyll . 16 NM56
Ben Hope: Suther. . 17 NC45
Ben Horn: Suther. . 17 NC80
Ben Klibreck: Suther. . 17 NC63
Ben Lawers: Perth. . 14 NN64
Ben Ledi: Perth. . 14 NN50
Ben Lomond: Stirl. . 14 NN30
Ben Loyal: Suther. . 17 NC54
Ben Macdhui: Aber. . 17 NN99
Ben More: Mull . . 14 NM53
Ben More: Perth. . 14 NN42
Ben More Assynt: Suther. 16 NC32
Benmore Head: Antrim. 18 J9
Bennane Hd.: Ayr . 14 NX08
Bennan Hd.: Bute. . 14 NR92
Ben Nevis: Inv. . . 16 NN17
Ben Resipol: Argyll . 16 NM76
Ben Rinnes: Banff . 17 NJ23
Ben Sgriol: Inv. . . 16 NG81
Benson: Oxon. . . SU 6191
Ben Stack: Suther. . 16 NC24
Ben Starav: Argyll . 14 NN14
Bentley: Hants . . SU 7844
Bentley: Yorks . . SE 5605
Bentworth: Hants . SU 6640
Ben Venue: Perth. . 14 NN40
Ben Vorlich: Dunb. . 14 NN21
Ben Vorlich: Perth. . 14 NN61
Ben Vrackie: Perth. . 17 NN96
Benwee Head: Mayo . 18 B7
Ben Wyvis: Ross&Crom. 17 NH46
Bere Alston: Devon. . 8 SX46
Bere Ferrers: Devon. . SX 4563
Bere I.: Cork . . 19 B2
Bere Regis: Dorset . SY 8494
Berkeley: Glos . . 11 ST69
Berkhampsted: Herts . 11 SP90
BERKSHIRE: Eng. . 7 SU—
Berkshire Downs . 9 SU47
Berneray: i., Inv. . 16 NL58
Berneray: i., Inv. . 16 NF98
Bernisdale: Skye . NG 4050
Berridale Water: r., Caith. 17 ND03
Berriedale: Caith. . ND 1223
Berriew: Montg. . . SJ 1801
Berrow Flats: Som. . 9 ST25
Berry Head: Devon. . 8 SX95
Berrynarbor: Devon. . SS 5546
Bertraghboy Bay: Gal. 19 B5
BERWICKSHIRE: Scot. 15 NT—
Berwick upon Tweed: Northumb. . 15 NT95
Berwyn: mtns., Mer. . 10 SJ03
Bessbrook: Armagh . 18 J7
Bessy Bell: mtn., Tyr. . 18 G8
Besthorpe: Notts . SK 8264
Bethersden: Kent. . TQ 9240
Bethesda: Caer. . . 10 SH66
Bettws-y-Coed: Caer. . 10 SH75
Bettyhill: Suther. . NC 7061
Beult: r. . . . 7 TQ84
Beverley: Yorks . . 13 TA03
Bewcastle: Cumb. . NY 5674
Bewcastle Fells: Cumb. 15 NY58
Bewdley: Worcs . . 11 SO77
Bewholme: Yorks . TA 1649
Bexhill: Sussex . . 7 TQ70
Bexley: Kent . . TQ 4973
Bibury: Glos . . 11 SP10
Bicester: Oxon. . . 11 SP52
Bicker: Lincs . . TF 2237
Biddulph: Staffs . 11 SJ85
Bidean nam Bian: Argyll 16 NN15
Bideford: & bay, Devon. 8 SS42
Bidford on Avon: War . SP 1052
Bigbury: & bay, Devon. 8 SX64
Biggar: Lan. . . 15 NT03
Biggin Hill: Kent . 7 TQ45
Biggleswade: Beds . 7 TL14
Bilbster: Caith. . . ND 2852
Billericay: Essex . . 7 TQ69
Billesdon: Leics. . . SK 7103
Billingborough: Lincs . TF 1134
Billingham: Dur. . 13 NZ42
Billinghay: Lincs . TF 1554
Billingshurst: Sussex . TQ 0825
Billington: Lancs. . SD 7235
Bill of Portland: Dorset 9 SY66
Bilston: Staffs . . 11 SO99
Bilton: War . . SP 4873
Bilton: Yorks . . SE 3157
Binbrook: Lincs . . TF 2093
Binegar: Som. . . ST 6149
Binevenagh: mtn., Antrim 18 H9
Bingham: Notts. . 11 SK73
Bingley: Yorks . . 13 SE13
Binham: Norf. . . TF 9839
Binnein Mor: Inv. . 16 NN26
Binnein Mor: R.&Crom. 16 NH26
Bintree: Norf. . . TG 0123
Birchington: Kent . TR 3069
Birdham: Sussex . SU 8200
Birdlip: Glos . . SO 9214
Birdoswald: Cumb. . NY 6067
Birkenhead: Ches. . 12 SJ38
Birmingham: War . 11 SP08
Birnam: Perth. . . 15 NO04
Birr: Offaly . . 19 F5
Birrens: Dumf. . . NY 2075
Birstall: Yorks . . 13 SE22
Birtley: Dur. . . 13 NZ25
Birtley: Northumb. . NY 8778
Bishampton: Worcs . SO 9851
Bishop Auckland: Dur. 13 NZ22
Bishopbriggs: Lan. . NS 6070
Bishop Burton: Yorks . SE 9839
Bishop Monkton: Yorks SE 3266
Bishop Rock: Scilly Is. 8 SV80
Bishop's Cannings: Wilts SU 0364
Bishop's Castle: Salop. 10 SO38
Bishop's Caundle: Dorset ST 6912
Bishop's Cleeve: Glos . SO 9527
Bishop's Lydeard: Som. 9 ST12
Bishop's Nympton: Devon. SS 7523
Bishop's Stortford: Herts 7 TL42
Bishop's Tachbrook: War SP 3161
Bishop's Tawton: Devon. SS 5630
Bishopsteignton: Devon. SX 9173
Bishopstoke: Hants . SU 4619
Bishopston: Glam. . SS 5889
Bishop Sutton: Som. . ST 5859
Bishop's Waltham: Hants 7 SU51
Bishopsworth: Som. . ST 5768
Bishopton: Renf. . NS 4371
Bisley: Surrey . . SU 9559
Bittadon: Devon.. . SS 5441
Blaby: Leics. . . SP 5697
Blackadder Water: r. . 15 NT74
Blackburn: Aber. . NJ 8212
Blackburn: Lancs . 12 SD62
Blackbushe: airport, Hants 7 SU85
Black Combe: Cumb. . 12 SD18
Blackcraig Hill: Ayr . 14 NS60
Blackdown: Sussex . 7 SU92
Blackdown Hills: Som. 9 ST11
Black Edge: Derby. . 13 SK07
Black Esk: r. . . 15 NY29
Blackford: Perth. . NN 8908
Blackford: Som. . . ST 4147
Black Hd.: Clare . 19 C5
Black Hd.: Corn. . 8 SW71
Black Hill: Ches. . 13 SE00
Black Hill: Dur. . 13 NZ05
Blackhill: Skye . . NG 3450
Black Hope Scar: Scot. 15 NT34
Black Isle: R. & Crom. 17 NH66
Blacklunans: Perth. . NO 1560
Blackmoor: Corn. . 8 SX05
Blackmoor: Hants . SU 7833
Blackmoor Vale: Dorset 9 ST71
Black Mount: Argyll . 14 NN24
Black Mountains: Breck. 10 SO22
Black Notley: Essex . TL 7620
Blackpool: Lancs . 12 SD33
Blackridge: W. Loth. . NS 8967
Blacksod Bay: Mayo . 18 A7
Blackstairs: mtns., Carlow 19 H4
Blackwater: Bute. . NR 8928
Blackwater: r., Essex . 7 TL81
Blackwater: r., Hants . 7 SU85
Blackwater: r., Meath . 18 H6
Black Water: r., Perth. 15 NO15
Blackwater: r., Wat. . 19 E3
Blackwater Forest: Banff NJ 3026
Blackwater Res.: Argyll NN 3059
Blackwood: Lan. . NS 7943
Blackwood: Mon. . ST 1797
Bladnoch: r. . . 12 NX36
Blaenau Ffestiniog: Mer. 10 SH74
Blaenau Morgannwg: Glam. . . 10 SN90
Blaenavon: Mon. . 10 SO20
Blaengarw: Glam. . SS 9093
Blaengwrach: Glam. . SN 8605
Blagdon: Som. . . ST 5058
Blaina: Mon. . . SO 2008
Blair, Mt.: Perth. . 17 NO16
Blair Atholl: Perth. . 17 NN86
Blairgowrie: Perth. . 17 NO14
Blakeney: Glos . . 11 SO60
Blakeney: & pt., Norf. 6 TG04
Blakesley: Northants . SP 6250
Blanchland: Northumb. 13 NY95
Blandford Forum: Dorset 9 ST80
Blane Water: r. . . 14 NS58
Blarney: Cork . . 19 D2
Blaven: mtn., Skye . NG 5321
Blaydon: Dur. . . 15 NZ16
Bleaklow Hill: Derby. . 13 SK19
Blencarn: Cumb. . NY 6331
Blencogo: Cumb. . NY 1947
Blenheim Palace: Oxon. 11 SP41
Bletchington: Oxon. . SP 5017
Bletchley: Bucks . 11 SP83
Blewburton: Berks . SU 5586
Blickling: Norf. . . TG 1728
Blidworth: Notts . SK 5855
Blisland: Corn. . . SX 1073
Blisworth: Northants . SP 7253
Blithe: r. . . . 11 SK03
Blockley: Glos . . SP 1634
Blofield: Norf. . . TG 3309
Bloody Foreland: Don. 18 E9
Bloxham: Oxon. . . 11 SP43
Blue Stack Mts.: Don. . 18 E8
Blundeston: Suff. . TM 5197
Blunham: Beds . . TL 1551
Blyth: Northumb. . 15 NZ38
Blyth: Notts . . SK 6287
Blyth: r., Norf. . . 6 TM47
Blyth: r., Northumb. . 15 NZ27
Blyth Bridge: Peeb. . NT 1345
Blythburgh: Suff.. . TM 4575
Blythe: r. . . . 11 SP17
Boarhills: Fife . . NO 5614
Boathmore: Ross&Crom. NH 5773
Boat of Garten: Inv. . 17 NH91
Bocking Churchstreet: Essex . . . TL 7525
Boddam: Aber. . . NK 1342
Boddin Point: Angus . NO 7153
Boderg, L.: Rosc./Leit. 18 F6
Bodiam: Sussex . . TQ 7826
Bodicote: Oxon. . . SP 4537
Bodmin: Corn. . . 8 SX06
Bodmin Moor: Corn. . 8 SX17
Bodnant: Denb. . . 10 SH87
Boggeragh Mts.: Cork. 19 D3
Bognor Regis: Sussex . 7 SZ99
Bog of Allen: Offaly . 19 G5
Bogrie Hill: Dumf. . 15 NX78
Bokerley Dyke: Dorset SU 0419
Bolam: Northumb. . NZ 0982
Bollington: Ches. . 11 SJ97
Bolney: Sussex . . TQ 2622
Bolsover: Derby. . 13 SK47
Bolt Head: Devon. . 8 SX73
Bolton: Lancs . . 13 SD70
Bolton Abbey: Yorks . 13 SE05
Bolton le Sands: Lancs. SD 4867
Bolt Tail: Devon. . 8 SX63
Bolus Head: Kerry . 19 Ins.
Bomere Heath: Salop . SJ 4719
Bonarbridge: R. & Crom. NH 6191
Bonby: Lincs . . TA 0015
Bo'ness: W. Loth. . 15 NT08
Bonnybridge: Stirl. . 15 NS87
Bookham: Surrey . TQ 1354
Boot: Cumb. . . NY 1700
Boothby Pagnell: Lincs. SK 9730
Bootle: Cumb. . . SD 1088
Bootle: Lancs . . 12 SJ39
Bordon Camp: Hants . SU 7935
Boreland: Dumf. . NY 1790
Boreraig: Skye . . NG 1853
Boreray: i., Inv. . . 16 NF88
Borgie: r. . . . 17 NC65
Borgue: Caith. . . ND 1325
Borgue: Kirkc. . . NX 6248
Boroughbridge: Yorks. 13 SE36
Borrowdale: Cumb. . NY 2514
Borth: Card. . . 10 SN68
Borthwick Water: r. . 15 NT30
Borve: Barra . . NF 6501
Borwick: Lancs . . SD 5273
Boscastle: Corn. . 8 SX09
Bosham: Sussex . . SU 8004
Bosherston: Pemb . SR 9694
Bosley: Ches. . . SJ 9165
Boston: Lincs . . 6 TF34
Boston Spa: Yorks . SE 4245
Bosworth Field: Leics. . 11 SK40
Botesdale: Suff. . . 6 TM07
Bothel: Cumb. . . NY 1838
Bothwell: Lan. . . NS 7058
Botley: Hants . . 7 SU51
Bottesford: Leics. . SK 8038
Bottisham: Cambs. . TL 5460
Botwnnog: Caer. . SH 2631
Boulsworth Hill: Lancs 13 SD93
Boultham: Lincs . . SK 956
Bourn: Cambs. . . TL 325
Bourne: Lincs . . 6 TF0
Bourne: r. . . . 9 SU1
Bournemouth: Hants . 9 SZ0
Bourneville: War . 11 SP0
Bourton: Salop . . SO 599
Bourton on the Water: Glos . . . 11 SP1
Bovey: r. . . . 8 SX7
Bovey Tracey: Devon. . 8 SX8
Bovington: Herts. . TL 010
Bovington: Dorset . SY 818
Bow: Devon. . . SS 720
Bowden: Rox. . . NT 553
Bowdon: Ches. . . SJ 758
Bowertower: Caith. . ND 236
Bowes: Yorks . . NY 991
Bowmore: Islay . . NR 315
Bowness: Cumb. . . NY 226
Bowness: Westmor. . 12 SD4
Box: Wilts. . . ST 826
Boxford: Berks . . SU 427
Boxford: Suff. . . TL 964
Box Hill: Surrey . 7 TQ1
Boyndie: Banff . . NJ 646
Boyne: r. . . . 18 J
Bozeat: Northants . SP 905
Bracadale: Skye . . NG 353
Brackley: Northants . 11 SP5
Braco: Perth. . . NN 830
Bracora: Inv. . . NM 719
Bradda Head: I. of Man SC 187
Bradfield: Essex . . TM 143
Bradfield: Berks . . 11 SU6
Bradfield: Yorks . . SK 269
Bradford: Yorks . . 13 SE1
Bradford on Avon: Wilts 9 ST8
Brading: I. of Wight . 7 SZ6
Bradninch: Devon. . 8 SS9
Bradnor Hill: Here. . 10 SO2
Bradshaw: Yorks . . SE 083
Bradwell: Bucks . . SP 833
Bradwell: Derby. . . SK 178
Bradwell on Sea: Essex TM 000
Bradworthy: Devon. . SS 321
Brae Doune: Ross&Crom. NC 460
Braehead: Lan. . . NS 955
Braemar: Aber. . . 17 NO1
Braemore: Caith. . . ND 063
Braeriagh: mtn., Scot. . 17 NN9
Braes of Angus . . 17 NO4
Brafferton: Yorks . SE 437
Bragor: Lewis . . NB 284
Braigo: Islay . . NR 236
Brailsford: Derby. . SK 254
Brain: r. . . . 7 TL7
Braint: r. . . . 12 SH4
Braintree: Essex . . 7 TL7
Braithwell: Yorks . SK 539
Bramber: Sussex . TQ 181
Bramford: Suff. . . TM 124
Bramhall: Ches. . 11 SJ8
Bramham: Yorks . SE 404
Bramhope: Yorks . SE 244
Bramley: Surrey . . TQ 004
Bramley: Yorks . . SE 253
Brampton: Cumb. . 15 NY5
Brampton: Hunts . TL 217
Brampton: Suff. . . TM 438
Brampton Bryan: Here. SO 367
Bramshaw: Hants . SU 261
Bran: r. . . . 16 NH2
Brancaster: Norf. . TF 774
Brancepeth: Dur. . NZ 223
Brandesburton: Yorks . TA 114
Brandon: Dur. . . NZ 234
Brandon: Suff. . . 6 TL7
Brandon Bay: Kerry . 19 A3
Brandon Mt.: Kerry . 19 A3
Brandsby: Yorks . SE 587
Branscombe: Devon. . SY 198
Branston: Lincs . . TF 016
Brant: r. . . . 13 SK9
Branthwaite: Cumb. . NY 052
Branxton: Northumb. . NT 893
Brassington: Derby. . SK 235
Bratton Clovelly: Devon. SX 469
Bratton Fleming: Devon. SS 643
Braughing: Herts . TL 392
Braunton: Devon. . SS 483
Bray: & hd., Wick. . 19 J5
Bray: r. . . . 8 SS6
Bray Head: Kerry . 19 Ins.
Breadalbane: Perth. . 14 NN5
Breage: Corn. . . SW 612
Breaksea Point: Glam. 10 ST0
Breamish: r. . . 15 NT9
Breamore: Hants . SU 151
Brean: Som. . . ST 305
Breasclete: Lewis . NB 213
Breaston: Derby. . SK 453
Brechfa: Carm. . . SN 523
Brechin: Angus . . 17 NO6
Breckland: Norf. . 6 TL7
BRECKNOCKSHIRE: Wales . . 10SN/SO
Brecon: & beacons, Breck. 10 SO02
Brecqhou: i., Chan Is. 9 Ins.
Brede: & r., Sussex . 7 TQ8
Bredenbury: Here. . SO 605
Bredgar: Kent . . TQ 886
Bredon: & hill, Worcs . 11 SO93
Breedon on the Hill: Leics. SK 402
Breidden Hill: Montg. 10 SJ21
Brendon: Devon . . SS 764
Brendon Hills: Som. . 8 ST0

G.B. & IRELAND

BRENISH — CHELFORD

Brenish: Lewis NA 9925
Brentford: Middx. 7 TQ17
Brent Knoll: Som. ST 3350
Brent Pelham: Herts TL 4330
Brentwood: Essex 7 TQ59
Bressay: i., Shet. Is. 17 HU54
Bretherton: Lancs SD 4720
Brett: r. 7 TL95
Bride: I. of Man NX 4501
Bridestowe: Devon SX 5189
Bridge: Kent TR 1854
Bridgend: Angus 17 NO56
Bridge End: Beds TL 0050
Bridgend: Glam. SS 9079
Bridgend: Islay NR 3362
Bridge of Allan: Stirl. 15 NS79
Bridge of Avon: Banff NJ 1420
Bridge of Balgie: Perth. 14 NN54
Bridge of Cally: Perth. NO 1351
Bridge of Dee: Kirkc. NX 7360
Bridge of Don: Aber. NJ 9409
Bridge of Dun: Angus NO 6658
Bridge of Earn: Perth. NO 1318
Bridge of Gaur: Perth. NN 5157
Bridge of Orchy: Argyll NN 2939
Bridgnorth: Salop 11 SO79
Bridgwater: Som. 9 ST23
Bridlington: Yorks 13 TA16
Bridport: Dorset 9 SY49
Brierfield: Lancs 13 SD83
Brierley Hill: Staffs 11 SO98
Brigg: Lincs 6 TA00
Brighouse: Yorks 13 SE12
Brightlingsea: Essex 7 TM01
Brighton: Sussex 7 TQ30
Brightons: Stirl. NS 9277
Brightwell: Berks SU 5790
Brig o' Turk: Perth. NN 5306
Brigstock: Northants SP 9485
Brill: Bucks SP 6513
Brimfield: Here. SO 5267
Brims Ness: Caith. 17 ND07
Brinklow: War SP 4379
Brinkworth: Wilts. SU 0184
Brisco: Cumb. NY 4251
Bristol: Eng. 11 ST57
Bristol Channel: Eng. 10 SS/ST
Brit: r. 9 SY49
Briton Ferry: Glam. 10 SS79
Brixham: Devon. 8 SX95
Brixworth: Northants SP 7470
Brize Norton: Oxon. SP 2907
Broad Bay: Lewis 16 NB53
Broad Cairn: Scot. 17 NO28
Broad Chalke: Wilts. SU 0325
Broad Clyst: Devon. SX 9897
Broadford: Skye NG 6423
Broad Haven: Mayo 18 B7
Broad Haven: Pemb SM 8713
Broadhembury: Devon. ST 1004
Broadhempston: Devon. SX 8066
Broad Hinton: Wilts. SU 1076
Broad Law: mtn., Scot. 15 NT12
Broadmayne: Dorset SY 7286
Broadstairs: Kent 7 TR36
Broadway: Worcs 11 SP03
Broadwindsor: Dorset ST 4302
Brochel: Raasay NG 5846
Brock: r. 12 SD53
Brockenhurst: Hants SU 2902
Brockhampton: Here. SO 6855
Brocklesby: Lincs TA 1311
Brodick: Bute. 14 NS03
Broker: Lewis NB 5536
Bromborough: Ches. SJ 3582
Bromfield: Salop SO 4876
Bromham: Beds TL 0051
Bromley: Kent 7 TQ46
Brompton: Yorks SE 4697
Brompton: Yorks SE 9482
Brompton Regis: Som. SS 9531
Bromsgrove: Worcs 11 SO97
Bromyard: Here. 11 SO65
Bronllys: Breck. SO 1435
Brooke: Norf. TM 2999
Brookland: Kent TQ 9825
Broom: War SP 0953
Brora: & r., Suther. 17 NC90
Broseley: Salop 11 SJ60
Brosna: r. 19 F5
Brotton: Yorks 13 NZ61
Brough: Shet. Is. HU 5564
Brough: Westmor. 13 NY71
Brough Head: Ork. Is. 17 HY22
Broughton: Hants SU 3132
Broughton: Lancs SD 5234
Broughton: Northants SP 8375
Broughton: Oxon. SP 4238
Broughton: Peeb. NT 1136
Broughton Astley: Leics. SP 5292
Broughton in Furness:
Lancs 12 SD28
Broughton Moor: Cumb. NY 0533
Broughty Ferry: Angus. NO 4630
Brown Cow Hill: Aber. 17 NJ20
Browney: r. 13 NZ24
Brownhills: Staffs 11 SK00
Brownsea I.: Dorset 9 SZ08
Brown Willy: mtn., Corn. 8 SX18
Broxa: Yorks SE 9491
Broxburn: W. Loth. NT 0872
Broxted: Essex TL 5727
Brue: r. 9 ST44
Bruernish Pt.: Barra 16 NF70
Brumby: Lincs SE 8909
Brunton: Fife NO 3220
Bruton: Som. 9 ST63
Bryanston: Dorset 9 ST80
Brydekirk: Dumf. NY 1870
Bryher: Scilly Is. 8 SV81
Brymbo: Denb. SJ 2953
Brynamman: Carm. SN 7114
Bryn Brawd: mtn., Card. 10 SN65
Bryn Celli Ddu: Anglesey SH 5170
Brynmawr: Mon. 10 SO11
Bryn-Siencyn: Anglesey SH 4867
Bualintur: Skye NG 4020
Bubwith: Yorks SE 7136
Buchan: Aber. 17 NJ95
Buchan Ness: Aber. 17 NK14
Buchanty: Perth. NN 9327
Buchany: Perth. NN 7202
Buchlyvie: Stirl. NS 5793
Buck, The: mtn., Scot. 17 NJ42
Buckden Pike: mtn., Yorks 15 SD97
Buckfastleigh: Devon 8 SX76
Buckhaven: Fife 15 NT39
Buckhurst Hill: Essex TQ 4193
Buckie: Banff 17 NJ46
Buckingham: Bucks 11 SP63
BUCKINGHAMSHIRE:
Eng. 7 SP—
Buckland: Herts TL 3533
Buckland: Kent TR 3042
Buckland Abbey: Devon. 8 SX46
Buckland Brewer: Devon. SS 4120
Buckland St. Mary: Som. ST 2713
Bucklesham: Suff. TM 2442
Buckley: Flint. 10 SJ26
Buckminster: Leics. SK 8722
Bucknall: Lincs TF 1668
Bucknell: Salop SO 3574
Bucksburn: Aber. NJ 8909
Buddon Ness: Angus 15 NO53
Bude: & bay, Corn. 8 SS20
Budleigh Salterton:
Devon. 9 SY08
Bugbrooke: Northants SP 6757
Bugthorpe: Yorks SE 7757
Builth Wells: Breck. 10 SO05
Bulford: Wilts. SU 1643
Bull Bay: Anglesey 10 SH49
Bull Pt.: Devon. 8 SS44
Bulmer: Yorks SE 6967
Bulphan: Essex TQ 6385
Bulwick: Northants SP 9694
Bunbury: Ches. SJ 5658
Buncrana: Don. 18 G9
Bundoran: Don. 18 E7
Bunessan: Mull NM 3821
Bungay: Suff. 6 TM38
Bunloinn Forest: Inv. NH 1608
Bunloit: Inv. NH 5025
Bunnahabhain: Islay NR 4374
Buntingford: Herts 7 TL32
Burbage: Leics. SP 4492
Burbage: Wilts. SU 2261
Bure: r. 6 TG41
Bures: Essex TL 9034
Burford: Oxon. 11 SP21
Burgess Hill: Sussex 7 TQ31
Burgh by Sands: Cumb. NY 3259
Burgh Castle: Norf. TG 4805
Burghclere: Hants SU 4657
Burghead: Moray 17 NJ16
Burgh le Marsh: Lincs. 6 TF56
Burghley House:
Northants 11 TF00
Burgh St. Margaret: Norf. TG 4413
Burham: Kent TQ 7262
Burhou: i., Chan. Is. 9 Ins.
Buriton: Hants 7 SU72
Burlescombe: Devon. ST 0716
Burley: Hants SU 2103
Burn: r., Yorks 13 SE17
Burnbank: Lan. NS 7055
Burneside: Westmor. SD 5095
Burneston: Yorks SE 3084
Burnham: Bucks SU 9382
Burnham Flats: North Sea 6 TF75
Burnham Market: Norf. 6 TF84
Burnham Crouch:
Essex 7 TQ99
Burnham on Sea: Som. 9 ST34
Burnham Overy: Norf. TF 8442
Burnhaven: Aber. NK 1244
Burnley: Lancs 13 SD83
Burnmouth: Ber. NT 9560
Burnopfield: Dur. NZ 1756
Burnsall: Yorks SE 0361
Burnswark: Dumf. 15 NY17
Burntisland: Fife 15 NT28
Burravoe: Shet. Is. HU 5178
Burray: Ork. Is. ND 4796
Burrelton: Perth. NO 2036
Burrow Head: Wig. 14 NX43
Burry Holms: Glam. 8 SS49
Burry Port: Carm. 10 SN40
Burscough: Lancs SD 4310
Burslem: Staffs 11 SJ84
Burstwick: Yorks TA 2228
Burton: Ches. SJ 3174
Burton: Westmor. 12 SD57
Burton Agnes: Yorks TA 1063
Burton Bradstock: Dorset SY 4889
Burton Joyce: Notts SK 6443
Burton Latimer:
Northants 11 SP97
Burton Pidsea: Yorks TA 2431
Burtonport: Don. 18 E8
Burton Salmon: Yorks SE 4827
Burton upon Stather: Lincs SE 8617
Burton upon Trent:
Staffs 11 SK22
Burtonwood: Lancs 12 SJ59
Burwarton: Salop SO 6185
Burwash: Sussex TQ 6724
Burwell: Cambs. TL 5866
Burwick: Ork. Is. ND 4384
Bury: Lancs 13 SD81
Bury St. Edmunds: Suff. 6 TL86
Bush: r. 18 H9
Bushey: Herts 7 TQ19
BUTESHIRE: Scot. 14 NS06
Bute Sound 14 NS05
Butleigh: Som. ST 5233
Butser Hill: Hants 7 SU72
Buttermere: Cumb. 12 NY11
Butterwick: Lincs TF 3845
Butt of Lewis 16 NB56
Buxey: Essex 7 TM10
Buxton: Derby. 13 SK07
Buxton: Norf. TG 2222
Byfield: Northants SP 5153
Byfleet: Surrey TQ 0461
Bylchau: Denb. SH 9762

Cabrach: Banff NJ 3826
Cadbury Castle: Som. 9 ST62
Cader Idris: mtn., Mer. 10 SH71
Cadgwith: Corn. SW 7214
Cadnam: Hants SU 2913
Cadoxton: Glam. ST 1269
Caergwrle: Flint. SJ 3057
Caerhun: Caer. SH 7770
Caerleon: Mon. 10 ST39
Caernarvon: & bay, Caer. 10 SH46
CAERNARVONSHIRE:
Wales 10 SH—
Caerphilly: Glam. 10 ST18
Caerwent: Mon. ST 4790
Caerwys: Flint. SJ 1272
Caha Mts.: Cork/Kerry 19 B2
Caher: Tip. 19 F3
Caher I.: Mayo 18 A6
Cahersiveen: Kerry 19 A2
Cahore Point: Wex. 19 J4
Cain: r. 10 SJ12
Caio: Carm. SN 6739
Cairndow: Argyll NN 1810
Cairngorm Mts.: Scot. 17 NH90
Cairnharrow: Kirkc. 14 NX55
Cairn Pat: Wig. 12 NX05
Cairnsmore: Kirkc. 14 NX69
Cairnsmore of Fleet:
Kirkc. 14 NX56
Cairn Table: Ayr./Lan. 14 NS72
Cairn Toul: mtn., Aber. 17 NN99
Cairn Water: r. 15 NX88
Caister on Sea: Norf. TG 5211
Caistor: Lincs 6 TA10
CAITHNESS: Co., Scot. 17 ND14
Caldbeck: Cumb. NY 3239
Caldecott: Rut. SP 8693
Calder: r. 13 SE02
Calderbank: Lan. NS 7662
Calder Bridge: Cumb. NY 0405
Caldercruix: Lan. NS 8167
Caldew: r. 12 NY34
Caldy I.: Pemb 10 SS19
Cale: r. 9 ST72
Calf of Man: I. of Man 12 SC16
Calgary: Mull NM 3751
Calgary Bay: Argyll 16 NM35
Calgary Point: Coll 16 NM15
Caliach Point: Argyll 16 NM35
Callan: Kilk. 19 G4
Callander: Perth. 14 NN60
Callanish: Lewis NB 2133
Callicvol: Lewis NB 5464
Callievar Hill: Aber. 17 NJ51
Callington: Corn. 8 SX36
Calne: Wilts. 11 ST97
Calshot Castle: Hants 7 SU40
Calstock: Corn. SX 4368
Calve I.: Argyll NM 5254
Calverton: Notts. SK 6149
Cam: r. 6 TL57
Camastianavaig: Skye NG 5039
Camberley: Surrey 7 SU85
Cambois: Northumb. NZ 3083
Camborne: Corn. 8 SW64
Cambrian Mts.: Wales 10 SH—
Cambridge: Cambs. 6 TL45
CAMBRIDGESHIRE:
Eng. 6 TL—
Cambus: Clack. NS 8593
Cambuslang: Lan. 14 NS66
Camel: r. 8 SX17
Camelford: Corn. 8 SX18
Camghouran: Perth. NN 5455
Cam Loch: Suther. 16 NC21
Camoge: r. 19 D4
Campbeltown: Argyll 14 NR72
Campseyash: Suff. TM 3356
Campsie Fells: Stirl. 14 NS68
Camrose: Pemb SM 9220
Camster: Caith. ND 2644
Camusteel: R. & Crom. NG 7142
Can: r. 7 TL61
Canewdon: Essex TQ 8994
Canisp Assynt: mtn.,
Suther. 16 NC21
Canna: i., Inv. 16 NG20
Cannich: Inv. NH 3331
Cannich: r. 16 NH23
Cannington: Som. ST 2539
Cannock: Staffs 11 SJ90
Cannock Chase: Staffs. 11 SJ91
Canonbie: Dumf. NY 3976
Canterbury: Kent 7 TR15
Canvey I.: Essex 7 TQ78
Capel: Surrey TQ 1740
Capel Curig: Caer. 10 SH75
Capel Garmon: Denb. 10 SH85
Capheaton: Northumb. NZ 0380
Caple St. Mary: Suff. TM 0938
Caputh: Perth. NO 0839
Cara: i., Argyll 14 NR64
Carbis Bay: Corn. SW 5339
Carbost: Skye NG 3731
Cardiff: Glam. 10 ST17
Cardigan: Card. 10 SN14
Cardigan Bay: Card. 10 SN48
Cardigan I.: Card. 10 SN15
CARDIGANSHIRE:
Wales 10 SN—
Cardington: Salop SO 5095
Cardross: Dunb. NS 3477
Careston: Angus NO 5260
Carew: Pemb SN 0403
Carey: r. 8 SX39
Carfin: Lan. NS 7758
Cargill: Perth. NO 1536
Carham: Northumb. NT 7938
Carie: Perth. NN 6157
Carisbrooke: I. of Wight 7 SZ48
Cark: Lancs SD 3676
Carlingford L.: Irel. 18 J7
Carlisle: Cumb. 12 NY35
Carlops: Peeb. NT 1656
CARLOW: Co., R. of
Irel. 19 H4
Carloway: Lewis NB 2042
Carlton: Notts. SK 6141
Carlton: Yorks SE 6423
Carlton in Lindrick: Notts. SK 5984
Carluke: Lan. 15 NS85
Carmarthen: Carm. 10 SN42
Carmarthen Bay: Carm. 10 SS29
CARMARTHENSHIRE:
Wales 10 SN—
Carmel Head: Anglesey 10 SH29
Carmyllie: Angus NO 5542
Carnaby: Yorks TA 1465
Carnan Iochdar: S. Uist NF 7847
Càrn Bàn: Inv. 17 NH60
Carnbee: Fife NO 5306
Carnbo: Kinr. NO 0503
Càrn-Coire nah Easgainn:
Inv. 17 NH71
Càrn Easgann Bàna: Inv. 17 NH40
Carneddau Hengwm: Mer. SH 6120
Carnedd Dafydd: Caer. 10 SH66
Carnedd Llewelyn: Caer. 10 SH66
Carnedd Wen: Montg. 10 SH90
Carnedd y Filiast: Wales 10 SH84
Càrn Eige: Ross&Crom. 16 NH12
Carnforth: Lancs 12 SD47
Càrn Glas-Choire: Inv. 17 NH82
Càrn Kitty: Moray NJ 0842
Càrn Mairg: Perth. 17 NN65
Càrn Mòr: Banff 17 NJ21
Càrn na Cairn: Inv./Perth. 17 NN68
Càrn na Loine: Moray. 17 NJ03
Càrn na Saobhaidhe: Inv. 17 NH61
Carnock: Fife NT 0489
Carnoustie: Angus 15 NO53
Carnsore Point: Wex. 19 J3
Carnwath: Lan. NS 9746
Carperby: Yorks. SE 0089
Carra, L.: Mayo. 18 C6
Carradale: Argyll NR 8138
Carrauntuohil: mtn., Kerry 19 B3
Carrbridge: Inv. NH 9022
Carreg Ddu: mtn., Caer. 10 SH24
Carregwasted Pt.: Pemb 10 SM94
Carrick: Argyll NS 1994
Carrick: Ayr. 14 NX39
Carrickfergus: Antrim. 18 K8
Carrickmacross:
Monaghan 18 H6
Carrick on Shannon: Leit. 18 E6
Carrick-on-Suir: Tip. 19 G3
Carron: r., Ross&Crom. 16 NG94
Carron: r., Ross&Crom. 17 NH59
Carron: r., Stirl. 15 NS78
Carrowmore Lake: Mayo 18 B7
Carsaig: Mull NM 5421
Carse of Forth: Stirl. 14 NS79
Carse of Gowrie: Perth. 15 NO22
Carshalton: Surrey 7 TQ26
Carsphairn: Kirkc. NX 5693
Carstairs Junc.: Lan. 15 NS94
Carter Bar: Eng./Scot. 15 NT60
Carthorpe: Yorks SE 3083
Cartmel: Lancs 12 SD37
Cary: r. 9 ST42
Cashel: Tip. 19 F4
Casquet Banks: Chan. Is. 9 Ins.
Casquets: i., Chan. Is. 9 Ins.
Cassley: r. 17 NC41
Castell Carreg Cennen:
Carm. 10 SN62
Castell Tomen y Mur:
Mer. SH 7038
Castle Acre: Norf. TF 8115
Castle an Dinas: Corn. SW 9462
Castle Ashby: Northants SP 8659
Castlebar: Mayo 18 C6
Castlebay: Barra 16 NL69
Castleblaney: Monaghan 18 H7
Castle Bolton: Yorks SE 0391
Castle Bytham: Lincs SK 9818
Castle Campbell: Clack. NS 9699
Castle Carrock: Cumb. NY 5455
Castle Cary: Som. 9 ST63
Castle Combe: Wilts. ST 8477
Castlederg: Tyr. 18 F8
Castle Donington: Leics. SK 4427
Castle Douglas: Kirkc. 14 NX76
Castle Eden: Dur. NZ 4338
Castleford: Yorks 13 SE42
Castle Hedingham: Essex TL 7835
Castleisland: Kerry 19 C3
Castle Loch: Wig. 12 NX25
Castlemartin: Pemb SR 9198
Castle of Mey: Caith. 17 ND27
Castlepollard: Westmeath 18 G6
Castlerea: Rosc. 18 E6
Castlerigg: Cumb. NY 2822
Castle Rising: Norf. TF 6624
Castleside: Dur. NZ 0748
Castleton: Derby. SK 1582
Castletown: Caith. ND 1967
Castletown: I. of Man. 12 SC26
Caston: Norf. TL 9598
Catcleugh: l., Northumb. 15 NT70
Cateran Hill: Northumb. NU 1023
Caterham: Surrey 7 TQ35
Caterthuns: Angus NO 5666
Catfield: Norf. TG 3821
Cat Law: Angus. 17 NO36
Caton: Lancs SD 5364
Catrine: Ayr NS 5225
Catsfield: Sussex. TQ 7213
Cattal: Yorks SE 4454
Catterall: Lancs SD 4942
Catterick: Yorks. SE 2397
Catterick Camp: Yorks 13 SE19
Catterline: Kinc. NO 8678
Catworth: Hunts TL 0873
Cauldcleuch Head: Rox. 15 NT40
Caulkerbush: Kirkc. NX 9257
Causamul: i., Inv. NF 6670
CAVAN: Co., R. of Irel. 18 G6
Cavendish: Suff. TL 8046
Cavenham: Suff. TL 7669
Caversham: Berks SU 7274
Cawdor: Nairn. 17 NH85
Cawood: Yorks 13 SE53
Cawston: Norf. TG 1324
Caxton: Cambs. TL 3058
Caythorpe: Lincs. SK 9348
Caythorpe: Notts. SK 6845
Cayton: Yorks TA 0583
Ceannanus Mor: Meath 18 H6
Ceann Riobha: Argyll. 14 NR38
Cefn-Einion: Salop SO 2886
Cefni: r. 10 SH47
Cefntilla Court: Mon. SO 4003
Ceiriog: r. 10 SJ23
Ceirw: r. 10 SJ04
Cellar Head: Lewis NB 5656
Cemaes Bay: Anglesey. 10 SH39
Cemaes Head: Pemb 10 SN15
Cemmaes: Montg. SH 8306
Ceres: Fife. NO 4011
Ceri: r. 10 SN34
Cerne: r. 9 SY69
Cerne Abbas: Dorset 9 ST60
Cerrigydrudion: Denb. SH 9548
Chaddesden: Derby. SK 3737
Chaddesley Corbett:
Worcs. SO 8973
Chadlington: Oxon. SP 3221
Chagford: Devon. 8 SX78
Chale: I. of Wight SZ 4877
Chalfont St. Giles: Bucks SU 9993
Chalford: Glos SO 8902
Chalgrove: Oxon. 11 SU69
Challacombe: Devon. SS 6941
Chanctonbury Ring:
Sussex 7 TQ11
Chandler's Ford: Hants SU 4320
Channel Islands 9 Ins.
Chapel en le Frith: Derby. SK 0580
Chapel of Garioch: Aber. NJ 7124
Chapeltown: Banff NJ 2421
Chapeltown: Lancs SD 7315
Char: r. 9 SY49
Chard: Dorset 9 ST30
Charing: Kent TQ 9549
Charlbury: Oxon. 11 SP31
Charlecote: War. SP 2656
Charles: Devon. SS 6832
Charlestown: Corn. SX 0351
Charlestown: Fife NT 0683
Charlestown of Aberlour:
Banff 17 NJ24
Charleville: Cork 19 D3
Charmouth: Dorset SY 3693
Charnwood Forest: Leics. 11 SK41
Charterhouse: Surrey 7 SU94
Chasetown: Staffs SK 0408
Chastleton: Oxon. SP 2429
Chatburn: Lancs SD 7644
Chater: r. 11 SK90
Chatham: Kent 7 TQ76
Chat Moss: Lancs 12 SJ79
Chatsworth House:
Derby. 13 SK27
Chatteris: Cambs. 6 TL38
Chatton: Northumb. NU 0528
Chawleigh: Devon. SS 7112
Chawton: Hants SU 7037
Cheadle: Ches. 13 SJ88
Cheadle: Staffs 11 SK04
Cheadle Hulme: Ches. SJ 8686
Cheddar: & gorge, Som. 9 ST45
Cheddleton: Staffs SJ 9651
Chedworth: Glos 11 SP01
Chelford: Ches. SJ 8174

G.B. & IRELAND

CHELLASTON — CYMMER

Chellaston: Derby. . *SK 3830*
Chelmer: *r.* . **7 TL62**
Chelmorton: Derby. . *SK 1169*
Chelmsford: Essex . **7 TL70**
Chelsea: London . **7 TQ27**
Cheltenham: Glos **11 SO92**
Chenies: Bucks . *TQ 0198*
Chepstow: Mon.. **11 ST59**
Chequers: Bucks. **11 SP80**
Cherhill: Wilts. . *SU 0370*
Cheriton: Hants . *SU 5828*
Cheriton: Kent . *TR 2036*
Cheriton Bishop: Devon. *SX 7793*
Cheriton Fitzpaine: Devon *SS 8606*
Cherry Burton: Yorks . *SE 9842*
Chertsey: Surrey. **7 TQ06**
Cherwell: *r.* . **11 SP44**
Chesham: Bucks. **11 SP90**
Chesham Bois: Bucks . *SU 9698*
CHESHIRE: Eng. **11 SJ—**
Cheshunt: Herts . **7 TL30**
Chesil Beach: Dorset . **9 SY58**
Chess: *r.* . . **11 SU99**
Chester: Ches. . **11 SJ46**
Chesterfield: Derby. **13 SK37**
Chester-le-Street: Dur. **13 NZ25**
Chesters: Northumb. **15 NY97**
Chesters: Rox. . **15 NT61**
Chesters, The: E. Loth.. *NT 5178*
Chesterton: Cambs. *TL 4560*
Chet: *r.* . . **6 TG20**
Cheveley: Cambs. *TL 6760*
Cheviot, The: *mtn.,* Northumb. **15 NT92**
Cheviot Hills: Eng./Scot. **15 NT70**
Chew: *r.* . . **9 ST66**
Chew Magna: Som. *ST 5763*
Chewton Mendip: Som. *ST 5952*
Chichester: Sussex . **7 SU80**
Chicken Hd.: Lewis *NB 5029*
Chiddingfold: Surrey *SU 9635*
Chideock: Dorset *SY 4292*
Chieveley: Berks *SU 4773*
Chigwell: Essex . **7 TQ49**
Chilham: Kent . *TR 0753*
Chillesford: Suff. *TM 3852*
Chillingham: Northumb. *NU 0625*
Chiltern Hills: Bucks **11 SU—**
Chinnor: Oxon. . *SP 7500*
Chippenham: Cambs. *TL 6669*
Chippenham: Wilts. **11 ST97**
Chipping: Lancs . *SD 6243*
Chipping Campden: Glos . . **11 SP13**
Chipping Norton: Oxon. **11 SP32**
Chipping Ongar: Essex **7 TL50**
Chipping Sodbury: Glos **11 ST78**
Chipping Warden: Northants . *SP 4948*
Chirbury: Salop . *SO 2598*
Chirk: Denb. . *SJ 2937*
Chirnside: Ber. . *NT 8756*
Chiseldon: Wilts. *SU 1879*
Chislehurst: Kent **7 TQ47**
Chitterne: Wilts. *ST 9843*
Chittlehampton: Devon *SS 6325*
Chobham: Surrey *SU 9761*
Chollerton: Northumb.. *NY 9372*
Cholsey: Berks . *SU 5886*
Chop Gate: Yorks *SE 5599*
Chopwell: Dur. . *NZ 1158*
Chorley: Lancs . **12 SD51**
Christchurch: Hants . **9 SZ19**
Christleton: Ches. *SJ 4365*
Christow: Devon. *SX 8385*
Christ's Hospital: Sussex **7 TQ12**
Chudleigh: Devon. **8 SX87**
Chulmleigh: Devon. **8 SS61**
Church: Lancs . *SD 7428*
Churchdown: Glos *SO 8819*
Church Fenton: Yorks *SE 5136*
Churchill: Oxon. *SP 2824*
Churchill: Som. . *ST 4359*
Church Lench: Worcs *SP 0251*
Church Minshull: Ches. *SJ 6660*
Church Stoke: Montg.. *SO 2694*
Church Stretton: Salop **11 SO49**
Church Town: Westmor. *SD 4491*
Churn: *r.* . . **9 SU09**
Churnet: *r.* . . **13 SK04**
Churton: Ches. . *SJ 4156*
Chwefru: *r.* . . **10 SN95**
Chysauster: Corn. *SW 4835*
Cilcennin: Card. . *SN 5160*
Cilfaesty Hill: Montg.. **10 SO18**
Cilgerran: Pemb . *SN 1943*
Cilycwm: Carm. . *SN 7540*
Cinderford: Glos . **9 SO61**
Cirencester: Glos . **11 SP00**
Cissbury Ring: Sussex . *TQ 1408*
Clachaig: Argyll . *NS 1281*
Clachan: Argyll . *NR 7656*
Clachan of Campsie: Stirl. *NS 6179*
Clachan of Glendaruel: Argyll *NR 9984*
Clach Leathad: Argyll. **14 NN24**
CLACKMANNAN: *Co.,* Scot. **15 NS99**
Clacton on Sea: Essex. **7 TM11**
Claerwen: *r.* . **10 SN86**
Claggain Bay: Islay **14 NR45**
Clanfield: Oxon. . *SP 2801*
Clapton: Northants *TL 0680*
Clara: Offaly . **19 F5**
Clare: Suff. . **7 TL74**
CLARE: *Co.,* R. of Irel. **19 D4**
Clare: *r.* . . **18 D6**
Clare I.: Mayo . **18 A6**
Claremorris: Mayo . **18 C6**
Clashindarroch Forest: Aber. *NJ 4634*
Clashmore: Suther. *NH 7489*
Clashnessie: Suther. *NC 0530*
Clatteringshaws Loch: Kirkc. . **14 NX57**
Clatworthy: Som. *ST 0530*
Claughton: Lancs *SD 5666*
Claughton: Lancs *SD 5242*
Clava: Inv. . *NH 7645*
Claverley: Salop . *SO 7993*
Claw: *r.* . . **8 SX39**
Claxby: Lincs . *TF 1094*
Clay Cross: Derby. **13 SK36**
Claydon: Suff. . *TM 1349*
Clay Head: I. of Man . **12 SC47**
Claypole: Lincs . *SK 8449*
Claythorpe: Lincs *TF 4179*
Clayton: Yorks . **13 SE13**
Clayton West: Yorks *SE 2511*
Clayworth: Notts. *SK 7288*
Cleadale: Eigg . *NM 4789*
Clear, Cape: Cork **19 B1**
Clear I.: Cork . **19 C1**
Clearwell: Glos . *SO 5708*
Cleator: Cumb. . *NY 0113*
Cleator Moor: Cumb.. **12 NY01**
Cleckheaton: Yorks **13 SE12**
Clee Hills: Salop . **11 SO58**
Cleethorpes: Lincs **6 TA30**
Clehonger: Here. *SO 4637*
Clent Hills: Worcs **11 SO97**
Cleobury Mortimer: Salop . . **11 SO67**
Cleobury North: Salop. *SO 6187*
Cletwr: *r.* . . **10 SN44**
Clevedon: Som. . **9 ST47**
Cleveland: Yorks . **13 NZ61**
Cleveland Hills: Yorks **13 NZ60**
Cleveleys: Lancs **12 SD34**
Clew Bay: Mayo . **18 B6**
Cley next the Sea: Norf. *TG 0444*
Cliburn: Westmor. *NY 5824*
Clifden: Gal. . **18 A5**
Cliffe: Kent . *TQ 7376*
Cliffe: Yorks . *NZ 2015*
Clifford: Here. . *SO 2445*
Clifford Chambers: War *SP 1952*
Cliffs of Moher: Clare. **19 C4**
Clifton Gorge: Bristol . **9 ST57**
Clifton Hampden: Oxon. *SU 5495*
Clifton upon Teme: Worcs *SO 7161*
Cliftonville: Kent. *TR 3770*
Clipston: Northants *SP 7181*
Clisham: *mtn.,* Harris . **16 NB10**
Clitheroe: Lancs. **13 SD74**
Clive: Salop . *SJ 5124*
Clogher Head: Louth . **18 J6**
Clonakilty: Cork **19 D2**
Clondalkin: Dublin **19 J5**
Clones: Monaghan **18 G7**
Clonmel: Tip. . **19 F3**
Clontarf: Dublin **19 J5**
Clophill: Beds . *TL 0838*
Cloughton: Yorks *TA 0094*
Clovelly: Devon. **8 SS32**
Clovenfords: Selk. *NT 4436*
Clowne: Derby. . *SK 4975*
Cluanie Forest: Ross & Crom. *NH 0409*
Clun: & *r.,* Salop **10 SO38**
Clunbury: Salop . *SO 3780*
Clun Forest: Salop **10 SO28**
Clunie Water: *r.* **17 NO18**
Clutton: Som. . *ST 6159*
Clwyd: *r.* . . **10 SJ15**
Clwydian Range: Wales **10 SJ17**
Clydach: Breck. . *SO 2213*
Clydach: Glam. . *SN 6801*
Clyde: *r.* . . **14 NS37**
Clydebank: Dunb. **14 NS47**
Clydesdale: Lanark **15 NS84**
Clynnog-fawr: Caer. *SH 4149*
Clyro: Rad. . *SO 2143*
Clyst: *r.* . . **8 SY09**
Clyst St. Mary: Devon. *SX 9890*
Clywedog: *r.,* Denb. **10 SJ05**
Clywedog: *r.,* Montg. **10 SN89**
Cnoc Moy: *mtn.,* Argyll **14 NR61**
Coal Aston: Derby. *SK 3679*
Coalbrookdale: Salop **11 SJ60**
Coalburn: Lan. . *NS 8034*
Coalisland: Tyr. **18 H8**
Coalville: Leics. **11 SK41**
Coatbridge: Lan. **14 NS76**
Coates: Cambs. . *TL 3097*
Coatham: Yorks **13 NZ52**
Cobbinshaw: Midloth. *NT 0257*
Cobh: Cork . **19 E2**
Cobham: Kent . *TQ 6768*
Cobham: Surrey . *TQ 1059*
Cock Bridge: Aber. *NJ 2509*
Cockburnspath: Ber. *NT 7770*
Cockenzie: E. Loth. **15 NT47**
Cockerham: Lancs *SD 4651*
Cockermouth: Cumb. **12 NY13**
Cockfield: Dur. . *NZ 1224*
Cockfield: Suff. . *TL 9054*
Cocking: Sussex *SU 8717*
Cock of Arran: Bute. **14 NR95**
Cockshutt: Salop *SJ 4329*
Coddenham: Suff. *TM 1354*
Codford: Wilts. . *ST 9639*
Codicote: Herts . *TL 2118*
Codnor: Derby. . *SK 4149*
Cod's Head: Cork **19 A2**
Coedpoeth: Denb. *SJ 2851*
Coggeshall: Essex **7 TL82**
Colchester: Essex **7 TM02**
Cold Ash: Berks . *SU 5169*
Cold Ashby: Northants *SP 6576*
Coldbackie: Suther. *NC 6159*
Cold Fell: Cumb. **12 NY65**
Cold Hesledon: Dur. *NZ 4146*
Coldingham: Ber. *NT 9065*
Coldstream: Ber.. *NT 8439*
Cole: *r.* . . **11 SU18**
Colebrook: Devon. *SS 7700*
Coleford: Glos . **11 SO51**
Colesborne: Glos. *SP 0013*
Coleshill: War . **11 SP18**
Coll: Lewis . *NB 4740*
Coll: *i.,* Argyll . **16 NM15**
Collafirth: Shet. Is. *HU 3482*
Collessie: Fife . *NO 2813*
Collieston: Aber.. *NK 0328*
Collingbourne Kingston: Wilts. *SU 2355*
Collingham: Notts. *SK 8261*
Collingham: Yorks *SE 3845*
Collington: Here. *SO 6459*
Collinstown: Dublin **18 J5**
Colmonell: Ayr . *NX 1586*
Coln: *r.* . . **9 SP10**
Colne: Lancs . **13 SD83**
Colne: *r.* . . **7 TL92**
Colne Point: Essex **7 TM11**
Colonsay: *i.,* Argyll **14 NR39**
Colsterworth: Lincs *SK 9224*
Colt Hill: Dumf.. **14 NX69**
Coltishall: Norf. . *TG 2620*
Colton: Staffs . *SK 0520*
Colton: Yorks . *SE 5444*
Colwich: Staffs . *SK 0121*
Colwyn Bay: Denb. **10 SH87**
Colyton: Devon . **9 SY29**
Combe Martin: Devon. *SS 5846*
Comber: Down . **18 K8**
Comberton: Cambs. *TL 3856*
Comeragh Mts.: Wat. **19 F3**
Commondale: Yorks *NZ 6610*
Compton: Devon. *SX 8664*
Compton: Surrey *SU 9547*
Compton Wynyates: War . . **11 SP34**
Comrie: Perth. . *NN 7722*
Cona: *r.* . . **16 NM97**
Congleton: Ches. **11 SJ86**
Congresbury: Som. *ST 4363*
Coningsby: Lincs. *TF 2258*
Conisbrough: Yorks **13 SK59**
Coniston: Lancs *SD 3079*
Coniston: Yorks . *TA 1535*
Coniston Cold: Yorks *SD 9054*
Conistone: Yorks *SD 9867*
Conistone Moor: Yorks **13 SE07**
Coniston Water: *l.,* Lancs . **12 SD39**
Conn, L.: Mayo **18 C7**
Connah's Quay: Flint.. **10 SJ26**
Connaught: *Prov.,* Irel. **18/19 —**
Connel: Argyll . *NM 9134*
Connel Park: Ayr *NS 6012*
Connemara: Gal. **18 B5**
Cononbridge: R. & Crom. *NH 5455*
Consett: Dur. . **13 NZ15**
Constantine: Corn. *SW 7229*
Constantine Bay: Corn. **8 SW87**
Contin: Ross & Crom.. *NH 4555*
Conway: & *bay,* Caer. **10 SH77**
Conway: *r.* . . **12 SH85**
Conwyl Elfed: Carm. *SN 3727*
Cooden: Sussex . *TQ 7207*
Cookham: Berks. *SU 8985*
Cookstown: Tyr. **18 H8**
Coomacarren: Kerry **19 A2**
Coombe Bissett: Wilts. *SU 1026*
Coombe Hill: Glos *SO 8827*
Cootehill: Cavan **18 G7**
Copinsay: i., Ork. Is. *HY 6101*
Coppins: Bucks . **7 TQ08**
Copplestone: Devon. *SS 7702*
Coquet: *r.,* & *dale,* Northumb. . **15 NZ19**
Corbridge: Northumb. **15 NY96**
Corby: Lincs . *SK 9925*
Corby: Northants **11 SP88**
Corfe: Som. . *ST 2319*
Corfe Castle: Dorset **9 SY98**
Corgarff: Aber. . *NJ 2708*
CORK: *Co.,* R. of Irel. **19 E2**
Cork Harbour: Cork **19 E2**
Corley: War . *SP 3085*
Corney: Cumb. . *SD 1191*
Cornforth: Dur. . *NZ 3034*
Cornhill: Banff . *NJ 5858*
Cornhill on Tweed: Northumb. *NT 8639*
Cornholme: Yorks *SD 9025*
CORNWALL: *Co.,* Eng. **8 SX—**
Cornwall, Cape: Corn. **8 SW33**
Corran: Argyll . **16 NN06**
Correen Hills: Aber. **17 NJ52**
Corrib, L.: Gal. . **19 C5**
Corrie: Bute. . *NS 0243*
Corrie Common: Dumf. *NY 2086*
Corringham: Lincs *SK 8691*
Corris: Mer. . *SH 7507*
Corrour Forest: Scot. *NN 4167*
Corsapool: Islay . *NR 2966*
Corse Hill: Lanark **14 NS64**
Corserine: Kirkc. **14 NX48**
Corsham: Wilts. **11 ST87**
Corsock: Kirkc. . *NX 7576*
Corston: Wilts. . *ST 9284*
Cortachy: Angus *NO 3959*
Corton: Suff. . *TM 5497*
Corve: *r.,* & *dale,* Salop **11 SO59**
Corwen: Mer. . **10 SJ04**
Coryton: Devon. *SX 4583*
Cosby: Leics. . *SP 5495*
Coseley: Staffs . *SO 9494*
Cosham: Hants . **7 SU60**
Cosheston: Pemb. *SN 0003*
Costessey: Norf. . *TG 1712*
Costock: Notts. . *SK 5726*
Cotehele: Corn. . **8 SX46**
Cotehill: Cumb. . *NY 4750*
Cotherstone: Dur. *NZ 0119*
Cothi: *r.* . . **8 SN63**
Cotswolds: *hills,* Glos . **11 ST/SP**
Cottenham: Cambs. *TL 4567*
Cottered: Herts . *TL 3129*
Cottesmore: Rut. *SK 9013*
Cottingham: Northants *SP 8490*
Cottingham: Yorks **13 TA03**
Coughton: War . *SP 0760*
Coul Point: Islay **14 NR16**
Coulin Forest: Ross & Crom. *NG 9954*
Coull: Aber. . *NJ 5102*
Coulsdon: Surrey **7 TQ35**
Coundon: Dur. . *NZ 2329*
Countesthorpe: Leics. *SP 5895*
Coupar Angus: Perth. **15 NO23**
Cour: Argyll . *NR 8248*
Courtmacsherry Bay: Cork . . **19 D2**
Cove: Hants . *SU 8555*
Cove: Kinc. . *NJ 9500*
Coventry: War . **11 SP37**
Cover: *r.* . . **13 SE07**
Coverack: Corn.. *SW 7818*
Covesea Skerries: Moray **17 NJ17**
Covington: Lan. . *NS 9739*
Cowal: Argyll . **14 NS09**
Cowbridge: Glam. **10 SS97**
Cowdenbeath: Fife. **15 NT19**
Cowdray Park: Sussex. **7 SU92**
Cowes: I. of Wight **7 SZ49**
Cowfold: Sussex . *TQ 2122*
Cowie: Stirl. . *NS 8389*
Cowie Water: *r.* . **17 NO88**
Cowley: Oxon. . **11 SP50**
Cowling: Yorks . *SD 9743*
Cowshill: Dur. . *NY 8540*
Coxhoe: Dur. . *NZ 3235*
Coxwold: Yorks . *SE 5377*
Coylton: Ayr . *NS 4219*
Craig: Angus . *NO 7055*
Craighouse: Jura. *NR 5267*
Craigie: Ayr . *NS 4232*
Craigiebar Castle: Aber. *NJ 5609*
Craigielands: Dumf. *NT 0802*
Craigmore: Bute. **14 NS16**
Craignure: Argyll *NM 7236*
Craigton: Angus . *NO 5138*
Crail: Fife . **15 NO60**
Crailing: Rox. . **15 NT62**
Crake: *r.* . . **12 SD28**
Cramlington: Northumb. *NZ 2776*
Cranborne: Dorset *SU 0513*
Cranborne Chase: Dorset . **9 ST91**
Cranbrook: Kent **7 TQ73**
Cranfield: Beds . *SP 9542*
Cranham: Glos . *SO 8912*
Cranleigh: Surrey **7 TQ03**
Cranshaws: E. Loth. *NT 6861*
Cranstackie: Suther. *NC 3555*
Crantock: Corn. . *SW 7860*
Cranwell: Lincs . **6 TF05**
Craster: Northumb. *NU 2519*
Crathes Castle: Kinc. *NO 7396*
Crathie: Aber. . **17 NO29**
Crathorne: Yorks *NZ 4407*
Craven: Yorks . **13 SD95**
Craven Arms: Salop **11 SO48**
Crawford: Lan. . *NS 9520*
Crawfordjohn: Lan. *NS 8823*
Crawick: Dumf. . *NS 7710*
Crawley: Hants . *SU 4234*
Crawley: Sussex . **7 TQ23**
Crawton: Kinc. . *NO 8779*
Cray: Breck. . *SN 8924*
Creach Bheinn: Argyll. **14 NN04**
Creagan: Argyll . *NM 9744*
Creag Meagaidh: Inv. . **17 NN48**
Creagorry: Benbecula *NF 7948*
Creag Riadhach na Graidhe: Suther. **17 NC62**
Credenhill: Here. *SO 4543*
Crediton: Devon. **8 SS80**
Cree: *r.* . . **12 NX37**
Creetown: Kirkc. *NX 4758*
Creran: *r.* . . **16 NN05**
Cressage: Salop . *SJ 5904*
Creswell: Northumb. *NZ 2993*
Creswell: Notts . **11 SK57**
Crewe: Ches. . **11 SJ65**
Crewkerne: Som. **9 ST40**
Crianlarich: Perth. **14 NN32**
Cribyn: Carm. . *SN 5251*
Criccieth: Caer. . **10 SH43**
Crich: Derby. . *SK 3554*
Crichton: Midloth. *NT 3862*
Crick: Northants. *SP 5872*
Crickadarn: Breck. *SO 0942*
Crickhowell: Breck. *SO 2118*
Cricklade: Wilts. **11 SU09**
Crieff: Perth. . **15 NN82**
Criffell: *mtn.,* Kirkc. **15 NX96**
Crimond: Aber. . *NK 0556*
Crimplesham: Norf. *TF 6503*
Crinan: Argyll . *NR 7894*
Cringleford: Norf. *TG 1905*
Crionaig: mtn., Lewis *NB 2906*
Croagh Patrick: Mayo. **18 B6**
Crocketford: Kirkc. *NX 8272*
Crockham Hill: Kent *TQ 4450*
Croft: Yorks . *NZ 2909*
Croglin Water: *r.* **12 NY64**
Croick: Ross & Crom.. *NH 4591*
Cromalt Hills: Suther.. **16 NC20**
Cromarty: R. & Crom. **17 NH76**
Cromarty Firth: Ross & Crom. **17 NH66**
Cromdale: Moray *NJ 0728*
Cromer: Norf. . **6 TG24**
Cromford: Derby. *SK 2956*
Crondall: Hants . *SU 7948*
Crook: Dur. . **13 NZ13**
Crookham: Northumb.. *NT 9138*
Crook of Alves: Moray *NJ 1362*
Crookston Castle: Lan. **14 NS56**
Cropredy: Oxon.. *SP 4646*
Cropton: Yorks . *SE 7589*
Crosby: I. of Man *SC 3279*
Crosby: Lancs . **12 SJ39**
Crossbost: Lewis *NB 3924*
Cross Fell: *mtn.,* Cumb. **12 NY63**
Crossford: Lan. . *NS 8246*
Crossgates: Fife . *NT 1488*
Cross Gates: Rad. *SO 0865*
Cross Hands: Carm. *SN 5612*
Crosshill: Ayr . *NS 3206*
Cross Hill: *mtn.,* Tyr. . **18 F8**
Crosshouse: Ayr . *NS 3938*
Cross in Hand: Leics. *SP 5083*
Cross Inn: Card. *SN 3957*
Crosskeys: Mon.. *ST 2292*
Crossmichael: Kirkc. *NX 7267*
Crossraguel Abbey: Ayr . . **14 NS20**
Croston: Lancs . *SD 4818*
Crouch: *r.* . . **7 TQ89**
Crowan: Corn. . *SW 6434*
Crowborough: Sussex *TQ 5130*
Crowcombe: Som. *ST 1336*
Crowe: Banff . *NJ 8266*
Crowland: Lincs . **6 TF21**
Crowle: Lincs . **6 SE71**
Crowlin Is.: R. & Crom. **16 NG63**
Croxton Kerrial: Leics.. *SK 8329*
Croy: Ross & Crom. *NH 7949*
Croydon: Surrey . **7 TQ36**
Cruden Bay: Aber. **17 NK03**
Crudwell: Wilts. . *ST 9592*
Crynant: Glam. . *SN 7905*
Cubbington: War *SP 3368*
Cubert: Corn. . *SW 7857*
Cuckfield: Sussex **7 TQ32**
Cuckmere: *r.* . **7 TQ50**
Cuddington: Ches. *SJ 5971*
Cudham: Kent . *TQ 4459*
Cudworth: Yorks **13 SE30**
Cuilcagh: Ferm. **18 F7**
Cuillin Hills: Skye **16 NG42**
Culbin Wood: Moray **17 NH96**
Culbokie: Ross & Crom. *NH 6059*
Culcabock: Inv. . *NH 6844*
Culgaith: Cumb. . *NY 6129*
Cullen: Banff . **17 NJ56**
Cullercoats: Northumb. *NZ 3571*
Cullin, L.: Mayo **18 C6**
Cullipool: Argyll *NM 7313*
Cullivoe: Shet. Is. *HP 5402*
Culloden Moor: Inv. **17 NH74**
Cullompton: Devon. **8 ST00**
Culm: *r.* . . **9 ST01**
Culmington: Salop *SO 4982*
Cul Mòr: R. & Crom.. **16 NC11**
Culmstock: Devon. *ST 1013*
Culnaknock: Skye *NG 5162*
Culross: Fife . **15 NS98**
Culter: Lan. . *NT 0233*
Culter Fell: Lan. **15 NT02**
Cults: Aber. . *NJ 8903*
Culworth: Northants *SP 5447*
Culzean Castle: Ayr **14 NS21**
CUMBERLAND: *Co.,* Eng. . **12 NY—**
Cumbernauld: Dunb. *NS 7676*
Cuminestown: Aber. *NJ 8050*
Cummertrees: Dumf. *NY 1366*
Cumnock: Ayr . **14 NS51**
Cumnor: Berks . **11 SP40**
Cumrew: Cumb. . *NY 5550*
Cumwhitton: Cumb. *NY 5052*
Cunningham: Ayr **14 NS34**
Cupar: Fife . **15 NO31**
Curragh, The: Kild. **19 H5**
Currane, L.: Kerry **19 A2**
Curraun Penin.: Mayo. **18 B6**
Currie: Midloth. *NT 1867*
Cushat Law: Northumb.. **15 NT91**
Cushendun: Antrim **18 J9**
Cutra, L.: Gal. . **19 D5**
Cwm: Mon. . *SO 1805*
Cwmbran: Mon. **10 ST29**
Cwmcarn: Mon. . *ST 2293*
Cymmer: Glam. . *SS 8596*

G.B. & IRELAND

CYNIN — EMSWORTH

Cynin: r. 8 SN21
Cynon: r. 8 SN90
Cynwyd: Mer. SJ 0541
Cywyn: r. 8 SN32

Dacre: Cumb. 12 NY42
Dacre Banks: Yorks SE 1961
Dagenham: Essex 7 TQ58
Dalbeattie: Kirkc. 15 NX86
Dalcross: Ross & Crom. 17 NH75
Dale: Pemb 10 SM80
Dale End: Yorks. NZ 7008
Daliburgh: S. Uist NF 7421
Dalkeith: Midloth. 15 NT36
Dalkey: Dublin 19 J5
Dallas: Moray 17 NJ15
Dalleagles: Ayr NS 5710
Dallington: Sussex TQ 6519
Dallowgill Moor: Yorks 13 SE17
Dalmally: Argyll 14 NN12
Dalmellington: Ayr NS 4705
Dalmeny: W. Loth. NT 1477
Dalmore: Ross & Crom. NH 6668
Dalry: Ayr. NS 2949
Dalry: Kirkc. NZ 6281
Dalrymple: Ayr NS 3514
Dalserf: Lan. NS 7950
Dalston: Cumb. NY 3750
Dalswinton: Dumf. NX 9385
Dalton: Dumf. NY 1173
Dalton in Furness: Lancs 12 SD27
Dalwhat Water: r. 14 NX79
Dalwhinnie: Inv. 17 NN68
Damerham: Hants. SU 1015
Dan, L.: Wick. 19 J5
Dane: r. 13 SJ86
Danebury Hill: Hants SU 3237
Darent: r. 7 TQ56
Darfield: Yorks SE 4104
Darlaston: Staffs 11 SO99
Darlington: Dur. 13 NZ21
Darnaway Forest: Scot. NH 9853
Darnick: Rox. NT 5334
Darowen: Montg. SH 8302
Dart: r. 8 SX76
Dartford: Kent 7 TQ57
Dartington: Devon. 8 SX76
Dartmoor: Devon. 8 SX68
Dartmouth: Devon. 8 SX85
Darton: Yorks SE 3110
Darvel: Ayr 14 NS53
Darwen: & r., Lancs 12 SD62
Datchet: Bucks SU 9876
Davenham: Ches. SJ 6570
Daventry: Northants 11 SP56
Davington: Dumf. 15 NT20
Daviot: Aber. NJ 7528
Dawley: Salop 11 SJ60
Dawlish: Devon. 8 SX97
Deal: Kent 7 TR35
Dean Water: r. 17 NO34
Dearham: Cumb. NY 0736
Dearne: r. 13 SE40
Deben: r. 6 TM26
Debenham: Suff. 6 TM16
Deddington: Oxon. 11 SP43
Dee: r., Aber. 17 NJ90
Dee: r., Ches. 10 SJ36
Dee: r., Kirkc. 14 NX75
Dee: r., Yorks 13 SD68
Deene: Northants SP 9492
Deeping Gate: Northants TF 1509
Deeping St. Nicholas: Lincs TF 2115
Deeps, The: Shet. Is. 17 HU33
Deer: r. 8 SS30
Deeside: Aber. 17 NO69
Deganwy: Caer. SH 7779
Deiniolen: Caer. SH 5863
Delabole: Corn. SX 0683
Denbigh: Denb. 10 SJ06
DENBIGHSHIRE: Wales 10 SJ—
Denby Dale: Yorks SE 2208
Denge Marsh: Kent 7 TR03
Denholm: Rox. NT 5718
Dennington: Suff. TM 2866
Dennis Head: Ork. Is. HY 7955
Denny: Stirl. 15 NS88
Dent: Yorks SD 7087
Denton: Lancs SJ 9295
Denton: Lincs SK 8632
Derby: Derby. 11 SK33
DERBYSHIRE: Eng. 11 SK—
Derg, L.: Don. 18 F8
Derg, L.: R. of Irel. 19 E4
Derravaragh, L.: Westmeath 18 G6
Derrynasaggart Mts.: Kerry/Cork 19 C2
Derryveagh Mts.: Don. 18 E8
Dersingham: Norf. TF 6830
Dervaig: Mull NM 4351
Derwent: r., Cumb. 12 NY03
Derwent: r., Derby 13 SK26
Derwent: r., Dur. 13 NY94
Derwent: r., Yorks 13 SE76
Derwent Water: Cumb. 12 NY22
Desborough: Northants 11 SP88
Desford: Leics. SK 4703
Deveron: r., Banff 17 NJ64
Devilsbit: mtn., Tip. 19 F4
Devil's Bridge: Card. 10 SN77
Devil's Dyke: Cambs. 6 TL66
Devils Water: r. 13 NY95
Devizes: Wilts. 9 SU06
Devon: r. 15 NS99
Devonport: Devon. 8 SX45
DEVONSHIRE: Eng. 8 SX—
Devoran: Corn. SW 7939
Dewsbury: Yorks 13 SE22
Dickleburgh: Norf. TM 1682
Didcot: Berks 11 SU59
Didmarton: Glos ST 8287
Diebidale Forest: Ross & Crom. NH 4584
Digby: Lincs TF 0754
Dighty Water: r. 15 NO33
Dilwyn: Here. SO4154
Dinas: & head, Pemb. 10 SN03
Dinas-Mawddwy: Mer. SH 8514
Dinas Powis: Glam. ST 1571
Dingle: & bay, Kerry 19 A3
Dingwall: R. & Crom. 17 NH55
Din Lligwy: Anglesey SH 4986
Dinnet: Aber. NO 4698
Dinnington: Yorks SK 5285
Dinton: Bucks SP 7610
Dinton: Wilts. SU 0131
Dionard: r. 16 NC35
Diptford: Devon. SX 7256
Dirleton: E. Loth. NT 5183
Dishforth: Yorks SE 3873
Disley: Ches. SJ 9784
Diss: Norf. 6 TM18
Distington: Cumb. NY 0023
Ditchingham: Norf. TM 3391
Ditchling Beacon: Sussex 7 TQ31
Ditsworthy Warren: Devon. 8 SX56
Ditton Priors: Salop SO 6089
Divis: mtn., Antrim 18 J8
Dizzard Point: Corn. 8 SX19
Dochart: r. 14 NN53
Docking: Norf. TF 7637
Doddington: Cambs. TL 3990
Doddington: Kent TQ 9357
Doddington: Lincs SK 8970
Doddington: Northumb. NT 9932
Dodleston: Ches. SJ 3661
Dodman Point: Corn. 8 SX03
Dodworth: Yorks 13 SE30
Dogdyke: Lincs TF 2055
Doirlinn Hd.: Barra NL 6299
Dolgarrog: Caer. 10 SH76
Dolgelley: Mer. 10 SH71
Dollar: Clack. 15 NS99
Dollar Law: Peeb. 15 NT12
Dolphinholme: Lancs SD 5153
Dolphinton: Lan. NT 1046
Dolton: Devon. SS 5712
Dolwyddelan: Caer. SH 7352
Don: r., Aber. 17 NJ81
Don: r., Yorks 11 SK49
Donaghadee: Down 18 K8
Doncaster: Yorks 13 SE50
Donegal: Don. 18 E8
DONEGAL: Co., R. of Irel. 18 F8
Donegal Bay: Don. 18 E8
Donhead St. Mary: Wilts. ST 9024
Donington: Lincs 6 TF23
Donington on Bain: Lincs TF 2382
Dooish: mtn., Tyr. 18 F8
Doon: r. 14 NS40
Dorbach Burn: r. 17 NJ04
Dorchester: Dorset 9 SY69
Dorchester: Oxon. 11 SU59
Dore: Yorks SK 3081
Dore: r. 9 SO43
Dores: Inv. NH 6034
Dorking: Surrey 7 TQ15
Dorn: r. 9 SP42
Dornie: Ross & Crom. NG 8826
Dornoch: & firth, Suther. NH 8089
Dornock: Dumf. NY 2366
Dorrington: Salop SJ 4703
DORSET: Co., Eng. 9 SY—
Dorstone: Here. SO 3142
Douglas: I. of Man 12 SC37
Douglas: Lan. NS 8330
Douglas: r. 12 SD41
Douglas Water: r., Lan. 15 NS83
Dougrie: Bute. NR 8837
Doulus Head: Kerry 19 Ins.
Dounby: Ork. Is. HY 2920
Doune: Perth 14 NN70
Doune Hill: Dunb. 14 NS29
Dounreay, Lower: Caith. 17 NX96
Dove: r., Derby. 11 SK22
Dove: r., Suffolk 6 TM17
Dove: r., Yorks 13 SE69
Dovedale: Staffs/Derby. 11 SK15
Dover: Kent 7 TR34
Doveridge: Derby. SK 1134
Dovestone Tor: Derby. 13 SK18
Dowally: Perth. NO 0047
Dowlais: Glam. SO 0607
DOWN: Co., N. Irel. 18 J7
Downderry: Corn. SX 3153
Downe House: Kent 7 TQ46
Downham: Cambs. TL 5284
Downham: Lancs SD 7844
Downham Market: Norf. 6 TF60
Downpatrick: Down 18 K7
Downpatrick Hd.: Mayo 18 B7
Downs, The: roadstead 7 TR45
Downside: Som. 9 ST64
Downton: Wilts. SU 1721
Draughton: Yorks SE 0352
Drax: Yorks SE 6726
Draycott: Derby. SK 4433
Draycott: Som. ST 4750
Draycott in the Moors: Staffs SJ 9840
Drayton: Norf. TG 1713
Drefach: Carm. SN 3538
Dreghorn: Ayr NS 3538
Drimnin: Argyll NM 5554
Drogheda: Louth 18 J6
Droichead Nua: Kild. 19 H5
Droitwich: Worcs 11 SO96
Dromore: Down. 18 J7
Dron: Perth. NO 1415
Dronfield: Derby. 13 SK37
Druid: Mer. SJ 0343
Druim Fada: mtn., Inv. 16 NN08
Drumbeg: Suther. NC 1232
Drumblade: Aber. NJ 5840
Drumburgh: Cumb. NY 2659
Drumclog: Lan. NS 6338
Drumelzier: Peebles NT 1335
Drumfearn: Skye NG 6716
Drumgask: Inv. NN 6193
Drumlithie: Kinc. NO 7880
Drummond Hill: Perth. 15 NN74
Drummore: Wig. NX 1336
Drumnadrochit: Inv. 17 NH53
Drumshanbo: Leit. 18 E7
Drybridge: Banff. NJ 4362
Dryburgh Abbey: Rox. 15 NT53
Dryfe Water: r. 15 NY18
Drygarn Fawr: Breck. 10 SN85
Drymen: Stirl. NS 4788
Duart Point: Mull 14 NM73
Dubh Artach: i., Argyll 14 NM10
Dubh Eilean: i., Argyll 14 NR38
DUBLIN: Co., R. of Irel. 19 J5
Dublin Bay: Dublin 19 J5
Duchray Water: r. 14 NN40
Duddington: Northants SK 9800
Duddo: Northumb. NT 9342
Duddon: r. 12 SD29
Dudley: Worcs 11 SO99
Duffield: Derby. SK 3443
Dufftown: Banff 17 NJ33
Dufton: Westmor. NY 6925
Dukeries, The: Eng. 13 SK67
Dukestown: Mon. SO 1410
Dulais: r. 10 SN80
Dull: Perth. NN 8049
Dullingham: Cambs. TL 6357
Dulnan: r. 17 NH82
Dulnanbridge: Moray NH 9925
Dulsie: Nairn. NH 9341
Dulverton: Som. 8 SS92
Dumbarton: Dunb. 14 NS47
Dumfries: Dumf. 15 NX97
DUMFRIESSHIRE: Scot. 15NX/NY
Dun: Angus NO 6659
Dunaff Head: Don. 18 F9
Dunalastair: Perth. NN 7058
Dunan: Skye NG 5828
Dunbar: E. Loth. 15 NT67
DUNBARTON: Co., Scot. 14 NS—
Dunbeath: Caith. ND 1629
Dunbeath Water: r. 17 ND13
Dunblane: Perth. 15 NN70
Duncannon: Wex. 19 H3
Duncansby Head: Caith. 17 ND47
Dun Carloway: Lewis NB 1941
Dunchurch: War SP 4871
Duncow: Dumf. NX 9683
Duncrievie: Kinr. NO 1309
Dundalk: & bay, Louth 18 J6
Dundee: Angus 15 NO43
Dundonald: Ayr. 14 NS33
Dundonald: Down 18 K8
Dundonnell Forest: Ross & Crom. NH 1181
Dundrennan: Kirkc. NX 7447
Dundrum Bay: Down 18 K7
Dunecht: Aber. NJ 7509
Dunfermline: Fife 15 NT08
Dungannon: Tyr. 18 H7
Dungarvan: & harb., Wat. 19 F3
Dungeness: Kent 7 TR01
Dunholme: Lincs TF 0279
Dunino: Fife NO 5311
Dunipace: Stirl. NS 8083
Dunkeld: Perth. 15 NO04
Dunkery Beacon: Som. 8 SS84
Dun Laoghaire: Dublin 19 J5
Dunlop: Ayr NS 4049
Dunmanway: Cork 19 C2
Dunmurry: Antrim 18 J8
Dunnet: Caith. ND 2171
Dunnet Hd.: & bay, Caith. 17 ND17
Dunnideer: Aber. NJ 6228
Dunning: Perth. NO 0114
Dunnington: Yorks SE 6652
Dunnottar Castle: Kinc. NO 8883
Dunoon: Argyll 14 NS17
Dunragit: Wig. NX 1557
Dun Rig: Peeb./Selk. 15 NT23
Dunrobin Castle: Suther. 17 NC80
Duns: Ber. 15 NT75
Dunscore: Dumf. 15 NX88
Dunsford: Devon. SX 8089
Dunstable: Beds 7 TL02
Dunstaffnage Castle: Argyll 14 NM83
Dunster: Som. 8 SS94
Duns Tew: Oxon. SP 4528
Dunston: Lincs TF 0663
Dunsyre: Lan. NT 0748
Dunure: Ayr NS 2515
Dunvegan: Skye 16 NG24
Dunvegan Head: Skye 16 NG15
Dunwich: Suff. TM 4770
DURHAM: Co., Eng. 13 NZ24
Durinish: Skye 16 NG24
Durlston Head: Dorset 9 SZ07
Durness: Suther. NC 4067
Durrington: Wilts. SU 1544
Dursey: i. & hd., Cork 19 A2
Dursley: Glos 11 ST79
Duthil: Inv. NH 9324
Duxford: Cambs. TL 4846
Dwyfor: r. 10 SH44
Dyce: Aber. 17 NJ81
Dyfi: r. 10 SN79
Dyke: r. 17 NC84
Dykehead: Lan. NS 8660
Dymchurch: Kent TR 0929
Dysart: Fife 15 NT39
Dyserth: Flint. SJ 0579
Dysynni: r. 10 SH60

Eaglesfield: Dumf. NY 2374
Eaglesham: Renf. NS 5751
Eakring: Notts SK 6762
Ealing: Middx. 7 TQ17
Earby: Yorks 13 SD94
Eardisland: Here. SO 4158
Eardisley: Here. SO 3149
Earith: Hunts TL 3875
Earlestown: Lancs SJ 5795
Earlish: Skye NG 3861
Earl's Barton: Northants SP 8563
Earls Colne: Essex 7 TL82
Earlsferry: Fife 15 NT49
Earl Shilton: Leics. SP 4697
Earl Soham: Suff. TM 2363
Earlston: Ber. NT 5738
Earl Stonham: Suff. TM 1058
East Allen: r. 13 NY85
Earn's Heugh: Ber. 15 NT96
Easdale: i., Argyll 14 NM71
Easington: Dur. NZ 4143
Easington: Yorks TA 3919
Easingwold: Yorks 13 SE56
Eask, L.: Don. 18 E8
East Barnet: Herts TQ 2794
East Barsham: Norf. TF 9133
East Bergholt: Suff. TM 0734
Eastbourne: Sussex 7 TV69
East Bridgford: Notts. SK 6943
East Budleigh: Devon. SY 0684
East Canisbay: Caith. ND 3673
Eastchurch: Kent TQ 9871
East Coker: Som. ST 5312
East Cottingwith: Yorks SE 7042
East Dean: Sussex SU 9013
Eastdean: Sussex TV 5598
East Dereham: Norf. 6 TF91
Eastern Cleddau: r. 10 SN01
Easter Ross: R. & Crom. 17 NH48
East Fen: Lincs 13 TF45
East Findhorn: r. 17 NH83
East Grinstead: Sussex 7 TQ33
East Haddon: Northants SP 6668
Eastham: Ches. 10 SJ38
East Ham: Essex 7 TQ48
East Hanney: Berks SU 4193
East Harling: Norf. 6 TL98
East Haven: Angus NO 5836
East Herrington: Dur. NZ 3654
East Hoathly: Sussex TQ 5216
East Ilsley: Berks 11 SU48
East Kilbride: Lan. 14 NS65
East Knoyle: Wilts. ST 8830
East Leake: Notts SK 5526
Eastleigh: Hants 7 SU41
East Linton: E. Loth. 15 NT57
East Loch Roag: Lewis 16 NB14
East Loch Tarbert: Harris 16 NG19
East Looe: Corn. 8 SX25
EAST LOTHIAN: Co., Scot. 15 NT—
East Markham: Notts SK 7472
East Neuk of Fife: Fife 15 NO50
East Norton: Leics. SK 7800
Eastoft: Lincs SE 8016
Easton: Dorset SY 6871
Easton: Suff. TM 2858
East Putford: Devon. SS 3616
East Quantoxhead: Som. ST 1343
East Retford: Notts 13 SK78
East Riding: Admin. Co., Yorks 13 SE84
Eastriggs: Dumf. NY 2465
Eastrington: Yorks SE 7929
East Rudham: Norf. TF 8228
Eastry: Kent TR 3155
East Stour: r. 7 TR03
East Suffolk: Admin. Co., Suff. 6 TM26
East Sussex: Admin. Co., Sussex 7 TQ62
Eastville: Lincs TF 4056
East Wemyss: Fife NT 3396
East Winch: Norf. TF 6916
East Witton: Yorks SE 1486
Eastwood: Notts SK 4646
East Wretham: Norf. TL 9190
Eaton: Ches. SJ 5763
Eaton: Norf. TG 2006
Eaton Socon: Beds TL 1658
Eau: r. 13 SK99
Eaval: mtn., N. Uist 16 NF86
Ebberston: Yorks SE 8983
Ebble: r. 9 SU02
Ebbw: r. 9 ST
Ebbw Vale: Mon. 10 SO10
Ebchester: Dur. NZ 1055
Ecclefechan: Dumf. NY 1974
Eccles: Ber. NT 7641
Eccles: Lancs 13 SJ79
Ecclesfield: Yorks SK 3393
Eccleshall: Staffs. 11 SJ82
Eccleston: Ches. SJ 4162
Eccleston: Lancs. SD 5216
Echt: Aber. NJ 7305
Eckford: Rox. 15 NT72
Eckington: Derby. 13 SK47
Eckington: Worcs SO 9241
Edale: Derby. SK 1285
Eday: i., Ork. Is. 17 HY53
Edderton: R. & Crom. NH 7184
Eddisbury: Ches. SJ 5669
Eddleston: Peeb. NT 2447
Eddleston Water: r. 15 NT25
Eddrachillis Bay: Suther. 16 NC13
Eddystone Rock: Eng. 8 SX43
Eden: r., Cumb. 12 NY54
Eden: r., Fife 15 NO21
Eden: r., Kent 7 TQ44
Eden: r., Mer. 10 SH72
Edenbridge: Kent 7 TQ44
Edenderry: Offaly 19 G5
Edenfield: Lancs SD 8019
Edenside: Cumb. 12 NY54
Edern: Caer. SH 2739
Edgbaston: War 11 SP08
Edgehill: War 11 SP34
Edgware: Middx. 7 TQ19
Edgworth: Lancs 13 SD71
Edinbain: Skye NG 3451
Edinburgh: Midloth. 15 NT27
Edington: Wilts. ST 9252
Edlingham: Northumb. NU 1108
Edmondbyers: Dur. NZ 0250
Edmonton: Middx. 7 TQ39
Ednam: Rox. NT 7337
Edrom: Ber. NT 8255
Edston: Peeb. NT 2239
Edzell: Angus NO 6068
Eggardon Hill: Dorset 9 SY59
Eggleston: Dur. NZ 0023
Egham: Surrey 11 TQ07
Eglingham: Northumb. 15 NU11
Egloshayle: Corn. SX 0071
Egloskerry: Corn. SX 2786
Eglwyswrw: Pemb SN 1438
Egremont: Cumb. 12 NY01
Egton: Yorks NZ 8006
Ehen: r. 12 NY00
Eigg: i., Inv. 16 NM48
Eilean an Roin Mor: i., Suther. 16 NC15
Eilean Donnan: Ross & Crom. 16 NG82
Eilean Mor: i., Coll 16 NM26
Eilean nan Each: i., Inv. NM 3981
Eilean nan Ròn: Argyll 14 NR38
Eilean nan Ròn: i., Suther. 17 NC66
Eilean Shona: i., Inv. 16 NM67
Eilean Trodday: i., Inv. 16 NG47
Elan: r. 10 SN87
Elan Village: Breck. SN 9365
Eldrig Village: Wig. NX 3247
Elerch: Card. SN 6886
Elford: Staffs 11 SK11
Elgin: Moray 17 NJ26
Elgol: Skye NG 5214
Elham: Kent TR 1744
Elie: Fife NO 4900
Elkesley: Notts SK 6875
Elland: Yorks 13 SE12
Ellen: r. 12 NY03
Ellesmere: Salop. 11 SJ43
Ellesmere Port: Ches. 11 SJ47
Ellingham: Norf. TM 3691
Ellingham: Northumb. NU 1725
Ellingstring: Yorks SE 1783
Elliott's Pike: mtn., Northumb. 12 NY58
Ellon: Aber. 17 NJ93
Elloughton: Yorks SE 9428
Elmdon Heath: War SP 1580
Elmstead Market: Essex TM 0624
Elmswell: Suff. TL 9964
Elphin: Suther. NC 2111
Elsdon: Northumb. NY 9393
Elsham: Lincs TA 0312
Elston: Notts SK 7548
Elstow: Beds TL 0547
Elstree: Herts TQ 1895
Elswick: Lancs SD 4138
Elsworth: Cambs. TL 3163
Elterwater: Westmor. NY 3204
Eltisley: Cambs. TL 2759
Elton: Derby. SK 2261
Elton: Hunts TL 0893
Elvanfoot: Lan. NS 9517
Elveden: Suff. TL 8279
Elvington: Yorks. SE 6947
Elwick: Dur. NZ 4532
Elworth: Ches. SJ 7361
Elwy: r. 12 SH97
Ely: Cambs. 6 TL58
Ely: r. 8 ST08
Emberton: Bucks SP 8849
Embleton: Northumb. NU 2322
Embo: Suther. NH 8192
Embsay: Yorks SE 0053
Emneth: Cambs. TF 4807
Empingham: Rut. SK 9408
Emsworth: Hants 7 SU70

G.B. & IRELAND

ENARD BAY — GOODWIN SANDS

Enard Bay: Suther. 16 NC01
Enborne: r. 11 SU56
Enderby: Leics. SP 5399
Enfield: Middx. 7 TQ39
English Channel 8/9 —
Ennell, L.: Westmeath 18 G5
Ennerdale Bridge: Cumb. 12 NY01
Ennis: Clare 19 D4
Enniscorthy: Wex. 19 H4
Enniskillen: Ferm. 18 F7
Ennistimon: Clare 19 C4
Enrick: r. 17 NH42
Ensay: i., Inv. 16 NF98
Enstone: Oxon. SP 3725
Enterkinfoot: Dumf. NS 8504
Enville: Staffs. SO 8286
Eoropie: Lewis NB 5264
Eorsa: i., Argyll 14 NM43
Epping: & for., Essex 7 TL40
Eppleby: Yorks NZ 1713
Epsom: Surrey 7 TQ26
Epworth: Lincs 6 SE70
Erch: r. 10 SH34
Erchless Forest: Scot. NH 4145
Erewash: r. 6 SK44
Eriboll: Suther. NC 4356
Ericht: r. 15 NO14
Eriskay: i., Inv. 16 NF71
Eriswell: Suff. TL 7278
Erith: Kent 7 TQ57
Erlestoke: Wilts. 9 ST95
Erme: r. 8 SX66
Ermington: Devon. SX 6353
Erpingham: Norf. TG 1931
Errigal: mtn., Don. 18 E9
Erris Head: Mayo 18 A7
Errogie: Inv. NH 5622
Escomb: Dur. NZ 1829
Escrick: Yorks SE 6243
Esha Ness: Shet. Is. HU 2178
Esher: Surrey 7 TQ16
Esholt: Yorks SE 1840
Esk: r., Cumb. 12 SD19
Esk: r., Cumb. 12 NY37
Esk: r., Midloth. 15 NT36
Esk: r., Yorks 13 NZ70
Eskdale: Dumf. 15 NY29
Eskdale Green: Cumb. 12 NY10
Essendine: Rut. TF 0412
ESSEX: Co., Eng. 7 TL—
Etal: Northumb. NT 9339
Etive: r. 16 NN14
Eton: & college, Berks 7 SU97
Ettington: War SP 2648
Etton: Yorks SE 9743
Ettrick: & r., Dumf. 15 NT21
Ettrickbridge End: Midloth. NT 3824
Ettrick Forest: Midloth. 15 NT32
Ettrick Pen: mtn., Scot. 15 NY10
Ettrick Water: r. 15 NT31
Etwall: Derby. SK 2732
Euchan Water: r. 15 NS70
Euston: Suff. TL 8978
Euxton: Lancs SD 5518
Evanton: R. & Crom. NH 6066
Evelix: r. 17 NH79
Evenley: Northants SP 5834
Evenlode: r. 11 SP22
Evercreech: Som. ST 6438
Evershot: Dorset ST 5704
Everton: Notts SK 6891
Evesham: Worcs 11 SP04
Ewell: Surrey TQ 2262
Ewelme: Oxon. SU 6491
Ewenny: r. 10 SS97
Ewenny Priory: Glam. 10 SS97
Ewes Water: r. 15 NY39
Ewhurst: Surrey TQ 0940
Exbourne: Devon. SS 6002
Exbury: Hants SU 4200
Exe: r. 8 SX99
Exeter: Devon. 8 SX99
Exford: Som. SS 8538
Exminster: Devon. SX 9487
Exmoor: Som. 8 SS74
Exmouth: Devon. 8 SY08
Exning: Suff. TL 6265
Exton: Rut. SK 9211
Exton: Som. SS 9233
Eyam: Derby. SK 2176
Eye: Suff. 6 TM17
Eyemouth: Ber. 15 NT96
Eye Peninsula: Lewis 16 NB53
Eye Water: r. 15 NT86
Eynsham: Oxon. SP 4309
Eythorne: Kent TR 2849

Fairbourne: Mer. SH 6113
Fairburn: Yorks SE 4727
Fairfield: Derby. SK 0673
Fairford: Glos 11 SP10
Fair Hd.: Antrim 18 J9
Fair Isle: Shet Is. 17 HZ27
Fairlie: Ayr NS 2155
Fakenham: Norf. 6 TF92
Fal: r. 8 SW94
Fala: E. Loth. 15 NT46
Falkenham: Suff. TM 2939
Falkirk: Stirl. 15 NS88
Falkland: Fife 15 NO20
Falloch: r. 14 NN32
Fall of Glomach: Ross & Crom. NH 0325
Falmer: Sussex TQ 3508
Falmouth: & bay, Corn. 8 SW83
Falstone: Northumb. NY 7287
Fanad Head: Don. 18 F9
Fangfoss: Yorks SE 7653
Fannich Forest: Ross & Crom. NH 1969
Faraid Head: Suther. 17 NC37
Farcet: Hunts TL 2094
Fareham: Hants 7 SU50
Faringdon: Berks 11 SU29
Farlam: Cumb. NY 5558
Farland Hd.: Ayr. 14 NS14
Far Moor: Lancs. SD 5304
Farnborough: Hants 7 SU85
Farnborough: Kent TQ 4464
Farndale East: Yorks SE 6697
Farndon: Ches. SJ 4154
Farndon: Notts SK 7651
Farne Is.: Northumb. 15 NU23
Farnell: Angus NO 6255
Farnham: Surrey 7 SU84
Farnhill: Yorks SE 0046
Farningham: Kent TQ 5566
Farnsfield: Notts SK 6456
Farnworth: Lancs SD 7305
Farr: Suther. NC 7163
Farrar: r. 16 NH33
Farringdon: Hants SU 7135
Farsley: Yorks 13 SE23
Farthinghoe: Northants SP 5339
Fashven: mtn., Suther. 16 NC36
Fastnet Rock: Cork 19 B1
Fauldhouse: W. Loth. NS 9260
Faversham: Kent 7 TR06
Fawley: Berks 11 SU38
Fawley: Hants SU 4503
Fazeley: Staffs SK 2001
Fearby: Yorks SE 1981
Fearnmore: R. & Crom. NG 7260
Feckenham: Worcs SP 0061
Feeagh, L.: Mayo 18 B6
Feetham: Yorks SD 9898
Felindre: Rad. SO 1681
Felixstowe: Suff. 7 TM33
Fell of Fleet: Kirkc. 14 NX57
Felpham: Sussex SZ 9599
Felsted: Essex 7 TL62
Felton: Northumb. NU 1800
Feltwell: Norf. TL 7190
Fenny Compton: War SP 4152
Fenny Stratford: Bucks 11 SP83
Fens, The: East Anglia 6 TL59
Fenwick: Ayr NS 4643
Feock: Corn. SW 8238
Feolin Ferry: Argyll NR 4469
Fergus: r. 19 D4
FERMANAGH: Co., N. Irel. 18 F7
Fermoy: Cork 19 E3
Fern: Angus NO 4861
Ferndale: Glam. SS 9997
Fern Down: Dorset SU 0700
Fernhurst: Sussex SU 9028
Ferryhill: Dur. NZ 2832
Ferryside: Carm. SN 3610
Fetlar: i., Shet. Is. 17 HU69
Fetterangus: Aber. NJ 9850
Fettercairn: Kinc. NO 6573
Fetteresso: Kinc. NO 8585
Fewston: Yorks SE 1954
Ffestiniog: Mer. 10 SH74
Fforest Fawr: Breck. 10 SN81
Fiaray: i., Inv. NF 7010
FIFE: Kingdom of., Scot. 15NT/NO
Fife Keith: Banff 17 NJ45
Fife Ness: Fife 15 NO60
Filey: Yorks 13 TA18
Filkins: Glos SP 2304
Fillongley: War SP 2787
Filton: Glos 11 ST67
Finaghy: Antrim 18 K/8
Finchingfield: Essex TL 6832
Finchley: Middx. 7 TQ29
Findhorn: Moray NJ 0464
Findochty: Banff NJ 4667
Findon: Sussex TQ 1208
Findon Ness: Kinc. 17 NO99
Finedon: Northants 11 SP97
Fingal's Cave: Argyll 14 NM33
Finghall: Yorks SE 1889
Finn: r. 18 F8
Finningley: Notts SK 6699
Finstown: Ork. Is. HY 3514
Fintona: Tyr. 18 G7
Fintry: Stirl. NS 6286
Fionn Loch: R. & Crom. 14 NG97
Fionphort: Mull NM 3023
Fire Beacon Point: Corn. 8 SX19
Firth of Clyde: Scot. 14 NS16
Firth of Forth: Scot. 15 NT49
Firth of Lorne: Scot. 14 NM72
Firth of Tay: Scot 15 NO32
Fishguard: & bay, Pemb 10 SM93
Fishlake: Yorks SE 6513
Fitful Head: Shet. Is. HU 3413
Fittleworth: Sussex TQ 0119
Five Penny Borve: Lewis NB 4157
Five Sisters: mtn., Ross & Crom. 16 NG91
Fladdabister: Shet. Is. HU 4332
Fladda-chùain: i., Inv. NG 3681
Flamborough Head: Yorks 13 TA27
Flannan Isles: Scot. 16 NA74
Flashader: Skye NG 3554
Flatford Mill: Suff. 7 TM03
Flat Holm: i., Som. 9 ST26
Fleckney: Leics. SP 6493
Fleet: Hants 7 SU85
Fleet: r. 17 NC70
Fleetwood: Lancs 12 SD34
Fletton: Hunts TL 1997
Flimby: Cumb. NY 0233
Flint: Flint. 10 SJ27
Flintham: Notts SK 7446
FLINTSHIRE: Wales 10 SJ—
Flitcham: Norf. TF 7226
Flitwick: Beds TL 0335
Flixborough: Lincs SE 8715
Flixton: Suff. TM 3186
Flodden Field: Northumb. 15 NT83
Flookburgh: Lancs SD 3675
Flotta: i., Ork. Is. ND 3593
Fobbing: Essex TQ 7183
Fochabers: Moray 17 NJ35
Fodderty: R. & Crom. NH 5159
Foel-fras: Caer. 12 SH66
Foel-Wen: mtn., Denb. 10 SJ03
Fogo: Ber. NT 7749
Foinaven: mtn., Suther. 16 NC35
Foleshill: War SP3582
Folkestone: Kent 7 TR23
Folkingham: Lincs TF 0733
Folkton: Yorks TA 0579
Font: r. 15 NZ09
Fontwell Park: Sussex SU 9504
Ford: Argyll NM 8603
Ford: Northumb. NT 9437
Ford: Salop SJ 4113
Forden: Montg. SJ 2201
Fordham: Cambs. TL 6370
Fordingbridge: Hants 9 SU11
Fordwich: Kent TR 1859
Fordyce: Banff NJ 5563
Foreland: I. of Wight 7 SZ68
Foreland Point: Devon 8 SS75
Forest Hall: Northumb. NZ 2869
Forest of Ae: Dumf. NY 0098
Forest of Alyth: Perth. NO 1755
Forest of Arden: War 11 SP17
Forest of Atholl: Perth. 17 NN77
Forest of Bere: Hants 7 SU61
Forest of Bowland: Eng. 12 SD65
Forest of Clunie: Perth. NO 0850
Forest of Dean: Glos 11 SO60
Forest of Glentanar: Aber. NO 5095
Forest of Harris: Harris 16 NB01
Forest of Knaresborough: Yorks 13 SE25
Forest of Rossendale: Lancs 13 SD82
Forest Ridge: Sussex 7 TQ62
Forest Row: Sussex TQ 4235
Forfar: Angus 17 NO45
Forgandenny: Perth. NO 0818
Formartine: Aber. 17 NJ82
Formby: Lancs 12 SD20
Formby Point: Lancs 12 SD20
Forncett St. Peter: Norf. TM 1695
Forres: Moray 17 NJ05
Forsbrook: Staffs SJ 9641
Forse: Caith. ND 2234
Forsinard: Suther. NC 8842
Fort Augustus: Inv. 16 NH30
Forteviot: Perth. NO 0517
Fort George: R. & Crom. NH 7656
Forth: Lan. NS 9453
Forth: r. 14 NS69
Forth Bridge: Scot. 15 NT17
Fortingall: Perth. NN 7447
Forton: Lancs SD 4851
Fortrose: R. & Crom. 17 NH75
Fortuneswell: Dorset SY 6873
Fort William: Inv. 16 NN17
Fosdyke: Lincs TF 3133
Foss: Perth. NN 7958
Foss: r. Yorks 13 SE66
Fossebridge: Glos 11 SP01
Fotherby: Lincs TF 3191
Fotheringhay: Northants 6 TL09
Foula: i., Shet. Is. 17 HT93
Foulden: Ber. NT 9355
Foulness: i., Essex 7 TR09
Foulness: r. Yorks 13 SE83
Foulness Point: Essex 7 TR09
Foulridge: Lancs SD 8942
Foulsham: Norf. TG 0324
Fountainhall: Midloth. NT 4349
Fountains Abbey: Yorks 13 SE26
Foveran: Aber. NJ 9824
Fowey: & r., Corn. 8 SX15
Fowlis Wester: Perth. NN 9223
Foxdale: I. of Man SC2778
Foyers: Inv. 17 NH42
Foyle: r. 18 G8
Foyle, L.: Irel. 18 G9
Foynes: Lim. 19 C4
Framlingham: Suff. 6 TM26
Frampton on Severn: Glos SO 7407
Framsden: Suff. TM 1959
Frankby: Ches. SJ 2486
Frant: Sussex TQ 5835
Fraserburgh: Aber. 17 NJ96
Freckleton: Lancs SD 4228
Freckleton: Lancs SD 4228
Freevater Forest: Ross & Crom. NH 3588
Freiston: Lincs TF 3844
Freshwater: I. of Wight 7 SZ38
Fressingfield: Suff. TM 2677
Freswick: Caith. ND 3667
Freuchie: Fife NO 2806
Friday Bridge: Cambs. TF 4605
Fridaythorpe: Yorks SE 8759
Frimley: Surrey SU 8758
Frinton: Essex 7 TM21
Friockheim: Angus NO 5949
Friskney: Lincs TF 4555
Friston: Suff. TM 4160
Fritton: Suff. TG 4700
Frizington: Cumb. NY 0316
Frodsham: Ches. SJ 5177
Frome: Som. 9 ST74
Frome: r., Dorset 9 SY69
Frome: r., Glos 11 SO90
Frome: r., Here. 11 SO64
Frome: r., Som. 9 ST74
Frosterley: Dur. NZ 0237
Froxfield: Wilts SU 2967
Fuday: i., Inv. 16 NF70
Fulbourn: Cambs. TL 5256
Fullarton: Ayr NS 3137
Fulwood: Lancs SD 5331
Fulwood: Yorks SK 3085
Funzie: Shet. Is. HU 6689
Furnace: Argyll NN 0200
Furness Abbey: Lancs. 12 SD27
Furness Fells: Lancs 12 SD29
Fyfield: Essex TL 5707
Fylde: Lancs 12 SD33
Fylingdales: Yorks NZ 9403
Fyne: r. 14 NN21
Fyvie: Aber. NJ 7637

Gade: r. 7 TL00
Gaick Forest: Inv. 17 NN78
Gainford: Dur. NZ 1716
Gainsborough: Lincs 6 SK89
Gairloch: R. & Crom. 16 NG87
Gairlochy: Inv. NN 1784
Gairn: r. 17 NJ20
Galashiels: Selk. 15 NT43
Gala Water: r. 15 NT44
Galgate: Lancs SD 4855
Gallan Head: Lewis 16 NB03
Galley Head: Cork 19 D2
Galloway: Scot. 14 NX—
Galmisdale: Eigg. NM 4784
Galston: Ayr 14 NS53
Galtee Mts.: Lim./Tip. 19 E3
Galtymore: mtn., Lim. 19 E3
GALWAY: Co., R. of Irel. 19 C5
Gam: r. 10 SH90
Gamblesby: Cumb. NY 6039
Gamlingay: Cambs. TL 2452
Ganstead: Yorks TA 1434
Ganton: Yorks SE 9877
Gara, L.: Sligo/Rosc. 18 E6
Garboldisham: Norf. TM 0081
Gardenstown: Banff NJ 7964
Gare Loch: Dunb. 14 NS28
Garelochhead: Dunb. NS 2491
Garforth: Yorks SE 4033
Gargrave: Yorks SD 9354
Garliestown: Wig. NX 4746
Garmouth: Moray. NJ 3364
Garn-Dolbenmaen: Caer. SH 4944
Garno: r. 10 SO09
Garrabost: Lewis. NB 5133
Garrisdale Point: Canna NG 2005
Garroch Hd.: Bute 14 NS05
Garron Point: Antrim 18 K9
Garron Point: Kinc. 17 NO98
Garry: r. 17 NN76
Garrynahine: Lewis NB 2431
Garstang: Lancs. 12 SD44
Gartan, L.: Don. 18 F8
Garthorpe: Lincs SE 8419
Gartly Stn.: Aber. NJ 5232
Gartmore: Perth. NS 5297
Gartocharn: Dunb. NS 4286
Garton on the Wolds: Yorks SE 9859
Garvald: E. Loth. NT 5870
Garve: Ross & Crom. NH 3961
Garvellachs: is., Argyll 14 NM61
Gateforth: Yorks. SE 5528
Gatehouse of Fleet: Kirkc. 14 NX65
Gateshead: Dur. 15 NZ26
Gattonside: Rox. NT 5435
Gatwick: airport, Surrey 7 TQ24
Gawsworth: Ches. SJ 8869
Gaydon: War SP 3654
Gayton: Norf. TF 7219
Geal Charn: mtn., Inv 17 NJ01
Geal-chàrn Mor: Inv. 17 NH81
Geary: Skye NG 2661
Geddington: Northants. SP 8983
Gedintailor: Skye NG 5435
Gedney Drove End: Lincs TF 4629
Gedney Hill: Lincs TF 3311
Geldie Burn: r. 17 NN98
Gelston: Kirkc. NX 7758
Gelt: r. 12 NY55
General Wade's Stone: Perth. NN 6972
Georgeham: Devon. SS4639
Georgemas: Caith. 17 ND15
Germoe: Corn. SW 5829
Gerrans: Corn. SW 8735
Gerrards Cross: Bucks 11 TQ08
Giant's Causeway: Antrim 18 H9
Gifford: E. Loth. NT 5368
Giggleswick: Yorks SD 8163
Gigha: i., Argyll 14 NR65
Gighay: i., Inv. 16 NF70
Gilberdike: Yorks SE 8329
Gilcrux: Cumb. NY 1138
Gilfach Goch: Glam. SS 9789
Gill, L.: Sligo/Leit. 18 E7
Gillamoor: Yorks SE 6890
Gilling: Yorks NZ 1805
Gillingham: Dorset 9 ST82
Gillingham: Kent 7 TQ76
Gilsland: Northumb. NY 6366
Gilwern: Breck. SO 2414
Gipping, r. 6 TM05
Girdle Ness: Kinc. 17 NJ90
Girthon: Kirkc. NX 6053
Girton: Cambs. 6 TL46
Girvan: Ayr 14 NX19
Gisburn: Yorks SD 8248
Glackbea: Inv. NH 5139
Gladestry: Rad. SO 2355
Glaisdale: Yorks NZ 7705
Glamis: Angus 17 NO34
GLAMORGAN: Co., Wales 10 SS—
Glanamman: Carm. SN 6713
Glandford: Norf. TG 0441
Glanton: Northumb. NU 0714
Glasbury: Rad. SO 1739
Glasgow: Lan. 14 NS56
Glas Maol: mtn., Angus 17 NO17
Glass: r. 16 NH33
Glasserton: Wig. NX 4238
Glasson: Lancs SD 4455
Glastonbury: Som. 9 ST43
Glatton: Hunts TL 1586
Glaven: r. 6 TG03
Glemsford: Suff. TL 8248
Glen: r. 11 TF11
Glen Affric: Inv. 16 NH12
Glen Almond: Perth. 15 NN83
Glen Artney: Perth. 14 NN71
Glenaruddery Mts.: Kerry 19 C3
Glen Avon: Banff 17 NJ10
Glenbarr: Argyll NR 6736
Glenbeg: Argyll NM 5961
Glenbervie: Kinc. NO 7680
Glenborrodale: Argyll NM 6060
Glenbuck: Ayr NS 7429
Glen Cannich: Inv. 16 NH23
Glencaple: Kirkc. NX 9968
Glencarse: Perth. NO 1921
Glen Cassley: Suther. 17 NC41
Glen Clova: Angus 17 NO37
Glen Coe: Argyll 16 NN15
Glencraig: Fife NT 1795
Glendalough: Wick. 19 J5
Glenddwr: Breck. SO 0743
Glen Devon: Perth. NN 9504
Glen Dochart: Perth. 14 NN53
Glendoe Forest: Inv. NH 4404
Gleneagles: Perth. 15 NN91
Glenelg: Inv. NG 8119
Glen Esk: Angus 17 NO57
Glenfarg: Perth. NO 1310
Glenfeshie Forest: Inv. NN 8790
Glenfinnan: Inv. 16 NM98
Glengarnock: Ayr NS 3253
Glen Garry: Inv. 16 NN19
Glenkens, The: Kirkc. 14 NX58
Glen Lednock: Perth 17 NN72
Glenlochar: Kirkc. NX 7264
Glenluce: Wig. NX 1957
Glen Lyon: Perth. 14 NN64
Glen More: Inv. 17 NH—
Glen Moriston: Inv. 16 NH31
Glen Nevis: Inv. 16 NN16
Glen of Aherlow: Tip. 19 E3
Glen Orchy: Argyll 14 NN23
Glen Orrin: R. & Crom. 16 NH34
Glen Oykell: Suther. 16 NC30
Glen Roy: Inv. 16 NN38
Glenshian: Inv. NM 7882
Glen Spean: Inv. 16 NN37
Glen Tarbert: Argyll 16 NM85
Glentham: Lincs TF 0090
Glenties: Don. 18 E8
Glen Trool: Kirkc./Ayr 14 NX47
Glen Urquhart: Inv. 17 NH43
Glenwhilly: Wig. NX 1771
Gleouraich: mtn., Inv. 16 NH00
Glossop: Derby. 13 SK09
Gloucester: Glos 11 SO81
GLOUCESTERSHIRE: Eng. 11 SO—
Gloup Ness: i., Shet. Is. HP 4905
Glyder Fawr: mtn., Caer. 10 SH65
Glyme: r. 9 SP42
Glyncorrwg: Glam. SS 8799
Glyndebourne: Sussex. 7 TQ41
Glyn Neath: Glam. SN 8806
Goat Fell: Arran 14 NR94
Goathland: Yorks NZ 8301
Gobowen: Salop SJ 3033
Godalming: Surrey 7 SU94
Godmanchester: Hunts 6 TL27
Goginan: Card. SN 6981
Gog Magog Hills: Cambs. 6 TL45
Gola I.: Don. 18 E9
Golcar: Yorks 13 SE01
Goldcliff: Mon. ST 3683
Golspie: Suther. 17 NH89
Gomersal: Yorks 13 SE22
Gometra: i., Argyll NM 3640
Gooderstone: Norf. TF 7602
Goodwick: Pemb SM 9438
Goodwin Sands: 7 TR45

Goodwood House: Sussex	7	SU80
Goole: Yorks	13	SE72
Goonhilly Downs: Corn.	8	SW72
Goosnargh: Lancs		SD 5536
Goostrey: Ches.		SJ 7770
Gordon: Ber.		NT 6443
Gordonstoun: Moray	17	NJ16
Gordonstown: Aber.		NJ 7138
Gorey: Wex.	19	J4
Goring: Oxon		SU 5980
Goring by Sea: Sussex		TQ 1102
Goring Gap: Berks/Oxon.	11	SU58
Gorleston: Norf.		TG 5204
Gorseinon: Glam.		SS 5998
Gort: Gal.	19	D5
Gorumna I.: Gal.	19	B5
Gosberton: Lincs		TF 2331
Gosforth: Cumb.		NY 0603
Gosforth: Northumb.	15	NZ26
Gosport: Hants	7	SZ69
Gotherington: Glos		SO 9629
Goudhurst: Kent		TQ 7337
Goulceby: Lincs		TF 2579
Gourdon: Kinc.		NO 8270
Gourock: Renf.	14	NS27
Govan: Lan.		NS 5464
Gower: penin., Glam.	10	SS59
Gowerton: Glam.		SS 5896
Gowna, L.: Long./Cavan	18	F6
Gowy: r.	12	SJ56
Grafton: Yorks		SE 4163
Graiguenamanagh: Kilk.	19	H4
Grain: Kent		TQ 8876
Grampian Highlands: Scot.	17	NN/NO
Grampound: Corn.		SW 9348
Grand Havre: Chan. Is.	9	Ins.
Graney, L.: Clare	19	D4
Grange: Cumb.		NY 2517
Grange: Lancs	12	SD47
Grangemouth: Stirl.	15	NS98
Grangetown: Yorks	13	NZ52
Grantham: Lincs	6	SK93
Granton: Midloth.		NT 2277
Grantown-on-Spey: Moray	17	NJ02
Grasby: Lincs		TA 0804
Grasmere: Westmor.	12	NY30
Grassholm I.: Pemb	10	SM50
Grassington: Yorks	13	SE06
Grass Point: Argyll	14	NM73
Graver: Lewis		NB 3815
Gravesend: Kent	7	TQ67
Grayrigg: Westmor.		SD 5797
Grays Thurrock: Essex	7	TQ67
Greasbrough: Yorks		SK 4195
Greasby: Ches.		SJ 2587
Great Altcar: Lancs		SD 3206
Great Asby: Westmor.		NY 6813
Great Ayton: Yorks		NZ 5510
Great Badminton: Glos	11	ST88
Great Bardfield: Essex		TL 6730
Great Barford: Beds		TL 1352
Great Bedwyn: Wilts.		SU 2764
Great Bernera: Lewis	16	NB13
Great Bircham: Norf.		TF 7632
Great Blasket: i., Kerry	19	Ins.
Great Budworth: Ches.		SJ 6677
Great Chalfield: Wilts.		ST 8763
Great Chesterford: Essex		TL 5042
Great Chishall: Cambs.		TL 4238
Great Clifton: Cumb.		NY 0329
Great Coates: Lincs		TA 2310
Great Cumbrae I.: Bute	14	NS15
Great Dalby: Leics.		SK 7414
Great Driffield: Yorks.	13	TA05
Great Dunmow: Essex	7	TL62
Great Easton: Leics.		SP 8593
Great Eau: r.	13	TF48
Great Eccleston: Lancs.		SD 4240
Great Gable: mtn., Cumb.	12	NY21
Great Gaddesden: Herts		TL 0211
Great Gidding: Hunts		TL 1183
Great Glen: Leics.		SP 6597
Great Gonerby: Lincs		SK 8938
Great Gransden: Hunts.		TL 2656
Great Haldon: Devon.	8	SX98
Greatham: Dur.		NZ 4927
Great Hampden: Bucks		SP 8403
Great Harwood: Lancs	12	SD73
Great Hatfield: Yorks		TA 1842
Great Haywood: Staffs.		SJ 9922
Great Langton: Yorks		SE 2996
Great Limber: Lincs		TA 1308
Great Livermere: Suff.		TL 8871
Great Longstone: Derby		SK 1971
Great Massingham: Norf.		TF 7922
Great Mew Stone: Devon.	8	SX54
Great Missenden: Bucks.		SP 8901
Great Mis Tor: Devon.	8	SX57
Great Oakley: Essex		TM 1927
Great Offley: Herts		TL 1427
Great Ormes Head: Caer.	10	SH78
Great Ponton: Lincs		SK 9230
Great Rissington: Glos		SP 1917
Great Rowsley: Derby		SK 2566
Great Russel: Chan. Is.	9	Ins.
Great Ryburgh: Norf.		TF 9527
Great Salkeld: Cumb.		NY 5536
Great Sampford: Essex		TL 6435
Great Shefford: Berks		SU 3875
Great Shelford: Cambs.		TL 4652
Great Smeaton: Yorks.		NZ 3404
Great Strickland: Westmor.		NY 5522
Great Tew: Oxon.		SP 3929
Great Thurlow: Suff.		TL 6850
Great Torrington: Devon.	8	SS41
Great Totham: Essex		TL 8511
Great Wakering: Essex		TQ 9487
Great Welnetham: Suff.		TL 8759
Great Whernside: mtn., Yorks	13	SE07
Great Whittington: Northumb.		NZ 0070
Great Wishford: Wilts.		SU 0835
Great Witley: Worcs		SO 7566
Great Yarmouth: Norf.	6	TG50
Great Yeldham: Essex		TL 7638
Greenfield: Flint		SJ 1977
Greenford: Middx.		TQ 1382
Greenhaugh: Northumb.		NY 7987
Greenlaw: Ber.	15	NT74
Greenock: Renf.	14	NS27
Greenodd: Lancs.		SD 3182
Greenore: Louth	18	J7
Greenore Point: Wex.	19	J3
Greensted: Essex.		TL 5302
Greenstone Pt.: Ross & Crom.	16	NG89
Greenwich: London	7	TQ37
Greetham: Rut.		SK 9214
Greetland: Yorks		SE 0821
Greian Hd.: Barra	16	NF60
Gresford: Denb.		SJ 3454
Greta: r., Cumb.	12	NY22
Greta: r., Yorks	13	SD67
Gretna: Dumf.		NY 3167
Gretna Green: Dumf.	15	NY36
Gretton: Northants		SP 8994
Greysouthen: Cumb.		NY 0729
Greystoke: Cumb.		NY 4330
Greystone: Angus		NO 5343
Greystones: Wick.	19	J5
Gribbin Hd.: Corn.	8	SX14
Griffithstown: Mon.		ST 2999
Grime's Graves: Norf.	6	TL88
Griminish Point: N. Uist	16	NF77
Grimley: Worcs		SO 8360
Grimoldby: Lincs.		TF 3988
Grimsay: i., Inv.		NF 8656
Grimsby: Lincs	6	TA21
Grimsetter: Ork. Is.	17	HY41
Grimspound: Devon.	8	SX78
Grimsthorpe: Lincs		TF 0423
Grimston: Norf.		TF 7221
Grindleford: Derby.		SK 2477
Grindon: Northumb.		NT 9144
Gringley on the Hill: Notts		SK 7390
Grinshill: Salop		SJ 5223
Gristhorpe: Yorks		TA 0882
Groby: Leics.		SK 5207
Grogport: Argyll.		NR 8044
Gronant: Flint.		SJ 0883
Grosmont: Mon.	11	SO42
Grosmont: Yorks		NZ 8205
Grosnez, C.: Jersey	9	Ins.
Grove: Berks	11	SU49
Grovely Ridge: Wilts.	9	ST93
Gruinard I.: R. & Crom.		NG 9494
Gruinart: Islay		NR 2767
Grundisburgh: Suff.		TM 2251
Guard Bridge: Fife		NO 4519
Guilden Sutton: Ches.		SJ 4468
Guernsey: i., Chan. Is.	9	Ins.
Guildford: Surrey	9	TQ05
Guilsborough: Northants		SP 6773
Guilsfield: Montg.		SJ 2111
Guisborough: Yorks	13	NZ61
Guiseley: Yorks	13	SE14
Gulland Rock: Corn.	8	SW87
Gullane: E. Loth.	15	NT48
Gulvain: mtn., Inv.	16	NN08
Gunby: Lincs		TF 4666
Gunnislake: Corn.		SX 4371
Gurnard's Head: Corn.	8	SW43
Gutcher: Shet. Is.		HU 5498
Guthrie: Angus		NO 5650
Guyhirn: Cambs.		TF 3903
Gwalchmai: Anglesey		SH 3975
Gwash: r.	11	SK 90
Gwaun: r.	8	SN03
Gweebarra: r.	18	E8
Gweebarra Bay: Don.	18	E8
Gweedore: Don.	18	E9
Gwennap: Corn.		SW 7340
Gwennap Hd.: Corn.	8	SW32
Gwili: r.	8	SN42
Gwyddelwern: Mer.		SJ 0746
Gwydderig: r.	8	SN83
Gwyrfal: r.	12	SH45
Gwytherin: Denb.		SH 8761
Gyffylliog: Denb.		SJ 0557
Gypsey Race: r.	13	TA07
Hackness: Yorks.		SE 9690
Hackney: London	7	TQ38
Haddenham: Bucks		SP 7408
Haddenham: Cambs.		TL 4675
Haddington: E. Loth.	15	NT57
Haddiscoe: Norf.		TM 4497
Haddon Hall: Derby.	11	SK26
Hadleigh: Essex		TQ 8087
Hadleigh: Suff.	7	TM04
Hadnall: Salop		SJ 5120
Hadrian's Wall: Cumb./Northumb.	15	NY66
Haerfauls, The: Ber.		NT 5750
Hagley: Worcs		SO 9181
Hagworthingham: Lincs		TF 3469
Haile: Cumb.		NY 0308
Haileybury College: Herts	7	TL31
Hailsham: Sussex	7	TQ50
Halberton: Devon.		ST 0012
Hale: Ches.		SJ 7768
Hale: Lancs		SJ 4682
Hales: Norf.		TM 3897
Halesowen: Worcs		SO 9683
Halesworth: Suff.	6	TM37
Halford: War		SP 2545
Halifax: Yorks	13	SE03
Halkirk: Caith.		ND 1359
Halkyn: mtn., Flint.	12	SJ27
Hallaton: Leics.		SP 7896
Halladale: r.	17	NC85
Hallaton: Leics.		SP 7896
Hallatrow: Som.		ST 6356
Hallington: Northumb.		NY 9875
Halstead: Essex	7	TL83
Halstock: Dorset		ST 5308
Halton: Ches.	11	SJ58
Haltwhistle: Northumb.	15	NY76
Halvergate: Norf.		TG 4206
Halwell: Devon.		SX 7753
Halwill: Devon.		SX4299
Ham: Shet. Is.		HT 9739
Hamble: Hants	7	SU40
Hambleden: Bucks		SU 7886
Hambledon: Hants	7	SU61
Hambledon: Surrey		SU 9638
Hambledon Hill: Dorset	9	ST81
Hambleton: Lancs		SD 3742
Hambleton Hills: Yorks	13	SE58
Hamilton: Lan.	14	NS75
HAMPSHIRE: Eng.	9	SU—
Hampshire Downs	9	SU55
Hampstead: London	7	TQ28
Hampton Court: Middx.	7	TQ16
Hampton in Arden: War		SP 2081
Hamsterley: Dur.		NZ 1131
Hanbury: Worcs.		SO 9663
Handa I.: Suther.	16	NC14
Handforth: Ches.		SJ 8883
Handley: Dorset.		ST 9917
Hanley: Staffs	11	SJ84
Hanmer: Flint.		SJ 4539
Hannington: Hants		SU 5355
Happisburgh: Norf.		TG 3731
Hapton: Lancs		SD 7931
Harberton: Devon.		SX 7758
Harbottle: Northumb.		NT 9304
Harbury: War		SP 3759
Harby: Leics.		SK 7431
Harby: Notts		SK 8770
Hardknott Castle: Cumb.		NY 2101
Hardwick Hall: Derby.	13	SK46
Harewood: Yorks	13	SE34
Harewood End: Here.		SO 5226
Harford: Devon.		SX 6359
Hargrave: Suff.		TL 7660
Harlech: Mer.	10	SH53
Harleston: Norf.	6	TM28
Harlosh: Skye		NG 2841
Harlow: Essex	7	TL41
Harome: Yorks		SE 6482
Harpenden: Herts	7	TL11
Harper: r.	11	SP98
Harper Town: Northumb.		NY 6758
Harpford: Devon.		SY 0890
Harpham: Yorks.		TA 0961
Harpley: Norf.		TF 7826
Harrapool: Skye.		NG 6523
Harrietfield: Perth.		NN 9829
Harrietsham: Kent		TQ 8753
Harrington: Cumb.	12	NX92
Harringworth: Northants		SP 9197
Harris: i., Inv.	16	NG19
Harrogate: Yorks	13	SE35
Harrold: Beds		SP 9456
Harrow: Middx.	7	TQ18
Hart Burn: r.	15	NZ08
Hartest: Suff.		TL 8352
Hart Fell: Dumf.	15	NT01
Hartford: Hunts		TL 2572
Hartington: Derby.		SK 1360
Hartland: Devon.	8	SS22
Hartlebury: Worcs		SO 8471
Hartlepool: Dur.	13	NZ53
Hartlip: Kent		TQ 8364
Hartshill: War		SP 3293
Hartwell: Northants		SP 7850
Harvington: Worcs		SO 8774
Harvington: Worcs		SP 0548
Harwell: Berks	11	SU48
Harwich: Essex	7	TM23
Hascombe: Surrey		TQ 0039
Haskeir Is.: Inv.		NF 6182
Haslemere: Surrey	7	SU93
Haslingden: Lancs	13	SD72
Hastings: Sussex.	7	TQ81
Hatch Beauchamp: Som.		ST 3020
Hatfield: Herts	7	TL20
Hatfield: Yorks		SE 6609
Hatfield Broad Oak: Essex	7	TL51
Hatfield Peverel: Essex		TL 7911
Hatherleigh: Devon.	8	SS50
Hathern: Leics.		SK 5022
Hatherop: Glos		SP 1505
Hathersage: Derby.		SK 2381
Hatton: Aber.		NK 0537
Haughley: Suff.		TM 0262
Haugh of Glass: Banff		NJ 4239
Haugh of Urr: Kirkc.		NX 8066
Haughton le Skerne: Dur.		NZ 3015
Havant: Hants	7	SU70
Haverfordwest: Pemb	10	SM91
Havergate I.: Suff.	7	TM44
Haverhill: Suff.	7	TL64
Haverigg: Cumb.		SD 1578
Hawes: Yorks	13	SD88
Hawes Water: Westmor.	12	NY41
Hawick: Rox.	15	NT51
Hawkhurst: Kent.		TQ 7630
Hawkinge: Kent		TR 2139
Hawkshead: Lancs	12	SD39
Haworth: Yorks.	13	SE03
Hawthorn: Dur.		NZ 4145
Haxby: Yorks		SE 6057
Hayburn Wyke: Yorks.		TA 0197
Haydock: Lancs	12	SJ59
Haydon Bridge: Northumb.		NY 8464
Hayfield: Derby.		SK 0386
Hayle: & r., Corn.	8	SW53
Hayling I.: Hants	7	SU70
Haynes: Beds		TL 0841
Hay-on-Wye: Here.	10	SO24
Hayscastle: Pemb		SM 8925
Hayton: Cumb.		NY 5057
Hayton: Yorks		SE 8145
Haywards Heath: Sussex	7	TQ32
Hazel Grove: Ches.	13	SJ98
Heacham: Norf.		TF 6737
Headcorn: Kent		TQ 8344
Headingley: Yorks	13	SE23
Headington: Oxon.		SP 5407
Headley: Hants		SU 8236
Heads of Ayr: Ayr.	14	NS21
Heanor: Derby.	11	SK44
Heart Law: Midloth.	15	NT 76
Heath and Reach: Beds.		SP 9228
Heathfield: Sussex		TQ 5821
Hebburn: Dur.		NZ 3265
Hebden: Yorks		SE 0263
Hebden Bridge: Yorks	13	SD92
Hebrides: Sea of.	16	NL/NG
Heckington: Lincs		TF1444
Hecla: mtn., S. Uist	16	NF83
Hednesford: Staffs		SJ 9913
Hedon: Yorks	13	TA12
Heighington: Dur.		NZ 2522
Heighington: Lincs		TF 0269
Helensburgh: Dunb.	14	NS28
Helford: Corn.		SW 7526
Hellifield: Yorks		SD 8556
Hell's Mouth: Caer.	10	SH22
Helmdon: Northants		SP 5843
Helmsdale: & r., Suther.	17	ND01
Helmsley: Yorks.	13	SE68
Helpringham: Lincs		TF 1340
Helsby: Ches.		SJ 4875
Helston: Corn.	8	SW62
Helvellyn: mtn., Cumb.	12	NY31
Helvick Head: Wat.	19	F3
Hembury Fort: Devon.		ST 1103
Hemel Hempstead: Herts	7	TL00
Hemingbrough: Yorks		SE 6730
Hemingby: Lincs		TF 2374
Hempnall: Norf.		TM 2494
Hempstead: Essex		TL 6338
Hemsby: Norf.		TG 4917
Hemswell: Lincs		SK 9290
Hemsworth: Yorks		SE 4213
Hemyock: Devon.		ST 1313
Hendon: Middx.	7	TQ28
Hendy: Carm.		SN 5804
Henfield: Sussex		TQ 2116
Hengoed: Glam.		ST 1495
Hengrave: Suff.		TL 8268
Henley in Arden: War.	11	SP16
Henley on Thames: Oxon	11	SU78
Henlow: Beds		TL1738
Hennock: Devon.		SX 8380
Henshaw: Northumb.		NY 7664
Hensingham: Cumb.		NX 9816
Henwick: Worcs		SO 8354
Hepple: Northumb.		NT 9800
Heptonstall: Yorks		SD 9827
Hepworth: Yorks		SE 1606
Hereford: Here.	11	SO54
HEREFORDSHIRE: Eng.	11	SO—
Herefordshire Beacon	11	SO73
Heriot: Midloth.		NT 3952
Herm: i., Chan. Is.	9	Ins.
Herma Ness: Shet. Is.	17	HP61
Hermitage: Berks		SU 5072
Hermitage Castle: Rox.	15	NY49
Herne Bay: Kent	7	TR16
Hernhill: Kent		TR 0660
Herriard: Hants		SU 6645
Herstmonceux: Sussex	7	TQ61
Hertford: Herts	7	TL31
HERTFORDSHIRE: Eng.	7	TL—
Hesketh Bank: Lancs		SD 4323
Hessle: Yorks	13	TA02
Heswall: Ches.		SJ 2682
Hethe: Oxon.		SP 5929
Hethersett: Norf.		TG 1505
Hethersgill: Cumb.		NY 4767
Hetton: Yorks		SD 9658
Hetton-le-Hole: Dur.	13	NZ34
Hetty Pegler's Tump: Glos		ST 7999
Heversham: Westmor.		SD 4983
Hewelsfield: Glos		SO 5602
Hexham: Northumb.	15	NY96
Hexworthy: Devon.		SX 6572
Heybridge: Essex		TL 8508
Heysham: Lancs.	12	SD46
Heytesbury: Wilts.		ST 9242
Heywood: Lancs	13	SD81
Hibaldstow: Lincs		SE 9702
Hickleton: Yorks		SE 4805
Hickling Broad: Norf.	6	TG42
Hidcote Boyce: Glos		SP 1742
Higham Ferrers: Northants	11	SP96
Higham on the Hill: Leics.		SP 3895
Highampton: Devon.		SS 4804
High Banks: Kirkc.		NX 7049
High Bentham: Yorks.	12	SD66
High Bickington: Devon.		SS 5290
High Blantyre: Lan.		NS 6756
High Bray: Devon.		SS 6934
Highbridge: Som.	9	ST34
Highclere: Hants		SU 4360
Highcliffe: Hants		SZ 2193
High Edge: Derby.	13	SK06
High Ercall: Salop		SJ 5917
High Halden: Kent		TQ 8937
High Ham: Som.		ST 4231
High Hesket: Cumb.		NY 4744
Highley: Salop		SO 7483
High Roding: Essex		TL 6017
High Seat: mtn., Westmor.	13	NY80
High Street: mtn., Westmor.	12	NY41
Hightae: Dumf.		NY 0979
Hightown: Lancs		SD 2903
Highweek: Devon.		SX 8472
High Willhays: mtn., Devon.	8	SX58
Highworth: Wilts.	11	SU29
High Wycombe: Bucks	11	SU 89
Hildenborough: Kent		TQ 5648
Hilgay: Norf.		TL 6298
Hill: Glos		ST 6495
Hillborough: Norf.		TF 8200
Hillington: Norf.		TF 7225
Hill of Fare: Aber.	17	NJ60
Hill of Fearn: R. & Crom.		NH 8377
Hill of Stake: Renf.	14	NS26
Hillsborough: Down	18	J7
Hillside: Angus		NO 7061
Hills of Cromdale: Banff	17	NJ12
Hillswick: Shet. Is.		HU 2877
Hilmarton: Wilts.		SU 0175
Hilpsford Point: Lancs.	12	SD26
Hilton: Westmor.		NY 7320
Hinckley: Leics.	11	SP49
Hinderwell: Yorks		NZ 7916
Hindhead: Surrey	7	SU83
Hindley: Lancs	12	SD60
Hindon: Wilts.		ST 9032
Hingham: Norf.	6	TG00
Hintlesham: Suff.		TM 0843
Hipperholme: Yorks		SE 1225
Hirnant: Montg.		SJ 0423
Hirwaun: Glam.		SN 9505
Hitcham: Suff.		TL 9851
Hitchin: Herts	7	TL12
Hobkirk: Rox.		NT 5810
Hockham: Norf.		TL 9592
Hockley: Essex		TQ 8293
Hockley Heath: War		SP 1572
Hockliffe: Beds		SP 9726
Hodder: r.	12	SD64
Hoddesdon: Herts	7	TL30
Hod Hill: Dorset		ST 8510
Hoe Hill: Lincs		TF 2197
Hoghton Tower: Lancs	13	SD62
Hogs Back: Surrey	7	SU94
Hogsthorpe: Lincs		TF 5372
Holbeach: & marsh, Lincs	6	TF32
Holbrook: Suff.		TM 1636
Holcombe Rogus: Devon.		ST 0519
Holderness: penin., Yorks	13	TA—
Holford: Som.		ST 1541
Holkham Hall: Norf.	6	TF84
Holland: Admin. Co., Lincs	6	TF22
Holland Fen: Lincs	13	TF24
Hollandbush: Stirl.		NS 7879
Hollesley Bay: Suff.		TM 3844
Hollingworth: Ches.		SK 0096
Holmbury: Surrey		TQ 1043
Holme: Hunts		TL 1987
Holme: r.	13	SE10
Holme next the Sea: Norf.		TF 7043
Holmes Chapel: Ches.		SJ 7667
Holmesdale: Surrey	7	TQ24
Holmfirth: Yorks	13	SE10
Holmrook: Cumb.		SD 0799
Holmwood: Surrey		TQ 1745
Holnicote Estate: Som.		SS 8944
Holsworthy: Devon.	8	SS30
Holt: Denb.		SJ 4053
Holt: Norf.	6	TG03
Holton le Clay: Lincs		TA 2802
Holtye House: Sussex	7	TQ43
Holwick: Yorks		NY 9026
Holyhead: Anglesey	10	SH28
Holy I.: Anglesey	10	SH27
Holy I.: Bute	14	NS03
Holy I.: Northumb.	15	NU14
Holyport: Berks		SU 8977
Holystone: Northumb.		NT 9502
Holytown: Lan.		NS 7760
Holywell: Corn.		SW 7758
Holywell: Flint.	10	SJ17
Holywood: Down	18	K8
Holywood: Dumf.	15	NX98
Homersfield: Suff.		TM 2885
Honing: Norf.		TG 3227
Honingham: Norf.		TG 1011
Honington: Lincs.		SK 9443
Honiton: Devon.	9	ST10
Honley: Yorks		SE 1311
Hoo: Kent		TQ 7872

Hook: Hants SU 7254
Hook: Yorks SE 7525
Hook Head: Wex. 19 H3
Hook Norton: Oxon. SP 3533
Hope: Devon. SX 6839
Hope: Flint. SJ 3058
Hopeman: Moray. NJ 1469
Hope under Dinmore: Here. SO 5052
Hopes, The: E. Loth. 15 NT56
Hopton: Suff. TG 5200
Horam: Sussex TQ 5717
Horbury: Yorks 13 SE21
Horden: Dur. NZ 4441
Horley: Surrey TQ 2843
Horncastle: Lincs 6 TF26
Hornchurch: Essex TQ 5487
Horndean: Hants SU 7013
Horn Hd.: Don. 18 F9
Hornsea: Yorks 13 TA24
Horrabridge: Devon. SX 5169
Horse House: Yorks SE 0481
Horsey: & mere, Norf. 6 TG42
Horsford: Norf. TG 1915
Horsforth: Yorks 13 SE23
Horsham: Sussex 7 TQ13
Horsham St. Faith: Norf. TG 2114
Horsington: Lincs TF 1868
Horsington: Som. ST 7023
Horsmonden: Kent TQ 7040
Horsted Keynes: Sussex TQ 3828
Horwich: Lancs 12 SD61
Hotham: Yorks SE 8934
Hot Hill: Rox. 15 NT41
Houghton le Spring: Dur. 13 NZ35
Houghton St. Giles: Norf. TF 9235
Hounslow: Middx. 11 TQ17
Housesteads: Northumb. 15 NY76
Houston: Renf. NS 4067
Hove: Sussex 7 TQ20
Hovingham: Yorks SE 6675
Howardian Hills: Yorks 13 SE57
Howden: Yorks 13 SE72
Howe of Fife 15 NO41
Howe of the Mearns: Kinc. 17 NO67
Howey: Rad. SO 0558
Howick: Northumb. NU 2517
Howmore: S. Uist NF 7536
Hownam Law: Rox. 15 NT72
Howth: Dublin 19 J5
Howtown: Westmor. 12 NY41
Hoxne: Suff. TM 1877
Hoy: i., Ork. Is. 17 ND29
Hoylake: Ches. 12 SJ28
Hoyland Nether: Yorks 13 SE30
Hucknall: Notts 11 SK54
Huddersfield: Yorks 13 SE11
Hudswell: Yorks NZ 1400
Huggate: Yorks SE 8855
Hughenden Manor: Bucks 11 SU89
Hugh Town: Scilly Is. 8 SV91
Huish Champflower: Som. ST 0429
Hull: see Kingston upon Hull
Hull: r. 13 TA04
Hullavington: Wilts. ST 8982
Hulme End: Staffs. 11 SK15
Humber: r. 13 TA21
Humbie: E. Loth. NT 4562
Humbleton: Yorks TA 2234
Hume: Ber. NT 7041
Humshaugh: Northumb. NY 9171
Hundleton: Pemb. SM 9600
Hundon: Suff. TL 7348
Hungerford: Berks 11 SU36
Hunmanby: Yorks 13 TA 07
Hunter's Quay: Argyll NS 1879
Huntingdon: Hunts 6 TL27
HUNTINGDONSHIRE: Eng. 6 TL—
Huntington: Yorks SE 6156
Huntingtower: Perth. NO 0924
Huntly: Aber. 17 NJ53
Hunton: Yorks SE 1892
Huntsham: Devon. ST 0020
Hurlers, The: Corn. SX 2672
Hurn: airport, Hants 9 SZ19
Hursley: Hants SU 4225
Hurstbourne Priors: Hants SU 4346
Hurstbourne Tarrant: Hants SU 3853
Hurstpierpoint: Sussex. 7 TQ21
Husbands Bosworth: Leics SP 6484
Husinish Point: Harris NA 9711
Husthwaite: Yorks SE 5175
Huttoft: Lincs TF 5176
Hutton: Ber. NT 9053
Hutton: Yorks TA 0253
Huyton: Lancs SJ 4490
Hyde: Ches. 13 SJ99
Hythe: Hants SU 4207
Hythe: Kent 7 TR13

Iarconnaught: Gal. 19 C5
Ibstock: Leics. SK 4010
Ickleton: Cambs. TL 4943
Icklingham: Suff. TL 7772
Iddesleigh: Devon. SS 5608
Ide: Devon. SX 8990
Ideford: Devon. SX 8977
Idle: Yorks SE 1737
Idle: r. 11 SK79
Idrigill Point: Skye 16 NG23
Iffley: Oxon. SP 5203
Ightham: Kent TQ 5956
Iken: Suff. TM 4155
Ilchester: Som. ST 5222
Ilderton: Northumb. NU 0121
Ilford: Essex 7 TQ48
Ilfracombe: Devon. 8 SS54
Ilkeston: Derby. 11 SK44
Ilkley: Yorks 13 SE14
Ilmington: War SP 2143
Ilminster: Som. 9 ST31
Imber: Wilts. ST 9648
Immingham: Lincs 6 TA11
Impington: Cambs. TL 4463
Inchbae Forest: Ross & Crom. NH 3876
Inchbare: Angus NO 6065
Inchcape: rock, Scot. 15 NO72
Inchkeith: i., Scot. 15 NT28
Inch Kenneth: i., Argyll. NM 4335
Inchmarnock: i., Bute. 14 NS05
Inchnacardoch Forest: Inv. NH 3009
Inchnadamph: Suther. NC 2522
Ingatestone: Essex 7 TQ69
Ingham: Suff. TL 8570
Ingleborough: mtn., Yorks 13 SD77
Ingleby Greenhow: Yorks NZ 5807
Ingleton: Yorks SD 6972
Inglewood Forest: Cumb. 12 NY44
Ingoldmells: Lincs TF 5668
Ingoldsby: Lincs TF 0030
Ingram: Northumb. NU 0116
Inishark: i., Gal. 18 A6
Inishbofin: i., Don. 18 E9
Inishbofin: i., Gal. 18 A6
Inisheer: i., Aran Is. 19 B5
Inishkea: is., Mayo 18 A7
Inishmaan: i., Aran Is. 19 B5
Inishmore: i., Aran Is. 19 B5
Inishmurray: i., Sligo 18 D7
Inishowen Head: Don. 18 H9
Inishowen Penin.: Don. 18 G9
Inishtrahull: i., Don. 18 G9
Inishturk: i., Irel. 18 A6
Inkberrow: Worcs SP 0157
Inkpen Beacon: Berks 9 SU36
Innellan: Argyll NS 1479
Inner Hebrides: Scot. 16 NM—
Innerleithen: Peeb. NT 3336
Inner Sound: Inv. 16 NG64
Innerwick: E. Loth. NT 7273
Inny: r., Corn. 8 SX37
Inny: r., Kerry 19 A2
Insch: Aber. NJ 6327
Insh: Inv. NH 8101
Inskip: Lancs SD 4537
Instow: Devon. 8 SS43
Inver: Ross & Crom. NH 8682
Inver Alligin: R. & Crom. NG 8457
Inverallochy: Aber. NK 0464
Inveran: Suther. 17 NH59
Inveraray: Argyll 14 NN00
Inverarity: Angus NO 4444
Inverbervie: Kinc. 17 NO87
Invercreran: Argyll NN 0147
Inver Dalavil: bay, Skye 16 NG50
Inverdruie: Inv. 17 NH91
Inverewe: R. & Crom. 16 NG88
Invergarry: Inv. 16 NH30
Invergordon: R. & Crom. 17 NH76
Inverharity: Angus NO 1963
Inverinate: R. & Crom. NG 9122
Inverkeilor: Angus NO 6649
Inverkeithing: Fife 15 NT18
Inverkeithny: Banff NJ 6246
Inverkip: Renf. NS 2071
Inverkirkaig: Suther. NC 0819
Inverlael: Ross & Crom. NH 1885
Inverliever Forest: Perth. 14 NM91
Inverlochy Castle: Inv. NN 1376
Invermoriston Forest: Inv. NH 3919
INVERNESS: Co., Scot. 17 NH64
Invershiel: R. & Crom. NG 9319
Invershin: Suther. NH 5796
Inverurie: Aber. 17 NJ72
Iona: i., Argyll 14 NM22
Ipplepen: Devon. SX 8366
Ipstones: Staffs SK 0249
Ipswich: Suff. 7 TM14
Irchester: Northants SP 9265
Ireby: Cumb. NY 2338
Ireland: Repub. of 18/19 —
Irfon: r. 10 SN84
Irish Sea 18/19 —
Irlam: Lancs 13 SJ79
Iron Acton: Glos ST 6783
Iron Bridge: Salop 11 SJ60
Irt: r. 12 SD09
Irthing: r. 13 NY66
Irthlingborough: Northants 11 SP97
Irvine: Ayr 14 NS33
Irvine: r. 14 NS33
Irvinestown: Ferm. 18 F7
Irwell: r. 13 SJ89
Ise: r. 6 SP88
Isla: r., Angus 15 NO13
Isla: r., Banff 17 NJ45
Island Magee: Antrim 18 K8
Island of Bute: Bute. 14 NS06
Island of Danna: Argyll 14 NR67
Island of Skye: Inv. 16 NG—
Islay: i., Argyll 14 NR36
Isle: r. 9 ST32
Isleham: Cambs. TL 6474
Isle Martin: R. & Crom. 16 NH09
Isle of Athelney: Som. 9 ST32
Isle of Axholme: Lincs 6 SE70
Isle of Ely: Cambs. 6 TL49
Isle of Ewe: R. & Crom. 16 NG88
Isle of Man: Irish Sea 12 SC38
Isle of May: Fife. 15 NT69
Isle of Oxney: Kent 7 TQ92
Isle of Purbeck: Dorset 9 SY98
Isle of Sheppey: Kent 7 TQ96
Isle of Thanet: Kent 7 TR36
Isle of Walney: Lancs 12 SD16
Isle of Whithorn: Wig. 14 NX53
Isle of Wight: Hants 7 SZ48
Isleornsay: Skye NG 6912
Islip: Oxon. SP 5214
Islivick: Lewis NA 9927
Itchen: Hants SU 4311
Itchen: r., Hants. 9 SU53
Itchen: r., War 11 SP45
Itchingfield: Sussex TQ 1328
Ithon: r. 10 SO06
Ivel: r. 11 TF13
Ivinghoe: Bucks SP 9416
Ivybridge: Devon. 8 SX 65
Ivychurch: Kent TR 0227
Iwade: Kent TQ 9067
Iwerne Minster: Dorset ST 8614
Ixworth: Suff. TL 9370

Jacobstow: Corn. SX 1995
Janetstown: Caith. ND 1932
Jarlshof: Shet. Is. 17 HU30
Jarrow: Dur. 15 NZ36
Jedburgh: Rox. 15 NT62
Jed Water: r. 15 NT71
Jeffreston: Pemb. SN 0806
Jemimaville: R. & Crom. NH 7165
Jersey: i., Chan. Is. 9 Ins.
Jervaulx Abbey: Yorks 13 SE18
Jethou: i., Chan. Is. 9 Ins.
John o'Groat's House: Caith. 17 ND37
Johnshaven: Kinc. NO 7966
Johnston: Pemb SM9310
Johnstone: Renf. 14 NS46
John's Town: Carm. SN 3919
Jordans: Bucks SU 9790
Joyce's Country: Gal. 18 B6
Jura: i., Argyll 14 NR 58
Jurby Head: I. of Man 12 SC39

Kaimes Hill: Midloth. 15 NT16
Kale Water: r. 15 NT81
Kames: Argyll NR 9771
Kanturk: Cork 19 D3
Keadby: Lincs SE 8311
Keady: Armagh 18 H7
Kearvaig: Suther. NC 2972
Kebock Head: Lewis 16 NB41
Kedleston: Derby. SK 3140
Keelby: Lincs TA 1610
Keen, Mt.: Angus 17 NO48
Keeper Hill: Tip. 19 E4
Kegworth: Leics. SK 4826
Keig: Aber. NJ 6119
Keighley: Yorks 13 SE04
Keil: Argyll NR 6707
Keiss: Caith. ND 3461
Keith: Banff 17 NJ45
Keld: Yorks NY 8901
Kelham: Notts SK 7755
Kellas: Angus NO 4535
Kellington: Yorks SE 5524
Kells: Kilk. 19 G4
Kells: Meath 18 H6
Kelmscot: Berks SU 2499
Kelsall: Ches. SJ 5268
Kelsey Head: Corn. SW 7660
Kelso: Rox. 15 NT73
Keltie Water: r. 14 NN61
Keltneyburn: Perth. NN 7749
Kelty: Fife NT 1494
Kelvedon: Essex TL 8618
Kelvedon Hatch: Essex. TQ 5698
Kemble: Glos ST 9897
Kemnay: Aber. NJ 7315
Kempston: Beds. 7 TL04
Kendal: Westmor. 12 SD59
Kenilworth: War 11 SP27
Kenmare: & r., Kerry 19 B2
Kenmore: Perth. NN 7745
Kenn: Som. ST 4168
Kennet: r. 11 SU16
Kennett: r. 6 TL66
Kenninghall: Norf. TM 0386
Kennington: Kent TR 0245
Kensaleyre: Skye NG 4251
KENT: Co., Eng. 7TQ/TR
Kent: r. 12 NY 40
Kentallen: Argyll 16 NN05
Kentford: Suff. TL 7066
Kentisbury: Devon. SS 6144
Kentmere: Westmor. NY 4504
Kenton: Devon. SX 9583
Kerloch: mtn., Kinc. 17 NO68
Kerrera: i., Argyll 16 NM82
KERRY: Co., R. of Irel. 19 B3
Kerry: Montg. SO 1490
Kerry Head: Kerry 19 B3
Kersey: Suff. TM 0044
Kessingland: Suff. TM 5286
Kesteven: Admin. Co., Lincs 6SK/TA
Keswick: Cumb. 12 NY22
Kettering: Northants 11 SP87
Ketton: Rut. SK 9704
Kew: Surrey 7 TQ17
Kexbrough: Yorks SE 2909
Kexby: Yorks SE 7050
Key, L.: Rosc. 18 E7
Keyingham: Yorks TA 2425
Keynsham: Som. 11 ST66
Keysoe: Beds TL 0763
Keyworth: Notts SK 6130
Kidderminster: Worcs 11 SO87
Kidlington: Oxon. 11 SP41
Kidsgrove: Staffs 11 SJ85
Kidwelly: Carm. 10 SN40
Kilbarchan: Renf. NS 4063
Kilberry: Argyll NR 7164
Kilbirnie: Ayr NS 3154
Kilbrannan Sound: Scot. 14 NR83
Kilbride: Argyll NM 8525
Kilchenzie: Argyll NR 6725
Kilchiaran: Islay NR 2060
Kilchoan: Argyll NM 4963
Kilchoman: Islay NR 2163
Kilchrenan: Argyll NN 0322
Kilchurn Castle: Argyll NN 1327
Kilconnell: Gal. 19 E5
Kilconquhar: Fife NO 4802
Kilcreggan: Dunb. NS 2380
KILDARE: Co., R. of Irel. 19 H5
Kildermorie Forest: Ross & Crom. NH4678
Kildonan: Bute. NS 0321
Kildonan: Suther. NC 9121
Kildrummy: Aber. NJ 4617
Kilfinan: Argyll NR 9378
Kilham: Northumb. NT 8832
Kilham: Yorks TA 0564
Kilkee: Clare 19 B4
Kilkeel: Down 18 J7
KILKENNY: Co., R. of Irel. 19 G4
Kilkerran: Argyll NR 7219
Kilkhampton: Corn. SS 2511
Kilkieran Bay: Gal. 19 B5
Killala: & bay, Mayo 18 C7
Killamarsh: Derby. 13 SK48
Killarney: Kerry. 19 C3
Killary Harbour: Irel. 18 B6
Killean: Argyll NR 6944
Killearn: Stirl. NS 5286
Killebegs: Don. 18 E8
Killegray: i., Inv. 16 NF98
Killichonan: Perth. NN 5458
Killiemore: Mull NM 4929
Killilan: Ross & Crom. NG 9430
Killin: Perth. 14 NN53
Killiney: Dublin 19 J5
Killinghall: Yorks SE 2858
Killyleagh: Down 18 K7
Kilmacolm: Renf. 14 NS36
Kilmallock: Lim. 19 D3
Kilmaluag: Skye NG 4374
Kilmany: Fife NO 3821
Kilmarnock: Ayr 14 NS43
Kilmartin: Argyll NR 8398
Kilmaurs: Ayr NS 4141
Kilmelfort: Argyll NM 8413
Kilmeny: Islay NR 3865
Kilmichael Glassary: Argyll NR 8593
Kilmichael of Inverlussa: Argyll NR 7785
Kilmore: Argyll 14 NM82
Kilmory: Bute. NR 9621
Kilmory: Rhum 16 NG30
Kilmuir: Ross & Crom. NH 6749
Kilmuir: Ross & Crom. NH 7573
Kilmuir: Skye NG 3770
Kilmun: Argyll NS1781
Kilninian: Mull NM 3945
Kilninver: Argyll 14 NM82
Kilnsea: Yorks TA 4015
Kilnwick: Yorks SE 9949
Kiloran Bay: Colonsay 14 NR39
Kilpatrick Hills: Dunb. 14 NS47
Kilrea: Lon. 18 H8
Kilrenny: Fife 15 NO50
Kilrush: Clare 19 C4
Kilsby: Northants SP 5671
Kilsyth: Stirl. 14 NS77
Kilsyth Hills: Stirl. 14 NS68
Kilvaxter: Skye NG 3869
Kilwinning: Ayr 14 NS34
Kilworth Mts., Cork 19 E3
Kimberley: Norf. TG 0704
Kimberley: Notts SK 4944
Kimblesworth: Dur. NZ 2547
Kimbolton: Hunts 6 TL06
Kimmeridge: Dorset 9 SY97
Kimpton: Herts TL 1718
Kinbrace: Suther. NC 8631
Kinbuck: Perth. NN 7905
KINCARDINE: Co., Scot. 17 NO—
Kincardine: Fife. NS 9387
Kincardine: R. & Crom. NH 6089
Kincardine O'Neil: Aber. NO 5999
Kinclaven: Perth. NO 1538
Kincraig: Inv. NH 8305
Kinder Scout: Derby. 13 SK08
Kineton: War SP 3351
Kinfauns: Perth. NO 1622
Kingairloch: Argyll 16 NM85
King Arthur's Cave: Here. 11 SO51
Kingham: Oxon. SP 2523
Kinghorn: Fife 15 NT28
Kingie: r. 16 NN09
Kinglassie: Fife NT 2298
Kingley Vale: Sussex SU 8111
Kings: r. 19 F4
Kingsand: Corn. SX 4350
Kingsbarns: Fife NO 5912
Kingsbridge: Devon. 8 SX74
King's Bromley: Staffs SK 1216
Kingsbury Episcopi: Som. ST 4320
King's Caple: Here. SO 5529
Kingsclere: Hants 7 SU55
King's Cliffe: Northants TL 0097
Kingscross: Bute. NS 0428
Kingsdon: Som. ST 5126
Kingsdown: Kent TR 3748
Kingskerswell: Devon. SX 8767
Kingskettle: Fife NO 3008
Kingsland: Here. SO 4461
Kings Langley: Herts TL 0702
Kingsley: Ches. SJ 5474
Kingsley: Hants SU 7838
Kingsley: Staffs SK 0047
King's Lynn: Norf. 6 TF62
Kingsmuir: Angus NO 4849
Kingsnorth: Kent. TR 0039
King's Norton: War SP 0478
King's Nympton: Devon. SS 6819
King's Seat: mtn., Angus 15 NO23
King's Somborne: Hants SU 3631
King's Sutton: Northants SP 4936
Kingsteignton: Devon. SX 8773
Kingston: Devon. SX 6347
Kingston: Moray. NJ 3365
Kingston Bagpuize: Berks SU 4098
Kingstone: Here. SO 4235
Kingston Lisle: Berks SU 3287
Kingston upon Hull: Yorks 13 TA02
Kingston upon Thames: Surrey 7 TQ16
Kingstown: Dublin 19 J5
Kingswear: Devon. 8 SX85
Kingswood: Glos ST 6473
Kington: Here. 10 SO25
Kingussie: Inv. 17 NH70
King Water: r. 12 NY56
King William's College: I. of Man 12 SC26
Kinlet: Salop SO 7180
Kinloch: Perth. NO 1444
Kinloch: Rhum 16 NM49
Kinlochbervie: Suther. 16 NC25
Kinlocheil: Inv. NM 9779
Kinlochewe: R. & Crom. 16 NH06
Kinlochleven: Inv. 16 NN16
Kinlochluichart Forest: Ross & Crom. NH 2570
Kinloch Rannoch: Perth. 17 NN65
Kinloss: Moray NJ 0661
Kinmuck: Aber. NJ 8119
Kinnairds Head: Aber. 17 NK06
Kinneff: Kinc. NO 8574
Kinnell: Angus NO 6050
Kinnel Water: r. 15 NY09
Kinrossie: Perth. NO 1832
KINROSS: & Co., Scot. 15 NO10
Kinsale: & harb., Cork. 19 D2
Kintail: Inv. 16 NG91
Kintbury: Berks SU 3866
Kintore: Aber. 17 NJ71
Kintra: Islay NR 3248
Kintradwell: Suther. NC 9308
Kintyre: Argyll 14 NR73
Kinver: Staffs SO 8483
Kippax: Yorks SE 4130
Kippen: Stirl. NS 6594
Kippford: Kirkc. NX 8355
Kippure: mtn., Irel. 19 J5
Kirby Muxloe: Leics SK 5104
Kirby Underdale: Yorks SE 8158
Kirkabister: Shet. Is. HU 4938
Kirkbampton: Cumb. NY 3056
Kirkbean: Kirkc. NX 9859
Kirk Braddan: I. of Man SC 3676
Kirkbride: Cumb. NY 2356
Kirkbuddo: Angus NO 5043
Kirkburn: Yorks SE 9855
Kirkburton: Yorks 13 SE21
Kirkby: Lancs SJ 4098
Kirkby in Ashfield: Notts 11 SK45
Kirkby Lonsdale: Westmor. 12 SD67
Kirkby Malham: Yorks SD 8960
Kirkby Mallory: Leics. SK 4500
Kirkby Malzeard: Yorks SE 2374
Kirkby Moorside: Yorks 13 SE68
Kirkby Stephen: Westmor. 13 NY70
Kirkby Thore: Westmor. NY 6325
Kirkcaldy: Fife 15 NT29
Kirkcambeck: Cumb. NY 5368
Kirkconnel: Dumf. NS 7312
Kirkcowan: Wig. NX 3260
KIRKCUDBRIGHT: Stewartry of, Scot. 14 NX—
Kirkcudbright: Kirkc. 14 NX65
Kirkham: Lancs 12 SD43
Kirkham: Yorks SE 7365
Kirkheaton: Northumb. NX 0177
Kirkhill: Inv. NH 5545
Kirkibost I.: Inv. NF 7564
Kirkinner: Wig. NX 4251

G.B. & IRELAND

KIRKINTILLOCH — LOCH LAXFORD

Kirkintilloch: Dunb. . NS 6573
Kirk Ireton: Derby. . SK 2650
Kirkland Hill: Dumf. . 14 NS71
Kirk Langley: Derby. . SK 2838
Kirkliston: W. Loth. . NT 1274
Kirkmaiden: Wig. . NX 1237
Kirkmichael: I. of Man SC 3190
Kirkmichael: Perth. . NO 0860
Kirknewton: Midloth. . NT 1166
Kirknewton: Northumb. NT 9130
Kirk of Shotts: Lan. . NS 8462
Kirkoswald: Ayr . . NS 2407
Kirkoswald: Cumb. . 12 NY54
Kirkpatrick: Dumf. . NY 2770
Kirkpatrick Durham: Kirkc. . . NX 7870
Kirk Smeaton: Yorks . SE 5116
Kirkstead: Lincs . . TF 1762
Kirkton: Ross & Crom. NG 8127
Kirkton of Culsalmond: Aber. . . . NJ 6432
Kirkton of Durris: Kinc. NO 7796
Kirkton of Glenbuchat: Aber. . . . NJ 3715
Kirkton of Glenisla: Angus . . NO 2160
Kirkton of Largo: Fife . NO 4203
Kirkton of Menmuir: Angus . . NO 5364
Kirkton of Skene: Aber. NJ 8007
Kirktown of Alvah: Banff NJ 6760
Kirktown of Auchterless: Aber. . . NJ 7141
Kirktown of Clatt: Aber. NJ 5325
Kirktown of Deskford: Banff . . . NJ 5061
Kirktown of Slains: Aber. NK 0429
Kirkwall: Ork. Is. . 17 HY41
Kirkwhelpington: Northumb. . . NY 9984
Kirk Yetholm: Rox. . NT 8227
Kirriemuir: Angus . 17 NO35
Kirtle Water: r. . 15 NY27
Kirtlington: Oxon. . SP 4919
Kirtomy: Suther. . NC 7463
Kirton: Lincs . . TF 3038
Kirton in Lindsey: Lincs 6 SK99
Kislingbury: Northants. SP 6959
Kit's Coty House: Kent TQ 7461
Knaik: r. . . 15 NN81
Knapdale: Argyll . 14 NR77
Knapton: Norf. . TG 3034
Knaresborough: Yorks 13 SE35
Knayton: Yorks . SE 4387
Knebworth: Herts . TL 2520
Kneesall: Notts . SK 7064
Knelston: Glam. . SS 4689
Knighton: Rad. . 10 SO27
Knightwick: Worcs . SO 7355
Kniveton: Derby. . SK 2050
Knock: Banff . . NJ 5452
Knock: Lewis . . NB 4931
Knockadoon Hd.: Cork 19 F2
Knockando: Moray. . NJ 1941
Knockanteagal: Benbecula . 16 NF75
Knockbain: Ross & Crom. NH 6255
Knockboy: mtn., Irel. . 19 C2
Knock Farril: R. & Crom. NH 5058
Knockfin Heights: Scot. 17 NC93
Knock Hill: Banff . 17 NJ55
Knockin: Salop . . SJ 3322
Knockmealdown Mts.: Tip. . . . 19 F3
Knocknagashel: Kerry 19 C3
Knottingley: Yorks . 13 SE52
Knowlton Circles: Dorset 9 SU01
Knowsley: Lancs . SJ 4395
Knowstone: Devon. . SS 8223
Knoydart: Inv. . . 16 NG80
Knucklas: Rad. . SO 2574
Knutsford: Ches. . 11 SJ77
Kyle: Ayr . . 14 NS52
Kyleakin: Skye . 16 NG72
Kyle of Durness: Suther. 16 NC36
Kyle of Lochalsh: Ross & Crom. . 16 NG72
Kyle of Tongue: Suther. 17 NC55
Kylerhea: Inv. . NG 7820
Kylesku Ferry: Suther. 16 NC23
Kyles of Bute: Bute. . 14 NS07
Kym: r. . . . 11 TF16

Laceby: Lincs . . TA 2106
Lacock: Wilts . . ST 9168
Ladder Hills: Banff . 17 NJ21
Ladhar Bheinn: Inv. . 16 NG80
Ladock: Corn. . . SW 8950
Ladybank: Fife . . 15 NO30
Lady Isle: Ayr . . 14 NS22
Ladykirk: Ber. . . NT 8947
Lagavulin: Islay . . NR 4045
Lagg: Jura . . NR 5978
Laggan: Inv. . . NN 6194
Laggan Bay: Islay . 14 NR25
Laggangarn: Wig. . NX 2470
Laich o' Moray: Moray 17 NJ16
Laindon: Essex . . TQ 6889
Lairg: Suther. . . 17 NC50
Lake District: Cumb./Westmor. . 12 NY11
Lakenheath: Suff. . TL 7182
Laleston: Glam. . . SS 8779
Lamachan Hill: Kirkc. 14 NX47
Lambay I.: Dublin . 18 J5
Lamberhurst: Kent . TQ 6735
Lambourn: & r., Berks 11 SU37
Lambourn Downs: Berks 9 SU38
Lamb's Head: Kerry . 19 A2
Lamerton: Devon. . SX 4476
Lamington: Lan. . . NS 9730
Lamlash: Bute. . 14 NS03
Lammermuir: Ber. . 15 NT75
Lammermuir Hills: E. Loth. . . 15 NT66
Lampeter: Card. . 10 SN54
LANARK: Co., Scot. . 15 NS84
LANCASHIRE: Eng. . 12 SD54
Lancaster: Lancs . 12 SD46
Lanchester: Dur. . NZ 1647
Lancing College: Sussex 7 TQ10
Landewednack: Corn. . SW 7012
Land's End: Corn. . 8 SW32
Lane End: Bucks . SU 8091
Lang Craig: Angus . NO 7048
Langdales: Westmor. . 12 NY30
Langford: Beds . TL 1841
Langford Budville: Som. ST 1122
Langham: Rut. . . SK 8411
Langholm: Dumf. . 15 NY38
Langley: Essex . . TL 4435
Langport: Som. . 9 ST42
Langstrothdale Chase: Lancs . . 13 SD87
Langthwaite: Yorks . NZ 0002
Langtoft: Lincs . . TF 1212
Langwathby: Cumb. . NY 5733
Langwell Forest: Caith.. ND 0325
Lanivet: Corn. . . SX 0364
Lanreath: Corn. . . SX 1756
Lanton: Rox. . . NT 6221
LAOIGHIS: Co., R. of Irel. . . 19 G5
Lapford: Devon. . SS 7308
Larbert: Stirl. . . NS 8582
Largs: Ayr . . NS 2058
Lark: r. . . 6 TL77
Larkhall: Lan. . NS 7651
Larkhill Camp: Wilts. . SU 1244
Larne: Antrim . . 18 K8
Larriston Fells: Rox. . 15 NY59
Lasham: Hants . SU 6742
Lasswade: Midloth. . 15 NT36
Lastingham: Yorks . SE 7290
Latchingdon & Snoreham: Essex . . TL 8800
Latheron: Caith. . ND 1933
Lauder: Ber. . . 15 NT54
Lauderdale: Ber. . 15 NT54
Laugharne: Carm. . SN 3011
Laughton: Sussex . TQ 5013
Launceston: Corn. . 8 SX38
Laurencekirk: Kinc. . 17 NO77
Laurieston: Kirkc. . NX 6864
Laurieston: Stirl. . NS 9179
Lavant: Sussex . . SU 8608
Lavendon: Bucks . SP 9153
Lavenham: Suff.. . 7 TL94
Lavernock: Glam. . ST 1868
Lawers: Perth. . . NN 6739
Lawshall: Suff. . . TL 8654
Laxay: Lewis . . NB 3221
Laxey: & bay, I. of Man 12 SC48
Laxfield: Suff. . . TM 2972
Laxford Bridge: Suther. NC 2347
Laxton: Notts . . 13 SK76
Layer de la Haye: Essex TL 9620
Layer Marney: Essex . TL 9217
Lazonby: Cumb. . . NY 5439
Lea: r., Essex . . 7 TL30
Lea: r., Herts . . 7 TL11
Leach: r. . . . 9 SP10
Leadburn: Midloth. . NT 2355
Leadenham: Lincs . SK 9452
Leaden Roding: Essex . TL 5913
Leadhills: Lan. . . NS 8814
Leadon: r. . . . 9 SO72
Leake: Yorks . . SE 4390
Lealholm: Yorks . . NZ 7607
Lealt: Skye . . NG 5060
Leam: r. . . . 11 SP56
Leamington Spa: War . 11 SP36
Leane, L.: Kerry . . 19 B3
Leannan: r., . . 18 F8
Leargybreck: Jura . NR 5471
Leatherhead: Surrey . 7 TQ15
Lechlade: Glos . . 11 SU29
Leckmelm: R. &Crom. . NH 1690
Ledaig: Argyll . . NM 9037
Ledbury: Here. . . 11 SO73
Lee: r. . . . 19 D2
Leebotwood: Salop . SO 4798
Leeds: Yorks . . 13 SE33
Leek: Staffs . . 11 SJ95
Leeming: Yorks . . SE 2989
Leen: r. . . . 13 SK54
Lee on the Solent: Hants SU 5600
Legbourne: Lincs. . TF 3684
Legerwood: Ber. . . NT 5843
Leicester: Leics. . 11 SK50
LEICESTERSHIRE: Eng. . . 11 SK—
Leigh: Dorset . . ST 6108
Leigh: Kent . . TQ 5546
Leigh: Lancs . . 12 SJ69
Leighterton: Glos . ST 8290
Leighton Buzzard: Beds 11 SP92
LEINSTER: Prov., R. of Irel. . . 18/19 —
Leinster, Mt.: Carlow/Wex. . 19 H4
Leintwardine: Here. . 11 SO47
Leiston: Suff. . . 6 TM46
Leith: Midloth. . . 15 NT27
Leith Hill: Surrey . 7 TQ14
Leitholm: Ber. . . NT 7944
LEITRIM: Co., R. of Irel. . . 18 E7
Len: r. . . . 7 TQ85
Lendalfoot: Ayr . . NX 1390
Lene, L.: Westmeath . 18 G6
Lenham: Kent . . TQ 8952
Lennox: Stirl. . . 14 NS49
Lennox Hills: Scot. . 14 NS68
Lennoxtown: Stirl. . 14 NS67
Lenzie: Dunb. . . NS 6571
Leochel-Cushnie: Aber. NJ 5210
Leominster: Here. . 11 SO45
Lepton: Yorks . . SE 2015
Leri: r. . . . 10 SN68
Lerwick: Shet Is. . 17 HU44
Lesbury: Northumb. . NU 2311
Les Ecrehou: is., Chan.Is. 9 Ins.
Leslie: Aber. . . NJ 5924
Leslie: Fife . . 15 NO20
Lesmahagow: Lan. . NS 8139
Letchworth: Herts . 7 TL23
Letham: Angus . . NO 5248
Letham: Fife . . NO 3014
Letterewe Forest: Ross & Crom. . NG 9772
Letterkenny: Don. . 18 F8
Lettermore I.: Gal. . 19 B5
Letterston: Pemb. . SM 9429
Leuchars: Fife . . NO 4521
Leurbost: Lewis . . NB 3725
Leven: Yorks . . TA 1045
Leven: & r., Fife. . 15 NO30
Leven: r., Yorks . 13 NZ40
Levens: Westmor. . SD 4886
Leverburgh: Harris . NG 0186
Leverton: Notts . . SK 7882
Lew: r. . . . 8 SS50
Lewannick: Corn. . SX 2780
Lewes: Sussex . . 7 TQ41
Lewis: i., Ross & Crom. 16 NB23
Lewisham: London . 7 TQ37
Lewiston: Inv. . . NH 5029
Lewknor: Oxon. . . SU 7197
Leyburn: Yorks . . 13 SE19
Leyland: Lancs . . 12 SD52
Leysdown: Kent. . TR 0370
Leyton: Essex . . TQ 3886
Lhanbryd: Moray. . NJ 2761
Liathach: R. & Crom.. 16 NG95
Libberton: Lan. . . NS 9943
Liberton: Midloth. . NT 2769
Lichfield: Staffs . . 11 SK10
Liddel Water: r. . 15 NY48
Liddisdale: Rox.. . 15 NH58
Lidgate: Suff. . . TL 7258
Liffey: r. . . . 19 J5
Lifton: Devon. . . SX 3885
Ligger Bay: Corn. . 8 SW75
Lilliesleaf: Rox. . . NT 5325
Limavady: Lon. . . 18 H9
LIMERICK: Co., R. of Irel. . . 19 D4
Limerick Junction: Tip. 19 E4
Limervay: i., Lewis . NB 3711
Limpsfield: Surrey . TQ 4152
Lincoln: Lincs . . 6 SK97
Lincoln Heath: Lincs . 6 SK98
Lincoln Marsh: Lincs . 6 TF—
LINCOLNSHIRE: Eng. 6 TF—
Lincoln Wolds: Lincs . 6 TF—
Lindale: Lancs . . SD 4180
Lindfield: Sussex. . TQ 3425
Lindsey: Admin. Co., Lincs . . 6 TF19
Ling: r. . . . 16 NG93
Lingay: i., Inv. . . NL 6089
Lingen: Here. . . SO 3667
Lingfield: Surrey . . TQ 3943
Linlithgow: W. Loth. . 15 NT07
Linney Head: Pemb . 10 SR89
Linslade: Bucks . . 11 SP92
Linton: Cambs. . . TL 5646
Linton: Rox. . . NT 7726
Linton: Yorks . . SD 9962
Lionel: Lewis . . NB 5263
Liphook: Hants . . SU 8431
Lisburn: Antrim . . 18 J8
Liscannor Bay: Clare . 19 C4
Liskeard: Corn. . . 8 SX26
Lismore: Wat. . . 19 F3
Lismore I.: Argyll . 14 NM84
Liss: Hants . . SU 7727
Listowel: Kerry . . 19 C3
Litcham: Norf. . . TF 8817
Litchfield: Hants . . SU 4553
Little Berkhampstead: Herts . . TL 2907
Littleborough: Lancs . SD 9316
Little Bowden: Leics. . SP 7487
Little Colonsay: i., Argyll 14 NM33
Little Cumbrae I.: Bute. 14 NS15
Little Dart: r. . . 8 SS71
Little Dunham: Norf. . TF 8613
Littleferry: Suther. . NH 8095
Littlehampton: Sussex. 7 TQ00
Little Harrowden: Northants . . SP 8771
Little Hinton: Wilts. . SU 2283
Little Hucklow: Derby. SK 1678
Little Loch Broom: Ross & Crom. . 16 NH09
Littlemill: Nairn.. . NH 9150
Little Milton: Oxon. . SP 6100
Little Minch, The: Scot. 16 NG—
Little Moreton Hall: Ches. . . SJ 8459
Little Ouse: r. . . 6 TL68
Littleport: Cambs. . TL 5686
Little Ross: Kirkc. . 14 NX64
Little Sark: Chan. Is. . 9 Ins.
Little Steeping: Lincs . TF 4362
Littlestone on Sea: Kent TR 0824
Little Stour: r. . . 7 TR15
Little Stretton: Salop . SO 4491
Little Sutton: Ches. . SJ 3777
Little Walsingham: Norf. 6 TF93
Little Waltham: Essex . TL 7012
Little Wenham: Suff. . TM 0739
Little Witley: Worcs . SO 7863
Litton: Derby. . . SK 1674
Liverpool: & bay, Lancs 12 SJ39
Lizard, The: Corn. . 8 SW71
Lizard Point: Corn. . 8 SW61
Llanaber: Mer. . . SH 5917
Llanaelhaiarn: Caer. . SH 3844
Llanafan: Carm. . . SN 6872
Llanafan-fechan: Breck. SN 9650
Llanallgo: Anglesey . SH 5085
Llanarmon: Denb. . SJ 1856
Llanarth: Card. . . SN 4251
Llanarthney: Carm. . SN 5320
Llanbadarn-fawr: Card. SN 6081
Llanbedr: Mer. . . 10 SH52
Llanbedr-goch: Anglesey SH 5180
Llanbedrog: Caer. . SH 3231
Llanberis: Caer. . . SH 5760
Llanbister: Rad. . . SO 1073
Llanboidy: Carm. . SN 2123
Llandaff: Glam.. . 10 ST17
Llanddarog: Carm. . SN 5016
Llandderfel: Mer. . SH 9837
Llanddeusant: Carm. . SN 7724
Llanddewi-Brefi: Card.. SN 6655
Llanddewi-Ystradenny: Rad. . . 10 SO16
Llanddona: Anglesey . SH 5779
Llandefeilog: Carm. . SN 4111
Llandilo: Carm. . . 10 SN62
Llandinam: Montg. . SO 0288
Llandissilio: Pemb . SN 1221
Llandovery: Carm. . 10 SN73
Llandrillo: Mer. . . SJ 0337
Llandrindod Wells: Rad. 10 SO06
Llandudno: Caer. . 10 SH78
Llandwrog: Caer. . SH 4556
Llandybie: Carm. . SN 6115
Llandysilio: Montg. . SJ 2618
Llandyssil: Montg. . SO 1995
Llandyssul: Card. . SN 4140
Llanegryn: Mer. . . 10 SH50
Llaneilian: Anglesey . SH 4692
Llanelidan: Denb. . SJ 1050
Llanelltyd: Mer. . . SH 7119
Llanelly: Carm. . . 10 SN50
Llanenddwyn: Mer. . SH 5823
Llanengan: Caer. . SH 2927
Llanerchymedd: Anglesey SH 4183
Llanfachraeth: Anglesey SH 3182
Llanfaelog: Anglesey . SH 3373
Llanfaethlu: Anglesey . SH 3186
Llanfair: Mer. . . SH 5729
Llanfair-ar-y-bryn: Carm. SN 8039
Llanfair Caereinion: Montg. . . SJ 1006
Llanfairfechan: Caer. . 10 SH67
Llanfair Talhaiarn: Denb. SH 9270
Llanfechell: Anglesey . SH 3691
Llanfihangel-ar-arth: Carm. . . SN 4839
Llanfihangel-Ystrad: Card. . . SN 5256
Llanfillo: Breck. . . SO 1133
Llanfrothen: Mer. . SH 6241
Llanfyllin: Montg. . 10 SJ11
Llanfynydd: Caer. . SN 5527
Llanfyrnach: Pemb . SN 2231
Llangadfan: Montg. . SJ 0010
Llangadock: Carm. . SN 7028
Llangain: Carm. . . SN 3815
Llangammarch Wells: Breck. . . SN 9347
Llangathen: Carm. . SN 5822
Llangefni: Anglesey . 10 SH47
Llangeitho: Card. . SN 6159
Llangemor: Glam. . SS 9187
Llangennech: Carm. . SN 5601
Llangerniew: Denb. . SH 8767
Llangian: Caer. . . SH 2928
Llanglydwen: Carm. . SN 1826
Llangoed: Anglesey . SH 6179
Llangollen: Denb. . 10 SJ24
Llangorse: Breck. . SO 1327
Llangower: Mer. . . SH 9032
Llangranog: Card. . SN 3154
Llangurig: Montg. . SN 9079
Llangwm: Denb. . . SH 9644
Llangwm: Pemb . . SM 9909
Llangwnadl: Caer. . SH 2033
Llangybi: Card. . . SN 6053
Llangybi: Mon. . . ST 3797
Llangynidr: Breck. . SO 1519
Llangynog: Montg. . SJ 0526
Llanharan: Glam. . . ST 0083
Llanharry: Glam. . . ST 0080
Llanidloes: Montg. . 10 SN98
Llanilar: Card. . . SN 6275
Llanmadoc: Glam. . SS 4493
Llanmorlais: Glam. . SS 5294
Llannefydd: Denb. . SH 9770
Llannon: Carm. . . SN 5408
Llanon: Card. . . SN 5167
Llanpumsaint: Carm. . SN 4129
Llanrhian: Pemb . . SM 8231
Llanrhidian Sands: Glam. . . 10 SS49
Llanrhystyd: Card. . SN 5369
Llanrug: Caer. . . SH 5363
Llanrwst: Denb. . . SH 7961
Llansannan: Denb. . SH 9365
Llansantffraed-in-Elwell: Rad. . . . SO 0954
Llansantffraid Cwmdeuddwr: Rad. SN 9668
Llansantffraid Glyn Ceiriog: Denb. . SJ 2038
Llansawel: Carm. . SN 6136
Llansilin: Denb. . . SJ 2028
Llanstephan: Carm. . SN 3511
Llanthony Abbey: Mon. 10 SO22
Llantilio-Crossenny: Mon. . . . SO 3914
Llantrisant: Glam. . ST 0483
Llantwit-Major: Glam.. SS 9668
Llanuwchllyn: Mer. . 10 SH82
Llanwddyn: Montg. . SJ 0219
Llanwnda: Caer. . . SH 4758
Llanwnen: Card. . . SN 5347
Llanwrthwl: Breck. . SN 9763
Llanwrtyd Wells: Breck. 10 SN84
Llanybyther: Carm. . SN 5244
Llanycefn: Pemb . . SN 0923
Llanymawddwy: Mer. . SH 9019
Llanystumdwy: Caer. . SH 4738
Llawhaden: Pemb . SN 0717
Llay: Denb. . . SJ 3356
Lleyn: penin., Caer. . 10 SH23
Lliw: r., Glam. . . 8 SN60
Lliw: r., Mer. . . 10 SH83
Llwyngwril: Mer. . SH 5909
Llynfi: r. . . . 9 SO13
Llysworney: Glam. . SS 9674
Loanhead: Midloth. . 15 NT26
Lochaber: Inv. . . 16 NN19
Loch a' Bharp: S. Uist NF 7822
Loch a' Chroisg: Suther. 16 NH15
Loch Affric: Inv. . 16 NH12
Lochaline: Argyll . NM6744
Loch Alsh: R. & Crom. 16 NG82
Lochan Fada: Ross & Crom. . 16 NH07
Locharbriggs: Dumf. . NX 9980
Loch Ard: Perth. . 14 NN40
Loch Arkaig: Inv. . 16 NN09
Lochar Water: r. . 12 NY07
Loch Assynt: Suther. . 16 NC22
Loch Awe: Argyll . 14 NM91
Lochay: r. . . 14 NN53
Loch Ba: Mull . . 14 NM53
Loch Boisdale: S. Uist. 16 NF71
Loch Bracadale: Skye . 16 NG23
Loch Brittle: Skye . 16 NG31
Loch Broom: R. & Crom. 16 NH19
Loch Brora: Suther. . 17 NC80
Loch Buie: Mull . 14 NM62
Loch Calder: Caith. . 17 ND06
Loch Caolisport: Argyll 14 NR77
Loch Carron: Ross & Crom. . 16 NG83
Loch Cluanie: Inv. . 16 NH10
Loch Creran: Argyll . 14 NM94
Loch Dee: Kirkc. . 14 NX47
Loch Doine: Perth. . 14 NN41
Lochdonhead: Argyll . NM 7333
Loch Doon: Ayr . 14 NX49
Loch Duich: R. & Crom. 16 NG92
Loch Dun Seilcheig: Inv. 17 NH63
Loch Dunvegan: Skye . 16 NG25
Loch Earn: Perth. . 14 NN62
Lochearnhead: Perth. . NN 5823
Loch Eck: Argyll . 14 NS19
Loch Eil: Inv./Argyll . 16 NN07
Locheil Forest: Inv. . NN 0889
Loch Eishort: Skye . 16 NG61
Loch Eriboll: Suther. . 16 NC46
Loch Ericht: Inv./Perth. 17 NN57
Loch Erisort: Lewis . 16 NB32
Loch Etive: Argyll . 14 NN03
Loch Ewe: R. & Crom. 16 NG88
Loch Eynort: Skye . 16 NG32
Loch Eynort: S. Uist . 16 NF82
Loch Fannich: Ross & Crom. . 16 NH26
Loch Fleet: Suther. . 17 NH79
Loch Frisa: Mull . 14 NM44
Loch Fyne: Argyll . 14 NR99
Lochgair: Argyll . . NR 9290
Loch Gairloch: Ross & Crom. . 16 NG77
Loch Garry: Inv. . 16 NH20
Lochgelly: Fife . . 15 NT19
Lochgilphead: Argyll . 14 NR88
Loch Glass: R. & Crom. 17 NH57
Loch Glencoul: Suther. 16 NC23
Loch Goil: Argyll . 14 NS19
Lochgoilhead: Argyll . NN 2001
Loch Harport: Skye . 16 NG33
Loch Hope: Suther. . 17 NC45
Loch Hourn: Inv. . 16 NG80
Loch Inchard: Suther. . 16 NC25
Lochinch Castle: Wig.. 14 NX16
Loch Indaal: Islay . 14 NR25
Lochindorb: l., Moray . 17 NH93
Lochinver: Suther. . 16 NC02
Loch Katrine: Perth. . 14 NN40
Loch Kishorn: Skye . 16 NG83
Loch Laggan: Inv. . 17 NN48
Loch Laxford: Suther.. 16 NC15

G.B. & IRELAND

LOCH LEVEN — MONIAIVE

Loch Leven: Kinr. 15 NO10
Loch Leven: Inv./Argyll 16 NN16
Loch Linnhe: Argyll 16 NM95
Loch Lochy: Inv. 16 NN29
Loch Lomond: Scot. 14 NS39
Loch Long: Scot. 14 NS29
Loch Loyal: Suther. 17 NC64
Loch Luichart: Ross & Crom. 16 NH36
Lochmaben: Dumf. 15 NY08
Lochmaddy: N. Uist NF 9269
Loch Maree: R. & Crom. 16 NG97
Loch Merkland: Suther. 16 NC33
Loch Mhor: Inv. 17 NH51
Loch Moidart: Inv. 16 NM67
Loch Monar: R. & Crom. 16 NH14
Loch Morar: Inv. 16 NM79
Loch More: Suther. 17 NC33
Loch Morie: R. & Crom. 17 NH57
Loch Muick: Aber. 17 NO28
Loch Mullardoch: Inv. 16 NH23
Lochnagar: Aber. 17 NO28
Loch Na Keal: Mull 14 NM53
Loch nan Clar: Suther. 17 NC73
Loch na Sheallag: Ross & Crom. 16 NH08
Loch Naver: Suther. 17 NC63
Loch Ness: Inv. 17 NH52
Loch Nevis: Inv. 16 NM79
Loch of Huxter: Shet Is. HU 5860
Loch of Stenness: Ork. Is. 17 HY21
Loch of Strathbeg: Aber. 17 NK05
Lochore: Fife NT 1796
Loch Ossian: Inv. 14 NN36
Loch Pooltiel: Skye 16 NG15
Loch Quoich: Inv. 16 NH00
Loch Rannoch: Perth. 17 NN55
Loch Resort: Lewis 16 NB01
Loch Rimsdale: Suther. 17 NC73
Loch Roag: Lewis 16 NB13
Loch Ryan: Wig. 14 NX06
Loch Scavaig: Skye 16 NG41
Loch Scridain: Mull 14 NM42
Loch Shiel: Inv./Argyll 14 NM87
Loch Shin: Suther. 17 NC41
Loch Snizort: Skye 16 NG35
Loch Striven: Argyll 14 NS07
Loch Sunart: Argyll 14 NM76
Loch Sween: Argyll 14 NR78
Loch Tarbert: Jura 14 NR58
Loch Tay: Perth. 14 NN63
Loch Teacuis: Argyll 14 NM65
Loch Torridon: Ross & Crom. 16 NG76
Loch Treig: Inv. 16 NN37
Loch Tuath: Mull 14 NM44
Loch Urigill: Suther. 16 NC21
Loch Watten: Caith. 17 ND25
Lochwinnoch: Renf. NS 3558
Lochy: r. 16 NN18
Lockerbie: Dumf. 15 NY18
Lockington: Yorks SE 9947
Lockton: Yorks SE 8489
Loddiswell: Devon. SX 7148
Loddon: Norf. 6 TM39
Lofthouse: Yorks SE 1073
Loftus: Yorks 13 NZ71
Logie Pert: Angus NO 6664
Logierait: Perth. NN 9451
Login: Carm. SN 1623
Lomond Hills: Scot. 15 NO20
Lonan: I. of Man SC 4383
LONDON: Co. & town, Eng. 7 TQ—
London Colney: Herts TL 1609
LONDONDERRY: Co., N. Irel. 18 G8
Longa I.: R. & Crom. 16 NG77
Long Ashton: Som. ST 5470
Longay: i., Inv. NG 6531
Long Barrow: Glam. 10 SS58
Long Bennington: Lincs. SK 8344
Long Buckby: Northants SP 6267
Long Burton: Dorset ST 6412
Long Clawson: Leics. SK 7227
Long Crag: Northumb. 15 NU00
Long Eaton: Notts 11 SK43
LONGFORD: Co., R. of Irel. 18 F6
Longformacus: Ber. NT 6957
Longhorsley: Northumb. NZ 1494
Long Itchington: War SP 4165
Longleat Park: Wilts. 9 ST84
Longmanhill: Banff NJ 7462
Long Marston: Yorks SE 4951
Long Meg: Cumb. NY 5737
Long Melford: Suff. TL 8646
Long Mountain: Salop. 10 SJ20
Long Mynd, The: Salop 11 SO49
Longniddry: E. Loth. NT 4476
Longnor: Staffs SK 0864
Long Preston: Yorks SD 8357
Longridge: Lancs 12 SD63
Longsdon: Staffs SJ 9554
Longside: Aber. NK 0347
Long Stratton: Norf. TM 1992
Long Sutton: Lincs 6 TF42
Long Sutton: Som. ST 4625
Longton: Lancs SD 4725
Longton: Staffs 11 SJ94
Longtown: Cumb. 15 NY36
Longtown: Here. SO 3225
Looe I.: Corn. 8 SX25
Loop Head: Clare 19 B4
Loppington: Salop SJ 4629
Lorne: Argyll 14 NN03
Loseley House: Surrey SU 9747
Lossie: r. 17 NJ15
Lossiemouth: Moray 17 NJ27
Lostwithiel: Corn. 8 SX15
Lothersdale: Yorks SD 9545
Loughborough: Leics. 11 SK51
Loughor: & r., Glam. 10 SS59
Loughrea: Gal. 19 D5
Loughros More Bay: Don. 18 D8
Loughton: Essex TQ 4296
Louth: Lincs 6 TF38
LOUTH: Co., R. of Irel. 18 J6
Lower Beeding: Sussex TQ 2227
Lower Bentham: Yorks SD 6469
Lower Dounreay: Caith. 17 NC96
Lower Heyford: Oxon. SP 4824
Lower Lough Erne: Ferm. 18 F7
Lower Milovaig: Skye NG 1550
Lower Peover: Ches. SJ 7474
Lower Slaughter: Glos SP 1622
Lowestoft: Suff. 6 TM59
Loweswater: Cumb. NY 1421
Lowick: Lancs SD 2986
Lowick: Northumb. NU 0139
Low Moor: Yorks 13 SE12
Lowther Castle: Cumb. NY 5223
Lowther College: Flint. 10 SH97
Lowther Hills: Scot. 15 NS90
Loy: r. 16 NN08
Lubenham: Leics. SP 7087
Lucan: Dublin 19 J5
Luccombe: Som. SS 9144
Luce Bay: Wig. 14 NX24
Lucker: Northumb. NU 1530
Ludborough: Lincs TF 2995
Ludford: Lincs TF 1989
Ludgershall: Bucks SP 6617
Ludgershall: Wilts. SU 2650
Ludgvan: Corn. SW 5033
Ludham: Norf. TG 3818
Ludlow: Salop 11 SO57
Lugar: Ayr NS 5821
Lugar Water: r. 14 NS52
Lugg: r. 10 SO26
Lugnaquillia: mtn., Wick. 19 J4
Lugwardine: Here. SO 5441
Luing: i., Argyll 14 NM71
Lumphanan: Aber. NJ 5804
Lumsden: Aber. NJ 4722
Lunan Bay: Angus 17 NO65
Lunanhead: Angus NO 4752
Lunan Water: r. 15 NO65
Luncarty: Perth. NO 0929
Lund: Yorks SE 9648
Lundie: Angus NO 2836
Lundin Mill: Fife NO 4102
Lundy I.: Devon. 8 SS14
Lune: r., Lancs 12 SD56
Lune: r., Yorks 13 NY82
Lunga: Treshnish Is. NM 2741
Lunga: i., Argyll. 14 NM70
Lurgan: Armagh 18 J7
Luss: Dunb. 14 NS39
Luthermuir: Kinc. NO 6568
Luthrie: Fife NO 3219
Luton: Beds 7 TL02
Luton Hoo Park: Beds TL 1018
Lutterworth: Leics. 11 SP58
Lutton: Northants TL 1187
Luxborough: Som. SS 9738
Luxulyan: Corn. 8 SX05
Lybster: Caith. ND 2435
Lydbury North: Salop SO 3486
Lydd: Kent 7 TR02
Lydford: Devon. SX 5084
Lydney: Glos 11 SO60
Lye: Worcs SO 9284
Lyme Bay: Dorset 9 SY38
Lyme Hall: Ches. SJ 9682
Lyme Regis: Dorset 9 SY39
Lyminge: Kent TR 1641
Lymington: Hants 7 SZ39
Lymm: Ches. 11 SJ68
Lympne: Kent 7 TR13
Lympstone: Devon. SX 9984
Lynas, Point: Anglesey 10 SH49
Lynchat: Inv. NH 7801
Lyndhurst: Hants 9 SU30
Lyne: r. 12 NY46
Lyneham: Wilts. SU 0179
Lynemouth: Northumb. NZ 2991
Lynher: r. 8 SX36
Lynmouth: Devon. 8 SS74
Lynsted: Kent TQ 9461
Lynton: Devon. 8 SS74
Lyon: r. 14 NN54
Lyonshall: Here. SO 3356
Lytchett Matravers: Dorset SY 9495
Lytham: Lancs 12 SD32

Maamturk Mts.: Gal. 18 B6
Maaruig: Harris NB 2006
Mablethorpe: Lincs 6 TF58
McArthur's Hd.: Islay 14 NR45
Macclesfield: Ches. 11 SJ97
Macduff: Banff 17 NJ76
Macgillycuddy's Reeks: Kerry 19 B2
Macharioch: Argyll NR 7309
Machers, The: Wig. 14 NX35
Machrihanish: Argyll 14 NR62
Machynlleth: Montg. 10 SH70
Macleod's Tables: mtn., Skye 16 NG24
Macnean, Lough: Ferm. 18 F7
Macroom: Cork 19 D2
Madderty: Perth. NN 9522
Madeley: Staffs SJ 7744
Madron: Corn. SW 4532
Maentwrog: Mer. 10 SH64
Maesgarmon: Flint. SJ 2165
Maesteg: Glam. 10 SS89
Maghera: Lon. 18 H8
Magherafelt: Lon. 18 H8
Maghull: Lancs SD 3702
Magor: Mon. ST 4287
Maiden Bradley: Wilts. ST 8038
Maiden Castle: Dorset 9 SY68
Maidenhead: Berks 11 SU88
Maiden Newton: Dorset 9 SY59
Maidens: Ayr. NS 2107
Maidens: rocks, Antrim 18 K8
Maidstone: Kent 7 TQ75
Maigue: r. 19 D4
Main: r., Antrim 18 J8
Mainland: i., Ork. Is. 17 HY31
Mainland: i., Shet. Is. 17 HU—
Malahide: Dublin 18 J5
Maldon: Essex 7 TL80
Malin Head: Don. 18 G9
Malinmore Head: Don. 18 D8
Mallaig: Inv. 16 NM69
Mallow: Cork 19 D3
Mallwyd: Mer. SH 8612
Malmesbury: Wilts. 11 ST98
Malpas: Ches. SJ 4847
Maltby: Yorks 13 SK59
Malton: Yorks 13 SE77
Malvern: Worcs 11 SO74
Malvern Hills: Eng. 11 SO74
Mamble: Worcs 11 SO67
Mamore Forest: Inv. 16 NN16
Manaccan: Corn. SW 7625
Manacles, The: Corn. 8 SW82
Manaton: Devon. SX 7481
Manchester: Lancs 13 SJ89
Manea: Cambs. TL 4789
Mangerton Mt.: Kerry. 19 C2
Mangotsfield: Glos 11 ST67
Manningtree: Essex 7 TM13
Manorbier: Pemb 10 SS09
Manor Water: r. 15 NT23
Mansell Lacy: Here. SO 4245
Mansfield: Notts 13 SK56
Mansfield Woodhouse: Notts 13 SK56
Manton: Rut. SK 8704
Manuden: Essex TL 4926
Maplin Sands: Essex 7 TR08
Mar: Aber. 17 NJ50
Marazion: Corn. 8 SW53
March: Cambs. 6 TL49
Marchington: Staffs 11 SK13
Marchwiel: Denb. 11 SJ34
Marchwood: Hants 7 SU30
Marden: Kent 7 TQ74
Mareham le Fen: Lincs 6 TF26
Maresfield: Sussex 8 TQ42
Mar Forest: Aber. 17 NO09
Margam: Glam. 10 SS78
Margaretting: Essex 7 TL60
Margate: Kent 7 TR37
Margery Hill: Yorks 13 SK19
Marham: Norf. TF 7009
Marhamchurch: Corn. SS 2203
Mariveg: Lewis NB 4018
Mark: Som. ST 3747
Market Bosworth: Leics. SK 4003
Market Deeping: Lincs 6 TF11
Market Drayton: Salop 11 SJ63
Market Harborough: Leics. 11 SP78
Market Lavington: Wilts. SU 0154
Market Rasen: Lincs 6 TF18
Market Warsop: Notts 13 SK56
Market Weighton: Yorks 13 SE84
Markinch: Fife 15 NO20
Marks Tey: Essex TL 9123
Markyate: Herts. TL 0616
Marlborough: Wilts. 11 SU16
Marldon: Devon. SX 8663
Marloes: Pemb SM 7908
Marlow: Bucks 11 SU88
Marnoch: Banff NJ 5950
Marown: I. of Man SC 3379
Marple: Ches. 13 SJ98
Marrick: Yorks SE 0798
Marsh, The: Glos 11 ST58
Marsh, The: Lincs 6 TF42
Marsh Baldon: Oxon. SU 5699
Marsh Chapel: Lincs TF 3598
Marshfield: Glos 11 ST77
Marsh Gibbon: Bucks SP 6423
Marske by the Sea: Yorks NZ 6322
Marston Magna: Som. ST 5922
Marston Moor: Yorks 12 SE45
Marteg: r. 10 SN97
Martham: Norf. TG 4518
Martin: Lincs TF 1259
Martinhoe: Devon. SS 6648
Martin Hussingtree: Worcs SO 8859
Martlesham: Suff. TM 2547
Martletwy: Pemb SN 0310
Martley: Worcs SO 7559
Martock: Som. 9 ST41
Marton: Lincs SK 8381
Marton: Yorks NZ 5115
Marwick Head: Ork. Is. HY 2225
Marwood: Devon. SS 5437
Maryborough: Laoghis 19 G5
Maryburgh: R. & Crom. NH 5456
Maryculter: Kinc. NO 8599
Marykirk: Kinc. NO 6865
Maryport: Cumb. 12 NY03
Marystow: Devon. SX 4382
Marytavy: Devon. SX 5078
Maryton: Angus NO 6856
Masham: Yorks 13 SE28
Masham Moor: Yorks 13 SE07
Mask, Lough: Mayo 18 C6
Matfen: Northumb. NZ 0371
Mathry: Pemb SM 8832
Matlock: Derby. 11 SK36
Matlock Bath: Derby. 11 SK25
Matterdale: Cumb. NY 3922
Mauchline: Ayr NS 4927
Maud: Aber. NJ 9247
Maughold Head: I. of Man 12 SC49
Maun: r. 13 SK56
Mawgan: Corn. SW 7024
Maxton: Rox. NT 6129
Maxwelltown: Kirkc. 15 NX97
Mayar: mtn., Angus 17 NO27
Maybole: Ayr 14 NS31
Mayfield: Sussex TQ 5827
MAYO: Co., R. of Irel. 18 C6
Mealasta I.: Lewis 16 NA92
Mealfuarvonie: mtn., Inv. 16 NH42
Meall an Fhuarain: mtn., Ross & Crom. NC 2802
Meall Dubh: mtn., Inv. 16 NH20
Meall Meadhonach: mtn., Suther. 17 NC46
Meall Mor: i., Suther. NC 1237
Meall nan Caoraich: Perth 15 NN93
Meall nan Con: Argyll. 16 NM56
Meare: Som. ST 4541
Mease: r. 11 SK21
Measham: Leics. SK 3312
MEATH: Co., R. of Irel. 18 H6
Meaul: mtn., Kirkc. 14 NX59
Medbourne: Leics. 11 SP79
Meden: r. 11 SK66
Medstead: Hants SU 6537
Medway: r. 7 TQ64
Meese: r. 11 SJ71
Meifod: Montg. SJ 1513
Meig: r. 16 NH35
Meigle: Perth. NO 2844
Meikle Millyea: mtn., Kirkc. 14 NX58
Meini Hirion: Caer. SH 7275
Meir: Staffs SJ 9342
Melbourn: Cambs. TL 3844
Melbourne: Derby. 11 SK32
Melbourne: Yorks SE 7543
Meldreth: Cambs. TL 3746
Melksham: Wilts. 11 ST96
Melling: Lancs SD 5970
Mellis: Suff. TM 0974
Mellon Charles: Ross & Crom. NG 8491
Melmerby: Cumb. NY 6137
Melmerby: Yorks SE 3376
Melness: Suther. NC 5862
Melrose: Rox. 15 NT53
Meltham: Yorks. 13 SE01
Melton: Suff. TM 2850
Melton Constable: Norf. TG 0433
Melton Mowbray: Leics. 11 SK71
Melvaig: R. & Crom. NG 7486
Melvich: Suther. NC 8864
Melvin, Lough: Leit./Ferm. 18 E7
Memsie: Aber. NJ 9762
Menai Bridge: Anglesey 10 SH57
Mendip Hills: Som. 9 ST55
Mendlesham: Suff. TM 1065
Menston: Yorks SE 1743
Meole Brace: Salop SJ 4811
Meon: r. 7 SU62
Meonstoke: Hants SU 6119
Meopham: Kent TQ 6466
Mepal: Cambs. TL 4481
Mere: Ches. SJ 7281
Mere: Wilts. ST 8132
Meriden: War SP 2482
MERIONETHSHIRE: Wales 10 SH—
Merrick: Kirkc. 14 NX48
Merriott: Som. ST 4412
Merrivale: Devon. SX 7555
Merse: dist., Ber. 15 NT74
Mersea Island: Essex 7 TM01
Mersey: r. 11 SJ68
Merthyr Cynog: Breck. SN 9837
Merthyr Tydfil: Glam. 10 SO00
Meshaw: Devon. SS 7519
Messingham: Lincs SE 8904
Metfield: Suff. TM 2980
Metheringham: Lincs TF 0661
Methil: Fife NT 3699
Methlick: Aber. NJ 8537
Methven: Perth. NO 0225
Methwold: Norf. 6 TL79
Mevagissey: Corn. 8 SX04
Mew I.: Down 18 K8
Mew Stone: Devon. 8 SX94
Mexborough: Yorks 13 SK49
Michaelstow: Corn. SX 0778
Micheldever: Hants SU 5138
Michelmersh: Hants SU 3426
Mickle Fell: Yorks 13 NY82
Mickleover: Derby. SK 3033
Mickleton: Glos SP 1543
Mickleton: Yorks NY 9623
Mickley: Yorks SE 2576
Mid Calder: Midloth. NT 0767
Middle Barton: Oxon. SP 4325
Middlebie: Dumf. NY 2176
Middleham: Yorks 13 SE18
Middlesbrough: Yorks 13 NZ42
MIDDLESEX: Co., Eng. 7 TQ28
Middlesmoor: Yorks 13 SE07
Middleton: Cork 19 E2
Middleton: Derby. SK 2755
Middleton: Lancs 12 SD45
Middleton: Lancs SD 8606
Middleton: Northumb. NU 1035
Middleton: Suff. TM 4267
Middleton: Sussex SU 9706
Middleton: War SP 1798
Middleton: Westmor. SD 6286
Middleton: Yorks SE 3027
Middle Tongue: mtn., Yorks/Lancs 13 SD88
Middleton in Teesdale: Dur. 13 NY92
Middleton Stoney: Oxon. SP 5323
Middleton Tyas: Yorks. NZ 2205
Middlewich: Ches. 11 SJ76
Midhurst: Sussex 7 SU82
Midlem: Rox. NT 5227
MIDLOTHIAN: Co., Scot. 15 NT—
Midsomer Norton: Som. ST 6654
Milborne: Dorset SY 8097
Milborne Port: Som. 9 ST61
Milbourne: Northumb. NZ 1175
Milburn: Westmor. NY 6529
Mildenhall: Suff. 6 TL77
Milfield: Northumb. NT 9333
Milford Haven: Pemb 10 SM90
Milford on Sea: Hants SZ 2891
Milk Hill: Wilts. 9 SU16
Millbrook: Corn. SX 4252
Miller's Dale: Derby. 13 SK17
Milleur Point: Wig. 14 NX07
Millom: Cumb. 12 SD18
Millstone Pt.: Bute. 14 NR94
Millton of Clova: Angus NO 3273
Milltown: Banff NJ 5447
Milnathort: Kinr. NO 1204
Milngavie: Dunb. 14 NS57
Milnrow: Lancs 13 SD91
Milnthorpe: Westmor. SD 4981
Milsted: Kent TQ 9058
Milton: Berks SU 4892
Milton Abbot: Devon. SX 4079
Milton Damerel: Devon. SS 3810
Milton Ness: Kinc. NO 7664
Milton Regis: Kent 7 TQ96
Miltownmalbay: Clare. 19 C4
Milverton: Som. 9 ST12
Minchinhampton: Glos 11 SO80
Minehead: Som. 8 SS94
Mine Head: Wat. 19 F2
Minera: Denb SJ 2651
Minety: Wilts. SU 0091
Minginish: Skye NG 4325
Mingulay: Inv. 16 NL58
Minnigaff: Kirkc. NX 4166
Minning Low: Derby. SK 2057
Minster: Kent TR 3164
Minster: Kent TQ 9573
Minsterley: Salop SJ 3705
Minster Lovell: Oxon. SP 3111
Minterne Magna: Dorset ST 6504
Mintlaw: Aber. NK 0047
Minto: Rox. NT 5620
Mirfield: Yorks SE 2019
Misbourne: r. 11 TQ08
Miserden: Glos SO 9308
Misson: Notts SK 6895
Misterton: Notts SK 7694
Mitcham: Surrey 7 TQ26
Mitcheldean: Glos. 11 SO61
Mitchelstown: Cork 19 E3
Mitford: Northumb. NZ 1685
Mizen Head: Cork 19 B1
Mizen Head: Wick. 19 J4
Moate: Westmeath 19 F5
Mochdre: Montg. SO 0788
Modbury: Devon. 8 SX65
Moel Fferna: mtn., Mer. 10 SJ13
Moelfre: i., Anglesey SH 5186
Moelfre: mtn., Carm. 10 SN33
Moelfre: mtn., Montg. 10 SN89
Moel Hebog: mtn., Caer. 12 SH54
Moel Seisiog: Denb. 10 SH85
Moel Siabod: mtn., Caer. 10 SH75
Moffat: & r., Dumf. 15 NT00
Moidart: Inv. 16 NM77
Mold: Flint. 10 SJ26
Mole: r., Som. 8 SS61
Mole: r., Surrey 7 TQ15
Molland: Devon. SS 8028
Monach Is.: Inv. NF 6264
Monadhliath Mts.: Inv. 17 NH91
MONAGHAN: Co., R. of Irel. 18 H7
Monar Forests: Ross & Crom. NH 1543
Monavullagh Mts.: Wat. 19 F3
Moneydie: Perth. NO 0629
Money Head: Wig. 14 NX04
Moneymusk: Aber. NJ 6915
Moniaive: Dumf. NX 7791

Monifieth: Angus . **15 NO53**
Monikie: Angus . NO 4938
Monk Fryston: Yorks . SE 5029
Monkland: Here. . SO 4557
Monkseaton: Northumb. NZ 3371
Monks Eleigh: Suff. . TL 9647
Monksilver: Som. . ST 0737
Monkstone Point: Pemb **10 SN10**
Monkton: Ayr . . NS 3527
Monkton Combe: Som. **9 ST76**
MONMOUTH: *Co.*,
Eng. . . . **11 SO51**
Monnow: *r.* . . **9 SO42**
Monreith: Wig. . . NX 3541
Montacute: Som. . **9 ST41**
Montgomery: Montg. . **10 SO29**
MONTGOMERYSHIRE:
Wales . . **10 —**
Montrose: Angus . **17 NO75**
Monzie: Perth. . . NN 8725
Moore: Ches. . . SJ 5584
Moorfoot Hills:
Midloth. . . **15 NT35**
Moors, The: Wig. . **14 NX26**
Morar: Inv. . . **16 NM78**
Moray Firth: Scot. **17NH/NJ**
MORAYSHIRE: Scot. **17 NJ15**
Morchard Bishop:
Devon . . SS 7607
Morda: *r.* . . **10 SJ32**
Mordiford: Here. . SO 5637
Morebath: Devon. . SS 9525
Morebattle: Rox. . NT 7724
Morecambe: Lancs **12 SD46**
Moresby: Cumb . . NX 9821
Morton: Ches. . . SJ 2589
Moretonhampstead:
Devon. . . **8 SX78**
Moreton in Marsh: Glos **11 SP23**
Moreton Pinkney:
Northants . . SP 5749
Morland: Westmor. . NY 6022
Morley: Yorks . . **13 SE22**
Morpeth: Northumb. . **15 NN28**
Morriston: Glam. . SS 6698
Morte Bay: Devon . **8 SS44**
Mortehoe: Devon. . SS 4545
Morte Point: Devon. . **8 SS44**
Mortimer's Cross: Here. SO 4263
Morton: Lincs . . TF 0924
Morvah: Corn. . . SW 4035
Morval: Corn. . . SX 2556
Morven: *mtn.*, Caith. . **17 ND02**
Morven: *mtn.*, Aber. . **17 NJ30**
Morvern: Argyll . **16 NM75**
Morville: Salop . . SO 6694
Morwenstow: Corn. . SS 2015
Mosedale: Cumb . . NY 3532
Moss: Denb . . SJ 3052
Mossley: Lancs . . **13 SD90**
Mostyn: Flint. . . **10 SJ18**
Mote of Urr: Kirkc. . **15 NX86**
Motherwell: Lan. . **15 NS75**
Mottingham: Kent . TQ 4272
Mottisfont: Hants . SU 3226
Moulin: Perth. . . NN 9459
Moulton: Ches. . . SJ 6569
Moulton: Lincs . . TF 3024
Moulton: Northants . SP 7866
Moulton: Yorks . . NZ 2303
Mound, The: Suther. . NH 7798
Mountain Ash: Glam . **10 ST09**
Mount Hawke: Corn. . SW 7147
Mountmellick: Laoighis **19 G5**
Mountnessing: Essex . TQ 6297
Mount's Bay: Corn. . **8 SW52**
Mountsorrel: Leics. . **11 SK51**
Mourne Mts.: Down . **18 J7**
Mousa: i., Shet. Is. . HU 4524
Mousehole: Corn. . **8 SW42**
Mouswald: Dumf. . NY 0672
Movile: Don. . . **18 G9**
Mow Cop: Ches. . SJ 8557
Moy: *r.* . . . **18 C7**
Moy Forest: Inv. . NN 4088
Moyle, The: Kirkc. . NX 8458
Muasdale: Argyll . NR 6840
Muchalls: Kinc. . . NO 9091
Much Birch: Here. . SO 5030
Muchelney: Som. . ST 4224
Much Hadham: Herts . TL 4319
Much Wenlock: Salop. **11 SO69**
Muck: *i.*, Inv. . . **16 NM47**
Muckish: *mtn.*, Don. . **18 E9**
Muckle Roe: Shet. Is. . **17 HU36**
Mugeary: Skye . . NG 4438
Muick: *r.* . . . **17 NO39**
Muine Beag: Carlow . **19 H4**
Muirdrum: Angus . NO 5637
Muirhead: Angus . NO 3434
Muirhead: Lan. . . NS 6869
Muirkirk: Ayr . . NS 6927
Muirnag: Lewis . . **16 NB44**
Muir of Fowlis: Aber. . NJ 5612
Muir of Ord: R. & Crom. NH 5250
Muker: Yorks . . SD 9197
Mulben: Banff . . NJ 3450
Muldoanich: i., Inv. . NL 6893
Mull: *i.*, Argyll . . **14 NM63**
Mullaghareirk Mts.: Irel. **19 C3**
Mullaghcarn: *mtn.*, Tyr. **18 G8**
Mullet Penin: Mayo . **18 A7**
Mull Hd.: Ork. Is. . **17 HY55**
Mullingar: Westmeath. **18 G6**
Mullion I.: Corn. . **8 SW61**
Mull of Galloway: Wig. **12 NX13**
Mull of Kintyre: Argyll **14 NR60**

Mull of Logan: Wig. . **14 NX04**
Mull of Oa: Argyll . **14 NR24**
Mumbles, The: Glam. . SS 6287
Mumbles Hd.: Glam. . **8 SS68**
Muncaster Castle:
Cumb. . . **12 SD19**
Mundesley: Norf. . TG 3136
Mundford: Norf. . TL 8093
Munlochy: R. & Crom. . NH 6453
Munslow: Salop . . SO 5187
Munster: *Prov.*,
R. of Irel. . . **19 —**
Munster: *r.* . . **19 G4**
Muntervary Hd.: Cork **19 B2**
Murdoch Head: Aber. . NK 1239
Murrow: Cambs. . TF 3707
Murton: Dur. . . NZ 3947
Murton: Westmor. . NY 7221
Musbury: Devon. . SY 2794
Musselburgh: Midloth. **15 NT37**
Muthill: Perth. . . NN 8616
Mutton I.: Clare. . **19 B4**
Myddfai: Carm. . . SN 7730
Myddle: Salop . . SJ 4623
Mydrim: Carm. . . SN 2921
Mydroilin: Card. . SN 4555
Mylor: Corn. . . SW 8135
Mynydd Bach: Card. . **10 SN66**
Mynydd Bwlch-y-Groes:
Breck. . . . **10 SN83**
Mynydd Ddu: Carm. . **10 SN71**
Mynydd Eppynt: Breck. **10 SN94**
Mynydd Hiraethog:
Denb. . . . **10 SH95**
Mynydd Pencarreg:
Carm. . . **10 SN54**
Mynydd Prescelly: Pemb **10 SN13**

Naas: Kild. . . **19 H5**
Naburn: Yorks . . SE 5945
Nadder: *r.* . . **9 SU03**
Nafferton: Yorks . TA 0559
Nagles Mts.: Cork . **19 D3**
Nailsea: Som. . . ST 4670
Nailsworth: Glos . ST 8499
Nairn: Nairn . . **17 NH85**
Nairn: *r.* . . . **17 NH74**
NAIRNSHIRE: Scot. . **17 NH84**
Nant-Ddu: Breck. . SO 0015
Nantwich: Ches. . **11 SJ65**
Nar: *r.* . . . **6 TF71**
Narberth: Pemb . **10 SN11**
Narborough: Leics . SP 5497
Narborough: Norf. . TF 7413
Nare Point: Corn. . SW 8025
Naseby: Northants . **11 SP67**
Nash: Bucks . . SP 7734
Nash Point: Glam. . **10 SS96**
Naunton: Glos . . SP 1123
Navan: Meath . . **18 H6**
Nave I.: Argyll . . **14 NR27**
Navenby: Lincs . . SK 9857
Naver: *r.* . . . **17 NC74**
Naworth Castle: Cumb. **15 NY56**
Nayland: Suff. . . **7 TL93**
Naze, The: Essex . **7 TM22**
Nazeing: Essex . . TL 4106
Neagh, L.: N. Irel. . **18 J8**
Neasham: Yorks . NZ 3210
Neath: *& r.*, Glam. . **10 SS79**
Necton: Norf. . . TF 8709
Needham Market: Suff. **6 TM05**
Needles, The: I. of Wight **7 SZ28**
Neenton: Salop . . SO 6487
Nefern: *r.* . . **10 SN13**
Nelson: Lancs . . **13 SD83**
Nenagh: *& r.*, Tip. . **19 E4**
Nene: *r.*, Hunts . . **6 TL08**
Nene: *r.*, Norf. . . **6 TF42**
Nenthead: Cumb. . NY 7743
Nenthorn: Ber. . . NT 6837
Nephin: *mtn.*, Mayo . **18 C7**
Nephin Beg Range:
Mayo . . **18 B7**
Ness: *dist.*, Lewis . **16 NB56**
Nesscliff: Salop . SJ 3819
Neston: Ches. . . **10 SJ27**
Netheravon: Wilts. . SU 1448
Netherbury: Dorset . SY 4799
Nether Kellett: Lancs . SD 5067
Nether Langwith: Notts SK 5371
Nether Poppleton: Yorks SE 5654
Nether Stowey: Som. . ST 1939
Netherton: Northumb. . NT 9907
Nether Wallop: Hants. **9 SU33**
Nether Whitacre: War . SP 2393
Netherwitton: Northumb. NZ 1090
Nethybridge: Inv. . NJ 0020
Netley: Hants . . SU 4508
Nettlebed: Oxon. . SU 7086
Nettleham: Lincs. . TF 0075
Nevern: Pemb . . SN 0840
Neville's Cross: Dur. . NZ 2643
Nevin: Caer. . . **10 SH34**
New Abbey: Kirkc. . NX 9665
New Aberdour: Aber. . NJ 8863
New Alresford: Hants . **7 SU53**
Newark upon Trent:
Notts . . . **11 SK75**
Newbiggin: Dur. . NY 9127
Newbiggin by the Sea:
Northumb. . **15 NZ38**
Newbigging: Lan. . NT 0145
Newbold on Stour: War SP 2446
New Bolingbroke: Lincs TF 3058

Newborough: Anglesey **10 SH46**
Newborough: Northants TF 2006
Newbridge: Kild. . **19 H5**
New Bridge: Kirkc. . NX 9478
Newbridge: Mon. . ST 2197
Newbridge on Wye: Rad. SO 0158
New Brighton: Ches. . **10 SJ39**
Newbrough: Northumb. NY 8767
New Buckenham: Norf. **6 TM09**
Newburgh: Aber. . NJ 9925
Newburgh: Fife . . **15 NO21**
Newburn: Northumb. . **15 NZ16**
Newbury: Berks . **11 SU46**
Newby Bridge: Lancs . SD 3685
Newbyth: Aber. . NJ 8254
Newcastle: Down . **18 K7**
Newcastle: Lim. . **19 C3**
Newcastle: Salop . SO 2482
Newcastle Emlyn: Carm. **10 SN34**
Newcastleton: Rox. . NY 4887
Newcastle under Lyme:
Staffs . . . **11 SJ84**
Newcastle upon Tyne:
Northumb. . . **15 NZ26**
Newchurch: Rad. . SO 2150
New Cumnock: Ayr . NS 6113
New Dailly: Ayr . . NS 2701
New Deer: Aber. . NJ 8846
Newdigate: Surrey . TQ 1942
Newent: Glos. . . **11 SO72**
New Forest: Hants . **9 SU20**
Newgale: Pemb . . SM 8522
New Galloway: Kirkc. **14 NX67**
Newhall: Derby. . SK 2821
Newhaven: Sussex . **7 TQ40**
New Holland: Yorks . **13 TA02**
New Hunstanton: Norf. **6 TF64**
Newick: Sussex . . TQ 4121
Newkirk: Aber. . . NJ 4304
New Luce: Wig. . . NX 1764
Newlyn: Corn. . . SW 4628
Newlyn East: Corn. . SW 8256
Newmarket: Lewis . NB 4235
Newmarket: Suff. . **6 TL66**
Newmill: Banff . . NJ 4352
Newmill: Rox. . . NT 4510
New Mills: Derby. . **13 SK08**
Newmilns: Ayr . . **14 NS53**
New Milton: Hants . SZ 2495
Newnham: Worcs . **11 SO66**
New Pitsligo: Aber. . NJ 8855
Newport: Essex . . TL 5234
Newport: Fife . . **15 NO42**
Newport: I. of Wight . **7 SZ48**
Newport: Mon. . . **10 ST38**
Newport: Pemb . . SN 0639
Newport: Salop . . **11 SJ71**
Newport Pagnell: Bucks **11 SP84**
New Quay: Card. . **10 SN36**
Newquay: Corn. . **8 SW86**
New Radnor: Rad. . SO 2161
New Romney: Kent . **7 TR02**
New Ross: Wex. . **19 H3**
Newry: Armagh/Down **18 J7**
New Scone: Perth. . NO 1325
New Silksworth: Dur. . NZ 3854
Newstead Abbey: Notts **6 SK55**
Newton: Yorks . . SE 8190
Newton: Yorks . . SD 6950
Newton Abbot: Devon. **8 SX87**
Newton Arlosh: Cumb. . NY 1955
Newton Ferrers: Devon. SX 5447
Newton Flotman: Norf. TM 2198
Newton Grange:
Midloth. . . NT 3364
Newton le Willows:
Lancs . . . **12 SJ59**
Newtonmore: Inv. . NN 7299
Newton St. Cyres:
Devon. . . SX 8797
Newton Stewart: Wig. . **14 NX46**
Newton Tony: Wilts. . SU 2140
Newton Tors:
Northumb. . . NT 9126
Newton Tracey: Devon. SS 5226
Newtown: Montg. . **10 SO19**
Newtown: Rox. . . NT 5731
Newtownards: Down . **18 K8**
Newtownbreda: Down **18 K8**
Newtown Forbes: Long. **18 F6**
Newtyle: Angus . . NO 2941
New Ulva: Argyll . NR 7080
Neyland: Pemb . . **10 SM90**
Nidd: *r.* . . . **13 SE35**
Nidderdale: Yorks . **13 SE16**
Niedpath Castle: Peeb. . NT 2340
Nigg: Ross & Crom. . NH 8071
Nine Maidens: Corn. . SW 4126
Ninfield: Sussex . . TQ 7012
Nissey: *r.* . . . **6 TL69**
Nith: *r.* . . . **15 NX97**
Nithsdale: Dumf. . **15 NX99**
Nocton: Lincs . . TF 0564
Noe: *r.* . . . **13 SK18**
Noirmont Point: Jersey **9 Ins.**
Nonington: Kent . . TR 2552
Norden: Lancs . . SD 8614
Nore: *r.* . . . **19 H3**
NORFOLK: *Co.*, Eng. **6TF/TG**
Norfolk Broads: Norf. **6 TG31**
Norham: Northumb. . NT 9047
Norland: Yorks . . SE 0622
Normanton: Yorks . **13 SE32**
Northallerton: Yorks . **13 SE39**
Northam: Devon. . SS 4429
Northampton:
Northants . . **11 SP76**

NORTHAMPTON-
SHIRE: Eng. . **11 SP—**
Northampton Uplands:
Northants . . **11 SP55**
North Beck: *r.* . . **13 TF04**
North Berwick: E. Loth. **15 NT58**
North Bovey: Devon. . SX 7483
North Brentor: Devon. . SX 4781
North Burton: Yorks . TA 0872
North Cadbury: Som. . ST 6327
North Carr: Fife . **15 NO61**
North Cave: Yorks . SE 8832
North Cerney: Glos . SP 0208
North Channel:
N. Irel./Eng. . **18 K9**
North Chapel: Sussex . SU 9529
North Coates: Lincs . TA 3400
North Crawley: Bucks . SP 9244
North Creake: Norf. . TF 8538
North Curry: Som. . ST 3125
North Dalton: Yorks . SE 9352
North Dorset Downs . **9 ST60**
North Downs: Kent . **7TQ/TR**
North Elmham: Norf. . TF 9820
Northern Ireland . **18 —**
North Erradale:
Ross & Crom. . NG 7481
North Esk: *r.* . . **17 NO57**
North Ferriby: Yorks . SE 9826
Northfleet: Kent . . TQ 6274
North Foreland: Kent. **7 TR46**
North Frodingham:
Yorks . . TA 1053
North Hill: Corn. . SX 2776
Northiam: Sussex . TQ 8324
North Kelsey: Lincs . TA 0401
North Kilworth: Leics. . SP 6183
Northleach: Glos . SP 1114
Northleigh: Devon. . SY 1995
Northleigh: Oxon. . SP 3813
Northlew: Devon. . SX 5099
North Lopham: Norf. . TM 0383
North Marston: Bucks . SP 7722
North Minch: Scot. . **16 NB—**
North Molton: Devon. . SS 7329
North Newbald: Yorks. SE 9136
Northolt: Middx. . TQ 1284
North Petherton: Som. . ST 2832
North Petherwin: Devon. SX 2889
North Queensferry: Fife NT 1380
North Riding:
Admin. Co., Yorks **13SD/SE**
North Ronaldsay:
i. & firth, Ork. Is. . **17 HY75**
North Scarle: Lincs . SK 8466
North Shawbost: Lewis. NB 2648
North Somercotes: Lincs TF 4296
North Sound: Gal. . **19 B5**
North Sound, The:
Ork. Is. . . **17 HY54**
North Sunderland:
Northumb. . NU 2131
North Tawton: Devon. **8 SS60**
North Thoresby: Lincs . TF 2998
North Tolsta: Lewis . NB 5347
Northton: Harris. . NF 9889
North Tyne: *r.* . . **15 NY78**
North Uist: *i.*, Inv. . **16 NF87**
NORTHUMBER-
LAND: *Co.*, Eng. . **15 —**
North Walsham: Norf. **6 TG23**
North Waltham: Hants SU 5546
North Weald Bassett:
Essex . . . TL 4904
North West Highlands. **16NH/NC**
North Wheatley: Lincs SK 7585
Northwich: Ches. . **11 SJ67**
Northwold: Norf. . TL 7596
Northwood: Middx. . TQ 0990
North Wootton: Som. . ST 5641
North Yorks. Moors **13SE/NZ**
Norton: Dur. . . NZ 4421
Norton: Rad. . . SO 3067
Norton: Yorks . . SE 7971
Norton St. Philip: Som. ST 7755
Norwich: Norf. . **6 TG20**
Noss Hd.: Caith. . **17 ND35**
Noss Mayo: Devon. . SX 5546
Nottingham: Notts. . **11 SK54**
NOTTINGHAM-
SHIRE: Eng. . **11 SK—**
Nuneaton: War . . **11 SP39**
Nunney: Wilts. . ST 7345
Nunnington: Yorks . SE 6679
Nunsthorpe: Lincs . TA 2606
Nutt's Corner: Antrim **18 J8**

Oa, The: Islay . . **14 NR34**
Oadby: Leics. . . SK 6200
Oakengates: Salop . **11 SJ71**
Oakford: Devon. . SS 9021
Oakham: Rut. . . **11 SK80**
Oakington: Cambs. . TL 4164
Oakley: Bucks . . SP 6412
Oakley: Hants . . SU 5650
Oakworth: Yorks . SE 0238
Oare: Kent. . . TR 0062
Oathlaw: Angus . . NO 4756
Oban: Argyll . . **14 NM83**
Ochil Hills: Perth. . **15NN/NO**
Ochiltree: Ayr. . . NS 5021
Ock: *r.* . . . **9 SU39**
Ockbrook: Derby. . SK 4235
Ockley: Surrey . . TQ 1439
Odiham: Hants . . **7 SU75**

Odstock: Wilts. . . SU 1426
OFFALY: *Co.*,
R. of Irel. . . **19 F5**
Offa's Dyke Path:
Wales . . **10SO/SJ**
Ogbourne St. George:
Wilts. . . SU 2074
Ogwen: *r.* . . . **12 SH66**
Oh Me Edge:
Northumb. . **15 NY69**
Okehampton: Devon. . **8 SX59**
Old Aberdeen: Aber. . NJ 9408
Oldany I.: Suther. . **16 NC03**
Old Bolingbroke: Lincs **13 TF36**
Oldbury: Worcs . . **11 SO98**
Oldbury Camp: Wilts. . **11 SU06**
Oldbury upon Severn:
Glos . . . ST 6092
Old Dalby: Leics. . SK 6723
Oldham: Lancs . . **13 SD90**
Oldhamstocks: E. Loth. NT 7470
Old Head of Kinsale:
Cork . . . **19 D2**
Old Howe: *r.* . . **13 TA15**
Oldland: Glos . . ST 6771
Old Leake: Lincs. . TF 4050
Old Mawbray: Cumb. . NY 0847
Oldmeldrum: Aber. . **17 NJ82**
Old Nene: *r.* . . **6 TL39**
Old Radnor: Rad. . SO 2559
Old Rayne: Aber. . NJ 6728
Old Romney: Kent . TR 0325
Old Sarum: Wilts. . **9 SU13**
Oldshore: Suther . . NC 2059
Old Weston: Hunts . TL 0977
Ollerton: Notts . . **13 SK66**
Olney: Bucks . . **11 SP85**
Olton: War . . . SP 1382
Olveston: Glos . . ST 6087
Omagh: Tyr. . . **18 G8**
Ombersley: Worcs . SO 8463
Onchan: I. of Man . SC 4078
Onich: Inv. . . . NN 0261
Onny: *r.* . . . **10 SO38**
Opinan: R. & Crom. . NG 7472
Orbliston: Moray. . NJ 3057
Orchy: *r.* . . . **14 NN23**
Orcop: Here. . . SO 4726
Ord: Skye . . . NG 6113
Ordie: Aber. . . NJ 4501
Ore: *r.* . . . **15 NT29**
Orford: Suff. . . **7 TM45**
Orford Ness: Suff. . **7 TM44**
Orkney Islands: .
& Co., Scot. . **17 Ins.**
Orleton: Here. . . SO 4967
Ormesby: Yorks . . NZ 5317
Ormiston: E. Loth. . NT 4169
Ormskirk: Lancs . **12 SD40**
Oronsay, *i.*, Argyll . **14 NR38**
Orpington: Kent . **7 TQ46**
Orrin: *r.* . . . **16 NH35**
Orrisdale: I. of Man . SC 3293
Orsett: Essex . . TQ 6481
Orston: Notts . . SK 7741
Orton: Westmor. . NY 6208
Orwell: Cambs. . . TL 3650
Orwell: *r.* . . . **7 TM14**
Osborne: I. of Wight . **7 SZ59**
Osbournby: Lincs . TF 0638
Oskaig: Raasay . . NG 5638
Osmington: Dorset . SY 7282
Osmotherley: Yorks . SE 4597
Osnaburgh: Fife . . NO 4117
Ossett: Yorks . . **13 SE22**
Osterley Park: Middx. . TQ 1577
Oswaldtwistle: Lancs . SD 7327
Oswestry: Salop . . **10 SJ22**
Othery: Som. . . ST 3831
Otley: Suff. . . TM 2055
Otley: Yorks . . **13 SE24**
Ot Moor: Oxon. . **11 SP51**
Otter: *r.* . . . **9 SY09**
Otterburn: Northumb. . NY 8893
Otter Ferry: Argyll . NR 9384
Otterham: Corn. . SX 1690
Otter Rock: Islay . **14 NR33**
Otterswick: Shet. Is. . HU 5185
Otterton: Devon. . SY 0785
Ottery: *r.* . . . **8 SX38**
Ottery St. Mary: Devon. **9 SY09**
Oughter, L.: Cavan . **18 G7**
Oughtmore: *mtn.*, Tyr. **18 H8**
Oulton: Cumb. . . NY 2551
Oulton: Yorks . . SE 3627
Oulton Broad: Suff. . TM 5292
Oundle: Northants . **6 TL08**
Ouse: *r.*, Bucks . . **11 SP53**
Ouse: *r.*, Norf. . . **6 TF60**
Ouse: *r.*, Sussex . . **7 TQ41**
Ouse: *r.*, Yorks . . **13 SE62**
Outer Hebrides: Scot. . **16NF/NA**
Ouzel: *r.* . . . **6 SP83**
Over: Ches. . . SJ 6366
Overbister: Ork. Is. . HY 6841
Overscaig: Suther. . NC 4222
Overseal: Derby. . SK 2915
Overstone: Northants . SP 8066
Overstrand: Norf. . TG 2440
Overton: Flint. . . **10 SJ34**
Overton: Hants . . SU 5149
Overton: Lancs . . SD 4357
Ovingham: Northumb. . NZ 0863
Ovington: Northumb. . NZ 0663
Owel, L.: Westmeath . **18 G6**
Owston Ferry: Lincs . SE 8000
Oxborough Hall: Norf. **6 TF70**

G.B. & IRELAND

OXENHOPE — ROBIN HOOD'S BAY

Oxenhope: Yorks SE 0334
Oxford: Oxon. 11 SP50
OXFORDSHIRE: Eng. 11 SP—
Oxhill: War SP 3145
Ox Mountains: Sligo 18 D7
Oxted: Surrey TQ 3852
Oxton: Ber. NT 4953
Oxton: Notts SK 6351
Oykell: r. 16 NC30
Oykell Bridge: Ross & Crom. NC 3801
Oyne: Aber. NJ 6725
Oyster Haven: Cork 19 E2

Pabay: i., Inv. NG 6727
Pabbay: i., Inv. 16 NF88
Pabbay: i., Inv. 16 NL68
Packwood House: War. SP 1772
Padbury: Bucks SP 7130
Paddock Wood: Kent TQ 6645
Padiham: Lancs 13 SD73
Padstow: Corn. 8 SW97
Paible: Harris NG 0299
Paible: N. Uist. NF 7367
Paignton: Devon. 8 SX86
Pailton: War SP 4781
Painscastle: Rad. SO 1646
Painswick: Glos 11 SO80
Paisley: Renf. 14 NS46
Pakefield: Suff. TM 5390
Palling: Norf. TG 4226
Palnackie: Kirkc. NX 8257
Palnure: Kirkc. NX 4563
Panbride: Angus NO 5635
Pangbourne: Berks 11 SU67
Pannal: Yorks SE 3051
Pant: Salop SJ 2722
Pant: r. 7 TL63
Pant Mawr: Montg. SN 8482
Papa Stour: i., Shet. Is. 17 HU16
Papa Westray: Ork. Is. 17 HY55
Paps, The: mtn., Kerry 19 C3
Parbold: Lancs SD 4911
Parham House: Sussex. TQ 0514
Park: dist., Lewis 16 NB31
Parkgate: Dumf. NY 0288
Parkham: Devon. SS 3821
Park Head: Corn. 8 SW87
Parracombe: Devon. SS 6744
Parrett: r. 9 ST33
Parsonstown: Offaly 19 F5
Partick: Lan. NS 5567
Partney: Lincs TF 4168
Parton: Kirkc. NX 6970
Partry Mts.: Mayo 18 C6
Parwich: Derby. SK 1854
Parys Mtn.: Anglesey SH 4390
Passage de la Deroute: Eng./Fr. 9 Ins.
Pass of Brander: Argyll 14 NN02
Pass of Killiecrankie: Perth. 17 NN96
Patchway: Glos ST 6082
Pateley Bridge: Yorks 13 SE16
Patna: Ayr NS 4110
Patrington: Yorks 13 TA32
Patterdale: Westmor. NY 3915
Paul: Corn. SW 4526
Pawlaw Pike: Dur. 13 NZ03
Pawlett: Som. ST 2942
Paxton: Ber. NT 9352
Peacehaven: Sussex 7 TQ40
Peak District: Derby. 13 SK18
Peasemore: Berks SU 4576
Peasenhall: Suff. TM 3569
Peckforton: Ches. SJ 5356
Peebles: Peeb. 15 NT24
PEEBLESSHIRE: Scot. 15 NT24
Peel: I. of Man 12 SC28
Peel Fell: mtn., Northumb. 12 NY69
Pegswood: Northumb. NZ 2287
Pegwell Bay: Kent 7 TR36
Pelynt: Corn. SX 2055
Pembridge: Here. SO 3858
Pembroke: Pemb 10 SM90
PEMBROKESHIRE: Wales 10SM/SN
Pembury: Kent TQ 6240
Penallt: Mon. SO 5210
Penally: Pemb SS 1199
Penarth: Glam. 10 ST17
Pen Brush: Pemb 10 SM83
Penbwchdy: Pemb 10 SM83
Pencader: Carm. SN 4436
Pencaitland: E. Loth. NT 4468
Pencarreg: Carm. SN 5345
Penclegyr: Pemb. 10 SM83
Pendeen: Corn. SW 3834
Pendine: Carm. SN 2308
Pendle Hill: Lancs 13 SD84
Penegoes: Montg. SH 7701
Penhale Point: Corn. SW 7559
Penicuik: Midloth. 15 NT25
Penifiler: Skye NG 4841
Penistone: Yorks 13 SE20
Penk: r. 11 SJ91
Penketh: Lancs SJ 5687
Penllech: Caer. SH 2234
Penmachno: Caer. SH 7950
Penmaen-Mawr: Caer. 10 SH77
Penmon: Anglesey SH 6381
Penn: Bucks SU 9193
Pennal: Mer. SH 6900
Pennan: Aber. NJ 8465
Pennines: range, Eng. 15 —
Pennine Way 13SD/SY
Penpont: Dumf. NX 8494
Penrhyn Bay: Caer. SH 8280
Penrhyndeudraeth: Mer. SH 6139
Penrhyn Mawr: Anglesey 10 SH27
Penrhyn Mawr: Caer. SH 1632
Penrith: Cumb. 12 NY53
Penruddock: Cumb. NY 4227
Penryn: Corn. 8 SW73
Pensarn: Denb. SH 9478
Penshurst: Kent TQ 5243
Pensilva: Corn. SX 2969
Pentire Point: Corn. 8 SW98
Pentland Firth: Scot. 17 ND38
Pentland Hills: Scot. 17 NT15
Pentland Skerries: Caith. 17 ND47
Pentraeth: Anglesey SH 5278
Pentre-Foelas: Denb. SH 8751
Pentre Ifan: Pemb. SN 0937
Pentrich: Derby. SK 3852
Penwith: penin., Corn. 8 SW43
Penybont: Rad. SO 1164
Pen-y-Ghent: Yorks 13 SD87
Pen-y-groes: Caer. SH 4753
Penzance: Corn. 8 SW43
Perran Bay: Corn. 8 SW75
Perranporth: Corn. 8 SW75
Perranzabuloe: Corn. SW 7752
Perry: r. 10 SJ32
Pershore: Worcs 11 SO94
Perth: Perth. 15 NO12
PERTHSHIRE: Scot. 15NN/NO
Peterborough: Northants 6 TL19
Peterchurch: Here. SO 3438
Peterculter: Aber. NJ 8400
Peterhead: Aber. 17 NK14
Peter Hill: Aber. 17 NO58
Peterlee: Dur. 13 NZ44
Petersfield: Hants 7 SU72
Peters Marland: Devon. SS 4713
Peterstow: Here. SO 5624
Petertavy: Devon. SX 5177
Petham: Kent TR 1251
Pettinain: Lan. NS 9542
Petworth: Sussex 7 SU92
Pevensey: Sussex 7 TQ60
Peveril Castle: Derby 11 SK18
Pewsey: Wilts. 9 SU15
Philleigh: Corn. SW 8639
Pickering: Yorks 13 SE78
Pickhill: Yorks 13 SE38
Picton: Yorks NZ 4107
Piddle or Trent: r. 9 SY79
Piddletrenthide: Dorset SY 7099
Piercebridge: Dur. NZ 2115
Pierowall: Ork. Is. HY 4348
Pike Rigg: Northumb. 13 NY75
Pill: Som. ST 5275
Pilleth: Rad. SO 2568
Pilling: Lancs SD 4048
Pillowel: Glos SO 6306
Pimperne: Dorset ST 9009
Pinchbeck: Lincs TF 2425
Pinhoe: Devon. SX 9595
Pinmore: Ayr NX 2090
Pint Stoup, The: Angus 15 NO64
Pirbright: Surrey. SU 9455
Pirnmill: Bute. NR 8744
Pirton: Herts TL 1431
Pitcaple: Aber. NJ 7225
Pitcarity: Angus NO 3265
Pitlochry: Perth. 17 NN95
Piscottie: Fife NO 4113
Pitsea: Essex TQ 7488
Pittenweem: Fife 15 NO50
Pladda: i., Bute. 14 NS01
Plaidy: Aber. NJ 7354
Plashetts: Northumb. NY 6690
Plas Newydd: Denb. 10 SJ24
Plockton: R. & Crom. 16 NG83
Pluckley: Kent TQ 9045
Plumbland: Cumb. NY 1438
Plumpton: Sussex TQ 3613
Plumtree: Notts SK 6133
Pluscarden Priory: Moray. NJ 1457
Plym: r. 8 SX56
Plymouth: Devon. 8 SX45
Plympton: Devon. 8 SX55
Plynlimon Fawr: Card. 10 SN78
Pocklington: Yorks 13 SE84
Point Lynas: Anglesey 12 SH49
Point of Air: Flint. SJ 1285
Point of Ardnamurchan: Argyll 16 NM46
Point of Ayre: I. of Man 12 NX40
Point of Knap: Argyll 14 NR67
Point of Stoer: Suther. 16 NC03
Polden Hills: Som. 9 ST43
Polegate: Sussex TQ 5805
Polesworth: War SK 2602
Polglass: Suther. NC 0307
Pollachar: S. Uist NF 7414
Pollaphuca Res.: Wick. 19 H5
Pollington: Yorks SE 6119
Polmaddie: mtn., Ayr 14 NX39
Polperro: Corn. 8 SX25
Poltalloch: Argyll NR 8196
Polwarth: Ber. NT 7450
Pontardawe: Glam. SN 7204
Pontardulais: Glam. SN 5903
Pontefract: Yorks 13 SE42
Ponteland: Northumb. NZ 1672
Pont-erwyd: Card. SN 7481
Pontesbury: Salop SJ 3905
Pontlottyn: Mon. SO 1206
Pontnewydd: Mon. ST 2896
Pontrilas: Here. SO 3927
Pontyberem: Carm. SN 4910
Pontypool: Mon. 10 SO20
Pontypridd: Glam. 10 ST09
Pool: Yorks SE 2445
Poole: & bay, Dorset 9 SZ09
Poolewe: R. & Crom. NG 8580
Pooley Bridge: Westmor. NY 4724
Pool of Muckart: Perth. NO 0000
Porlock: & bay, Som. 8 SS84
Portadown: Armagh 18 J7
Portaferry: Down 18 K7
Port Ann: Argyll 14 NR98
Port Appin: Argyll 14 NM94
Portarlington: Laoighis 19 G5
Port Askaig: Islay NR 4369
Port Bannatyne: Bute. NS 0767
Port Carlisle: Cumb. NY 2461
Port Charlotte: Islay NR 2558
Portchester: Hants SU 6105
Port Dinorwic: Caer. 10 SH56
Port Ellen: Islay 14 NR34
Port Elphinstone: Aber. NJ 7719
Port Erin: I. of Man 12 SC16
Port Errol: Aber. 17 NK03
Portesham: Dorset SY 6085
Portessie: Banff NJ 4466
Port Eynon Pt.: Glam. 10 SS48
Port Glasgow: Renf. 14 NS37
Portgordon: Banff NJ 3964
Porthcawl: Glam. 10 SS87
Porthcurno: Corn. SW 3822
Porthleven: Corn. SW 6225
Porth Neigwl: Caer. 10 SH22
Porthscatho: Corn. SW 8735
Porthtowan: Corn. SW 6847
Portinnisherrich: Argyll NM9711
Portinscale: Cumb. NY 2523
Port Isaac: & bay, Corn. 8 SW98
Portishead: Som. 9 ST47
Portknockie: Banff NJ 4868
Portlaoighise: Laoighis 19 G5
Portland Bill: Dorset 9 SY67
Portlethen: Kinc. NO 9396
Portloe: Corn. SW 9339
Portmadoc: Caer. 10 SH53
Portmeirion: Mer. SH 5937
Portnacroish: Argyll NM 9247
Portnahaven: Islay NR 1652
Port nan Long: N. Uist. NF 8978
Portobello: Midloth. 15 NT37
Port of Menteith: Perth. NN 5801
Porton: Wilts. SU 1836
Portreath: Corn. SW 6545
Portree: Skye 16 NG44
Portrush: Antrim 18 H9
Port St. Mary: I. of Man SC 2067
Portskerra: Suther. NC 8765
Portskewett: Mon. ST 4988
Portslade by Sea: Sussex TQ 2506
Portsmouth: Hants 7 SU60
Portsonachan: Argyll NN 0420
Portsoy: Banff 17 NJ56
Portstewart: Lon. 18 H9
Port Sunlight: Ches. 10 SJ38
Port Talbot: Glam. 10 SS79
Portumna: Gal. 19 E5
Port Victoria: Kent TQ 8773
Port William: Wig. NX 3343
Portyerrock: Wig. NX 4839
Post Rocks: Islay 14 NR47
Potter Hanworth: Lincs TF 0566
Potter Heigham: Norf. TG 4119
Potters Bar: Middx. TL 2501
Potterspury: Northants. SP 7543
Potton: Beds 7 TL24
Poulter: r. 11 SK67
Poulton le Fylde: Lancs 12 SD33
Poundstock: Corn. SX 2099
Powis Castle: Montg. 10 SJ20
Prawle Pt.: Devon. 8 SX73
Prees: Salop SJ 5533
Preesall: Lancs 12 SD34
Prescot: Lancs SJ 4692
Prestatyn: Flint. 10 SJ08
Prestbury: Ches. SJ 8976
Prestbury: Glos SO 9624
Presteigne: Rad. 10 SO36
Preston: Ber. NT 7957
Preston: Lancs 12 SD52
Preston: Rut. SK 8602
Preston: Yorks TA 1830
Preston Candover: Hants SU 6041
Preston on the Hill: Ches. SJ 5780
Prestonpans: E. Loth. 15 NT37
Prestwich: Lancs 13 SD80
Prestwick: Ayr 14 NS32
Prestwood: Bucks SP 8700
Prickwillow: Cambs. TL 5982
Priest I.: R. & Crom. 16 NB90
Princes Risborough: Bucks 11 SP80
Princethorpe: War SP 3970
Princetown: Devon. 8 SX57
Priors Marston: War SP 4857
Probus: Corn. SW 8947
Provan Hall: Lan. NS 6766
Prudhoe: Northumb. 15 NZ06
Prysor: r. 10 SH63
Pucklechurch: Glos ST 6976
Puddington: Devon. SS 8310
Puddletown: Dorset SY 7594
Pudsey: Yorks 13 SE23
Puffin I.: Anglesey 10 SH68
Puffin I.: Kerry 19 Ins.
Pulborough: Sussex TQ 0418
Pulham St. Mary: Norf. TM 2185
Pumpsaint: Carm. SN 6540
Puncheston: Pemb SN 0029
Puriton: Som. ST 3241
Purleigh: Essex TL 8301
Purton: Wilts. SU 0887
Puxton: Som. ST 4063
Pwllheli: Caer. 10 SH33
Pylewell Park: Hants SZ 3595
Pyworthy: Devon. SS 3102

Quadring: Lincs TF 2233
Quainton: Bucks SP 7420
Quantock Hills: Som. 9 ST13
Quarff: Shet. Is. HU 4235
Quarry Hills: Kent 7 TQ85
Quarter: Lan. NS 7251
Quatford: Salop SO 7390
Quatt: Salop SO 7588
Queenborough: Kent 7 TQ97
Queensberry: Dumf. 15 NX99
Queensbury: Yorks SE 1030
Queensferry: W. Loth. 15 NT17
Quendon: Essex TL 5130
Quernmore: Lancs SD 5160
Quinag: mtn., Suther. 16 NC22
Quinnish Pt.: Mull 16 NM45
Quirang: mtn., Skye 16 NG46
Quorndon: Leics. SK 5616

Raasay: i., Inv. 16 NG54
Raby Castle: Dur. 13 NZ12
Race of Alderney: Chan. Is. 9 Ins.
Rackenford: Devon. SS 8418
Radcliffe: Lancs 13 SD70
Radcliffe on Trent: Notts SK 6439
Radlett: Herts TL 1600
Radley: Berks 11 SU59
Radnor Forest 10 SO26
RADNORSHIRE: Wales 10 SO06
Radstock: Som. 9 ST65
Radway: War SP 3648
Rafford: Moray. 17 NJ05
Raglan: Mon. SO 4107
Ragstone Ridge: Kent. 7 TQ55
Rainford: Lancs SD 4700
Rainham: Kent TQ 8165
Rainhill: Lancs 12 SJ49
Rait: Perth. NO 2226
Ramasaig: Skye NG 1644
Rame Head: Corn. 8 SX44
Ramor, L.: Cavan 18 G6
Ramsbottom: Lancs 13 SD71
Ramsbury: Wilts. SU 2771
Ramsey: Essex TM 2130
Ramsey: Hunts 6 TL28
Ramsey: & bay, I. of Man 12 SC49
Ramsey I.: Pemb 10 SM62
Ramsgate: Kent 7 TR36
Ramsgill: Yorks SE 1170
Rams Ness: Shet Is. HU 6086
Randalstown: Antrim 18 J8
Rankinston: Ayr NS 4513
Rannoch Moor: Perth. 17 NN35
Ranskill: Notts SK 6587
Ratby: Leics. SK 5105
Rathdrum: Wick. 19 J4
Rathfriland: Down 18 J7
Rathlin: i., Antrim 18 J9
Rathluirc: Cork 19 D3
Rathmell: Yorks SD 8059
Rathmullan: Don. 18 F9
Ratho: Midloth. NT 1370
Rathven: Banff NJ 4465
Ratlinghope: Salop SO 4096
Rattray: Perth. 17 NO14
Rattray Hd.: Aber. 17 NK15
Raunds: Northants 11 SP97
Ravenglass: Cumb. 12 SD09
Ravenscar: Yorks NZ 9801
Ravenstonedale: Westmor. NY 7203
Ravensworth: Yorks NZ 1407
Rawcliffe: Yorks SE 6822
Rawmarsh: Yorks 13 SK49
Rawtenstall: Lancs 13 SD82
Ray: r., Oxon. 11 SP62
Ray: r., Wilts. 9 SU19
Rayleigh: Essex 7 TQ89
Raynham Park: Norf. 6 TF82
Rea: r., Salop 10 SJ30
Rea: r., Worcs 11 SP08
Reading: Berks 11 SU77
Rearsby: Leics. SK 6514
Reay: Caith. NC 9664
Reay Forest: Suther. NC 3840
Reculver: Kent TR 2269
Redbourn: Herts TL 1012
Redcar: Yorks 13 NZ62
Redding: Stirl. NS 9178
Redditch: Worcs 11 SP06
Redesdale: Northumb. 15 NY89
Redesmouth: Northumb. NY 8681
Redgorton: Perth. NO 0928
Redgrave: Suff. TM 0478
Redhill: Surrey 7 TQ25
Red Hills: Skye 16 NG52
Redlake: r. 10 SO37
Redmire: Yorks SE 0491
Redpoint: R. & Crom. NG 7369
Redruth: Corn. 8 SW74
Red Wharf Bay: Anglesey 10 SH58
Redwick: Glos ST 5485
Redwick: Mon. ST 4184
Ree, L.: R. of Irel. 18 F6
Reedham: Norf. TG 4201
Reepham: Lincs TF 0373
Reepham: Norf. 6 TG12
Reeth: Yorks 13 SE09
Reiff: R. & Crom. NB 9614
Reigate: Surrey 7 TQ25
Relugas: Moray. NH 9948
Rempstone: Notts SK 5724
Rendcomb: Glos SP 0109
RENFREW: Co., Scot. 14 NS56
Renish Point: Harris NG 0481
Rennibister: Ork. Is. HY 4010
Rennington: Northumb. NU 2118
Renvyle: Gal. 18 B6
Repton: Derby. 11 SK32
Rescobie: Angus NO 5152
Resolis: R. & Crom. NH 6765
Resolven: Glam. SN 8202
Reston: Ber. NT 8861
Rettendon: Essex TQ 7698
Rey Cross: Yorks 13 NY91
Reynoldston: Glam. SS 4890
Rhayader: Rad. 10 SN96
Rheidol: r. 10 SN67
Rheola Forest: Glam. 10 SN80
Rhiconich: Suther. NC 2552
Rhidorroch Forest: Ross & Crom. NH 2497
Rhinns, The: penin., Wig. 14 NX05
Rhinns of Islay: Islay 14 NR25
Rhinns of Kells: Kirkc. 14 NX48
Rhinns Pt.: Islay 14 NR15
Rhinog Fawr: mtn., Mer. 10 SH62
Rhiw: Caer. SH 2227
Rhiw: r. 10 SJ10
Rhobell Fawr: Mer. 10 SH72
Rhondda: Glam. 10 SS99
Rhonehouse: Kirkc. NX 7459
Rhoose: Glam. 10 ST06
Rhoscolyn: Anglesey SH 2675
Rhosllanerchrugog: Denb. SJ 2946
Rhosneigr: Anglesey SH 3172
Rhossilli: Glam. SS 4188
Rhu: Dunb. NS 2783
Rhu Coigach: Ross & Crom. 16 NB91
Rhuddlan: Flint. 10 SJ07
Rhum: i., Inv. 16 NM39
Rhunahaorine: Argyll NR 7048
Rhyddhywel: Montg. 10 SO07
Rhyl: Flint. 10 SJ08
Rhymney: Mon. 10 SO10
Rhymney: r. 10 ST28
Rhynd: Perth. NO 1718
Rhynie: Aber. NJ 4927
Rib: r. 7 TL32
Ribble: r. 13 SD63
Ribble Head: Yorks SD 7678
Ribblesdale: Yorks 13 SD85
Ribchester: Lancs SD 6435
Riccall: Yorks SE 6237
Riccarton: Ayr NS 4235
Riccarton: Rox. NY 5397
Richards Castle: Here. SO 4969
Richborough: Kent 7 TR36
Richmond: Surrey 7 TQ17
Richmond: Yorks 13 NZ10
Rickarton: Kinc. NO 8188
Rickmansworth: Herts 7 TQ09
Riddings: Cumb. NY 4075
Riddings: Derby. SK 4252
Ridgewell: Essex TL 7340
Ridingmill: Northumb. NZ 0161
Ridlees Cairn: Northumb. 15 NT80
Ridsdale: Northumb. NY 9084
Rievaulx Abbey: Yorks 13 SE58
Rigside: Lan. NS 8734
Rigton: Yorks SE 2749
Rigton: Yorks SE 3743
Rillington: Yorks SE 8574
Rineanna (Shannon Airport): Clare 19 D4
Ringford: Kirkc. NX 6857
Ringmer: Sussex TQ 4412
Ringstead: Norf. TF 7040
Ringway: airport, Ches. 13 SJ88
Ringwood: Hants 9 SU10
Ringwould: Kent TR 3648
Ripley: Derby. 11 SK35
Ripley: Surrey TQ 0556
Ripley: Yorks 13 SE26
Ripon: Yorks 13 SE37
Rippingale: Lincs TF 0927
Ripponden: Yorks SE 0319
Risby: Suff. TL 7966
Risca: Mon. 10 ST29
Riseley: Beds TL 0463
Rishton: Lancs 12 SD72
Risley: Lancs 12 SJ69
Rivington: Lancs SD 6214
Roade: Northants SP 7551
Roag: Skye NG 2744
Roan Fell: Dumf./Rox. 15 NY49
Roaringwater Bay: Cork 19 B1
Roberton: Lan. NS 9428
Roberton: Rox. NT 4314
Robertsbridge: Sussex TQ 7323
Robin Hood's Bay: Yorks NZ 9505

G.B. & IRELAND

ROBOROUGH — SKEGIRSTA

Roborough: Devon. SS 5717
Rocester: Staffs. SK 1039
Roch: Pemb **10 SM82**
Rochdale: Lancs. **13 SD81**
Roche: Corn. SW 9860
Rochester: Kent **7 TQ76**
Rochester: Northumb. NY 8397
Rochford: Essex. **7 TQ89**
Rockbeare: Devon. SY 0195
Rockcliffe: Cumb. NY 3561
Rockcliffe: Kirkc. NX 8553
Rockingham: Northants **11 SP89**
Rockland All Saints: Norf. TL 9896
Rode Heath: Ches. SJ 8056
Rodel: Harris **16 NG08**
Roden: *r.* **11 SJ53**
Roding: *r.* **7 TL50**
Rodings, The: Essex **7 TL51**
Rogan's Seat: *mtn.*, Yorks **13 NY90**
Rogart: Suther. NC 7303
Rogiet: Mon. ST 4687
Roineval: *mtn.*, Skye **16 NG43**
Rois-Bheinn: Inv. **16 NM77**
Rokeby: Yorks NZ 0714
Rollesby: Norf. TG 4415
Rolleston: Notts SK 7452
Rollright Stones: Oxon. **11 SP23**
Rolvenden: Kent TQ 8431
Romaldkirk: Yorks NY 9921
Roman: *r.* **7 TL92**
Rombalds Moor: Yorks **13 SE04**
Romford: Essex **7 TQ58**
Romney Marsh: Kent **7 TR03**
Romsey: Hants **7 SU32**
Rona: *i.*, Inv. **16 NG65**
Ronaldsway: I. of Man **12 SC26**
Ronas Hill: Shet. Is. **17 HU38**
Ronay: *i.*, Argyll **16 NF95**
Rookhope: Dur. NY 9342
Roos: Yorks TA 2830
Ropley: Hants SU 6431
Ropsley: Lincs SK 9834
Rora Head: Ork. Is. ND 1799
Rosapenna: Don. **18 F9**
ROSCOMMON: *Co.*, R. of Irel. **18 E6**
Roscrea: Tip. **19 F4**
Rosedale Abbey: Yorks SE 7296
Rosehall: Suther. NC 4701
Rosehearty: Aber. **17 NJ96**
Rosemarket: Pemb SM 9508
Rosemarkie: R. & Crom. NH 7357
Rosemullion Hd.: Corn. **8 SW82**
Roskhill: Skye NG 2745
Roslin: Midloth. NT 2663
Rosneath: Dunb. NS 2583
Rossal School: Lancs **12 SD34**
ROSS & CROMARTY: *Co.*, Scot. **16 NH—**
Rosses, The: Don. **18 E8**
Rossett: Denb. SJ 3657
Rossington: Yorks SK 6298
Rosslare Harbour: Wex. **19 J3**
Ross of Mull: Mull **14 NM31**
Ross-on-Wye: Here. **11 SO62**
Rosyth: Fife **15 NT18**
Rothbury: *& forest*, Northumb. **15 NU00**
Rother: *r.*, E. Sussex **7 TQ82**
Rother: *r.*, W. Sussex **7 SU82**
Rother: *r.*, Yorks **13 SK48**
Rotherfield: Sussex TQ 5529
Rotherham: Yorks **13 SK49**
Rothes: Moray. **17 NJ24**
Rothesay: Bute. **14 NS06**
Rothiemurchus: forest, Inv. NH 9206
Rothienorman: Aber. NJ 7235
Rothwell: Lincs TF 1499
Rothwell: Northants **11 SP88**
Rothwell: Yorks. **13 SE32**
Rottingdean: Sussex TQ 3702
Roughtinglinn: Northumb. NT 9737
Roughton: Norf. TG 2136
Roughty: *r.* **19 B2**
Round Hill: Yorks **13 SE15**
Rousay: *i.*, Ork. Is. **17 HY43**
Rowde: Wilts. ST 9762
Rowington: War SP 2069
ROXBURGH: *Co.*, Scot. **15 NT63**
Roxton: Beds TL 1554
Roxwell: Essex TL 6408
Roy: *r.* **16 NN39**
Royal Leamington Spa *see* Leamington Spa
Royal Tunbridge Wells *see* Tunbridge Wells
Roybridge: Inv. NN 2781
Royston: Herts **7 TL34**
Royston: Yorks **13 SE31**
Royton: Lancs SD 9207
Ruan Minor: Corn. SW 7115
Rubery: War SO 9777
Rudby: Yorks NZ 4706
Ruddington: Notts SK 5733
Ruel: *r.* **14 NS08**
Rudgwick: Sussex TQ 0934
Rudha Ardvule: *c.*, S. Uist **16 NF73**
Rudha Dubh: *c.*, Tiree. **16 NM04**
Rudh' a' Geodha: *c.*, Argyll **14 NR49**
Rudha Hunish: *c.*, Skye **16 NG37**
Rudh' a' Mhail: *c.*, Argyll **14 NR47**
Rudha na Faing: *c.*, Islay **14 NR15**
Rudha nan Leacan: *c.*, Islay **14 NR34**
Rudh' an Dùnain: *c.*, Skye **16 NG31**
Rudha Ruadh: c., Suther. NC 1651
Rudha Shamhnan Insir: *c.*, Rhum **16 NG30**
Rudh'Re: *c.*, R. & Crom. **16 NG79**
Rudston: Yorks TA 0967
Rudyard: Staffs SJ 9557
Ruel: *r.* **14 NS09**
Rue Point: I. of Man **12 NX40**
Rufford: Lancs SD 4515
Rugby: War **11 SP57**
Rugeley: Staffs **11 SK01**
Ruislip: Middx. **7 TQ08**
Rumblingbridge: Kinr./Perth. NT 0199
Rumney: Glam. ST 2179
Runcorn: Ches. **11 SJ58**
Runnel Stone: Corn. SW 3720
Runnymede: Surrey **7 SU97**
Runswick: Yorks NZ 8016
Rush: Dublin **18 J6**
Rushall: Staffs SK 0201
Rushden: Northants **11 SP96**
Rushen: I. of Man SO 2169
Rushton Marsh: Staffs SJ 9362
Rustington: Sussex TQ 0502
Ruswarp: Yorks NZ 8809
Rutherglen: Lan. **14 NS66**
Ruthin: Denb. **10 SJ15**
Ruthven: Perth. **17 NO24**
Ruthwell: Dumf. NY 0067
RUTLAND: *Co.*, Eng. **11 SK90**
Ruyton of the Eleven Towns: Salop SJ 3922
Rydal: Westmor. NY 3606
Ryde: I. of Wight **7 SZ59**
Rye: *& bay*, Sussex **7 TQ92**
Rye: *r.* **13 SE58**
Ryhall: Rut. TF 0311
Ryhill: Yorks SE 3814
Ryhope: Dur. NZ 4152
Ryton: Dur. NZ 1564
Ryton: *r.* **13 SK67**

Sabden: Lancs SD 7737
Sacriston: Dur. NZ 2447
Saddell: Argyll NR 7832
Saddle, The: *mtn.*, Inv./Ross & Crom. **16 NG91**
Saddleback: *mtn.*, Cumb. **12 NY32**
Saddleworth: Yorks SE 0005
Saffron Walden: Essex. **7 TL53**
St. Abb's Head: Ber. **15 NT96**
St. Agnes: *& head*, Corn. **8 SW75**
St. Albans: Herts **7 TL10**
St. Alban's Head: Dorset **9 SY97**
St. Andrews: *& bay*, Fife **15 NO51**
St. Anne's on the Sea: Lancs **12 SD32**
St. Anns Head: Pemb **10 SM80**
St. Arvans: Mon. ST 5196
St. Asaph: Flint. **10 SJ07**
St. Aubin: Jersey **9 Ins.**
St. Austell: Corn. **8 SX05**
St. Bees: *& head*, Cumb. **12 NX91**
St. Blazey: Corn. **8 SX05**
St. Boswells: Rox. **15 NT63**
St. Breward: Corn. SX 0977
St. Briavels: Glos SO 5504
St. Bride's Bay: Pemb **10 SM71**
St. Bride's Major: Glam. SS 8975
St. Catherines: Argyll NN 1207
St. Catherine's Hill: Hants **7 SU42**
St. Catherine's Point: I. of Wight **7 SZ57**
St. Clears: Carm. SN 2716
St. Cleer: Corn. SX 2468
St. Columb Major: Corn. **8 SW96**
St. Combs: Aber. NK 0563
St. Cyrus: Kinc. NO 7464
St. David's: Pemb **10 SM72**
St. Day: Corn. SW 7242
St. Dennis: Corn. SW 9558
St. Donat's: Glam. SS 9368
St. Erme: Corn. SW 8449
St. Erth: Corn. SW 5435
St. Ervan: Corn. SW 8870
St. Ewe: Corn. SW 9745
St. Fagan's Castle: Glam. **10 ST17**
St. Fergus: Aber. NK 0951
St. Fillans: Perth. NN 6924
St. Finan's Bay: Kerry **19 Ins.**
St. George's Channel **19 J3**
St. George's: *i.*, Corn. **8 SX25**
St. Germans: Corn. **8 SX35**
St. Goran: Corn. SW 9942
St. Govan's Head: Pemb. **10 SR99**
St. Harmon: Rad. SN 9872
St. Helens: I. of Wight SZ 6288
St. Helens: Lancs **12 SJ59**
St. Helier: Jersey **9 Ins.**
St. Hilary: Glam. ST 0173
St. Ishmael's: Pemb. SM 8307
St. Ives: *& bay*, Corn. **8 SW54**
St. Ives: Hunts **6 TL37**
St. John Beckermet: Cumb. NY 0106
St. John's: I. of Man SC 2781
St. John's Chapel: Dur. **13 NY83**
St. John's Point: Don. **18 E8**
St. John's Point: Down **18 K7**
St. Just: Corn. **8 SW33**
St. Keverne: Corn. SW 7821
St. Leonards: Sussex **7 TQ80**
St. Leonard's Forest: Sussex **7 TQ13**
St. Magnus Bay: Shet. Is. **17 HU26**
St. Margaret's at Cliffe: Kent TR 3644
St. Margaret's Hope: Ork. Is. **17 ND49**
St. Martin's: *i.*, Scilly Is. **8 SV91**
St. Martin's Point: Guernsey **9 Ins.**
St. Mary Cray: Kent TQ 4767
St. Mary's: Ork. Is. HY 4701
St. Mary's: Scilly Is. **8 SV91**
St. Mary's L.: Selk. **15 NT22**
St. Maughan's Green: Mon. SO 4617
St. Mawes: Corn. **8 SW83**
St. Mawgan: Corn. SW 8765
St. Mellons: Mon. ST 2281
St. Merryn: Corn. SW 8874
St. Michaels: Kent TQ 8835
St. Michael's Mt.: Corn. **8 SW53**
St. Monance: Fife NO 5201
St. Neot: Corn. SX 1867
St. Neots: Hunts **6 TL16**
St. Nicholas: Pemb SM 9035
St. Nicholas at Wade: Kent TR 2666
St. Ninians: Stirl. NS 7891
St. Ninian's Cave: Wig. **14 NX43**
St. Paul's Walden: Herts TL 1922
St. Peter Port: Guernsey **9 Ins.**
St. Peter's: Jersey **9 Ins.**
St. Teath: Corn. SX 0680
St. Tudwal's Is.: Caer. **10 SH32**
St. Vigeans: Angus NO 6443
St. Weonards: Here. SO 4924
Salcey Forest: Northants **11 SP85**
Salcombe: Devon. **8 SX73**
Sale: Ches. **13 SJ79**
Salem: Card. SN 6684
Salen: Argyll NM 6864
Salen: Mull NM 5743
Salford: Beds SP 9339
Salford: Lancs SJ 7796
Salhouse: Norf. TG 3014
Saline: Fife NT 0292
Salisbury: Wilts **9 SU13**
Salisbury Plain: Wilts **9ST/SU**
Sally Gap: Wick. **19 J5**
Saltash: Corn. **8 SX45**
Saltburn by the Sea: Yorks **13 NZ62**
Saltcoats: Ayr **14 NS24**
Saltee Is.: Wex. **19 H3**
Saltfleet: Lincs TF 4593
Salthouse Broad: Norf. **6 TG04**
Sanda: *i.*, Argyll **14 NR70**
Sandal Magna: Yorks SE 3418
Sanday: *i.*, Inv. **16 NG20**
Sanday: *i.*, Ork. Is. **17 HY74**
Sandbach: Ches. **11 SJ76**
Sandbank: Argyll NS 1580
Sand Bay: Som. **9 ST36**
Sandgate: Kent **7 TR23**
Sandhaven: Aber. NJ 9667
Sandhurst: Berks **7 SU86**
Sandhurst: Kent TQ 7928
Sand Hutton: Yorks SE 6958
Sandlings, The: Suff. **7 TM35**
Sandness: Shet. Is. **17 HU15**
Sandown: I. of Wight **7 SZ58**
Sandray: *i.*, Inv. **16 NL69**
Sandringham: Norf. **6 TF62**
Sandsend: Yorks NZ 8512
Sandwich: Kent **7 TR35**
Sandy: Beds TL 1649
Sanquhar: Dumf. **15 NS71**
Santon: I. of Man SC 3171
Sapcote: Leics. SP 4893
Sarclet: Caith. ND 3443
Sark: *i.*, Chan. Is. **9 Ins.**
Sark: *r.* **12 NY37**
Satley: Dur. NZ 1143
Sauchen: Aber. NJ 7010
Saughall: Ches. SJ 3569
Saundersfoot: Pemb SN 1304
Saval Beg: mtn., Suther. NC 3742
Savernake Forest: Wilts. **9 SU26**
Sawbridgeworth: Herts **7 TL41**
Sawdde: *r.* **10 SN72**
Sawel Mt.: N. Irel. **18 G8**
Sawtry: Hunts TL 1683
Saxby All Saints: Lincs. SE 9816
Saxilby: Lincs SK 8875
Saxlingham Nethergate: Norf. TM 2397
Saxmundham: Suff. **6 TM36**
Saxthorpe: Norf. TG 1130
Saxton: Yorks SE 4736
Sca Fell: Cumb. **12 NY20**
Scalasaig: Colonsay NR 3894
Scalby: Yorks TA 0090
Scaleby: Cumb. NY 4563
Scalford: Leics. SK 7624
Scalloway: Shet. Is. SU 4039
Scalpay: *i.*, Harris **16 NG29**
Scalpay: *i.*, Skye **16 NG63**
Scamblesby: Lincs TF 2778
Scapa Flow: Ork. Is. **17 HY30**
Scar: *r.* **14 NS70**
Scarba: *i.*, Argyll **14 NM60**
Scarborough: Yorks **13 TA08**
Scarfsferry: Caith. ND 2673
Scariff I.: Kerry **19 A2**
Scarinish: Tiree NM 0444
Scarisbrick: Lancs SD 3713
Scarp: *i.*, Inv. **16 NA91**
Schichallion: *mtn.*, Perth. **17 NN75**
Schole Bank: Chan. Is. **9 Ins.**
Scilly Is. **8 SV—**
Scole: Norf. TM 1579
Scolt Hd.: Norf. **6 TF84**
Sconser: Skye NG 5232
Scorton: Lancs SD 5048
Scorton: Yorks NZ 2400
Scotforth: Lancs SD 4759
Scothern: Lincs TF 0377
Scotstown: Argyll NM 8263
Scotter: Lincs SE 8800
Scourie: Suther. NC 1544
Scrabster: Caith. **17 ND17**
Scratchbury: Wilts. *ST 9144*
Scruton: Yorks SE 3092
Sculthorpe: Norf. TF 8931
Scunthorpe: Lincs **6 SE81**
Scurdie Ness: Angus **17 NO75**
Scurrival Point: Barra **16 NF60**
Seaford: Sussex **7 TV49**
Seaham Harbour: Dur. **13 NZ44**
Sea Houses: Northumb. NU 2232
Seale: Surrey SU 8947
Seamer: Yorks NZ 4910
Seamill: Ayr NS 2047
Seana Bhraigh: Ross & Crom. **16 NH28**
Sea of the Hebrides: Scot. **16 —**
Seascale: Cumb. **12 NY00**
Seaton: Devon. **9 SY29**
Seaton: Rut. SP 9098
Seaton: *r.* **8 SX26**
Seaton Delaval: Northumb. NZ 3075
Seaton Ross: Yorks SE 7741
Seaton Sluice: Northumb. NZ 3376
Sea View: I. of Wight SZ 6291
Sedbergh: Yorks **12 SD69**
Sedgebrook: Lincs SK 8537
Sedgefield: Dur. **13 NZ32**
Sedgeford: Norf. TF 7136
Sedgemoor: Som. **9 ST33**
Sedlescombe: Sussex TQ 7818
Seghill: Northumb. NZ 2874
Seil: *i.*, Argyll **14 NM71**
Selborne: Hants **7 SU73**
Selby: Yorks **13 SE63**
Selker Bay: Cumber. **12 SD08**
SELKIRK: *Co.*, Scot. **15 NT42**
Sellafield: Cumb. **12 NY00**
Sellindge: Kent TR 0938
Selling: Kent TR 0356
Selsey Bill: Sussex **7 SZ89**
Selston: Notts SK 4553
Selworthy: Som. SS 9146
Semley: Wilts. ST 8926
Sence: *r.* **11 SK60**
Sennen: Corn. SW 3525
Sennybridge: Breck. SN 9228
Seph: *r.* **13 SE59**
Setchey: Norf. TF 6313
Settle: Yorks **13 SD86**
Settrington: Yorks SE 8370
Seven: *r.* **13 SE78**
Seven Heads: Cork **19 D2**
Sevenoaks: Kent **7 TQ55**
Seven Sisters: Glam. SN 8108
Seven Stones: Corn. SW 0524
Severn: *r.* **11 SO82**
Sgarbh Breac: *mtn.*, Argyll **14 NR47**
Sgeir a' Mhill: c., Uist NF 8312
Sgreadan Hill: Argyll **14 NR72**
Sgùman Còinntich: *mtn.*, Ross & Crom. **16 NG93**
Sgùrr a' Chaorachain: Ross & Crom. **16 NH04**
Sgùrr a' Choire Ghlais: Inv. **16 NH24**
Sgùrr Alasdair: Skye NG 4520
Sgùrr a' Mhaoraich: Inv. **16 NG90**
Sgùrr a' Mhuilinn: Ross & Crom. **16 NH25**
Sgùrr Bàn: R. & Crom. **16 NH07**
Sgùrr Mòr: R. & Crom. **16 NH27**
Sgùrr na Ciche: Inv. **16 NM99**
Sgùrr na Lapaich: Inv. **16 NH13**
Sgùrr Ruadh: Ross & Crom. **16 NG95**
Shader: Lewis NB 3854
Shaftesbury: Dorset **9 ST82**
Shalbourne: Wilts SU 3163
Shandon: Dunb. NS 2586
Shandwick: R. & Crom. NH 8574
Shanklin: I. of Wight **7 SZ58**
Shannon: *r.* **19 D4**
Shannon Airport (Rineanna): Clare **19 D4**
Shap: *& fells*, Westmor. **12 NY51**
Shapinsay: *i.*, Ork. Is. **17 HY51**
Sharlston: Yorks. SE 3818
Sharnbrook: Beds SP 9959
Sharpness: Glos SO 6702
Sharpnose Points: Corn. **8 SS21**
Shaugh Prior: Devon. SX 5463
Shaw: Lancs **13 SD90**
Shawbury: Salop SJ 5521
Sheaf: *r.* **13 SK28**
Shebbear: Devon. SS 4309
Sheelin, L.: R. of Irel. **18 G6**
Sheep Haven: Don. **18 F9**
Sheep I.: Argyll **14 NR70**
Sheep I.: Pemb **10 SM80**
Sheep's Head: Cork **19 B2**
Sheepstor: Devon. SX 5567
Sheepwash: Devon. SS 4806
Sheerness: Kent **7 TQ97**
Shee Water: *r.* **17 NO16**
Sheffield: Yorks **13 SK38**
Shefford: Beds **7 TL13**
Sheffry Hills: Mayo **18 B6**
Shehy Mts.: Cork **19 C2**
Sheigra: Suther. NC 1960
Sheldwich: Kent TR 0156
Shelf: Yorks **13 SE12**
Shelve: Salop SO 3399
Shenfield: Essex TQ 6094
Shenstone: Staffs SK 1004
Shepherdswell: Kent TR 2548
Shepreth: Cambs. TL 3947
Shepshed: Leics. **11 SK41**
Shepton Mallet: Som. **9 ST64**
Sherborne: Dorset **9 ST61**
Sherborne: Glos SP 1714
Sherborne St. John: Hants SU 6155
Sherburn: Dur. NZ 3142
Sherburn: Yorks SE 9576
Sherburn in Elmet: Yorks **13 SE43**
Shere: Surrey *TQ 0747*
Sherfield upon Loddon: Hants SU 6757
Sheriff Hutton: Yorks SE 6566
Sheringham: Norf. **6 TG14**
Sherington: Bucks SP 8846
Sherkin I.: Cork **19 C1**
Sherston: Wilts. ST 8585
Sherwood Forest: Notts **11 SK55**
Sheshader: Lewis. NB 5534
Shetland Islands: Scot. **17 Ins.**
Shiant Is.: R. & Crom. **16 NG49**
Sheildaig: R. & Crom. NG 8154
Shieldhill: Stirl. NS 8976
Shifnal: Salop **11 SJ70**
Shilbottle: Northumb. NU 1908
Shildon: Dur. **13 NZ22**
Shillay: i., Inv. NF 8891
Shillingstone: Dorset ST 8211
Shincliffe: Dur. NZ 2940
Shingles, The: Essex **7 TR28**
Shipdham: Norf. TF 9607
Shipley: Yorks **13 SE13**
Shipston on Stour: War **11 SP24**
Shipton: Glos SP 0318
Shipton: Yorks SE 8543
Shipton under Wychwood: Oxon. SP 2717
Shira: *r.* **14 NN11**
Shirebrook: Derby. SK 5267
Shirenewton: Mon. ST 4793
Shobdon: Here. SO 3961
Shoeburyness: Essex **7 TQ98**
Shoreham: Kent TQ 5261
Shoreham by Sea: Sussex **7 TQ20**
Shorwell: I. of Wight SZ 4582
Shotley Bridge: Dur. NZ 0752
Shotley Gate: Suff. TM 2434
Shottermill: Surrey SU 8732
Shotton: Dur. NZ 4139
Shotton: Flint. **10 SJ36**
Shouldham Thorpe: Norf. TF 6607
Shrawardine: Salop SJ 3915
Shrawley: Worcs. SO 8064
Shrewsbury: Salop **11 SJ41**
Shrewton: Wilts. SU 0643
Shrivenham: Berks **11 SU28**
SHROPSHIRE (Salop): Eng. **11SO/SJ**
Shuna: *i.*, Argyll **14 NM70**
Shuna: *i.*, Argyll **14 NM94**
Sible Hedingham: Essex TL 7734
Sibsey: Lincs TF 3551
Sidbury: Devon. SY 1491
Sidcup: Kent **7 TQ47**
Sidlaw Hills: Angus/Perth. **15 NO34**
Sidmouth: Devon. **9 SY18**
Sigglesthorne: Yorks TA 1545
Sighty Crag: Cumb./Northumb. **15 NY68**
Silchester: Hants **7 SU66**
Sileby: Leics. SK 6015
Silecroft: Cumb. SD 1281
Silloth: Cumb. **12 NY15**
Silsden: Yorks **13 SE04**
Silverdale: Lancs. SD 4674
Silvermine Mts.: Tip. **19 E4**
Silverstone: Northants **11 SP64**
Silverton: Devon. **8 SS90**
Simonburn: Northumb. NY 8773
Simonsbath: Som. SS 7739
Sinclair's Bay: Caith. **17 ND35**
Singleton: Lancs SD 3838
Singleton: Sussex SU 8713
Sion Mills: Tyr. **18 G8**
Sittingbourne: Kent **7 TQ96**
Skara Brae: Ork. Is. **17 HY12**
Skateraw: Kinc. NO 9193
Skeffling: Yorks TA 3619
Skegirsta: Lewis NB 5461

G.B. & IRELAND

SKEGNESS — TANNADICE

Skegness: Lincs 6 TF56
Skeirinoe: i., Inv. NG 3092
Skellig Rocks: Kerry 19 Ins.
Skellingthorpe: Lincs SK 9272
Skelmersdale: Lancs SD 4605
Skelmorlie: Ayr NS 1967
Skelpick: Suther. NC 7256
Skelton: Cumb. NY 4335
Skelton: Yorks SE 5656
Skelton: Yorks 13 NZ61
Skendleby: Lincs TF 4369
Skenfrith: Mon. SO 4520
Skerries: Dublin 18 J6
Skerryvore: i., Hebrides 14 NL92
Skibbereen: Cork 19 C2
Skidby: Yorks TA 0133
Skiddaw: mtn., Cumb. 12 NY22
Skinidin: Skye NG 2247
Skipness: Argyll NR 8957
Skipness Point: Bute. 14 NR95
Skipsea: Yorks TA 1655
Skipton: Yorks 13 SD95
Skipwith: Yorks SE 6538
Skirfare: r. 13 SD97
Skirling: Peeb. NT 0739
Skirwith: Cumb. NY 6132
Skokholm I.: Pemb 10 SM70
Skomer I.: Pemb 10 SM70
Skulamus: Skye NG 6823
Skull: Cork 19 B2
Skye: i., Inv. 16 NG—
Slaggyford: Northumb. NY 6752
Slaidburn: Yorks SD 7152
Slaithwaite: Yorks 13 SE01
Slamannan: Stirl. NS 8573
Slaney: r. 19 H4
Slapton: Devon. SX 8244
Slaugham: Sussex TQ 2528
Slayley: Northumb. NY 9757
Slea: r. 6 TF04
Sleaford: Lincs 6 TF04
Slea Head: Kerry 19 Ins.
Sleat: Skye 16 NG60
Sledmere: Yorks SE 9364
Sleights: Yorks NZ 8607
Sliabh Gaoil: Argyll 14 NR87
Slieve Anierin: Leit. 18 F7
Slieve Aughty: Gal. 19 E5
Slieve Beagh: Ferm. 18 G7
Slieve Bernagh: Clare 19 D4
Slieve Bloom: Laoighis 19 F5
Slieve Car: Mayo 18 B7
Slieve Donard: Down 18 K7
Slieve Elva: Clare 19 C5
Slievefelim: Lim. 19 E4
Slieve Gallion: Lon. 18 H8
Slieve Gamph: Sligo 18 D7
Slieve Gullion: Armagh 18 J7
Slieve Mish: Kerry 19 B3
Slieve Miskish: Cork 19 B2
Slieve More: Mayo 18 A7
Slievenaman: Tip. 19 F3
Slieve Rushen: Cavan/Ferm. 18 F7
Slieve Snaght: Don. 18 G9
Sligachan Inn: Skye 16 NG42
SLIGO: Co., R. of Irel. 18 E7
Sligo Bay 18 D7
Slindon: Sussex SU 9608
Slinford: Sussex TQ 1131
Slingsby: Yorks SE 6974
Slioch: mtn., R. & Crom. 16 NH06
Slough: Bucks 11 SU97
Slyne Head: Gal. 19 A5
Smailholm: Rox. NT 6436
Smallburgh: Norf. TG 3324
Small Hythe: Kent TQ 8930
Smethwick: Staffs 11 SP08
Snaefell: mtn., I. of Man 12 SC38
Snainton: Yorks SE 9182
Snaith: Yorks 13 SE62
Snape: Suff. TM 3959
Snape: Yorks SE 2684
Snodland: Kent TQ 7061
Snowdon: mtn., Caer. 10 SH65
Soa I.: Mull 14 NM21
Soar: r. 11 SK 42
Soay: i. & sound, Skye 16 NG41
Soham: Cambs. 6 TL57
Soke of Peterborough: Admin.Co., Northants 6 TF10
Solent, The: chan., Hants 9 SZ49
Solfach (Solva): r. 10 SM82
Solihull: War 11 SP17
Sollas: N. Uist NF 8074
Solva: Pemb 10 SM82
Solway Firth: Eng./Scot. 15 NY05
Somersby: Lincs TF 3472
SOMERSET: Co., Eng. 9 ST—
Somersham: Hunts TL 3677
Somerton: Som. 9 ST42
Sonning: Berks SU 7575
Sopley: Hants SZ 1596
Sorbie: Wig. NX 4346
Sorisdale: Coll NM 2763
Sorn: Ayr NS 5526
Soulby: Westmor. NY 7410
Sound of Arisaig: Inv. 16 NM68
Sound of Barra: Outer Hebr. 16 NF70
Sound of Canna: Inv. 16 NG30
Sound of Eigg: Inv. 16 NM38
Sound of Gigha: Argyll 14 NR64
Sound of Harris: Harris 16 NF98
Sound of Islay: Argyll. 14 NR46
Sound of Jura: Argyll. 14 NR98
Sound of Monach: Outer Hebr. 16 NF76
Sound of Mull: Argyll. 14 NM64
Sound of Raasay: Inv. 16 NG55
Sound of Rhum: Inv. 16 NM49
Sound of Shiant: Lewis 16 NG39
Sound of Sleat: Inv. 16 NG70
Souter Head: Kinc. NJ 9601
Southall: Middx. TQ 1280
Southam: War 11 SP46
Southampton: Hants 7 SU41
South Bank: Yorks 13 NZ52
South Barrule: I. of Man 12 SC27
South Benfleet: Essex TQ 7785
South Boisdale: S. Uist NF 7417
Southborough: Kent 7 TQ54
South Brent: Devon. SX 6960
South Cave: Yorks 13 SE93
South Clifton: Notts SK 8270
South Creake: Norf. TF 8536
South Cuil: Argyll NM 9956
South Darenth: Kent TQ 5669
Southdean: Rox. NT 6308
South Dell: Lewis NB 4961
South Dorset Downs 9 SY69
South Downs: Sussex 7SU/TQ
South Elmsall: Yorks SE 4711
Southend: Argyll. NR 6908
Southend on Sea: Essex 7 TQ88
Southern-down: Glam. SS 8874
Southerness Point: Kirkc. 12 NX95
Southern Uplands 14/15 —
Southery: Norf. TL 6294
South Esk: r. 17 NO55
South Foreland: Kent 7 TR34
South Gate: Card. SN 5879
Southgate: Middx. TQ 3093
South Hams: Devon. 8 SX65
South Hayling: Hants SZ 7299
South Hetton: Dur. NZ 3745
South Kirkby: Yorks SE 4410
South Kyme: Lincs TF 1749
South Lee: mtn., N. Uist 16 NF96
South Lopham: Norf. TM 0481
South Milton: Devon. SX 7042
South Mimms: Middx. TL 2200
South Molton: Devon. 8 SS72
South Ockendon: Essex TQ 5982
South Perrott: Dorset ST 4706
South Petherton: Som. ST 4316
South Petherwin: Corn. SX 3182
Southport: Lancs 12 SD31
South Ronaldsay: i., Ork. Is. 17 ND48
South Shields: Dur. 15 NZ36
South Skirlaugh: Yorks TA 1439
South Sound: Clare 19 C5
South Stoke: Oxon. SU 6083
South Tawton: Devon. SX 6594
South Tyne: r. 12 NY65
South Uist: i., Inv. 16 NF73
Southwell: Notts 11 SK75
Southwick: Dur. 12 NZ35
Southwick: Hants SU 6208
South Wingfield: Derby SK 3755
South Witham: Lincs SK 9219
Southwold: Suff. 6 TM57
South Wootton: Norf. TF 6422
South Zeal: Devon. SX 6593
Sow: r. 11 SJ82
Sowe: r. 11 SP37
Sowerby: Yorks SE 0323
Sowerby: Yorks SE 4381
Sowerby Bridge: Yorks 13 SE02
Sowton: Devon. SX 9792
Spalding: Lincs 6 TF22
Spaldwick: Hunts TL 1272
Sparkford: Som. ST 6026
Spean Bridge: Inv. 16 NN28
Speeton: Yorks TA 1574
Speke: Lancs 12 SJ48
Speldhurst: Kent TQ 5541
Spennymoor: Dur. 13 NZ23
Sperrin Mts.: N. Irel. 18 H8
Spettisbury: Dorset ST 9002
Spey: r. & bay, Moray. 17 NJ35
Spilsby: Lincs 6 TF46
Spital: Caith. ND 1654
Spithead: roadstead, Hants 9 SZ69
Spittal: Pemb SM 9723
Spittal of Glenshee: Perth. NO 1169
Spofforth: Yorks 13 SE35
Spondon: Derby. SK 3935
Spreyton: Devon. SX 6996
Springfield: Fife NO 3411
Sprint: r. 12 NY50
Sprouston: Rox. NT 7534
Sprowston: Norf. TG 2412
Spurn Head: Yorks 13 TA41
Spynie: Moray. NJ 2265
Stack Is.: Inv. NF 7807
Stackpole Head: Pemb 10 SR99
Stack Rocks: Pemb 10 SM81
Stacks Mts.: Kerry 19 B3
Stadhampton: Oxon. SU 6098
Staffa: i., Argyll 14 NM33
Staffin I.: Skye NG 4969
Stafford: Staffs 11 SJ92
STAFFORDSHIRE: Eng. 11 SJ/S6
Stagsden: Beds SP 9849
Staindrop: Dur. NZ1220
Staines: Middx. 11 TQ07
Stainforth: Yorks SD 8267
Stainforth: Yorks SE 6411
Stainland: Yorks. SE 0719
Stainmore: Westmor./Yorks 13 NY91
Stainton: Yorks NZ 4714
Staintondale: Yorks SE 9898
Staithes: Yorks NZ 7818
Stalbridge: Dorset 9 ST71
Stalham: Norf. 6 TG32
Stalybridge: Ches. 13 SJ99
Stamford: Lincs 6 TF00
Stamford Bridge: Yorks 13 SE75
Stamfordham: Northumb. NZ 0772
Standish: Lancs SD 5610
Standlake: Oxon. SP 3902
Standon: Herts TL 3922
Stanford in the Vale: Berks SU 3493
Stanford le Hope: Essex TQ 6882
Stanhope: Dur. 13 NY93
Stanley: Dur. 13 NZ15
Stanley: Perth. NO 1033
Stanley: Yorks 13 SE32
Stannington: Northumb. NZ 2179
Stansted Mountfitchet: Essex TL 5124
Stanton: Suff. TL 9673
Stanton Harcourt: Oxon. SP 4105
Stanton Moor: Derby. 11 SK26
Stanton upon Hine Heath: Salop SJ 5624
Stanway: Glos SP 0532
Stanwick: Yorks NZ 1811
Stapleford: Notts SK 4837
Stapleford: Wilts. SU 0637
Staplehurst: Kent TQ 7843
Starcross: Devon. SX 9781
Start Bay: Devon 8 SX84
Start Point: Devon. 8 SX83
Start Point: Ork. Is. 17 HY74
Stathern: Leics. SK 7731
Staughton: Hunts TL 1364
Staunton on Wye: Here. SO 3645
Staveley: Derby. 13 SK47
Staverton: Glos 11 SO82
Staverton: Northants SP 5461
Steart Flats: Som. ST 2647
Stebbing: Essex TL 6624
Steep Holme: i., Eng. 9 ST26
Steeping: r. 13 TF46
Steeple: Essex TL 9303
Steeple Bumpstead: Essex TL 6741
Steeple Claydon: Bucks SP 6927
Steeple Morden: Cambs. TL 2842
Steeton: Yorks SE 0344
Stenhousemuir: Stirl. 15 NS88
Stenton: E. Loth. NT 6274
Stepps: Lan. NS 6668
Stevenage: Herts 7 TL22
Stevenston: Ayr NS 2624
Steventon: Berks. SU 4691
Stewarton: Ayr 14 NS44
Stewkley: Bucks SP 8525
Steyning: Sussex. 7 TQ11
Stichill: Rox./Ber. NT 7138
Sticker: Corn. SW 9750
Stickford: Lincs TF 3560
Stickney: Lincs TF 3456
Stiffkey: & r., Norf. 6 TF94
Stillington: Yorks SE 5867
Stilton: Hunts 6 TL18
Stinchar: r. 14 NX29
STIRLING: Co., Scot. 14 NS79
Stithians: Corn. SW 7336
Stob a Choin: mtn., Perth. 14 NN41
Stobo: Peeb. NT 1837
Stock: Essex TQ 6998
Stockbridge: Hants 7 SU33
Stockport: Ches. 13 SJ88
Stocksbridge: Yorks 13 SK29
Stocksfield: Northumb. NZ 0561
Stockton Heath: Ches. SJ 6185
Stockton on Tees: Dur. 13 NZ41
Stockwith: Notts/Lincs. SK 7996
Stoer: Suther. NC 0428
Stogursey: Som. ST 2042
Stoke by Clare: Suff. TL 7443
Stoke by Nayland: Suff. TL 9836
Stoke Climsland: Corn. SX 3574
Stoke Ferry: Norf. TF 7000
Stoke Fleming: Devon. SX 8648
Stoke Gabriel: Devon. SX 8457
Stoke Goldington: Bucks SP 8348
Stokeinteignhead: Devon. SX 9170
Stoke Mandeville: Bucks SP 8310
Stokenchurch: Bucks SU 7596
Stokenham: Devon. SX 8042
Stoke on Trent: Staffs 11 SJ84
Stoke Point: Devon. 8 SX54
Stoke Prior: Here. SO 5256
Stoke Prior: Worcs SO 9467
Stoke Rivers: Devon. SS 6335
Stoke St. Mary: Som. ST 2622
Stokesay: Salop 11 SO48
Stokesley: Yorks 13 NZ50
Stone: Bucks SP 7812
Stone: Glos ST 6895
Stone: Staffs 11 SJ83
Stonefield: Argyll 14 NR87
Stonehaven: Kinc. 17 NO88
Stonehenge: Wilts. 9 SU14
Stonehouse: Glos. SO 8005
Stonehouse: Lan. 15 NS74
Stoneleigh: War SP 3272
Stoney Stanton: Leics. SP 4894
Stoneywood: Aber. NJ 8910
Stonybreck: Fair Isle 17 HZ27
Stonyhurst College: Lancs 12 SD63
Stony Littleton: Som. ST 7456
Stony Stratford: Bucks 11 SP74
Stopsley: Beds TL 1023
Stormont: Perth. 17 NO15
Stornoway: Lewis 16 NB43
Storr, The: mtn., Skye 16 NG45
Storrington: Sussex TQ 0814
Stort: r. 7 TL42
Stotfold: Beds TL 2136
Stottesdon: Salop SO 6782
Stoughton: Sussex SU 8011
Stour: r., Dorset 9 ST80
Stour: r., Essex 7 TL83
Stour: r., Kent 7 TR15
Stour: r., War 11 SP23
Stour: r., Worcs 11 SO88
Stourbridge: Worcs 11 SO88
Stourhead: Wilts. 9 ST73
Stourport-on-Severn: Worcs. 11 SO87
Stow: Lincs SK 8781
Stow: Midloth. NT 4644
Stowe School: Bucks 11 SP63
Stowmarket: Suff. 6 TM05
Stow on the Wold: Glos 11 SP12
Strabane: Tyr. 18 G8
Strachan: Kinc. NO 6792
Strachur: Argyll NN 0901
Stradbroke: Suff. TM 2373
Stradishall: Suff. TL 7452
Stradsett: Norf. TF 6605
Strait of Dover 7 TR32
Straiton: Ayr NS 3804
Straloch: Perth. NO 0463
Strang: I. of Man SC 3777
Strangford: & l., Down 18 K7
Stranraer: Wig. 14 NX06
Strat: r. 8 SS20
Strata Florida: Card. 10 SN76
Stratfield Turgis: Hants SU 6960
Stratford St. Mary: Suff. TM 0434
Stratford upon Avon: War 11 SP25
Strathan: Inv. NM 9891
Strathaven: Lan. 14 NS74
Strath Avon: Banff 17 NJ12
Strathblane: Stirl. NS 5679
Strathbogie: Aber. 17 NJ53
Strath Bran: R. & Crom. NH 2460
Strath Carron: Ross & Crom. 17 NH59
Strath Conon: Ross & Crom. NH 4055
Strath Dearn: Inv. 17 NH82
Strathdon: Aber. NJ 3513
Strath Earn: Perth. 15 NN81
Strath Ettrick: Inv. 17 NH52
Strathfarrar: Inv. NH 3038
Strath Fleet: Suther. 17 NC70
Strath Glass: Inv. NH 3734
Strath Halladale: Suther. 17 NC95
Strath Kanaird: Ross & Crom. 16 NC10
Strathkinness: Fife NO 4516
Strathmiglo: Fife. NO 2109
Strathmore: Scot. 15 NO45
Strathmore: r. 17 NC44
Strathmore Water: r. 17 ND04
Strath Nairn: Inv. 17 NH73
Strath Naver: Suther. 17 NC75
Strath of Kildonan: Suther. 17 NC82
Strath Oykell: R. & Crom./Suther. 16 NC40
Strathpeffer: Ross & Crom. 17 NH45
Strath Spey: Inv. 17 NH91
Strathvaich Forest: Ross & Crom. NH 3276
Strathy: r., Suther. 17 NC85
Strathy Pt.: Suther. 17 NC86
Strathyre: Perth. NN 5617
Stratton: Corn. 8 SS20
Stratton Audley: Oxon. SP 6026
Stratton on the Fosse: Som. ST 6550
Street: Som. ST 4836
Strensall: Yorks SE 6360
Stretford: Lancs 13 SJ89
Stretham: Cambs. TL 5174
Stretton: Ches. SJ 6182
Stretton: Rut. SK 9415
Strichen: Aber. NJ 9455
Stripple Stones: Corn. SX 1374
Stroma: i., Caith. 17 ND37
Stromeferry: R. & Crom. 16 NG83
Stromness: Ork. Is. 17 HY20
Stronsay: i., Ork. Is. 17 HY62
Strontian: Argyll NM 8161
Strood: Kent TQ 7369
Stroud: Glos 11 SO80
Struan: Perth NN 8065
Strule: r. 18 G8
Strumble Head: Pemb. 10 SM84
Struy: Inv. NH 4039
Stuartfield: Aber. NJ 9745
Studland: Dorset. SZ 0382
Studley: War SP 0763
Stuley: i., Inv. NF 8323
Sturminster Marshall: Dorset SY 9499
Sturminster Newton: Dorset 9 ST7
Sturry: Kent TR 176
Sturton: Lincs SK 888
Stutton: Suff. TM 1434
Suck: r. 19 E
Sudbury: Derby. SK 163
Sudbury: Suff. 7 TL8
Sueno's Stone: Moray. NJ 055
SUFFOLK: Co., Eng. 7 TM—
Suie Hill: Kirkc. 15 NX7
Suilven: mtn., Suther. 16 NC1
Suir: r. 19 G
Sulby: I. of Man SC 399
Sulby: r. 12 SC4
Sulgrave: Northants 11 SP5
Sumburgh Hd.: Shet. Is. 17 HU4
Summer Bridge: Yorks. SE 206
Summer Isles: Ross & Crom. 16 NB9
Sunart: Argyll 16 NM7
Sunderland: Dur. 13 NZ3
Sundridge: Kent TQ 485
Sunk Island: Yorks TA 261
Sunningdale: Berks SU 956
Surbiton: Surrey. 7 TQ1
Surfleet: Lincs TF 252
SURREY: Co., Eng. 7 TQ—
SUSSEX: Co., Eng. 7 TQ—
Sutcombe: Devon. SS 341
SUTHERLAND: Co., Scot. 17 NC—
Sutterton: Lincs TF 283
Sutton: Beds TL 224
Sutton: Cambs. TL 447
Sutton: Surrey 7 TQ2
Sutton Bridge: Lincs TF 482
Sutton Coldfield: War. 11 SP1
Sutton Courtenay: Berks SU 509
Sutton in Ashfield: Notts 11 SK5
Sutton Lane Ends: Ches. SJ 937
Sutton le Marsh: Lincs. TF 528
Sutton on Hull: Yorks TA 113
Sutton on Sea: Lincs TF 528
Sutton on the Forest: Yorks SE 586
Sutton on Trent: Notts SK 796
Sutton Place: Surrey TQ 025
Sutton St. James: Lincs. TF 391
Sutton Scotney: Hants. 9 SU4
Sutton Valence: Kent TQ 814
Swadlincote: Derby. 11 SK3
Swaffham: Norf. 6 TF8
Swaffham Prior: Cambs. TL 576
Swainby: Yorks NZ 470
Swalcliffe: Oxon. SP 373
Swale: r. 13 SE2
Swale, The: Kent 7 TQ9
Swaledale: Yorks 13 NZ1
Swallow Cliff: Som. 9 ST3
Swanage: Dorset 9 SZ0
Swannington: Norf. TG 131
Swansea: & bay, Glam. 10 SS6
Swanton Morley: Norf. TG 011
Swanwick: Derby. SK 405
Swardeston: Norf. TG 200
Swaton: Lincs TF 133
Sway: Hants SZ 279
Swayfield: Lincs SK 982
Swilly: l. & r., Don. 18 F
Swift: r. 11 SP5
Swimbridge: Devon. SS 612
Swinderby: Lincs. SK 866
Swindon: Wilts. 11 SU1
Swinefleet: Yorks SE 762
Swineford: Mayo 18 D
Swineshead: Beds TL 056
Swineshead: Lincs TF 234
Swinford: Leics. SP 567
Swinton: Ber. NT 844
Swinton: Lancs SD 770
Swona: i., Ork. Is. ND 388
Swords: Dublin 18 J
Sybil Pt.: Kerry 19 Ins
Syderstone: Norf. TF 833
Sykehouse: Yorks SE 621
Symington: Ayr NS 383
Symington: Lan. NS 993
Syre: Suther. NC 694
Syresham: Northants SP 624
Syston: Leics. SK 621
Syston: Lincs SK 924

Tadcaster: Yorks 13 SE4
Taddington: Derby. SK 147
Tadley: Hants SU 606
Taf: r. 8 SN2
Taff: r. 10 ST1
Tain: Ross & Crom. 17 NH7
Talaton: Devon. SY 069
Talgarth: Breck. SO 153
Talisker: Skye NG 323
Talla: l., Selk. 15 NT1
Talladale: R. & Crom. NG 927
Talley: Carm. SN 633
Talybont: Card. SN 658
Tal-y-llyn: Mer. 10 SH7
Tamar: r. 8 SX4
Tame: r. 11 SP2
Tamerton Foliot: Devon. SX 476
Tamworth: Staffs 11 SK2
Tanat: r. 10 SJ1
Tanera More: i., Ross & Crom. 16 NB9
Tannadice: Angus NO 475

G.B. & IRELAND

TANTALLON CASTLE — WATH

Tantallon Castle: E. Loth. 15 NT58
Tanworth: War SP 1170
Taplow: Bucks SU 9182
Tap o'Noth: mtn., Aber. NJ 4829
Tara Hill: Meath 18 H6
Taransay: i., Inv. 16 NB00
Taransay Glorigs: is., Inv. NA 9606
Tarbat Ness: Ross & Crom. 17 NH98
Tarbert: Argyll NR 8668
Tarbert: Harris 16 NB10
Tarbert: Jura NR 6082
Tarbet: Dunb. NN 3104
Tarbolton: Ayr NS 4327
Tarbrax: Lan. NT 0255
Tarfside: Angus NO 4979
Tarf Water: r., Perth. 17 NN98
Tarf Water: r., Wig. 14 NX26
Tarland: Aber. NJ 4804
Tarporley: Ches. SJ 5562
Tarrant Gunville: Dorset ST 9212
Tarskavaig: Skye NG 5809
Tarves: Aber. NJ 8631
Tarvin: Ches. SJ 4867
Tas: r. 6 TM19
Tattenhall: Ches. SJ 4858
Tattershall: Lincs TF 2157
Tattingstone: Suff. TM 1337
Taunton: & vale, Som. 9 ST22
Tavistock: Devon. 8 SX47
Tavy: r. 8 SX58
Taw: r. 8 SS52
Tawe: r. 8 SN70
Tay: r. 15 NO13
Tayinloan: Argyll NR 6945
Taynuilt: Argyll NN 0031
Tayport: Fife 15 NO42
Tayvallich: Argyll NR 7386
Tealby: Lincs TF 1590
Teangue: Skye NG 6609
Tebay: Westmor. NY 6104
Tedburn St. Mary: Devon. SX 8194
Tees: r. 13 NZ01
Teesdale: Yorks/Dur. 13 NY92
Teifi: r. 10 SN24
Teifiside: Card. 10 SN44
Teign: r. 8 SX88
Teignmouth: Devon. 8 SX97
Teise: r. 7 TQ63
Teith: r. 14 NN60
Teme: r. 11 SO85
Templand: Dumf. NY 0886
Temple: Midloth. NT 3158
Temple Combe: Som. ST 7022
Temple Ewell: Kent TR 2844
Templemore: Tip. 19 F4
Templeton: Devon. SS 8813
Templeton: Pemb SN 1111
Tenbury Wells: Worcs. 11 SO56
Tenby: Pemb 10 SN10
Tendring: Essex TM 1424
Tenterden: Kent 7 TQ83
Ter: r. 7 TL71
Terling: Essex TL 7715
Terrington: Yorks SE 6670
Terrington St. Clement: Norf. TF 5520
Test: r. 7 SU33
Tetbury: Glos ST 8993
Tetford: Lincs TF 3374
Tetney: Lincs TA 3101
Tetsworth: Oxon. SP 6801
Teviot: r. 15 NT40
Teviotdale: Rox. 15 NT41
Tewkesbury: Glos 11 SO83
Texa: i., Argyll 14 NR34
Thame: & r., Oxon. 11 SP70
Thames: r. 7 —
Thatcham: Berks SU 5167
Thaw: r. 8 ST07
Thaxted: Essex 7 TL63
Theale: Berks SU 6371
Thet: r. 6 TL88
Thetford: Norf. 6 TL88
Thetford Chase: Norf. 6 TL88
Theydon Bois: Essex TQ 4598
Thirkleby: Yorks SE 4778
Thirsk: Yorks 13 SE48
Thomastown: Kilk. 19 G4
Thorganby: Yorks SE 6841
Thornaby on Tees: Yorks 13 NZ41
Thornborough: Bucks SP 7433
Thornbury: Glos 11 ST69
Thornby: Northants SP 6675
Thorncombe: Dorset ST 3703
Thorndon: Suff. TM 1469
Thorne: Yorks 13 SE61
Thorner: Yorks SE 3740
Thorney: Cambs. TF 2804
Thornhill: Dumf. 15 NX89
Thornhill: Perth. NS 6699
Thornhill: Yorks SE 2418
Thornley: Dur. NZ 3639
Thornton: Lancs 12 SD34
Thornton: Yorks SE 1233
Thornton Dale: Yorks SE 8383
Thornton in Craven: Yorks SD 9148
Thornton le Beans: Yorks SE 3990
Thornton le Fen: Lincs TF 2849
Thornton Steward: Yorks SE 1787
Thorpe: Derby. 11 SK15
Thorpe le Soken: Essex TM 1822
Thorpeness: Suff. TM 4759
Thorpe on the Hill: Lincs SK 9065
Thorpe Thewles: Dur. NZ 4023
Thorrington: Essex TM 0920
Thor's Cave: Staffs SK 0954
Thorverton: Devon. SS 9202
Thrapston: Northants 11 SP97
Threave Castle: Kirkc. 15 NX76
Three Bridges: Sussex TQ 2837
Threekingham: Lincs TF 0836
Threlkeld: Cumb. NY 3225
Threshfield: Yorks SD 9963
Thropton: Northumb. NU 0202
Thrumster: Caith. ND 3345
Thrushel: r. 8 SX48
Thurcroft: Yorks SK 4888
Thurlby: Lincs TF 0916
Thurles: Tip. 19 F4
Thurlestone: Devon. SX 6743
Thurmaston: Leics. SK 6109
Thurnscoe: Yorks SE 4605
Thursby: Cumb. NY 3250
Thursley: Surrey SU 9039
Thurso: & r., Caith. 17 ND16
Thurton: Norf. TG 3200
Thwaite: Yorks SD 8998
Tibbermore: Perth. NO 0523
Tibenham: Norf. TM 1389
Tibshelf: Derby. SK 4360
Tibthorpe: Yorks SE 9555
Ticehurst: Sussex TQ 6930
Tickhill: Yorks 13 SK59
Tideford: Corn. SX 3459
Tideswell: Derby. SK 1575
Tidworth: Hants. 9 SU24
Tighary: Uist NF 7171
Tighnabruaich: Argyll NR 9772
Tilbury: Essex 7 TQ67
Tilehurst: Berks SU 6673
Till: r., Lincs 11 SK88
Till: r., Northumb. 15 NT93
Tillicoultry: Clack. 15 NS99
Tillingham: Essex 7 TL90
Tillyfourie: Aber. NJ 6412
Tilney St. Lawrence: Norf. TF 5414
Tilshead: Wilts. SU 0347
Tilstock: Salop SJ 5337
Tilt: r. 17 NN86
Timberland: Lincs TF 1158
Timberscombe: Som. SS 9542
Tincleton: Dorset SY 7691
Tingewick: Bucks SP 6533
Tinkinswood: Glam. ST 0973
Tintagel: & head, Corn. 8 SX08
Tintern Abbey: Mon. 11 SO50
Tinto Hills: Lan. 15 NS93
Tinwald: Dumf. NY 0081
TIPPERARY: Co., R. of Irel. 19 E4
Tipton: Staffs SO 9592
Tiptree: Essex TL 8815
Tiree: i., Argyll 16 NL94
Tirga More: mtn., Harris 16 NB01
Tirry: r. 17 NC51
Tisbury: Wilts. ST 9429
Titchfield: Hants SU 5305
Titchmarsh: Northants TL 0279
Titley: Here. SO 3360
Titterstone Clee: Salop 11 SO57
Tiumpan Head: Lewis 16 NB53
Tiverton: Devon. 8 SS91
Tivetshall: Norf. TM 1787
Tobermory: Mull 16 NM55
Toberonochy: Argyll NM 7408
Toddington: Beds TL 0129
Todhead Point: Kinc. NO 8676
Todmorden: Yorks 13 SD92
Toe Head: Cork. 19 C1
Toe Head: Harris NF 9594
Tollerton: Yorks SE 5164
Tollesbury: Essex TL 9510
Tolleshunt D'Arcy: Essex TL 9312
Tolpuddle: Dorset 9 SY79
Tolsta Head: Lewis 16 NB54
Tolstachaolish: Lewis NB 1938
Tomatin: Inv. NH 8028
Tomcrasky: Inv. NH 2512
Tomdoun: Inv. NH 1501
Tomintoul: Banff NJ 1618
Tomnavoulin: Banff NJ 2227
Tonbridge: Kent 7 TQ54
Tondu: Glam. SS 8984
Tone: r. 9 ST32
Tong: Yorks SE 2130
Tongue: Suther. NC 5957
Tonna: Glam. SS 7798
Tonypandy: Glam. 10 SS99
Tonyrefail: Glam. ST 0188
Topcliffe: Yorks SE 4076
Topsham: Devon. 8 SX98
Tor Bay: Devon. 8 SX95
Tormarton: Glos ST 7678
Torne: r. 13 SE70
Torness: Inv. NH 5727
Torphichen: W. Loth. NS 9672
Torphins: Aber. NJ 6202
Torpoint: Corn. 8 SX45
Torquay: Devon. 8 SX96
Torran Rocks: Argyll 14 NM21
Torridge: r. 8 SS41
Torridon: R. & Crom. 16 NG95
Torrin: Skye NG 5720
Torrisholme: Lancs SD 4464
Torryburn: Fife NT 0286
Torthorwald: Dumf. NY 0378
Torver: Lancs SD 2894
Tory I.: Don. 18 E9
Toscaig: R. & Crom. NG 7138
Totland: I. of Wight SZ 3286
Totnes: Devon. 8 SX86
Tottenham: Middx. 7 TQ39
Tottington: Lancs SD 7712
Tottington: Norf. TL 8995
Totton: Hants SU 3513
Tove: r. 11 SP74
Toward Point: Bute. 14 NS16
Towcester: Northants 11 SP64
Tower Point: Pemb 10 SM71
Towie: Aber. NJ 4412
Tow Law: Dur. 13 NZ13
Townhill: Fife NT 1089
Town Yetholm: Rox. NT 8228
Towthorpe: Yorks SE 9062
Towton: Yorks SE 4839
Towyn: Mer. 10 SH50
Tralee: & bay, Kerry 19 B3
Tramore: & bay, Wat. 19 G3
Tranent: E. Loth. 15 NT47
Traprain Law: E. Loth. NT 5874
Traquair: Midloth. NT 3334
Trawden: Lancs SD 9138
Trawsfynydd: Mer. SH 7035
Trealaw: Glam. ST 0092
Trecastle: Breck. 10 SN82
Tredegar: Mon. 10 SO10
Treen: Corn. SW 3923
Trefeglwys: Montg. SN 9690
Trefignath: Anglesey 10 SH28
Trefilan: Card. SN 5457
Trefnant: Denb. SJ 0570
Trefonen: Salop SJ 2526
Tregaron: Card. 10 SN65
Tregoney: Corn. 8 SW94
Tregothnan: Corn. SW 8541
Tregynon: Montg. SO 0999
Treharris: Glam. ST 1097
Trelleck: Mon. SO 5005
Tremadoc Bay: Caer. 10 SH53
Trent: r. 11 SJ92
Trentham: Staffs SJ 8640
Trentishoe: Devon. SS 6448
Treorky: Glam. SS 9596
Tre'r Ceiri: Caer. 10 SH34
Tresco: Scilly Is. 8 SV81
Treshnish Isles: Argyll NM 2841
Tresmeer: Corn. SX 2387
Tressait: Perth. NN 8260
Tre-Taliesin: Card. SN 6591
Trethevy Quoit: Corn. SX 2569
Tretower: Breck. SO 1821
Trevelgue: Corn. SW 8464
Trevor: Caer. SH 3746
Trevose Head: Corn. 8 SW87
Trim: Meath 18 H6
Trimdon: Dur. NZ 3634
Trimingham: Norf. TG 2738
Trimley: Suff. TM 2736
Tring: Herts 11 SP91
Trochrie: Perth. NN 9739
Troon: Ayr 14 NS33
Troon: Corn. SW 6638
Trossachs, The: Perth 14 NN50
Trostan: mtn., Antrim 18 J9
Trotternish: Skye 16 NG45
Troup Head: Banff 17 NJ86
Troutbeck: Westmor. 12 NY40
Trowbridge: Wilts 9 ST85
Trumpan: Skye NG 2261
Trumpington: Cambs. TL 4455
Trundle, The: Sussex SU 8810
Truro: Corn. 8 SW84
Trusham: Devon. SX 8582
Trwyn Cilan: Caer. 10 SH22
Trwyn y Tal: Caer. 10 SH34
Tryweryn: r. 10 SH84
Tuam: Gal. 18 D6
Tud: r. 6 TG01
Tuddenham: Suff. TL 7371
Tullamore: Offaly 19 G5
Tulliemet: Perth. NO 0052
Tullow: Carlow 19 H4
Tullynessle: Aber. NJ 5519
Tummel: r. 17 NN95
Tummel Bridge: Perth. NN 7659
Tunbridge Wells: Kent. 7 TQ54
Tunstall: Lancs SD 6073
Tunstall: Staffs 11 SJ85
Tunstall: Suff. TM 3655
Tunstall: Yorks SE 2195
Tupton: Derby. SK 3965
Tur Langton: Leics. SP 7194
Turnberry: Ayr NS 2005
Turnditch: Derby. SK 2946
Turnhouse: Midloth. 15 NT17
Turriff: Aber. 17 NJ74
Tusker Rock: Glam. 10 SS87
Tutbury: Staffs SK 2129
Tuxford: Notts 13 SK77
Tweed: r. 15 NT94
Tweeddale: Peeb. 15 NT24
Tweedmouth: Northumb. NT 9952
Tweedsmuir: Peeb. 15 NT12
Twelve Pins, The: Gal. 18 B6
Twickenham: Middx. 7 TQ17
Two Bridges: Devon. SX 6075
Twomileborris: Tip. 19 F4
Twrch: r., Carm./Breck. 8 SN71
Twrch: r., Montg. 10 SH91
Twycross: Leics. SK 3605
Twyford: Berks SU 7975
Twyford: Hants SU 4724
Twyford: Leics. SK 7210
Twymyn: r. 10 SH80
Twynholm: Kirkc. NX 6654
Tydd Gote: Lincs/Cambs. TF 4518
Tydd St. Giles: Cambs. TF 4216
Tyldesley: Lancs. 12 SD60
Tyndrum: Perth. NN 3330
Tyne: r., Dur. 13 NY96
Tyne: r., E. Loth. 15 NT57
Tyne Gap: Northumb. 12 NY66
Tynemouth: Northumb. 15 NZ36
Tynewydd: Glam. SS 9399
Tynron: Dumf. NX 8093
TYRONE: Co., N. Irel. 18 G8
Tysoe: War SP 3343
Tywardreath: Corn. SX 0854
Tywi (Towy): r. 10 SN62

Uckfield: Sussex 7 TQ42
Udny: Aber. NJ 8726
Uffculme: Devon. 9 ST01
Ufford: Suff. TM 2953
Ugie: r. 17 NK44
Ugthorpe: Yorks NZ 7911
Uig: Lewis NB 0433
Uig: Skye NG 3963
Ulbster: Caith. ND 3241
Ulceby: Lincs TA 1014
Uldale: Cumb. NY 2536
Uley: Glos. ST 7898
Ulgham: Northumb. NZ 2392
Ullapool: R. & Crom. 16 NH19
Ulleskelf: Yorks SE 5140
Ullesthorpe: Leics. SP 5087
Ullock: Cumb. NY 0724
Ullswater: l., Cumb./Westmor. 12 NY42
Ulpha: Cumb. SD 1993
Ulster: Prov., N. Irel. 18 —
Ulva: i., Argyll 14 NM43
Ulverston: Lancs 12 SD27
Unst: i., Shet. Is. 17 HP60
Unstone: Derby. SK 3777
Upavon: Wilts. SU 1354
Uphall: W. Loth. NT 0571
Upham: Hants SU 5320
Upholland: Lancs SD 5105
Uplyme: Devon. SY 3293
Upminster: Essex TQ 5686
Upper Arley: Worcs SO 7680
Upper Broughton: Notts SK 6826
Upper Chapel: Breck. SO 0040
Upper Corris: Mer. SH 7408
Upper Langwith: Derby. SK 5169
Upper Lough Erne: R. of Irel. 18 F7
Upper Tean: Staffs SK 0139
Uppingham: Rut. 11 SP89
Upsall: Yorks SE 4587
Upton: Berks SU 5186
Upton: Ches. SJ 4069
Upton: Ches. SJ 2687
Upton upon Severn: Worcs. 11 SO84
Upwell: Cambs. TF 5002
Upwey: Dorset SY 6684
Upwood: Hunts TL 2582
Urchfont: Wilts. SU 0356
Ure: r. 13 SE46
Urie: r. 17 NJ72
Urmston: Lancs 13 SJ79
Urquhart: Moray. NJ 2863
Urquhart Castle: Inv. 17 NH52
Urra: Yorks NZ 5702
Urr Water: r. 12 NX77
Usk: Mon. 10 SO30
Usk: r. 10 ST39
Usworth: Dur. NZ 3057
Uttoxeter: Staffs 11 SK03
Uxbridge: Middx. 7 TQ08
Uyea: i., Shet. Is. HU 6098
Uzmaston: Pemb SM 9714

Valentia I.: Kerry 19 Ins.
Vale of Aylesbury: Bucks 7 SP70
Vale of Belvoir: Notts 13 SK74
Vale of Berkeley: Glos 11 SO70
Vale of Clwyd: Denb. 10 SJ06
Vale of Conway: Caer. 12 SH76
Vale of Evesham: Worcs. 11 SP04
Vale of Glamorgan 10 SS07
Vale of Gloucester 11 SO81
Vale of Kent 7 TQ93
Vale of Llangollen: Denb. 10 SJ23
Vale of Pewsey: Wilts. 9 SU16
Vale of Pickering: Yorks 13 SE77
Vale of Powis: Montg. 10 SJ20
Vale of Sussex 7 TQ21
Vale of Taunton: Som. 9 ST22
Vale of Wardour: Wilts. 9 SU02
Vale of White Horse: Berks 11 SU39
Vale of York 13 SE47
Valle Crucis Abbey: Denb. 10 SJ24
Valley: Anglesey 10 SH27
Valtos: Lewis NB 0936
Vange: Essex TQ 7287
Vaternish: & point, Skye 16 NG25
Vatersay: i., Inv. 16 NL69
Vaynor: Breck. SO 0410
Ventnor: I. of Wight 7 SZ57
Ver: r. 11 TF10
Vernham Dean: Hants SU 3356
Verwood: Dorset SU 0908
Veryan Bay: Corn. 8 SW93
Vidlin: Shet. Is. HU 4765
Vorran I.: Inv. NF 7235
Vowchurch: Here. SO 3636
Vyrnwy: r. 10 SJ21
Vyrnwy, L.: Denb. 10 SH92

Waddesdon: Bucks SP 7416
Waddingham: Lincs SK 9896
Waddington: Lincs SK 9764
Waddington: Yorks SD 7243
Wadebridge: Corn. 8 SW97
Wade's Causeway: Yorks 13 SE89
Wadhurst: Sussex TQ 6431
Waenfawr: Caer. SH 5259
Wainfleet All Saints: Lincs 6 TF45
Wakefield: Yorks 13 SE32
Wakes Colne: Essex TL 8928
Walberswick: Suff. TM 4974
Walcot: Lincs TF 1256
Waldon: r. 8 SS30
Walgrave: Northants SP 8071
Walkden: Lancs SD 7303
Walkern: Herts TL 2926
Wall: Northumb. NY 9168
Wall: Staffs SK 0906
Walland Marsh: Kent 7 TQ92
Wallasey: Ches. 12 SJ39
Wallingford: Berks 11 SU68
Walls: Shet. Is. HU 2349
Wallsend: Northumb. 15 NZ26
Walmer: Kent 7 TR35
Walpole St. Peter: Norf. TF 5016
Walsall: Staffs 11 SP09
Walsden: Yorks SD 9322
Walsham le Willows: Suff. TM 0071
Walsoken: Norf. TF 4710
Waltham: Lincs TA 2503
Waltham Abbey: Essex 7 TL30
Walthamstow: Essex 7 TQ38
Walton: Cumb. NY 5264
Walton: Surrey 7 TQ16
Walton: Yorks SE 4447
Walton le Dale: Lancs. 12 SD52
Walton on the Naze: Essex 7 TM22
Walton West: Pemb SM 8713
Wamphraygate: Dumf. NY 1295
Wangford: Suff. TM 4679
Wanlockhead: Dumf. NS 8712
Wansbeck: r. 15 NZ08
Wansford: Northants TL 0799
Wansford: Yorks TA 0656
Wanstead: Essex TQ 4087
Wanstrow: Wilts. ST 7141
Wantage: Berks 11 SU38
Wappenham: Northants SP 6245
Warboys: Hunts TL 3080
Warbstow: Corn. SX 2090
Warcop: Westmor. NY 7415
Warden: Northumb. NY 9166
Ward Hill: Ork. Is. 17 HY20
Wardington: Oxon. SP 4946
Wardle: Lancs 13 SD91
Ward's Stone: Lancs 12 SD55
Ware: Herts 7 TL31
Wareham: Dorset 9 SY98
Warehorne: Kent TQ 9832
Wargrave: Berks SU 7878
Wark: Northumb. NY 8576
Warkworth: Northumb. NU 2306
Warmington: War SP 4147
Warminster: Wilts 9 ST 84
Warrenpoint: Down 18 J7
Warrington: Lancs 12 SJ68
Warter: Yorks SE 8750
Warton: Lancs SD 4972
Warwick: Cumb. NY 4656
Warwick: War 11 SP26
WARWICKSHIRE: Eng. 11 SP—
Wasbister: Ork. Is. HY 3932
Wasdale Head: Cumb. 12 NY10
Wash, The: bay, Eng. 6 TF53
Washbrook: Suff. TM 1242
Washburn: r. 13 SE15
Washford: Som. ST 0441
Washington: Dur. 13 NZ35
Washington: Sussex TQ 1212
Wast Water: l., Cumb. 12 NY10
Watchet: Som. 9 ST04
Waterbeach: Cambs. TL 4965
Waterbeck: Dumf. NY 2477
WATERFORD: Co., R. of Irel. 19 G3
Waterford Harbour: Wat. 19 H3
Watergate Bay: Corn. 8 SW86
Waterhouses: Dur. NZ 1841
Wateringbury: Kent TQ 6853
Waterlooville: Hants SU 6809
Water Newton: Northants TL 1097
Water of Ae: r. 15 NX99
Water of Feugh: r. 17 NO59
Water of Fleet: r. 12 NX56
Water of Leith: r. 15 NT16
Water of Luce: r. 12 NX16
Water of Milk: r. 15 NY28
Waterside: Ayr NS 4308
Watford: Herts 7 TQ19
Wath: Yorks SE 3277

Wath: Yorks SE 1467
Wath upon Dearne: Yorks 13 SE40
Watlington: Oxon. 11 SU69
Watten: Caith. ND 2454
Watton: Norf. 6 TF90
Watton: Yorks TA 0150
Watton at Stone: Herts TL 3019
Waun-oer: mtn., Mer. 10 SH71
Waveney: r. 6 TM39
Waver: r. 12 NY24
Wawne: Yorks TA 0836
Weald, The: Kent 7 TQ—
Wear: r. 13 NZ35
Weardale: Dur. 13 NZ03
Weardley: Yorks SE 2944
Weare: Som. ST 4152
Weasenham All Saints: Norf. TF 8522
Weaver: r. 11 SJ64
Weaverham: Ches. SJ 6173
Weaverthorpe: Yorks SE 9670
Wedmore: Som. ST 4347
Wednesbury: Staffs 11 SP09
Wednesfield: Staffs SJ 9400
Weedon: Northants SP 6259
Week St. Mary: Corn. SX 2397
Weem: Perth. NN 8449
Weeting: Norf. TL 7788
Weldon: Northants SP 9289
Welford: Northants SP 6480
Welland: r. 6 TF33
Wellesbourne Mountford: War SP 2755
Wellingborough: Northants 11 SP86
Wellington: Here. 11 SO44
Wellington: Salop 11 SJ61
Wellington: Som. 9 ST12
Wellington College: Berks 7 SU86
Wellow: Notts SK 6666
Wells: Som. 9 ST54
Wells next The Sea: Norf. 6 TF94
Wells of Ythan: Aber. NJ 6338
Welney: Norf. TL 5294
Welshampton: Salop SJ 4334
Welshpool: Montg. 10 SJ20
Welton: Lincs TF 0079
Welwyn: Herts 7 TL21
Welwyn Garden City: Herts 7 TL21
Wem: Salop 11 SJ52
Wembley: Middx. 7 TQ18
Wemyss Bay: Renf. NS 1969
Wemyss Castle: Fife 15 NT39
Wendling: Norf. TF 9213
Wendover: Bucks 11 SP80
Wendron Moors: Corn. 8 SW63
Wenhaston: Suff. TM 4275
Wenlock Edge: Salop 11 SO59
Wenning: r. 13 SD66
Wensley: Yorks SE 0989
Wensley Dale: Yorks 13 SD89
Wensum: r. 6 TG01
Went: r. 13 SE51
Wentnor: Salop SO 3892
Wentworth: Yorks SK 3898
Wenvoe: Glam. 10 ST17
Weobley: Here. SO 4051
Werrington: Northants TF 1703
West Adderbury: Oxon. SP 4735
West Allen: r. 13 NY75
West Auckland: Dur. NZ 1826
West Barnes: E. Loth. NT 6578
West Bay: Dorset SY 4690
West Bergholt: Essex TL 9527
Westbourne: Sussex SU 7507
West Bridgford: Notts. 11 SK53
West Bromwich: Staffs 11 SP09
West Burra: i., Shet. Is. 17 HU33
Westbury: Bucks. SP 6235
Westbury: Salop SJ 3509
Westbury: Som. 9 ST44
Westbury: Wilts. ST 8751
West Calder: Midloth. NT 0163
West Chevington: Northumb. NZ 2297
West Chiltington: Sussex TQ0918
West Clandon: Surrey TQ 0452
West Cleddau: r. 8 SM92
West Dean: Sussex SU 8512
West Down: Devon. SS 5142
Westerdale: Yorks NZ 6605
Westerham: Kent 7 TQ45
Wester Ross: Ross & Crom. 16 NH16
West Felton: Salop SJ 3425
West Fen: Lincs 6 TF35
Westfield: Caith. ND 0564
West Firle: Sussex TQ 4707
Westgate on Sea: Kent 7 TR37
West Grinstead: Sussex TQ 1721
West Haddlesey: Yorks SE 5526
West Haddon: Northants SP 6371
West Hallam: Derby. SK 4341
West Ham: Essex 7 TQ48
West Hanningfield: Essex TQ 7399
West Harptree: Som. ST 5556
West Hartlepool: Dur. 13 NZ53
West Heslerton: Yorks SE 9175
West Hoathly: Sussex TQ 3632
West Ilsley: Berks SU 4682
West Kirby: Ches. 12 SJ28
West Langwell: Suther. NC 6908
West Lavington: Wilts. SU 0052
Westleton: Suff. TM 4469
Westlinton: Cumb. NY 3964
West Linton: Peeb. NT 1551
West Loch Roag: Lewis 16 NB03
West Loch Tarbert: Argyll 14 NR86
West Loch Tarbert: Harris 16 NB00
West Looe: Corn. 8 SX25
WEST LOTHIAN: Co., Scot. 15 NT07
West Lulworth: Dorset 9 SY88
West Malling: Kent 7 TQ65
WESTMEATH: Co., R. of Irel. 18 F6
West Meon: Hants SU 6424
West Mersea: Essex TM 0112
Westmill: Herts TL 3627
West Moors: Dorset SU 0802
WESTMORLAND: Co., Eng. 12 NY—
Westnewton: Cumb. NY 1344
Westonbirt: Glos 11 ST88
Westoning: Beds TL 0332
Weston on the Green: Oxon. SP 5318
Weston Subedge: Glos SP 1240
Weston-Super-Mare: Som. 9 ST36
Weston Underwood: Derby. SK 2942
Westonzoyland: Som. ST 3534
West Pennard: Som. ST 5438
Westport: Mayo 18 B6
West Putford: Devon. SS 3515
Westray: i., Ork. Is. 17 HY44
West Riding: Admin. Co., Yorks 13 SE23
West Runton: Norf. TG 1842
West Saltoun: E. Loth. NT 4667
West Suffolk: Admin. Co. Suff. 6 TL86
West Sussex: Admin. Co., Sussex 7SU/TQ
West Tytherley: Hants. SU 2729
West Walton Highway: Norf. TF 4912
Westward Ho!: Devon. 8 SS42
West Water: r. 17 NO57
West Wellow: Hants SU 2818
West Wickham: Kent TQ 3866
West Wittering: Sussex SZ 7999
West Wratting: Cambs. TL 6052
West Wycombe: Bucks 7 SU89
Wetheral: Cumb. NY 4654
Wetherby: Yorks 13 SE44
Wethersfield: Essex TL 7131
Wetton: Staffs SK 1055
Wetwang: Yorks. SE 9359
WEXFORD: Co., R. of Irel. 19 J3
Wexford Bay: Wex. 19 J3
Wey: r. 7 SU94
Weybourne: Norf. TG 1143
Weybridge: Surrey 11 TQ06
Weymouth: Dorset 9 SY67
Whaley Bridge: Derby. 13 SK08
Whalley: Lancs SD 7335
Whalsay: i. Shet Is. HU 5663
Whalton: Northumb. NZ 1281
Whaplode: Lincs TF 3224
Wharfe: r. 13 SE14
Wharfedale: Yorks 13 SE05
Whatton: Notts SK 7439
Whauphill: Wig. NX 4049
Wheatley: Oxon. SP 5905
Wheelock: Ches. SJ 7458
Wheldrake: Yorks SE 6744
Whernside: mtn., Yorks 13 SD78
Wherwell: Hants. SU 3840
Whickham: Dur. 13 NZ26
Whiddy I.: Cork. 19 B2
Whimple: Devon. SY 0497
Whipsnade: Beds 11 TL01
Whissonsett: Norf. TF 9123
Whitbeck: Cumb. SD 1184
Whitburn: Dur. NZ 4061
Whitburn: W. Loth. 15 NS96
Whitby: Ches. SJ 3975
Whitby: Yorks 13 NZ81
Whitchurch: Bucks 11 SP82
Whitchurch: Devon. SX 4972
Whitchurch: Glam. 10 ST18
Whitchurch: Hants 9 SU44
Whitchurch: Here. SO 5417
Whitchurch: Salop 11 SJ54
Whitchurch: Som. ST 6167
White Castle: Mon. 11 SO31
White Coomb: mtn., Dumf. 15 NT11
White Esk: r. 15 NY29
Whiteford Point: Glam. 10 SS49
Whitehaven: Cumb. 12 NX91
Whitehead: Antrim 18 K8
White Hill: Angus 17 NO37
Whitehills: Banff. NJ 6565
Whitehorse Hill: Berks 11 SU38
Whitehouse: Argyll NR 8161
Whitekirk: E. Loth. NT 5981
Whitemire: Moray. NH 9854
Whiten Head: Suther. NC 5068
Whiteparish: Wilts. SU 2423
Whiterashes: Aber. NJ 8523
White Roding: Essex TL 5613
Whitesand Bay: Corn. 8 SW32
Whitesand Bay: Corn. 8 SX35
Whitesand Bay: Pemb. 10 SM72
White Waltham: Berks SU 8577
Whitfell: Cumb. 12 SD19
Whitfield: Northumb. NY 7758
Whitgift: Yorks SE 8022
Whithorn: Wig. 14 NX44
Whiting Bay: Bute. NS 0425
Whitland: Carm. SN 1916
Whitletts: Ayr NS 3622
Whitley Bay: Northumb. 15 NZ37
Whitney: Here. SO 2647
Whitsome: Ber. NT 8650
Whitstable: Kent 7 TR16
Whittingham: Northumb. NU 0611
Whittington: Derby. SK 3975
Whittington: Lancs SD 5976
Whittington: Salop SJ 3230
Whittington: Staffs SK 1508
Whittle le Woods: Lancs SD 5721
Whittlesey: Cambs. TL 2797
Whittlesford: Cambs. TL 4748
Whitton: Suff. TM 1447
Whitwell: Derby. SK 5276
Whitwick: Leics. 11 SK41
Whitworth: Lancs 13 SD81
Whixall: Salop SJ 5034
Wiay: i. Skye 16 NG23
Wick: & r., Caith. 17 ND35
Wicken: Cambs. TL 5770
Wicken: Northants SP 7439
Wickford: Essex TQ 7593
Wickham: Hants. SU 5711
Wickham Market: Suff. 6 TM35
WICKLOW: Co., R. of Irel. 19 J4
Wicklow Hd.: Wick. 19 K4
Wicklow Mts.: Wick. 19 J4
Wickwar: Glos 11 ST78
Wid: r. 7 TL60
Widdrington: Northumb. NZ 2595
Widecombe in the Moor: Devon. 8 SX77
Wide Firth: Ork. Is. 17 HY41
Widford: Herts TL 4115
Widnes: Lancs 12 SJ58
Widworthy: Devon. SY 2199
Wigan: Lancs 12 SD50
Wigginton: Staffs SK 2106
Wighill: Yorks SE 4746
Wighton: Norf. TF 9339
Wigmore: Here. SO 4169
Wigston Magna: Leics. 11 SP69
Wigton: Cumb 12 NY24
Wigtown: & bay, Wig. 14 NX45
WIGTOWNSHIRE: Scot. 14 NX—
Wilbarston: Northants SP 8188
Wilberfoss: Yorks SE 7350
Wilby: Northants SP 8666
Wilkhaven: R. & Crom. 17 NH98
Willand: Devon. ST 0310
Willaston: Ches. SJ 6752
Willenhall: Staffs 11 SO99
Willerby: Yorks TA 0230
Willersey: Glos SP 1039
Willesborough: Kent TR 0441
Willesden: Middx. 7 TQ28
Willingdon: Sussex TQ 5902
Willingham: Cambs. TL 4070
Willingham: Lincs SK 8784
Willington: Derby. SK 2928
Willington: Dur. 13 NZ13
Williton: Som. 9 ST04
Willoughby: Lincs TF 4772
Willoughby: War SP 5167
Willoughby on the Wolds: Notts SK 6325
Willoughton: Lincs SK 9293
Wilmcote: War SP 1658
Wilmslow: Ches. 11 SJ88
Wilnecote: War SK 2201
Wilpshire: Lancs SD 6832
Wilsden: Yorks SE 0935
Wilsford: Lincs TF 0043
Wilton: Rox. NT 4914
Wilton: Wilts. 9 SU03
Wilton: Yorks SE 8582
WILTSHIRE: Eng. 9ST/SU
Wimbish: Essex TL 5936
Wimbledon: Surrey 7 TQ27
Wimblington: Cambs. TL 4192
Wimborne Minster: Dorset SZ 0199
Wimpole Hall: Cambs. TL 3351
Wincanton: Som. 9 ST72
Wincham: Ches. SJ 6675
Winchcombe: Glos 11 SP02
Winchelsea: Sussex 7 TQ91
Winchester: Hants 9 SU42
Windermere: & l., Westmor./Lancs 12 SD39
Windrush: r. 11 SP21
Windsor: Berks 11 SU97
Winfarthing: Norf. TM 1085
Winford: Som. ST 5364
Winforton: Here. SO 2947
Wing: Bucks SP 8822
Wingate: Dur. NZ 4036
Wingates: Northumb. NZ 0995
Wingham: Kent TR 2457
Wingrave: Bucks. SP 8718
Winkleigh: Devon. SS 6308
Winscombe: Som. ST 4157
Winsford: Ches. 11 SJ66
Winsford: Som. SS 9034
Winsham: Som. ST 3706
Winsley: Wilts. 9 ST76
Winslow: Bucks 11 SP72
Winster: Derby. SK 2460
Winster: Westmor. 12 SD49
Winstone: Glos SO 9609
Winterborne: Abbas: Dorset SY 6190
Winterborne Monkton: Dorset SY 6787
Winterborne Stickland: Dorset ST 8304
Winteringham: Yorks SE 9222
Winterton: Lincs. SE 9218
Winterton: Norf. TG 4919
Winton: Westmor. NY 7810
Wirksworth: Derby. 11 SK25
Wirral: Ches. 10 SJ38
Wisbech: Cambs. 6 TF40
Wishaw: Lan. 15 NS75
Wisp Hill: Rox./Dumf. 15 NY39
Wistanstow: Salop SO 4385
Wiston: Lan. NS 9531
Wiston: Pemb SN 0218
Wistow: Hunts TL 2781
Wistow: Yorks SE 5835
Witchford: Cambs. TL 5078
Witham: Essex 7 TL81
Witham: r. 13 TF16
Witham Friary: Wilts. ST 7440
Witheridge: Devon. 8 SS81
Withern: Lincs TF 4282
Withernsea: Yorks 13 TA32
Withersfield: Suff. TL 6547
Witherslack: Lancs SD 4384
Withiel: Corn. SW 9965
Withington: Glos. SP 0315
Withington: Here. SO 5643
Withypool: Som. SS 8435
Witley: Surrey SU 9439
Witney: Oxon. 11 SP31
Witton Gilbert: Dur. NZ 2345
Witton le Wear: Dur. NZ 1431
Wivelscombe: Som. 9 ST02
Wivenhoe: Essex 7 TM02
Wnion: r. 10 SH71
Woburn: Beds 11 SP93
Woden Law: mtn., Rox. 15 NT71
Woking: Surrey 7 TQ05
Wokingham: Berks 7 SU86
Wold Newton: Yorks TA 0473
Wolfhill: Perth. NO 1533
Wolf Rock: Corn. 8 SW21
Wollaston: Northants SP 9062
Wollaston: Salop SJ 3212
Wolsingham: Dur. 13 NZ03
Wolstanton: Staffs SJ 8448
Wolston: War SP 4175
Wolverhampton: Staffs 11 SO99
Wolverton: Bucks 11 SP84
Wolviston: Dur. NZ 4525
Wombourn: Staffs SO 8793
Wombwell: Yorks 13 SE30
Womersley: Yorks SE 5319
Wooburn: Bucks SU 9187
Woodbridge: Suff. 7 TM24
Woodbury: Devon. SY 0087
Woodchester: Glos SO 8302
Wood Green: Middx. TQ 3191
Woodhall Spa: Lincs 6 TF16
Woodland: Dur. NZ 0726
Woodplumpton: Lancs SD 4934
Woodside: Perth. NO 2037
Woodstock: Oxon. 11 SP41
Woodville: Derby. SK 3119
Wookey: Som. ST 5145
Wool: Dorset SY 8486
Woolacombe: Devon. 8 SS44
Wooler: Northumb. 15 NT92
Woolfardisworthy: Devon. SS 3321
Woolhampton: Berks SU 5766
Woolpit: Suff. TL 9762
Woolsington: Northumb. 15 NZ17
Woolstaston: Salop SO 4498
Woolsthorpe Manor: Lincs 6 SK92
Woolwich: London 7 TQ47
Wootton: Lincs TA 0815
Wootton: Northants SP 7656
Wootton Bassett: Wilts. 11 SU08
Wootton Wawen: War SP 1563
Worcester: Worcs 11 SO85
WORCESTERSHIRE: Eng. 11 SO—
Worfield: Salop SO 7595
Workington: Cumb. 12 NX92
Worksop: Notts 13 SK57
Worlaby: Lincs TA 0113
Worlingworth: Suff. TM 2368
Wormbridge: Here. SO 4230
Wormit: Fife NO 3925
Worms Head: Glam. 10 SS38
Worsborough: Yorks 13 SE30
Worsley: Lancs 13 SD70
Worth: Kent TR 3356
Worth: Sussex TQ 3036
Worthen: Salop SJ 3204
Worthing: Sussex 7 TQ10
Worthington: Leics. SK 4020
Wotton Under Edge: Glos 11 ST79
Wotton Underwood: Bucks SP 6815
Wouldham: Kent TQ 7164
Wragby: Lincs 6 TF17
Wrangle: Lincs TF 4250
Wrath, Cape: Suther. 16 NC27
Wreak: r. 11 SK71
Wreay: Cumb. NY 4348
Wrekin, The: Salop 11 SJ60
Wrelton: Yorks SE 7686
Wrentham: Suff. TM 4982
Wrexham: Denb. 11 SJ34
Wribbenhall: Worcs SO 7975
Wrington: Som. ST 4662
Wroot: Lincs SE 7102
Wrotham: Kent 7 TQ65
Wroughton: Wilts. SU 148
Wroxeter: Salop 11 SJ50
Wroxham: Norf. TG 2917
Wroxton: Oxon. SP 4141
Wye: Kent. 7 TR04
Wye: r., Derby. 13 SK26
Wye: r., Glos 11 SO50
Wyke: Yorks SE 1526
Wykeham: Yorks SE 9683
Wyke Regis: Dorset SY 6677
Wylam: Northumb. NZ 1164
Wylye: Wilts. SU 0037
Wylye: r. 9 ST94
Wymeswold: Leics. SK 6023
Wymondham: Leics. SK 8518
Wymondham: Norf. 6 TG1
Wyre: r., Card. 10 SN67
Wyre: r., Lancs 12 SD33
Wythall: Worcs SP 0675
Wythburn: Cumb. NY 3214
Wyvis Forest: R. & Crom. NH 467

Yafforth: Yorks SE 349
Yalding: Kent TQ 705
Yar: r. 9 SZ5
Yarburgh: Lincs TF 349
Yarcombe: Devon. ST 240
Yardley Hastings: Northants SP 865
Yare: r. 6 TG0
Yarm: Yorks 13 NZ4
Yarmouth: I. of Wight 7 SZ3
Yarmouth: Norf. see Gt. Yarmouth
Yarnbury Castle: Wilts. 9 SU0
Yarnscombe: Devon. SS 552
Yarrow: Midloth. NT 352
Yarrow Water: r. 15 NT2
Yarty: r. 9 ST2
Yate: Glos ST 708
Yattendon: Berks SU 547
Yatton: Som. ST 426
Yatton Keynell: Wilts. ST 867
Yaxley: Hunts TL 189
Yeadon: Yorks 13 SE2
Yealm: r. 8 SX6
Yealmton: Devon. SX 575
Yeaton Pevery: Salop SJ 431
Yeavering Bell: mtn., Northumb. NT 932
Yell: i., Shet. Is. 17 HU4
Yelvertoft: Northants SP 597
Yelverton: Devon. SX 526
Yeo: r., Devon. 8 SS6
Yeo: r., Devon. 8 SS8
Yeo: r., Devon./Som. 8 SX8
Yeo: r., Som. 9 ST4
Yeo: r. Som. 9 ST3
Yeovil: Som. 9 ST5
Yester Mains: E. Loth. NT 556
Yetminster: Dorset ST 591
Y Gaer: Breck. SO 002
Y Llethr: mtn., Mer. 10 SH6
Ynysdeullyn: Pemb 10 SM8
Ynys Lochtyn: Card. 10 SN3
Yoker: Renf. NS 516
York: Yorks 13 SE6
YORKSHIRE: Eng. 13 —
Yorkshire Dales 13 SD9
Yorkshire Wolds: Yorks 13SE/T
Youghall: & bay, Cork. 19 F
Youlgreave: Derby. SK 216
Yoxall: Staffs SK 14
Yoxford: Suff. TM 39
Yr Eifl: mtn., Caer. 10 SH3
Ysbyty Ystwyth: Card. 10 SN7
Yscir: r. 10 SN9
Ysgubor-y-coed: Card. SN 68
Ystalyfera: Glam. SN 76
Ystrad: r. 12 SJ0
Ystradgynlais: Breck. SN 78
Ystrad-Meurig: Card. SN 70
Ystwyth: r. 10 SN7
Ythan: r. 17 NJ

Zeal Monachorum: Devon. SS 71
Zeals: Wilts. ST 77
Zennor: Corn. SW 45
Zetland: i., Shet. Is. 17 HU
Zone Point: Corn. 8 SW

THE NATIONAL GRID

(as used on pp. 6-17, and in the Gazetteer of the British Is.)

The National Grid is a network of imaginary lines covering Great Britain and beginning at a point in the sea off Land's End. These lines are numbered in metres, first to the east, and then to the north.

Grid references in the Gazetteer, e.g. '**ST 36**' are made up of three elements :

1. The first letter ('**S**' in the example). The diagram shows how the letters '**S**', '**T**', '**N**', and '**H**' fall in relation to England, Wales, and Scotland.

2. The second letter ('**T**' in the example). The second diagram shows how each big square is divided into twenty-five 'second letter' squares, each being 100 × 100 kilometres.

3. The Figures. Each of these 100 kilometre squares is subdivided by lines running at 10 kilometre intervals. Distance is calculated from the SW corner of the square, first to the east (eastings) then to the north (northings). The diagram shows the position **36** approximately.

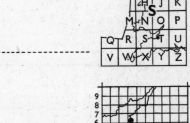

To define the position more exactly the 10 kilometre squares may be further subdivided into 1 kilometre squares. The two eastings distances—**32**—are given first ; followed by the two northings distances— **61**—to produce the " four figure reference " **ST 3261**

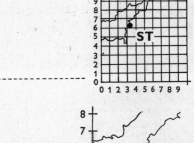

With larger-scale maps—e.g. 1 inch to the mile— the process of subdivision goes further and " six figure references " or even eight figure references are used to indicate positions more precisely.

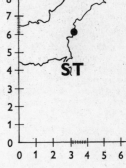

(1 kilometre = ·62 mile, and 1 mile = 1·61 kilometres)

The National Grid is used in this atlas with the sanction of the Director General, Ordnance Survey, and of H.M. Stationery Office.

COUNTRIES OF THE WORLD

COUNTRIES	POPULATION (nearest thousand) a	DENSITY (per sq. mile) a÷b	AREA (in sq. miles) b	Arable & orchard	Permanent meadow & pasture	Forest & woodland	Waste, city areas etc.
Aden, Colony & Protectorate	681,000	6	112,100	0·4	–	–	99·6
Afghanistan	12,000,000	48	250,000	1·9	*	1·7	96·4
Albania	1,394,000	130	10,629	12·3	29·6	34·5	23·6
Algeria	8,876,000	10	847,552	2·6	18·7	1·4	77·3
Arabia	10,000,000	11	947,000	–	–	–	100·0
Argentina	18,907,000	18	1,079,965	10·7	41·0	17·3	31·0
Australia	8,539,000	3	2,974,581	1·5	47·9	4·0	46·6
Austria	6,934,000	214	32,369	22·1	27·9	36·6	13·4
Belgium	8,654,000	736	11,755	33·7	24·7	18·7	22·9
Belgian Congo & Ruanda Urundi	15,000,000	16	930,554	20·7	37·0	42·3	*
Bermuda	38,000	1728	22	5·0	16·7	33·3	45·0
Bolivia	3,019,000	7	415,000	0·3	*	44·0	55·7
Brazil	52,633,000	16	3,288,050	2·2	15·6	46·5	35·7
British Borneo							
North Borneo	352,000	12	29,387				
Sarawak	550,000	12	47,000	18·0	1·0	75·0	6·0
Brunei	41,000	20	2,226				
British Central Africa see *Federation of Rhodesia & Nyasaland*							
British East Africa							
Kenya	5,410,000	25	219,730	2·7	20·6	2·5	74·2
Tanganyika	7,408,000	22	342,706	3·2	14·1	41·5	41·2
Uganda	4,994,000	62	80,292	11·5	–	8·3	80·2
Zanzibar & Pemba	264,000	258	1,020	38·3	14·8	0·4	46·5
British Honduras	67,000	8	8,867	8·7	0·3	78·9	12·0
British Somaliland	700,000	10	68,000	1·1	95·4	1·7	1·8
British Southern Africa							
Basutoland	564,000	48	11,716	12·4	86·8	0·3	0·5
Bechuanaland	296,000	2	275,000	–	98·0	*	2·0
Swaziland	185,000	28	6,704	14·0	78·0	1·2	6·8
British West Africa							
Cameroons	1,080,000	32	34,081	39·3	32·8	27·2	0·7
Gambia	280,000	70	4,005	21·3	–	39·1	39·6
Gold Coast & Togoland	4,112,000	45	91,843	17·2	*	51·9	30·9
Nigeria	23,920,000	71	338,593	7·4	*	43·7	48·9
Sierra Leone	2,005,000	67	30,169	55·5	30·4	4·1	10·0
British West Indies							
Bahamas	85,000	19	4,404	1·2	–	25·4	73·4
Barbados	212,000	1277	166	60·0	15·6	–	24·4
Jamaica	1,472,000	334	4,411	15·0	21·1	17·7	46·2
Leeward Is.	110,000	251	438	15·6	14·7	9·2	60·5
Trinidad & Tobago	650,000	328	1,980	39·0	*	54·2	6·8
Windward Is.	295,000	359	821	24·5	11·8	47·2	16·5
Bulgaria	7,290,000	170	42,796	38·7	2·3	33·2	25·8
Burma	18,675,000	71	261,789	12·9	*	33·7	53·4
Canada	14,009,000	4	3,845,144	3·8	3·1	35·0	58·1
Ceylon	8,104,000	320	25,332	21·6	*	53·8	24·6
Chile	5,932,000	21	286,397	8·0	9·2	22·0	60·8
China	†600,000,000	173	3,490,301	9·4	19·9	8·6	62·1
Formosa	6,250,000	452	13,808	23·9	1·7	59·5	15·0
Colombia	11,768,000	27	439,829	1·9	33·1	63·2	11·8
Costa Rica	801,000	41	19,695	14·9	4·3	78·4	2·4
Cuba	5,807,000	134	44,206	17·2	34·0	26·2	22·6
Cyprus	450,000	126	3,572	46·9	10·2	18·1	24·8

This table is taken from The Oxford Economic Atlas of the World which should be consulted for further information

* Included in other groups.   – None.   † Estimate.

COUNTRIES	POPU...
Czechoslovakia	12,
Denmark	4,
Dominican Republic	2,
Ecuador	3,
Egypt	18,
El Salvador	1,
Ethiopia	11,
Federation of Rhodesia & Nyasaland	
N. Rhodesia	1
S. Rhodesia	2
Nyasaland	2
Fiji Is.	
Finland	4,
France	42,
French Equatorial Africa	4,
Cameroons	3,
French Morocco	8,
French Overseas Departments	
French Guiana	
Guadeloupe	
Martinique	
Réunion	
French Overseas Territories	
Comoro Is.	
French Oceania	
French Somaliland	
Madagascar	4,
New Caledonia	
St. Pierre & Miquelon	
French West Africa	16,
Togo	1
Germany, East	18
Germany, West	49,
Greece	7,
Guatemala	2
Haiti	3,
Honduras	1
Hong Kong	2
Hungary	9
Iceland	
India	356,
Indo-China (Cambodia, Laos & Viet Nam)	27,
Indonesia	81,
Iran (Persia)	19,
Iraq	4,
Ireland, Republic of	· 2
Israel	1
Italy	47,
Japan	83,
Jordan	
Korea, North	8
Korea, South	20,
Lebanon	1
Liberia	2
Libya	1
Liechtenstein	
Luxembourg	
Malaya & Singapore	5,
Malta	
Mauritius	
Mexico	25,
Mongolia	1,
Netherlands	10,